Wild Side Adventures

— A Memoir —

Nan Williams

by Nan Williams

Illustrated by Mary Jo Phelps

Acknowledgements:
My thanks to Trish Crapo for proof reading these stories and
making suggestions for smoother reading;
special thanks to Lynne Rudié for the layout and design
and her patience with changes to get it just right;
and to Eugene Michalenko of Adams Specialty & Printing
for taking on the final production of a real book.
Most of all my appreciation to my husband Jack
whose support and encouragement has made this all happen.

ISBN # 13: 978-0-615-14983-7

Published by
Nancy N. Williams
36 Brown Road
Rowe, MA 01367

These stories first appeared in the Rowe, Massachusetts Town Newsletter,
Rowe Goal Post, over a period of years from 1982-1994.

Photographs are from the archives of the author unless otherwise credited.

To Ted Taylor

My very first hiking partner who guided me on an expedition up and over the heights of Todd Mountain a very long time ago when I was 11. My thanks to him for being my childhood inspiration for a life-long love of trekking through the woods and sailing downhill on skis.

Nan Williams

Mary Jo Phelps

Wild Side Contents

Introduction

During the first years I was involved as an editor of the *Rowe Goal Post*, news was sometimes scarce. To make the newsletter a little more interesting and fill out a couple of pages, I began to write about my favorite subject - the wonderful natural world found all around us in Rowe.

The first story was very short, but as townspeople began to enjoy these essays, they grew in length and scope and went on almost monthly for thirteen years from 1982 through 1994. They became known as the *Wild Side* and in answer to many requests, here is the collection. Dates of publication end each story.

This is generally a record of hikes I took in and around Rowe at all times of the year. I used the "editorial we" but on many hikes I was alone. Other times my delightful companion was the late Mary Liz Snively. My favorite hiking guide was son Rob Williams. Son Rick Williams and his wife Laurie introduced me to the joy of cross-country skiing and took me to the mountains of Utah. My flower searching partner was daughter-in-law Sue Williams. Daughter Sue and son-in-law Den Pollock took us hiking in the White Mountains and joined me searching for Rowe boundaries. Assorted other adults occasionally came along and various young people joined on major expeditions. You will all recognize yourselves!

Eventually, I wrote about other trips, and the *Wild Side* crossed this great country and ventured into such places as Mexico, Ireland, Europe and the Bahamas.

Many of the essays feature the history of Rowe and include autobiographical memories of Rowe in my youth. It is interesting even now to realize both the continuity and the changes in our natural world and the varying inventory of plant and animal life.

When I was having trouble finding photographs to illustrate these stories, Mary Jo Phelps offered to do some drawings. After seeing her first one I knew they would be a wonderful addition to the book and eagerly awaited each new rendition. Now this is her book too!

These stories should not be read all at once! It will be more interesting to read one every so often when you feel like taking off to the woods. If you read all the spring ones together you will get awfully sick of digging leeks! There is much repetition, but remember, they were written over a period of years. Also, please try to read them in chronological order as there are often references or continuations from previous stories.

For those of you who encouraged me through the years, I hope you enjoy these adventures a second time around. To new readers, happy Wild Siding with me in the hills of Rowe and beyond.

Nan Williams
Rowe Highlands Farm
August 2008

1982

Amidon Ravine on Pelham Brook

Tunnel Road power line, looking west

April has been a month of extremes – from wallowing in waist-deep snow getting to the beach one week, to shirtsleeve hiking in seventy-degree sunshine the next. The latter hike took us to a remote ravine in west Rowe where the hillside was covered with tiny yellow violets, blue and white hepaticas, the dainty leaves of squirrel corn, the scent of wild leek and our first sight of the weird blue cohosh. If one can experience the thrill of spring, this was it. All that beauty hiding away from civilization!

Looking for a *Goal Post* story, we later walked down into Deb Truesdell's old sugar house off Tunnel Road and wondered how

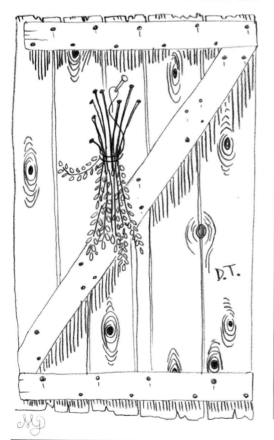

many kids will remember tramping down there in the spring to be treated with a taste of warm maple syrup in a Dixie cup. It was sad to see the old rusty popcorn popper and a bouquet of pussy willows still hanging on the wall.

Hearing a waterfall, we investigated further to find a small pool surrounded by rocks near the source of Steele Brook. There we found at our feet a dead red-shouldered hawk. Such a beautiful bird, brown with bands of black and white on the wings and tail, and soft rust and white under parts with reddish shoulders. These birds are usually found in swampy woods sitting on a low perch watching for snakes or frogs, also eating small mammals and insects. Although sorry to see the loss of such a young bird, we appreciated the chance to have a closer look at one of our wild citizens.

Another thrill this week was the discovery of a small bog containing three pitcher plants. These uncommon, strange-looking carnivorous plants have hollow curved leaves which collect water into which are attracted various insects. These insects drown and are eventually digested as food for the plant. **5/82**

Looking for wildflowers this last month took us up through the tall ponderosa pines and cedars on Moscow Mountain where we found pure white trillium, mariposa tulips and to our great joy, calypso orchids. Descending into the open area, we were suddenly flushing pheasants from the bright green winter wheat fields of the fertile rolling Palouse country under the Big Sky of Northern Idaho. All such a contrast to our meadows, woods and stone walls of Rowe.

Out there they call the place between two hills a "draw" and grow wheat on thousand-acre fields, dusting their crops by airplane. Monster machines ride the steep side hills with their cabs straight up and the only trees are on the mountaintops. All part of our great wild land.

* * * * *

Meanwhile, back in Rowe "green up" has really come as well as our usual crop of mayflies, which for a few weeks make us wish we lived on the moon!

Flowers are blossoming now so fast that we have lost count. Our most recent hike to a favorite spot just outside Rowe rewarded us with a hillside of purple and white showy orchids and our "find of the year," a rock covered with the rare walking fern.

In the bird department, the village area has a resident broad-winged hawk while the back woodsy roads are resounding at evening with the song of the hermit thrushes. **6/82**

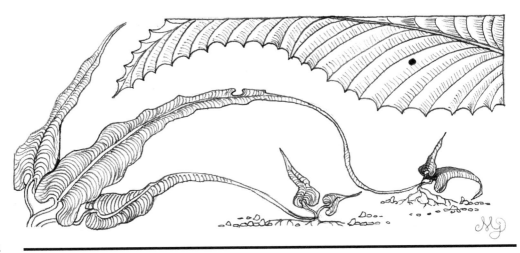

Lots of "wild" activity this month. A mother bear with two cubs was seen on Zoar Road below the Carse house, a single doe and a mother and fawn are frequent visitors in the village, rather large snapping turtles are busy laying eggs in many sandy areas around the lake, wild turkeys come and go, an almost albino skunk found himself in a squirrel trap and just took a nap, a Canada goose has been a resident on the village green, a baby skunk and a baby porcupine were found, several families of bluebirds are raising young and the mosquitoes are fierce.

Even through the haze, it's that magical time of year when the twilight lasts past nine, and the old bull frogs are saying, "Too deep, too deep" and "Go round, go round." And it's time every child had the experience of catching fireflies in a jar to keep and watch by their bedside all night. It's also the daisy and buttercup and paintbrush time. Our fields are beautiful with these New England wildflowers.

Two short hikes have not produced any startling discoveries this month but have been enjoyable. There are some interesting large round-leaved orchids on the Park trails. These and the pitcher plants are fairly rare. They should NOT be picked. It's also quite easy to come upon a thrush's nest in

the woods. You find them near the ground with lovely blue eggs.

Perhaps the most fun to watch was a chipmunk village. There must have been several generations with aunts, uncles and cousins darting in and around and over rocks and tree stumps. They seemed to have hundreds of holes and peered at us from all angles. Then on command, everyone changed places. It was better than a Walt Disney cartoon! **7/82**

Orchids, Flowers and Other WildLife

Orchids are the flower find this month. Small woodland orchids are all around the lake with at least one ragged fringed, and most beautiful of all, six large purple-fringed orchids on the Park Trail. Helleborine is just coming out in the woods. All of these are exceptionally interesting flowers especially when looked at through a magnifying lens.

Woodland orchid

On the lake surface are yellow bladderworts, red watershield, yellow and white water lilies, and in the water, bur reeds, and white arrowheads with blue skullcap around the edges and on rocks and logs, round-leaved sundew.

Several trout have been caught at Pelham Lake with large tooth marks in their bellies indicating perhaps they are being attacked by larger bass, contrary to expectations.

Have no doubts, this is Bear Country! They have been seen lately on the east end of Ford Hill Road, Hazelton Road near the village and a mother and cub at Bear Swamp. A male bear will range fifteen miles, mother and cub somewhat less so this may be only one bear seen several times. Now is the time to watch the power lines with binoculars and try to spot a bear eating blackberries. Although primarily nocturnal, they seem to be about quite often at midday.

Skunks are also in great abundance with a mother and four babies roaming the village. Little holes scratched in your lawn indicate a skunk has been by looking for grubs.

Although he's not telling the exact location, the $10\frac{1}{2}$ pound brown trout caught by Henry Dandeneau, Sr. in the Deerfield River recently must have been from the Rowe shore!

Dismantling the Woodward house on Browning Hill last month left clouds of homeless bats, many with babies hanging to their wings. We hope some of you have given them homes for they are great insect eaters for your yard. **8/82**

Ragged-fringed orchid

Goldenrod and Earthstars, Fall Arrives

Earthstar mushrooms

As mysteriously as they appeared in the spring, they have gone again. Our songbirds, migrating mostly at night, seem to disappear without our realizing it, and suddenly the woods are quiet except for an occasional jay, a few starlings collecting in the treetops, and the scream of a red-tailed hawk from his perch along the Deerfield. It is hard to believe that the bobolink who spent the summer in our fields will be wintering on the "pampas" in Brazil, and the little spotted sandpipers, having raised their families along Pelham Brook, will be wintering with some of our other residents on the coast of Florida. And perhaps most amazing of all will be the flight to Mexico of the Monarch butterfly now in the pupa stage, hanging on our milkweed.

The woods are great this time of year. Most of the bugs have gone and many of the wildflowers have become bright berries or interesting seedpods. A pretty sight on Davis Mine Road is a patch of bunchberries with their bright red clusters of berries scattered in with the blue berries of the corn lily. The trillium has a large red berry, each little wild lily-of-the-valley has a cluster of red-spotted tan berries and even the little starflower has two tiny-segmented gray berries. The white baneberry has become a collection of "doll's-eyes" (especially on Potter Road), the fireweed sports cotton from its seedpods, and the fruitdots are ripening to a rich dark brown on some of the ferns. You can't help but appreciate the little row of seed boxes on mad-dog skullcap in wetlands.

Goldenrod and asters are everywhere. But how much more interesting is life when you realize that the numerous varieties of each do not look at all alike. One slender stalk of goldenrod is white and called silverrod, and the New England aster is the very deepest purple. Now is the time to look for the pretty little white spiral orchid called ladies' tresses. Consider yourself lucky if you find them with blue fringed gentians.

Many mushrooms appear this time of year, NONE of which should be sampled unless you are a real expert – but observed and enjoyed, yes. They come in many shapes and colors. Our exciting "first find" this month was a clump of "earth stars" on the old Noyes Wheeler land north of Yankee. (When wet, they open to a most unusual star shape surrounding a puffball.)

Another "Wild Side day" took us a short distance out of Rowe to the Floating Island in Sadawga Lake at Whitingham, Vt. What a "squishy" experience that was! It's a reddish sphagnum moss bog covered with wild cranberry, pitcher plants and bog rosemary and is definitely floating on water, as we learned when one boot went through the moss and filled with water!

Right here at home one of the prettiest and most interesting walks is up the Pelham Brook Ravine (called the Amidon Ravine on old Rowe post cards) from the bottom of Browning Hill to the Mill Pond Dam. There are rocks, ferns, waterfalls and pools with intriguing old foundations from the several mills that used that short section of Pelham Brook for waterpower during the first one hundred and fifty years of the Town of Rowe before the switch to our other stream, the Deerfield, as a source of waterpower.

The Park Department has a new trail from the bridge below Pelham Lake dam, south along the brook connecting with the west end of the Base Trail. These trails are really great and many people are enjoying them. Fall is here for sure. August 22 marked an early frost in the lower sections of town and a few trees have spots of red. Go out hiking on the Wild Side! This is the most beautiful and most enjoyable time of the year! **9/82**

Floating Island in Sadawga Lake

Discovery of the Rare Orchid

From one year to the next, we forget what glorious things happen to our Rowe hills during September and October. The color seems early this year (no real killing frost yet), but perhaps we say this every year. It must have been a wonderful fall for bees as some fields have been heavy with the scent of goldenrod honey.

We took a rather unexpected hike the other day up the mountainside east of the Soapstone area. Curiosity about an old wood road, what looked like a cellar hole and this and that kept us going up and up until it became no small problem to get out by daylight! The road stopped, but the "cellar hole" proved rather interesting. It was a natural collection of large rocks around which many grape vines had grown pulling down all the trees, which then had become a series of natural arbors under which you could walk. This left an open circle of daylight in an otherwise heavily forested area, and all the tall trees around the circle were totally covered with grape vines! Once we satisfied ourselves it was not manmade, we appreciated it as quite a feat of nature (or a creeping menace headed toward town!) At least, it was a great haven for birds and animals.

Further on there was a beautiful stone wall only about 150 ft. long on the side hill in the middle of nowhere. Did old Jessie King build that in the late 1700's? His ghost seemed to be about walking the hillside with us on his old property that day.

We found lots of maidenhair fern, but with the angle of the sun getting lower, we didn't spend too much time flower hunting. However, there was one different looking specimen right in our path, which we quickly decided to pick and put in our knapsack for future identification. Later we regretted our decision to pick when we discovered it to be a badly mangled but very fragrant and very rare "three-birds orchid" (Triphora trianthophora) which can be dormant for many years between blossomings.

Another "find of the month" will interest the Fire Department. Somewhere on that hillside we stumbled across an old fire hose lost in a forest fire battle many years ago.

Eventually, the way out was down across a deep trough proving to be the path of one of the big landslides that took a train off the track back in the 1930's. Anyone have any pictures of that? The night freight went past us as we finally made our way out of the woods, content to know that we'd really gotten acquainted with another side of Rowe.

* * * * *

Curiosity brought us back to this area once more for a closer look at the Deerfield Arch, which is quite impressive when you're standing inside. This rock formation is in the Deerfield River (in Charlemont) just above the Florida Bridge and right below the old bridge abutments that mark one of the corners of Rowe's boundaries. Dates of the selectmen's perambulation of town lines were carved in the bridge rocks and just upriver in Rowe a pretty little clump of bluebells of Scotland had attached itself to a large boulder. This narrow Deerfield Gorge is spectacular with many potholes and unusual rock formations. Stop and look again when you pass by, in case you've been taking this scenery for granted along with our beautiful fall foliage! **10/82**

Ginseng

This October has been beautiful! The fall colors seem to have lasted longer than usual, and it was not until our first hard frost on Oct. 23rd that the leaves came tumbling down by the bushel. The beech and oak trees have turned that lovely bronze and will grace our hillsides for a while longer.

But why are the wild geese avoiding us this year? Pelham Lake has always been a stopping place for several flocks as they wing their way southward, but this year not a one has been seen on the lake and only a few overhead. Do they know something we don't about the weather soon to descend upon us?

One October hike on the border of Heath and Rowe turned up fresh bear droppings, but when we heard something crashing through the woods some time later our thoughts were on deer. "Must have been a moose," I thought, as the quick, long distance glimpse was very dark colored. A few minutes later we finally put two and two together and realized it must have been a bear!

An earlier hike in West Rowe was a typical fall day with sunshine, wind, clouds and the first snow flurry of the season leaving small white particles on the moss we were examining. The next morning the top of Greylock stood out white and clear. This was the hike when we finally found fringed gentians in Rowe. Without bright sun they were closed, but their beautiful blue color and delicate fringe was just as lovely. These are not to be confused with the bottle gentians which never open (except by the bumble bee that pollinates them) and are much more numerous. The fringed gentians are biennial,

Fringed gentians

Frank Knight Photo

taking two seasons to flower then dying.

Several times we have been enthused to find a single ginseng plant on one or another hillside in Rowe. We knew that ginseng was a prized herb of Chinese culture dating back four thousand years as the "Herb of Eternal Life," or the "Elixir of Life," an aphrodisiac and general cure-all.

Natural food stores in this country carry several ginseng products and many old-timers in Rowe speak of digging and selling ginseng years ago. The plant has become fairly rare and takes many years to grow to full size. Is it still locally hunted and dug today? Here's a little story.

Ginseng

Steve Autio, returning to Rowe after several years' absence, was looking forward to visiting his old haunts around these hills he used to tramp as a teen-ager. One spot on a very remote hillside that Steve was especially anxious to see was "his" ginseng patch that he had watched through the years, carefully planting the seeds in the fall to ensure new plants. Hiking up the mountainside, camera in hand, Steve expected to record a spectacular patch of ginseng. What he found was a very large area of newly turned ground.

So the answer is "yes," people are still combing the hillsides in remote areas of Rowe to dig and probably sell ginseng. A Health Food Store in Brattleboro said that there is a good market for ginseng in Boston and San Francisco, but this particular store would not deal in local wild roots for they are considered an endangered species.

One more Rowe story with a happier ending. To protect the catch, the names and places will remain anonymous. Once upon a time, two small boys took great pains to transfer a six-inch trout they had caught in a brook to a far off spring in the woods. The incident, long forgotten, was recalled by the same two men as they had occasion recently to visit said spring and found to their surprise one very lonely eighteen-inch trout!

By the time you read this it will be November. Some people have bumper stickers that say, "I love New York" or Vermont. Well, I want one that says, "I hate November!" Now that's a terrible attitude! Our Wild Side always has something intriguing to observe, but I still have to admit a real prejudice against November! Happy Thanksgiving!   **11/82**

Ginseng in fruit

Well, November is over and our comment against that particular month certainly produced some feedback. At least half the population must have birthdays or anniversaries in November, which makes for a special month, no matter the weather. Others called our attention to the beautiful silver gray color of the mountains, the quiet peacefulness of this time of year and even the glorious absence of bugs. Certainly this has been an exceptional fall with prolonged good weather and sunshine. However, one bumper sticker was seen with a vote for our side.

No Flowers, No Leaves, November

The light fall of snow the day after Thanksgiving has created a whole new world, sparkling in the sun and gleaming in the moonlight. It is time for winter. The barred owl is still hooting on Adams Mountain and a snowy owl was reported near the ledges on Zoar Road. The foxes are around and healthy. A bear was heard prowling around the village recently and another seen at the top of Joe King hill. June Brown tried to entice this one by calling "Here bear, come bear" but Sir Bear, highly insulted with that treatment, walked off into the woods.

A mid-November hike took us to Pulpit Rock on Rowe's high west rim and brought to mind all the picnics enjoyed there by generations of Rowemans. In years gone by, a summer was never complete without at least a few picnics at Pulpit Rock, also known as Prospect Rock. It appears on a map as early as 1858 and has been the subject of many poems and legends through the years.

Even without the picnic, the area was impressive. The new power lines to Bear Swamp make the approach different from the old days, but the final break through the bushes onto open ledge with the Deerfield River nearly a thousand feet below, and the wild mountains of Florida and Monroe beyond is still spectacular.

In a recent Wild Side story, we mentioned hiking across the old landslide on Negus Mountain. In response to our question, Ellen Peck Powell former resident on whose father's land the slide occurred sent us a B&M booklet containing pictures of the slide and derailed cars. It happened during New England's famous hurricane September 21, 1938. Another large slide occurred under Pulpit Rock but nothing more in recent years.

Don't forget to fill your bird feeders. It seems to be a never-ending job this fall due to a bumper crop of blue jays. **12/82**

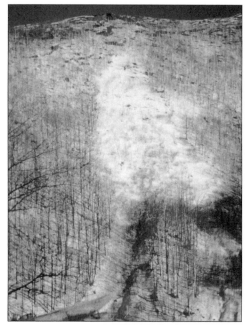

**1938 Landslide below Pulpit Rock
picture circa 1950**

Looking toward Adams Mountain and the "big mowing"

Janet Littlefield with Jim Lively's horses

The year was fast coming to a close, and we wanted to take one last hike for 1982. Dressing (too warmly) for the occasion on one of the final days of December, we started out on the park trail from Pond Road, just letting curiosity take us where it would.

Veering from the path in the "big mowing" toward Soule's, we wound around large trees and through underbrush, following a deer trail in the leaves. Thinking back, there really had been a beautiful "mowing" there, and Mederic Lively from Heath used to mow it using his mules. What a view sitting on the hay wagon looking down the valley into "the hopper" and west toward Greylock. Time passes and for want of a mule, trees grow.

We climbed over the stone wall on the hill and down into a small swamp with uprooted trees. The moss had frozen some but not the water underneath. It was a funny feeling underfoot as the moss tipped and floated with your footsteps but did not break through. It took waving arms to stay upright, and a flock of chickadees gathered in the trees above, darting about to get a better view of this intruder and discussed the matter quite fully. There was much fresh evidence of deer, and following the trail, it seemed they must surely be over the next rise.

We crossed the park trail that goes to the Sibley Cabin and followed an interesting stone wall straight up the hillside to the left. The lovely mosses and lichens on the rocks were especially noticeable, perhaps standing out more without the usual flowers, plants and mushrooms to distract us. Much appreciated at this time of year are the evergreen ferns, marginal and spinulose woodferns fresh as summer and the leathery Christmas and polypody standing tall and green.

We followed the stone wall up and up, wondering why a wall here and who were the men who built it? It was just an ordinary wall, but each stone was still in place where it had been laid perhaps two hundred years ago. Once in a while there was a break in the wall, stones scattered to make a roadway, and in other places a real bar-way built into the original wall. There was a noticeable lack of chipmunks darting in and around the rocks. They had all gone to bed for the winter, not to be fooled by a few warm days.

The wall finally reached a level spot and went on through the woods, but we turned to climb a ridge to the right, reaching a narrower level spot quite steep on three sides, sort of the nose of the mountain. One tends to think "What a place for a house!" as the view opens up through the trees, but thank goodness there was no house, for we wouldn't have been here enjoying the wind in the trees, the deer paths in the leaves, and the tumbles of rocks now and then sheltering a porcupine den.

Further up the mountain, it became very steep under an enchanting little hemlock forest. Suddenly we were very tired and out of breath and pulled ourselves up to lean against a tree facing up the hill. It felt so good to lean against that tree! After catching our breath and resting a while, we marveled at all the beautiful little places such as this that are here every day with no one to see them. Perhaps it is like the tree cracking in the woods, there is no sound if no one is there to hear it.

The top of Adams Mountain doesn't sit straight. It's on sort of an angle, running southwest to northeast so that front and back aren't where they should be. We scuffed around a little, wondering again where the old wooden tower used to be and tried to picture how it had looked. That set us to wondering whatever happened to the bronze tablet that was installed on top of the tower pointing the direction of other mountains seen from there. It mysteriously disappeared not long after being placed up there in 1929. Do you suppose it rests in some far-off antique shop, some attic or was it melted down for scrap? Or maybe it is still hiding under a rock somewhere on the mountain, victim of a long-ago prank? Wouldn't it be great if it mysteriously appeared on the museum steps some day?

Wanting to head back along the ridge of South Mountain, we started down in the logical direction – mainly concerned that we not get too far around and land down at Davis Mine as we did once upon a time! When it did not level out at all, we looked carefully through the trees until we spotted a building, the

Unitarian Church. We were off course about 90 degrees. Maybe the next glacier will move Adams Mt. square to north and south.

Climbing back up to our left, the walking was easy along the ridge and once again we were hot on the deer trail, finding where several had bedded down in the leaves. We should have kept closer watch and stepped more quietly instead of letting our mind wander over the stone wall that came straight up the mountainside and crossed the ridge from the right. It was the top of the old sheep pasture, and it reminded us of the sheep bell we have that must have been carried over a good deal of this mountainside. The bell has the initials of its owner J. H. * (for Starr, an old Rowe sheep farmer). What a pretty sight, those sheep grazing on the open hillside and the sound of the bells. The latter is my earliest memory.

You have to pay attention to the present! When we looked up from our thoughts, a good-sized deer just ahead of us jumped up and bounded off through the brush, waving an especially large white flag in greeting. We ran a ways to see him again, but he was long gone over the hill.

We began to wonder if we had missed King's Highway that crosses the mountain in the saddle, but soon a

Stone wall on top of Adams Mountain

path led downhill, intersecting with the familiar trail over the ridge. The "lay of the land" was as we remembered, but on quick count, it had been sixteen years since we'd last made this pilgrimage.

Here at the top of the trail is a large tall flat-sided boulder beside the path. It looks too uniquely situated to be natural but too large to have been "placed" there. After some contemplation on this matter, we arrived at the conclusion the path had been "placed" there because of the rock and not the reverse. King's Highway was the route from Deerfield and Charlemont to Fort Pelham in the seventeen forties, and the route taken by the troops going to Bennington in the Revolutionary War. If only rocks could talk.

The path back was an easy downhill jaunt and feeling our pockets we realized we'd picked up the usual assortment of rocks, mosses and what have you.

* * * * *

December has been a balmy month with unusual temperatures in the sixties a couple of times. A small snowstorm gave us a white Christmas, and at least there were no "Grasshoppers on Christmas Day" as the Recorder evidently headlined about Rowe in 1911.

Browns and grays are the colors just now but somehow they are more friendly shades than those of November. Even though real winter hasn't arrived yet, we are "over the hump"; the days are getting longer, the Christmas trees are out for the birds, and the seed catalogues have arrived. The bluejays have thinned out some but the evening grosbeaks are here in huge flocks. There are mourning doves, woodpeckers, chickadees, both species of nuthatches, goldfinches and a few purple finches in the bird population.

In the animal department, at least two white weasels have been seen. These are nosy little creatures and quite fun to watch as they seem to be playing games with you, darting here and there, hiding for a minute then always coming up for another look.

* * * * *

In the book *Picturesque Franklin – 1891* by Clifton Johnson, there are several local pictures, one of which is a house shown on the east bank of Pelham Brook between Rowe and Zoar. The only way to prove the location is to stand in the brook, picture in hand, and identify a rock. One out of hundreds in the picture is still in the same place, the rest have been tossed and tumbled like marbles by the tremendous force flowing down that rocky ravine during all the floods since 1891.

Once the location is proved, the next step is to find the cellar hole, and sure enough, across the brook, there it is in a small level area hanging on the hillside. The tiny barn foundation is there, too. A little further investigation discovers the two end rocks with anchor cables that held the footbridge in the picture.

Take a look on your next trip to Zoar. All this is just below the watering trough. The house would have been in Charlemont, for the line follows the brook on the east side to a spot up the hill above the ledges.

Happy New Year and here's to January! Any special place you'd like to hike this month? **1/83**

Snow, beautiful snow, arrived mid-January and accumulated to fifteen inches or so. Some of us are happy about it! A hike across the power lines in North Rowe in the sunshine after new fallen snow was a glorious treat well worth waiting for. A special sight that day was Jim Lively coming over the hill with his team of horses, drawing logs on a sled. Using a cant hook, he rolled the logs onto the pile while we made friends with the horses. It seemed that there must be something very satisfying about a day's work performed in this manner.

Before the deep snow, we took one of our favorite hikes around Yankee and up the old HT&W railroad bed. This always entails an update on the small beaver dam behind the Yankee fence. A new generation of beaver must be helping out, for the dam was considerably higher, flooding our usual path. The fox tracks we had been following went out onto the ice, and we wondered if a small beaver had been contemplated as lunch.

The old Noyes Wheeler cellar hole doesn't change much through the years, but we always have to check it out and marvel at the old stone culvert on the brook. With great authority, we quote Clifford Sibley and tell our hiking companions about the once beautiful front lawn, the fish-fries, and the cattle to be salted up on the hill. And we promise on the next trip to take them up to the Wilcox pasture, the small graveyard and down by our favorite waterfall.

On up the tracks (or where the tracks used to be) we cross the Vermont line and check to be sure Rowe's northwest boundary marker is secure. Going into Whitingham, we find a gravel bank on our right and wonder if this is of Yankee construction vintage or something earlier.

Next comes the Lime Kilns Area, and we climb up into the old quarry, half expecting to see those beautiful bulblet ferns of summer draping down over the rocks in the snow. Of course, they are much too fragile to survive the cold. Climbing to the top, we find even our sturdy goldies and narrow-leaved spleenwort ferns are brown and matted under the snow. This makes the miracle of spring to come even more unreal.

Further on, we take a side trip up the brook to the Mayan Temple-like structure which was to be the "Carbide Operation." This amounted to a stock selling fraud from all hearsay (very few facts can be found), and our friend Celso Marchegiani of Readsboro told us recently that his father was the one who brought the never-used lumber from there to build his house in Readsboro, Vt.

Back out now in the open field, we find where the Power Company has excavated a large amount of fill for the recent raising of the level at Harriman Dam. As we are discussing this project, a large red-tailed hawk flies off his perch on the hillside and circles out over the river. A red-tail is about twenty plus inches long with a wingspread of forty-eight inches and lives mostly on small rodents. These hawks are fairly common along the Deerfield.

Coming to the end of our hike across the suspension bridge at Harriman Station, we find ourselves like the nickname of the old railroad – Hungry, Tired and Weary. **2/83**

Spring has arrived! The first clue was a call from Chris Tower of Zoar Road on February 15th at 7:10 a.m. to report a robin. By the next morning it had worked its way a little farther north and we could hear him singing in our treetop. A check with the glasses showed the bird to be plump and fit in spite of Rowe's worm shortage at the present time.

Although snow covers our ground, it softens in the noon sunshine and somehow the air is different. It SMELLS like spring! (We didn't tell you this until April last year!) The trees have come alive, and you can just feel the sap rising to those red buds. The crows are back, and the chickadees are using their sweet little "fee-bee" call. This always SOUNDS like spring.

One recent Saturday our favorite hiking guide was around, and we purposely provoked an argument concerning the variety and size of "big" trees in town, hoping it would bring forth the response, "Want to see the largest ash tree in Rowe?" It did, and we were soon parked just above the lower truck escape on Monroe Hill and donning snowshoes for the pilgrimage.

We should have known from past experience that this guide has no mercy for the middle-aged. We headed straight up – on the run! The first encounter was with a steep brook gully – down one side, across the water and up the other bank. If we hadn't "cried uncle" by this time, we were judged fit for the rest of the mountain.

Big boulders loomed up ahead, and we wove in and around the most intriguing ones, surprised to find just how maneuverable our "bear paws" were between trees and up the ledges. The only problem was that our ski poles went through the soft snow and wouldn't hold on rock.

From up ahead, our guide called down, "If you can make it around Devil's Curve there, come on up and see the porcupine." We were hanging on for dear life, nearly uprooting a small hemlock, and by the time we reached the porcupine, he had disappeared into a hole in the snow. At this vantage point, we were allowed to catch our breath and while doing so, examined some odd formations of white quartz under an overhanging rock and observed several trough-like paths made by the porcupine. He had dropped several branches (for later consumption) from the top of a hemlock and gnawed the bark around the base of another tree. We hoped he didn't savor ash trees.

Next we climbed off to the left and out into a bowl-shaped area facing south with beech and birch trees and little underbrush. It was time to shed one layer of clothing, put hat and gloves in the knapsack, soak up the beautiful sunshine of late February and look up through the lacy treetops to the bright blue sky. We felt happy to be alive and fortunate to be out "on the Wild Side" this glorious winter day.

Approaching a small, rounded hilltop covered with spruce and hemlock, we found a congregating spot for deer. Many tracks and depressions in the snow showed where deer had bedded down – leaving imprints of their front legs as they had gotten up on their knees. In several places they had pawed the snow down to earth and green ferns. We followed one track right out to the brow of the hill, where a deer had stood – for no other obvious reason than to enjoy the view.

By this time our guide was far over the

other side of the hill and called directions to a "monster tree." This was not the object of our trip, but was certainly a monarch to be noted – a sentinel, tall and stately, on the north side overlooking Yankee Atomic, Sherman Pond and a view to Haystack in the distance. It was a hemlock with cinnamon-red bark – the circumference of the trunk measuring eleven feet, three inches at shoulder height. Inaccessible to loggers of the past, we hoped it would stand proudly guarding this hillside for generations to come.

Doubling back now, we climbed above the "bowl" to investigate a huge overhanging cliff. Here, we literally pulled ourselves up by trees to reach a shelf under the cliff. A large birch tree grew in front with its upper branches reaching over the top. Animal tracks of the cat nature, greatly enlarged by melting snow, crossed the shelf while a partially burned log lay rotted on the ground – seeming to indicate a lightning strike rather than a campfire. Ice poured out of a huge split in the cliff. Poking at some debris in a small hole in the rock, we found an "owl pellet" – a regurgitated ball of fur and bones – probably carried there by a chipmunk or mouse.

Getting up to the next level was no easy task. We hugged the cliff as the shelf got narrower and tracked across steep, slanting ground trying not to go down in an avalanche. Almost – Whoops – Hang On – Up Off Your Knees – We Made It!

Just then a roar from the south, and we were treated to an air show, courtesy of two A-10's doing acrobatics over our heads, climbing and diving around the mountain tops. When the show was over, we got back to the business at hand – approaching the largest ash tree in Rowe.

Two prominent boulders sitting on a knoll marked the outer boundary of Its territory. We were quiet and walked with reverence – after all, this ancient tree deserved our respect. You could feel the presence of Something – the air was electrified. Then the undisputed "Lord of the Wilderness" reluctantly showed Itself. An ash of giant proportions!

It was awesome, but not perfect – measuring fourteen feet, six inches as we stretched the tape around its girth at shoulder height. A "pasture ash," so called, splitting into seven branches high above our heads. Denied in youth the privilege of standing straight and tall, this tree had grown large and lived long, becoming the elder statesman of the forest. We ran our fingers over its diamond-shaped bark, reached for its limbs, peered into its crevices and finally sat and rested our backs against its trunk, feeling its strength and stature.

As we left this Giant's domain and followed the small brook down through the pretty little hemlocks of the Monroe State Forest land, we felt it had been both a privilege and an honor to have made the acquaintance of this ancient resident of Rowe.

P.S. Of course, if we have missed, in some far corner, an ash tree of greater stature, we stand corrected and wish to be informed!   **3/83**

Lemuel Truesdell's Cellar Hole

Until the wildflowers really begin to appear (coltsfoot is already blossoming near Ledge Lane on the way to Charlemont), we take off on a hike with much more gusto with a "search" in mind. This month we have been involved with stories about early settlers in Rowe for the Historical Society Bulletin. Lemuel Truesdell came to Rowe by ox cart from Buckland in 1822, settling in a house near Steele Brook Road on the old "Merrill Lot." A little research in the Registry gave the dimensions of this lot and a few later names, but no clues as to just when the house existed. If we could see the actual cellar hole, this Truesdell story would come to life, and the whole idea seemed a good excuse to explore new territory. Were we looking for a few rocks or a real cellar hole? We did not know, but, somewhere within the bounds of this seventy-acre lot, families had lived in a house and carried on a farm. The search was on.

We parked by the old Bent/Veber place on Steele Brook Road and walked a short distance down to a corner of two walls on the east side of the road. This was the lot in question, but immediately did not look like a house site – a few old apple trees, many rocks and a small brook with a swampy area on both sides – a woodlot maybe, but certainly not the place for a house.

A thin sheet of ice had formed on all the quieter pools of the small brook, and we stopped to admire the lovely crystal patterns. The whole wet, muddy area seemed to have risen up with ice formations that crunched back down as we walked. The shadier spots had snow, but as we climbed the hillside across the brook, the sun had melted many patches of bare ground and each rock and

depression became a possible cellar hole! Reaching the top of the hill, we had our site picked out – a pretty level area with small tree growth showing that this had been open field within the last thirty years. It would have had a beautiful view down the valley. The cellar hole must be here. The snow cover was heavy, but being crusty, you could walk on top. We looked over large rocks, stone walls and followed deer tracks on up the slight incline, wondering just how far this "high meadow" extended but we found no cellar hole.

A large boulder in the wall drew us down the hillside, and an appointment at home finally took us back to the car, scaring up a partridge on the way. It always amazes us how fast they can fly off through the dense woods without hitting anything.

It was disappointing to end the search without success, and we took a minute to walk over to see if the ice was thundering on Bent's lonely little fire pond.

Appointment met, frustration and curiosity set in. Where was that cellar hole? We checked the geodetic map, the lot description, and finally the History of Rowe. Percy Brown had said, "There is one cellar hole upon the heights some fifty rods to the southwest of this old road which marks the site of the Carpenter Bliss homestead." The old road, in this case, swung left from Tunnel Road just past the power lines and came out at the big bend on Steele Brook Road some distance below the Bent/Veber place. Off and running once again.

We parked on the level area by the turn of Tunnel Road on the hill going up to the junction of Steele Brook Road. If we followed the edge of the ridge from here, we'd surely find the cellar hole.

The snow cover was again deep but walkable. We followed several strange sets of tracks but came to no conclusions except that deer had also passed through. Melting snows distort tracks, and we vowed to take more hikes after new fallen snow – such occasions not too plentiful this year. Snow might now be distorting cellar hole sites, too.

We soon came to a stone wall which seemed to have some magic pull, other than our love of rocks, drawing us to follow it downhill in spite of Percy Brown's phrase in our mind, "upon the heights." Down and around we followed, coming to a corner where the remains of a huge old maple tree had stones piled over its roots – a long ago property boundary.

Walking along this wall, we began to feel as if we had come upon an ancient graveyard where the old ones stood like statues – gnarled, rugged, weather-beaten – having endured for generations whatever nature had to offer, and finally dropping limb by giant limb to be mossed into the ground beneath. These old maples had been here longer than the town and before the first settlers. Touching them meant reaching back in time – a stone endures, but a tree is a living thing.

Feeling far from the modern world as we walked around one of these treasures, it came as rather a shock to find there beside this tree a wad of aluminum foil. Some city hunter had eaten his lunch here with no appreciation for this wilderness or sensitivity for the backrest he was using. We knew this, for otherwise he surely would have carried home his sandwich wrapper. We continued on and found that his friend had been sitting by the next tree.

By now, quite a hillside was between us and the "heights" to the west. Steele Brook valley was deepening to the east. As the stone wall turned down again we went through an opening or gateway into an area forming an increasingly wider shelf on the hillside – a rather pleasant level area. We investigated a square pile of rocks but by no stretch of the imagination could it have been a cellar hole. Beginning to be convinced we were way off-course, we started to look around for the most logical escape route without totally retracing our original path back to the car, by now a long way behind us. We contemplated being lost, but ruled that out – we could always drop down to Steele Brook and follow it out to Mike Cascone's. He had been good enough to transport us back to our car when we emerged at the end of another off-course safari. While mulling this decision, we kept walking forward just a ways further.

The whole farm layout unfolded so naturally in front of us that we couldn't believe our eyes. The house was on the left at the edge of the hill, and the barn on the right with stonewalled barnyards leading back to the rather steep sidehill. There was a huge boulder behind the barn, and the largest yet of the remaining ancient maple trees sprawled over the outcropping of ledge.

"There on the heights" – not the top, but certainly high above the valley and road below. "We" got so excited, which in itself was frustrating, because this time, "we" were alone. We suddenly needed someone with whom to share the joy of this discovery.

We looked over the cellar hole first, climbing down inside and putting our arms around the two ash trees growing there. Our fingers just touched on one and not within a few inches on the other. Four good-sized birches were in another corner. This house had been gone at least a century. Looking around, we decided this homestead had been quite elegant for those early times, or its builder a fine stone mason by trade. Walls were built around three sides of the house site with what looked like steps down from the front door to a lower terrace. The lilacs were gone, if there ever had been any, but perhaps the summer would reveal some other bits of floral decoration. We wished the builder could know we were appreciating his talents so many years hence.

We toured the area once again finally sitting in the warm afternoon sun on the edge of the cellar hole. Putting ourselves back one hundred and sixty-one years, we watched Lemuel Truesdell come up the lane in his oxcart with his family and possessions, and we could just faintly hear his wife saying "Oh Lem, this is a beautiful spot," as the children ran off to see who could be first to climb up the big boulder by the barn. **4/83**

"Cabin fever" seems to have been the "in" thing this winter. Several recent magazines featured articles on how to avoid or rid yourself of said disease. With the exception of our usual "Novemberitis," we've always been able to breeze through the rest of the year without a trace of this malady. However, after two heavy snowstorms the third week of April and continuous rain before and since, we finally succumbed to a terrible case of cabin fever.

One day we found ourselves, almost delirious, over on Tunnel Road in back of the old Ethier/Peck place madly pawing at the snow trying to uncover any evidence of those first little spring beauties which should have been up and dressed in pink and white long before this. We found them, budded and matted flat under the heavy snow. Even hepaticas had been budded, but the weight and iciness of the late snow had bent their heads over, and they would blossom facing the earth beneath instead of showing their cheery little faces to the sky. Spring was doomed this year! After some further restless wanderings, we went back to the car, discouraged, and headed home, our cabin fever worsening.

Almost at the foot of the hill just above the Switching Station Road, we focused on a small brook rushing down the mountainside on our left. This evidently pretty well dries up in the summer for we hadn't noticed it before. From the road, we judged it must pour out of a spring as the hill was steep and the top almost in sight. Parking the car on the roadside, we headed up for a quick look. The ground was bare, and we were very soon rewarded with the sight of tiny new violet leaves and furled spikes of trillium about six inches high. Our spirits lifted and our cabin fever subsided.

It was a friendly little stream tumbling down through moss covered rocks and tree roots and around boulders on its way to join Steele Brook down in the valley to the east. On up the hill, which proved to be a landing and not the top, the main brook came from off to the left while a small tributary cascaded down from the next ridge, where a small swamp seemed to be its source.

We were now in snow and looking back at our tracks going from rock to tree to wall. We wondered what impression we might give to someone trying to follow in our footsteps. This thought occurred at this moment because we could hear voices – but just who else would be out in this wilderness? We walked a ways toward the sound and stopped to listen, a series of loud weird calls from the lower swamp which fed our brook. We ran down the bank and followed the brook up to the level swampy area, the sound growing louder and louder. WOOD FROGS, not peepers, were issuing their mating calls from various choice locations. We stepped from tuft of grass to fallen limb and once in a while lost our footing into the soft sphagnum moss as the water poured over our boot tops. Try as we might, it was impossible to spot those little creatures, only two or three inches long, who were creating such a racket. We listened for several minutes, marveling at nature's unique "carryings-on."

Skirting the wide swampy area, the hillside ahead seemed more open and spotted with large rocks. A stone wall to the west drew our attention and following it down a ways, we came upon an old foundation near a large boulder with an iron pin in the side. Odd pieces of old machinery were scattered about, well rusted with years of exposure to the elements. This must have been the remains of Merritt Peck's sawmill, circa early 1900. We walked around and tried to visualize the operation with logs and lumber piled high, sawdust flying, and the buzz of the saw as Merritt guided a spruce log down the track. How important these old sawmills were to the early farmers who harvested their own trees, sawed their own lumber and built their own houses and barns – and here on the Peck farm – cabins for summer boarders.

Taking stock of our situation, we decided to head west for the Bear Swamp Road above the Switching Station. As was our custom, we poked our nose into any and all rock or downed tree formations that might be bear dens, but no such luck. Porcupines seemed to be plentiful for many trees had been gnawed around the base and hemlock branches were strewn around. Every intriguing den seemed to be thick with porcupine droppings.

The road we expected to be "just over the knoll" proved nowhere in sight. We checked the sun and continued heading west through another swamp to see an old maple tree. True to form, someone had been here before us and built a platform across a limb with ladder steps nailed on the tree trunk. We climbed up to have a look at this hunter's station still filled with snow. It overlooked a likely deer trail and bedding down place under the evergreens, but alas there were no deer in sight for our eyes.

By this time, we were really trudging in the snow, and as the road appeared through the trees, we breathed a sigh of relief that it would be all smooth downhill back to the

Small yellow violets

car. We stamped the snow off our, by now, very wet boots and decided it was too much trouble even to go the short distance uphill to overlook the Upper Reservoir.

We had sort of forgotten what had prompted us to have arrived in this location in the first place. It had something to do with spring fever – or was it cabin fever? Whichever, we were tired, and we'd seen no blossoms. Looking ahead of us, high up on the ridge were the microwave towers. We wished we were younger with the energy to climb up there and see the world, but in our present condition it was totally out of the question. We even gave ourselves a small argument on not leaving anything unclimbed, but all muscles said no, and we resigned ourselves to advanced age and our present affliction, which had once again gained control.

Another small brook was making a pleasant sound coming down the ravine to the left, and we stopped to see where it went through a culvert under the road. Looking up toward the woods ahead, large rocks seemed to hang down from the top, forming a sort of cave. Quickly, we left the road and pushed through the first brushy section into a more open area with big trees.

The snow had melted on this eastern facing slope, and it was covered with generations of dead leaves. Suddenly stems of dainty new green leaves appeared at our feet, and we were on our knees identifying them as Dutchman's breeches and squirrel corn. Up a little further, we ran to see Virginia waterleaf just out of the ground and, beyond by a big maple, the bright red spots in the leaves were new scarlet cup mushrooms, harbingers of spring for sure. The hill was steep, but it took no effort to climb once we spotted the strange blue cohosh high above us. Then holding on with our toes, we reached up between the ledges to unfurl the leaves of a tiny new wild ginger plant. How could the world suddenly have so much to offer in so small an area!? It WAS SPRING and everything was coming up after all. As we pulled ourselves up the last few feet, there before our eyes were the first real blossoms, several tiny yellow violets hardly an inch high were more glorious to us on this day than a dozen red roses with long stems!

As we sat on the highest ledge by the microwave towers, happily enjoying our reward of having seen flowers and being on top of the world in the spring sunshine, feeling the refreshing breezes blowing up from the Deerfield River far below, and looking out on Adams and Negus, and Steele Brook Valley, and all our beloved hills of home, we glanced back down on the road and could hardly remember the poor tired woman with cabin fever we had left behind, the one who couldn't possibly climb the highest mountain.   **5/83**

Looking down on the Deerfield River from Switching Station Hill

The Joy of Discovering Swamp Life

A swamp is just a swamp or so we thought before this morning. We had been told about the "Day Swamp" off Cyrus Stage Road several weeks ago, and it had been intriguingly in the back of our mind ever since. "Don't go there alone," we were advised. "It's easy to get lost back there, and years ago the area was said to contain quicksand in which horses and cattle were lost." But it was such an unexpectedly beautiful morning, frighteningly near the *Goal Post* deadline, and our curiosity, of course, had gotten the best of us.

The sun had not long been over the horizon when we started off through the grass, our footsteps leaving a path in the heavy morning dew. Once into the woods, morning birdsongs greeted us from all directions, an ovenbird saying, "teacher, teacher, teacher," an eastern wood pewee calling, "pee-a-wee," and then a white throated sparrow chiming in, "we praise thee O Lord" – appropriate, we thought – this was Sunday morning.

Looking down, we found ourselves walking on a carpet of tiny white violets, and in the woods on either side were clumps of goldthread blossoms standing above their flat shiny clover-like leaves. We resisted the urge to poke our fingers in the earth to find their tiny golden roots.

The path was on an incline headed down and patches of wet moss were becoming more frequent. We veered off the path to the left to see where something had been digging, then on further to enjoy a lovely clump of painted trillium, typical of this obviously acid soil. Just ahead through the trees was the first little swamp, a primeval looking spot with old moss covered dead trees, some horizontal across a beautiful bed of bright green sphagnum moss. We stood there quietly taking in the scene and listening to the sound of an early morning frog while checking all corners for any new flowers.

All of a sudden, from somewhere in the distance ahead of us, came such a loud honking and squawking and beating of wings that we were sure we'd found the secret summer haven of hundreds of Canada geese. We sailed across that little swamp on a mossy log, swinging from tree to tree and finally ducking under a mass of fallen branches to crawl up the next bank. From that vantage point, we could see a huge complex of grassy swamp in the foreground and a beaver pond full of dead gray trees in the background. There were still too many trees to see the geese, but their racket continued.

Down the bank we slid, only to find that this grassy swamp looked too deep to cross and too big to go around, but we were too anxious to see what was going on to be fussy. Frustrated, we quickly decided to get our footing from one clump of grass to the next, all the while thinking about possible quicksand and quagmire! The louder the geese squawked, the less judgment we used. After going in circles a couple of times, trying to find footing, we walked right straight across foot-deep grass, water and mud! Once on the other side, we crawled through another big old fallen tree and up onto the center strip of higher land tightly forested with small balsam trees and bordering the greater part of the beaver pond.

Standing close to the water's edge, we balanced ourselves against a dead tree and just looked and listened. "Save our wetlands for wildlife" had never been so real to us before. The next half hour was one of the most joyous "Wild Side" occasions we have ever spent.

The sun was shining just over the top of the tall evergreens on our right, a slight breeze was blowing across the pond from the northeast, and there were the geese, not a hundred, just two pair, honking, flapping, talking, preening, playing and just generally being happy to be alive. They swam around the dead trees fairly close to where we were standing and finally quieted down to contented low conversation among themselves.

It seemed as if every known bird was singing from some favorite corner of the swamp as we stood there entranced. As if right on cue, a great blue heron with his beautiful wide wingspan flew into view from the far corner, coming gracefully to light on top of a dead tree in the center. This was the Wild Side in all its stark glory, far from human disturbance.

A large hawk rose from his perch high in the evergreens, circled the pond and flew off toward the sunrise, the morning sun spotlighting him in his flight. The dew was still glistening on the greenery along the shore, and a catbird, oblivious to our presence, lit close by on a limb and sang his special mimicking song. Two king birds were darting back and forth catching the first insects of the day while a swallow flew past with a mouthful of grass, headed for a nesting place in one of the dead trees. Every so often, the old gander revved up his voice like a siren and the wing beating ritual began again.

At first we wished we had brought a camera or field glasses or at least a paper and pen to record the variety of this scene, but then we were glad to be free and empty-handed, having only to absorb in memory the pleasure of this experience. After a long while, we moved on down this rise of land to see if we could get to the backside of the pond. The underbrush was so thick, we literally crawled on our hands and knees for some distance until the smaller trees thinned out.

To our left, another pond opened up to view on the east side of the high ground. The morning sun was now focused on the open, sloping bank, sparkling on the drops of dew that accentuated an unbelievably beautiful carpet of red and green. Hundreds of checkerberry plants, each holding five or six large berries, covered the slope. We picked a handful of the wintergreen-tasting fruit and knew we would not starve if we became marooned on this faraway island. We looked closer at the last berry in our hand and marveled at the perfect five-pointed star impression on the bottom. A rose-breasted grosbeak took this time to fly past us, light on a dead tree in the water and burst into song.

Certainly beavers had been here in years past but were not now in evidence, although when we reached the end of the land, a beaver dam still in good shape kept the level of water in the upper pond on our left higher than the lower one to the right. A small waterfall fell through the sticks in the center with a happy sound. We tested the ground and decided we'd try a flying leap across this dam rather than return through the underbrush on our hands and knees. Quicksand, perhaps, underwater on either side of this dam? Fortunately, we didn't prove that theory one way or another. The water was flowing northeastward toward Heath and must make its way to the Deerfield via West Branch Brook and Colrain.

The northwest bank and hillside became a totally different world of bright sunny beech and maple woods. One huge tree sat in the swampy area just across from the dam. Its very heavy, shaggy bark covered a straight trunk up to the spreading branches on the forest ceiling, too high for us to identify the leaves. Whatever its species, it had sprouted in this swamp long before Rowe was settled. Following a beaver trail up the first bank, we found all the early spring plants which indicate good rich soil. Always hoping to discover a new variety, we continued on up this hill rather than circling the pond as we had intended.

Thinking of Robert Frost's poem about the path not taken, we wondered what hand guides us this way or that, enabling us to come upon some treasure of rock, flower or citizen of the Wild Side.

We wandered from this to that, listening to a least flycatcher who says "che-bek" and reminds us of a geometry exam on a beautiful May day long ago when such a bird sang constantly outside an open window in our exam room. Angles and theorems have been forgotten but never that little "che-bek." A vireo was singing as we came across an old wood road to follow, then we turned off through the woods to examine the large boulders and outcroppings of ledge now becoming more numerous.

Walking over a small knoll, listening to all the kinds of warblers singing, we were certainly surprised to find in front of us a large fireplace with chimney. Although never having seen this before, we knew at once it was the so called "Indian Chimney," about which there are several legends and no facts except that its existence has been known back many generations. Located in a strange place on a ledge, under a hill, and among rocks where no house would have been built,

Indian Chimney

Rowe Historical Society

its use and date are a mystery and certainly not typical of Indian custom. Perhaps a similar structure in some neighboring area will someday give us a clue. We had been promised a guided trip to see this early relic and had been looking forward to it, but perhaps there is more of a thrill coming upon something unexpectedly, like exploring an ancient city by yourself instead of being shown the sights on the motor coach tour.

We spent time investigating the surrounding area and taking stock of our bearings. Leshure Road, like Middletown Hill, runs north and south but somehow in our thinking, east has always been where west should be in north Rowe.

Knowing the approximate location of the chimney, we had to draw a little map in the leaves to convince ourselves that we needed to go north to the power line and then toward the sun to get back to our car on Cyrus Stage Road!

Out on the power line, the walking was relatively easy, the sunshine warm and a field sparrow entertained us with song. It had been a glorious morning, and we were anxious to return and share our joys of the Wild Side.   **6/83**

A Rare Day in June

"Oh what is so rare as a day in June?" To fully experience this feeling, we came up here to the old Ethier/Peck house site on Old Tunnel Road. It's near noon on a bright sunny day. The sky is blue - a rather hazy blue because it is hot and humid - not real Rowe weather. Here on the grass facing north, there is a slight breeze and puffy little white clouds are just above the horizon. In the woods close by, a hermit thrush is singing, such beautiful clear notes, perfect every time, no discords, no mistakes. After a while the thrush fades into the distance and a chestnut-sided warbler takes over with "Little Miss Richee," sounding coarser and more monotonous, but he's obviously happy. A woodpecker is drumming, and there are other warblers which we still do not know by song.

June is the time of year when our fields of flowers rival in color our autumn hills. Daisies, buttercups, clover, red and yellow paintbrush (hawkweed), yellow cinquefoil, white yarrow, dainty white madder cover the fields and in the marshy spots, blue flag and ragged robin. Here on the hill behind us, a purple-flowering raspberry, looking like a lovely wild rose, marks this old house site.

Now a towhee down in the field is saying, "Drink your tea, drink your tea", and we wish we had brought our lunch and planned to spend the whole day in this one spot.

Every so often it is totally quiet, and we can hear the bees in the flowers and once in a while a big old bumblebee zings past our face. We think for a moment how important he or she is in pollinating some of the "hard to get at" flowers like the lady's-slippers. Lying back on the ground with a piece of hay (you can't say grass anymore) in our mouth, we contemplate the little white clouds which are becoming more numerous. Isn't this what you dream of when the snow is blowing in your face in January?

* * * * *

Our thoughts drifted back to early this morning when the sun was first streaming in our east window and seemed to be calling us for a hike - one like the Park Trail up Todd Mountain. As we drove past the Lake, the morning mist was rising, and we thought of stopping for a while, but for some reason we had Todd Mountain on our mind. We could always see the lake.

Peck Field circa 1900

30

Well, we had to stop anyway. Two large snapping turtles were out to lay eggs in the sand beside the road. One poor lady was trying to dig a hole in the grass, and it looked like a long process. The other seemed to be having better luck in some soft sand almost on the road and had gotten right down to business. But the chance of survival of little ones in this location was pretty slim. If cars didn't run over them, the skunks would certainly have a feast on the eggs. If they do survive the first few weeks, these turtles live a long, long time and grow quite large. Each year at this time, they come out and lay up to forty eggs somewhere in sand or dirt and cover them, but then never go near them again. If and when the young hatch out, they are totally on their own. The turtles around Mill Pond have a little better chance in the big sand pile by the town garage. Although we feared for their survival once traffic started, we decided to leave these two turtles alone. After all, we wouldn't want to be bothered at a time like this.

Starting our hike at the Base Trail from the Mine Road, we immediately heard several unusual birds of the same species singing back and forth, and, of course, had to go chasing off into the brush with the glasses trying to identify them. The mosquitoes were fierce or starved and attacked us in swarms. We always wait with the "bug juice" until absolutely necessary, and the time had come! The bird must have been a ventriloquist for even though it kept singing, we couldn't spot it. Expecting to stay on the trail, we had come out in clean white sneakers, but soon, jumping off a rock while looking up, we landed one foot ankle deep in mud – so much for white shoes. It did make

us look down and see all the pretty wood-sorrel blossoming under the ferns. These little white flowers, some needing more sun to open up for the day, always look like a man's old-fashioned pink striped shirt and seem to call for a bow tie. Finally, our elusive little bird flew through the trees and landed on the wall where we could get a good look as it gave another rendition of its high, clear sweet song. It was a tiny winter wren with a perky little tail straight up. We remembered having watched one on the ground, probably near a nest, issuing its loud call note and running around like a mouse.

* * * * *

Back here in the grass at our hilltop site, we are aware of a small noise and moved only our eyes to see what is coming out of the woods. It's a partridge making a funny little clucking sounds and picking here and there at the ground, coming quite close, completely oblivious that there is an intruder in its feeding ground. We hope the clucking is for young ones but none appear, and the bird makes its way across the hill and into the woods. A pretty yellow swallowtail butterfly seems to be following the partridge and finally finds a flower to light upon.

* * * * *

This morning, after identifying the bird, we came around the old Todd house cellar hole. Someone had dug for bottles in the old dump and left the broken pieces of china and glass. We picked up a piece of a plate, sort of off-white with a blue edge. What do you suppose the table looked like when this plate was last used? What members of what family were there and what had their life been like that day? Was it a beautiful June day like today? There was part of a pretty little glass sauce dish – perhaps that meal had been homemade bread and applesauce.

It is difficult for us to stay on the trail – something more intriguing always distracts us, and we go bushwhacking off to the side as we did this morning climbing Todd. Reaching the top was both nostalgic and disappointing. Nostalgic because Todd was the first "real mountain" we had climbed as a kid. A friend had decided it was time we learned to hike and at that age we remember doing our best to "keep up" with him and from then on we have always looked at that mountain with a sense of accomplishment and respect. We were now disappointed because the nice open flat ledges with grass and apple trees had finally all grown up. After all, it had been a good many years since that first ascent! The ledges were still there and would always create an opening to the sky, but the rest was brush. We began to get a sense of claustrophobia.

We started down the trail to the lake, but remembering that our first trip so long ago was down the back side and home via Davis Mine Road, we went looking for the huge open cliffs we remembered telling everyone about. We soon came to the conclusion that what might have so excited us as a child might not be as impressive to us today – at least we didn't find anything on that scale. The back of Todd is steep, and we held onto trees and finally just sat and slid down the rock. Coming into a basin area, there was a large outcropping of rock which formed a high wall on one side. We went over and got acquainted, putting our hand against it, feeling its strength and coolness. Large trees were trying to grow on the tiny bit of soil on top and some had succeeded in splitting the rock as they grew – such force in a living organism. Pink lady's slippers were scattered in our path as we went on.

Eventually we came upon an old wood road which we knew would lead us somewhere. It soon went past an old cellar hole, one more for our collection. This one puzzled us for it didn't match any locations we could remember on the old maps. This had been a good-sized house, but there was nothing especially unique about it or the surroundings. It had been someone's family home, and the wood road must have been the old 1792 road to Charlemont. We looked forward to some research that might produce a story and scene we could visualize. Out on the Davis Mine Road, it was easy walking back in the hot morning sun.

* * * * *

Up in the sky here on Ethier/Peck Hill, the little white clouds are now casting shadows on Whitcomb Mountain and those hills to the north where the power line crosses. A dull increasing sound in the distance behind us is soon identified by a train whistle as a freight lumbers up the Deerfield Valley. When the noon siren from the village interrupts our reverie, we head home.

* * * * *

Still thinking about greater heights and wide open spaces, we seemed to need that trip to "Old Smokey" after the claustrophobic feeling on Todd. The *Goal Post* and lesser things could wait a little longer. We headed down Steel Brook Road. In spite of liking to hike, we thought it necessary to drive the car up through the field to the traditional parking spot at the foot of the trail. The field was no longer, and the bushes scratched against the car as we carefully drove up the old grassy road. Even the parking area was hardly discernable, and we missed our usual visit with the Bents telling them we were going berrying on their hill. The trail looked the same up across the ledges but showed evidence of recent heavy rains. How many times we'd climbed this trail with blueberry pails clinking, anticipating the sweet juicy fruit, and the thrill of the spectacular mountaintop scenery. Nothing would ever change "Old Smokey!" Of course, lack of fires in recent years has diminished the blueberry crop, but the view would always be the same!

Or would it? We nearly ran up the last grade. Familiar rocks appeared and we threw down the knapsack ready to sit – but we couldn't sit, we had to stand on tiptoes to see the view over the trees. First Todd and now Old Smokey – didn't Rowe have any open mountaintops left? We stewed awhile then climbed another hundred feet.

Always give life a second chance, climb a little higher, rewards are just around the corner! It would take another glacier to rearrange this beautiful Deerfield Valley canyon on Rowe's western edge and wear away the mountains of Savoy and Greylock, and the Green Mountains to the north, all visible from this spot. A place to renew the spirit and soar with the birds and become part of the Wild Side of this great corner of the earth we call home.

We sat for a long time on this mountaintop in the midst of lovely pink and white laurel, looking at the hills and valleys and the river, at the expanse of the sky and the clouds and wondered how Heaven could be any more beautiful.   **7/83**

Mountain laurel on Negus

Chuck Blackler Photo

Great Blue Heron's Nest Discovered

Little did we suspect back in May when we wrote about the great blue heron coming gracefully to light on top of a dead tree in the center of the Day Swamp that we would come to know this particular bird so well. Recently, returning to the same vantage point on the east side of the swamp, we realized that the nest in that dead tree was not clearly visible from where we had been and that in spite of our observation of much activity that day, we had missed the most dramatic event – the nesting of a pair of great blue herons.

After finding an easier entrance path, this swamp drew us back many times – always revealing something new and exciting on the Wild Side. Several more blue herons and the smaller green heron soon appeared. There were huge bull frogs, black ducks, many swallows, and then one day, when mother heron flew out of that cluster of sticks about twenty feet above the water in the dead tree, we suddenly realized that she was nesting.

We saw the young ones about the first of July and have literally spent hours and hours quietly watching from the wooded hillside nearby. We looked for bird books giving nesting habits and feeding schedules of blue herons but could find no details. We had to discover for ourselves.

Our first observation of the feeding took place about an hour after our arrival. A parent (mother or father as both parents feed) flew in squawking over the trees and came to light on the top of the dead tree and carefully stepped down the branches to the nest. It held its head up and then put it down where the chicks grabbed on to its beak. This process was repeated several times. The bird was obviously regurgitating partially digested food into their mouths. It stayed perhaps ten minutes – finally climbing back up the tree, standing for a while, then flying off over the trees again.

There must have been at least five eggs. Three fluffy babies, looking like herons, could cuddle in the nest and hardly be seen. Another was dead and laying partially over the back of the nest. Still another was alive but very weak, and the others would pick at it when the parent arrived – poignant moments – it seemed as if they were trying to tell it to get up and take food. The parent did nothing (while we were watching) to remove the dead one or to prod the one still alive - the job seemed only to feed those who could grab for it. On the next visit, one scrawny dried up dead one was hanging upside down outside the nest, and the other was gone. It seems cruel to even mention this, but it showed survival of the fittest – one of the first rules in the wild.

In these early visits to the swamp, the young herons were settled and quiet most of the time, but would then get up and walk around the edges, preen their fluff and carefully woops over the edge never seeming to foul the nest. When the parent arrived, they got excited and made little squawking noises, but often just talked among themselves when all were awake and walking around.

One day we went into the swamp about 9 a.m. watching a heron fly off as we approached. Walking through a bit of underbrush, we settled ourselves in a more or less concealed location on the hillside, and sat with the binoculars, watching the nest and the whole area. It was warm

The Swamp

and comfortable and most relaxing. The anticipation of the parent's arrival kept us alert. What a wonderful place to be – so near and yet so very far from the mad, busy world. The swallows were rushing to catch bugs for their hungry young, who were now large enough to be peering out of various holes in the dead trees. The blackbirds were there, too, and the grackles. A few cedar waxwings had arrived with their pleasant soft calls and seemed to be feeding on bugs also.

The water now was mostly covered with the lily pads of water-shield and their little red flowers standing above the surface. Tiny yellow snapdragon-like flowers were scattered over the water standing up from their inflated long pouches like the rays of a star floating on the water. These are swollen bladderworts – too pretty and dainty to be known by such a name. Papa bullfrog ground out his call from the western edge and was soon answered by another across the swamp. Then the smaller frog varieties with their heads and bugging-out eyes above the water croaked in unison from every section. The chorus lasted a few minutes, and then all was quiet again except for an occasional frog bark.

The sun grew warmer and the bees buzzed in and around the tiny flowers of the bristly sarsaparilla which seemed to be in clusters all around us. Along the shore, the swamp candles or yellow loosestrife were at their height, so pretty among the ferns. On the edge of the old beaver dam the wild calla lily had grown large and started forming fruit. Low dewberries were blossomed white most everywhere. The old gravelbank floor was covered with little red sundew leaves and a few low blueberries were turning purple. The partridgeberry in small patches along the hillside was blossomed with its little twin flowers and very fragrant.

But where was the parent heron? We had been there three and a half hours, and she had not returned. We were greatly concerned although we had seen her fly out as we arrived. Do herons normally leave their babies this long? The chicks seemed content, but it was comical to watch them all look up and follow the flight of a small airplane. Regretfully, we had to leave before we knew the answers.

Not much else mattered that day – our mind was on the herons and possible solutions to "what if." The babies did seem pretty safe from predators and were totally ignored by the resident hawk. But the parents in their search for food elsewhere were vulnerable.

Evening. Surely parent herons come back to the nest to roost. The only way we would know this for sure was to be there. We sat on the log in the more open area watching and listening. The babies were fine - not squawking for food as we expected. We began to look at other things.

The sun was making a bright reflection

across the water as it slowly sank behind the trees. Ducks swam within sight, picking at bits of green in the water then noiselessly moved on around the dead trees and lily pads. Through the binoculars, a strange shape appeared in focus in the water – a small head, two eyes and a nose formed a circle with its own reflection – not a ripple to mark its presence. It came fairly close, then disappeared underwater without a trace. A beaver. No wonder the dams were holding so well. We had seen no evidence of this fellow earlier in the spring. Perhaps he had just claimed this pond as a new home. Whatever the reason, we were happy to see him.

It became quite dusky and still no parent herons. Our fears were mounting, but the babies stretched, slept, walked and gave no evidence of worry. The frogs kept up a continual barking, croaking chorus and suddenly the beaver flopped down into the lower pond with an enormous splash. The clouds became gold, pink and finally grey. Venus appeared in the western fading glow and Jupiter rose high over our heads to the south.

Our herons must be roosting elsewhere for they should have come back by now – they do not feed at night. Or do they? Leave the babies alone? This doesn't seem logical, but we are here and they are not. We wonder many things as we slowly pick our way out by flashlight. We wish we had all the answers, but that would probably lessen the joy of discovering the Wild Side for ourselves.

The next morning, we were back in the

Heron nests at The Swamp

swamp quite early, giving the whole swamp a quick sweep with our eyes before focusing the binoculars on the nest fully expecting to see three dead chicks. They were cuddled down in the nest, and we strained our eyes for any sign of life while waving one arm to swat the deer fly buzzing around our head. While all this was happening, something large nearby on our right pulled large feet out of the mud with a loud suction sound and went crashing off into the woods. Squinting through the glasses and worried about the birds, it took a few seconds to change focus and thoughts. We were not fast enough to see the intruder. Knowing we had scanned the area and seen nothing as light as deer and remembering the sound in the mud, it had to have been a black bear catching frogs!

If we'd only seen him! How could we have missed this sight? Someday we would see a bear other than the small one that ran across the road several years ago.

We didn't have long to wait. Just a few nights later out on Cyrus Stage Road, there was Father Bruin looking noble and sleek and beautiful in the late afternoon sun, standing on all fours in the middle of the road, stopping us dead in our tracks. He was lord of that area and we would pass at his convenience. What a wonderful sight! It made our day. There is nothing quite like seeing for yourself and knowing for sure that this great animal lives among us.

We had not been in that swamp long that morning when the familiar honking and squawking sounded over the trees and there was the heron bringing food as usual, completely oblivious to all the worry she had

Young herons

caused us. Another adult showed up that day standing for a long time in the very top of a pine.

On our last visit, the heron family was doing fine. Parents may have trouble surviving the attacks of the hungry children. The little ones are almost full grown, feathered out, standing tall, flapping their wings and with a vengeance grabbing the parent's beak and neck to get the food when they arrive, making up for lost time, perhaps! Their voices are louder, and they are generally more active pacing the nest in circles. There is still no evidence of the younger generation taking to the air. That season is yet to come.

The swamp has changed with the seasons. The swallows have gone, but the waxwings are still there. The bluejays make a racket and chase the hawk. The beaver does a good bit of splashing and has matted down the grass in paths all around the pond. The woodland orchids have come up and blossomed, the blueberries are ripe, the calla lily fruit is pinky, the checkerberry is blossomed with six or seven flowers on one stem, the corn lily has large blue berries, the bunchberry has beautiful red clusters of berries and along the path, the narrow-leaved blue gentian is in bloom. A whistling, snorting deer has claimed the area and objects loudly to our intrusion.

Our herons were picking out their nest when the trillium and goldthread covered the ground; their young were hatched when the swamp candles first budded; and the family all left the nest when... Only another passing of a season will finish our story. And next year when the trillium is in blossom... **8/83**

"Looks like quite a canyon up the top end of Cold River. Good possibility of getting completely lost. Want to go?"

"How soon?"

"Now."

"Want to take sandwiches?"

"Five minutes!"

So it goes when our favorite guide is willing to include us in some new adventure. It never pays to say "no" or "wait" – we might not get another invitation. We're not timid, but we just might not venture four and a half miles up a lonely valley in the wilds of Savoy and Florida by ourselves.

This was a two car trip. One car was left at a bridge on South County Road in Florida where Cold River first leaves civilization for its long winding course down through the wilderness, finally coming close to the Mohawk Trail under "Dead Man's Curve" where we started our trek.

As we parked the second car, we could look up on the mountainside and see some of the towering hemlocks known to be near four hundred years old. Another day, we had climbed to locate these trees and found that two of us could not touch hands with our arms outstretched around them. The University of Massachusetts Forestry Department has examined this ancient stand and taken test borings to determine their age. Judging from the similar size, the sentinel hemlock on the mountain above Yankee must be close to the same vintage. Four hundred years ago – that's 1583! How much of the world has come and gone since then – yet something here in our midst is still alive and growing.

Today we climbed down the steep bank to the small brook which shortly flowed into the Cold River where it widens out of the ravine in the mountains. Looking at the map earlier, we judged our total climb to be roughly five hundred feet in elevation and four and a half miles back to the bridge. As always, anticipation and curiosity overcome many obstacles and soothe sore muscles that, if given any attention, could suddenly require our being carried home.

Anticipation was high as we started up the course and rounded the first bend along the sandy shore, coming to a secluded swimming area that had obviously been enjoyed by the public for many years. This section of the river is within the bounds of Mohawk Trail State Forest. Further upstream it forms the boundary with Savoy State Forest and at top flows out of Florida State Forest. We soon became very appreciative of our State Forest System and the knowledge that this wilderness had been and would be preserved.

This lower section of the river in its winding rocky course deep in the narrow ravine is spectacular. This was a beautiful, hot but very windy day and as the river turned, the air was either dead calm or wild with the valley funneling the wind down its course, whipping the trees and rippling the pools of water. Around other bends, as the mountains rose in height, the roar of the wind could be heard across their very tops high above us. And as the river wound its way through the mountains, the sun seemed to play tricks – first casting our shadows behind us, then to the side and sometimes ahead.

The riverbed was very rocky – a few large boulders but mostly smaller ones – and the easiest method of travel was from rock to rock, weaving from shore to shore, depending on the availability of the next foothold. Some were too close for normal stride, like the ties on a railroad track, and others were spaced farther apart, requiring some momentum and a well-aimed jump. It was hard to look ahead when you had to look down at your footing. At times we found ourselves surrounded by a wide pool and had to run around and retrace our leaps and pick another route. We tended to hold our breath negotiating some of these maneuvers and sometimes had to stop and enjoy the surrounding view while we breathed again – but not for long.

Often an outcropping of ledge would form a wall along the water's edge and create a long narrow pool – dark and cool with overhanging trees. We had a great urge to take a dip but remembering another long walk in wet dungarees after falling in an old beaver channel, we decided to stay dry.

Flowers? Yes, they were speeding by – Joe-Pye-weed, asters, goldenrod, jewelweed, ferns of all kinds – but as we had suspected from the start, this was not to be a flower finding trip unless we stumbled on something really special and yelled STOP or UNCLE to slow down the parade.

Our first discovery was of the man-made variety. As we came to the first confluence – Gulf Brook flowing in from the left – we spotted a trail and bridge. But what strange construction it was – a normal approach on one shore but coming to an abrupt stop high off the ground on the other side – all well secured with cables. We sat (thank goodness) for a time to contemplate this relic and study the maps as to our whereabouts. We certainly must be pretty nearly back to the first car. It had been a great hike – wild beautiful country – and we could have lunch in the grassy field by the bridge.

Wait a minute! Even our trusty guide pretended surprise as we looked at the map, although we suspect he knew all along. Behind us it was about a mile back to our starting point – ahead to the car, three and a half more! Already strange muscles were sore from rock hopping on the balls of our feet and our shoulders ached from waving our arms for balance. But turn back – never!

We could make no sense out of the suspended bridge although someone had spent a lot of effort constructing it. As we started on, another platform appeared with a cable across the river. On the other side was what seemed to be a snowmobile cable car, rather a clever contraption for winter crossing. The first bridge could have been the original landing and now it had been moved upstream.

The river above here was cluttered with bigger rocks and seemed to split around an island. We walked up the center of this island and welcomed the relief of stepping on solid ground for a few minutes. And now what's ahead? A log cabin in this wilderness! It was a spooky sort of place, even reminded us of the movie "Deliverance," giving the impression of a hermit having "holed up" for the winter. The cabin was built of logs and rested on six stumps. It had no windows except a small hole covered with burlap. Inside it was not tall enough to stand up in but had a stove and cooking facilities. Remains of candles were scattered around and old sleeping bags were hanging on the outside for insulation. This hide-out had been abandoned for some time, and we created all sorts of stories concerning its history.

Our idea was lunch, and we suggested it at several ideal locations, but our guide had no thoughts for food just yet. We were consuming a good quantity of river water that may or may not have been of the purest quality. It certainly was not cold as the name would imply; this was a hot August day and the water level was very low. What a torrent this must become in the spring – tumbling rocks and trees in all directions and overflowing its banks to create the level flood-washed areas along the sides especially on the curves.

Tiny fish were abundant in small isolated pools, and we wondered what would happen to them if the water level receded any further. One very deep pool was created between ledges and boulders, and the grandfather of all area fish slid under the rock. We watched for several minutes hoping he would venture back in the sunshine, but he was wise to movements on the shore. We suggested lunch again but no response.

By now we seemed to be out of the deepest section of the valley. The riverbed alternately widened out to open sunshine and narrowed to a tree covered stream. In places, large trees had fallen across the rocks, and we climbed up and over not only the logs but all the debris that had washed downstream and collected behind them. Once in a while an old wood road followed along the edge then disappeared where high water had washed into the bank. It was by one of these roads that we finally announced that WE were going to eat a sandwich! Our guide seemed finally convinced that the food wouldn't need to be saved for midnight sustenance and joined in. As always on such occasions, anything would have tasted like a gourmet meal. We did realize after sitting a short time that muscles stiffen quickly and with a long trek ahead it was wisest to keep moving.

Further on, Bog Brook came down a gorge to the left. This intrigued our guide who had a sudden burst of energy to run up the rocks to investigate. We could look for flowers in the meantime. In the deep shade, a zigzag goldenrod indicated very rich soil, but by the time we thought of looking for companion plants, our guide was back and already ahead of us upriver.

Soon on the right, an unusual outcropping of ledge followed up the side of the mountain with a small brook flowing underneath. We climbed up to see a tumble of huge rocks all packed in together as if each was waiting for the other to go first down the steep ravine. Pursued further this could have been a shorter but more difficult climb out to the road, but we followed the original plan and climbed or slid back to the river.

From here on was just a long, long trek from rock to rock to rock with the view ahead looking more or less the same whenever we dared take our eyes off our feet. Even our eyes were tired from staring at rocks, which when viewed closer were really very colorful with an abundance of the pinkish-red variety. One looked like our idea of a meteor and took some further investigation. We have already planned in our next life to come back as a geologist.

On and on and on! We seemed to be walking mechanically now. The sides were getting steeper again. The whole river took a very gradual climb. We were aware of the distance but not so much the sense of climbing. We had really been pushing for the last hour, and when we came to the confluence of Tower Brook we all flung ourselves on the sandy shore with moans and groans. The remaining fruit from lunch was a lifesaver. As we recuperated, we wondered about the Indians who must have come up or down this stream in their search for a trail across Hoosac Mountain. In our imagination, they could still be lurking in the hills around us for this upper river valley remained on the true Wild Side with no evidence of change created by man.

The final three-quarters of a mile was covered in anticipation of seeing that bridge around the next corner. The sun had already set behind the high sides of our valley for this was not exactly big sky country.

Nothing ever looked or felt quite as refreshing as the pool below the bridge where we finally took off our hiking boots

and socks and waded to our knees in the now cold Cold River.

"Sure is quite a canyon up Cold River. Ever walked up through there?"

"Yes, we remember it well!"

* * * * *

When the blackberries were first turning ripe, and the everlasting was blossomed full, we visited the swamp late on the afternoon of August 10th. The young herons were pacing the nest as always and climbing up and down the tree branch. The parents were both there in different parts of the swamp stalking fish, and we saw each one make a catch. And then as naturally and gracefully as if they had always known how, the young birds flew from the nest for the first time. Somehow, after weeks of watching, we had chosen the perfect moment to return once again.

One young bird flew across the swamp to a maple limb on the far side and put up a terrible squawking later when the adult flew past and ignored her. The second bird went about half the distance to the very top of a tall dead tree and remained there like a statue. The third child flew about ten feet to a close tree and teetered and wobbled, often having to quickly spread its wings to regain balance. This must have been the youngest needing perhaps one more day to gain confidence.

Bon voyage young herons! You have provided us with a great deal of joy and appreciation on the Wild Side. We will be watching for your return even before the trillium opens its buds in the spring. **9/83**

Our final destination had been neatly planned as the "Bogeyman Road," but for want of a right hand turn in the right place, we didn't come out that way. Instead, we emerged across "Cookie's Bridge" by the church, took a long cool drink at the watering trough, and then worried about retrieving two cars at far distant locations.

For several different reasons, we have recently focused our attention on "The Northwest." The first mystery was the name. Certainly an area on Rowe's South Mountain and southern boundary doesn't deserve the name "Northwest." Logically northwest of Charlemont, the area is labeled on the geodetic map as being both in Rowe and Charlemont. "The Basin," source for Legate Hill Brook, is in Charlemont, but the headwall of the basin is in "The Northwest," in the southern part of Rowe.

Confused? So were we and never did make that right hand turn by "a clump of sticks" to pick up the trail south to Blueberry Hill and ultimately the Bogeyman Road where we had already left a car. And now there's another name – "Bogeyman Road." Probably the people there today wouldn't choose it – "Ledge Lane" is much more poetic – but back in our childhood, the steep mountain road just above the Mohawk Trail was known by that name and you watched for it next beyond "The Cave" on the way to Charlemont, after closing your eyes and holding your breath around the big ledge that made the road hang out over the river. One winter in Charlemont, a stately elderly gentleman with long white whiskers took to walking down Tea Street most every day. He walked with a sprightly gait and always threw his cane forward before placing it

firmly on the ground. He looked like a kindly old grandfather and as he always came from that hill direction, we assumed him to be the "Bogeyman" in person.

Today's map, drawn by a good authority, showed us most of the trails leading in and out of The Northwest with such detail as "deer stand," "painted rock," "tree across," "rock with quarter on top," and yes, "Bogeyman Road." This map along with lunch, binoculars and compass was packed in the knapsack, and we were off and running at 9:30 a.m. up the old wood road by the bridge just over the town line in Charlemont. It was a beautiful September day after the change to cooler weather – the kind of day you dream about all through the hot, muggy, buggy summer!

That we were going up the side of the mountain was evident in our very quick reduction in pace. The climb to the first ridge took us from about 800 ft. elevation at the bridge to 1500 ft. in a series of small plateaus mixed with steeper climbs. The sunny level areas were covered with lovely New York ferns which at this time of year intermittently lose chlorophyll, turning some a soft creamy white, while others remain green. The lack of old stone walls here seemed to indicate this mountainside to have been a series of woodlots rather than pasture land. How many generations of men have left the warmth of home fires to log these hills?

We were examining a blue-stemmed goldenrod along the path when movement in the woods ahead drew our attention. Our eyes were peeled for a deer, or even a moose, to come bounding down the path when four strangers passed us by looking for the bridge.

Assuring them of their course, we each went our opposite ways.

Soon two birch logs had neatly placed themselves across the path breaking a small sapling in the process. We tried to fathom from whence they had fallen thus but could not match log with proper stump and continued on to cross "Floyd's Trail," an old wood road from Floyd Veber's up over the mountain to connect with the Todd Road into Zoar.

The land here near the ridge widens out and becomes a very pleasant grassy knoll with exposed ledges and pretty birch trees. We dreamed of having a cabin here and spending our time clearing the hilltop and watching the western sunsets from a favorite ledge. Off to the south is a small nub of a hill called "Todd." (Not the Todd Mountan by Pelham Lake.) We climbed its prominent boulder – which looks artificially placed at just the right spot – and looked west toward Whitcomb Summit and Spruce Hill in Florida. The latter is a spectacular point of interest with which we have just this week become acquainted. The mile or so hike and short climb on a trail in Florida State Forest is one of the least publicized treasures in our area. The 360 degree view overlooks the North Adams/Adams valley, south to Savoy Mt. and Pittsfield, east to the Deerfield Valley, Rowe, Heath, Monadnock Mt. and around to Vermont and Clarksburg.

Back on Todd, we looked for the benchmark that should be there but could not be found – covered with moss, perhaps, or years of fallen leaves. Behind this hill, our map described a "boulder with a quarter on top." Again we met with little success in locating the coin in spite of attempts with a "divining rod." Perhaps hobblebush doesn't make the best forked stick or else we gave up the project too soon realizing there were many other sights to see.

Coming down to "Deb's Trail" or the old Todd Road, we had a swamp to check out and detoured south. This was Deb's Trail, so called, because farther down was the old Todd/Truesdell cellar hole where the late Gerald Truesdell of Rowe was born. We crisscrossed between the road and the dry brook bed looking for evidence of an old beaver dam. We had now come to farmland with good substantial stone walls which led to the farmyard and a nice old cellar hole with large trees in the center. Huge cut rocks in the foundation were most intriguing. Not realizing there had been two houses in this area, we wondered now from which had come the old pair of hand-made snowshoes that the late Roy Lincoln had given us. Somewhere hereabouts a sapling had been cut, bent and carved for the frames, and a deer had been killed – adding meat to the larder – and whose hide had been cut in strips and woven around the frames to make the snowshoes. We could picture the man working on these, perhaps sitting right here on this very hearthstone.

The sad remains of the recently burned Truesdell house were farther down on a bend in the road, and we remembered the story of how much young Sadie Truesdell had loved her first little mountain home. Out behind, we tramped through a large brushy swamp – quite dry with crunchy-soft sphagnum moss – and found no evidence of any beaver dams although, with water, it would make an ideal spot. Bushwhacking through the alders and brush brought the reward of seeing beautiful stands of tall bronze cinnamon fern, leathery little blue-green clumps of crested fern and a varied collection of sensitive fern.

All these details having been checked out, we headed back up the road and on to the path to "The Northwest." Another long plateau and even a dip downward stretched out before the next climb. This trough thick with lush green ferns we distinctly remember. Having tagged along this far last year as "assistant brush picker-upper" for the motorcycle trail clean-up boss, we had hoped it would work into a guided tour of "The Northwest." Prospects were good until one faint clap of thunder over Greylock sent us flying back down the mountain, hitting the ground only every so often. It was a fast moving storm and a long flight back to the car. On the last descent, thunder and lightning were already crashing around us. (Unfortunately, we grew up liking snakes and such things, but not being too fond of thunder showers!)

Well, today was different, and we continued on, starting now to look for the right hand turn at the fork where there were "sticks standing up." Chipmunks were everywhere, and we thought they must be playfully following us. Here and there a flower, mostly asters, or a mushroom or a weird this or that kept us going strong, up and up. When we came into an old logged section and promptly lost the path, we suddenly realized we'd been climbing a long time, and the lay of the land for a right hand turn down the ridge didn't look possible.

When in doubt, it's time for lunch. We climbed a short way to the highest point and found a sunny ledge with a view through the trees. Sitting down to a well earned picnic in

the woods on a warm September afternoon – for what more could you ask? And, yes, we did know one thing for sure; we were in "The Northwest" at last. It was one o'clock.

We had a little difficulty with juicy tomatoes and hungry yellow jackets and often set everything aside to look through the glasses or study the maps, hoping to determine our exact location by a particular land mark. We were in Rowe, on the north headwall of "The Basin" with Blueberry Peak far down to the right and Legate Hill closer to our left. "The Basin" certainly resembled its name – round, deep and we might add, wild. Chipmunks were making their funny little fall sounds and here and there a bird was rustling in the leaves. It was tempting to curl up and take an after lunch nap in the soft moss and grass around us.

Then there was the noise! Something once, loud and close – like metal sliding – just over the hill in front of us. We waited quietly for another sound but nothing more was heard. It seemed like a "civilization" noise and not a "wild" one, but we could not really describe it. With wilderness a long ways in either direction, it was certainly strange, and we are still mystified.

Wondering if there was day enough left to cover the ground that might be ahead of us, we regretfully left our perch. Shortly we came down around to a "T" and considered this might be our right hand turn. We pondered for awhile, walking down a long ledge to get a better view of the Basin. Ruling out the right turn as being too steep and illogical, we continued on the trail. Soon we could look off directly north and spotted a red barn and open land through the trees. The woods were too thick to see anything else, but we finally

identified Johnson's barn on Ford Hill Road. It seemed amazingly close.

Eventually we came onto "Intermountain 91" or so it seemed – wide, muddy logging roads and brush everywhere. Modern logging equipment seems so cruel to the land compared to the little grassy wood roads left from fifty or a hundred years ago.

Why we didn't step right in the open wasp's nest, we're not sure. We had stopped to look at a tiny clump of mushrooms and almost mistook the nest for a funny looking ground fungus until we saw the yellow jackets. We had not disturbed them and stood back a reasonable distance, observing them through the binoculars. The nest was a beautiful piece of artistry tucked under a large muddy rut. The alternating shades of grays and greens in little swirls were fascinating. Wasps of this kind collect bits of rotted wood and green stems of plants which they chew and mix with their saliva to form a sort of papier-mâché that becomes firm when dry. The colors reflect the materials they have chewed, but they must make the swirls for the sheer beauty of the finished product, which is seldom seen underground. We felt very fortunate that this one had been open to our view.

The way home took us farther up to 1950 ft. as we crossed under the power lines, but it was all easy downhill from there back to the village. We had been to the South and seen "The Northwest" and it was only 2:30 p.m. **10/83**

The Old Readsboro Road

It had been fifteen years – before the great popularity of cross-country skis – since that nice spring day in March when we had packed up some hamburgers, the usual picnic supplies and outfitted a variety of kids and adults with shortie and regular skis for a ski-hike-picnic down the Old Readsboro Road from a place in Vermont called Plumb's Camp to the top of Middletown Hill. It's basically all downhill, but there were just enough uphill jaunts to be murder on the feet of those of us wearing heavy downhill ski boots. A savior named Lenny Laffond, as we remember, came by on a snowmobile and picked up the little ones who were by that time asking "How much farther?" But that's ancient history.

Today, in mid-October, we had also packed a lunch but wore comfortable walking shoes as we started our trek once again down the Old Readsboro Road, starting at the power line on Lone Pine Road in Whitingham, Vermont. Sometimes called the Bennington Road, the Rowe section was established as a town road in 1787 although it must have been in existence earlier. It is thought that this was the route taken by Sergeant Nathaniel Corbet on August 14, 1777 as he marched a group of men from Myrifield to the Battle of Bennington. From our starting point today, the road must have continued north down the slope to Lime Hollow and on up the Deerfield valley.

This has not been a spectacular year for foliage, but in the October sunshine you realize that even a dull season is glorious in these hills. A lovely carpet of leaves covered the road as we started down the hill, removing windfall branches in our path. Immediately, we had to stop and examine an Indian cucumber root with its two whorls of leaves, now turned yellow, and cluster of berries on top. These berries seem to bleed their color into the upper four leaves giving them a pretty red center. The woods around us were a world of ferns of various shades, some already turned brown and shriveled like the hayscented while others were green, brown or white, waiting for the ultimate frost to lay them on the ground. But the Christmas fern, marginal, and other wood ferns seemed to be taking on new life, knowing they would still be standing tall and green even after the winter snows covered all else.

Before circling around to Plumb's camp, the "road less traveled" went straight on south, and we pursued our course that way exploring for a short ways another pathway leading down the steeper bank to the right. Soon a small level area spread out to the west with drop-offs on three sides. The loss of a few more leaves would open the view across the Deerfield valley to the mountains of South Readsboro. Underfoot were small forked stalks topped with a single three-sided pod of seeds – now all dry and rattley. Our lovely little wild oats of spring! The fruits and seeds of fall sometimes take on such strange forms that it is often difficult to recognize even our most familiar flowers. Those little pods so perfectly shaped and marked had evolved from a little yellow bell flower which covers the woodlands in early May.

Although there is no official stone marker, a torn paper sign on a tree told us we were crossing the Massachusetts border. We now began our search for the several old cellar holes known to be along this way. A

The Old Readsboro Road

Wheeler-Wilcox chimney on Old Readsboro Road

memory purely for the size of the stone chimney with three fireplaces rising from a large square stone base in the center. As we rounded the next bend, this structure, known as the Wheeler-Wilcox place, came in sight on the west side of the road. The cellar hole remained as we remembered, but "My how the trees have grown!" This had been the open site of our winter picnic fifteen years ago. In more recent times, it must have been Boy Scouts who had made this a winter campsite. Piles of firewood, remains of several campfires and various shelters built of pine branches were scattered over the area. We walked farther afield and found the old barn foundation out in the back. A good sized white birch had been rigged with a platform high in the branches — either a deer hunter's stand or more likely the Scouts "Indian Look-out."

A stand of tall goldenrod was between the house and barn sites and a long level outcropping of ledge probably indicated a very thin layer of soil keeping trees from growing at least in one spot. What a beautiful farm this must have been when the land was clear and open to the southwestern view. Several old apple trees reminded us that there probably had been dried apples hanging in

stone wall running east and other groups of rocks near a wet area gave us pause to stop and look around. Something looked like a lilac bush and was not, but there was an old apple tree. Ferns were the highlight here – many clumps of crested fern and a good specimen of a very tall slender fern which we picked to identify at home and had to fold over three times to fit in the knapsack.

This road so far was very easy walking and just continuously pretty, looking ahead under the canopy of yellow leaves and following between two, at times, very impressive stone walls. These were wagon roads made for a time less hurried when the physical labors of eking out an existence on and from the land were the rewards of life in these hills.

Among Rowe cellar holes there is one that, once seen, remains uppermost in the kitchen and a good barrel of cider in the cellar. This house was listed as J. Wheeler on the 1858 map but gone by 1871. It had been one of the early ones. Do you suppose some young man from here joined Sergeant Corbet as he marched by to Bennington on that August day so long ago?

Moving on, we tried to keep on the straight and narrow and leave further investigation of intriguing side roads to another time. Somewhere now on the east side of the road was one of the boundaries of the Monroe State Forest. This was land that was sold to the state by the Bolton family years ago when the State was buying forest land for $5 an acre. Near this boundary we crossed a branch of Wheeler Brook and recognized a turnaround point in another hike when we were climbing up the brook which flows past the Noyes Wheeler farm behind Yankee.

The next long gradual climb reminded us of those miserable ski boots not meant for this type of thing – the blisters had healed but not the memory. As the land leveled we came out to the Yankee power line. It had been pleasantly cool in the woods and the bright sunshine of the open hill felt good. We must soak up as much as possible now before winter! Here we turned west for a side trip to the top of the ridge for lunch, stopping to sample the fruit from an old-fashioned apple tree on the edge of the woods. The apples were a lovely yellow color with red cheeks – and delicious!

At the top, we chose a flat ledge, spread out our sandwiches, fruit, maps, and binoculars and shed a few layers of jackets and sweaters no longer needed in the warm autumn sunshine. What a beautiful wild world we looked out upon toward the hills of Monroe, Florida and on to Greylock. Hills and valleys and power lines but not a house in sight. The only visible human activity was once in a while the glint of the sun on a car climbing the last open stretch to the top of Greylock and a friendly small plane passing just above us.

Wildlife was a little scarce – several crows made noises in the trees behind us and a funny little caterpillar was traveling hell-bent across the ledge as if mighty late for an important appointment. We did torment him a little to see if we could change his course, but like the indicator of a compass he kept heading north. We wished him luck as he took off through a forest of grass beyond the rock. He's probably in Canada by now! Seeing several dried scats prominently placed on a ledge at the top of this hill made us hope that it had been an eastern coyote that had thus marked his trail crossing. Authorities say that although a cross between a dog and coyote is possible, the animal we see here is a true eastern coyote and not a "coy dog."

High thin clouds moved across the sky during our lunch and slightly muffled our sunshine, but made pretty patterns in the sky. Reluctantly we finally packed our gear, tied our shoes and returned to the old road from whence we had departed. Here starts the major descent which drops this road nearly three hundred feet in the next half mile – a great little run on skis! Many a rainstorm, since the road was discontinued in 1874, had eroded this road to bedrock and stones. We had walked from Potter Road across the power lines and down this section one rainy day in recent years and can vouch for the rather treacherous slippery walking under those conditions.

After this dry summer, the road now gave us no problem, and we spent a good bit of time off to either side trying to locate at least three known cellar holes. Of the Langdon place on the east side, we found no trace. But further down, the two high walls of a building on the Pike place were beside the road. Was this near where our early minister, Rev. Preserved Smith had lived in 1797? The story goes that as the Smiths were driving to the Meeting House at the Old Centre one Sunday morning, they looked back over the hill and saw their house on fire. Their home was destroyed as well as all the early church records. Fire then, as now, was a heart breaking experience.

At the bottom of this hill, the road now swings southwest, but the original went more to the southeast crossing a brook (now an interesting little beaver pond) and connecting to Middletown Hill above the Williams farm. Following the present road still between good stone walls, we were searching for one more cellar hole – that of the Hunt-Allard-Gates place torn down by Yankee when they had to acquire the property surrounding the plant. We eventually turned off on a road to the west and came upon

remains of many walls, a large evergreen tree and a small brook, all well guarded by a huge porcupine that hid his head in the wall upon our intrusion. He had done well in tramping down the Japanese bamboo bush and grass, but once again the woods had taken over and it was hard to discern what had been where. But among the rocks, the day lilies and other remains of earlier flower gardens still showed the love and care that had been put into this homestead.

Finishing our hike on down this old Readsboro Road, we wished we could skip back in time and ride in a horse and carriage back up this way, visiting each house and family in their time. But then again, it was pretty nice in today's world – having the time to take a leisurely walk on the Wild Side under October's bright blue skies. **11/83**

Old Readsboro Road

The morning of "The Day After," we took to the woods. Actually, we spent the day before "The Day After" there, too. If we were to be subjected (out of curiosity) to this much publicized television movie about a devastating nuclear attack upon the face of the earth, we needed to get out on the Wild Side and contemplate ourselves as an endangered species. We feel endangered, anyway, in the woods during the November and December hunting season. Safety in numbers they say, so we did not hike alone.

On the day before, we chose the dramatic – Rowe's western ridge. Turning down the dirt section of Tunnel Road is usually considered already on the Wild Side, but today it looked like a KOA campground with five trucks and campers of bow hunters.

Knapsacks went over our shoulders at the Peck Cemetery, and we headed west. November was outdoing itself this year to be kind to those of us who tend to be critical. It was a beautiful day, warm to the point of having to shed jackets for shirtsleeves when we revved up our inner heaters climbing hills.

Rowe's second lake was surprisingly low. Covering about 118 acres when full, the Bear Swamp Upper Reservoir is one of Rowe's attractions not often seen by the general public. Bear Swamp was a natural mountaintop basin now diked on three sides and filled with river water which is run through the power house in the mountain to produce 600 megawatts of electricity at peak demand times. The water level fluctuates daily between here and the Deerfield River reservoir about 700 feet below.

This morning as the waters sparkled in the sunshine, we remembered seeing the summer resident cormorant around these waters and thought what a haven this would be for a loon, an osprey or even an eagle. We would keep watch.

While climbing the rocks to higher ground, we admired all the British Soldier lichens with their red caps just clearing the top of the snow. Next we passed through sort of a basin full of rocks with beech and maple trees. So intent were we looking for items on the Wild Side that we walked right past a camouflaged hunter with bow and arrow in hand. When we exchanged conversation, he had a complaint – not about our intrusion but concerning the prevalence of the wrong kind of game. He had seen a bear, but he was hunting deer! We were happy to hear of his misfortune. Perhaps we would have the same bad luck.

Once on the hillside in back of the reservoir, we had to circle to the north to find the ridge or razorback which we would follow down to our outlook destination. Away from the southern exposure, the little bit of snow had settled in for the winter, covering the slippery carpet of recently fallen leaves. Looking at birds in the trees and the remains of asters and goldenrod on the ground, we walked along the big paw prints for several feet without focusing on them. Sure enough, the hunter's bear had passed this way. But the tracks were yesterday's and the bear could now be miles away, scouting out a winter home for he would be denning in a couple of weeks.

From this point, the land drops in a series of steps down over rock cliffs. These can best be visualized as they are silhouetted against the sky from the River Road south of the Bear Swamp Information Center. Most of the larger rocks are peppered with small marble-sized garnets. These, of course, are the garden variety garnet and not gemstones, but, nevertheless, interesting.

As we swung down over the rocks, the trees became smaller and weather-stunted while the spectacular valley view opened before us. Although this is the same Deerfield Valley as under Pulpit Rock, it is a closer and more exciting view overlooking the lower Bear Swamp dam and spillway with the steep narrow canyon of Fife Brook and Raycroft Lookout directly across the valley. Having flowed south from Vermont, this is the point at which the Deerfield River starts its peculiar twisting route around the Big Bend at Hoosac Tunnel and heads easterly toward the Connecticut. Like a toy, the B&M Railroad bridge spanned the river just outside the Tunnel, and the route of the old HT&W Railroad bed could be seen coming up the east side of the River, reminding us of the importance of the railroad for access to this valley before the turn of the century. This access built industries such as pulp, paper and power. But our valley remains wild, and the old Indian name meaning "Forbidden Mountain" still seems to fit its remote valleys and heights.

Looking at the holes in the ledge

At the outer edge of our ridge is a small drop-off – perhaps ten feet at the highest. This vertical cliff face has many holes into which you can put your fist and sometimes part of your arm. Obviously some chemical has dissolved out of these rocks with years of weathering, but we have not yet seen its likeness elsewhere in the area.

Our destination reached, granola bars and apples consumed, we decided on the more challenging way home down another cliff face and across the mountainside back up to the original heights. On the way, a smaller set of tracks crossed our path, but were difficult to distinguish – except, in that area, it was a good bet the animal was not domestic. As we were approaching the top, the usual Saturday afternoon roar came down the valley, and we watched two A-10's flying perpendicularly below the horizon down the Deerfield Valley, whipping around the Big Bend and out of sight. Maneuverability is certainly the name of the A-10 game. We thought we weren't doing too badly ourselves!

* * * * *

Twenty-four hours is all that's really necessary to recuperate from one escapade to another. The morning of "The Day After" and the day after the last hike, a crew of five of the younger generation, plus dog, rushed on the scene and declared to us their destination was Dunbar Brook – immediately – join them or be left behind. We joined!

This is really the story of "Buddy", the dog – greatest little sheep herder of all time – racing this trail many times over in his obsessed desire to keep six hikers in view and on the path. Dunbar Brook is in the State Forest in the town of Florida and Monroe with trail access on the River Road at the town lines. Buddy performed his first feat right off the bat by the dam at the start of the trail. He was racing around everyone and suddenly darted under a walkway. Here he found himself on the edge of a ravine with too much momentum to stop and leaped through the air to the other bank – landing in a U shape, hind end first! If he didn't run headlong into a porcupine, this character would certainly keep our crew in line. He had a tough time. No one would stay on the trail.

Our first observation was the clarity of Dunbar Brook. With a greenish tinge, the water acted as a glass, magnifying the rocks and sand on the bottom of a small pond set back from the bank. Noise ahead indicated rapids and a fast moving stream – no lack of water here even after a dry summer. The well-worn and relatively easy uphill path is mostly high above the brook, and we quickly detoured down the bank to get better acquainted.

Dunbar Brook, in a narrow valley, is fast, full and literally choked with some of the largest boulders we've seen – yes, even bigger than Pelham Brook's collection on its last fling to the river. We wanted to pursue

our course up around the rocks, but this crew was as fast moving up the path as the brook water was coming down the gorge – and not wanting to get Buddy absolutely exasperated, we followed the rest.

To our left, the mountainside was covered with a continuous carpet of beautiful green spinulous ferns. This mat spread all around the large moss covered rocks that seemed to be tumbling down the hillside – each boulder sporting a toupee of polypody fern.

Before long, one trail branched off to Raycroft Road while the main one crossed the brook and continued up a somewhat level plane beside the stream. A sign declared "under cultivation about 1800." We had come to a mountain farm of an early settler, and we began to "smell" a cellar hole. Many very old tall and straight pine trees grew along this brook. Eventually a bridge on the left took us across Haley Brook which had branched off Dunbar. On the hillside in the V of the streams was a State Forest Shelter and fireplace. We, including Buddy, lined up on the platform, opened knapsacks and lunched on crackers, cheese and fruit.

Knowing this crew was apt to take off in a hurry, we became fidgety and used most of this lunch break to explore. This was just such an ideal location – there had to be a cellar hole. A stone wall of large rocks followed across the back and sure enough there was the cellar hole nestled against the hill. Stone steps dropped into a small cellar beside the big stone chimney base in the center. Large slabs of rock had evenly spaced, chiseled out notches for some unknown reason. We were in the "Gore" section of Monroe, but probably too far west for this area to have been part of Rowe in the

Rob, our favorite hiking guide

early days. Nevertheless, we had the usual intriguing questions of who, when and what had taken place here where pioneers had tried to settle this wilderness. Happily for us, their efforts had been in vain, and it was wilderness once again.

Here's where the crew and the one we thought was leader got separated, and even Buddy couldn't remedy the situation. Wanting to see more of Dunbar Brook Gorge which was becoming narrower and totally filled with rocks, the crew spread out along the lower path. At one point, raving about a gigantic boulder in the middle of the stream, we were suddenly startled to see "The Hermit of Dunbar Brook" sitting cross-legged in the shadows far under the carved out lower side. Buddy, of course, recognized one of his charges and quickly ushered him back to the path.

We finally came to the end of this route. The path was disappearing, and the brook becoming impossible to climb. Where was our leader when we needed him? We all realized we had to get ourselves out of this predicament and, with Buddy's help, we crawled through the brush up the steep bank and back to the real path. Here we all war-whooped for our supposed leader with no response. Buddy even ran out of sight down the path, but came back alone. There was to be some change of direction at the power line so we continued on.

It was really no surprise to find our lost leader standing on the highest rock under the power line looking at us with the question, "Where have you been?" Buddy was so overjoyed that he ran continuous circles around the group to celebrate how well he had done collecting everyone together. We gave him another piece of cheese for his efforts.

This junction of the power line and path opens up a wider vista to the high mountains on either side and reinforces our sense of remoteness from civilization. Although the line had been kept clear of trees, it was a tangled mass of brush and blackberry brambles and caused a few groans of "Are you sure?" when our enthusiastic leader said, "We're going up that side!" It looked like good rabbit country and a supermarket for bears in berry season.

Everyone found his own way up through the brush and Buddy had to make wider and wider circles. We ourselves opted for the north side in the woods, looking carefully at the vegetation hoping for the dried up remains of a new find. It all looked pretty ordinary.

Down in Haley Brook valley, we could see our guide waiting for us to come in sight. He stayed only long enough to shout our instructions, "Go down the brook," as he went off up the hill on the run. We stood looking at what we had been told to do with mixed emotions. Down ahead of us were rocks, pools, rows of icicles hanging from the bank and steep waterfalls – no one else in sight – even Buddy had forsaken us.

We felt a little like an old bobcat left to prowl the Wild Side all alone. But then a thought occurred to us, and we picked our way down the rocky gully with joy in our heart. It might be "The Day After" in terms of our youth, but no one in this group was yet considering this old Bobcat an "endangered species." They knew we could still survive full well on our own. **12/83**

1984

Overlooking Beaver Island in the Deerfield River from Negus Mountain

View south from Negus Ridge toward Charlemont

Anticipation is often half the joy of events in our lives, and when we were promised a birthday hike in the early part of December, we relished the thought for several days. To be "taken" on a hike, you see, would get us to places out of our category on our own.

"Pine Cobble, " in the Town of Florida, rises steeply to 1700 ft. on the south side of Fife Brook northwest of the Big Bend in the Deerfield River. It is the next mountain south of Raycroft Lookout. Pine we understood but "what's a cobble?" Well, it's a "naturally rounded stone, something bumpy as if paved with cobblestones." Sure enough, looking at our destination from the road upriver, we could see this mountain rising in a series of bumps or cobbles, each one higher than the last.

The gang assembled by Fife Brook just below the Lower Reservoir dam. Because of "Buddy"s notoriety from last Wild Side hike, we have a waiting list of dogs requesting to join us. Negus and Tucker, two labs, won the toss this time.

We had some idea what was in store for us as we had crawled up the canyon of Fife Brook a couple of summers ago – to our thoughts, that's one of the most challenging, picturesque and unusual bits of territory in this area. Today we started up the left bank but gradually worked our way around to ascend the front of this ridge up and down the series of cobbles.

The first discovery was the remains of downed poles and crossbars of an old telephone or electric line – probably service into the area when the power stations were being built back around 1916.

It was a beautiful warm day with some

snow in the woods, but as we attained the top of each cobble, the outcroppings of rocks were clear. We shed jackets as we sat and looked out across the Deerfield Valley to the great wall of Rowe on the other side.

Behind each cobble was a depression or small valley, and we swung down into these areas, hanging onto trees and examining ledges full of garnets. From these tiny valleys we could more easily look down toward Fife Brook whose canyon was becoming deeper and deeper to our right.

Negus and Tucker were gone from the start, racing ahead chasing everything that moved including partridges and snow balls. As ice pieces fell from our footsteps down the mountainside, the dogs went bounding after them down to the very edge of cliffs amid our shouts for their return before a final leap.

After the third cobble and valley, we were struggling up through thick laurel trees toward an open rock face. We came upon a loose rock that looked like a petrified stump. We had to pull it out of the ground to examine it more closely. In so doing, it got away from us and went shooting down over rocks, snow and around trees. Far out of sight, we could still hear it tumbling. Thinking immediately of the dogs in the line of fire, brought to mind an old legend about neighboring Hunt Hill. It seems that back in the early days, two old natives named Hunt and Raycroft were prospecting along the ridge of that hill. Hunt was on the upper side chipping away and loosened a large rock. He turned around quickly and yelled to his friend below, "Raycroft, Look out!" And that's why Hunt Hill to this day has a place called Raycroft Lookout. We'd remember Pine Cobble with its "Negus and Tucker Lookout."

True to other observations, we picked up deer tracks near the top and found where they had stood overlooking the valley. On another open level ledge was evidence of previous human occupation – a broken-handled shovel. Someone had probably been camping on these remote heights. We wished we could do likewise. The trees were scrubby and over the tops we spotted a lone cleared field toward Florida Mountain. We finally located it as being west of Reed Brook Valley and Torrey Mountain Road near the Mohawk Trail.

Another valley and cobble brought us close to the top. From this vantage point we looked over and beyond "the wall" to see Adams and Negus Mountains rising in the distance. Downriver, the view extended to the bend by the tunnel and upstream to the rock quarry on the Lower Reservoir which came first in line of view before the swing of the mountain south of Pulpit Rock. What a tremendous valley right here in our own backyard!

With only one more notch to go to reach the ultimate cobble, someone remembered the time and our need to be home at an appointed hour. We had taken longer than expected just admiring the valley from each new height. It took a little consultation with the geodetic map and everyone's advice to settle on a way back. Retracing our steps was never an option. The final choice was the shortest, the quickest and we might add the most exciting – scaling the edge to the west and then straight down! It was a drop of some 800 ft. to the valley floor behind the Laird house.

We wonder how we get ourselves in these predicaments! In this case, sliding down through the laurel, it was hard to tell ahead of time whether we might land on the top of a cliff. Fortunately, we could just slalom around trees and down gullies between rocks and never came to that dreaded point of no return. Talking the dogs back from the edge of nowhere seemed to be the hardest problem.

Approaching the bottom, we came across an old road which was easily followed back around the hill to our starting point picking up again the path of the old power line. Another enjoyable hike exploring our Deerfield Valley.

* * * * *

New England weather changes while you're watching, so the fact that the day after Christmas was a whole new world was not surprising. The temperature stood at 10 degrees, and the sun, even at noontime, was low on the southern horizon. The jackets we'd shed two weeks before were tightly belted and our under-garments were of the long red variety, top and bottom. Hats and gloves were a must. It was cold!

If the last hike was a birthday present, this one we found in our Christmas stocking. Still exploring the Deerfield Valley, the plan was to move upstream to the State line where we left a car, hoping our calculations would return us to that location. Looking west to the high ridge described as our destination, we knew this would be another hike finished by the seat of our pants.

Our starting point was the State boundary on the South Readsboro Road between Readsboro and Monroe, and our intentions were to follow the State line crosslots back to the car – as the crow flies about a mile, but the change in elevation would be from 1936 ft. to 1121 ft. Once out of the car, it took some stomping of feet and waving of arms to muster enough internal heat and courage to take off. Jumping over the snow bank, we tested the footing and all took off on the run down across the open power line to the woods. The snow depth varied from six to twelve inches depending on the drifting and was not bad walking. A thin layer of crust under the powder made our footsteps sound like winter. Although we did not shed any clothes, it proved a glorious day to be out on the Wild Side.

Following wood roads, we soon picked up an old fence line with early blazed trees which we assumed to be the route to follow. This should also be the boundary of the Green Mountain National Forest on the Vermont side.

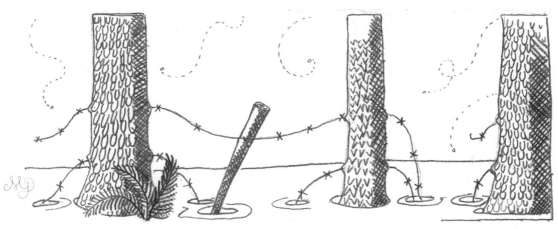

The woods were still and quiet under their blanket of snow and one wondered how all those delicate little plants and flowers of spring could survive. Under the beech and maple forest the low hobble bush poked up through the snow and seemed already to have its furled brown leaves in place for spring.

The old fence appeared and disappeared, grown well into the center of many of the line trees. As the land began to slant downward, we crossed a small upland swamp, now a circle of ice. Rocks and boulders became greater in number and we paused to walk around the base of one, brushing off the snow to see the ferns and moss still green but well matted under the snow. A small hole near the rock was surrounded by ice crystals. We judged some small animal to be wintering under this rock and breathing just enough to form the crystals in the cold air.

With this diversion, we got far behind the rest of the crew and picked up their tracks on the run to catch up! This path traced down around another swampy place and eventually followed a small brook well hidden under a thick cover of ice. On the next bend, the brook revealed itself as a small waterfall plunging into an icy pool. Suddenly there was motion in an otherwise still world, and the motion made lovely water music.

In the woods, the snow was smooth and powdery and showed off little animal tracks to good advantage. In one spot, lines of deer mice tracks traveled between holes near the base of trees and into a tiny playground where the snow had not fallen on the soil beneath an overhanging tree. It would be fun just to sit still and watch these goings on. Off in another direction a larger mouse had been in a hurry for he jumped, creating a series of imprints, tail and all, a little deeper in the snow.

We could now see the rest of the crew gathered at something interesting down under the next hill. We spotted the large rocks on top and walked around them, completely missing the fact that the brook under ice had swung left and disappeared between the rocks. From the underside, everyone was admiring a beautiful tall ice-covered waterfall over the rocks into a natural basin or pool – solid with ice. At the base of the falls, beside a rock in the pool was a hole in the ice surrounded by many pretty ice crystals – a larger version of what we had seen earlier. Putting our hand in the opening, we encountered a current of warm air. Consultation, once again, produced this explanation: the fast moving water was drawing cold air in from an opening in the ice at the top of the falls. Below the ice blanket, the water – above 32 degrees – was warming the air and forcing it out through the only hole in the basin. This air, being warm and full of moisture like the breath of an animal, formed the ice crystals as it met the ten degree air at the opening.

By this time, we had lost the fence line and as the brook flowed more southward, there was a discussion as to whether this was Tower Brook or another not listed on the map. The consensus was to head in a more northerly direction around the hill to the left. The landscape had become quite steep and littered with slash piles from logging operations. As the snow had drifted around these piles it was difficult walking, and we often fell through the brush and had to maneuver our way up and out. The rocks, too, were different. Climbing up to an outcropping of ledge, we found it looked like a large wall of huge slabs cut with square corners.

Into the evergreen trees now, it became apparent that we were near our intended destination of open rocks overlooking Sherman Pond. As the hill faced east, the crusty part of the snow became more solid and walking was slippery. We could see an opening in the trees and tried a higher route, separating from the crew. Thus we gained the summit but not the view. About a hundred feet below, we could hear the rest exclaiming over the grand view of Yankee, Sherman and the old Wilcox hill to the east while we examined an old hemlock hanging on to the very edge of the ridge. Looking down, we momentarily thought we might have to be rescued by helicopter, but with luck we hung onto a small tree and let ourselves down over rocks – then took a good slide to the lower level. The view was well worth the effort, and we enjoyed it from all angles. Looking down at the car by the State marker, we seemed to be standing exactly with one foot in Vermont and the other in Massachusetts.

And then the fun began. We realized we were standing on top of a perpendicular wall at least four hundred feet above the road with great rocks and trees cluttering our path and the footing icy crust! Carefully picking our way to the right, we could look down to even more intriguing walls of rock. We would find an easier way down and double back to see those rocks. But there was not an easier way! Coming to a real point of no return, we had to slide. It was tricky. You had to swerve to the right to land on a ledge and avoid a large tree or oblivion further down. Sliding on cardboard as a kid was never like

this. The only casualty was a lost mitten of the last one down. This required a volunteer to climb back up and try it again!

To our right, the brook was now coming down a steep gully and to our left were boulders and ancient trees. Some of the rocks were still of the square cut variety and covered the hill. The giant old hemlock trees were treasures to behold. This virgin growth in among the rocks could easily be four or five hundred years old. Three of us spread our arms around one tree and upon our return measured fourteen feet, six inches.

The age, the strength and the beauty of these giants right here on our own Wild Side made some of our petty everyday concerns seem very trivial in the scheme of things. These ancient trees, the stars above us on these winter nights and thoughts of the miracle of tiny flowers appearing from under the snow on these hillsides in the spring all gave us an incredibly good feeling about our being part of this mysteriously beautiful world in which we live.

Down now on the edge of the open power lines at the bottom of the hill, someone spotted a nut wedged between two branches of a small maple tree. We found the nut to be from a nearby butternut tree. Then we saw another, and another and another. Squirrels had taken all the butternuts they could find and hidden them in very obvious places in every tree around – crazy antics of our furry friends.

Crossing the open hill we picked a winter bouquet of dried asters, goldenrod and bottle gentians which to us had their own special beauty even in December.

Now from the Wild Side, Happy Hiking for 1984. **1/84**

Happy New Year 1984, Overlooking Zoar

January 1st, 1984 was a day to remember – clear crisp air, beautiful blue sky and a shiny crusty snow underfoot. It was definitely not a day to be inside on the couch recuperating from New Year's Eve. Instead, it was a day to climb mountains, to see the world from the top, to proclaim the New Year and look 1984 straight in the eye.

Turning the corner at Zoar and crossing Pelham Brook for the third time, you head in a southeasterly direction toward Charlemont. Looming up ahead is the lower plateau of Blueberry Peak. Its balding front is covered with steep ledge, loose rocks and laurel bushes. The sparse trees hang on for dear life and those nearer the top have been stunted by the perpetual west wind. A couple of pine trees front and center have grown to a reasonable height and conveniently retain their branches for climbing. This mountain and those pine trees give us a real good feeling now every time we rush off down through Zoar on the way to the city.

That good feeling is perhaps first a sense of accomplishment. We did it! It was a struggle to be sure, but then again isn't everything? It was a struggle just to get the crew beyond the first roadway up around the new metal cribbing. Here the crust had created a beautiful slide to be enjoyed on your seat, your knees or your stomach and everyone had to try it all ways. The real struggle, however, started about the middle of the cribbing, heading straight up. Every step was a challenge

to break through the crust and find solid footing. Our knees ached, and we leaned against various trees catching our breath after each long hassle through thick laurel and rocks. Rewards came with each step. The view through the bare trees was exciting from the start as we looked out over the road to the Deerfield River and watched the valley deepen as we gained altitude.

Reaching the open section nearer the top, we became more and more impressed with and dependent upon the now small, rugged laurel bushes which grew in every nook and cranny of soil. Their roots went deep to support our full weight as we pulled ourselves up over the faces of the outcropping ledge. Resting now was pure joy, leaning back against the mountain and looking west out over the river valley and the wilderness of Todd Mountain where climbs the old Indian Trail en route from Deerfield across Forbidden Mountain down into the

Looking down on the Deerfield River and Zoar Village many years ago

Hoosac valley. (The area has lots of Todd Mountains!)

The crest of our hill was soon attained and opened to a view of mountains beyond mountains and valleys into deeper valleys, a truly spectacular sight well worthy of New Year's Day 1984. The miniature village of Zoar was nestled below us by the river, a seemingly toy railroad running along its edge. Tiny cars drove past little box houses and cemetery stones lined up like match sticks. The mighty river came in a sweeping curve from the west around the solid fortress of Negus Mountain. Behind this rose the Hoosac Range with the sun highlighting the white spire of Florida Church. Another valley joined the Deerfield at the bend where the waters of Pelham Brook carried rocks and silt into the larger stream, and the road turned into the hills toward Rowe. Here joined Steele Brook's narrow cascade above which another tiny road made its way up the ravine. Rugged Coon Hill stood guard over these passages to the north. And to the west, other mountains were creating long shadows into the valley below.

The Grand Canyon of Western Massachusetts! We pictured a paved parking area over the deer tracks where we were standing and a concrete and iron observation platform with directional signs to Negus, Todd and Coon and a bronze plaque with raised drawings describing the geological ages that were responsible for forming this great valley and another picturing the early Indians camping by the river – and then we saw all the tourists with cameras and the busses with their motors running, throwing diesel exhaust in our faces. No! No! No! We shuddered from the bad dream. We wanted to share this spot with others but hopefully always by the same route we came this morning – step by step, with the only observation platform being the upper limbs of the pine tree where we climbed today and initialed NNW with our fingernail in the soft pine bark and proclaimed the arrival of 1984.

We'd like to leave you in the top of that pine tree to watch the changing patterns of sunlight and shadow across this valley, but there are some hibernating wild creatures in the rock crevices of this mountain and perhaps you'd like to join us finding them.

The view toward Charlemont through denser tree cover was pleasant but not spectacular and provided a more gradual slope for our descent. It actually prompted a little running and jumping, but soon a ledge looked too steep to jump, and we looked for an escape route. A curious one opened up. A monster piece of rock had split from the main ledge, leaving a three foot crack all around. If we let ourselves down six feet or so into this crack we could crawl down and around to ground level. It was a tight squeeze on the exit, but we managed. Now we could look back and see the extent of the cliff in both directions. Without the crack, we would have been retracing our steps a good way back.

Below us now, huge rocks had fallen in a tumble all around. A small passageway was maneuverable under the cliff between rocks and trees. Each overhang or large split had something interesting to investigate including porcupine dens, strange icicles and green lichens. Then we came upon a larger formation like a cave into which one could walk. We first noticed swallow nests perched on the high shelves, and then we spotted two thin, vertical cracks into the interior of the ledge. These were surrounded full length by ice crystals. As we knew from our last hike, something was breathing inside, and we reached our fingers in to feel real warmth. Only bats could be tucked into this narrow crevice in the mountain. We had found a Wild Side Condominium! Some creatures had holed up for the cold months; others were out and about enjoying the snow while the rest, like their human friends, had flown south for the winter.

And so we meandered down the mountain, thinking on all we had seen and experienced on this Happy New Year hike.

* * * * *

Life in the Day Swamp has not been monitored by us since the three young blue herons fledged the nest and took to life on their own. As we sat by the shore so many summer days, we had dreamed of walking through the swamp once the winter ice was solid.

The date for a hike was set a couple of weeks in advance, but when the day arrived, it was cold and damp with heavy clouds threatening snow. Our enthusiasm was nil until we changed the destination from a mountain top to the swamp. This particular swamp in summer had never failed to produce something new and fascinating on the Wild Side. Would it continue to cheer our mood on a dark day in winter?

After the discovery of the nesting herons, our approach to this swamp was always made in great anticipation, and once on course, today was no exception. Entering through the beech woods, we found the north side of

each tree covered with a smooth icy coating from the recent storm. Various bark colors and textures were highlighted and magnified by this glassy cover. Beech nuts still hung like tiny cones high in the branches. Further along under the evergreens, rabbit tracks bounded back and forth across our path while the straight line of fox tracks led the way ahead of us. Overhead, chickadees darted among the limbs, speaking softly.

Turning the last familiar corner, we came into the open area of the old gravel bank and soon saw the swamp in its winter dress. The old dead trees were standing frozen into smooth ice with a light covering of snow. The stumps and fallen logs created weird forms and shapes under the ice. We looked immediately toward the heron's nest and saw nothing at all clinging to the tree tops. We carefully made our way out onto the ice toward the trees we had looked at so many times. Standing like coon dogs under a treed animal, we went round and round looking for some evidence. The big nest of sticks between these two trees had fallen, blown away in the wind leaving no trace. Nearly two months of heavy birds tromping around had taken its toll. We hoped it would not discourage the return of the birds in the spring.

Following some smaller tracks, we went past the big beaver house (completely missing the air hole on top that signifies beaver occupation for the winter) and headed for the series of dams where the tracks disappeared down a hole into the water – a mink or an otter was in residence feasting on the heron's summer supply of catfish and frogs. In the lower pool was a section of open water near the dam.

Recent heavy rains had caused flooding. Here something was moving, swimming in this water over the ice. It looked for all the world like a huge tadpole, but certainly not in January! But we all verified that that was exactly what we were seeing and anticipated reporting to herpetological authorities the strange January phenomenon in a Rowe swamp. Consulting reference books at home, we found that bullfrogs stay as tadpoles for two and sometimes three years. But shouldn't they be under the mud in January? Authorities later assured us we had observed a perfectly common occurrence in open pond water anytime during the winter. Live and learn! This swamp had proved to be a learning experience every time we visited.

Traversing the rest of the pond, we peeked into nesting holes of summer swallows, saw new beaver gnawings on a big maple and found evidence of more otter antics sliding down the inclines by the back dam. Climbing onto the level of the second pond, we again followed tracks, admiring along the way a large stand of cattails. We couldn't resist pulling apart the heads and watching the mysterious way the tightly packed seeds gently curled around our hand, displaying the lovely soft reddish brown fur inside.

So intrigued were we with all these attractions that the grey clouds and lightly falling snow did not matter in the least. Only when we misjudged the channel area of the second pond and stepped far down into moving water and mud did we become aware of the day's temperature, but it did not dampen our enthusiasm.

Climbing up out of the swamp, the woods were strewn with very short hemlock branches and many tiny cones. First suspecting a porcupine at work, a glossy tree trunk reminded us of the recent ice storm and we realized this was the resulting damage to tender tips. We collected a pocketful of cones ready for some future project.

The paw prints that now crossed our path were large and had broken through the crusty surface − a coyote or bobcat perhaps. They led us through a lovely young balsam forest interspersed with the remains of big old, decayed hardwood trees covered with fungus. Near these trees we suddenly noticed the thousands of tiny, tiny snow fleas or springtails. We later learned that they live on pollen and fungus spores.

Moments before we rejoined the regular path, we had come to a more open area and thought for sure we were lost. A large mountain had now loomed up behind the swamp. From this spot and without leaves, a whole new perspective was gained of the hillside rising to the north. It is the continuous rise of land which culminates in Porter Hill in North Rowe − a mountain indeed. Back on the path we found our entrance tracks full of snow fleas.

Out among the beech trees, we came upon an unusual old yellow birch that had grown bent over about ten feet off the ground for almost twenty feet at which point all the limbs grew vertically. It made our back ache just to look at it. Dried delicate little beech drops (a small brown, branched plant parasitic on beech roots) peeked out from the snow cover as we made our way back to the car, happily trying to remember everything we'd seen on this short tramp through the woods on a very cold grey day in January. **2/84**

The Lentil Soup Gang and the Last Frontier

If you don't LIKE lentil soup and sour pickles, this hike is not for you. From the description of our destination, lunch didn't seem necessary, but who were we to veto a good winter picnic even at nine in the morning. Our contribution of lentil soup seemed quite acceptable, and we signed on with the rest of the crew. Seriously studying the geodetic map, the trail boss declared our destination as "The Last Frontier." Had we really climbed every mountain, viewed Rowe from every angle and followed every stream? Hardly, but there can't be many more hilltops from which to view the Deerfield River!

Today's conditions, varying from bare ground to three feet of snow, required equipment, and we strapped into various types of snowshoes with one brave soul on cross-country skis. Trail boss and Buddy, the dog, were left to follow on foot.

We entered the woods at the top of Monroe Hill heading west. As you might suspect, Buddy bounded from here to there in flying leaps to get himself out of one drift into the next, and trail boss was soon out of sight ahead of everyone. Our picnic was to be at the top of the power line east of Monroe Bridge – just a stone's throw from our starting point, by our estimation. It was a warm, very hazy day, and the heavy jackets should have been left behind.

There is a real art to walking on snowshoes and not getting tangled up in brush and undergrowth. We used ski poles which probably aren't legitimate to the sport but sure help the amateur. Uphill went quite well but down was another story. Some were fortunate enough to find a steep spot and slide like a skier, but often the second man down didn't fare as well. Sitting and sliding proved either disastrous or needed wax to get started. Needless to say, the terrain was a challenge. If there was an easier way, it was always the wrong direction. After much kidding, the man on cross-country skis was the envy of all, taking the ups and downs well in stride.

The first item of interest was a piece of iron (like an axe head) wedged into a crack in a small ledge. Well now, there must be a story here. We gathered around for speculation. "The old settler got so mad at these bony hills that he threw his axe into a rock – so mad at his wife that he went

The Lentil Soup Gang

out and cracked rocks – swung his axe at a tree and missed." No? We suspect there is an old deed that reads, "...bounded at the northwest corner by an iron wedge in a rock." What a pretty sheep pasture this must have been when cleared and used years ago. Matted over rocks, fallen trees, and small bushes were hundreds of dry strings of climbing false buckwheat vine coming up out of the snow.

Our steps quickened when we spotted two huge boulders, wearing hats of snow, sitting on top of the hill. Going through our usual ritual we checked around each one. Finding a small porcupine den under the second one, we tried to kneel down to look inside. Kneeling, we found, does not come easy on our snowshoes, and we had to bend in the middle and hang our head low, only to find no one home.

Meanwhile, the crew was having a conference as to directions, and the verdict seemed to be "down the back side." In hindsight, we must have been standing on a half grapefruit kind of hill and went down and around the side. The trail boss didn't admit to being lost, but he and Buddy did a lot of tramping around ahead with shouts of "Over this way!" and "Come on back here!" Out of the more open hardwoods, we had come into a section of spruce and hemlock where the porcupine had had a feast and dropped many small branches for later use. The deer, too, had crisscrossed the area and found shelter under the evergreens.

The terrain now became vertical and each one picked his own route through the obstacle course that descended into the upland valley below. Our cross-country skier made a few wild runs and quick sit-downs and finally settled on a safer traverse. On snowshoes, we put our poles ahead and leaned on them as we maneuvered our webbed feet through the brush and trees down the hill. One of our poles went further down than expected, and we landed head over teakettle with our face in the snow. Buddy seemed to enjoy this stunt more than we did trying to untangle trees, arms and snowshoes.

The idea of lunch suddenly came to mind – not such a bad idea after all as our stomach growled in anticipation. Our trail boss could certainly make a ten minute hike into a three hour adventure with a little help from "Grapefruit Hill." And there goes Buddy off in a new direction, his tracks simply big round holes in the snow every four or five feet where he landed and took off.

As this Wild Side story was intended to be a more visual hike, with pictures, we'll get you right out on the power line to see the view. And there's that meandering Deerfield River, here flowing over the dam and around the little village of Monroe Bridge – some of the river water going from the dam by tube and open canal to feed Number Five Hydro Station further downstream. When the original covered bridge spanned the river here, connecting two parts of Rowe in the early 1800s, it was referred to as "a wild and picturesque spot."

Once again we marveled at the geology of this area – the uplifting and wearing down of mountains which created this beautiful gorge in our backyard. Today it is hazy – a real summer haze hangs up and down the valley obscuring the distant mountains. We climbed up the snowmobile trail to the right, reaching the highest point on the power line and looked north to see the river dammed again creating Sherman Pond, still used by the tiny Sherman Hydro Station for which it was created and in recent years by Yankee Atomic. Below us to the left, a wide valley has eroded, tilting toward the river between this mountain and the Pulpit Rock range which is the eastern wall of the river valley from here to Hoosac Tunnel. Actually very little of the river is in view because of the smaller hills in front of us. We examined all points with the field glasses, picked out vertical Kingsley Hill Road across the valley and wondered at the foot tracks along side the snowmobile trail on the opposite side of Monroe Hill Road.

Shedding the big feet, it was good to be footloose for a few minutes to appreciate this windswept hillside on the edge of the woods. Where the ledge was visible, moss encircled rose-colored rocks along with some bright red British Soldier lichens and green staghorn club moss in the deeper soil of the bank. This power line, built ten years ago for transmission from the new Bear Swamp Hydro Station, still showed scars of construction with decaying uprooted trees along the edge. The roots of these provided dry sticks for the fire in the stone fireplace now being built by the crew on the top ledge. A discarded metal piece of some machine, found close-by, provided an ideal grate. The lentil soup was soon bubbling and boiling, well seasoned with the usual ashes of a campfire. Meanwhile, the volunteer cook was on her knees making cheese and tomato sandwiches for everyone including Buddy who stood by waiting for his share.

As everyone arranged themselves on rocks and stumps and consumed a large portion of hot lentil soup, sprinkled with Parmesan cheese and accented with a homemade sour pickle, we continued to feast our eyes on the dramatic terrain of the Wild Side before us.

We couldn't help but wonder if Cornelius Jones himself had not stood on this very spot to survey the rugged beauty of the northwest corner (Monroe) of the "parallelogram of 10,000 acres" which he had purchased in 1762 and called Myrifield. (Myrias means 10,000 in Greek.) And as we enjoyed the comforts of our feast on this warm hazy day, we thought back to the cold, starvation and hardships experienced by the seventy returning soldiers who had lost their way, almost two hundred and twenty-six years ago to the day, on what must have been the first "Wild Side" hike down this Deerfield Valley, chronicled by the young nineteen-year-old veteran, Rufus Putnam. And we also remembered their dog whose life was sacrificed in desperation to save the famished men as they camped here below us in this wild gorge on that stormy night in February so long ago.

And so on this pleasant February day in the latter part of the twentieth century, we dismantled our fireplace, watched a helicopter come out of the haze and fly over our heads to the east, spotted two high A-10s passing south, with their usual maneuvers through our valley, and finally headed down across the power line through the blackberry brambles and dried mullein stalks.

The Last Frontier? Never! With the coming of spring, every nook and cranny will be a new frontier with fresh and exciting treasures on the Wild Side.   **3/84**

Rowe's North Boundary and Early Settlers

Looking down Potter Road, North Rowe

We never knew them, of course, those early settlers who made their way across Massachusetts and took their chances on Myrifield. Capt. William Taylor came from Worcester about 1770 and was one of Rowe's first Selectmen. He settled in and made his home on land either side of Potter Road at the present Shields farm. Next west, arriving about 1784, was Joseph Cressy from Connecticut. His sons moved on down to Tunnel Road creating the "Cressy Neighborhood." Today we started off across Capt.Taylor's land.

All through March we'd been waiting for a nice spring day when the snow had melted enough to walk comfortably in the woods. We tested it yesterday up the front of Todd Mountain. It was a one up, two down situation and tough on the knees – much more fun going down the back side with a little momentum pulling us from our sunken footsteps. Today we used snowshoes.

By mid-morning we made the decision to go. There were no takers for our last minute plans, so we were deposited alone at the Town Line marker on Potter Road. Our game plan called for heading west, ten degrees north, along the State Line to the Old Readsboro Road following along Capt. Taylor's north wall and on across Cressy's land. No one told us Taylor never built a north wall!

The road crew had plowed a good turnaround spot, but on snowshoes it was a Chinese puzzle to climb over the big snow chunks and down the short steep bank. We walked around a few times like an animal trying to jump a fence and finally made it over the hurdle. Down on solid ground, the snow surface held firm and walking was comparatively easy.

Heading west, ten degrees north, from our precise starting point would have taken us precisely to the intersection of the Vermont line and the Old Readsboro Road, but that didn't take into consideration Peter Cottontail, a beautiful swamp and other interesting side shows along the way.

The first rabbit tracks soon crossed our path and went into the sheltered hole in the snow under a large downed tree limb. Hopefully, this was a good omen for today's Wild Side collection. The land sloped west for a short distance then leveled out into a huge swamp hidden slightly by the evergreens around the edge. According to the geodetic map, this neighboring piece of Vermont was quite possibly the largest section of flat land in the area, rivaled only by the "Great Swamp" (now Pelham Lake) of Capt. Taylor's time two hundred years ago.

Always anticipating the possibility of another heron rookery, we went out on the swamp to explore. Certainly underfoot were pockets of water, sphagnum moss and swamp bushes, but now, securely covered with ice and layers of snow, it was all quite passable with snowshoes. Come spring and summer, our passage would be around and no longer across.

A true swamp and not presently a beaver pond, this area was totally fascinating – wide and open and bright in the March sunshine, full of stately dead trees in various degrees of decay – and absolutely quiet. Not a sound anywhere – not a blackbird vying for territory or a jay screaming, not even a chickadee. Eerie silence in this far-off white desert land.

Walking across to the center of the swamp, we found small bushes with washed-out looking red berries and tall remains of trees drilled with woodpecker holes. Some trees had overturned, pulling out of the water large circles of roots and dirt. Along one edge, we finally heard what sounded like the slow intermittent tapping of a woodpecker. Some small bit of life, at last. But looking closer with the binoculars, we found the

well-worn limb of a maple tree intertwined with a spruce very gently creaking as a soft breeze passed over our head.

In search of life, we poked holes in the iced pools of water and found only mud and decayed leaves. Systematically, we scanned the treetops for evidence of herons. Nothing. Yet there was life here. You could feel it ready to burst forth in the spring sunshine – bugs and birds and frogs and flowers and all the wonderful intriguing life in a swamp. Wild Side treasures.

Capt. Taylor and Joseph Cressy must have identified their mutual corner with a suitable marker, but we suspected we'd passed that point, lost beneath mounds of drifted snow. The land rose up enough to circle the swamp and then gently sloped southward as we tramped westerly. Soon the evergreens – hemlock, spruce and balsam – became so thick that passage was almost

impossible. We continually found ourselves in a cage of trees from which there was no obvious exit.

We must have climbed into rabbit heaven! Tracks ran in every direction with single telltale pellets along the way. Grouse were here, hiding in small circular shelters of leaves under low branches. Every so often one would sail out of its roosting point at great speed, somehow avoiding all interfering branches. Red squirrels lived here, too, evidenced by the ends of spruce branches dropped on the ground after their cones had been removed and squirreled away in some nifty hiding spot. One such hungry creature had taken a cone and sat in the snow by his hole, carefully extracting the seeds and leaving a heap of cone petals called a midden.

Without a compass, we probably would have taken our direction from the sun, but at high noon in one of those cages it was easy to become disorientated. Whether we were anywhere near the Vermont line was now anybody's guess. The land sloped more to the south, and we came upon apple trees, usually an indication of a nearby cellar hole. With snow deep enough to distort ground objects, we did not try to locate a house site, but couldn't resist inspecting two large boulder erratics. Just rock rocks, but we love 'em all. Further down on the side hill, near a brook gully was one huge mound covered with snow. We detoured down. Instead of a rock under the snow, we found a large decayed pile of slabs from an old sawmill. The rabbits loved this and tracks led to the large open end where we found a real apartment house. Our snow-blinded eyes could not see in the dark crevices, and we mentally added a

flashlight as a new piece of equipment for our knapsack.

Good hunting ground for a larger predator! The scattered soft hairs of rabbit remains were in the nearby snow. The tracks of this hunter crossed our path, and we followed them some distance trying to determine positive identification. There were claw marks on the two top toes, of these side by each tracks, which according to our reference indicates canine rather than feline varieties. We guessed a coyote.

We could see the brook gully widening out onto the Old Readsboro Road, and we emerged just north of there, recognizing the spot from previous hikes up Wheeler Brook. We walked the short distance to the Vermont line on snowmobile tracks. We had headed "west, ten degrees South," evidently, with all the detours, our calculations weren't bad after all.

Homeward bound, we chose to head directly southeast in hopes of picking up the crossroad to the old Bolton cellar hole on Potter Road. Abandoned in 1835, and neither end very precise on the old maps, this road's location would be difficult to trace. However, with luck, aiming southeast would bring us back near the car waiting at the end of Cross Road.

It seemed we were running an obstacle course starting with the deep ravine of the small brook followed by a wall of dead branches at the base of evergreens on the other side. We soon ventured into a tiny beaver pond, now drained, on another small flowing stream. These were all mountain sources for Wheeler Brook joining the Deerfield at Sherman Pond. Southeast tracked very gradually up a rather wet hillside where several large trees had overturned. We looked over a couple rather carefully, hoping to find buried in the uplifted soil some relic of Joseph Cressy. Instead we found holes leading to small bird's nests hidden among the roots.

More apple trees and just the pleasant open lay of the land took us on a short detour up to the south. The early 1780 dwellings in Myrifield were generally log huts marked only by a slight depression in the ground or a collection of rocks hardly discernable in summer. But here, somewhere on this hundred acre plot, the Cressys raised their sons and somehow this seemed like a good location. Mirages of lilac bushes and cinnamon roses came across our vision. We retrieved an apple from our knapsack and munched as we circled back on course, passing new piles of rotted slabs.

Down nearer the brook, we spotted an east-west wall and gave some thought to following it, but realizing it could not be an original property boundary, we continued southeast. Nothing intersected our course with any resemblance to the old crossroad path we were seeking.

The sun had passed its zenith and was casting our shadow in longer proportion. We hurried on up through an endless beech wood hillside and suddenly realized we had

ceased to "stop and smell the flowers." Our curiosity had waned as our body fatigued. We picked out a sturdy tree and leaned to rest. Looking up through the red buds of springtime to the clear blue sky above was a lovely treat. How often we plod through life with our heads down oblivious to the canopy of sky and clouds and stars above.

Rested and refreshed, we now saw the tiny snow fleas, the remains of an ancient tree trunk and heard the soft voices of chickadees feeding in the evergreens ahead. Here a modern wood road came to our rescue and we followed, soon to realize that we were back with Capt. Taylor emerging behind the Dennington barn. We had tracked a good many degrees east of south, but it did not matter – we were not competing for an orienteering badge. We were out hiking on the Wild Side and remembering the courage of our forbearers who created a town in this wilderness and served it well two hundred years ago. **4/84**

Dennington barn

Spring Wildflowers and Happy Easter

Spring is arriving slowly this year. It is having difficulty dodging the raindrops and pushing new shoots through the remaining snow in the woods. But when the calls came that the herons were back, we knew Mother Nature had everything under control.

Easter Sunday dawned bright and cool, but by midday it was shirt-sleeve hiking weather. Knowing the north woods still had snow, we thought up a good excuse to hike over west to find the two cellar holes near the source of Steele Brook. We parked the car by Sparky's Corner and headed down inside the stone wall on the right.

Richard Mason had sold this land to Ephraim Hill in 1780 for thirteen hundred Spanish milled dollars and Bartholomew Bartlett and Christopher Page had owned it before that. We hoped they were respectable men for we were walking with them today, in spirit, asking questions and hoping they would guide us to the old homesteads. However, they seemed to fade into the woods as we quickly became more intrigued and surprised with the large rocks and bits of ledge that veered our course up a hill to the north.

Steele Brook has many sources we realized as we crossed areas where the spring run-off appeared and disappeared among the leaves and rocks. In all, an insignificant-looking stream to have been responsible for carving this valley we now traversed. Eroding waters from higher mountains in our geologic past had played their part.

Now far beyond the cellar holes, we let curiosity take us along a wood road which led through a park-like stand of hemlocks. Such trees, usually devoid of underbrush, remind us of an old world cathedral with the soft choir of wind singing overhead. As we left the cool dimness of the woods to emerge on the open power line, the sun beat down with that welcome warmth that only spring can produce. We wanted to stretch out on the dry mossy hill and absorb every ray.

But it was not yet time to relax. We had to climb over a small knoll to see the fast moving, tiny stream which was probably the largest tributary of Steele Brook. Rewards awaited along its edge – the bright yellow blossoms of spring's earliest flower, the coltsfoot. Looking like a dandelion or hawkweed about four inches high, this plant blossoms early and goes to seed. Later, many large leaves appear on single stems and their shape resembles a colt's hoof. Nearby, the brown fertile stems of horsetails were just coming through the moss. What sheer joy these weeds can generate on an April day in New England when snow still covers the north side of the hills.

We stood for several minutes looking down at the pretty pebbles in the brook bed. Their colors – slate blue, quartz white and rusty orange – gleamed in the sunshine. We removed one and found that as it dried off in our hand it was not nearly as pretty as it had been under the sparkling water. We were tempted to follow this stream back down through the woods, but a huge white rock further down the power line seemed to have a stronger pull.

"Rugged" best describes this land under the power line along the eastern side of our western boundary mountain – Pulpit Rock Ridge, for want of a better name. Hills and vales, boulders and large faces of ledge are still surrounded by disturbed land from the newer power line even though most of the scars have healed. It's hard to imagine this as a sheep pasture in the old days.

The beautiful white quartz boulder should be transported to the Village Green! It sits partway down a hill, protected by blackberry bushes with a carpet of coltsfoot on the roadway passing alongside. A slight bit of mossy soil has collected in a depression on top and sports a lovely collection of red topped British Soldier lichens. Circling the rock, as seems to be our custom, we found this was not just white but very clean and very hard, showing no signs of wear like our other rocks. Touching it was a shock. It was very cold even on the sunny side. White rocks don't absorb heat – our lesson for today. Looking back toward the brook, a small whirlwind had funneled leaves up above the power line, and they were slowly floating back to earth.

The microwave towers came into view high ahead of us, and we could not pass them by without climbing to one of our favorite spots. Then we could relax! Arriving at the top, we'd have gladly traded the contents of our knapsack – maps, compass, binoculars, etc. – for one swallow of water. Our Easter lunch of ham had created a tremendous thirst after the climb. We sat looking longingly at the white rapids in the Deerfield far down in the valley below.

The hillside just south of where we had been sitting is evidently made of good rich woodsy soil for it contains all the spring plants that need that environment. We suspect this was our destination all along, but it was more fun arriving there unexpectedly by this devious route. We knew just where to look for the Dutchman's-breeches and squirrel-corn, whose leaves look just alike, and it is always a thrill to really see them again. The dainty white and yellow pantaloons and heart-shaped flowers were not yet visible, but the clumps of green leaves had already come up in all the familiar places.

Climbing down the bank on that special hillside, we found ourselves first in a patch of early saxifrage with tightly budded blossoms ready to spring forth. Some small animal had nibbled all the leaves on these tasty morsels. The seemingly water-stained leaves of the Virginia waterleaf were well on their way, and there were the spring beauties! Those little pinkish white flowers with darker pink veins usually litter the woods but seemed late this year. It was good to see them again! And that funny blue cohosh was up and budded, looking like some grotesque creation for a horror movie. It soon loses this identity and becomes green with dark blue and yellow flowers. We searched for a tiny yellow violet but in vain. We found the leaves of the larger Canada violet but not the tiny round-leaved yellow which blossoms before the leaves are very large. The wild ginger, too, was still sleeping under the carpet of last year's leaves.

We climbed the ridge again and came down by the Upper Reservoir to see what birdlife might be about. A killdeer greeted us with his song and four ducks were quietly swimming in the distance while eight more circled overhead. We remembered last week's early morning visit when we saw about fifty black ducks in a cove and watched a flock of Canada geese winging north in their familiar V shape. Soon afterwards, we followed the flight of two blue herons intent on their own particular destination. Were these our special

The folded and faulted rock

through the woods. As much as we ached in all joints by then, there was always the possibility of finding something else new and interesting. The terrain was level and rather swampy until it began to climb to an outcropping of ledge – our reward for this detour. Looking for an example of the folding and faulting and squeezing of our rocks as they were formed into these mountains millions of years ago, here was our exhibit. Some were even rippled rocks like the edge of a hard muddy shore. Another spot to add to our collection of favorites!

Our short cut was the long way around as always, but if not taken we would have missed the turkey feathers strewn on the ground. We looked for other remains but found nothing but feathers. Nearby in a tiny patch of snow was the unmistakable paw print of the predator in this woodland drama.

Back to the car seemed like the longest mile we had ever walked. Bent over and dragging our feet in winter boots, we trudged up the road with only a nod to old Ephraim Hill sitting on his stone wall. Afraid the car was a mirage, we ran the last few feet with key in hand. As we settled with a great sigh of relief behind the wheel and opened the window, our eyes focused on two big arrows and a cheery message scratched on the dirt road beside us –   **5/84**

pair returning to nest in the Day Swamp?

The afternoon sun was warm on our back as we headed east toward Tunnel Road, realizing how far we had wandered from the car. Strange frog noises came from the little swamp below the reservoir, and we stopped to listen. These were not the spring peepers but big old frogs. With the glasses we counted fifteen and watched them thrash around in that tiny pond. As we walked on, their funny voices suddenly stopped and all was quiet.

Instead of taking the access road, we thought it would be shorter to go cross-lots

The Leek Tradition

Once you've tasted them, you may immediately become a life-long convert. You'll always remember the first time you came upon them in that rich woodsy spot – a colony of fresh green leaves among the brown debris of winter on the forest floor of early spring. You can smell them, too – their pleasant oniony scent surrounds you as you dig with your fingers far down in the moist earth to uncover your first wild leeks.

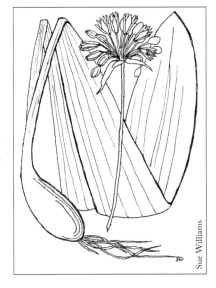

Sue Williams

By mid-May we could wait no longer. It was high time to introduce another friend to our annual spring ritual of leek hunting! A field sparrow greeted us from over the hilltop as we left the car just above the junction of Steele Brook and Tunnel Roads. It was a beautiful morning, a bit on the cool side, and the breeze was brisk as we started down Tunnel Road through the old "Cressy neighborhood" at a rather fast pace in anticipation of all the good things to come.

The first warbler stopped us in our tracks, and we walked back and forth with binoculars trying to locate the little ventriloquist high in the maple tree. He eventually flew off into the woods leaving us frustrated in our attempts to identify, but in his place a chestnut-sided warbler obliged very nicely on the other side of the road, then a redstart with his flash of black and orange and an unmistakable black-throated green warbler both came by to be seen and heard. As we stopped to look at the old Southwest School foundation, a veery thrush flew from rock to ground to tree and on into the woods. We wondered if on early spring mornings long ago the pupils walking to this little one room school had taken time to listen to these same bird songs along the way.

Poking on down the road, we admired the new little long beech ferns whose fronds tip over backwards on their stems. Blue violets, too, were numerous and came in many varieties which we must learn to distinguish instead of just enjoying. As the Bear Swamp dike loomed up on the west side of the road, the wind whipped over the edge and quickened our pace into the shelter of the woods. We soon appreciated the advantage of the wind in keeping at bay the now overly numerous black flies – "The Bugs" of New England spring. But if there were no bugs, so too would disappear our lovely songbirds, and we stopped to listen to the clear flute-like song of a hermit thrush in the distance. This music was soon overpowered by the ovenbird loudly singing, "teacher, teacher, teacher."

We passed the first old Cressy farm with its many walls and foundations, a fairly level spot in this mountainous countryside. Mats of gill-over-the-ground surrounded the yard and grapevines tugged at the trees. Along here where the road starts down again, we crossed the old boundary of "Fulham's Grant" – a five hundred acre plot which was originally incorporated along with Myrifield into the Town of Rowe. Beyond here had been the unincorporated section called Zoar – this western portion of Zoar was annexed to Rowe in 1838.

Coming to the small road into the "Clay Pit", we walked up to a log where we could sit and overlook this wide open expanse of land where clay had been removed for use in the Bear Swamp dikes. In ten years, the scars had healed by being re-seeded with bushes and grasses. Native plants were filtering in, and this now was one of our favorite haunts especially in the fall.

Although we had covered only a short distance on our intended route, we found ourselves eagerly dipping into the knapsack for cheese, bread, and apples realizing it was already lunchtime. The tiny deep purple violets at our feet intrigued us, and we forgot the food for a moment to examine them more closely. Even with our heads down and thoughts on violets, the distant song of the bluebird brought us to our feet, binoculars in hand. That lovely first song of spring from our childhood memories was now a rare treat to hear. We spotted him some distance away, and as if he knew our wishes, he flew to the top of the tree behind us and for a minute or so sang only to us. Leek hunting could be forgotten – the bluebird had made our day! As we finished our lunch, a chestnut-sided warbler happily sang beside us, a flicker called across the hill and a flycatcher puzzled us in the poplar tree ahead. High above, a turkey vulture floated over the landscape looking for carrion remains.

Headed down the road once again, we looked for the usual pink lady's-slippers, but could only find the leaves of one, not yet budded. These are erratic in their growing habits and may appear and disappear from year to year. In the little brook by the old Cressy/Doubleday house, bright yellow coltsfoot still blossomed. We remembered the lovely open view from here years ago as it stretched off toward Negus Mountain. This was the second old Cressy farm whose bounds were laced with sturdy old stone walls. Neighboring to the south was yet another Cressy cellar hole with interesting barnyard walls and many large circular piles of excess rocks in the pasture. Now this old Cressy neighborhood had returned to the Wild Side from whence it originated long ago.

Timber cutting in recent years has cluttered the land with slash along the lower section of Tunnel Road, but also has opened up new views across the Deerfield Valley, so lovely today with the mountains clad in soft spring greens. As the road steepened into its cliff-hanging section over the brook ravine, large clumps of blue and white violets grew among the heaps of brush, and birds once again filled the trees. A pair of orioles delighted us with color and song, a black and white warbler seemed very friendly and a black-throated blue warbler sang to us all along the way. Numerous others eluded our identification.

Having descended now to our intended destination, we began observing more carefully. The always spectacular huge rock cliffs and jumbles of boulders in this area of serpentine and talc certainly make for a most interesting landscape. Here we left the road to bushwhack down toward the old Soapstone Quarry where we had a suspicion there might be some wild leeks – we could almost smell them!

It's hard to remember just what we saw first – perhaps it was the large clumps of hepaticas whose blossoms had gone by but whose soft new growth of leaves felt cottony to the touch, or the red columbine growing high up in tiny rock crevices. Suddenly the ground was covered with tall stemmed violets – the downy yellow and the Canada whose white flower has a touch of purple on the back. White toothwort was in blossom everywhere, and there were frequent patches of the beautiful little dwarf ginseng with perfectly round little balls of white flowers. In particularly moist areas grew colonies of wild ginger, now blossomed with a rusty red, bell-shaped flower at the base of two leaf stems almost on the ground. In among all these were the dainty fronds of maidenhair fern.

So intrigued were we with this unending array of springtime that we were standing knee deep in the leeks before we really looked for them. With a shout of joy, we were on our knees digging down with our fingers to come up with the first leek of the season, reeking with that wonderful earthy onion smell that draws you back year after year. The earth was soft and damp and we had our small plastic bags full in no time and tucked away in our knapsack. But leeks are like berries, you have to shut your eyes and leave them because you want to dig just one more, and thus we found ourselves back on our knees once again. It's really all part of the ritual!

Finally, standing and rearranging our bulging knapsacks, we turned to look around this little dell of rocks. Across the way was a sight we shall not soon forget. A large outcrop of ledge had collected a little soil on the lower end and in various cracks and crevices. From our vantage point, the sun was highlighting the side toward us where grew first a line of miterwort – the tall single stems of tiny fringed white blossoms – then surrounding these were the white flowers of early saxifrage scattered between leaves of the earlier Dutchman's-breeches. On a tiny ledge above grew the bright red columbine and here and there along the rock were stands of maidenhair fern, while dainty whorls of maidenhair spleenwort fern grew along the lower cracks. Summer and winter could come and go, and we would still vividly remember this treasured spot.

As we meandered down the hill, still more flowers were scattered along the way, and we found it hard to take a step without damaging something fragile in our path. We came down by the Soapstone Quarry and eventually back on the road. Happy with our leeks and our memories of lovely birds and flowers, we were homeward bound.

One more treasure, however, was in store. This time it was a small ravine between cliff walls where new ferns looked especially lush. Here we found lovely patches of toothwort, three unusual yellow trillium and a large stand of silvery spleenwort fern above which early saxifrage covered the rocks. Jack-in-the-pulpits were here and there and an occasional fragrant heart-shaped squirrel corn was still in bloom. Fresh bear droppings added to the excitement as we stumbled onto our real find of the day – one circular cluster of fairly rare narrow-leaved spleenwort fern. Although we have seen this in the area, it is always a joy to add a new item to our "Found in Rowe" collection!

So as you can see, my friends, the leek hunting tradition hath many rewards.   **6/84**

Peck's Field on a Rare June Day

If twice repeated establishes a tradition, we are setting one now by again writing the July Wild Side up at the old Ethier house site, known in earlier years as a favorite spot on the Peck farm. It's a lovely June day with a good breeze and lots of fluffy flat-bottomed clouds between here and Greylock on the western horizon. On the way over, we stopped for a drink at the familiar roadside spring and listened to a hermit thrush very close by. As we walked downhill a bit to look for the dainty pink herb Roberts along the side, a tiny winter wren burst forth in song and treated us to several choruses of his sweet music.

Once settled here on the hill, we walked around to enjoy the several laurel bushes in full bloom. We bent to smell an especially pink cluster and found it lovely to look at but having no perfume. Soon we became aware of a noise in the distance back toward Negus – sort of sounded like a fox barking. The sound grew louder and closer and we realized it was coming over the trees and not through the woods. Just then four young ravens flew croaking by and went down off toward the switching station. The racket went on for a long time and every so often an adult raven would pipe up with a much deeper guttural squawk. Perhaps these are the family from the nest down on Coon Hill in Zoar, but hopefully they are Rowe natives. It is good to know the ravens still consider this a wilderness area. A towhee is singing "drink your tea" down in the field. If life doesn't quiet down up here, we may never get to tell you about our early morning venture!

* * * * *

It was shortly after sunrise when we entered the woods off Cyrus Stage Road, wearing our heavy wool sweater which felt good in the morning dampness. The woods seemed strangely dark with only low rays of sunlight coming from the east. All the birds were up and singing and especially noticeable was a happy little chickadee following along with us. Somehow the chickadee song seems unusual in the summertime. The meadow rue was blossomed along the path to the Swamp, and the woods on either side were carpeted with new shiny leaves of the goldthread. Bluets were still scattered here and there, the pyrola was already budded under the hemlock tree, and the little swamp was full of wild calla lilies.

We knew what awaited us in the Day Swamp. The joy of discovery had come about a week ago. The great blue herons had returned to the area, but with last year's nest gone, it was a question whether they would choose this spot again. Having checked there for several weeks, we had sort of given up hope. From the first viewpoint we had seen nothing, but as we had walked around the edge, there the heron was high in a tree on the far side. How could we have missed it! The nest looked small and flimsy and what could be holding it to that high limb? The heron sat head up like a queen surveying all around her. It had been several minutes before we saw the second nest lower and to the right with its occupant cuddled right down tending to business. We had a heronry!

When we arrived this morning, both birds were barely visible and perhaps had not yet realized it was daybreak. Very soon, two other herons flew in from downstream, circled the nests and lighted in the tall hemlocks to the left. We expected they were there to change places with the setting parents and take their turn, but the ones on the nest never moved. To be sure, these two flew around once more, decided they were not yet needed and took off for some early morning fishing.

We walked around the old gravel bank to examine the numerous holes in the sand. Our first thought was that turtles had been digging holes to lay eggs, but there was not an egg to be found. Perhaps skunks or bears were after ants, but these were such little ants that that didn't seem logical. Then we found the egg shells – sort of soft and rubbery. Skunks or raccoons had had a feast and not a turtle would hatch. Looking back at the floor of the gravel bank, it was glistening red in the morning sun with the bright new leaves of the sundew plants. The sheep laurel was in bright pink bud and ready to open. Around the edge of the Swamp, the bunchberry flowers were just turning brown and dropping petals while their centers were beginning to form fruit. The Canada mayflowers already had their tan-colored berries. This morning the swallows were flying high while the frogs jumped for insects in the water and now and then barked from their various stations. Pretty turquoise dragonflies flitted over the water.

Looking up, we caught sight of the heron in flight from the high nest to the tallest treetop on the far side. We were surprised it left the nest without the other bird being there to take over. Don't eggs get cold? Or cooked in the sun? We noted the time as 7:25. It was funny to watch. The bird stood on one foot and then another looking all around as if to say, "It's your turn, so now where are you?" She (we think it was "she") preened her feathers – this was really needed for she looked pretty ragged – stretched her wings a few times and then proceeded to stand still for the next hour and twenty minutes while we worried! We stood on one foot and then another until finally settling on a log with our back against a tree and a good view of both nests. Heron number two never moved a muscle.

A chipmunk ran around us a few times and then decided we were intruding on his territory and scolded us from a nearby log. Eventually he braved the run and came around behind us darting into a hole we hadn't even noticed right by our feet. He scrambled in, turned around and from the safety of his hole stuck his nose out and watched us, speaking sociably every so often. We didn't want to take our eyes off the heron but couldn't resist the chipmunk antics. Something new seems to always turn up every time we visit this Swamp, and today a mother black duck and six little fuzzy followers went paddling by. We had seen many ducks but never the babies.

After the long wait, mother heron simply flew off and disappeared. We guessed she'd gone to round up her delinquent fisherman and get him to tend the eggs. But still heron number two was tending to business on her/his own. From our calculations last year, the young herons should hatch about the time the swamp candles are budding (a little before Rowe Old Home Day). We'll return then to learn the possible ill effects of the seemingly careless nesting habits of the first blue heron!

We had really come out early for a long hike, and now we had spent over two hours sitting in the Swamp. It was time to move on. We packed up and headed north by the compass. Our intention was to explore further this northwestern section of the "Green and Walker" Grant. Back in 1741 four men, merchants of Boston, were granted a tract of 8,575 acres of land "northeast of the Deerfield." They also wanted more acreage toward the river, but that would later go to Cornelius Jones, our founder of Rowe. Most of the Green and Walker Grant became Heath at their incorporation in 1785, but at the same time a strip two hundred rods wide was added to Myrifield's eastern border to become Rowe, also in 1785. This land was surveyed in 1796 and divided into fourteen lots, which were then purchased for resale by Nathan Rice of Hingham. It is interesting to note that several lots were purchased by area innkeepers – Robert McClellen of Colrain, Thompson Smith of Heath and Joel Hall of Charlemont. Land in those days must have

been considered a good investment.

We headed north along a swampy brook where the swamp buttercups highlighted the thick green growth. Our course soon crossed the power line where blackberry bushes were in full bloom. We stopped to look at something and noticed that we were surrounded by low brown ferns. A stand of the delicate marsh fern had all been frosted on a recent cold night. We tend to think of vegetable gardens and forget that wild things, too, are killed by late frosts.

As we crossed the old fence lines, we thought of those early men who had walked this land in 1800 to determine its value and finally settled for $450 a lot, each including about one hundred acres. The land rises to the west and going north is not necessarily always up, as would seem logical. Our compass was handy. We detoured here and there looking at boulders and were intrigued with a large three-cornered pile of rocks – boundary marker or maybe just a fancy way to get rid of the pasture stones. Two pink lady's slippers caught our eye – it is rather late for them in bloom, and these were unusually deep pink. We examined them carefully and found they had a stem leaf as well as the two familiar base ones. Every flower book says "no stem leaves", but in all other respects these were normal, proving there is always one exception to every rule.

Walls and paths now looked familiar, and we knew we must be on Green and Walker Lot #12 where it's our guess that Humphrey Taylor built the first house in this section sometime after 1801. It's a beautiful old cellar hole – in recent years known as the Crittenden place – and surrounded by big old maples in the lee of the hill. A substantial barn foundation is lost below a lovely side hill stand of hayscented fern, now spotlighted with patches of sunlight. The old chimney had several fireplaces, and the yard was still scattered with bloodroot, baneberry and dainty oak fern. A comfortable sheltered spot and we thought of Caty Taylor's invalid daughter whose support was provided for in his will probated in 1847. She was to be cared for by her sister and brother-in-law in this house. Caty willed her his best bed with six linen sheets and two calico quilts. He also had twelve old chairs and a painted bureau, but only six knives and forks. Rowe pioneers.

The view was clear and bright back on the power line atop Porter Hill, and we were glad we had an apple to call lunch as we sat on a rock looking eastward over the contours of Heath and beyond.

Again by compass we headed south along the border of Myrifield and the Green and Walker Grant where an occasional ancient tree probably marked the line. We finally drifted eastward where curiosity took us. Huge granite boulders were scattered through the woods as the hill steepened and porcupines had found every hiding place under them. Patches of wood sorrel were here and there with shamrock-like leaves and dainty pink-veined white flowers. One large round-leaved orchid had produced nice flat leaves, but no flower. These are often victims of slugs and even deer.

Coming down now on the back side of the Swamp, we looked with the glasses through the trees and saw the heron standing on the highest nest carefully turning the eggs with its beak and then settling down over them. The second bird was still snuggled and quiet.

All was well and we breathed a sigh of relief – we could stop worrying. Suddenly the wind broke off a limb high in a tree between us and the water, and it crashed noisily down through the leaves. This was enough to disturb the herons, and they both rose up and flew off. It was now well after noon, and we could not wait again, but we did circle out around the southern end of the Swamp, looking with the glasses whenever a view opened through the trees. Our final sighting still showed empty nests. But not to worry, these creatures all seem to survive and increase even though the turtle eggs are eaten, and the herons are erratic in nesting behavior – that's the wonder of the Wild Side.

We stopped to cut a few cattails to cook the "hearts" and walked through a beautiful carpet of sphagnum moss where the deer had eaten the flower tops off the tall swamp saxifrage, and the seeds of the marsh marigolds had formed a strange new decoration. Looking back at the Swamp once more, the trees were full of cedar waxwings, and we could hear the soft sound of their calls.

* * * * *

As we leave this lovely spot on Ethier-Peck Hill, the sun is lowering toward Whitcomb Mountain, and the gentle breeze has increased. A sparrow hawk or kestrel is performing its special fete hovering in the wind over the field. A bird about eleven inches long, it flies into the wind then remains stationery often beating its wings but never moving. Occasionally it makes a floppy quick flight around and tries it again. They do this to scan the ground for grasshoppers and mice. A "Windhover", he's called, and we joined him in spirit. **7/84**

Sadly neglected on our tours of the surrounding hills and vales of Rowe has been the Southeast corner in the Davis Mine section of town. Because of a jog in the line with Heath, Rowe has three boundary markers in this corner. Our search for them made a good excuse for a hike. With luck, we might stumble on at least one of these.

It was a lovely morning and we were on our way bright and early. Davis Mine Road – one of the few real country dirt roads left – was patterned with patches of early morning sun filtered through the overhanging trees. Passing first the little quaking bog beside the road, we noticed the two or three pitcher plants had blossomed, turned green and gone to seed while blue flag still blossomed beside the lush stands of cinnamon fern. Often we've seen a red-shouldered hawk sitting on the dead tree in the center.

Driving on past Tuttle Brook, we stopped to appreciate the patch of bunchberry on the right. A low spring flower resembling the dogwood blossom, each had now become a cluster of bright red berries. Surrounding these were the taller stems of the yellow clintonia sporting bright blue berries. And all along the way, ferns of many varieties softened the roadsides with their lovely lacy hues of green.

Farther down the road just before a tiny stream, we knew there was hidden in the trees a few remains of an old foundation where one of the Davis Mine families had lived. We had recently talked with a woman (now in her eighties) who had been born in that "Little Yellow House" beside the road.

Although the existence of certain ore deposits had been known for forty years, it was after Herbert Davis's discovery of valuable iron pyrites in 1882 that Davis Mine was opened and soon became a thriving operation – lasting twenty-nine years, "*Most successful mine in Massachusetts and one of the finest in the country*" had been said of it. A community of well over two hundred people formed around the mine and along with the company buildings there were many houses, boarding houses, a store, post office and school – even street lights some forty years before Rowe village even had electricity! All that remains now are some holes in the ground and one original house. Tall primroses and mullein mark the roadside where bustling activity once filled the roads, and the smell of sulphur was in the air. Old Davis Mine – now just a ghost town in the woods.

Exploring the mine area itself was not our intention and is not recommended for the operation ended with huge cave-ins around the shafts. We left the car at the bend in the road ("Devil's Elbow") where, after the Great Hurricane in the fall of 1938, the old Davis Mine Road to Charlemont had to be abandoned and a new one made, curving north to connect with the Davenport Road which leads on to Charlemont further west.

Hermit thrushes have claimed this territory, and their lovely music surrounded us as we started down the old road. Our first detour was to explore a small rise in the ground to the left where stood some larger old trees. With our first step into the roadside ferns and grass, a bird flew up from our feet and there exposed was a hermit thrush's nest with three beautiful blue-green eggs. We quickly moved some distance away, hoping we had not permanently disturbed this nesting thrush. Other birds would chatter and scold at such an intrusion, but the shy hermit totally disappeared from sight, awaiting our removal.

Looking over this small level area, we soon came upon a large cellar hole and remembering old pictures presumed this to have been the Stranahan house. Over fifty years of abandonment had produced good-sized trees inside the stone foundations. In western mining areas, ghost towns still have remaining buildings because of the dry climate, but here, although many buildings were torn down, our New England rains and humidity have decayed the rest and left us with only stone foundations lining old cellar holes. And time has now taken from us all but a few "children" who remember growing up at Davis Mine.

Moving on down the road, we came out into the open under the power line. The morning had been cool, and the sunshine felt good, but its warmth already predicted a hot day. Looking east up the hill, spots of orange caught our eye. Looking with binoculars, we found the hillside spotted with wood lilies. How pleased we were to see such a stand of one of our favorite flowers! Back into the woods again the road soon joined the brook which was a rich rusty color from the iron in the mine further back. The rocks are slimy and slippery and the acid water does not appeal to fish. However, the ledges and stones are rather pretty as the sun sparkles on the water flowing around them.

A lovely stand of dainty oak fern and lots of long beech fern (that bends over backward) was growing along the moist roadside and kept us looking for plants rather than an indication of the Town Line. In hindsight we're sure we passed the line early on, but curiosity about what was around the next

corner and a vague memory of hiking this road a couple summers after the hurricane, kept us going on into Charlemont some distance. Off and on the road disappeared into the brook bed and from there we could see all the large rocks used in building up this road to make it passable for the huge Studebaker ore wagons which each carried from seven to eleven tons of ore from the mine down this mountain on the way to Charlemont and the railroad. We could almost hear the wheels churning along the muddy road.

Plants new to us often quickly stand out as something different in the usual mass of foliage around us, and we are soon on our knees. Thus we saw here for the first time the rosy bells or twisted stalk with red berries. We had looked for this in the spring and not been really sure if we had found it. Easily confused with Solomon's-seal, the rosy bell stalk is twisted, branched, and the little stems of the flowers and berries also have a crook in them. So once again we had the joy of discovering a new flower for our collection. We would have to return in the spring to see the pink bell-shaped blossoms.

If we were ever to find the Town cornerstones, we must change directions, cross the brook and head east up the ravine. As we left the road, the plentiful helleborine orchid, just in bud, lined the edge, and on the hillside across the brook were scattered the northern green orchids. These, like many other flowers, need to be observed close-up with a hand lens to appreciate the tiny orchid flowers. The heat of the day seemed to have sunk into this ravine and livened up the mosquitoes which were attacking us from all directions.

As we climbed the hill in rather open

woods, there were many patches of the pretty little stem of white flowers called round-leaved pyrola. The leaves are leathery and shiny and the several drooping blossoms on a stem have long curving pistils hanging from their flowers. Often in the same area could be found the blossoming pipsissewa – three or four white waxy flowers with pink and green tinges growing on small stems with two shiny leathery whorls of evergreen leaves.

Suddenly in this acidic soil we came upon a moist area with more ferns and grasses, including rich soil plants like maidenhair fern and white baneberry (doll's-eyes). Hiking up a little above this spot, the rocks were strewn around as if someone had been prospecting and, strangely, they felt a little talc-like, probably accounting for the variation in plants. Somewhere in this southeast corner is a piece of land owned by the Town of Rowe, but at that moment we were still not sure if we were in Rowe or Charlemont. We spent some time speculating on the boundaries we had set out to find, but too many other interesting things distracted us from a serious search. We could always come back now that we knew the way. Soon we picked up an old wood road and had to follow it to see where it went.

With many twists and turns and very good walking, this wood road led us back out to the power line down a ways from the top of the hill. Now we knew for sure we were back in Rowe! We could now examine the lovely wood lilies close at hand and pick handfuls of ripe wild raspberries as we climbed to the top. It was now hot mid-morning, almost time for lunch but not quite. We found a comfortable rock and enjoyed the breeze at this height, looking over the far horizons with the binoculars.

* * * * *

Thinking back to last week's hike into the Day Swamp, we reminisced again about the three fuzzy baby herons that had hatched in the lower nest we had been watching. Unfortunately, as we had suspected from the erratic behavior of the parents tending the high nest, no eggs had hatched and the nest was abandoned. Settling in the grass with our backs against the trees, we had waited for a visit from the feeding parents. Waiting, one has to be as quiet and patient as the birds themselves when they are stalking fish. Nothing happens for a long time! The frogs bark and croak singly and in unison, the cedar waxwings make soft calls as they fly among the dead stumps and trees, and occasionally a pair of kingfishers will chase each other down the length of the water. Then something interesting happens – almost always, if you wait long enough.

That day it began with the strange feeling that someone was watching us. The doe was lying in the tall grass just around the next little cove. Her head was up and she was quietly observing us funny humans sitting by the trees, staring at bird's nests! We co-existed for some time until she felt the pangs of hunger and got up, stretched and, like a moose, walked into the water way above her hips, put her head totally underwater and came up with a long dangle of water-shield – a slimy water plant with small, red flowers growing like water lilies on the surface of the pond. Having devoured the first, she ducked for another and continued the process for a least a half an hour when she finally emerged and sauntered off into the woods. Rowe's

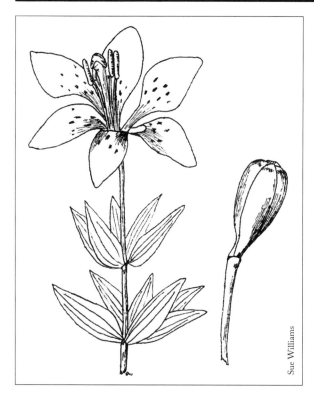

Sue Williams

of the hill just where the map indicated. Down the line of larger trees which must be the Town line, we spotted several rattlesnake plantains in full bud. These are small stems of orchids with checkered leaves in a rosette at the base.

Walking back toward the Davis Mine, we thought about the early traffic over this road between the available Blacksmith Shop at the Mine on the Rowe side and the Gristmill and Sawmill of Dell in Heath. Down in the valley by the brook, the humidity of the day had settled in, and we found ourselves trudging up the other side with thoughts of ice water and a cool breezy place for lunch – like back on our own deck at home.

The sandwiches were a bit mangled from being carried, but good nevertheless, for by this time we were hungry. We had not found the cornerstones, but as

"moose-deer" had been discovered! In the meantime, father heron had come back and landed on the nest, checked the sleeping babies and flown off again without even offering anyone a tasty morsel. Perhaps we should check out the heron's progress on the way home today – a good place for lunch.

* * * * *

Old maps indicate that a road existed from the Davis Mine area of Rowe to the Dell in Heath. We walked down the back side of the power line to see if we could find any remains of this old road. Another road took us into the woods to the north where we soon connected with the one we were looking for. The old stone wall was on top

we said, there was always another day. Our assorted woodland and rock treasures were spread out on the picnic table, and the breeze across the deck was heavenly.

The stage was set, and the timing was perfect. The mother deer came out first, going directly to center stage in the field below. As if it could hardly wait for its cue, the little spotted fawn entered from off by the brook, leaping and bounding through the high grass to the mother's side. A quick nudge to mother, and it was off again, running in ever widening circles like a playful dog teasing his master. It was a good long performance, and when it finally ended both actors exited gracefully over the stone wall in the rear. **8/84**

A Nostalgic Trip to Old Smokey

Dear to the hearts of many Rowe-mans are memories of hikes, picnics, early morning breakfasts or just the hours spent picking blueberries on Rowe's Negus Mountain, Blueberry Hill or by whatever term you fondly remember it. Rowe's firemen, through the years, remember it as "Old Smokey" and are now known to be nostalgic about the nights and days they have spent fighting the forest fires set by the railroad in the valley below. Fires have been scarce in recent years, the brush and trees are growing up, and thus the blueberry crop has dwindled. But the expansive views of the Deerfield River valley are still as spectacular and as close to Heaven as one can imagine.

It was early Sunday morning when we looked out across the "Hopper" and saw the fog rising from the river behind the knob of Negus. And in the east the sun was greeting us from just above Todd Mountain, its rays highlighting the red leaves of an early-turning tree. Between the two sights was spread a beautiful clear blue sky with a tinge of fall in the air. This was our lucky day – we were due for a Wild Side hike.

To traverse the length of Negus would require two cars, and we were soon parking the first by Florida Bridge, noting that already the river fog had dissipated in the clear morning air. We took a minute to walk on the bridge and see the sky reflected in the clear pools of water as the river ambled down this gorge. The Deerfield River, regulated by the New England Power dams above us, was at the moment very low, and the beauty and fury of high water, which we had seen in this spring's flood, was now hard to imagine.

The shortest route back to our starting point was to drive up Steele Brook Road – in itself an adventure! This tiny narrow dirt road hugs the mountainside above the brook ravine and gradually climbs onto wider ground through the old sheep pastures of long ago farmers who settled this wilderness. Today we aren't chasing cellar holes, but we're aware that several exist in this old southwest neighborhood of Rowe.

We came to the road through the field that takes you to the bottom of the first climb to Negus and automatically drove in the now overgrown tunnel-like passage, and then wondered why we hadn't left the car on the road and walked that short distance. Tradition had prevailed. You always drove in, scratching the car on the hardhack and bushes – but then remember what a welcome sight the car was when you came back carrying the blueberry pails? As always in recent years, we missed the stop at the Bents to ask if we could climb their hill. For some of us Rowe-mans, other memories of this mountain go back long before the Bent's arrival to when it was the Herbert Veber farm. Now all is owned by the New England Power Company.

Today as we climbed the first ridge, the anticipation grew, and we hoped once again that the stiff, wintery west winds had stunted the growth of trees which otherwise would block a glorious view. Blueberries were few and far between, but the whorled asters and goldenrods lined our path.

Hiking across Negus is more than a view, a picnic, blueberries or flowers. It is an experience – a renewal of spirit – a feeling of contentment that our rugged mountain world remains the same. There it was before us – the wide expanse over the Deerfield Valley with mountains folding one on another westward to Greylock, northward over the Bear Swamp Reservoir to Vermont and south far beyond the ridge where followed the old Indian Mohawk Trail.

The canopy of sky above us held wisps of high cirrus clouds – long streamers of ice crystals, they tell us in the description of these "Mare's Tails" – and several jet trails were woven in various directions. As the jet trails widened and intersected the clouds, the resulting pattern was like frost on a window pane. We lay on the ground and watched these changing patterns with the binoculars – like looking into a giant white kaleidoscope.

As the trail winds across the hill, each vantage point gives a different perspective. Between the views, we stopped to watch some flickers and chased another large brown bird with the binoculars and listened to his call all along the way – a call so familiar to that area, but one we had never bothered to identify. It was a towhee – probably a female or young bird without the distinctive orange marking of the male or the usual familiar song of the breeding season. Waxwings and chickadees were numerous as were the songs of several warblers not in sight. A pewee gave his plaintive call in the distance. From the open field, we headed back into the woods to the trail, climbing the knob of the mountain. At the edge of the woods were marsh ferns which immediately caught our eye. Marsh ferns on a mountaintop! A hidden spot of moisture must have caught their spores, and they seemed to be thriving.

From past experience, we remembered we could bushwhack to the eastern edge of this knob and overlook Rowe through the trees with the strange perspective of the school on Pond Road sitting just above the Leger house on Zoar Road. Today we stayed on the trail, coming out to the interesting open ledge facing south. This rock is a good example of the folding and faulting of various layers in our geologic past. Here we explored a bit and came out in a more open area facing west. What a treasure house of plants and colors! The low blueberry bushes had started to turn a dark red while a few remaining berries hung on dry stems. Thickly scattered in between were hundreds of bunchberry plants bright with their red berries. Again, a plant we have always seen in the wet swampy areas of the lowlands. The good acid soil of blueberry country must be its requirement, too. What a lovely mingling of colors and textures. Large patches of the low sheep laurel had a special green hue with the dried blossoms still remaining. The regular laurel bushes were contrasting darker green, and we were quickly drawn to a low area of plants the color of western sage. It was the lycopodium called ground cedar, a lovely bluish green.

We never did really like to pick berries – straw, black or blue – but in our youth, a pail of berries for the household always got us the opportunity to roam the fields and hillsides in their search. We soon learned to pick fast, eat none and spend the time searching. We were reminded of that today as we dropped our knapsack on a rock and started searching further and further down the hill. The rewards are great and long-remembered. We wandered down toward three old dead birch trees and beside one found a ledge on the brink of the drop to the river some eight or nine hundred feet below us.

This new perspective was more exciting as we looked directly down on the river, just below Beaver Island – a landmark on even the earliest maps of the area. Two curves of the railroad were visible as it snaked along by Soapstone Switch, which regulates a sidetrack allowing two trains to pass at this point. Across to the north, we could just see the water over the dike at the Upper Reservoir, and as our eyes followed along that ridge, Doubleday's Cliffs stood out in the morning sun. We thought of the variety of plants we had found in the good rich soil on that mountain and down the brook ravine to Beaver Island, so close and yet all so different from the ones

Looking down on the Deerfield River from Negus Mountain

the westbound train in the valley to our left. The first train was slowing to a stop on the sidetrack. We would watch Soapstone Switch in action.

The high cirrus clouds had drifted eastward by now and were replaced by clear blue sky and little puffy, fair weather clouds casting pretty shadows on Whitcomb Mountain. Three turkey vultures floated lazily on the currents along the ridge behind us. The long freight trains passed each other while we watched, fascinated to be able to see this action from

here in this thin acid soil. This was not a spot to be taken in with a short visit – it needed time to be appreciated and experienced to the fullest. The first thing we wanted was the camera in the knapsack back on the top of the hill – and maybe even lunch.

No sooner had we returned from the quick sprint up the hill than that lovely nostalgic sound came drifting down the valley. A train whistle. As the engine came into sight in the distance, it seemed to be laboring and smoking. It's all downhill from the Hoosac Tunnel entrance just out of sight, and the train should be coasting. The mystery was soon solved by the whistle of

our new-found perch on the mountainside. When all was quiet again, two ravens flew across our view toward the Reservoir, croaking their own strange calls.

In our less occupied moments, we checked the ground around us and found a small branching plant with tiny yellow and white blossoms. New to our collection, it was cowwheat and seemed to be growing everywhere once we noticed it. With miles to go, we thought of leaving, but there were still things unseen – birds to bring us to our feet, binoculars in hand, or clouds with new shapes or just the warm sunshine and blue sky to soak into our memory – to be recalled on some gloomy November day. Hours drifted by as minutes while we watched someone tubing in the river, followed another freight train down the valley and finally consumed the cheese and crackers and fruit from our knapsack lunch.

When the decision was finally made to pack up and leave, we did it reluctantly and slowly – fortunately. One more treat was in store for us from this vantage point. But when it appeared, we doubted our senses and thought perhaps we had truly drifted back to those early childhood berry picking days. But it WAS a passenger train – at least eight shiny silver cars rolled around the bends and disappeared toward the Tunnel. Passenger service was discontinued in December of 1958 – one of those dates we especially remember, having made great effort to ride one of the last trains. There is usually a fall foliage trip by one train, but this is only August. (A group of 550 railroad buffs, we learned later, on a trip from Boston to North Adams and back). We had been at the right place at the right time to see this one.

We spent the rest of the day completing our tour across the mountain path through sweetfern (which is not a fern at all) and many varieties of goldenrod to the other summit overlooking Zoar and into Charlemont – where the river makes another big bend and

you can stand and see it on both sides. This is spectacular, too, and perhaps even more dramatic, but by the time you spend a day on Negus, the dramatic seems ordinary and you come to expect to be thrilled by yet another sight. This razorback ridge is rocky and treeless except for some scrub oaks and lots of the pretty yellow false foxglove, parasitic on the oaks. The Rowe line crosses diagonally here down to the old bridge abutment above Florida Bridge. One huge glacial boulder sits along a shelf partway down, and below this there is a trail through the woods to the bridge – so they say – we missed it again!

So we retraced our steps back the old trail to the car on Negus. The flat-topped white asters were full of bees and grew as high as our head in the sun, but in the woods it was cool and quiet and a shy hermit thrush came by to welcome us back from our journey. **9/84**

Glacial erratics on Negus

Death of a House

By Rob Williams
From West County News
May 15-28, 1980

The people of Rowe were taught a lesson this month that times do change and that these are not the old days.

To understand the emotions that people in Rowe expressed, one first needs to know the history of the town and its love for blueberries. Especially important is knowing the relationship between electricity, the railroad, and a red house at the top of the mountain. A history lesson seems to be in order.

Smoke in the sky over west Rowe can mean one of two things: Either it is a sign that local fire fighters are in for a day of work on "Old Smokey" or it's just fog rising off the Deerfield River.

"Old Smokey?" That's just another - and a well-deserved - name for Negus Mountain. It went up in smoke with clockwork regularity almost every time the Boston and Maine sent a fire-breathing locomotive upriver west of Charlemont, between Zoar and the Hoosac Tunnel. Sparks that flew from the exhaust or from the brake shoes landed in the ties and ignited the creosote. Then, depending on the wind, the Rowe fire department headed for the tracks or the top of the mountain.

In 1939, an especially dry year, "Old Smokey" burned for ten days. In 1949, a four-and-a-half-day fire was brought under control after authorities "made plans to evacuate the little village of 180 residents" some three miles away.

When the wind was right, smoke from the forest fires in this remote section would be wafted over much of the town, acting as the best fire alarm the town could afford in those days.

Though newspaper headlines had told of the "whole town ready to flee," no house in town had more cinders land on its roof than the Herbert Veber farmhouse, on the east flank of "Old Smokey." Roy and Kathleen Bent bought the place in 1953, the same year that the Town of Rowe spent nearly $2,000 in firefighting wages for one fire on that mountain. The Veber farm had been abandoned for many years and narrowly escaped many sweeping forest fires, thanks to every "able-bodied" person in town. Roy and his wife saw a future in the place, and spent ten years of weekends flushing the porcupines from the premises and slowly restoring the one-and-a-half-story cape.

In 1956, a four-day fire came dangerously close to the house and prompted Roy to have a waterhole dug in his backyard to preserve his house as well as his peace of mind.

It was "deep snow still lying in high sheltered areas" in April of 1959 that saved the Roy Bent place and kept "the season's worst fire from becoming a major conflagration." That fire burned 125 acres.

In 1963, Roy retired and brought his wife, Kathleen, and his mother to live in Rowe. Although the Bents lived approximately two miles from their nearest year-round neighbor, they had plenty to keep them busy. Virtually the entire mountain was covered with blueberry bushes which were renewed periodically, courtesy of the incendiary B & M Railroad 1,000 feet down in the valley.

The Bents got their burning blueberry patch on CBS News during a 1968 fire which was the biggest in recent history. The

Death of a House

spectacular fire line could be seen heading towards the Bent's house from many points in town.

A haven for hungry firefighters was Kathleen Bent's kitchen, which served town truck drivers in winter just as it did firemen in summer. Kathleen must have served a ton of cookies back then.

When Roy was not picking blueberries for Kathleen, or hunting, or fighting fires, he worked on his house. It was amazing how the quaint red house was revived after being so dilapidated as to be taken off the tax rolls. The work around the house involved everything from sanding the wide floor boards to fixing the masonry around the outside. For fifteen years, every time Roy heard a train "down in the valley he turned his eye towards the western sky for signs of fire that could destroy his work with one shift of the wind.

With track fires occurring weekly in the summer and a major forest fire approximately every ten years, surrounding fire departments gradually became more efficient at "Old Smokey." In the most recent major fire there, in April of 1975, three bulldozers, a helicopter and an airplane were used to aid the firemen on the ground and the fire was out in a day and a half.

At the same time that the forest fires seemed less of a threat to the Bents, the hospital seemed further away and the winters seemed much longer. Times were changing. In the late 70s, it had been a little while since Roy backed his red Willys out of his garage and drove up the mountain to survey his blueberry patch.

The New England Power Company, which built the nearby Bear Swamp Pumped

Storage project, had bought all of neighbor Leo Ethier's land by this time. The company listed the last parcel of 480 acres, which abutted Roy's land, as an alternative site for the twin nuclear plant proposed (and cancelled) for Charlestown, R.I. In the spring of 1977, the power company made an offer to the Bents that they could not refuse.

That fall, the townspeople gave a potluck supper at the Rowe School in honor of the Bents. Soon they were on their way to Virginia, to live near their son.

In the last year before the Bents moved on, there were 17 fires down on the railroad tracks. The following spring, the railroad finally got the money to pick up all the old ties that had been dumped beside the tracks. There were only four track fires that year.

Everything in that area seemed different after the Bents left. It was a different drive down Steele Brook Road toward the Bent house. There were no hound dogs to make known, your arrival as soon as you rounded that special corner on the three-mile-long dirt road. The grass was not cut and the American flag no longer flew on the high white flagpole, but the house stood ready, "apparently, for some big wheel in the company" to make it a summer home.

On, April 3 of this year, smoke appeared in the western sky. There had been no real track fires in two years and it was too early in the season for one to start. The ominous black smoke was definitely not fog. So where was the smoke coming from?

The power company had decided that they had no use for these buildings in such a remote area and that any vandalism would make them an eyesore. With this decision, contracted workmen had poured fuel on the wide varnished floor boards and throughout the house and then had ignited it. The power company was doing what the railroad had nearly done, inadvertently, many times over the past hundred years. A portable pump took suction from the historical fire pond only to protect the large tree which stood near the house. Eight-foot flames leaped out of the upstairs windows as the men retreated from the heat. Soon, it was over and the shocking news found its way around town.

How ironic that this house could be destroyed in this way. The house that for so many years was seriously threatened by raging forest fires and every time had stood its ground rescued by so many volunteer fire fighters working and hoping for rain now was burned from within - on purpose.

It rained the next day on the smoldering pile that was once Veber's farm, then Bent's cherished retirement home. Sound carried especially well in the fog rising off the river valley. A west-bound freight rumbled past the foot of "Old Smokey" sounding its horn as if in sad protest that the century-long game was over.   *

The Hoot, Toot and Whistle of the old Hoosac Tunnel and Wilmington Railroad engines, traversing the tracks for six miles in Rowe along the Deerfield River, have been silent now for some thirteen years. Harold Lowe, Engineer, of North Adams, took the last train down through the valley on August 31, 1971, ending eighty-six years of that railroad's interesting career, spanning the time from the hauling out of pulp wood from the virgin forests of southern Vermont to the hauling in of the 175 ton reactor vessel for Yankee Atomic. The building of Bear Swamp Pumped Storage project finally signaled its last run.

Nan and Sue ready for hike

It was time we took a hike up that old railbed from Hoosac Tunnel past the flag stops at Logan's and Heywood's to the Bear Swamp lower dam where new construction has changed the terrain. We dropped off a car on Tunnel Road by the Switching Station Road on top of the mountain, and our chauffeur delivered us to the railroad bridge over the river just outside the Hoosac

Tunnel entrance. It was a beautiful mid-September day – the kind of day you look forward to all year.

Railroads, one soon learns, were not made for walking! The ties are too close for normal stride and too far apart for stepping on every other one. Balancing on the rails is not the solution either. Crossing the bridge, we tried to avoid looking down through the cracks to the river far below and stepped quickly for fear a train would come roaring out of the Tunnel behind us. Once we were safely off the tracks on the Rowe side, we looked around among the goldenrod and asters and tried to visualize the old Switching Yard for the electric cars that took trains through the Tunnel – back before diesels, when the steam engines created too much smoke. One of our earliest memories is of the lightning flashes in the night sky caused by the cables on those electric engines.

Two wide rails veered off for a short distance into the sumac bushes to the left, following the old HT&W roadbed up the river, and we headed that way. Another well-worn dirt road came in from the other direction and both soon merged into a good, clear path along the shelf above the river, hugging, for a while, the steep wall of rock that was the mountainside. Along here we made our first discovery, investigating lots of trailing vine-like runners. They all traced back into the foam flower leaves, still holding dried flower stems and seeds. In other areas these runners were underground, but the soil was sparse here on the rocks and the roots were out in the open. The bedrock wall soon gave way to a stone wall as the land widened out on a terrace where the river took another big bend to the northwest. Here must have been the flag stop called Logan's. With no houses past Hoosac Tunnel, why a stop here? (We learn later that these stops were only on paper and never existed.)

Leaving the terrace, the sides became steep once again, both up the mountain on our right and down to the river on the left. What a journey this must have been on the original old narrow gauge track! Perhaps this good path is now maintained by the fishermen who use this "Catch and Release" area of the Deerfield. Several of them were now scattered along the opposite bank enjoying the fall sunshine on the shore or standing mid-river in a likely pool. We thought of a recent suggestion that "Wild Side" should go fishing sometime, and we made a mental note for next spring. One of the largest flower stalks we've seen soon appeared beside the path. As tall as our heads, the Canada Lily now had three stems with large seed pods forming a sort of cup on the top. These would have been a beautiful yellow cluster of blossoms in summer. Beyond this we came into a rich soil area where white snakeroot grew in great profusion along with zigzag goldenrod, baneberry and maidenhair fern. At one point, we stopped to look at something in among the asters a little off the path, and a woodcock suddenly flew up, barely missing our head in flight.

Our path was cool and shaded, but the sun was bright on the river and highlighted now and then an early-turning soft maple in lovely shades of red. Along this old railbed were still the remains of the telephone poles, but all traces of track were gone. Once in a while we found large rocks in the path that had rolled down the mountain, and it reminded us that that was one of the serious problems of the old HT&W – landslides. As we rounded another bend, a large section of land seemed to be in the normal course of the river. Sure enough, on the mountain side were the scars of just such a disaster – probably dating back to the 1938 hurricane which nearly put this line out of business.

Something orange was hanging in a bush just ahead of us and, coming closer, we could see the remains of a balloon. Ah, one from Rowe Library, no doubt. No. This one had a large tag advertising a "Double Feature" – free safety inspection and a free movie admission at Midas Dealers from Woodbridge and Edison, New Jersey! We decided it would be a little costly to take advantage of their free offer.

As Raycroft Lookout Mountain loomed up just ahead of us, the brush began closing in, and we realized we were coming to the end of the cleared path – by a strange rocked-up muddy spring on the hillside. Here the climb would begin, for we had planned to go up the ridge to the high point overlooking the Lower Reservoir Dam, across the valley from the Lookout – a climb of about nine hundred feet by the time we would see the Upper Reservoir. Climbing up a short distance and resting on a rock to plot our course, we decided it was time for lunch. Real tart new Macintosh apples and some cheese and crackers seemed like a feast.

In hindsight, if we had headed straight up the mountain, we would probably have avoided the laurel, but we went sideways, thinking it would be easier and also give us a closer glimpse of the dam. Thick, tangled, steep, miserable and a few more adjectives hardly describe the situation we found ourselves in. Only the vague idea that the whole mountain couldn't be like this, kept us headed up — literally crawling on our hands and knees! Having passed such a large section of rich soil, this acidic area was surprising. Daylight ahead seemed to indicate different terrain and gave us courage to continue. The laurel ended as quickly as it had started, and we came out on a wide area of pleasant open woods — a sort of plateau on the mountainside. What a relief! Laurel, lovely in the spring, is the most miserable kind of foliage to penetrate on foot.

Nearing the back of this plateau as we started to climb again, three huge oak trees loomed up. They were in a row, surrounded by stones, and probably had been left as boundary markers for this mountain lot since it was first plotted out in the unincorporated tract called Zoar in 1800. Hopefully, in the Registry of Deeds we would someday find the reference to "Three Oak Trees in a Row."

Open rocks and ledge were in the sunshine ahead, and we thrilled to each new perspective of the river valley widening to our view as we climbed. Arriving at a perfect spot, we sat down to soak in the warm fall sunshine and imprint that lovely view on our minds. We have seen this valley from many angles, but sometimes one is special and this one was. The white steeple of Florida Church was high across the valley, and to the west, the tower atop Whitcomb Summit just visible between Pine Cobble and Raycroft Mountain. The sky was that bright blue of autumn with only a few clouds on the far horizon. We examined everything interesting with the binoculars and realized once again what a wild and beautiful country we live in. Although reforested with now large trees, clearly visible south on the mountain above the railroad was the outline of the old landslide which had started high up and taken a wide path down across the tracks, ending, trees and all, in the river.

It would have been fun to look down and see that little old train again coming up its winding narrow course above the river, but that is now only a memory of days gone by in the ongoing history of the hills of Rowe. We reluctantly left our perch and continued the climb up and around rocks that seemed to always have a toehold where we needed one. At one point, we watched a person across the way enjoying the view in our direction from the Raycroft Lookout. At another spot we admired the brilliant red berries of a mountain ash which was clinging to the rocks. At our feet were several ant hills in the sparse soil of the mountaintop. From somewhere below ground, the ants were bringing up real red soil making an unusual contrast with the grey rocks around. Moss and lichens came in many varieties and here created a beautiful varied carpet of grays and greens.

Reaching the end of the ridge where we had been before, we looked again for the holes in the vertical ledge where some mineral has been washed away leaving several strange holes – some large enough to put our arm in up to the elbow. Nearby rocks were measled with garnets. Tiny rainwater ponds had formed on the ledges, looking like miniature Japanese gardens with mosses and lichens and mushrooms growing in and around them. Feeling suddenly cool, we looked at the sky and realized the clouds on the horizon had come quite swiftly in our direction, carried on a cold breeze, gradually blotting out the lovely sunshine.

Heading up with more determination, we quickly climbed the rocks and spent less and less time gazing at the view – except

Bear Swamp Upper Reservoir

where we could finally look far down and see the railroad bridge spanning the river where we had first crossed, and there contemplated our distance traveled. Nearer the top it was woods again, and the ground was covered with the low foliage of the wild oats, now turned a burnished yellow as if the sun was again streaming through the trees. Bear droppings proved the area was still home to the bruin in spite of man's rearrangement of his habitat. As we finally glimpsed the Upper Reservoir, the unmistakable call of a raven greeted us as the cold wind blew stronger. Once out around the Reservoir, we walked fast, shivering as we wondered what had happened to our beautiful day.

But the weather did not discourage us from checking all our familiar flower friends of summer, now gone to seed. The tiny dwarf snapdragons had each developed two seed pods which had opened at the top, exposing a minute black seed in each. Tall mullein stalks with now and then a single yellow flower, milkweed pods not yet open, goldenrods, silver-rod, and asters of every variety, both pearly and sweet everlasting, several lovely purple thistles still in bloom, Joe-Pye-weeds, clusters of big leaves of the earliest spring flower, the coltsfoot, and new cattails – all of these grew along our path.

The heavy black cloud now overhead began to spit rain as we jogged down the Switching Station Road to the waiting car. Even in the rain, it was a very special treat to see the fringed gentians and ladies' tresses growing together beside the road. Then finally we realized that, like the old railroad's nicknames, we were also, "Hungry, Tired and Weary" and probably needed some "Hot Tea and Whiskey." **10/84**

The long climb into the hills of Rowe begins in Zoar as you twice cross Pelham Brook, leaving the Deerfield and heading east to face the bulwark of Coon Hill which then turns your path northward through the pines to the town line. Here we started, at the intersection of Zoar and Steele Brook Roads with Pelham Brook, just six and a half miles from the car waiting at our destination – the Vermont line at Whitingham. For this Wild Side hike, we have come out of the woods and off the mountains to take a stroll through the town.

Perhaps it was a little more vigorous than a stroll, but we stopped often to inspect the wayside plants, to discuss the way things used to be or just to listen to the brooks which flowed along beside or

crossed our path as we made our way in a northeastwardly direction across the town. Here at the southern entrance, the maps indicate the elevation at 800 feet and after a short level stretch, the real climb begins at the old watering trough. The frost had finally taken the pretty flowers which graced the rusty tub (moved from the opposite side of the road) whose cool waters, in years gone by, had revived many a tired horse on its way to and from the train at Zoar.

Pelham Brook has here created a rocky gorge with the endless rushing of its waters toward the Deerfield. Huge boulders, one famous as a face, others with potholes like the one that was taken from here for the town hall memorial, and other rocks with sharp edges, worn smoother with time, that were blasted from the ledges when the road was first widened in 1936 – all clogged the brook to create swirls and still pools collecting the newly dropped autumn leaves and reflecting the bright midday sun. Here in this gorge, the sun rises late and sets early behind the surrounding mountains. In honor of a man who once lived at the top, this hill is still known as Joe King Hill. We were pleased with our progress when we attained this first summit.

Around the bend, we came in sight of the refuse garden and stopped across the way to examine some graceful stalks of mugwort with aromatic lacy leaves. Along the level, the sun was warm on our backs and as the view widened out, the beautiful October colors shone in all their glory – the maroon oaks, bronze beech and especially lovely yellow aspen (locally known as poplar) along with the traditionally beautiful red and yellow maples. This has been a long and glorious fall, and today it was a joy to slowly observe our town from bottom to top.

It always intrigues us to wonder how the glacier formed the two little hills as the road turns between them around the corner by the Vebers. Irene called a cheery greeting to us from her doorway. Potatoes all dug, Floyd's garden is now cleaned and ready for the winter's rest. We miss the big old maple tree at the foot of Brittingham Hill as we look toward the steep path of the power line to the east. Passing under the power line, we crossed the southern boundary of the original Myrifield Grant of Cornelius Jones. Part of an old wall in the woods to our left marks the line. Then came County Brook, hardly a trickle, but some townspeople can remember when its raging waters completely washed out this road during the 1938 hurricane.

We walked on past the old Starr farm where sheep had been raised on the surrounding mountainsides and farmers had mowed a field now grown to woods between us and the brook. The old house, too, has memories of many State children who found a good home within its walls, and of guests who came to spend summers at Pelham Brook Farm. Further along on the left, we looked toward the old cellar hole which dates back as the Isaac Cooper house mentioned in the description of this road as it was first laid out by the selectmen in 1795. The large stand of cinnamon fern has now been frosted to a lovely cinnamon brown. From here the woods close in on either side and tall pines shed their needles in the gentle breeze.

We stopped to look at new blazes on trees beside the road and recounted the recent mystery finally solved by a call to the U.S. Forestry Service. Off on the hill

to our left, unbeknownst to the landowner, was one of the New England testing plots of the Forestry Service, checked in 1953, 1971 and again last month to determine the growth and condition of the forests and their soil. Newly marked by renewing old blazes, the trail to the plot and the circle around it created a spooky atmosphere which spawned all manner of stories from buried treasure to weird Druid ceremonies – until finally the truth was known. Someday you will read a statistic that "proves" the New England forests are declining – take it with a grain of salt, it's only because your neighbor has cleared his favorite hilltop up above Zoar Road! Two ravens called as they flew over the trees, but we really didn't hear them say "nevermore."

Down the small dip and up again, we admired the big droopy evergreen tree with long cones and crossed over Sam Rice Brook. Wonder what those old timers would think to know their names were perpetuated on roads and brooks around the town? As we walked along the dugway over the brook, we were reminded of the first fulling mill which stood here by a dam and pond on Pelham Brook. Now the Community Church came into sight, its whiteness accentuated by the bright trees along yet another brook named for the Shippee family. On we walked through the snug little village, once known as Slab City – probably for the piles of slabs used in the old talc mill which dominated this village around nineteen hundred. The old school, flooding us with memories, now is a museum preserving a wealth of the tangible history of Rowe. The old store, once the heart of town activity, has moved through the years from the Old Center at the top of Middletown

Hill to the upper village by the library, then over the hill by the dam and here where modern travel has finally caused its doors to close for lack of business.

Blanche Veber greeted us as we went by and apologized for not asking us if we wanted a ride when she passed us earlier. Not yet, but thanks, we were doing quite well so far! The climb of Browning Hill was ahead, but the beautiful sight of the afternoon sun highlighting an orange maple by the brook took our minds from any aching muscles. Now like a park, this roadside bordering the cascade of Pelham Brook in the center of town has become a pleasant memorial to all the industries which perched along this waterpower in the early eighteen hundreds. Starting at the bottom, there had been Eddy's casket and cabinet shop, Scott's boot and shoe, the tannery, the fulling mill, a house and lumber barn and across the brook at the top, a grist mill and dam beside the blacksmith shop. And finally on this side of the dam, the big saw mill. A busy little hill in our early history.

Today Bernice Foster's lovely flower garden still had late blossoms, and we paused to discuss the neighboring wildlife (bear) with Bill and Bernice as we passed their yard. On the other side, only a little water was dripping over the dam for this has been a dry fall. Another orange tree marked the top of the hill, and from there we looked out across the Village Green and the Mill Pond toward the old weathered Knowlton barn at Soules and on to Adams Mountain, which is placed solidly on our eastern horizon as if standing guard over our little mountain town. Such a glorious world of color will be imprinted on our minds all winter. The old owl still

stands proudly on the library weather vane and could tell of many changes since arriving on that perch, amid a typical small town controversy, back in 1935. The town hall looks about the same as when it was built in 1895, and we think of the many unsuccessful efforts of Walter Bates to have shutters put on its windows. The attractive hydrangea bushes, almost trees, still flank the pretty stone Unitarian Chapel.

Leaving the village, we started up the Pond Road with renewed vigor for we had a long stretch of gently climbing roadway before the real hills begin again. Basking in the warmth and beauty of Indian summer, we realized this day was very special to have come when we were free to be out with a friend hiking on the Wild Side. The red Williams barn was silhouetted against the blue sky on the hill to our left as we crossed the path of the old flume, built in the early eighteen thirties to carry water to the big satinet factory, on whose site now proudly stands the new fire station. Then we went over the culvert through which flows a little no-name brook. It always had a trout ready to snap up the worm on our bent-pin fishhook back in our childhood when we were too small to be allowed to fish in the "Big Brook."

Pelham Lake sparkled in the sunshine, and we tended to linger thinking of the early reference to this area as the Great Swamp or the Great Meadow. Privately owned with dam sadly in need of repair, Percy Brown rescued the Lake in 1927, and thirty years later gave it to the townspeople of Rowe. What better day to enjoy and be grateful. Crossing the causeway, we scanned the little pond where muskrats have been busy making paths through the rushes and building house mounds for winter. Pelham Brook here empties into this little pond, flowing down from the north close by the site of old Fort Pelham from which it long ago derived its name. Other tributaries come through the lake channel to join Pelham Brook in sight of the Fort

Pelham Lake reflections

built on the overlooking hill back in 1744.

Rounding the curve by the school, the flag was flying high in the breeze with a particularly beautiful grove of yellow aspens as background. Summer's last flowers, the smooth hawksbeard, like little yellow dandelions, were blossoming in great profusion by the beach road and along the school lawn. A few birds flew up ahead of us, and we finally identified tree sparrows flitting among the branches.

Now for the discovery of the day! As we looked for the ladies' tresses growing along the left bank, we came upon quantities of red berries. Thinking at first we had found the largest ever partridge berries, to our great surprise closer examination proved them to be cranberries. We tasted their tart holiday flavor and mentally added a new find to our Rowe list.

The climb begins again at the corner above Tuttle's Flat, so called, where in olden

times many a baseball game was won or lost, depending on your team. From here we looked over a field of dried goldenrod and asters back toward Adams Mountain. At the foot of Ford Hill, we remembered another watering trough, long gone to progress and the convenience of wider roads, but appreciated, only yesterday it seems, when Bill Upton delivered the daily mail by horse and buggy. Tiny pink/red flowers, gone to seed, covered the roadside. We identified sand jointweed by later looking at it with the magnifying glass.

Passing the Leshure Farm of old, we admired Mr. Beaumier's land clearing project, and thought back to the old mansion and lovely gardens that once graced this site. A fall such as this twenty-six years ago, saw the dismantling of the old house. From those gardens we remembered the armfuls of daffodils we used to bring back to boarding school after what became a traditional Spring Saturday bringing friends to visit Rowe. A whole dorm of girls would have daffodil corsages for Sunday morning church.

Another brook, Potter, crossed under the bridge, as we decided to munch the apples from our knapsack, vetoing the idea of sitting down for this snack as we still had hills to climb and more than a mile to go. With renewed determination, we started the last long climb to Vermont. As we gained altitude, more flowers seemed to have survived the frosty nights, and we found buttercups, red clover and numerous asters still in bloom. Near the old Henderson farm, we detoured off the road to the left to examine the tall dried stalks of angelica and collect a few seeds for our garden. Here Jane Gracy and Evelyn Soule went by and, seeing no car, backed up to be sure we were not in need of help. Once again, thanks, but our destination is just up the hill!

One of the most remembered sights of the day was from the top of Shumway Road looking west toward Pete and Norma Brown's – a real New England pastorale. The cows were on the hillside, and Pete was mowing the last of the hay with the tractor. The long dirt road stretched down the hill by the pasture, curving across the brook and up to the house. Behind the grey barn, a beautiful red and orange maple was spotlighted in the long rays of the sun. After enjoying this scene to the fullest, we went a little further on and picked fresh blueberries beside the road.

The last mile is always the longest, and our pace was slowing. Under the power line, we spent time looking at the variety of cones on the clump of evergreens. This seems to be a banner year for cones. Squirrels and birds should be happy, but is it an old New England weather indicator of the long cold winter to come? Never mind, the wind and snow may blow, but we can always curl up by the fire and dream back to this beautiful day in October when we were out on the Wild Side strolling across the Town of Rowe.

Crossing the Vermont line to make it official, we were now at elevation two thousand twenty, and, after three hours of nearly steady climbing, it felt very, very good to sit down in the waiting car.   **11/84**

1985

Pelham Lake beach

Nan with Bea Sibley and Mederic Lively

A Mountain Climb at Last

Sometimes you just have to climb a mountain! Being denied access to the woods and hills for two months (holidays, weather, colds) has been like a jail sentence, and when the day arrived that we were free, we had to climb a mountain. What better one than Adams, which had been challenging us every morning from our kitchen window?

We arrived home from a necessary shopping trip about one in the afternoon realizing that our moment had finally come, and we ran and changed into warm hiking clothes like we had done as a kid after school, rushing to go out and play in the snow. The temperature was a warm twenty degrees, the sky was blue, and the sun was shining brightly – a rare day for cold January 1985. As we bounded down the back steps, a chickadee flew into the neatly stacked pile of drying wooden fence posts behind the barn. What a great idea for a winter bird shelter, we thought as a junco hopped into the bottom layer. We should build one every year.

With a run and a jump, we slid a good distance down the back hill. It was sheer joy to be starting for a hike, and we looked up to the notch just south of Adams Mountain's peak where we fully expected to be very shortly. The lower field was white with new snow, sparse as it was, and old tracks could easily be seen. Overhead, the sky had wisps of high cirrus clouds, which told us to enjoy the day for Weather was on the way. We crossed by the recently repaired stone wall, and knowing that it was on one of the original Myrifield property lines, wondered if Seth Howard or Ambrose Stone had first gathered and placed those stones along their mutual boundary back in the late 1700s.

In the woods now, we routed our steps to the Base Trail and listened to the sounds of Pelham Brook and followed its ice patterns up and down stream as we crossed the small footbridge. No new fox tracks on the ice today. So often a fox barks from here in the summer and tracks across the ice in winter, but we have yet to find their den close by. Already the chickadees were calling from the treetops as they quietly picked away at seeds and bark. Our theory for their absence at the feeders this winter is the abundance of food in the woods rather than the dire prediction of some that they have succumbed to environmental hazards. We had stopped to listen longer than necessary, because the path had suddenly turned uphill and our housebound knees were objecting. If the mountain had not been our determined goal, we would have turned back right then!

Our spirits and enthusiasm carried us on. It was a glorious day. The woods were beautiful with the soft dry new-fallen snow on the evergreens. Deer tracks soon crossed our path and we left the Base Trail, following the tracks off through the brush and swampy area to the right. Here, tree club moss tops were popping out of the snow like a grove of miniature Japanese bonsai. A small yellow birch shone silver in the sunshine as the little rolls of bark peeled around the trunk. We crossed the fence line of our Big Mowing – hard to imagine that those fun hayrides of our youth, behind Mederic Lively's mule team, took place here where there is now a forest of pine and birch. We could still feel the coarse dry hay on our legs as we stood on top of the hay wagon, leaning on the pitchfork looking off toward the western view of Greylock on a hot summer day and thinking we (probably two or three kids) were being such a big help with the haying. We always get nostalgic crossing this area.

Deer tracks became more numerous and some were quite fresh. As we hiked across the little mounding hills, hobblebush was prevalent with its three yellow-brown, tightly furled leaves at the ends of the low branches. The deer had feasted here and there. A small brook drained off the hillside from the left, and we descended into a tiny valley to cross the ice-covered stream gurgling under solid ice. We stopped to examine a rock – flat and roundish on its side in the further edge of the brook. It seemed covered with whitish lichens but these quickly brushed off with our mitten to reveal a pinkish gray rock underneath. Our first mistake – we had come out with no knapsack containing the usual hand lens, glasses, maps and other paraphernalia useful along the way. We wanted to follow the brook out into the swampy beaver dam, but decided we had better keep to our original course. We were bound for the mountaintop!

Just above the brook we found remains of the old woven wire sheep fence which always sends us into reverie about the long ago pastoral of Rowe with hundreds of sheep (2,847 by assessors count in 1832) grazing on its open hillsides. Soon we came out on the Sibley Cabin Trail along which we remember seeing the mottled leaves of the orchid called rattlesnake plantain back in the fall. Walking on the trail was easy and someone had already been through with cross-country skis. The afternoon sun was streaming through the trees and ahead was a Christmas card scene of several small hemlock trees laden with snow either side of the path. Here again we could hear the chickadees in the trees.

The path through the old Sibley lane turned off to the right, and we kept on the trail ahead, stopping to look at some hardy leathery leaves of trailing arbutus lifted above the snow. As the trail finally turned right across the brook toward the Sibley cabin, we chose to go up the brook where we could walk on the iced pools and climb up the little waterfalls frozen to double and triple their size. Mosses along the edges were still green and tiny-footed animals (mice, voles etc.) had established paths from their hiding places under the bank. Climbing around a fallen tree, we got out of the brook and back on the left bank which was in the sunshine while the brook was already in the shadow of South Mountain looming up on our right.

We hastened our steps, thinking of the setting sun and the distance still ahead. As the climb began, the footing became slippery, not from the snow but from the quantity of dry leaves – beech and oak – under the snow. Our knees rebelled again and we leaned against a tree to survey the hillside. The tiny dried beech drops (parasitic on beech roots) created little bouquets here and there up through the snow. Boulders were scattered on the hill and we spotted the huge flat-topped one known in earlier times as Poet's Seat. We detoured up to the left long enough to climb on top and pick out Greylock and Whitcomb Mountain through the trees to the west. Jumping off the side of this monumental rock, we ran a ways along the hill to get back nearer the valley of the stream we were first following. This valley is in the fold of the two mountains where you always see the fog rising after a summer storm.

Looking now toward the setting sun,

which we seemed to be racing to keep above the mountain, it was very hazy and already covered by the fast moving high cirrus cloud cover coming in from the west. But the warmth was still there and we watched the water of melting snow trickle down the front of a rock. It would soon freeze into a long wavy icicle. Here the deer had collected and made circular tracks as they browsed on tender young shoots, helping to keep the woods fairly clear of heavy underbrush. Looking up through the trees, we could see the multitude of seed cones on all the birches. Near the high stump of a big old tree we found a sign with a yellow star and the code "eleven, three and fifty degrees." It was probably an orienteering guide for some adventurous group.

A tumble of rocks and ledge took us more to the left, where we climbed around porcupine paths and found a sheltered three-cornered place to sit if we had been caught in the rain. Higher up, another ledge had beside it a frozen waterfall coming like a glacier down over the rocks. We looked at the various lichens that would ultimately help dissolve this ledge into grains of sand as the mountain erodes away in eons of geologic time. Empty brown gypsy moth cases were attached in several places along the rock. Large holes in trees indicated the presence in the area of the shy and beautiful red-headed pileated woodpecker.

Nearing the top now, we found the

Adams Mountain after an ice storm

yarding place of deer under the hemlock trees. Deer seem to like mountaintops. Again water had poured out of the ground and frozen the earth so that we had to detour way to the left to keep our footing. Our knees ached as we quickened our pace up along the old stone wall to the level area of the narrow ridge. We had made it! Our sense of accomplishment was dwarfed as we looked at that stone wall. Why had men, with the help of animals, found it necessary to build a wall up the side of this mountain, across the ridge to a stopping place near a ledge, now marked with an iron stake and ribbon? Was this the corner of Park land or an old internal boundary? No knapsack, no maps. We did know that in 1801 this whole mountain and six hundred acres were deeded from Cornelius Jones to John Adams, for whom the mountain acquired its name. John was living on the property much earlier, and he may have built the wall, or perhaps his son, Isaiah, who had twenty-three cattle in 1832.

Having arrived at our destination, we had to make some decision as to the return trip. We had never gone over the backside from this angle, and we considered dropping down into Davis Mine and walking home via the road. The back side was very steep, we did not have binocs to sight landmarks, and just now the thought of a five mile hike home was enough to discourage us from that plan. If we were going to do something like that and probably get lost in the process, this was too late in the afternoon to start. We would follow along the backside of the ridge just to be different – we'd been along the front – and eventually cross King's Highway and follow that back down to the village. But then all good plans can go astray.

We beat the sun and could now watch it descend to a lower western horizon as we hiked in that direction. It was exhilarating to be on top of the mountain, and our curiosity took us from one interesting thing to another. Deer tracks and pawed leaves were everywhere. And finally new tracks – squirrels in a real heaven of oak trees and acorns had scampered from tree to tree along the ground. Another unfamiliar track we suspect might have been a fisher. This was good porcupine hunting ground and only the fisher has the real knack of killing them without getting full of quills. Certainly there were no rabbits to provide food for predators. We listened for birds but heard none. Rocks, too, kept us busy climbing down to look at and back up to be sure we stayed on the ridge. Up here somewhere we hope to locate the ledge where it is said some blasting was done in search of a vein of copper back in the mining days. The snow – clean, white and beautiful – was a little deeper here on the top.

Remembering a hike along this ridge a couple of years ago, the distance had been further than we had anticipated so we were not looking for the down path yet, in spite of knowing we were already mighty tired. Soon some big old oak trees took our interest, and we investigated each, finally seeing some orange marks and wondering if they marked the edge of an old woodlot where the line trees had been saved all these years. We realize now that in our vision a hill was looming up in an unnatural place, but we were busy looking at trees and not mountains. A green park sign on a tree ahead assured us everything was fine – except the green sign was signed "J.C. Van Itallie!" Panic was immediate!

Lost in our own back yard? We were certainly not where we thought we were! Quickly coming to our senses, we looked at the bright spot that had been the sun, now at our back. We had turned completely around and were merrily heading east toward Davis Mine. How could we be so dumb or was it absentminded? It had been easy and rather fun, but visions of finding our way home in the dark made us stop, look and think. Somehow tracing along the back of the ridge, we had slowly descended an unknown ridge bearing off to the south. With the absence of binocs, we weren't checking far-off terrain either. Fortunately, the power line was visible across the valley, and we quickly put it and the setting sun at our left shoulder and fairly flew back up the mountain, catching our breath only after making positive identification of our whereabouts.

Safely in command again, we climbed to the pass at the top of King's Highway or Norton's Trail as it was earlier known. John Norton was the chaplain of the forts in 1746, and we know from his diary that he passed this way on August 1, 1746 going to Fort Massachusetts, where he was captured when the fort was attacked and surrendered to the French and Indians. Norton was marched to Canada and held captive for a year while his wife and children endured the hardships of life at Fort Shirley in Heath.

We had climbed up to see again the perfect Glacial erratic – the big flat-sided rock that was conveniently dropped beside this old path, the path taken by Moses Rice with timbers to build Fort Pelham in 1744, the same path Cornelius Jones traveled in 1762 with his family in an oxcart to settle on his ten thousand acre plantation he called Myrifield, the path that felt the tramp of soldiers from Deerfield to the battle at Bennington in 1777, and we dare say the route of hundreds of barrels of rum that kept these men alive in this wilderness. If only we could sit quietly and watch them all parade by.... Yes, there goes Archibald Thomas in 1783 carrying the petition for incorporation of a new town to be named Exeter... Didn't they like Jones's name, Myrifield? (Meaning a field of ten thousand acres.) Thomas is on his way to Boston... That's quite a trip! He has spent many hours composing and writing this petition for the last one was turned down. We wish him well. Do you suppose anyone will remember and appreciate his efforts in two hundred years?

Time goes quickly as we sit here on the trail. It's early 1785 and a messenger on horseback is coming up from Charlemont... Good day, sir. Any news from Boston? Really? February 9th, you say. And signed by John Hancock himself. That will be good news for the folks who have been waiting to hear. But you say the new town is to be called Rowe... That's strange, wonder why? Politics perhaps...   **2/85**

Finding the Cold Spring on a Winter Day

*"*T*urn back O man, Forswear thy foolish ways..."* The strains of that old favorite chapel hymn strangely came to mind as we stood knee deep in crusty snow, still in sight of the road, knowing full well that we should turn back and go home for snowshoes, but... once under way it's hard to rearrange our thoughts backwards.

It was a lovely, 1985 February day. Our front lawn had bare spots and surely the woods would be the same. It was cool, not cold, and the wind was still. This hike has been on our list for a long time since we researched some old deeds concerning the Noah Brown farm that later became known as Rainbow Hill. Little things intrigue us and this time it was two references to a northwest corner being near a "cold spring." A spring is a spring but why phrased a "cold spring?" We pictured a walled-up spring, long ago the supply to an old house and probably located on the north side of the hill where the water remained especially cool on a hot July day.

We must admit we had not looked at those old deeds for over a year, but the plan had been in our mind. We would walk east from the top of Monroe Hill, follow along a fairly level course and come out on the Old Readsboro Road. There might be a change of plans taking us up to the power line, but we would see when the time came.

Fifty feet into the woods we knew we had made a mistake. It was still winter on these hills. And in fact, in this location, it seemed that all the snow from neighboring Florida Mountain had blown across the valley and settled under these trees – like the tall red pine under which we were standing. We usually start off with such gusto that our enthusiasm takes us a long ways before

we really size up the situation. But today we knew right off that we were in trouble. That old hymn goes on to say, *"Yet now her child whose head is crowned with flame, still wilt not hear thine inner God proclaim, Turn back O man, Forswear thy foolish ways."* Of course, a difficult hike in the woods was not the original interpretation of the "foolish ways of man" but today the words seemed appropriate to our situation.

We have given you ample warning to turn back, but if you insist on coming along, you must be prepared – this may be the worst hike we will ever take! Be sure your long underwear is tucked into your socks because every time your boot goes, with a push, into the crust on top of the snow, the crust, against the front of your leg, will rub all clothing up and drop snow into your socks. Once one foot is through the crust, the boot will sink into snow up to your knee. And then there is the other leg that must be withdrawn from its knee-deep location and with effort pushed into the crust ahead and sunk to the same depth. Beginning to get the feel for it? Why not walk on the crust, you say? It's just not quite strong enough, so the extra push to get through it to start with is better than the jolt of thinking it will hold and falling through anyway.

You have to learn these things by trial and error and by the time we perfected all the techniques, we were some distance into the woods. It would be so great on snowshoes! We quickly calculated the time it would take to retrace our steps, turn the car around, drive home, find the snowshoes, answer the phone, look for the binocs which we had forgotten again, answer the phone, read the mail, answer... Oh, let it ring, restart the car, drive back... It wouldn't be worth it, the day would be gone. It was so beautiful there in the woods, so quiet and peaceful listening to the birds. We took one more step and simply sat in the snow. That's what we would do – sit in this nice open spot, listen to the birds and just see what happened here on a beautiful February day.

The sun was warm and we spotted pine siskins, goldfinches and chickadees in the trees over our head. A nuthatch made his familiar call from another direction. The trees were really full of birds darting here and there. A cheery little "chick-a-dee-dee" came from a limb close by. South of us, we could now see a boundary wall of the State Forest land that we were on and Walter Miller's orange signs on the trees on the other side. We were thinking now and trying to remember at which junction of boundaries was that cold spring. Of course, we should have up-graded our homework before this field trip. If we went back for the snowshoes, we could read that old deed...

Our body heat and the snow soon had us on our feet again. It was wet sitting in the snow. We brushed off and wondered what ever happened to those good old gabardine ski pants we used to wear out sliding as a kid – they never soaked through. Or had we forgotten? A small hilltop was just ahead and looked as through there might be a view. We would go that far and then back out to the road along the wall. The snow on the way to the hill was deeper than ever, but suddenly up under the trees it was soft. Heavenly, with this we could go miles. No view, but the wall was interesting – large spaces between the rocks and we wondered if it had been built that way or heaved in the winter frosts.

The snow had made strange drift patterns as the wind had blown through the holes. Had Jeddiah Barrett built this wall or was it Reuben Clark? The old hymn goes on to say, *"Age after age their tragic empires rise, Built while they dream..."* Many men had built their own little empires on these hill farms in Rowe and in memory of their dreams we still admire these old stone walls.

Deer trails were numerous, and we began to realize that following one eliminated the process of breaking through the crust. The trail at the moment took us away from the wall and off into thicker woods. But deer seem to go under and around and through all kinds of brush, and we finally found ourselves crawling on hands and knees to get under some hemlocks. Enough of that, we would go back to our own ways. So up and over a ledge and into deeper snow we went, then slid down the backside, first exploring a big old uprooted tree expecting to find someone "at home" in its shelter. Lots of red squirrels lived in these woods. We came across many of their middens where they had pulled apart cones, eaten the seeds and left the heaps of refuse. Holes in the snow indicated where they had hidden piles of treasure. It seemed unnecessary to hide any for the trees were unusually full of cones and there would be no trouble picking a fresh one for lunch.

Through a small valley we trudged and on up the next hill, still wondering why we were torturing ourselves and where exactly we thought we were going. Deer tracks now led to a sheltered area of softer snow near the top of this hill, and on the way we picked up another track obviously not a deer. Long strides made depressions in the snow though not as deep as the deer's sharp hooves. No real paw print could be distinguished. Later over the top of the hill in deeper snow the animal had bounded on down into the woods. A bobcat perhaps – certainly not a dog. Here on top it was quite open and again the birds were active. Partly because it was so pleasant in this spot and mostly because we just dropped from sheer exhaustion into the snow, we sat again and looked and listened. A marked boundary line went downhill to the north, and we plotted our location on the geodetic map that we did remember to bring. We could go downhill to the south a short distance and probably find our way to Brown Road without much trouble – but the car was way back on Monroe Hill and just maybe the downhill to the north was more interesting. We were crazy enough to have come this far...

We contemplated lunch but it was still early, and we knew we could not stay in the snow for long, although wondered if we could ever move again. We ached in muscles we didn't even know we had. Then a bird began to sing, and we listened intently trying to make it sound like a goldfinch or purple finch but it was not. It was sort of a three part song beginning like a chipping sparrow and ending with two rather pretty series of notes. This was repeated quite often but not continually – a happy musical sound. It was a common redpoll singing praises to the sky on this lovely day. *"Earth shall be fair,"* the old hymn chanted, *"And all men glad and wise."*

It was hard to take ourselves away from this location, but once on our feet, we looked at the old wood road downhill and thought we would do our own bounding to beat the nasty walking – we landed with a thud on our knees on crust that suddenly held our weight.

It would have been so simple to turn back at the very beginning! This would rate, along with the one in the snow through the brush in the old field above the lake along Potter Brook, as one of the worst hikes we have ever taken! But that bird song was lovely and the sunshine and the woods...

The trees along the State Forest line were well marked and we planned now to follow this to a corner then go directly west to Monroe Hill. An old dead tree gave us an excuse to pause and observe all signs of life under the loose bark. Old spider webs caught the sawdust from the decaying wood, and we were fascinated with the egg tunnels of the tiny bark beetles, which had turned this old tree into an artistic wood engraving. Woodpeckers had probably had a feast picking out the beetle larvae. Perhaps an owl lived in the big hole nearer the top. From here we followed deer tracks to the top of a small ledge where the deer had nibbled the fungi all around an old decaying birch.

Several times we lost the line trees and had to search for the red and blue marks, taking no chances on confusing our location. The snow on this side was very inconsistent with easy places, heavy crust or in general the same knee-deep misery. A nice outcropping of ledge had a thick cover of soft, very green moss sprinkled with dry remains of little spinulous ferns taking root. On down the hill, we seemed to be coming into a little ravine, and we could finally see the well-marked corner where the Forestry land turned east. By the corner a small brook formed, flowing down a steeper ravine beyond. This was a nice little sheltered area with the sun streaming down on an open greenish spot of moss from which the brook seemed to be flowing. We walked up to it, looked around and decided to cross and eat our lunch here before going west to the road.

The mossy spot to cross was double our stride so we planted one foot in the middle of the moss, and as we put our weight on that foot to reach across with the other, our step sank into soft wet moss way over our fairly high boot. The exceptionally cold water oozed down around our toes and swished

back up our leg as we put the other foot on solid ground. Right in the midst of the step, the light dawned! We had not only found the "cold spring" but we had unintentionally tested its contents and found the name to be all too true. As we sat on a stump overlooking this northwest corner of Noah Brown's land, eating our sandwich and apple, we wondered if he, too, had first walked these bounds on a lovely February day and been foolish enough to step right in the middle of his, indeed, very cold spring? As we headed downhill along the brook, we looked back at that spot in the sunshine and watched a big hemlock

limb drop its load of snow directly on the stump where we had been sitting.

From here on, the snow depth was getting close to impossible, becoming in places more like waist deep, and we were now hauling one soggy foot. It seemed logical to follow the stream downhill, but a quick look at the map proved this to be the long way home and even though our path to the west was uphill, the shortest distance appealed the most. Our mind was soon taken off our troubles as we discovered the existence of rabbits – their tracks in the fine snow here covering the crust and nibbled twigs and pellets all along the hillside. As we wallowed in the snow to get up the hill, we were happy to think that at least a few rabbits were coming back into the area. On the hill under big trees were many deer beds where they had pawed away the snow down to leaves and rested in little hollows on dryer ground. In the distance we could hear the noisy flight of a partridge from a tree. These lovely woods were enchanted with so many wild creatures all making their home together. Turn back? Never! See what we would have missed! Suddenly the walking didn't seem as bad even though the road was still a long way away.

We came out of the woods just below where we had entered some two hours earlier, and as we walked slowly but happily back to the car, the final lines of that old hymn came to mind once again...

"Now, even now, once more from earth to sky, Peals forth in joy man's old undaunted cry, Earth shall be fair and all her folk be one." **3/85**

There were three hikes in all, and we were party to two of them. The third, of course, was the most rewarding, and we had to participate in that one vicariously... but we are getting a little ahead of the story.

It was a windy but sunny day in mid-March when our favorite hiking guide succeeded in riling up our curiosity by asking if we had ever seen the old "lining towers." Where and for what were our first questions answered by "Florida Mountain" and "for the surveying of the Hoosac Tunnel." There was a quick decision to "go see", and we were off to Whitcomb Summit – parking the car beside the Mohawk Trail just north of where the power line crosses below the Summit. There used to be a sign just south of the power line indicating that you were then passing over the famous Hoosac Tunnel.

As on other mountain tops we've experienced recently this one was covered by a heavy crust (walkable) with three or four inches of new snow – quite disproving our theory that all the snow from Florida Mountain had blown over to Monroe Hill in Rowe.

We started off on the run, uphill, as always with this particular guide. The beech and maple woods were open and pretty with

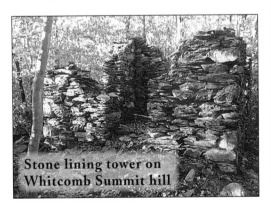

Stone lining tower on Whitcomb Summit hill

scattered small evergreens in clean fresh snow. We soon cut out onto open land under the power line, and as we climbed, the view back toward Rowe grew more dramatic and interesting. A monster granite boulder was placed appropriately partway up in the center of our trail. With a little encouragement and boost from our guide, we climbed the rock and sat looking over the wild terrain of the hills of Rowe. Strangely, very little civilization was visible in Rowe. Adams Mountain was placed to the right of center view and slightly to its left was the Krumm house, off Davis Mine Road, clearly standing out in the open with New Hampshire's Mount Monadnock rising to heights directly behind it. Tucked along the side hill on the lower left was the yellow house of the Williams Farm on Middletown Hill. Above the Deerfield valley was the red and white tower along the rim of the Upper Reservoir of Bear Swamp. Other than those few landmarks, the rest of the hills seemed deserted – hiding well their three hundred and some human inhabitants.

The high tension lines over our heads hummed a tune in the wind, and as we approached the top of the mountain, Greylock loomed up to the west with the afternoon sunshine highlighting the tower on its snow covered round hump. From there we could overlook the Central Shaft of the Hoosac Tunnel. Dug for ventilating purposes, this shaft, 1028 feet deep and 600 feet west of the actual center, houses huge fans which help clear the tunnel of smoke and fumes. Going north along the ridge we followed a snowmobile trail some little distance into the woods and slightly downhill. Here we found the object of our hike – the tall square remains of the old twelve by twelve foot stone lining tower with carefully arched doorways looking like a Mayan Temple erected to appease some strange gods. Mortar still held rocks together although it was crumbling badly from having withstood more than a century of weather on this mountaintop. From here there had to have been a line of sight to "Rowe's Neck" opposite the tunnel's eastern portal, but such a view was now well obscured by dense treetops.

A lonesome train whistle carried on the wind over the hills from North Adams, and we flew back down through the trees to the car for the purpose, our guide said, of meeting the train as it came through the eastern portal of the tunnel. We arrived in time to see clouds of yellow diesel smoke billowing out of the tunnel and being carried up the brook ravine – perhaps the strong west wind was blowing right through the tunnel. While waiting we examined Rowe's Neck across the way and tried to determine just where the next lining tower had been placed. No train appeared, and we finally took off back up the mountain top to see if the fans were still running at the Central Shaft. As we stopped along the way, the train emerged from the tunnel below us, sounding its whistle as it rumbled out across the bridge into Rowe.

* * * * *

The next chapter in the lining tower quest involved phone calls to anyone who might know where and what exactly was located in Rowe. Yes, there was "something" there – prompting one long ago rumor that "it" was for gun emplacements during World War ll – but no one we could find had any firsthand knowledge. Careful study of the mountain

with binoculars at least convinced us that there was no such stone tower as we had seen in Florida. We reread the few words in Carl Byron's book about Hoosac Tunnel, *Pinprick of Light*, which was our only authority, *"Doane resurveyed the tunnel line and replaced Edward's grooved iron markers with six stone lining towers during 1866, one on each peak of Hoosac, one at each portal, and one on Rowe's Neck to the east and Notch Mountain to the west. The crews cast a line from that tower to the 25 foot high red and white iron pole at the peak of the sloped roof on the next tower in line, or into the black portals where it was carried forward on plumb bobs driven into wooden plugs in the cavern's roof. The line was extended by sighting down all the plumb bobs toward a tiny light glowing in the blackness. This light was moved and sighted, moved and re-sighted, until the line was straight as an arrow. Then a miner's lamp flashed once, and the drillers went back to work."* Thus we spent the week building our curiosity to the peak. The first free day we would go exploring.

That day soon arrived. Checking the maps, we prepared for a long hike. Perhaps sometime we should purposely take a Wild Side hike on a foggy rainy day to give a rest to the words beautiful, lovely, warm, and ideal; for once again we have to repeat them. The blue skies of spring were overhead as we started around the top of Bear Swamp Upper Reservoir shortly after noon. We were headed for the area of Doubleday's Cliffs and had to go cross-lots as the road to our usual starting place was still snow-covered and muddy. The reservoir water was very low, and we searched the surface for ducks. None were found just then, but other things of interest took our attention like the bank of pretty pink lichens. Lichens, like mushrooms, have technical

Latin names and very few common ones so pink lichens are just that to us. Shortly, two black ducks came winging in, settling on the far side. We watched them, marveling once again at the yearly cycle which brings back our birds to nest in these hills. On the return trip we would see a flock of blacks and a pair of mallards.

From this vantage point, we could look down on the lower side of the big bend in the Deerfield valley to the rapids above the Florida bridge where the river takes yet another turn through its gorge in the mountains. Off on the hills, the remains of old wood roads were prominent as snow still lined their courses on otherwise bare slopes. To the west rose the rounded hill of Doubleday's Cliffs and over it towered the white spire of the Florida church across the valley. We picked our way down the dike rocks and onto the road to the "clay pit." We passed the little swamp where a family of black ducks had raised their young last year. It was still covered with solid ice. Our path alternated snow and mud with numerous blackberry canes from last summer. On a southern exposure, the ground was bare, but a good bit of snow remained in the shaded woods. At the edge of the wide-open hillside where the clay had been removed for the reservoir dikes, we turned right into an old wood road trail that would take us nearer the ridge. The road had become a small brook bed, and we hopped back and forth trying to keep our feet reasonably dry. Chickadees, goldfinches and pine siskins flitted now and then in the trees above. The brook finally drained off into the mossy swamp on our left, and we climbed to slightly higher and dryer ground.

Here were lovely hillside woods with beech, maples and oaks. Large white birches lifted strong arms skyward, and their lacy tops were beautiful against the blue sky. We investigated an old beech that had years of bear claw marks up and down the bark. Remains of civilization crossed our path in the form of an old stone wall. The whole area was a series of hills, rocks and cozy, sheltered basins. We left the path in one of those basins to go toward the ridge past the remains of an old stone house. Large trees now grew in the cellar hole, indicating its abandonment in the early 1800s. We have not researched this property but have heard the name Granger associated with it. What a wonderful time children must have had growing up here with all the rock walls and outcroppings with nooks and crannies to aid their imagination in child's play.

The ridge was snowy and many deer paths criss-crossed the hill with other smaller tracks clearly outlining the paws of a wandering porcupine. Once in a while, earlier tracks had remained as packed snow while the rest of the snow had melted around them, leaving a series of raised mounds instead of depressed tracks. Mosses on various rocks and decaying logs were beautiful bright green or yellow green in contrast to the white snow. This land along the ridge was a series of gradually rising small hills and valleys, some of which led us to points of ledge too high to descend and we had to detour around the side. It seems as if the Cliffs must be on the next rise, but there was always one more. Lunch just couldn't be put off any longer! A dry ledge outcropping seemed the ideal spot in the sun – and even if not ideal, we were suddenly too hungry to be fussy. Delicious ham sandwiches, cheese and pickles appeared from our partner's knapsack, and we added an apple and orange. A feast, as always, on a picnic.

We can think of so many pretty spots in the woods just waiting to be enjoyed but so seldom seen. We considered ourselves the lucky ones and took our time enjoying everything in our path like the shining bark on the yellow birch trees, the several kinds of lycopodium – wolf's claw, princess pine, and tree club moss – and the occasional small round mounds of pincushion moss. From the next little hill, we walked out onto a large, flat open ledge totally covered with beautiful gray and light green reindeer lichens. The view was spectacular, as it is all along this ridge above the Deerfield. We were looking north to Raycroft Lookout, which rises directly behind the Lower Reservoir dam where all was quiet with the Fife Brook Hydro Station evidently not generating. The only clouds in the sky were two jet contrails making a large "V" from the western horizon. In the woods behind us a huge tumble of rocks cluttered a knoll and must have been home to many wild creatures.

Soon the land looked more familiar, and we knew at last we were approaching the final climb to the Cliffs. On the heights, closer, it seemed, to the sky, we stood with our heads back watching the unusual pattern being made by the two contrails we had seen earlier. Like cirrus mares tails they had become a series of wispy lilies, each growing on a stem from inside the previous blossom. From the camping spot on the eastern ledge, we looked to the left, over the Upper Reservoir to Adams Mountain, then out toward the length of Negus and down to the top trails

of Thunder Mountain, and finally around to the right, over parts of Florida, to the tower in Savoy (actually Borden Mountain fire tower) and out upon all the houseless wilderness in between. A train could be heard echoing between the hills as it rolled down the river valley but could not quite be seen. Staying there only long enough to admire the view, we were anxious to explore for we had made this trip for a purpose – the search for the lining tower there on Rowe's Neck.

Roaming around the knob of this hill, we tried to find a viewpoint from one of the numerous rocks. We could sight to the power line on Florida Mountain but not through the trees to the tunnel. We moved around some more to the south, climbing down to the next level. Still not able to get a bearing, we continued down around a length of cliff, hoping for an opening in the trees. Finally, we came out on a long, sloping open ledge with the tunnel entrance directly in front of us, and the power line stretching over the mountain high above it. The perfect site for the lining tower! But search as we might, there was nothing man-made in sight – no bolts, no holes, no piled rocks. The view again was spectacular and delighted us especially as it was a whole new angle of the Deerfield valley, sighting straight down the river to the railroad bridge. Noticing that the sun, in our eyes, was nearing the horizon, we checked the time. It was four p.m. We had found too much of interest on the Wild Side along the way!

The nagging thought lingered that our position, the tracks into the tunnel and the stone lining tower to the right of the power line above all had to line up perfectly. We took a few more minutes to climb up and

Old roadway by Doubleday's Cliffs

the setting spring sun as we walked on a field of bright red British soldier lichens, and listened to robins in the trees. To our minds, the hike had been a great success.

* * * * *

Our bubble was burst the next day when the instigator of this search reappeared on the scene and declared our efforts to have been in vain. The third hike, for which we were too weary, was his alone and from the bottom up. As a result, we are happy to report that the four rock bolts, being all that is left, which were used to hold the old lining pole on Rowe's Neck are still secure in the ledge and are located within a stone's throw north of our supposed site! We had been so close.

In 1866 and for the next two years, the engineers sighted by their lining towers, from the west portal to Notch Mountain, over the two Hoosac ranges to Rowe's Neck and back to the east portal, performing a survey so exact that when the borings met they were only 7/16th of an inch off center on the four and three quarter mile tunnel that would remain the longest tunnel in North America until 1916.

Although the building of the Hoosac Tunnel was plagued with problems, the engineering is still recognized with pride as a feat of national historic significance by the Society of Civil Engineers. And in this great drama of the last century, Rowe played a part. **4/85**

down further to our right, but as things lined up the lay of the land didn't lend itself to positioning of towers or guns. We returned to the ledge and decided somehow that that had to be "it" – at least for today. We did not linger on our return trip along the old walled-up road under the Cliffs (had this road been built to provide access to the tower?) down to Tunnel Road, joining a porcupine en route, and back up across the clay pit. Our bodies cast long shadows in

This One Is a Cliffhanger

Be careful folks, this nice little flower story ends as a cliffhanger! Aunt Martha Henry would have called it an "open and shet" day – some clouds, some sun. When we first started out, stalking the visiting loon on the backside of the lake, it was a pretty "shet" morning, rather chilly and damp. We might have had second thoughts about further hiking, but today was the day and we seldom give up.

Our destination was west Rowe, back to the lovely ravine which inspired the creation of one of our first "Walks on the Wild Side" three years ago after discovering the hillside full of yellow violets and all the other rich soil treasures hidden away over there in the spring. Today was April 23, and we parked near the dike on Tunnel Road and walked down to the old wood road along the upper side of the brook. Contrary to our usual nearly empty knapsack, we were carrying a camera, tape recorder and the binocs, all of which would prove to be a pain before the day was over.

Our first stop was at the site of an old talc prospect. Here on the Peck property, someone had dug for talc and there remained a small hole filled with water and green slime (a lovely soft color). Nearby was another scooped-out area and various small piles of dirt and rocks – some of which felt soft and slippery like talc. The extent of the operation here is unknown, but it looks of very short duration. We continued down the pretty little tumbling brook, investigating various slabs of rock. A red squirrel chattered at us and ran off up a hemlock tree. Looking for the first yellow violets, we crossed the brook to the west and then began chasing rocks. There seemed to be several scattered around, and we finally had to climb a little rounded knoll to look at another, and one more beyond. One special boulder must have been an old property boundary for it was topped by a conspicuous smaller white rock with a short stone wall just below. We climbed up to look around. This was all nice open beech and maple woods and must have been lovely pasture on the Cressy farm years ago, and also the southern boundary of the old Fulham grant.

Here we realized we hadn't seen a flower, and the brook we had intended to follow was already descending into the ravine to the east. We turned our course that way via another rock, and as we did so there was the first little round-leaved yellow violet just waiting to be noticed! These tiny violets appear before the leaves, but when the leaves do come, they grow bigger and bigger and by June you can't believe they really belong to those first tiny flowers. Nearer the rock, we noticed it was split by a five- or six-inch curved crack, and as we approached a little chipmunk was sitting in the center watching us. He finally ducked inside for safety but couldn't resist peeking back out to get another look at this strange intruder. By the time we had the camera set for his next appearance, he had scampered out the other side and scolded us from the distance. No problem, we discovered the camera wasn't loaded properly anyway!

Here we really turned downhill and were suddenly in the midst of everything! A lovely little clump of white hepaticas was almost gone by, and the shamrock-like leaves looked fresh and new. Another step and we were surrounded by the dainty leaves of squirrel corn (we always stick our finger down in the earth once to find the little yellow kernel that gives it the name) and here and there, a red trillium blossoming among the yellow wild oats springing up everywhere. Collections of dwarf ginseng were up and budded. One of the loveliest blossoms of spring is that dainty little ball of flowers coming out of the center of three sets of three leaves of the dwarf ginseng. Clusters of sweet cicely leaves mingled with new little fern fronds. We hardly had time to appreciate all these things when one of our favorite birds that hides away in wilderness brook valleys burst into song – a sweet little winter wren only four inches long. How can such a tiny thing have such a musical song? And it is a long song for he goes through the whole verse each time.

Trying to catch the wren's voice, we took out the tape recorder, but the breeze was just enough to overpower the song. We then decided to record what we were seeing as we went along and talked the whole rest of the trip! It's an interesting document to listen to, but as we got ourselves into more and more difficulties later on, we tended to think of it as the "black box" they would retrieve after the crash! We decided it was more fun to train our own mind to remember sights and sounds as we had always done without artificial aids and things to carry.

Looking down that lovely ravine, we spotted dark green patches and caught a whiff of that wonderful spring smell – leeks! Between here and there were new shoots of delicate maidenhair fern, rather pinkish with the tops just unfolding, and more squirrel corn which seems to grow everywhere between little clusters of Dutchman's breeches whose leaves look just the same but which seem to grow in clumps rather than scattered. The squirrel corn flowers are fragrant and blossom

as little fancy elongated hearts with a pinkish tinge while the Dutchman's are little white pantaloons with yellow waists. And then there was blue cohosh that we always term "weird" because it comes up a strange gray-blue color with matching tiny star-shaped flowers with yellow centers. This grows two or three feet tall and turns perfectly normal green later on.

We had resisted the leeks long enough! It was time to put down our paraphernalia, take out our plastic bag, get down on our hands and knees and push our fingers down in the soil to dig the leeks. From past experience we knew there were good and bad places to dig leeks, and we do remember this was not the ideal spot. Leeks have strong roots and tend to grow deep down around fern roots, stones, logs etc. and, unless the soil is really wet, can be very frustrating to remove whole. One usually digs, scrapes and wiggles and finally, in exasperation, pulls the leek that then breaks off just above the nice tasty bulb on the end. But when they are the first leeks of the spring, you sure try very hard to extract them whole. That hillside was quite dry, and we did give up rather easily the first time, scrubbing our hands in the cool brook water. As we put this powerful smelling cargo in the knapsack, we noticed the stems of budded miterwort with its two little leaves just under the flower head. Everything looks so different and intriguing when first coming out of the ground.

Remembering some early saxifrage on a rock, we climbed a little higher and across the hill to investigate a tall ash tree which had toppled and showed how depressions are made in a hill over the years when trees grow and fall, lifting a good chunk of soil with the roots and depositing it on the down side of the resulting hole. We sat a minute and found the ground strewn with small blue, great-spurred violets. And there on the rock was the first array of saxifrage – a rosette of soft fuzzy leaves in the center of which grows a stem several inches high with tiny white flowers. Such a lovely view of this deep V-shaped ravine with the brook sparkling in the sun as it flowed over lush green moss on rocks and ledge along which grew great patches of toothwort. Stands of Christmas fern dotted the hillside opposite where the old wood road was well defined. This side of the ravine, as we have described, was covered with all the spring flowers. Close your eyes and picture it. Can you smell the leeks on the gentle breeze coming up the brook? And hear the train just rounding the curve by Soapstone and rolling down the valley. The hill below was steep, and we sat and slid down past a large rock to get back to the brook, passing one lonely little pine seedling in this otherwise hardwood forest.

Back nearer the water, we found yellow trout-lilies (adder's tongue) blossomed among the leeks. It was interesting to see the dry clusters of old leek blossoms with seedpods fallen among the new growth. Sometimes flowers (even the little yellow violets) push right up through dry leaves and blossom with a leaf still attached around their neck. Here we began to find Canada violets – white flowers tinged on the back with purple and leaves on the same stem. As we went on down the ravine, we found the toothwort blossomed, and all the flowers in various stages repeated again and again. A section of downed trees on the hillside forced us to cross the brook. As the little wren continued to sing, we thought of birds and hadn't really heard many others. Nests, too, came to mind and looking back to the hill we had just descended, spotted a large nest in the top of one of the tall trees. Nothing seemed to be at home just then. Yesterday it had been a different story when we walked through the woods to look at a high nest. Its occupant protested fiercely and literally dive-bombed us until we withdrew! It was a fairly rare goshawk protecting his own corner of Rowe. Today a red-tailed hawk flew lazily over the ravine with its tail flashing in the afternoon sun.

Three years ago when we had been here the first time, we had turned around and hiked back up the hill. Today we had anticipated continuing down to the railroad and walking back to Florida Bridge with another car waiting, but after three phone calls, found no one to share our hike. So with no special plans, we continued on down the brook, discovering beautiful long rambling waterfalls over the exposed ledges as the hill grew very steep. On our side, it became squashy moist as we went across slanting ledge covered with years of decayed leaves soaked by the runoff from a side-hill spring. The leeks loved it here, too, but we spotted more down in a basin area across the brook. Also in the distance, we were anxious to see blossomed cut-leaved toothwort. As we stood enjoying the brook, a friendly black and white butterfly flew by and then returned to circle several times around our head. We crossed the brook again and in so doing wished we could be dropped in this spot to watch this lovely falls after a good flooding storm. (But please, no thunderstorms today!)

There certainly was cut-leaved toothwort all over the hill, but when we bent down to see the blossoms, we discovered that they came from saxifrage growing in between! The toothwort was not yet blossomed. A host of red trillium looked down and laughed at us from the hill just above. Here we attacked the leeks again and were more successful – at least enough to flavor our scrambled eggs for a few mornings. A rock was nearby and we decided to call this lunch break although there was no food in our pack – we had mistakenly thought an early peanut butter sandwich before we left would carry us through. We shed the wool sweater and studied the map.

Largest boulder in Rowe?

On our way again, we shortly recognized another old road coming around the hill from the right, crossing another small ravine and the brook and going on down toward the old landslide area. We remembered that road and how it had ended in briars and laurel. Even knowing what was in store, we left the brook and continued that way, expecting to pick up the old wood road back up to the car.

Well, it didn't happen that way! We went out around the bend to a point where we could see the river through the trees and came up with a totally insane impulse – to explore the hill of jumbled huge boulders that appeared behind us. Steep, thick with prickly berry bushes, a tangle of vines, laurel, and dead charred trees from a long ago forest fire – If anyone had said we had to climb that hill… Curiosity does strange things to our good judgment and aching joints! We talked into the tape recorder and complained bitterly at our choice. Fortunately, the wrong button was pushed so we don't have to suffer through that again!

For the third time, we think we have found absolutely the largest boulder in Rowe. This one loomed through the trees high above us, and we somehow made our way through the maze to its base. The downhill side was vertical, flat and towered over our head. It seemed to be resting on a collection of small rocks, and we hoped there would be no earthquake to suddenly start it moving in our direction. The rock had interesting markings, including some that could be glacial grooves going opposite the grain. Walking around this one would be difficult, but as we went to the right and squeezed between other rocks, we found that the next side had a large overhang. Once around this lower corner, the steep side was not apparent and you could easily walk up the slanted backside to the top. WOW! What a view! It looked directly down the river toward the rapids above Florida Bridge and of course the whole mountainside of Negus, Nelson Flats and the hills of Florida. Worth every groan during our miserable approach. Behind us, we were surrounded by a wonderful collection of ledges, boulders, rocks – all with intriguing nooks and caves from which we were sure we were being watched by some denizen of the wild. Our only companion was the little winter wren who had followed us and was now running around the rocks and grass below. Her mate was still singing in the trees not far away.

The lovely "open" sunshine had changed to "shet," and we looked up to see still half the mountain to climb. The rocks gave way to more ledge and laurel, and we began pulling ourselves up by bushes and pieces of grass. To keep us climbing – other than the question of what else could we do at that point – we remembered old pictures from the Percy Brown family taken on the Peck farm overlooking the Deerfield at a favorite place they called "Trunket." The old pictures and the present view were looking more and more alike. We had always wanted to find this spot, but never expected to approach it from below! We became more enthused as the camera and binocs banged around our neck, and we still talked into the non-running tape recorder. We started right up a steeper ledge, pulling on trees and finding toe holes for the next step until . . .

We were stopped in our tracks at a point of no return – too far up to go back down and nothing to get hold of above us! Good grief now what? We quickly scanned the sky for turkey vultures expecting them to hover in anticipation. Perhaps the smell of leeks would hold them off for a while. At last we had really gotten ourselves into a situation we didn't expect to get out of – by ourselves! If we didn't have all that junk around our neck and the recorder in our hand... We leaned our knees against the ledge and tried to enjoy the view over our shoulder. A cold shiver came over us as we looked down the cliff.

The only answer was to stay put and wait to be rescued. But can you imagine the embarrassment? The women home making sandwiches for the search crew because they couldn't find us by daylight and who in the world would dream of looking here for anybody? And the question being "Where on the Wild Side did she go?" And it surely would have to appear in the *Goal Post!*

All these things went through our mind as we hung there, but suddenly looking westward, we realized the clouds were really rolling in, and the wind had picked up. Maybe there was a thundershower in the offing like yesterday. That did it! With a thundershower coming we can get out of anywhere in a hurry! We took a deep breath, stuck our fingers in the moss and walked right up the front of that ledge, tape recorder and all!!

We wish to report that the view from "Trunket" is splendid overlooking the whole valley from Florida Bridge up around the bend by Soapstone and the old King place with all of Beaver Island in full view below – well worth a return trip... but this time from the top! As we crossed the Peck field on the way back to Tunnel Road, a white-throated sparrow was singing his special song, "We Praise Thee O Lord." "Amen," we said. **5/85**

Just Over the Line in Vermont

It was a long leisurely hike in the late May (25th) sunshine, two miles as the crow flies, but by the time we had gone sideways, up and down and backward we must have tramped a few more miles. Ever since we discovered them three years ago, our traditional Memorial Day excursion to see the showy orchids at the Whitingham Lime Quarry is anticipated as one of the highlights of spring. The showy orchid is found only in rich woods mostly in limestone regions, and unfortunately, although close, we have not yet discovered this treasure within the boundaries of Rowe.

The day dawned a bit cloudy, but the prospects for sun were good and we were not disappointed. It would possibly be a two-car trip so we left one at the Yankee Information Center and drove on past Sherman Reservoir to our starting point at the footbridge across from Harriman Hydro Station over the border in Vermont. It took us a few minutes just to cross the bridge for below us in the river was a school of large perch jumping for bugs on the surface. A yellowthroat was singing in the bushes on the other side and a pair of kingbirds darted here and there.

The lilacs were lovely on the New England Power Company's park-like lawn. Harriman Station was built in the early twenties and one is surprised to focus on the ornate gargoyles extending from the upper corners of the building. The turbines were humming with two outlets discharging water rushing back to the river – water that had originated in one of the branches of the Deerfield above Wilmington, drained into sixteen mile Harriman Reservoir, come through the mountain in the two and a half mile long tunnel into the turbines at Harriman Station and returned to the riverbed only to be used again and again for power as it flowed on down the Deerfield to the Connecticut.

As we climbed the hill to the old Hoosac Tunnel and Wilmington rail bed, now a Power Company road, we picked and smelled a piece of spicy thyme growing wild along the road, then stooped to examine the wood-betony, almost gone-by on the hillside. Turning south along the road, the wild geranium was in blossom near the early bloodroot whose leaves have now grown huge and awkward. Orioles were singing near us and another could be heard further down the road. A tiny hummingbird came and lit on the wire above our head, showing off his pretty, iridescent green back in the bright sun. Green was the theme for this day – all shades and hues. The coolness of the trees already felt good as we progressed along the road, stopping now to appreciate the lovely spiral song of the veery thrush and then to try and find the elusive warblers – surely all ventriloquists – in the dense tree branches along the river.

What a glorious day to be out on the Wild Side! We would have been content just sitting there on the open hillside, looking downriver to Yankee, watching and listening to all the birds. A flicker echoed from the edge of the woods and every bird seemed to be singing in chorus. The honeysuckle trees planted by the Power Company to fill in the disturbed area were heaven for nectar seeking, tiger swallowtail butterflies, bees and other insects and, following them, the bug-eating birds. Activity in the open gravel area drew our attention, and we focused on a spotted sandpiper picking at the ground and flicking his stubby, pointed tail. Swallows, too, seemed to have found a home here and were probably bank swallows nesting in the top of gravel bank nearer the river.

The constant song of the red-eyed vireo broke into our consciousness every so often as we walked on through wild strawberry and little yellow cinquefoil blossoms. The usually marshy area was dry and only a few purple violets were thriving. The greens of the trees at various stages of leaf were beautiful against the clear blue of the sky and the darker blue of the river now widened into Sherman Reservoir. A catbird had us puzzled for a few minutes. His song was strange, and we were never quite sure if we were seeing him and hearing a mockingbird or brown thrasher with similar, mimicking notes. Closer to the river we watched a yellow warbler who seemed to stay put and be friendlier than others of his kind.

Here we left the sunshine to pursue our course into the woods following the path of a wood road around the old lime kilns and foundations. To our left, further up in the woods along the brook was the strange-pillared, half-finished structure of the Sherman Carbide Promotion, which never got off the ground and seems to have ended with a Sheriff's deed in 1922. The Lime Quarry, on the other hand, was a large and profitable operation back around the turn of the century and one or two of the area's very senior citizens can remember drawing spruce logs there which were used by the wagonload to burn the lime in the kilns before it was bagged much like talc and sent off to market, a carload a day by railroad. The Rowe Historical Society has a letter concerning the lime used in building the stone Unitarian Chapel in the village. The December 2, 1907 letterhead reads *"The Vermont Lime Company, Inc. The Strongest Lime in the World, Whitingham Brand, Green Mountain Brand and Chemical Brand. Kilns at Sherman, Vermont. Readsboro office."* That property and the several other farms and homes in the area were purchased by New England Power Company about 1924.

The Lime Quarry in operation circa 1900 Whitingham, Vermont

Readsboro Historical Society

Now a lovely shade of green moss covers the walls, hiding the old foundations while chipmunks dart between the long cold bricks of the old kilns. But today we are looking for flowers – those that are so special to this rich lime soil, and we are thankful that the commercial operation has ceased and the area has gone back to mysterious ruins and wilderness for our special enjoyment. As the road turned uphill, we could see in the filtered sunlight the beautiful display of thin spikes of miterwort flowers, a sight worth coming to see a week earlier in the season. Now the sweet cicely with its pretty, fernlike, lacy leaves was just bringing forth its tiny dainty white blossoms, and the baneberry plants each had their little ball of tiny flowers. Foamflower was at its height with clusters of small frothy white flowers and pretty leaves. Knee deep in flowers, we had to locate a Canada warbler singing close-by and identify for sure his black necklace on a bright yellow breast. Wild ginger was draping itself over the top of the old kiln on the left and long beech fern tipped over backward, looking at the new fronds of the Christmas fern in patches all along the hill. In the small gully to our right, the Virginia waterleaf was uncurling its funny flower buds on plants surrounding more kiln ruins.

Turning now onto the level of the quarry itself, our path was dotted with rattlesnake fern, a light green, lacy leaf with a fertile stalk rising in the center. This quarry is dry and you walk into the bottom, surrounded by a semicircular high wall of rock. A strange appearing and disappearing brook cascades (this year dribbles) out of the rock into the quarry over bright, beautiful green moss on the left, flows a ways and disappears into the silted floor just outside the quarry. Some years we have seen this flowing almost out to the drop-off on the hill, but now with our land so dry, it disappears into the porous sand near the bottom of the cascade. And the quarry, too, shows signs of the drought. It is usually moist underfoot and rather humid and steamy, with long tiers of bulblet ferns growing out of the limy rocks. Now the ferns seem stunted and dry and lack the lushness of other years. But still this is a beautiful spot, and we circled around to see our specially remembered first station of Goldie's fern, the numerous clumps of marginal fern among the prolific silvery spleenwort, and the delicate accents of maidenhair and fragile ferns.

When all had been inspected, we began the traditional climb up by the cascade to find our first glimpse of the orchids in their hiding places. Appropriately today, our first find was a green orchid – the long-bracted orchis growing in its familiar spot under a tree. The second find was a bit more dramatic and exciting – fresh bear droppings! But so goes our luck, old bruin never showed his face. And then the showy orchids! Those are beautiful, three or four inch stems of hooded flowers with rose-purple tops and white lips, each flower a miniature orchid as we examined them closely with the magnifying glass. Our first specimen was lovely but finding others, we realized that many were past their prime or had turned brown because of the dry weather. But these were all treasures, and we appreciated each in turn, including the special all white one that still bloomed in its own particular location.

At the top of the rise, we came to a narrow level area that seemed to be a man-made dam across the dry gulch of the old brook bed – before it disappears underground. Whatever its origin, this tabletop now has lovely stands of the noble Goldie's fern, and a patch of leeks. We remember this fondly, too, as the first leeks we ever found. Today we pounced upon them for a special treat to eat raw with our sandwiches. Already the bright green leaves of early spring had died down and the single-pointed red bud of the flower was standing above the nearly white, dried leaves. One patch seemed to be near the surface, and we easily dug six and put them in the knapsack. Wow, did they smell good!

Here we took a circle around a little knoll to the left to first check out the progress of the single large, round-leaved orchid that we watch for each year. It was up and the leaves were still small, but the bud, about four inches high, had turned brown and a small spider had draped a web around what would have been greenish-white orchid blossoms. The forest floor here was covered with the soft cottony catkins from the poplar trees and the large, deep green leaves of the earliest tiny yellow violet. We climbed and then descended into the gulch through a mass of beautiful dainty maidenhair fern to the spot where grew the not-often-found, narrow-leaved spleenwort fern – a little later than others and just unfolding its slender light green fronds. Both sides of the gulch were covered with all of these varieties of ferns in their lovely array of spring greens. We hated to walk up the hill, or for that matter anywhere here, for something beautiful would be crushed. As we climbed up and around, more orchids were scattered everywhere along with Canada violets and one little bit of wild life, a small snake, slithered off into the leaves.

On the top of the quarry, we found lots of blossoming yellow roundleaf ragwort also typical of limy soil areas. Our real purpose of this tour over the top was to visit once again the rare walking fern that grows on several rocks on the northwest outside of the quarry. Looking poorly at this time of year anyway, the first mat of fern seemed very dry but alive, and the lower stand was indeed still "walking" to new locations. It is such fun to know where to find these very special plants in their natural habitat and return year after year to check their progress and to visit special flowers at blossom time.

Back in the quarry, we washed the leeks and headed out to a perfect picnic spot sitting high up on an old cement wall of the kiln buildings, overlooking the reservoir through the treetops. As soon as we were seated, a pair of black and orange redstarts flew into the trees in front of us and, although flying about, remained within sight and sound all during lunch. Our partner produced two delicious turkey and lettuce sandwiches on pumpernickel, and we crunched the leeks along with them. Apples and grapes made dessert. A meal and atmosphere no restaurant could boast!

* * * * *

As we ate lunch, we talked about another choice hike this week through a field in Cyrus, listening to the song of the bobolinks and then a quick detour to check for herons in the swamp and the progress of a setting Canada goose. Disappointed at seeing neither, we had become rather vocal as we scanned the water surface with the glasses. Then, when we turned around, father and mother goose were sitting in the grass just across the small beaver dam, calmly watching and listening to our rantings. As we watched, then stone still, six little soft goslings not two days old poked their heads up and eventually all took a swim guarded by mother in front and father behind. Later the parents guided and talked the little fellows up over the dam and slowly zigzagged their way through the grass and weeds to the far shore blending well into the background. Luck had placed us at the right place at the right time!

* * * * *

Today we discussed the homeward options. Rested and refreshed, we chose the longer more difficult course again, heading up by the cascade to follow an intriguing old wood road along a stone wall. Hoping to go over the top of the mountain back into Massachusetts down through the old Wilcox pasture to the Wheeler cellar hole behind Yankee, we could then circle the fence to the car. The road and the wall came to naught, and this is where we added miles, so it seemed, of bushwhacking through the underbrush along the side of the hill high above Sherman Reservoir. Our good sport partner must have quietly questioned our sanity, but as we finally came over the top into lovely open woods and picked up another old wood road where we found the familiar sugarhouse foundation, confidence was restored! And the sight of a pair of scarlet tanagers close-by in the trees was reward enough for climbing any mountain.

It was fitting, too, that we should have chosen to pass this way on Memorial Day week-end and visit the two lone graves placed so long ago on that remote hillside in northwest Rowe. Carved on one slate gravestone was the name of Thomas Wilcox who died in 1814, age 77. On the other stone was carved Renewed, his wife, who died in 1824 at the age of 85. The small, oval foot markers have the initials T.W. and R.W. Now in the midst of woods, the first gravesite for Thomas chosen one hundred and seventy-one years ago was likely then in the corner of a beautiful open sheep pasture. We had not brought flowers, for these graves rested among the wildflowers of the woods, but in this Bicentennial year we had climbed the mountain and taken a moment of time to honor and remember this unknown early pioneer couple. Further down the road are monumental stone walls full of huge rocks drilled and dragged into place. We like to think of these walls as a lasting accomplishment of Thomas Wilcox, late of Rowe.

Looking back as we were nearing our final destination around Yankee fence, a beautiful fluffy white cloud rose gracefully behind the old Wilcox pasture, and a lovely bright green beetle resting on the grass in our pathway reflected the late afternoon sun. **6/85**

Yankee behind the fence

Pelham Lake Park, For the Love of Rowe

With Rowe's Bicentennial Old Home Day celebration fast approaching and all the deadlines for projects to be met, time has become a very precious commodity. And time and weather have not coincided for us as we waited for that rare day in June to take you on a hike to some far-off corner of Rowe. But then something very special happened at the Bicentennial Community Picnic at the beach. Sandy Lively, for the park commission, read the dedication of the new flagpole and tribute to Percy Whiting Brown, donor of Pelham Lake Park. How often we take our surroundings and good fortune for granted! It was a moving experience to look out over the lake and Adams Mountain and realize that, as Sandy said, our generations will come and go, leaving behind examples of changing material culture for our museum, but our mountain will remain constant. Our Adams and Todd mountains, thanks to Percy Brown, will be "forever held in their natural wild state" for our Rowe children's children and their children and on to future generations. Next morning (Sunday June 23rd), we went out to enjoy our own Pelham Lake Park.

It was not a rare June day. It was a misty, hazy, cloudy morning, typical of June 1985, with only breeze enough to occasionally blow the early morning raindrops off the leaves onto our shoulders. But we headed down our hill with special joy in our hearts for we were to trek first the newly named Williams Trail from Pond Road through the park along the old Base Trail up behind the lake. This honor had been bestowed upon the Williamses at the park ceremonies yesterday for "Jack's assistance to Percy Brown in creating Pelham Lake Park" and for our own "Wild Side interpretations." It was a totally unexpected tribute for which we were both most sincerely touched and appreciative.

This was to become a day of ferns and thrushes and memories. Tall stately clusters of interrupted and cinnamon ferns guarded the entrance to the trail and then gave way to the smaller prolific New York ferns that carpet the trailsides and woods. We immediately disturbed a nesting robin for she chirped her distress calls and told us to hurry on. A wood thrush was more sociable and sang to us all along the trail. Crossing the footbridge on Pelham Brook, we remembered being told that the old stone abutments here once held a covered bridge in years gone by and that this had been a well-traveled bridle-way.

The story came to mind of Pauline Hicks and her marriage here in 1917 with the reception at the present Gracy house. The young couple had carefully planned a get-away with their horse and buggy hitched and ready in the old barn at the bottom of Middletown Hill. When the appropriate time came, their friends expected to give them a rousing send-off down through the village, but instead the newly married Stones drove off through the covered bridge and out the old bridle-way to Davis Mine and on down to Charlemont, outsmarting their mischievous friends.

And there were men like George Stanford who walked this road daily for a time to work at Davis Mine, and others from the Mine who came this way to fish for bullheads at night at Rowe Pond. Percy Brown, too, must have known this road as a young eleven-year-old boy when he spent his first summer in Rowe in 1898. And then there are our own recollections of walks as a small child on a father's hand along this trail and through the woods to the back side of the lake – all the while being made aware of plants and trees and birds. We can still remember our fascination with the little red berries on the low wild yew bushes. As we said, this was to be a day of memories with the "new" Williams Trail already dear to our hearts.

We followed the path out through the big mowing now disguised with trees, brush and large bracken fern. Detouring over a small hill by our old campsite, we stopped for a moment to enjoy the first slanting rays of morning sun, beaming through the trees in the mist. We walked on up the hill by the hemlocks where we have often disturbed a family of deer under their shelter and then listened while a sapsucker tapped loudly on a tree. We couldn't resist taking the old familiar short course through the woods to the water's edge on the Lakeside Trail. The area seemed more open than usual, and we suspected beaver, but huge splinters told the story. A tall hemlock tree had been struck by lightning and exploded into limbs and chips in all directions.

We came to the opening near the water and, looking directly across the misty lake, saw the new Bicentennial flagpole high above the school, framed in trees, with the flag flying gently in the morning breeze. An old bullfrog croaked his deep "go round" and we took his advice and continued along the shore. Splashes and enlarging circles in the water indicated fish jumping for their breakfast, and we finally caught sight of a good-sized one in the act. Coming again close to the water, we stood totally amused, watching the little whirligig beetles darting in circles and chasing each other around and

Painted trillium

around on the surface of the water. We fully expected them to gobble each other up like the little Pac-man computer monsters.

Large, low hobblebush covers the area around the lake, and in the acidic soil grow painted trillium with three leaves and a blossom, now gone to seed and in the process of producing a bright red berry for fall. The lovely little starflowers above a whorl of leaves are also producing seeds and each stage is worth looking at with the hand lens. Their final fruit is a tiny, round gray berry with quarter section lines. Pink lady's slippers love this soil, but those have also blossomed and left behind their two large leaves and tall stem with a pointed hat. We looked at pretty royal ferns along the shore and stepped in the soft wet sphagnum moss that's always such a lovely shade of green. A darning needle buzzed past us on his morning rounds, catching mosquitoes as we stooped to examine the spotted St. Johnswort starting to come up along the mossy shore. We crossed several tiny streams draining from the heights of Adams now towering above us. Wood sorrel was in blossom in many places – a small white flower with pink stripes like an old-fashioned shirt on top of shamrock leaves. And then we remembered the purple-fringed orchids and knew we were near their hiding place. If left undisturbed, the constancy of the plant world is one of the recurring joys of summer – to return to special spots and find again and again a particular flower. It was a joy this morning to find this beautiful orchid just where we expected, healthy and well budded for blossoming in the not too distant future.

We looked out over the lake once more before heading up the path. A few lovely white, fragrant water lilies could be seen and near them a beaver had just come down the channel for a look around his domain. The swallows were flying low for bugs and a duck took flight from among in the reeds. Back up on the Williams Trail, we went for a short distance and turned up Notch Trail. We must have been walking at a good pace for we missed the two stations of the large round-leaved orchid and arrived at the notch quite out of breath and ready to lean against a tree and relax. A scarlet tanager was singing in the treetop and fortunately the constant song of the vireo had stopped in honor of the tanager's more unusual voice. The breeze blew gently and the leaves shed more raindrops that felt good against our heated body.

Another fork in the trail turned us up the side of Adams Mountain. Last night we had re-read some correspondence from Percy Brown in which he had stated that in the 1920s John Davenport, with a team of horses, was the one who drew the planks

for the old tower on top of this mountain up a wood road from the Davis Mine schoolhouse to the notch where we were at the moment. From there he had "cleared up the north side to the top." We looked at the fairly steep terrain and wondered just where he had started "up". Perhaps in the winter with the leaves gone that old path might be located or could the present trail be his path? Today we climbed a short distance up and then took the trail off to the right across the mountain to the northwest lookout that was our destination today.

As we approached the lookout opening, the first sight through the trees was the reflection of the library in the Mill Pond. This brought to mind that just fifty years ago on Old Home Day, Percy Brown was master of ceremonies at Rowe's One Hundred and Fiftieth Birthday when the town was celebrating the completion and dedication of the new library building. We crossed the clearing and found a rock where we gladly sat to rest and overlooked our village. As if precisely planned, we were seated comfortably with time to catch our breath, when the Community Church bell pealed out the call to morning service in the valley to the south.

The air was hot and hazy, and we could not see beyond our immediate hills, but there was a certain beauty in the mistiness. We could trace brooks like Pelham, from its source in North Rowe down through a valley, crossing Ford Hill Road and passing by the bluff site of old Fort Pelham of the 1740s. Likewise with Shippee Brook. Both valleys were created by the run-off from much higher mountains in our geologic past, but the present landscape, although scraped by the glaciers, has been constant for thousands of years. We followed Middletown Hill up to the woods behind the Williams farm and envisioned the Centennial parade as it marched to that grove for the "Speaking and Ceremony of 1885." Do you suppose some of our descendants will sit on this very rock one hundred years hence and try to imagine what took place at the Bicentennial in 1985? Will they still look down on the flag flying in the breeze on the hill behind the school? Hopefully, for the 300th there will be another re-dedication and tribute to Percy Brown for his wisdom and generosity in preserving this park "to be forever held" for the future generations of the townspeople of Rowe. May they still know that he gave it "For the Love of Rowe."

Our fondness for new terrain led us bushwhacking our way back down the surprisingly steep mountainside to our left and eventually into a beautiful area of waist-high spinulose and hayscented fern along an old stone wall. Crossing the Sibley Cabin Trail, we went again cross-lots toward home. In a small swamp we found hundreds of tiny seedlings taking root, each with three needles and a tiny spot of light green in the center. This mystified us, but with the hand lens we could see that they were miniature hemlock trees sprouting as thick as grass.

Our present detour back home was a temporary stop for lunch and a pause while threatening weather passed. We had one more trail in mind. At the dedication on Saturday, the east portion of the old bridle-way to Davis Mine was re-named the "Sabrina Rice Trail" in honor of a fourteen-year-old Rowe girl who last year, by a fatal accident, was deprived of her share of a lifetime of enjoyment of Pelham Lake Park. We wanted to take a walk for Sabrina down her trail.

We were delivered to the Davis Mine Road and given a new safari hat, which we were instructed to wear – something with loops through which we could stick our various collected ferns, flowers and whatnot. Although not liking hats, we agreed to try it and must admit it kept the mosquitoes out of our hair and, as we would later find, disguised us as well.

At the entrance to Sabrina's Trail is an appropriately pretty stand of bunchberry with dogwood-like flowers, in their prime earlier in June. A treat later in the fall will be their display of bunches of bright red berries. Going on down this lovely woodland trail, we passed the old walls and moss-covered cellar hole of the Todd farm of yesteryear. The old dump behind the house has been well-picked for treasure and a heap of broken pieces of blue glass bottles is about all that remains of human occupation. Small royal ferns, most often found in wetter places, have seeded along this path, and Indian cucumber root adds interest to an otherwise ferny world. As you would guess, cucumber root, so named for its crunchy cucumber-tasting root, was a favorite food of the Indians. It has two tiers of whorled leaves, the bottom of which resembles the starflower, and three or four greenish-yellow flowers dangle from the top. In the fall, these flowers become blue berries, which stand up above the leaf and shed a blue/red dye in the center of the top whorl. Further on in the deeper woods, a hermit thrush was singing its lovely, clear, flute-like song as if in special tribute to Sabrina. We stood and listened for several minutes.

Pelham Lake Park, For the Love of Rowe

His song continued as we passed the Todd Mountain Trail and descended the hill. Sabrina would have loved her woodsy trail. Now others will especially appreciate it when they walk this way and listen to the thrushes singing in Sabrina's memory.

As we turned down the Beach Trail, the mood changed, as did the terrain. Now becoming more moist, the land sprouted sensitive fern and false hellebore and a veery thrush supplied the music with his spiral song. We crossed Tuttle and Potter Brooks and immediately stopped to see the stand of dainty oak fern. Moving on toward the beach, we heard voices quickly approaching from behind, and we expected runners. Sure enough, two girls, who knew us well, were close behind. We stepped aside and watched them pass with no recognition. We were just a strange, little old lady in tennis shoes and a funny hat! Suddenly they stopped short, looked back and shouted, "Oh, it's you!" (We'll just carry that hat in the knapsack for emergencies next time.)

We sat for a moment on the new park bench and looked out over the pretty little quiet cove off across the lake to the mountain. We thought of Percy Brown and what a treasure Pelham Lake Park is for our town.

That he had given it to us "For the love of Rowe" there was no doubt. We recalled two sentences Percy had written in a winter 1957 letter to us – "First, let me express keen pleasure at reading your description of the walks and get-togethers thereafter... your letter gave me a thrill, and were it not mid-winter I should be tempted to take the next train east and join you." Percy was obviously pleased and enthused that a newer generation was sharing his interest and real love of Rowe, and he suggested more old roads and cellar holes to be explored. He would have truly enjoyed visiting with townspeople at Saturday's Community Picnic and been most appreciative of Sandy's dedication. For Percy Brown's love of Rowe, we shall all be forever grateful and may all future generations share his love of this beautiful quiet little country town with its unique Pelham Lake Park.   **7/85**

Pelham Lake Cove

It is good to be home! After all is said and done, the hills of New England and especially those of Rowe are very dear to our heart. But sometimes it takes a jolt to our senses to further appreciate that which is under our very noses and before our eyes every day. To go was a spur of the moment decision like a good many of our treks have been, but this one involved a car, eight thousand miles, and twenty-eight beautiful days of vagabonding across twenty-one states in this vast country of ours.

"Trails West" we called it as we talked to our companion tape recorder. What a wild feeling of freedom we had as we drove off on that August Monday morning – like the young girl we had been thirty-two years before, starting out on a similar trip to follow "Route #66" west. Looking at Zoar and the surrounding hills, we already saw them with different eyes, knowing that for some time we would not be rushing through that valley on some errand to Greenfield. As we turned at the Mohawk Trail, it seemed fitting that our first "trail west" should follow a part of the old Indian Trail that had led the early Indians and soldiers and settlers over the mountains into and out of the Deerfield valley. We stopped at the eastern summit and took a last look at our own beautiful country. The sun was well up in the morning sky, and each Rowe hill was accentuated with an unusually lovely, misty haze. We looked fondly at all the spots we knew so well. Adams Mountain was standing guard while the sun played on the waters of the Upper Reservoir, tucked in a pocket of hills, and long shadows reached to the Deerfield River where high mountains still delayed the sunrise. Was anything more beautiful to be in store for us? Perhaps "beautiful" was to be a matter of interpretation and feeling. We knew that within us a "love of Rowe" gave this scene a special beauty.

Just before leaving, we had called our favorite hiking guide to see if he had any advice for other parts of the country. "Go to Knoxville, Tennessee," he said after some thought, "and turn right. Look for another town which uses the nuclear symbol with an acorn in the center." Rowe's Bicentennial emblem carries the nuclear symbol in celebration of Yankee Atomic's twenty-five years of generation of electricity by nuclear energy, the peaceful use of the atom. The town of Oak Ridge was born for another purpose and yet historically, it was on the trail leading to "Rowe 1985." So with our first destination in mind, we rolled along the highways, always scanning the roadsides for the flowers of the season – purple loosestrife, Queen Anne's lace, early goldenrod, viper's bugloss, black-eyed Susans, Joe Pye weed, bladder campion and sweet clover, the roadside "weeds" of New England. As the landscape changed, we made quick stops to pick new flowers and soon our day's collection called for several evening hours with the flower guides and eventual frustration in not having adequate reference material or pressing space!

By our standards, it was already hot. The car air-conditioner was going full tilt and was comfortable, but as we climbed up the Skyline Drive in the Shenandoah National Park in Virginia, it was good to be in the mountains again with the windows open and a real breeze blowing. We had inquired at the motel about the Drive. "Well you can go up there, but once you've seen the view on one side and then on the other, you've seen it all. Now down here a ways, you take this route west and you'll come to a big shopping mall. That's pretty nice. My wife likes that." "Thank you sir, but I'm out on the Wild Side," I felt like saying, but then he wouldn't have understood. Up on the mountain, we were excited to find our first nodding wild onion in bloom and stopped at the Park center to look at charts of flowers and animals and hear a ranger tell of the early settlement. Time – we thought yesterday we had all the time in the world, but if we stopped there for the afternoon looking and hiking and becoming familiar with the history of Virginia, what would happen to all the other places? And, we finally told our self, Virginia was pretty much like home. We wanted to spend some time on the prairies in the Big Sky Country. As the motel man had advised, we took the short trip on the Drive, but not for his reasons. It really was lovely. We exited Virginia on the superhighway after a nice afternoon visit with former Rowe residents, Kathleen and Roy Bent in Salem.

Forty years ago to the day, August 6, 1945, the first atomic bomb was dropped on Hiroshima, Japan. Regardless of each of our personal feelings concerning this matter, it is a fact of history. And that wartime history began in the U.S. on December 2, 1942 at the University of Chicago with the world's first initiated and controlled self-sustaining nuclear chain reaction. Subsequently was born the super-secret "Manhattan Project" which ultimately produced the first atomic bombs, ending World War Two.

A tremendous industrial complex and the city of Oak Ridge were created in 1942-1945 by the federal government, in extreme secrecy, out of 92 square miles of rural backwoods in Tennessee, for the research and production of enriched uranium that would produce the tiny grams of plutonium needed for the new bomb. The horrendous job of creating a livable "city" and three huge industrial complexes, quickly and secretly, is an amazing story of engineering, construction, the building hundreds of houses of cement and asbestos, frustration, mud, severe hardships on families, and final achievement of purpose on August 6, 1945. Originally planned as a town for 2,800, Oak Ridge had a wartime population of 75,000, most of whom did not know the project's purpose.

At the heart of Oak Ridge and the Manhattan Project was the Graphite Reactor (X-1O) the world's oldest nuclear reactor. Originally built to produce the first grams of plutonium, it was soon switched to creating "atoms for peace" and became the prime producer for the world's supply of radioisotopes and a valuable research tool for studying the effects of radiation on matter. Fondly revered (by Enrico Fermi and those men who knew her well) as the "Loyal Lady" or the "Graphite Queen," the reactor served twenty years to the day, ending her career on November 4, 1963. Three years later "she" was designated as a National Historic Landmark. Located in the midst of the Oak Ridge National Laboratory, the control room and mammoth loading face are now open to the public, along with an excellent energy exhibit.

We, too, stood in awe before "The Queen" and in awe of all the technology created by the minds of pioneers in all fields. Fitting Rowe Yankee's own "Loyal Lady" into this time span, "She" was first planned in 1953 and went "on line" in 1960 as the second commercial reactor producing "atoms for peace" in this country – the daughter, perhaps, of Oak Ridge's Graphite Queen.

Oak Ridge today (population 26,000 and an independent incorporated city since 1959), is a famous "Energy Capital" and houses the American Museum of Science and Energy as well as three major research and production installations for the Department of Energy. Their Gaseous Diffusion Plant, one of the world's largest industrial complexes on a 1500-acre site, separates fissionable uranium to fuel nuclear reactors used for the generation of electricity, naval propulsion and research, and for advanced isotope separation. The research and development center has become the National Energy Laboratory for all means of energy production and conservation. Born under pressure in wartime, this "Science City" has now become an outstanding center of research and high technology complexes for both the federal government and private industry. Only the remaining "cemesto" houses give away its origin.

Steeped in technology and overwhelmed by the size of the complexes, we went searching for simpler things like wildflowers along country roads – marked (for tourist purposes) with signs depicting a jumping deer in front of a nuclear symbol. We found such new things as butterfly weed, partridge pea and rose pinks, and watched Canada geese as we ate a picnic lunch by the Clinch River. Our afternoon hike was on the trails of the University of Tennessee's Arboretum where one could marvel at the stumps and three foot thick logs of old fallen chestnut trees.

And when we were rested, we took to the road again across and then up and out of the great valley of East Tennessee through pretty country with strange rows of bumpy hills. We stayed off the superhighways and meandered west via the less traveled roads, less traveled by tourists but always by folks in their pick-up trucks who were never, never in a hurry. We excited to the widening landscape and fields of the silage crop milo, soybeans and beautiful diked, wet green fields of rice. Signs read "watermelon and catfish." We stopped at a stand and bought cantaloupe, mainly to talk to the farmer and ask a few questions about his crops and the weather. Questions! We always had questions.

Unexpectedly, the Mississippi River proved to be quite an obstacle in our path. Looking for the unusual, we had chosen a winding route through northwestern Tennessee to the Tiptonville Ferry. With visions of Huck Finn, we were half expecting to find a raft with a man to pole us across. In our path was a stop at Reelfoot Lake. We were intrigued with the huge patches of water-lilies called American lotus which had yellow blossoms and leaves sometimes two feet wide, and with tall cypress trees growing in the water. Park signs gave some interesting facts about the fourteen by five mile lake. It had been created in Mississippi bottomland by monster earthquakes in 1911 and 1912. Firsthand accounts of early settlers said the earthquakes "roiled the Mississippi River bed and the waters flowed backwards." This year the lake water level had been purposely dropped to try and kill some of the vegetation (including lotus) that was choking the lake – famous to sportsmen for its fish and waterfowl.

At Tiptonville the signs simply said "To the River." We followed them across more bottomland and finally on an old dirt

Snow-on-the-mountain

store gathering, we followed Route #7 up on the mountain south of Jasper. None of the folks had been there (maybe twenty miles away) for many years, but they knew it was a sightly place for a stranger to go! They were right, and we enjoyed several viewpoints. Because of the extreme heat even on the mountain, we indulged ourselves and bought our first restaurant meal (we had been eating from our cooler thus far) at a shop perched on the edge of a scenic slope. The Tennessee ham sandwich was extra tasty and the young Conservation Officer at the next table gladly answered all our questions and mentioned that they were trying to start an elk herd there in the mountains. He directed us to Pruitt on the Buffalo National River where hiking trails and canoeing were available. With great anticipation of some athletic activity, we drove down into the valley to the Park area called Pruitt.

The HEAT hit us in the face as we opened the car door, and by the time we had walked the short distance under the trees to the swimming hole on the river, we were totally exhausted. The temperature was in the high nineties, and the humidity must have been twice that. Oppressive heat such as we had never experienced before. We trudged along the river trail and waved to the friendly canoeists who looked broiled limp in the sun. Suddenly we came to our senses and realized that we could be spending our time in the cool mountains of Colorado and that we were under no obligation to tour Arkansas! With our last strength we made it back to the car and took off right up past Dog Patch, through Missouri and by nightfall were listening to the cicadas outside our motel in Baxter Springs, Kansas – back on the old

road up onto the dike. The idea of a raft seemed more of a possibility if the road to the ferry was that bad but, looking up and down the river, we saw nothing but trees. The river was muddy and full of sand bars, and we wondered how it could have depth enough for the coming tug to push its barges downstream. We walked to the water's edge and threw pebbles in as the cargo passed. The mighty Mississippi was deeper than it looked. Back in town, it took inquiries at two garages before we could fathom the southern drawl and learn that no ferry had existed for five years – a new one was still "in the talk'n stage." So we went fifty miles down the road and crossed with all the other tourists on the superhighway on one of only three Tennessee bridges across the Mississippi. On the other side, Missouri was FLAT! The world was now half land and half sky.

A sojourn in the Ozark Mountains sounded good, and we drove across the state of Arkansas like we hike, following whatever path took our fancy, enjoying high plateau scenery of wooded hills and lovely, open brown pastures. On advice of a small town

Route #66 in a town we remember well as the place with good lemonade and a friendly locksmith who helped us get back into our '49 Chevy after closing the door on our keys thirty-two years before!

Kansas had some interesting things in store for us. From the old days, we missed the Burma Shave signs to keep us amused along the road. Kansas immediately obliged with something similar. "You know you are short when your hair has more body than you do" and "God feeds all birds, but he doesn't throw it in the nest." Then there appeared to be tall apple trees here and there with grapefruit-sized fruit, and we were introduced to the Osage orange whose fruit is liked by horses, squirrels and rabbits. A tall green and white flower bugged us until we finally pulled into a field road to take a closer look and a picture. We were in luck, we thought, for the farmer was also just approaching. We asked our question almost before saying hello. The answer, "Around here, all we call 'em is weeds." Weed or not, it was snow-on-the-mountain, very pretty and unusual and a contrast to the constant crop of small roadside sunflowers. Oil wells, too, seemed to grow in Kansas, and they looked like giant black grasshoppers scattered in the fields. We learned about the huge irrigation systems necessary in that dry land and that thousand foot wells had to be dug and pumped as the rivers were already exhausted. Corn required irrigation but wheat fields could lie fallow for a year to absorb moisture. Farmers planted "sections" (640 acres) usually to a farm. All of Rowe could fit on some Kansas farms! One stop

Nan wading in the Pacific

for coffee was simply to ask about a giant field of sunflowers, "That one is 320 acres (a half section), and do you know, when the sun goes down at night that field glows in the dark." We could easily believe it.

Thus we came to the real prairie land. There isn't much of this country that looks like Middletown Hill in Rowe, but by the time we had rolled past Moline, Kansas, it was a whole new world. The great state of Kansas rises from less than 1000 feet on the eastern boarder to over 3,600 feet at the western edge – a gentle sloping rise that is only apparent in the occasional popping of eardrums. Kansas had now become a vast and lonely grassland. We pulled off on a side road for lunch. Getting out of the car, we experienced something very strange. This new world was absolutely quiet. A soft wind could be felt against our face, but it made no noise – there were no trees, no bushes, just grasslands as far as the eye could see. Grass and sky and quiet. There were flowers, too, and we took half our sandwich and walked along the road to examine each in turn.

When we returned, the second half of the sandwich, sitting on the hood of our car was totally toasted in the HOT and very dry air of Kansas in August.

Three days we took to cross the state of Kansas through Winfield along the southern half and on up through Dodge City. A monument to Spanish explorer Francisco Vasquez de Coronado, who led the first white men into this territory in June, 1541 looking for 'cities of gold', Fort Dodge, now a soldiers' home, and Dodge City itself gave us pause to stop, visit attractions and contemplate the history along the old Santa Fe Trail.

Over a ten year period, five million cattle passed from Texas to the stockyards and railhead here. A section of the old wagon tracks have been preserved just west of the city, and on that quiet hill you could almost hear the wheels turning. Known as the trail of commerce, cast iron implements (hoes, axes, kettles) went south to Mexico while wool, gold, silver and cattle came north. Today, the area is still the center of cattle dealing with thousands of head in feedlots and tall grain elevators along the railroad, and Dodge City has a mock gun battle awaiting any tourist who walks down restored Front Street.

Our "trails west" continued on into Colorado where the last stop on our solo trek was a morning walk out into a field appreciating the quiet wide open grasslands, freshly plowed wheat fields, and in the distance the first sight of the snow-capped Rocky Mountains. We met our mate at the Denver airport and continued up into the mountains where the air was cold and the scenery was beautiful at ten thousand feet, and then drove down across the desert of Utah and Nevada where it was hot and dry with a different kind of beauty. We felt the soft fog and the salt spray of the Pacific, and then climbed the tree-clad hills surrounding Lake Tahoe.

Reaching our destination in the high valley of Payette Lake in Idaho, we thought back on this grand and glorious country of ours – the cities and towns and villages and farms, and all the wonderful friendly people of those places who had answered our many questions, and the natural beauty of the big sky, the lakes and mountains and prairies, and the faces of so many wildflowers that had gladdened our passage. And we remembered the awesome technology of Oak Ridge, and in contrast, the wondrous, quiet splendor in the natural Cathedral Grove of the ancient giant redwoods at Muir Woods in a canyon north of San Francisco. The words of "God Bless America" still linger in our heart. **10/85**

Nan at Muir Woods

Our own special feeling for the month of November is not a very well-kept secret. To say the least, it is not our favorite time of year from the last of the leaves to the first of the snow. Sometimes the snows of December come in mid-November and then we are happy. We had been trying to decide on a new place for this Wild Side hike – somewhere that might really enthuse us about November, when along came Saturday, November 16th – cold, raw and bleak. It was one of those days that takes you places you hadn't really intended to go.

It started with an unexpected early morning trip to Yankee. On the way, we noticed "Little Niagara," better known as the spillway from Sherman Pond, steaming and spraying in full splendor on that frosty morning. All hydroelectric stations must have been generating for the volume of water was spectacular. We had seen these falls recently from the top of the mountain but had never taken a closer look. Quickly going home for the camera, it made our day, even sweetened November, to have found a new sight to enjoy. Actually the town line is in mid-river, so this landmark is half in Monroe. Along the riverbank, we walked amid the lovely red berries of bittersweet nightshade, a common viney plant all along the Deerfield, and then we stood for some time watching the might and power of the water as it thundered down over the rocks. We would remember it as an exciting morning in bleak November!

Returning home up Monroe Hill, we thought of a cellar hole we had been meaning to explore on the knoll just beyond the end of the upper truck escape. Now was as good a time as any, so we pulled off the road. Fortunately, we had thrown on a red jacket and hat, as this is bow season for deer hunting and not the time to be out in brown. That section of land is in the Monroe State Forest and had, at some time, been planted with narrow rows of softwoods. The dead lower limbs and windfalls made walking a Chinese puzzle, but we soon saw the circular depression containing some foundation rocks. It had been a small house tucked in the mountains, and seemed to have omitted a barn. We walked down toward a brook and up around the back side of the cellar hole. The original road went behind this house site, but we have a suspicion that this house, known years ago to old-timers as "Brooks' Shanty," was not of the 1790 vintage.

Now the cellar hole is nearly filled with soil, a fallen tree and years of needles shed from the surrounding trees. A large rock in the backyard was split and lifted horizontally, making ideal shelter for squirrels that had carried in many cones and left middens on their "front porch." We followed an old woods road for a ways, but then the November air seemed to penetrate our jacket and we did not linger. Perhaps we were thinking all the time of something more interesting we had found the day before in the Franklin County records.

The original tax maps of Rowe define the earliest County road here in 1771 – before Rowe was incorporated. This intrigued us, and we found in the Court House the original Hampshire County description of the layout of this road in 1771 – surveyed but surely never built for the straight lines seem oblivious to land contours. Starting on the north line of the Province at a maple tree marked "CI:ND GC:SB:DB" (for the men who surveyed), this road was to go

Rowe's Little Niagara — spillway from Sherman Pond

south to stones and a stump in the "Hoosack Road" (early name for the Mohawk Trail) in Charlemont. From the Province Line the road ran "south 608 perch by a line of marked trees (Potter Road) to a heap of stones on a rock in Mr. Jones' lane about eighteen rods west of this barn" (somewhere near the bottom of Potter Road) then "south 34 degrees east 300 perch onto the north side of a hill to a birch marked H.W. (highway) and stones by it," (somewhere on the lower slopes of Todd Mt.) then made a series of zigzags across the present Mine Road by a variety of marked trees, one near "Mill Brook," and finally ran over the hill in Rowe's present southeast corner (into Dell) past some mentioned dwellings and on down to East Charlemont.

So on that cold miserable day in November, we went home for more suitable wool sweaters and a heavier jacket and set out for the place we must have had in mind all the time – that "North side of the hill" where a birch tree had had "stones by it" in 1771. Nothing else but our insatiable curiosity could have taken us out on this wild goose chase! On the Pond Road, we were first distracted by a lonely great blue heron standing on the thin ice around the rushes of the little causeway pond. He had his head extended for some time as if he was about to crack the ice and come up with lunch in one quick swoop. We watched for a while but knowing how patiently herons can stand for hours, we decided not to wait. By the beach, we watched ducks on the back side of the lake – three or four small white buffleheads had stopped by to dip and dive in the far corner. More toward the center of the lake, several larger ducks (probably mergansers)

were swimming in the slightly choppy water of that dreary November day.

We skipped along the beach path in a great spirit of anticipation, stopping a moment by the new seat and lookout to try to appreciate "the lovely silver tones of November trees." A breeze chilled us right through the wool sweater and a blue jay screeched overhead. We moved on. It was not long before we detoured into the woods to our left thinking there might be an old tree or something on the "line." Instead we found black globs of frozen decayed mushrooms, crunchy, frozen pale green sphagnum moss, black stems of dried Indian pipes, and an array of dark evergreen ferns. Stepping through the moss in a swampy area, we realized we had dressed for winter in all but our feet – we were still wearing thin and now wet summer sneakers. We came to the brook farther up than expected by the remains of an old mill dam. We thought of crossing the brook but decided to go back to the trail bridge which was nearer our "line" where we wanted to follow a compass reading to find our "rocks piled up." Along the brook we could see where the hurricane's high water had spread debris and flattened the grass.

Bridge? What bridge? There HAD BEEN a substantial bridge across Potter Brook by the trail and a lesser one over Tuttle Brook where the trail continues. The brooks come together there and flow as one becoming the channel of Pelham Lake. But the bridges were both gone! All gone! Well, we'd find them – they probably floated down a ways on the high water. We walked along the brook edge toward the lake noticing beaver trails through the grass to the woods. Bright red spots in this otherwise gray atmosphere excited us. They were the stalks of red berries from numerous Jack-in-the-pulpits there along the brook. What a pretty sight in November. We were standing on tiptoes now trying to look all the way down the channel to spot a bridge. None was in sight nor were there any remains of the recent beaver dam. Sandy silt covered the brookbed and the water was still high.

It began to occur to us that we were not going to find a place to cross. We were easily distracted from this thought first by a fallen spruce tree which had lots of the bright orange fungus called "Witches Butter." This expands and contracts according to the moisture – like a sponge – and when dried up can not be distinguished from the branch it is on, but then pops out on a rainy day. We like to have a collection of this "butter" on hand to show off a little natural magic – by putting the seemingly ordinary, dry piece of wood into water and watching it soon produce a strange yellow/orange growth.

We jumped some small beaver channels and got over to the tree, but as we tried to pull off the fungus we found it frozen solid and could not pull it free. Instead we climbed on the fallen tree and balanced ourselves while we "looked out to sea" – there were still no bridges in sight! How could they totally disappear?

We continued walking toward the open area by the lake and were finally stopped by flooded inlets too wide to jump. The thin ice had beautiful patterns interwoven with the grasses draped across. Stalks of summer vervain and purple loosestrife stood among the old dry cattails. There were, after all, things of beauty in gray November. We shivered again as the wind carried the sound

of a Zoar train which seemed to be coming up the Pond Road by the dam. It was that awful penetrating cold that felt like snow! We turned and headed back, knowing full well that we must retrace our steps back up to the old mill dam to cross the brook.

By the time we swung across on the rocks of the old dam, grabbing a small hemlock for balance, we felt a little foolish. Why didn't we turn around right there and go home? At what point in life will our age and infirmities and good sense overtake our curiosity? But it was easy walking now, and we were soon back at the fork in the brooks expecting to walk straight across Tuttle Brook on the shallow rocks as we did in the summer. Wrong again! The water was just a little too high, and we didn't really want to completely soak our sneakers in fifteen degree weather. We started up the brook, knowing there were plenty of rocks to take us across but as we approached each likely spot the stride was just a bit too wide or the rock too slippery. Frustration set in! We made many starts and wisely changed our mind. We became like a caged beast trying to escape! At one point, a long tree trunk lay beside the brook, and we thought we could roll that into the brook and walk across. We kicked, pushed, shoved and kicked. It was frozen solid. This is really a tiny little brook – very pretty, tumbling down a small incline over mossy green rocks. That day every branch and twig near the water had acquired a row of icicles and in quiet pools ice had attached itself in strange formations to the rocks. We finally relaxed and enjoyed the sight.

We made our crossing easily much further up the brook and reversed our direction back down the other side. We also convinced ourselves that the trail ahead was to be via Davis Mine Road and not back the way we had come. Finally reaching the appointed place on the east side of the confluence of the two brooks, we took our compass reading south thirty-four degrees east and started off, convinced for sure that those men in 1771 were merely following orders and not using any common sense whatsoever in the layout of a new road through the wilderness. We could easily follow the compass but had no way, except by our line drawn to scale on the geodetic map, to know where the end of the three hundred perch measurement would be. The dreary November atmosphere had gotten to us, and we were about to declare this trip "mission unaccomplished."

Strangely enough a small "hill" appeared before us in the approximate location we had drawn on the map. We climbed it and then searched the "north side" – up, down and around. There were no ancient trees but there were birches as the old marked tree had been. In our mind we had expected to find a real cairn a few feet high but there was no such thing. But there was under our feet a mound of earth covered with leaves and soil. A small rock shifted under our step. We immediately dug down under the soil and leaves to find that the mound was not a ledge outcrop but probably a huge old stump, well decayed. On the north and downhill side, we removed the rock that was loose under our feet, and then another and another – enough to feel certain that they were not a natural collection, but that they had been hastily gathered from the surroundings and placed long ago beside a "birch tree marked H.W. on the north side of a hill." We dug further, expecting to find a time capsule

or something, but those early surveyors and chainmen had no time for such trivial pursuits to delight future generations. And this had to be just one of hundreds of trees sighted and marked in the slow and steady development of civilized roads in the "new world."

We could see no particular obstacles causing the zigzags from there on and without a chainman of our own, could not further plot the course. We climbed the hill, crossing one stone wall, to reach Sabrina's Trail at the base of the Todd Mountain Trail where an old birch tree did have a nearby pile of rocks. But this was now the Todd farm where two cellar holes, many walls and piles of rocks cluttered the hill.

A happy November day after all, we thought, as we briskly walked down Davis Mine Road, noticing a patch of pipsissewa we had never seen and checking the still reddish remains of the pitcher plant flowers in the little bog. From there, we went on to Pond Road where we were delighted with a little bouquet of ice crystals that had gracefully pushed up through a sandy spot on the bank, and with the multitude of yellow fall dandelions that were still in blossom. Finally, in honor of the season, we sampled the lovely red and juicy wild cranberries growing beside the road. A few minutes later, we watched with real joy as the first snowflakes began to fall.   **12/85**

1986

Fringed gentians

Frank Knight Photo

Although there is no story, here is the final discovery of the Town Bounds in the Northwest in 1989

Den with upper stone marker

DP & NNW 89 initials on nearby tree

Lower marker (C for Charlemont)

Old beech tree with many years of initials of perambulators

Perambulating Town Lines

There was a lot of perambulating going on during the year of 1985! Greenfield and Bernardston were doing it, Heath was doing it, Charlemont and Hawley and Colrain were doing it, and, yes, even Rowe was doing it! The state law says the town boundaries must be perambulated every five years by the selectmen or their representatives and judging from the dates on the stones, this is traditionally done in the years ending with 5 and 0. To perambulate in our book says, "to walk through and examine." What is required is that the cornerstones be found and marked. In city areas it means driving to a street corner, but in these hilltowns it can involve long hikes into the wilderness!

We started out one December day to perambulate the easy markers first, traveling by car with the three selectmen, George Riggan, Tim Snyder, and Ellen Foberg with her young daughter, Kirsten. The stone beside Pelham Brook just above the ledges on Joe King Hill is the boundary with Charlemont where the line comes up the middle of Pelham Brook from line bridge and turns east to the so-called Northwest – a strange angle left over from the annexing of Zoar by Charlemont and Rowe in 1838. Having examined the rock and sprayed it with identifying paint, we went on down by the mouth of Steele Brook where the 1938 hurricane raised havoc with the lay of the land and the area doesn't quite fit the description listed in the 1914 Massachusetts Atlas of Boundaries which was our authority. Nevertheless, the stone is there.

From there, the town line goes straight southwesterly over Negus Mountain to the next point at water level on the Deerfield River where the mark is on the abutment

Nan by boundary marker on the Deerfield River

of the old Florida Bridge upstream of the present bridge 665 ft. The covered bridge on the old site was washed out by a flood in 1869, and the new one located downriver to avoid the railroad (accounting for Rowe's owning one third of the present bridge). Here we walked along the railroad past the hole in the rock (made famous in 1838 by Hawthorne as the Deerfield Arch) and climbed down a precarious slope to the river where the last chiseled date in the rock was 1950 and must have been the handiwork of John Bond, Ellsworth Veber and William Baldrachi, Rowe Selectmen of that year. Had it been summer, we would have looked for the delicate bluebells growing on a large rock in the river. Today an assortment of strange poles was hanging on wire high over the water in the gorge. They were later described as slalom poles for canoeists who run the rapids in high water.

The town line follows the river around Rowe's portion of Zoar to the next corner where the towns of Florida, Monroe and Rowe (across the River) come together. This stone is over the bank near the mouth of Dunbar Brook in the State picnic area. There is puzzlement here on how Rowe lost (without any mention or documentation) this southwest corner of the Myrifield Grant, which was incorporated into Rowe but later listed as within Florida's boundaries when that town was incorporated in 1805 – before Monroe was created from Rowe lands west of the Deerfield.

Next in the western line is the boundary marker above Yankee, about three-quarters of a mile on the old HT&W Railroad bed beside Sherman Pond on the Deerfield River. Rowe's northwest corner is actually in the middle of the river (as the whole western boundary is), but that being inaccessible, the witness mark on land is the official stone. This corner is partway between Yankee and Harriman Station and can be approached by walking down from Harriman or by going around Yankee fence and walking up the rail bed. Both seemed needlessly long and strenuous when a short walk through the Yankee yard would be quick and easy – or would it?

In the spirit of cooperation and due to the official nature of our mission, Yankee agreed. We, of course, would go via the guardhouse to be checked in and out. This immediately eliminated one selectman with a small child. Due to the large number of cars in the parking lot, it also necessitated our walking from the info center down to the guardhouse – no less strenuous than walking around the fence hill we were avoiding! We hardly even hike with a wallet and this nearly eliminated us, for a social security number was needed and ours was not impressed in memory. But after phone calls, searches, signings, issuance of dosimeters and hard hats and several other official acts, the three of us were cleared and led the few steps across the yard to the back gate, by a guard who would stand by and await our return.

It was a lovely morning to hike up the old railroad bed in the fall sunshine, but our pace was more urgent, knowing that the guard was waiting. We refrained from our usual practice of collecting dried flowers, rocks and mushrooms and stuffing them in our pockets. The boundary marker was soon found (directly across from the small island in Sherman Pond), examined, marked, and photographed. Thus, with our official act completed, we returned to the gate – wishing

Boundary stone above Yankee

we could just take a minute to run up to the old Wheeler cellar hole and look for the unique earthstar mushrooms which grow there. Although we appreciated Yankee's cooperativeness, we realized that we could have walked the fence in half the time and saved the embarrassment of them having to call an extra female guard to come out to the back gate and search us before we reentered! Nevertheless, it was a Rowe experience, and we were grateful to know that our neighbor on the River was well protected – even from perambulating selectmen!

From that northwest corner the boundary joins Whitingham, Vermont in a straight line all across the top of Rowe. Along the old Whitingham Road, which goes by the Carey yard, there is another marker on the Vermont border known as the Jilson Corner. There the line makes a slight change of angle. A short hike to this spot found the marker north of a stone wall and a little southeast of a Vermont cellar hole. It is on land Cornelius Jones sold to Mathew Barr back in 1781 and where Stephen Gleason settled in 1784.

Rowe's northeast corner is shared with Heath and Whitingham. Several calls to Heath (and Charlemont) produced no joiners for treks to our mutual corners and with the year drawing to a close, we continued on our own. On Stone Hill Road just over the line in Heath, we started the climb east of the brook up through the open field where some previous selectmen had directed us (selectmen can forget a lot in ten years, it seems!). The 1914 directions show the bound beside a brook that is a little deceiving for it is not the main Burton Brook, which we thought, but an eastern tributary. We crossed an old stonewall into a larger field and headed for the northwest corner finding an old wood road which we traced to a small brook – looking over all the knolls as possible

**Jilson stone,
North boundary**

sites for this elusive marker, now already further north than we expected. Following the brook seemed the only logical path, and we climbed a hill on the west side, looking everywhere for the three and a half foot granite monument which could easily blend into the gray beech woods. It was finally spotted on the brow of the hill, well hidden in the trees west of the vague remains of the specified old wire fence. And just above it a few feet was the old crude boundary stone with earlier dates. We are not sure why the Vermont line was slightly changed here. Our trek took longer than expected, and we were identifying the road marker on Stone Road by car headlights. And so we rounded another corner in the great 1985 perambulation.

* * * * *

The next five boundaries to complete the circuit are those hidden high in the hills of east and south Rowe and are probably not seen for years at a time by human eyes unless, perhaps, those of a stray hunter. The Northwest rises up four hundred feet out of The Basin west of Legate Hill in Charlemont. The far-off sounding name refers to the area that holds the northwest boundary of Charlemont and is a vast mountaintop wilderness behind Coon Hill in Zoar – partially in Rowe and part in Charlemont. There lie two Rowe bounds

– one is the northwest corner of Charlemont where it intersected the Rowe line after a strip of Charlemont was incorporated into Rowe in 1785, and the other was made when the strange shape of Zoar was divided between the towns.

On a crisp Sunday morning in December, three of us set out to find those Northwest bounds – to do the searching before involving the selectmen in a wild goose chase! Previous selectmen remembered things like "Old Will Pierson from Charlemont took me in. He knew the way. I didn't pay much attention," or "It's off that old wood road out of the Basin. You can't miss it," etc., etc. We made it a two-car trip, leaving one at the line bridge in Rowe and starting our trek on the old wood road below the Blakeslee house on Legate Hill in Charlemont. New snow in the woods made for pretty country and not bad walking as we quickly descended into the Basin below a large well-hidden chalet on the hill. Its wide rolling garage door solved a two-year-old mystery noise that we heard one fall day while having a picnic on the mountaintop on the west side of the Basin. Thinking there was not another house for miles, we were suddenly surprised by the seemingly close crashing of metal and then silence. Across the valley, that garage door being rolled down fit the bill perfectly.

The Basin is, as you might expect, a rather swampy place, collecting the run-off from three hillsides and eventually channeling into one brook that meanders down and around to join the Deerfield near the Buttonball Tree in Charlemont. Large pine trees made a canopy overhead and small hemlocks grew along our path that steadily climbed to the back of the Basin and

then steeply up the hill as it gently curved to the west near the heights. At that point, the sun shone through the icy branches of every tree and created a winter wonderland. Limbs near the ground had developed a covering of ice over a collection of snow – but the snow had melted, leaving the ice hanging strangely on each branch. Deer tracks crossed our path several times and as the road turned downhill, we veered off and took another path up onto a plateau where three deer could be seen running across the hillside ahead.

It was time to seriously study the map and there was much speculation about our exact location in relation to the bounds we sought. The consensus was to follow the deer up the next ridge. We crossed a tiny solidly frozen swamp and came up onto a familiar path – back down which we had flown one summer day when a faint clap of thunder in the distance caught us far from shelter in that wild Northwest! But the path only proved that we knew the way home, not that we knew what town we were in or where to look for boundaries. Continuing on up the ridge, we came upon a Peck Lumber Company well-marked line. At first we thought we were in luck, but then realizing that they might also have property in Charlemont, it proved nothing.

Finally on top of the ridge, we separated and searched in various directions – the challenge was on! The woods were really lovely with new clean snow and sparkling ice above. A small cabin would be nice, with a big fireplace and large windows looking off toward Thunder Mountain. We began to look more for nature signs than we did for boundaries. And then the setting sun penetrated our senses, and we shouted for the others to give up the search. We had started too late on a short December day, and now must make tracks for home before early darkness stranded us in the Northwest. Chalk one up for mission failure, but it was a joy to be in the woods on such a perfect winter day. We had covered some territory all told, and during the long steep, bushwhacking descent down the western slope to the car at line bridge we had begun to favor a knee that dislikes the downhill run. But we were already looking forward to the challenge of next time!

* * * * *

Next time came the following weekend when we persuaded our two companions to join in the hopefully shorter search for Rowe's southeast corner – located in 1914 in "a partly open pasture with young pines" on a level area about 1,000 feet east of a point on the old Davis Mine Road. Continuous snow flurries had accumulated a few inches of fluffy new snow, and again it was a privilege to be in the woods. We parked the car at the Devil's Elbow, and continued down the old road on foot past the cellar hole of the Stranahan house and the spot where we once had found a hermit thrush's nest.

The first encounter was with fresh tracks in the snow. It was hard to judge them in such soft snow. The prints were singly in a straight line but they meandered over, around, and under all sorts of things and puzzled us all until, in thinner snow, the turkey foot was obvious! They had certainly combed the area, criss-crossing the tracks of a small deer. Mice tracks were in abundance and being of so lightweight the

Sue, Den and Nan at Southeast boundary stone

mice made interesting patterns on top of the snow, often disappearing in tiny holes. A tall wild lettuce, goldenrod and other dried specimens were propped in the snow under the power line. Looking up the open hill to the east we remembered the beautiful sight of wood lilies growing there in the summer. Later, a small gurgling brook and an old trail joined in from the west.

Soon our road disappeared into the brook – thanks to the 1938 hurricane. We walked around rocks on rather thin ice in one channel and occasionally broke through, giving our boots a good washing in the orange water. This is one road that was abandoned after that devastating storm and never rebuilt. It had been a sturdy road as evidenced by the shored up center that still remained. All the heavy Davis Mine Studebaker ore wagons pulled by four-horse teams had traveled this road to ship the sulphur ore by the railroad at Charlemont. A man could make two trips a day if the weather and mud permitted and he didn't dally. For twenty-nine years an historic road where now all is quiet save the murmuring of the rusty acidic mine water under the ice. Trying to judge distance to an unmarked town line, we decided we had gone too far and retraced a few steps before crossing the thicker ice chunks on the main brook to climb the hill to the east. Ice crystals on flat rusty-colored rocks along the brook were beautiful and could have kept us happy for the rest of the day.

On the hill the crew spread out, finally arriving on a flat area at the top. We again began looking at things like bright orange witches' butter on a dead cherry tree, listening to soft-spoken chickadees in the hemlocks, and watching a brown creeper searching up and down a tree for grubs. Soon a snowmobile trail crossed our path, and we gladly followed in a northerly direction where, at a junction, we all followed the trail marked Peter's Store, although we were far from that destination! The power line was soon seen through the trees and a well-marked corner revealed the north-south old wire fence for which we were searching.

After consulting with the map and observing the land contours, we decided to turn and follow the fence remains to the south. It seemed a long way down through the brush along a well-marked boundary line to another level area. Our crew boss was way ahead, and when he was finally

in sight, we saw him leaning against a tall stone, grinning like a Cheshire cat. We were not totally convinced it was a Rowe bound until we saw the R as well as the H and C carved on the appropriate sides of the marker. But the puzzling fact was that the 1914 description of the stone as a foot and a half high. Uncovering surrounding snow revealed the older stone carved with 1885 plainly in sight. Sometime since 1914, a new marker has been erected.

The tall stone had been well carved and painted orange on top. For the lack of tools or paint, we hung several orange ribbons in the surrounding trees. Then to satisfy our curiosity, we took a compass heading and marked an approximate line back to the Mine Brook. Shortly, it crossed the snowmobile trail on the old wood road. The selectmen, if they so desire, could be carried to the site of this southeast marker. At the Mine Brook, we found ourselves further down the Davis Mine Road than we had walked, at a leaning yellow birch tree. The pine on the east side of the brook had fence wire around the base. Perhaps we were right on the property line. This fifty-acre corner lot belongs to the Town of Rowe – being part of the old Winchell farm taken on Tax Title from the Arthur Farrington Estate for non-payment of taxes back in 1959. We shall return and look it over for springtime goodies come April.

And so passed the winter days of sunshine and perambulating – following an old New England custom.

A Happy New Year to all our friends on the Wild Side! **1/86**

*"Something hidden, Go and find it.
Go and look behind the Ranges
Something lost behind the Ranges.
Lost and waiting for you. Go!"*

– Rudyard Kipling
The Explorer

S tanding on the far side of Florida Mountain beyond the first range of mountains as you look west from Rowe, our guide told the assembled group of eight that we would be hiking down a lost valley in search of general adventure and a hidden family cemetery. Our anticipation had been building all week. A phone call early in the week had asked our plans for Saturday the 18th of January and although we hinted that we still had town boundaries to find, we could not turn down a challenge from our favorite hiking guide.

Our crew included an old favorite, Buddy the dog, who, you may remember, escorted us up Dunbar Brook a couple of years ago; a forester from Idaho, fresh out of Ponderosa Pine country; and a new recruit-in-training, eight-month-old Arolyn Anne, riding high in her red backpack on our guide's shoulders. It was a two-car trip. The first car was left on Black Brook Road in Savoy where the Mohawk Trail crosses the Cold River. We were to come down Wheeler Brook valley across the way, but there certainly wasn't any valley that we could see. Loading the second compact car to the hilt (barking dog in the rear), we drove slowly up the trail past Dead Man's Curve and turned down South County Road at the Mobil station. We parked at the end of the plowed road and suited-up for the trek ahead.

It was a relatively warm afternoon with hazy sunshine, and we needed neither hat nor gloves. However, we could have used some padded pants for the downhill later on! We started up the road that was now just a snowmobile trail through fairly deep, soft, drifted snow, and we found it easier for everyone to walk in the same footsteps. Our first treat was a spectacular and different view of Rowe from the top of a long steep open field which always stands out when looking toward Florida from many places in west Rowe. Because of the haze, the scene was a rather flat blue but still uniquely beautiful, looking over the rugged terrain of Rowe's Neck – that odd shape of our southwest corner carved by the Deerfield River whose drainage system, we have learned from Norman Hatch's new *Geologic History of Rowe*, was formed not from the recent glaciers but millions of years ago by the gradual erosion of mountains here that were once several miles high.

Among the cliffs and rocks that were moved and scraped by the glacier, we could see crossing the old Tunnel Road, a long stone wall made by early settlers who invested in land and tried to tame this wild mountain country and make it profitable farmland. Their walls in the wilderness are now silent monuments to the eventual failure of those efforts. But man has tamed the river, and we could look over to the Upper Reservoir of Bear Swamp where man-made dikes stored the river water for the production of electricity with huge turbines deep inside the mountain. Far below, the railroad snaked its way up the river and disappeared into the mountain to our left where another venture of man, the 4¾ mile Hoosac Tunnel, still bears daily rail traffic, and is a continuing monument to the ingenuity and persistence of our forefathers.

We must move on! We could spend days marveling at all the angles and history of the Deerfield Valley, but also tucked away amid these hills are other sights and sounds equally as amazing but seldom seen, and to ferret out something new was the purpose of our venture today – so let's be on with it! We continued the climb up the road through woods that obscured the view and quickened our pace. At the top of the hill (elevation about 1,720 feet) just before the road heads down into open fields by a couple of summer houses, we went into the woods to the right. But before leaving that road, we took time to see where Samuel Rice's Road went down the mountain to our left to join the River Road just past Florida Bridge.

Rice was given a grant by the General Court to build a road from the mouth of Cold River in Charlemont over Clark Mountain to the road we were on (then known as Hawley's Road) and it was completed in 1768. Also here along this road, Joshua Locke was given a grant in 1771 to build a tavern to accommodate the travelers. A new road called the Second Massachusetts Turnpike and Stage Road was built with a better grade up Whitcomb Mountain (in the present location) in 1785, but became a toll road in 1797 with a Toll House on the Krutiak or Nelson Flats. This prompted people to use Rice's Road again as a shunpike – although steep and winding, it was free. Although the only traffic here now is an occasional snowmobile, in the days gone by this was a popular and well-traveled road.

The woods were nice and fairly open and although the snow was drifted in spots, we usually sank to just above our ankles. Once in a while it was closer to our knees. There were lots of low laurel bushes and for once it was a good feeling to be able to walk on top of instead of crawling on our hands and knees under them, as we have been known to do. The snow was cluttered with lots of debris – seeds, pine needles, pieces of bark

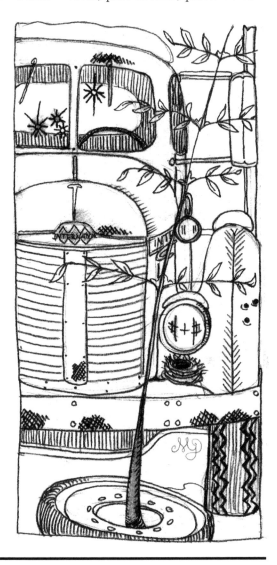

and twigs, and cones – all victims of several ice storms and windy weather with no fresh new snow. Deer tracks were everywhere and in many places it seemed as if a whole herd had been digging through the snow into the leaves beneath, looking for beechnuts, acorns and tasty twigs. Over the first hill we came upon a graveyard, but not the one we were looking for. This one was for several old farm trucks of the 'twenties and 'thirties vintage. Tires had rotted, metal had rusted, stuffing was hanging from old seats, and hunters had fired holes in the remaining windows of vehicles, which at one time had been a farmer's pride and joy and daily necessity. Only squirrels and mice now appreciated them. Buddy had a ball sniffing out their hiding places.

We soon found the beginnings of a tiny stream as the land began to slope downward, and we investigated a small stone dam that might have made an ice pond in years past. The deer had come here to drink and in each hoof print one dry yellow beech leaf had lodged, making bright yellow trails to the brook. Beech leaves often stay on all winter, rustling in the wind and making a pretty sight in the woods on young smooth-barked, light gray trees.

We spent time trying to identify trees for our own benefit and to acquaint our forester friend with the charms of New England woods – here comprised of beech, maple, birch, cherry, and oak. We found a witch hazel bush and examined its flower remains (they blossom in November) and several open seedpods. These eject their seeds with force when they open and then remain as hard little twin cups on the tree. Tree barks are fascinating and especially lovely in winter when various colors and textures stand out against a blue sky in the bright winter sunshine.

Our guide took us around the back of the hill and on down toward the bottom of a long, narrow open field, the top of which was out of sight back by the car. Here we turned south on the remains of another old road. At this point the field ended and there was a marked distinction in the nearby woods. We had entered the Mohawk Trail State Forest land, and it had been planted with various softwood trees, mostly red pine, but never cared for and trimmed, so trees were too close together with some surviving and some dead. The effect was to create a solid upper canopy that let in little light and an under story that was nothing but brushy, dead lower limbs.

It took some careful thought to maneuver the red backpack and small child's face through the underbrush. Her favorite position seemed to be listing to the right – perhaps to get a better view of the coming attractions around her Dad's favorite old green hat. When the way opened up a little better, we found something new to us, pointed out by our western friend – a series of bear trees where the animal had clawed several red pines and pulled off the bark to get at the juicy pitch inside. Claw and tooth marks were prominent. Old bruin had had a feast.

We were still basically following the old road even though it was brushed in and had been sometimes washed out by the small brook, which had come along side from the right. Soon there was a trail crossing and our guide stopped at the intersection to welcome us to "Todd's Mobil" – the local identification of a snowmobile/motorcycle trail. This again has a history in that it follows or closely parallels, in this section, the old Indian Mohawk Trail which came across the top of Florida from the west, crossing here and following the ridge down toward Todd Mountain and descending to the Deerfield valley by the present state camping area on Cold River – a trail well-traveled by both Indians and soldiers. Shortly after examining a small square cellar hole and identifying several tall Norway spruce with cones, our guide declared, "Here it is!"

At the junction of two streams forming Wheeler Brook and in a somewhat more open area, was the little cemetery. Drifted with snow, only two stones were visible and may be all that are there. A small wall formed the lower end and perhaps can be found under the snow all the way around. The tallest stone was square and perhaps four feet high. The family name was Gillette. His first name was Collins, and he died in 1890. She was born in 1808 and died in 1887 and under the delicate line carving of a rose, her name was engraved – Freelove Rose.

The companion stone was a flat marble slab with the prominent carving of a finger definitely pointing toward Heaven. This was in memory of Amoretta, daughter of Collins and Freelove Rose. There had also been a son, Oliver, and daughter, Sarah. Here was a family who had lived and struggled and died on this farm on the side of Florida Mountain, and now rested peacefully here in the woods beside these small singing brooks. So many thoughts went through our minds. Who were they? What was life like back then? Did they enjoy a good life here on their hillside? And most of all we wondered who were her parents and how did

FREELOVE ROSE

they happen to choose the hauntingly lovely name Freelove Rose?

Oddly enough, we found later, searching the Berkshire Registry of Deeds that Collins Gillette first bought his house site (the cellar hole by the cemetery) from Samuel Negus in 1832 and another piece of land from Nathan and Freelove Drury. Not her mother, but there must be some connection – or more likely we've somehow missed seeing a very common early name! Perhaps they all valued their independence for across the brook on the other side dwelt Freeborn Wheeler. Before moving on, we repacked baby in knapsack, lengthening the seat so perhaps her listing could be improved, but we soon learned that although she looked uncomfortable it was her preference. She was not sleeping, but wide-eyed, not wishing to miss a trick. And from there on the view from her vantage point was to grow more exciting.

We crossed the left-hand brook and meandered steadily downhill through more natural woods, stopping here and there to examine pretty fungus growth on dead trees, to look at the fanciful ice formations along the brook and now and then to call Buddy, who seemed to be racing off hither and yon in all directions and not rounding up his crew at all – a feat which gained him such fame on his last jaunt with us. One quick fall into a small swampy hole brought him up shaking off water from head to toes. Back near the brook, we came upon a monster grandfather white pine tree – certainly one of the tallest, straightest and biggest pines in the area. We made due recognition of it and looked around to point it out to our western friend who, we discovered, had already walked under it totally unimpressed. Although he did

not volunteer the comparison with western trees, you could sense that in the face of our excitement he was thinking, "I'd REALLY like to show these New Englanders a BIG tree!"

It is hard to remember now just where the ravine began. We crossed the stream once again and soon picked up what looked like a channel high on the side of the hill over the deepening brook. This we followed for some distance until it ended near a bend in the brook. Our guide ahead looked puzzled and was peering down into the rocky ravine when suddenly he shouted, "Hey, look at this!" as he bounded down the steep bank, knapsack, baby and all. We saw nothing but rocks, but he had spotted several stone pillars, which on closer examination were the foundation of a large mill to which the channel had been directed. Gradually we all slid down the bank and crossed the gurgling brook as it raced down the ravine – dropping steeper just beyond the mill site.

The stones in one pillar were all frost, and we stuck our hand between the rocks to feel real warm air flowing out. The earth behind or some small animals within were definitely breathing! Once again we were speculating – was this Collins Gillette's mill, or that of Sam Negus or maybe Freeborn Wheeler whose family name seemed to have been attached to this brook. What kind of mill and when was it built? Heavy snow covered any further clues that might have been there waiting for us. Deep in the ravine at the curve of the brook, this spot was not exactly easily accessible by foot or wagon! Our short search in the Registry turned up no answers, but a visit with Edwin Wheeler in Florida did. He was grandson of Freeborn, who owned all the land on the west side of the brook. A Wheeler uncle owned the other side. The mill had been owned by Gilbert Mann of Zoar (large house now gone on the Cronk property) who was the area "wheeler and dealer" in lumber, property and mortgages in the late 1800s. Mr. Wheeler, now in his eighties, remembered that as a child he used to sneak down to the mill pond and try to catch their fish. There had been a cabin and several shanties in the area that were used into the 'twenties. All houses including the Gillettes' and Wheelers' had burned before the State took over the land, but Gil Mann's mill was moved. When lumbering was going on, the men drew the logs up the hill and then down Torrey Mountain Road to be loaded on the trains at Hoosac Tunnel. As for the stone pillars, Mr. Wheeler seemed puzzled, too. It sounded as though they predated the Mann Mill to when they used to make scythe snathes there. More than likely that remote spot in the ravine was early known as a natural source of power and has more history than can be remembered by the present generation. Stories forever "lost behind these ranges!"

From the mill site, the crew separated and descended both sides of the ravine, weaving back and forth as the brook dropped in steps about four hundred feet in elevation down to the Cold River. Strange forestry markings with blue paint and ribbons, padded trees and circle bark cutouts kept us investigating here and there. Baby protested slightly that it was long past her dinner time, but was soon overwhelmed by the dizzying heights she seemed to be subjected to as our guide stood along the bank's edge looking down on steep ice-covered waterfalls that played muted

music as they swirled around the rocks and fell to the pools below, repeating the process time after time down the rocky steps of the ravine. Meanwhile the rest of us were trying to maneuver the downhill with reasonable safety – at times swinging from tree to tree and at others just sitting and sliding. The winter icy dress of these falls was beautiful, but we kept thinking of summer and green moss and overhanging ferns or spring run-off increasing the beauty of fast moving water. We would return!

Our last brook crossing before the final eastward twist of the ravine was precarious as we picked our way single file across an ice ledge. A crossing nearer Cold River threatened more open, deep water, and we chose the ice instead. Fortunately, the river just below the bridge was shallow, and the ice there held our weight. As we walked under the big metal and concrete bridge (with 950 ft elevation marks), we could look upstream and see the remaining half of the graceful arch which had been the much photographed "Cold River Bridge on the Mohawk Trail" before the 1938 hurricane tore apart man's handiwork all along this valley.

Traffic could be heard rolling over our heads, and we knew we were back near civilization. From the road, we looked back toward the ravine which, from that vantage point, was still not giving to casual onlookers any hint of its existence, yet we had gone and found its hidden treasures. **2/86**

A Glorious Winter Day

Once every few years there comes the rare privilege of experiencing a day so glorious and memorable that it makes all petty problems in life seem insignificant. A day on which our Wild Side is so radiant and beautiful that it is really beyond description. The morning of Saturday, February 22nd was just such a day, and we were ready and waiting.

It was the most brilliant morning of the entire winter – more so perhaps because of the previous week of dreary rain and clouds. Friday morning we decided it was never going to clear, and we would don our heaviest jacket and rain hat and go to the woods trying to find something interesting to tell you about raindrops. When the afternoon arrived, it was pouring. Our enthusiasm for the wet and cold Wild Side was nil. We would put off our hike until tomorrow, and take whatever that day had to offer. It couldn't be much worse.

When the first light of Saturday dawned, we knew it was a different kind of day – it was light - in fact, bright! With daylight proclaiming the glory of winter in New England, we could hardly wait to finish breakfast and call a friend to join us for a snowshoe hike. Our destination often depends on the day, and today we made a quick mental review of the town and decided on North Rowe. The rain of the last few days had frozen and thawed and frozen again on every

limb and twig, and just before dark the evening before, the rain had changed to huge snowflakes, creating a fresh white blanket on the ground and over every icy branch. As the sun rose over Adams Mountain Saturday morning, the world became a sparkling pure white wonderland. North Rowe seemed to be calling us.

Leaving one car on Shippee Road, we drove the other to the power line on Potter Road where we harnessed up and headed west on the snowmobile trail. Not having snowshoed for a couple of years, we weren't too adept at straps while standing on one foot and took at least one humorous tumble. We started off pigeon-toed and clumsy, but a little tightening of straps set us straight. We always use ski poles that are taboo with the purist but very satisfactory for our style. And our pace was leisurely for we could not rush through this wonderland without admiring everything in sight. The power lines hummed as they marched across the hill, and

North Rowe power line

the wind made a strange crackling sound as the icy trees swayed to the gentle breeze. The sun was warm on our backs and as we watched the wind in the tops of the trees, we looked through the white birches and spruces to a clear deep blue sky. Every small bush on the ground was a beautiful sculpture; the old blackberry brambles arching to the ground with the berry hulls still remaining; the delicate wheat-brown grasses bent with the weight of ice; swamp pink bushes still holding up their collections of tiny, vase-like dry seed pods; and the lowly goldenrod gleaming with ice as the snow on its dried blossoms resembled cotton ready to pick.

The astonishing thing about that pure white world was the color it contained. Blue sky, dark evergreens, silver gray yellow birches and all shades of browns and grays in the bark of the trees bordering the open power line. Everything was accented by the iridescent flashes of rainbow colors as the sun's rays reflected off every piece of ice. The ice on the tall spruces had melted faster than on the hardwoods trees and thus developed icicles on each branch, making them look like individually decorated Christmas trees. An old apple tree gleamed red through its icy cover, and shadows across the ground made us look up to see a small flock of evening grosbeaks flashing bright yellow as they flew off to the woods behind us. We had a camera with us but no picture could do justice to this world nor could it interpret the feeling and privilege of being there hiking in the warm sunshine with so much beauty all around us and so much fresh air to breathe. It was truly exhilarating!

The power line sloped gently to the west from Potter Road to a height of 2,000 feet before it dropped down two hundred feet into the wide open basin, where collected the headwaters of Shippee Brook, and then up again before its final drop into the Deerfield valley. From the first height we looked westward to Greylock, north to the hills of Monroe, and southwest toward Savoy, which, from that vantage point, towered over Negus and the other layers of mountains between. Fields and houses took on strange proportions. In the foreground the house and barn of Bill Brown on Shippee Road and surrounding fields were quite apparent, and above that was the colony of houses and pastures along Hazelton Road by the Foberg's, Sibley's and Thoung's.

But then, just beyond Sibley's was a huge open field (we knew there was nothing there but woods) with a house and barn along a curving road and another house at the top of the field. Even with binocs this arrangement puzzled us, and not until later when we laid out a map at home could we visualize Tunnel Road past Sparky Truesdell's house to the Taylor's on Petrie Road. Distances, heights and angles are deceiving from mountaintops! Also visible on the distant hills of Florida, was the steep open field from which we had looked back toward Rowe on last month's Wild Side hike.

Icy mountains and hills created altogether different perspectives and one of the loveliest was the effect of the dark black/green evergreen trees standing out against the white hills. Unreal, something in a painter's imagination, we would think if we saw it on canvas. We lingered at the hilltop, making sure we were missing nothing in that strange and lovely wonderland. With the heat of the sun, pieces of ice melted on the highline poles and often came crashing down, breaking the silence as they smashed against the wood and metal structures below. Reluctantly, we started down the hill, glad of the ski poles to brace ourselves against the steep descent. Soon a noise could be heard coming from the west, and we spotted two snowmobiles weaving their way down the opposite side of the basin. They soon passed us with a cheery wave and glided up the steep slope where we had just come down. Then all was quiet again except the gentle crackling of the trees along the side.

The protected bottom of the little valley seemed even warmer, and we crossed a small area of open running water – the start of Shippee Brook. The grasses along the water were almost green and the snow had melted along the bank to reveal the dry fertile fronds of last year's sensitive ferns. Old hayscented ferns were crumpled above the snow, lending yet another hue of brown to the colorful world.

We spent some time looking over a small tree with twin twigs of seeds that looked like dried-up chokecherries but it defies identification until we can see the leaves in the spring. In the woods here were scattered beech trees with their bronze leaves still in place, and further up, a pine tree had a heavier burden of ice and snow than its neighbor, the spruce, perhaps because each long pine needle was individually iced. Occasional dry leaves still on the bushes out in the open looked like balls of iced fruit, and we checked them out to be sure. With the effort of climbing up the next ridge, our down jacket became much too warm and at the first opportunity, when we stopped to identify the open hillsides now looming in

the distance to the east in Heath, we shed the coat and stuffed it in the knapsack, continuing on much more comfortably with only a wool sweater. The hillside in Heath was the power line we had crossed on the great Bicentennial trek from Fort Shirley.

We were approaching the intersection of the old Readsboro Road, which we intended to take south. The trail had been used to the north but not to the south. We noted its entrance at the woods but wanted to go on to a favorite hilltop a little further west and find a place for lunch. After poking the snow off a perfect rock, we decided to lean against rather than sit on the rock, leaving our snowshoes in place on our feet. This was easier said than done for we tried to spread our jacket against the rock to keep dry and then back up to it sideways and lean with our feet at right angles to our bodies. The downhill side was even more awkward, but when you are hungry, position sometimes doesn't matter! That was not the only hardship to annoy our picnic.

Two more snowmobiles came roaring up and across the summit just above us. Another trail branched south from there, and we assumed they were headed that way. But they stopped and, when we were spotted, one came roaring down off the trail to talk with us and inquire about trail directions. This was fine except that he managed to get the snowmobile stuck and had to rev and roar a goodly cloud of exhaust across our lunch and in our faces before he could head back up the hill. They eventually continued on the path south that we then imagined was a detour back to the Readsboro Road. We could hear them still going westward for a long way although they never came in sight back on the power line. We would remember this fact as the day progressed!

Needless to say, we did not linger over lunch. Our hastily made sandwiches were not the greatest and the grapes were mighty sour, but our partner's offer of a hunk of good chocolate drastically improved the situation. The air had cleared and we were again admiring the scenery. To the west, thin high clouds were on the way while a few low wispy puffs sat over the valleys. Suddenly realizing that our next lap was to be in the woods, we hated to leave the open sunshine and contemplated continuing down the power line to Monroe Hill, but that was steep and a long hike back to the car. We finally cut across the power line up to the woods on the south side where our curiosity led us to the trail where the snowmobiles had disappeared under the low-hanging icy branches. It looked so inviting that we had to follow – placing small bets on our resulting destination. We said back on the Readsboro Road, but our partner opted for Monroe Hill. We privately hoped our own intuition was correct! It would indeed be a long walk back up Monroe Hill.

Once in the woods, it was even more beautiful with the sun shining thru the icy canopy of branches over our heads. The variety of trees created additional hues and shades of color – none more beautiful than the lovely green and white striped bark of the moose maple whose branches culminated in bright red tips and buds. Behind the moosewood, an unoccupied squirrel's nest was the first sign of life in these woods. The snow was smooth and clean with nary a track to be seen. The trail did lead westward along a more or less level ridge, and it was a long time before we had any confidence that our destination bet was possibly correct. No matter the outcome, it proved to be a lovely trail, and we quietly thanked the snowmobilers for forging our path. The woods, we soon realized, had many more charms to slow us down – investigating this and that or just standing in awe of a particularly beautiful spot, a wall, a brook, or just a ray of sunlight through an ancient, craggy beech tree.

North Rowe after ice storm

The path was variable and kept us in suspense as to which direction we were really headed. Our mind was more at ease as we turned south down a small ravine beside a growing brook. Here one small deer track finally crossed our path. The woods were alive as well as beautiful! Looking up, we saw a large shelf fungus growing out of the top of a small dead birch like a street light on top of a pole. We crossed the brook and stopped to admire the old trunks of gnarled maple trees – perhaps an old sugar orchard long abandoned – and several large burls on the cherry trees. Overhead we watched fast moving jet contrails and looking ahead of the noise spotted the ghostly jets against the blue. A slight thinning of the trees to the left convinced us we were finally tipped toward the east and we soon declared ourselves winner of the bet. We no sooner spoke the words than the path made a sharp hairpin turn to the seeming northwest and up the mountain. We were doomed and surely headed for Monroe Hill – no doubt about it! Fortunately, some tracks distracted those thoughts. The tracks were a close series of about six-inch round depressions in a straight line crossing our path and disappearing under trees on both sides. Well distorted and filled with new snow, they would remain a mystery – their closeness and symmetry still puzzling.

We started up the hill at a faster pace out of wonderment and curiosity at the turn of the trail. We expected soon to be back on the power line – perhaps the trail was one big loop – but we remembered that the snowmobilers had not returned in sight. That was one possible clue that all was well. Our pace was slowed again to appreciate a collection of snow and ice-covered baby spruce trees. All lower branches were bent downward, and the very tops formed a perfect cross on each tree – a series of miniature green church steeples in the white snow. And then there began to be stone walls – short ones and long ones well hidden under the crusty snow. We must be in the vicinity of the old cellar holes, Pike and Hunt, and pastures along the old

Readsboro Road. A dead tree sported rows and rows of small white fungus up and down the bark and another tall spruce had a super crop of cones at its very tip.

Nearing the top of a small hill, we came onto a fairly level area with towering pines. We suddenly felt that we had been there before – on the way down from our hike over Round Hill. If we were correct, a stonewall and property sign would soon mark Bill Brown's land, and sure enough, we could see it in the distance. Even though we described the rest of the trail as passing a corner of Rainbow Hill field and doubling back to cross a brook, our partner was not totally convinced to give up the bet until we came out in the field behind Brown's on the Readsboro/Shippee Road. One last lovely musical sound awaited us walking through tall pines. It was raining under a bright blue sky! Our crystal world was melting in the warm afternoon sun – but only under the dark pines trees. Out in the open, the same wonderland of ice sparkled on the hardwood trees. They would need warmer sun than that to shed their glamour.

Thinking back, our curiosity had won again! And thanks to the snowmobilers for the great new trail that had intrigued us. As we sat at home with a relaxing cup of tea, the clouds thickened and obscured the blue while the setting sun was veiled in white. We had captured in memory four of the most glorious hours of the winter, and we would treasure them for years to come. **3/86**

In search of Spring, we waited until the very last possible moment, the 29th, to take our March Wild Side hike. By then we could report all sorts of frogs and herons and growing things! And we sort of had "swamp fever," knowing that life would certainly be stirring there. We were happy to learn that our favorite hiking guide was to be around, and he would know where to show us the real signs of Spring! When the day arrived, he was suddenly talking about glacial grooves on rocks in Heath. "But," we countered, "what about the swamp? What about Spring?" His reply didn't come directly, but before the day was over we had learned the answer.

Our crew was small but enthusiastic, and we headed out in early morning, making our way toward Heath with two cars. Our first sign of Spring was a pair of Canada Geese walking on the edge of the water along Pelham Lake. With the ice still frozen, they hardly had room to swim, but for better or worse, they were here! We left the car on the bend just this side of the Heath Fairgrounds. First crossing a brown-colored field where the matted grass was just beginning to feel free again after the heavy weight of winter snows, we joined the muddy path of Ledges Road and headed down the hill to the South. Closed in the winter, this road went from mud to snow drifts still two or three feet deep. But first we had to stop and admire the wide expanse of view west toward Rowe.

Like looking at Adams Mountain in a mirror, Todd was on the right and Adams on the left and their familiar rounded shapes were backward to our vision. The almost one hundred and eighty degree Rowe view started on the right at Sullivan's on Cross Road in North Rowe where the sun highlighted their white house and continued with the houses down Potter Road before the mountains interfered. The yellow Williams house just peeked through the trees directly over the Davis Mine Road cut, and then the next Rowe dwelling was the Monroe house and field far to the left at the Charlemont line on Legate Hill. Highlines stood out, as did the eastern lookout on Adams Mountain. At about eighteen hundred feet, we were enjoying one of the nicest views in the area, looking from one hilltown over the valley to another. Greylock, still white with snow, rose in the far distance.

A warm wind was blowing from the southwest, and we trudged through the rotten snow, which held us on one step and buried us to the knees with the next. The winter winds, uninterrupted from Greylock to the west, had drifted the snow particularly high in that spot. Soon in the shelter of the woods and a southern exposure, the road and ground were bare, and we began to examine the ledges for the reported glacial marks. Sure enough, on close examination we found several places where a north-south channel or small grooves dissected the natural grain of ledge. Time and climate, creating a slow and steady wearing away of the rocks, had all but destroyed those markings left by the mile high glaciers which twice covered our towns and wiped away our soils, dragging boulders and stones across the remaining bed rock which we were examining.

In the course of checking ledges, we also became aware of the varieties of lichens growing on rocks. The lichens produce an acid, which plays a part in the slow disintegration of the rocks, and together they help rebuild the soil in eons of time. With the small hand lens we were on our knees looking closer at all the wondrous shapes in this miniature world we seldom see. Tiny red/orange insects were roaming around – some looked like mites and others like beetles, and a raft of tiny spiders scurried here and there after their winter naps. The shades of greens, grays, yellows, and browns of the lichens and their odd shapes created a weird world under glass. Lichens are a mysterious plant – a combination of algae and fungus that grow together in a kind of partnership (symbiosis). Not requiring soil, they grow on all kinds of surfaces like rocks and trees. The alga makes the food, and the fungus lives on it and produces the main bulk of the new plant, the thallus.

Out on the power line now, we left the road and turned west as two broad-wing hawks sailed on the air currents over our heads and a brown creeper seemed to follow us singing a dainty sweet song but blending with the tree barks so we never could pick him out. The lay of the land was rough and rocky – some bare ground, some knee-deep ponds, running brooks and deep snow drifts. We traced a strange path, looking closely at all the bare ledges, avoiding the ponds and drifts and some of us investigated every interesting lichen, dried weed and spot of greenish grass which might be sending forth something spring-like.

Spring was in the air but not on the ground. The bright fresh spring greens turned out to be last year's spinulous ferns and shamrock-like goldthread leaves, both of which retain their color and shape all winter. Standing in the snow were the twisted tops of the lovely dark cinnamon-colored, hayscented ferns now crumbling and blowing in the wind. Soon we were picking a bouquet – dry but beautiful even though we had our heart set on springtime. Starting with the lovely open dry "flowers" of the swamp pinks so prolific on the power lines, we added the dry meadowsweet and hardhack which was a new treat to explore with the hand lens, and then came the curlicue shreds of cotton candy on a stick – the strands of white silken threads from the long narrow seed pods of the pretty pink fireweed.

Our guide was now far ahead, entertaining baby in backpack and allowing us to stroll along at our own pace. He soon called for us to see some writing in the cement under the highline tower. It clearly said "Billy Gibson, Aug. 9, 1936, Millbury, OH." Well now, there was a mystery! Was

Billy Gibson a worker on the construction crew when the power line went through or was he just a visitor who liked to carry a pail of cement to properly mark his trail? And where was Billy now after the intervening fifty years, and would he like to know that his name is still readable on a hillside in Heath, Massachusetts? We later tried to contact him, but the Gibsons in Millbury, Ohio didn't know anything about one of their clan (grandfather, maybe?) by the name of William!

Next we looked closely at the snow mold on the ground. Under the lens it was covered with tiny seeds or spores and all seemed to disappear if we tried to touch it. A reference book on molds? Not yet in our collection! And then came something else very intriguing – straw-colored cocoons attached to branches. The first we tried to open, and although the material resembled a leaf, it was very tough and almost needed a knife to pull apart. When we finally tore it open, there was inside a very hard, dried chrysalis of a caterpillar/butterfly. From the texture, it must have been one of the giant silkworm moths that overwinter in this stage, spinning a tough cocoon. This one had obviously not survived to hatch, but why? Looking around, we found three of them in one general area, and wondered if the line spraying or maybe just the cold weather had destroyed them. One more mystery to add to our growing list!

Another rock in the open sunshine had a collection of small bleached bones. Something had feasted on something else that had long legs and a small rounded rib cage, but the predator had taken away the major portion of his lunch. Under another tree, we pulled apart an owl pellet full of fur and tiny bones.

Owls regurgitate these balls to get rid of indigestible animal parts. So much evidence of interesting Wild Side activity around us! But no signs of Spring!

We were still thinking about the swamp, and the fact that things were probably going on THERE right that minute. Our guide had taken us on an interesting exploring hike, but he knew we were REALLY LOOKING FOR SPRING! From the top of the power line hill we looked at the long steep descent to the road below and prepared for the "brakes-on" climb down after enjoying once more the view off to the west and the warm (70 degree) sunshine of that near-perfect summer day in March. No sooner had we gone a few feet down and found a dried fertile frond of the sensitive fern as a final addition to our tightly clutched bouquet, when our second car on Long Hill Road appeared from under the hill just below us. The road in the distance at the very bottom was 8A, far beyond our destination. Our lovely hike was over all too soon!

* * * * *

Lunch and things at home kept us busy for a few hours, and by three o'clock we still couldn't get rid of our "swamp fever." The only cure was to grab the binocs and head out Cyrus Stage Road, and, as always, it was in great anticipation. We hadn't even found a spring beauty on our morning hike, and we knew we had seen them blossomed when there was still snow on the ground! Our guide was great, but this time he just hadn't understood – we wanted to see Spring!

Once off the road, the ground was wet – very wet – but we pushed on quickly until we finally stopped and realized we were out of breath, trying to hurry through the deep snow! Spring? The very warm day had not made a dent in the snow cover in the woods, but we continued to climb up and down, following some kind of a weaving path made weeks earlier by a human on snowshoes or a snowshoe rabbit on the run. Tracks at this late date were so completely distorted and the snow was black with needles from the hemlocks and bits of bark and debris from the woods. As we pulled one foot after another out of the snow, our boots were wet and then totally soaked for we were in a hurry and didn't pick and choose our steps very carefully. Strange air currents began to hit us – the first was hot and then suddenly we turned a corner, and it was very cold, which really felt good at that point! It might be snowy on the way, but we bet there would be so much life at the swamp! Small trees were bent over the path and still covered with snow. Laid low by the ice storms, they were still frozen in the ground and covered with snowdrifts! Spring? We stopped to listen for frogs, but had to move on quickly for the path on the old road was a small river of meltwater.

Reality did come as a considerable shock when we finally reached the totally ice-covered swamp. Although the ice looked too soft to walk on, it nevertheless was thick and white and forbidding. There were no frogs croaking and no herons looking for frogs. The only sound was an occasional redwing honking in the distance. We were dumfounded. And then slowly it dawned on us why our guide had taken us to look at glacial grooves on rocks. This was that awkward time of year when warm days seem like Spring, but no matter what, in the hills of Rowe and Heath, it just needs a couple more weeks to really BE Spring – and no matter how anxious, you still

have to find something else of interest (like glacial grooves in rocks) on the Wild Side while waiting for the flowers and ferns and herons! Our guide knew this all along, but at the end of March you just cannot come out and say, "Not yet, wait a couple of weeks!" We were "rushing the season" and we knew this, too, but we seem to have to prove it to ourselves every year!

Looking across the swamp we saw bare ground on the far hillside, and we could close our eyes and see that hillside as it was covered with spring beauties last year. With that many, just one must be up and blossomed ahead of schedule, and we would find it! Sustaining our energy with a few mangy checkerberries along the shore, we walked around to our usual crossing log. High water made it difficult to reach and precarious to walk on – requiring a final leap to reach the shore. We'd never make it back the same way!

We searched the hillside for a spring beauty blossom. Not a one! Finally, on our knees, we carefully pulled back the leaves, and there they were – tiny fragile white shoots from small corms culminating with two brown/green leaves about a half-inch long and several tightly closed buds. One cluster had a real pink bud, and we carefully pulled it out of the leaves and wrapped it in a Kleenex to carry home. Yes, for Easter Sunday morning, our tiny pink spring beauty bud was, to our mind, the most beautiful Easter lily we had ever seen.

As we walked back across the beaver dam, a robin in the distance was calling for rain, and, although we did not know it at the time, the herons had already returned to Mill Pond. **4/86**

In our dreams of faraway places, there will always be a field sparrow singing. We've never even seen a field sparrow, but they are one of our favorite birds. Faraway places like Peck's field in west Rowe or the top of Old Smokey always have field sparrows singing just over the hill and out of sight. Our Audubon Field Guide describes their song as "a series of soft, plaintive notes, all on the same pitch, accelerating to a trill at the end." We hope we never hear a field sparrow at home for it would spoil our dream of faraway places.

April was nearly at the end (the 27th) before we could take a day for our excursion into the wilderness. We have two favorite spots in the spring, both between Tunnel Road and the Deerfield River. Last year we took you down through the ravine. This year it was time to return to the Soapstone area. We delayed an early morning start because the clouds were black and heavy and full of dropping rain, but the weatherman chanted a different tune. When we picked up our partner, she was confident we could find beauty in the rain. It was a two-car trip and, having exchanged family cars in the morning, we left our "borrowed" one by the river at the lower end of Tunnel Road. Clouds apparently made a good day for fishermen for they lined the shore.

As we drove back up the mountain to Rowe, we began to dream of the faraway places we were soon going to see, where the sun always shines from a blue sky dotted with puffy white clouds, and there is a field sparrow singing just over the hill. It was hard to realize where the reality of dark clouds disappeared and the dream of sunshine began. But like magic, we stepped out of the car in Peck's field into a brilliant world of a perfect summer day and the first sound was the plaintive call of the field sparrow just beyond our sight.

With a light heart and a quick step, we started off down Tunnel Road. It was a little too early to be delayed by migrating warblers, but new green shoots of most everything keep us scanning the roadside and admiring tiny new, bent over backward fiddleheads of long beech ferns, red stems of sensitive fern, the delicate brown wrapping of the larger marginal clumps, and the every which way collection of new light green Christmas ferns. We strolled past the old schoolhouse foundation, which brought to mind that our faraway place was once well populated with townspeople of Rowe. And then there were the early folding sprouts of pink lady's-slippers! We were very excited to see three right together. Then across the road there must have been twenty-five! It does take a while to come to our senses after a long cold winter – lady's-slippers they were not, but instead a healthy clump of clintonia.

The lovely yellow trout lilies reflected the sunshine as we searched in vain for the familiar small clump of hepaticas. Our reward was blossoming hobblebush here and there in the woods, and further along by the Cressy cellar hole, the gill-over-the-ground was everywhere and already in bloom. There we detoured to investigate a couple of lovely white rocks a ways down the old hillside pasture. The rocks were very cold, as are all white rocks, and covered with a pretty green and gray moss and lichen combination, which we promptly examined under the glass. Such a beautiful miniature world we so seldom see!

On down the road, we thought the place had been booby-trapped. A thin white thread was strung across the road, and we almost hesitated to investigate. It seemed to follow all along the side of the road here and there wound around a bush or stick. The only answer was some sort of surveying device, and either the power company or the Doubledays were measuring their acreage. The string led us through a cluster of pretty pink mayflowers and, as we stuck our nose down to smell, we found two beautifully marked bumblebees enjoying the nectar in each fragrant blossom. This of course reminded us of food, and we decided to stop off and overlook the clay pit while we had a snack. We settled for a little wine and a cookie, for the sandwiches must be saved to have with the fresh leeks that would soon be in our path. Hunger got the best of us though, and we snitched half a sandwich, too. As we munched, a field sparrow sang to us from the back corner of the open hillside.

The little brook by the old Doubleday house was singing its way down over the rocks around the brightly blossomed yellow coltsfoot. Such a cheery bright weed in the spring! Or was it summer? The air was very warm, and the bugs were out! That's not fair – they are two whole weeks early this year! But not even the bugs could discourage our first quest for those very special spring wildflowers, and the early saxifrage greeted us, clinging to the ledge just below the first old Cressy cellar hole – pretty little flowers with yellow centers and lightly wooly stems.

On down the road we passed the old rock bridge through which tumbled the waters of another mountain brook along whose steep ravine grew stands of huge red trillium. They say there is another cellar hole hidden there somewhere over the bridge, and we must stop and find it some day.

Our stony path was strewn with acorns with bright red coloring on the "meat" inside, and as we progressed down the hill, something moved quickly through the leaves ahead of us. A big turkey was blending in so well with the forest around, it was hard to focus on the lovely bronze feathers. Violets now began to greet us on every side – blue ones, deep purple ones, the tiny yellow ones,

and white ones. Violets and goldenrod and asters all give us fits for they are so hard to identify exactly. We often just give up and enjoy them. Some dainty white violets are fragrant, and we had just found a patch and were down on our knees looking close when the intruders came upon us – two characters on four-wheelers! What had happened to our dream of faraway places? Well, we have to forgive those two for disturbing our sanctuary, for they were on a mission of mercy looking for us. It seemed the car we had been assigned was nearly out of gas the day before, and to ward off any dire catastrophe of our having to walk home, the boys were sent to get the keys from us so the gas could be delivered! Some people we know are always out of gas!

With the commotion over, we continued on down by those wonderful huge ledges and rocks covered with rock tripe which they say would sustain us if we were starving which we were, and just over the hill and off the path was our real treat of the season – the first leeks! We eagerly dug a few and devoured them on the spot, stating that they were the sweetest and crispiest and most delicious we had ever eaten! Far, faraway places always have leeks!

We were soon stepping on numerous downy yellow violets and Canada violets, both of which are "stemmed" and grow in rich woods, and we were certainly in rich woods for all the spring flowers were there – a heavenly collection – and we hardly knew what to admire first. The special little bowl-shaped glade was full of bright green leeks, wild ginger with its funny little reddish purple blossom right on the ground, blue cohosh now green and gone well past its weird

Miterwort

stage, very delicate fronds of maidenhair fern not yet unfurled, red trillium, Dutchman's-breeches with white and yellow pantaloons, and squirrel corn with fragrant little hearts – the delicate little leaves of the last two looking exactly alike.

The high ledge on one side hid in its crevices the dainty maidenhair spleenwort fern, saxifrage and red columbine and most delicate and lovely of all, the miterwort, sporting tiny little fringed caps as flowers and two opposite leaves on the stem. We could scarcely contain ourselves and had to see everything at once, checking to be sure that each flower was growing as we remembered. For a minute we thought we had lost the lovely clump of hepaticas, but a little searching found them multiplied to three and now full with the new growth of cottony soft leaves, the flowers having been very early bloomers. The kidneyleaf buttercup grew along the rock path and the baneberry was budded, looking confusingly like cohosh.

Only one favorite was missing, and we continued searching until the lay of the land looked right, and sure enough the dwarf ginseng was just bursting its tiny flowers into perfect round balls above three sets of leaves like its larger namesake. The "Arolyn flower," we shall always call it now, for we picked it to bring to her mother on the day our granddaughter, Arolyn, was born.

Leeks were calling, and we had to dig our spring's supply. Scrambled eggs and leeks, fried cold baked potato and leeks, leek soup, leek hamburgers, but best of all a picnic in the woods on a beautiful spring day with ham sandwiches filled with as many leeks as would fit between the slices – now that's living! The local red-tailed hawk was screaming down over the river as we sat on the rock with our gourmet meal.

We had to move on and carefully climbed over the old decayed log covered with porcupine quills in our special little glade where the chipmunks were peering at us from every hiding spot. Down over the hill we always admire the big old wolf tree with strange-shaped limbs, and marvel that it escaped the loggers saw which seemed to have girdled all the old "useless" trees. Two more special places were waiting for our visit, and we had to climb back up the road along the brook among the spring beauties to look for the stations of the rare Goldie's fern. The

silvery spleenwort seemed to be growing everywhere, and we began to worry that something had happened to Goldie's. We had scrambled up the hill to inspect another green clump when our partner shouted to "Come see"!

We sort of slid down the moist hillside and wondered what there was to be found under the brushy place where she was looking. Blending nicely into the grass were the largest and strangest looking green, gray, black, brown-colored fiddleheads we had ever seen, but then we had never seen Goldie's in that stage before! That was excitement enough to carry us on to the next ravine where we found the same single stand of narrow-leaved spleenwort fern right where it always grows, and the special yellow trillium in among still more of everything we had seen before including toothwort in every direction.

Sooner or later we had to return from our faraway dreamland, and find our way back to the real world as we walked along the old road high above the railroad where many a wagon had passed on a trip from west Rowe down to meet a train at the Hoosac Tunnel Station. So much has changed since then – life is now so different and continues to change every day, but on the hillside above the Soapstone quarry the same leeks still grow and the columbine still finds a niche on the rock and the Goldie's fern is rooted deep in the soil. Human life may change, but there is great constancy out there on the Wild Side.

Again driving back up the hill to Rowe, we were refreshed and renewed knowing that some things never change – like the field sparrow who always returns to those faraway places. **5/86**

Old postcards of Rowe with pictures taken by Charlie Canedy in the early 1900s reveal many rocks and rills on the surface of our hilltown that have been lost beneath the canopy of eighty years of forest growth unhindered by the grazing cows and sheep of yesteryear. We've been intrigued with an old postcard picture taken from Pulpit Rock looking northeast back up toward the highest point on the mountain. Three ladies posed on the rocks for perspective. Although the picture shows most of the mountain as open ledge, the intriguing thing is a triangular shaped boulder prominently

OLD ROWE POST CARD OF PULPIT ROCK
Notice the ladies and the triangular shaped rock in the upper right.

sitting near the top. We meant to find it someday, just for fun.

Part of our New Hampshire crew was in town on May 25th, and we planned a hike, mainly to show our transplanted westerner a little more of his adopted hometown. It was also a good chance to finally check out that rock triangle sitting above Pulpit Rock. We started off without the "Off" or any bug juice because someone had left it in the other car, but as long as we kept our bodies and arms moving, life was bearable. As we entered the trail west by the old Massachusetts Talc Mine on Monroe Hill Road, our first mission was to swing by the soapstone ledge to check for any new plants in that different soil. Cottony catkins of the poplar trees were on the ground as we walked in, and we could see why in recent days, the air had been full of this fluff as the spring winds carried the tiny seeds to be scattered to new locations throughout the town. The new green maidenhair spleenwort ferns were daintily tucked in every nook and cranny of the mossy soapstone ledge, and the round-leaved yellow ragwort was in blossom. We especially wanted to keep track of a Solomon's seal which we hoped was a special larger variety, but examining it this time, we determined the plant to be ordinary.

A thrush was singing close by, and it seemed a good opportunity to give our theory for learning the New England thrush songs. We recommend one rule - if you have to stop and wonder if it is a hermit thrush, then it isn't! This one was, and its song was clear and beautiful and unmistakable. The wood thrush is lovely and lives nearer civilization, but it does not have the clear flute-like tones of the hermit. The veery thrush has a very different, spiraling song. The woods were full of warblers, but it would have slowed the hike considerably if we had taken time to find and identify each one. Instead, we watched red salamanders wiggling and squirming in all the muddy places.

A beautiful sunny day after a couple weeks of rain highlighted the still wet, green mosses and endless array of new leaves as well as the dark, damp, variegated tree barks. And for once, the woods were quiet underfoot. We walked noiselessly like Indians in moccasins, now and then unavoidably stepping on a bouquet of violets in our path. Two large round leaves on the ground sidetracked us for a minute, and we were disappointed to find that the orchid was not to blossom this year. Examining the leaves, they were very shiny underneath, indicating the large round-leaved orchid that is found occasionally in more acid woods. Unfortunately, slugs find this plant very attractive, and often eat leaves and stem before the flowers have a chance to develop.

The trail soon brought us to the open power line and a lovely view toward the upper end of Sherman Pond and on toward Haystack Mountain in Vermont. In spite of having to look through wires, the power lines are great places for views and give some idea what it must have been like in the old, close-cropped sheep pastures on our rocky hillsides. According to assessors' records, in 1832 twenty-eight hundred sheep, over nine hundred cattle, and nearly two hundred oxen and one hundred forty horses fed on the grasses of Rowe! And everyone burned wood for fuel. No wonder the hills were open.

We turned left on the power line and then followed the trail up through the woods on the west side. This trail came out near the top of the highest hill where we had once had a winter picnic, and opened an even wider expanse of view northward and back over Rowe where we could see the top of Foberg's barn and a corner of the Rowe Camp building on the mountain – otherwise, it seemed as if we were in the midst of wild, uninhabited country. Sunshine and blue sky persuaded us to sit for a minute and enjoy the scene.

From there we expected to bushwhack into the woods a little higher to the top and then down to find the rock triangle and continue on to Pulpit Rock. Simple to find our way. (It is always a mystery why we take crucial things like geodetic maps out of our knapsack!) The first diversion was to what looked like a blazed trail into the woods behind us. Of course, our curiosity led us right up that path – and around, and down and around – until logic said to go left or you'll be off the ridge. This we did, but one of our members wanted to go "just a bit further" on the trail. We had come to the conclusion that it was a snowmobile trail and probably led back to Monroe Hill Road. We wanted to look for the rock!

Going along the ridge, the first thing we found was a small swampy pond tucked between the rocks. Strange thing on a mountaintop. As we crossed around this and went further toward interesting rocks on the downside, our wandering member shouted that she had found a "hunting camp." Well, if she was at the Lenth cabin, we were totally off mark. Following her shouts, we turned back and hiked further down the mountain. The tree cover was so thick with the new summer growth that there was no way to look out at any point for bearings, and we wondered just where we were going. Nothing looked familiar. But we finally arrived at the "camp." What a wonderful hide-a-way between two ridges!

The ground was clear of brush but covered with a carpet of leaves, and two makeshift lean-tos made of brush, some with freshly wilted leaves, passed for "hunting lodges." But this was not hunting season. We suspected we had happened on the favorite campsite of the present generation of Rowe boys who like to take to the woods. There are other sites scattered around town from other generations of Rowe boys who loved the woods and still fondly remember their youthful nights in the wild. We wondered if the recent campers had also found the fresh collection of bear droppings that we came upon just over the hill!

Deciding that we didn't really have time to search for the bear den, we climbed back up what seemed to be the main ridge and found ourselves on a huge open ledge in the sunshine. The trees still covered the view of the valley below us, but we could see Florida Church, Greylock towering in the distance, and the fold of mountains at the end of the lower Bear Swamp Reservoir – reminding us of the painting of this view by the famous artist, John Marin, who recorded his interpretation of our hills in watercolors back in 1918. So we were finally where we wanted to be, but we were surprised to find two larger swampy "ponds" between the rocks. One was filled with sphagnum moss and cinnamon ferns and grasses with swamp pink bushes in blossom around the edge. We ran up and down the various open ledges and

wished we could spend a few days exploring the rocks and enjoying the solitude of this sunny mountaintop – pictured as completely open and without trees on our old postcard.

Our mission continued, looking for the triangular rock on the hill below. We came upon it fairly quickly, but it was not nearly as large or impressive as we had expected from the postcard picture. Now surrounded by trees, we would have passed it by if it had not been the object of our search! Being the only large rock to be seen, we must have found the right one. In the days of our postcard, any boulder stood out in the open country. On down the hill, the little Lenth cabin was to the right, and we paused a moment to remember young David, who had loved this mountain and its every mood and season and had known and appreciated all of its wild creatures.

Reaching Pulpit Rock, the whole valley below unfolded before our sight, and we sat on the rock in the sun, feeling no apologies were needed to our western friend who might again be silently comparing this New England scene with ones from Idaho. We still consider the Pulpit Rock view of the Deerfield Valley as spectacular – fit to hold its own with any other suggested! Of course, a glorious warm "Real Rowe Day" in May adds to our prejudice. The background music for this dramatic view was the sweet notes of several hermit thrushes in the wild country between us and the river nearly a thousand feet below. A rose-breasted grosbeak flew across our view, and several warblers sounded happy in the woods behind us. Tiny matchstick people were having a picnic at the New England Power Company grounds down by the river while others had parked their toy cars to walk the Dunbar Brook Trail in the valley across the way.

Further plans called for hiking across the ridge and picking up the new trail coming in from the south end. We had promised to show the crew a few pink lady's slippers which should be in bloom along with more swamp pink.

"Where are they? I don't see any," the others kept saying. "Wait," we said, "they are here somewhere I'm sure." A towhee kept singing "drink your tea," as it followed us through the laurel and various bushy trees stunted by the westerly winds which whip up the Deerfield valley and the winter snows which bombard this mountaintop. Then suddenly they were there – one, two, ten, dozens in singles and clumps – the beautiful moccasin flower, squirrel shoes or Venus's slipper. This lovely, deep pink orchid can not be transplanted successfully because it requires a symbiotic relationship with a special fungus not often found in our flower gardens. And picking the flower keeps it from seeding itself for future years. Best left to be enjoyed in the wild where they thrive under the right conditions, this flower is pollinated by the bumblebee that seems to know just how to walk into one end of the little pink shoe and out the other, spreading pollen as he goes. But alas, he gets no reward for most orchids do not produce nectar. We pushed up through the thickest laurel bushes already in pink bud, and found our way back on the main trail. Like walking through a lovely park, this "Lady's Slipper Trail" was an unforgettable treat to be treasured in memory.

The south view lookout was equally dramatic, overlooking the Upper and Lower Bear Swamp Reservoirs, Greylock, Savoy Mountain and the various landmarks on the eastern summit of the Mohawk Trail. The spring shades of green on our New England hills rival their fall spectacular. The lovely hues of soft colors and the lush foliage make us appreciate our rainy days which make it all possible. As we watched, two swallowtail butterflies chased each other across the rocks. We were reluctant to leave, but it was already past noon, and we had not packed a lunch.

The trail back took us past bright green moss in the little swampy area on the back side of the rocky ridge, down a little brook bed, and then through the Russian-like white birch woods (resembling the scenery for a Chekhov play) to the open power line where we could once again see off to the east toward Adams Mountain, and then down the Steele Brook valley toward Coon Hill in Zoar, surrounding us in all directions with our beloved "hills of home." We hoped our westerner was feeling a new sense of belonging in New England. A bright, iridescent green beetle flew across our path as we started down the rocky road on the trail back to the car. The woods at the bottom were refreshingly cool after the hot, mid-day sunshine. An oven bird called, "teacher, teacher, teacher," and there were ferns, lovely ferns everywhere.

On the last trail through the old, open pasture, a thrush sounded her distress call as we walked too near a nesting site, and along our path, a small clump of blue-eyed grass delighted us all. So once again, this time thanks to an old Rowe postcard, we had a mission which took us on an adventure to new territory amid our Rowe hills and, along the way, thrilled us with beautiful sights and sounds on the Wild Side. **6/86**

"Promises, promises!" has been our flippant response to our younger friends who, for several years now, have been telling us of the great rafting on the Deerfield River and how they were going to take us along "next time!" "Been rafting lately?" we would hint, but there was always some excuse about the water not being up. On June 14th, the water was up, the day was gorgeous, and the invitation finally came. We were ready before they could finish the sentence.

The water on the Deerfield is regulated by the New England Power Company, and the normal everyday flow, other than after a rain, is too low for rafting. "Water up" is dependent upon generation at various hydro stations upriver – Harriman, Sherman, Number Five, Bear Swamp and Fife Brook – all controlled from Harriman Station in Whitingham, Vermont. A call to them or friends along the river will give the pertinent information. It takes about three hours for the water from Harriman to reach Florida Bridge. Someone seemed to think the river would be going down at three o'clock, so there was some sense of urgency to get in the water before that time. It was 2:58 as we finally set sail.

Having, for all these years, climbed the mountains to look down on our Deerfield Valley, it was a strange experience to actually be on the river surface looking up. We put in on the Florida side

off the road just below the Bear Swamp Dam, climbing down the path on a sharp incline to the rocks by the river. The crew, numbering eleven, lifted down various pieces of equipment, including the six passenger rubber raft, a canoe and two kayaks. All had donned life jackets making a colorful scene of orange, yellow and green. From water level, we looked back to see the powerful spillway of the dam towering above us, and a turkey vulture riding the currents of air overhead. The raft loaded first, and we paddled into an eddy just downriver to wait for the other boats to be launched and catch up. Concern for the water level led to several shouts to make haste. As we held our location by a tree branch, we all imagined the rocks to be showing more and more water mark above the surface of the river. The level can go down as quickly as it rises, and we fully expected to be riding the last waves down the river.

"Here they come!" and we were off amid shouts of excitement and challenge! Suddenly

Launching the boats below Fife Brook dam

the others were all ahead of us into the first small rapids, as the river started its hundred foot drop from our starting point to the landing site by the Nelson Flats above Zoar Gap almost five miles downstream. Six in the raft traveled at a slower pace than the others, but not by much! The river had a swift current, and we floated and swooshed over the smaller rocks and paddled quickly to get around the larger ones, falling into the resulting swirling pools ahead. Those experienced on the river said to go left of the islands quickly coming up in center river, and more frantic paddling by our captain in the rear and first mate perched with one leg over the bow on the port side whirled us unto deeper water along the shore. Two sandpipers flew upriver with their funny flight close to the water.

With the first excitement over, there was time to look up and up and see the mountains surrounding that wild and spectacular narrow valley through which the river had carved its course over eons of geologic time. There being no shore landmarks in that first area, it was confusing to envision just where we were among the mountains – certainly miles from civilization! A power line crossing the mountaintop loomed into our vision ahead, and we realized it was the one near Whitcomb Summit close by the old lining tower used for the Hoosac Tunnel engineering – the corresponding lining pole having been high on the mountain wall rising to our left.

The river water was clear and sparkling silver in the sunshine over the predominantly orange and white rocks of the riverbed. The shore foliage was lush in a great variety of spring greens, while the sky overhead was bright blue. With the water fluctuation, grasses have a chance to grow on the little hummocks,

and these swayed in the breezes or floated forward on the water surface. Lovely ferns lined the shore with one particularly tall stand of graceful, tropical-looking ostrich ferns. Looking back, we could see Raycroft Lookout and the heights of Pine Cobble where we had once taken a winter hike which ended with a wild slide down the mountain through the laurel and trees.

Even from high altitude satellite photos you can pick out the familiar big bend in the course of the Deerfield River as it flows around the southwestern corner of the town of Rowe. Along that course are many smaller curves, and we were well into the first one at the top of Rowe's Neck as we sailed along below the old HT&W railroad bed hanging on the mountainside to our left. Fifty years ago, several landslides down the steep sides of this mountain wiped out the tracks and created the mid-river islands like the one we just passed. The scars are healed now and one would never know such horrendous natural disasters happened along our peaceful valley. And peaceful it was today, as we lazed along the straightaway in the sunshine.

Whoops – we weren't ready for that one! But the cool water felt good as it splashed over the side. Ahead of us, the river actually went downhill and narrowed the channel as it turned another sharp bend to the left and then calmed into a slow-moving eddy where we all gathered to discuss the approach to the next curve. Although we had momentarily been beneath the River Road, our course soon disappeared into the wilderness once again.

Ah, what a life! It reminded us of the old song popular back in our day – "Cruising Down the River on a Sunday Afternoon" or perhaps "On a Slow Boat to China." Oh, no, it wasn't so slow! "Hang on! Here comes a big potato (local slang for a sizable river rock). Paddle quick to the right! Hang on! Wooooow, that was a wet one! Hey, that was fun! Can't we turn around and take that one again?"

And then came another bend, and we saw in the woods on the left the old foundation for the rock crib dam built back in 1866 for water power to run the air compressors for the drills during the Hoosac Tunnel construction. The Rowe museum has a good picture of this dam for otherwise it would be hard to realize it ever existed on this site. Back near the railroad bed again on the Rowe side, we remembered the date of the last train on this precarious line. It was August 31, 1971 with engineer Harold Lowe at the controls.

The old Hoot, Toot and Whistle, a twenty-four mile spur line to Wilmington, was started in 1885 to haul pulp, supplies and passengers for the mills in Monroe, Readsboro and Wilmington. Its demise came, after being rebuilt to haul in the Yankee reactor and machinery in the 1950s, when Bear Swamp construction in the early 1970s had to do away with the rail bed. We were in a wilderness valley which probably has seen more major activity in the last one hundred and fifty years than any other area in the county. We all waved to the fisherman casting his line from a nearby rock. This upper area is the "Catch and Release" section of the Deerfield.

Looking up as the mountains seemed to be closing in around us, a huge steel structure appeared, spanning the river high over our heads. The main line Boston and Maine Railroad coming out of the Tunnel crosses this trestle as it passes into Rowe. Underneath on the bank were the crumbling remains of the

compressor house where the water had been channeled from the dam upriver. Someone shouted "Watch out for the whirlpool!" as we rounded the point of the greatest bend in the Deerfield where deep pools swirl around the narrow gap to head eastward through these rugged mountains which refuse to erode and hold the river to this strange, bending course.

The Hoosac Tunnel. The Great Bore. What can we say quickly as we glide by? Just a few facts for the newcomers. The Hoosac Tunnel was started in 1851. The first train ran in February, 1875. At four and three quarter miles, it was the longest tunnel in North America until 1916. It prompted the first American use of a pneumatic drill and the first testing and use of nitroglycerin as an explosive. The cost was over 14 million dollars, one hundred and ninety-five lives and a great deal of political intrigue. It was an American engineering feat at the time with an error of only 9/16th of an inch in line of meeting for the headings. If a train had obliged us by passing toward the tunnel, its lonesome whistle for the road crossing above would have echoed up and down the valleys as it crossed this trestle. Today all was quiet except for the music of a party going on in the woods on the Rowe side. A cowboy-hatted participant came to the clearing to check our passage. They had a monster big tire tube tied on a rope, floating in the river.

The stream seemed to jog along a little faster once we had made the bend. Lovely laurel was growing at the water's edge with both pink and white blossoms. On the Florida side by the old Hoosac Tunnel store building was a great collection of the big plant with white flat-topped blossoms called cow parsnip. More rocks were nearer the

Talc shaft at
Soapstone Quary

Nan at old
Jessie King cellar hole

surface here, and we could feel them under the raft. Although we were in a long section of more or less straight course, it seemed to require constant alertness and careful navigating around the rocks showing above the water level. However, this only added to the excitement, and there was banter back and forth between the various ships in the convoy. "How'd you like that one?" "Let's take the next one right down the center!" "How come you keep changing captains there in the canoe?" And then the shout, "Hey, look who's on the bridge!" as the iron bridge across the river to the Hoosac Tunnel section of Rowe came into view. Our favorite hiking guide had volunteered to baby-sit so wife and grandmother could join the crew. "Where's Arolyn?"everyone called as we approached. "Asleep in the car, of course," was the answer as we quickly swirled under the bridge and out of earshot.

Now only two houses are reached by that bridge to Rowe – the covered bridge pictured in last month's *Goal Post* was in this spot – but in times gone by there had been a busy railroad station called "Hoosac Tunnel" (even though in Rowe). And from here the road went east to the old Soapstone Quarry and on up the heights to the Cressy and Peck neighborhoods and on over to Rowe center. This was a busy road when West Rowe folks depended on the railroad to take their produce to the markets in North Adams. Many a person has walked or driven a horse and buggy up or down the old road to the train. Now returned to wilderness, we wonder how many animals roam the mountainsides which loom above us on either side. One of the kayaks now came along side, and we rode in tandem for

a while, discussing the intricacies of the sport of kayaking compared to the more forgiving tendencies of the raft.

In the vicinity of old Jesse King's cellar hole, the river begins to narrow and the downhill angle becomes more apparent. We wondered what this valley must have looked like back in the late 1700s when Jesse purchased three thousand acres of Zoar that would later become Rowe. What drove men to speculate on vertical land? Vertical was almost the term for the next set of rapids! Well, not really, but for us novices, it was pretty exciting! In fact, it began to get in our blood, and we secretly hoped the next ones would be bigger as we war whooped with the rest when the water came over the bow in the biggest splash yet on the downfling around a big potato.

Two fishermen on the rocks watched our antics. The mountains seemed to be closing in on us from all sides again, and we knew why Thoreau on his trip through this valley in 1844 called it the "most remarkable and pleasing scenery" he had ever seen. Neither would we dispute the 1841 description of the valley in a book called *Scenographical Geology* which says, "*As one goes westward, these hills approach nearer and nearer to the river, become bolder in their outlines, and steeper in their declivinities, till at length, in Zoar and Florida, they shoot up, sometimes a thousand feet high, in a variety of spiry and fantastic forms, and the traveler, as he looks forward, can often see no opening through which the river can find its way. The murmuring of its waters, however, at the bottom of the gulf, sometimes swelling into a roar, as they rush through some narrow defile, tell him that they have found a passage.*"

We had found the passage in 1986 and amid the roar and swirling waters we came round yet another bend, and shouting for pure joy, went directly into the mainstream of the next rapids like someone on horseback charging into battle! Around and around, whirling now with a little help from the captain, we tossed by a huge boulder and into the resulting whirlpool below! Cheers mingled with the roar of the river while we quickly shed our shoes and used them as instruments to bail the raft! Being first in line for that thrilling ride, we paddled into calmer water and watched the fate of our companions who were coming around a slightly lesser challenge, we thought, nearer the shore. The current suddenly took the canoe and hurled it toward the shore cliff while its crew paddled frantically to swing out into center river once again. Crash! Loud boos from the rest of the crew, and then cheers as the feat was finally accomplished without further mishap.

"Beaver Island coming up!" This seemed a good place to pull ashore, dump the water out of the raft and stretch our legs for a minute. As we were already wet, it didn't matter that we walked through water along the island's edge to look at the local floral varieties. We found tall angelica and had a chance to examine its blossom clusters at close hand, and then made a new discovery for our Rowe collection – a plant that looked like dogbane but slightly different. It was called Indian hemp, a bushy, weedy type of plant with a pretty blossom.

Beaver Island is an interesting ten acre piece of Rowe land in the midst of the river, probably created in the long distant past by the silt and wash coming down the ravine brook from the mountain on the left. The island gets washed every flood time and has lots of tall trees but little underbrush. It was part of the estate of Jesse King in 1839 and has been the object of many transfers down through the years until the final one to New England Power in 1911.

Back underway again, Old Smokey came into view. The fire scars from last year are still prominent, and we were flooded with memories of berry picking up there on Bent's mountaintop. There was a gathering of turkey vultures near a high cliff and a strange, duck-like bird was flying high. The river widened and was shallower, and they say that somewhere under us, was still buried a railroad car lost in the three landslides of 1938, which wiped a train right off the track.

Nearing our destination now, we treasured every last minute of beauty and excitement – a promise had been fulfilled in good measure! The water was still up and sparkling as we beached just short of the descent into the treacherous Zoar Gap – that was kayak territory. **7/86**

S cared to death and running for our lives! Bears? No way! The monsters were over our heads! It had been a hot, humid day getting around to late afternoon before we could settle the little one for a nap and dare to run off down the railroad tracks on our continuous search for all the wildflowers in Rowe. Lovely flowers grow in rich soil in the woods, but many more,

Purple-flowering raspberry and chicory

often considered weeds, grow in "waste places" like the B&M tracks which snake along the Deerfield River for three miles on Rowe's southern boundary. We left one car at the "Thunder Bridge" and were delivered to the railroad trestle just outside the Hoosac Tunnel at a little after three o'clock on the afternoon of July 15th. The parting shot from our chauffeur was, "I'll bet you're going to get caught in a shower!" "Never!" we shouted back, "You know we'd both DIE of fright if we REALLY got caught out in a thundershower!" It turned out to be not one but two "monster" showers!

We walked the trestle slowly, looking through the wide cracks at the river far below until we realized a train could come out of the tunnel pretty quickly, and we didn't want to be on the trestle when that happened! Safe on the Rowe side, we soon were admiring a field full of wildflowers! There were the lovely blue blossoms with red stamens on the ugly bristly stems of viper's bugloss, a beautiful weed which grows particularly

in limestone soil. Although that area isn't listed as limy, it does produce some of the same plants along the tracks and near the Soapstone area. The yellow sweet clover was growing in great profusion mixed with white sweet clover, chicory, butter and eggs, and bouncing bet, the phlox-like flowers which seem to love railroads and other roadsides at this time of year. The purple-flowering raspberry was in bloom on the riverbank as we went back toward the woods to check some unblossomed, tall leafy stems. We were enjoying it all but particularly looking for something new and different to add to our ever-growing list of Rowe flowers. Round-headed bush-clover started us off.

Coming back toward the tracks, we stumbled on the rusted, folded remains of one of the towers which had carried the wires for the old electric engines. Before diesels, these engines pulled trains through the tunnel, eliminating some of the choking smoke from the steam engines. One of our early childhood memories was of the night flashes of light in the west as the wires connected these engines. It was always such a comforting realization that the flash was from the trains and not an approaching thundershower, although we were never quite sure! You see we were programmed early in life to dread summer's pyrotechnic delights.

That lovely field of flowers had been the switchyard for the electric trains and the top of the "Y" where the old H T&W tracks came down the river and joined the B&M – one branch of the "Y" going toward North Adams, and the other riding along the hillside down behind the Hoosac Tunnel station where it joined the track going toward Zoar.

Choosing to stay nearer the woods, we followed along the old roadbed and were soon on our knees, looking over some gone-by avens plants. Tall and slightly different, we finally declared them yellow avens with a note to check for sure when they were in blossom next year. Our project could be a fulltime summer activity, and we try to crowd so much territory into one free afternoon! The other plants around us were a variety of wormwood or artemisia – those we must see again later in the summer when they have their peculiar green blossoms.

Our thoughts kept wandering to the weather conditions and we often looked skyward, where the white clouds in the beautiful blue sky were turning darker on the bottoms, especially as they came over the mountain above the tunnel behind us. But really nothing to worry about... There were two Rowe houses ahead of us, and they would give us shelter in an emergency, but what about further on? It is a long lonely way back to Florida Bridge!

Our path criss-crossed back and forth across the tracks between the riverbank and the woods on the mountain side – we didn't want to miss a thing. At times, flowers took a back seat to our curiosity about the old HT&W rail bed now paralleling the B&M tracks but on a higher level as the eastern stem of its "Y" swung toward Zoar. The rusted machinery of something still rested in an old odd-shaped foundation. Somewhere along here had been an old hotel when the railroad ended at that mountain wall, and the passengers had to be taken by stagecoach over the mountain to continue their rail trip west from North Adams. We climbed the hillside to investigate the rugged stone walls built to protect the tracks, but then made a quick return, as our partner called for consultation on some curious plant she had found on the lower level.

Rounding the gradual bend, we came in sight of the road crossing to the two Rowe houses. Here we listened to a yellowthroat singing "wichity, wichity, wichity" in a tree by the river and looked over the plentiful showy tick-trefoil, a bushy weedy plant with pink blossoms. Ahead in the distance, we admired a beautiful, pinkish cumulonimbus cloud billowing up over Negus Mountain. How could you call such a thing of beauty a "thunderhead?" Here again was a small field of wildflowers – a lovely garden where the old

The monsters overhead

Hoosac Tunnel station had been. "Pinks" gave a pretty accent among the blues and whites, and we found them to be Deptford pinks – a new one for our list! As we wandered further along the way, we realized that we had passed the point of no return and, come what may, our destination was the Florida Bridge.

As we were pondering some old violet leaves on one side, our partner shouted, with more urgency than before, that she had found something across the tracks. Certain "finds" are more exciting than others, and we had long been looking for something else in the onion family – wild leeks were already a favorite. Sure enough, there were the tall clusters of pink blossoms on slender stems, indicating one of four native varieties in the onion family. They proved to be field garlic by name, and after tasting a clove of the bulb there was no doubt at all! The few specimens we put in our knapsack were more powerful than spring leeks, and we didn't think anything could top those for strong aroma.

That find kept us discussing our good fortune for some time as we proceeded on down the tracks, forgetting even to look up and see what was gradually happening over our heads. White snakeroot grew along the side of the path, but that was not new to our collection. However, something near it was – white vervain – not nearly as pretty as the blue and purple varieties.

A noise in the distance caught our attention, and we listened while a train labored up the valley. Remembering the frequency of wrecks on this line in years past, we thought it best to seek higher ground to wait the passage of the freight. From our hillside perch, we waved to a startled engineer who looked surprised to see two women peering out of the woods in the middle of nowhere. As the cars rattled along, we thought of the tales of men and boys (anyone remember?) and hobos who rode the trains by grabbing on and climbing to the top. Tunnels often had warning devices for just such hitchhikers, who might otherwise have been wiped off the cars. We thought of a favorite story called "Boxcar Adventure", that we read as a serial in the old "Child Life" magazine. It was about a family who lived in an old abandoned boxcar and survived on blueberries. To a child, it sounded like the ideal way to live. Boston and Maine, Great Northern, B and O, Southern Pacific- they all rattled by and were gone, ending with a little less magic now that the caboose is a thing of the past. We could hear the whistle of the engine as it signaled the road crossing outside the tunnel, and we knew the train would soon be passing through that "Great Bore" in what the Indians called "Forbidden Mountain" when they first roamed this river valley long, long ago.

Once the commotion of the train had subsided, we had to come to grips with the reality of our situation. A thundershower was clearly approaching from behind – a rumbley sort of thunder that didn't yet sound too threatening. We had time to calmly discuss the situation as we continued along the tracks. When the time came, it would be the sensible thing to seek some sort of shelter. With our watch reading long after five, we didn't want to hide out for too long or we would be faced with darkness as well! Wanting to search for flowers nearer the river edge, perhaps we could get into the safety of the woods by the old Jesse King cellar hole where the land flattened and jetted out toward the river for some distance as the railroad track made a big curve in a northeasterly direction.

SNAP, CRACKLE, CRASH!!! Like baseball players running for home plate, we took off down the tracks, jumping and sliding into the shelter of a gully off to the right at the very beginning of the old King property. FLASH! BANG! Whew, that was a close one, but the shelter of the bushes and trees gave us great confidence! When we finally uncovered our heads, the first thing we could

see was an old, old tall tree stump with huge branches decaying on the ground – looking for all the world as if it had been struck and shattered by lightning years ago.

It was the big, dark, moving lump on the ground that quickly took our mind off the weather. A big old granddaddy snapping turtle was lumbering inland from the river. A little late in the season for her to be laying eggs, or was he, too, seeking shelter from the storm?

He seemed to ignore our intrusion and refused to snap at the stick we teased in front of his nose continuing slowly and steadily about his business. A small spring was hollowed out of the ground at the bottom of the little gully and large boulders and a ledge were at the river edge. The song of high water over small rapids seemed to drown out the thunder and lulled us into thinking all was well, as we sat hiding on a rock under the bushes watching the river flow by.

Curiosity soon had us on our way again, as the dry thunder continued to rumble but did not crash around us. We explored the two old King cellar holes – one, still a well-built foundation of square cut stones, and the other, perhaps the older of the two, tumbling into obscurity. Someone had dug and raked the old dump and set out broken pieces of glass and pottery. From Jesse King's homestead in the 1790s to the Hoosac Quarry activities of the 1880s, this piece of land had seen much activity, and must have made a pretty farm site along the river. We tramped down across the lower level, finding beds of shinleaf in the woods and fringed loosestrife and budding Joe Pye weed in the more open land along the river. Again watching the flowing water, our partner suddenly shouted, "Look!" There, almost in the river, was one of our special "hope-to-finds" – the white spikes of Canadian burnet. She had found this on the river in East Charlemont and expected it might also be in Rowe. Today's good fortune was increasing! Or was it?

After a session on our knees, identifying pointed-leaved tick-trefoil (not the highest priority on our list but something new), we pushed on through the jungle of tall bushes which were good cover from the storm but miserable to penetrate. We emerged on the tracks to see again the beautiful cloud over Negus still ahead. The thunder had subsided somewhat, and we walked our normal pace, finding alfalfa here and spotted knapweed there. BOOM! And we were off on the run again – going as far as this grandmother's breath would take us – not very far! We tried to convince our partner, a runner by choice, that she should go on ahead to safety – so at least one of us would come out of this alive! But thinking ahead, we still had a long way to go, and it seemed charitable to stay together! While maintaining a fast walking pace, we opened the knapsack and passed the small plastic water bottle back and forth. Ah, good for another mile!

Finally, rounding the bend by Beaver Island, we at least felt we could ignore the waysides from there on, for we had recently come down the ravine and continued home there along the tracks. We also knew it was another mile to the bridge! By then it was seven o'clock. We pictured those at home really worried, but having no way to rescue us from the road across the river. They were worrying, weren't they? Looking back, the sky was very threatening, and we could see a lightning flash over the mountain. But wait! Look at this wicked, six-foot-tall thistle just over the bank! Out came the flower book and told us it was a bull thistle. A bit further on, there was one blossomed a beautiful purple. We wanted to cut the blossom and bring it home in the knapsack, but the idea of waving even a small metal knife at the streaking lightning seemed suddenly very unwise. We kept feeling the top of our head to see if our hair was standing on end (we were told this happens when lightning is about to strike). The river noise was louder as the waters roared around the lower side of Beaver Island, and the sound of another train whistle was muffled on the ever increasing wind as our route turned directly south along the base of Negus mountain.

As the engine came in sight, we seemed to be torn between the devil and the deep blue sea! We did not want to walk beside the train, but at that moment it was more important to keep ahead of the monster that was trailing us at the rear. The engineers in the several engines were friendly and the train was going very slowly. There was some comfort in seeing other human beings, but all this metal to attract lightning! Did you ever hear of a train or track being struck? We guessed not, but with no explanation. Either we were walking faster or the train was stopping. Sure enough it ground to a halt. Great! One less worry, we thought, until the ragged-bearded man appeared ahead and seemed to be doing something between the cars. A bandit! Unhitching the cars for the great train robbery! And us suddenly appearing as witnesses to the fact! The monster behind or the bandit in front – either way, we'd never get out of this alive!

The trainman smiled, looked at the sky, and said, "You're going to get wet", as we passed him almost on the run. "No problem," we thought, "that's the least of our worries!" Soon under way again, the train then speeded up and was really going a good clip right beside us, the piggyback cars swaying with the motion. Maybe we should grab on and let it carry us back to the safety of the tunnel, but by that time it was really rolling. And without so much as the old friendly wave of a caboose man, it was gone.

Then it happened! Not a big boom to start with but from a different direction. We automatically started to run, but with the next CRASH and the raindrops, it dawned on us that we were running toward the storm! That big beautiful monster cloud over Negus was indeed a thunderhead, and we were right under it! CRASH! BOOM! We were sitting ducks or running ducks – doing just what they tell you not to do. If only we could make the car. It now seemed so close yet so very far. FLASH! BANG! We dove for the side. Last year's fire had burned all excess foliage along there, and it was a mighty slim bush we were hiding under. STREAK! FLASH! CRACKLE! BOOM! We could see the jagged streaks against the mountain across the river. Our partner put her head between her knees, and we leaned flat back on the hillside crushing everything in the knapsack which made the garlic reek more than ever. In spite of the danger, we somehow wanted

to keep one eye open to see what was going on – we'd be dead soon enough. BOOM!

That monster roared around us in that narrow river valley for fifteen or twenty minutes before there was any lull in the activity overhead. When the lull came, we could then concentrate on the other ever growing monster that had been chasing us down the tracks in the first place. The next BOOM upriver convinced us that we should take advantage of the lull overhead and make a dash for it. The adrenalin was flowing, and we got up and ran for our lives! A quarter mile maybe, until another bright FLASH chased us under a cliff. We could hardly breathe and our legs were like rubber. With shaking arms, we reached for the water bottle without which we would have died of parched throat. Again the sound from upriver was ugly and threatening, and once again we decided to run for our lives. It is amazing what the old body can do when the need arises! Just as we reached the car, with one of us totally exhausted and the other pretty shaky, that beautiful monster cloud had the last word – issuing one final resounding BANG!

As we drove up the hill toward the village, the slight rain had stopped and the sun was almost shining – as if there had never been a shower there at all. "You're back," they said nonchalantly with nary a trace of concern in their voices. As we both sat reviving ourselves on the deck with wonderful tall, cool glasses of iced tea, there appeared over Adams Mountain the most beautiful double rainbow we had ever seen. We thought for sure the monsters had really gotten us, and we had been ushered into heaven after all. **8/86**

Triphora trianthophora, they call it in botanical circles where technically all flowers are known by their Latin names. We prefer to know our resident wildflowers by their common names, and this one is a "nodding pogonia" or "three-birds orchid." It is an insignificant little plant, three to eleven inches high, with a succulent-looking stem and one to three very fragile, small white flowers which blossom one at a time for one day only! The important and history-making news about these little residents is that they are an endangered species and Rowe's colony is, at present, the only known location of this plant in the state of Massachusetts!

The discovery was made, if you remember, quite by accident on a September Wild Side hike back in 1982. (Have we really been doing this for four years?!) With a partner, we were walking the railroad beyond the Soapstone area and curiosity took us into the woods and up the mountain where, at dusk, we were suddenly rushing to get out before total darkness descended. Along the way, we literally stumbled across a small unknown plant in our path. We quickly picked it (usually a botanical no-no) and stuffed it in the knapsack for future identification. The trip back was rugged through the brambles and brush across the old landslide area and back onto the railroad track. By the time we got home, the poor little flower was badly mangled but still very fragrant. After hours of study with nearly every book in our collection, we pronounced it a very rare three-

Three-birds orchid

birds or little bird orchid - a plant that may stay dormant underground for several years. It seemed incredible to have found it at all and especially right here in Rowe!

We marveled at the find but did not notify any authority until this last spring when Botany Professor Barre Hellquist from North Adams State College took a look at our pressed collection. He spotted our tiny three-birds specimen and enthusiastically told us that our find was indeed very important. As the plant flowers in late August or September, we recently made preliminary arrangements to guide Barre and Bruce Sorrie, State Botanist, from the Massachusetts Natural Heritage Program, to the site in early September. And that's what took us on our first Wild Side venture this month!

Because the site was so inaccessible, we felt we should go in alone and try to find a reasonable approach to the area and possibly the flower itself before taking the authorities on a wild goose chase. We started early in the morning with lots of energy and total confidence that there were no thunder showers in the offing. The maps and old pictures showed it to be an easy climb down from the top, and we parked by the Cressy cellar hole on the old Tunnel Road, planning to follow the stone wall down the mountain to eventually meet up with the remains of an old wood road where we thought we had first picked our tiny specimen.

Following the wall was the easy part. Although seemingly on an angle, it was a north-south wall, well defined until its abrupt end at the brow of the steep decline. As we were looking for a plant of rich soils, we perked up upon finding maidenhair fern – a good indication of rich soil – and started our search fairly high on the mountain.

Of course, after four years, we were not exactly sure what we were looking for! We combed every inch of the hill where the fern grew but nothing out of the ordinary came into view. Our ears were more in tune. It reminded us of the old adage that there is no noise from a tree crashing in the woods if no one is there to hear it. We were there and several unexplained crashes had us expecting a bear to approach head on, or at least a startled deer, but nothing materialized. The screech of a red-tailed hawk overhead did take us by surprise.

Water poured out of ledges and mysteriously from under a huge tree and soon created a mountain stream, along which we found several varieties of plants and mushrooms. This is certainly the year for mushrooms! All colors and sizes abound, but tiny reddish-orange ones seem to predominate. We stooped to investigate them – are they gilled? pored? spined? – appreciating each and every one, but becoming proficient in their Latin names, is something we may never achieve. A few have everyday names like the "old man of the woods" which is a big old, dark brown mushroom with a warty top and white spores. They seem so much friendlier when they have English names.

Perhaps we still haven't forgiven our high school Latin teacher who flunked us in Latin III, so we had to spoil our "Summer of '47" by taking the train at Zoar every morning to Shelburne Falls, where a dear little lady did her best to teach us all about Cicero in a morning and afternoon session punctuated only by a delightfully friendly lunch. Upon returning to school, we felt that passing that exam was a major accomplishment in our lives. But the gall of having wasted a whole summer learning something we really didn't want to know still wells in our throat when we are confronted with the likes of Triphora trianthophora or Strobilomyces floccopus – the real name of our old man mushroom.

A road of sorts crossed our little stream, and we expectantly followed it to the left. At the junction, we found spotted coralroot, a strange yellow-reddish stem with tiny purple-spotted yellow flowers. Did this look something like our orchid? We were not quite sure. We knew our road had not been used by man in several generations, but deer seem to make their own superhighways in the woods and this one was well traveled but hardly wide enough for hoofs to navigate, as it clung to the mountainside. Back in the maidenhair fern belt we thought we recognized the area where we had stumbled on the flower of our quest four years ago. We put down the knapsack and spent nearly an hour searching every inch of the area. Nothing. We even broke off a V-shaped branch to see if we could perform the magic of a divining rod. No luck. Or perhaps it told us the truth – there were no three-birds orchids in that spot.

Finding nothing in our knapsack to mark the spot, we investigated a bright orange glob on the hill. It was not a mushroom but a decayed balloon! We picked it up and hung it in a sapling to mark the spot. How disappointing it was going to be to bring our Natural Heritage botanist way in there only to say, "This is where the flower was, honest!" We were dejected and hungry and had thrown only a banana and a piece of cheese in the pack for lunch. We went back toward our stream and stood eating our meager repast. Finishing our banana, we flung the peels down the mountain with a vengeance to match our mood. The peel caught nicely high in a tree and hung there mocking us!

Curiosity kept us following the road back across the mountain. Every so often it would just disappear, and we would bushwhack off in another direction on the track of something interesting – usually another mushroom. We found the strange, short span of stone wall on a fairly level shelf which we had passed by four years ago, so we still knew approximately where we were. Our mission had been to find an easy way into that area, and already we knew that one did not exist. Tramping a bit further, we could hear a brook ahead. Ah, that must be Doubleday's Brook! Our plan then changed.

If that was the brook, Tunnel Road must not be far over the hill. We might not be in such bad shape after all! We ran down one bank of the small ravine and up the other – and there stopped dead in our tracks! At our feet, between two boulders, were about seven fragile, light green stems with tiny oval clasping leaves and little white blossoms! It had to be our orchid! What a thrill! On our knees, we looked into the throat of the tiny, three-quarter inch flowers with the magnifying lens and saw the distinct three green lines on the lower lip. The woods were dark even though the sun was shining, and it was difficult to take a picture, but we tried. Even though we felt we were committing a real crime, we did pick two plants which would identify our find to the authorities and

provide one good pressed specimen for our collection. As we did this, we noticed one more flower above us on the rock.

Two things came to mind. The flower, in blossom for only a day, was in its prime, and it would be urgent for the Natural Heritage people to come in within the next few days rather than later in September. And we must find our way out to Tunnel Road on a route that we could find again on the return trip. If only we had some orange tape! We started off with gusto, up over big rocks, around ledges, over downed trees and up the mountainside, thinking all along that Tunnel Road was practically in sight. Our great good fortune in finding the orchid keep our spirits high, and we breezed past one more isolated blossom. It was heavy shade in the woods but very humid, and when we finally stopped to rest, we realized we had been tramping fast and furiously through pretty rugged terrain. Looking around, there was a large area where grapevines had pulled down trees and another tree had been hit and burned by lightning. Ahead was a ridge full of rocks and large trees, and we thought if we climbed, we would be further up Tunnel Road and not have such a great walk back to the car. A train rumbled down the tracks toward Zoar, and its closeness indicated that we did have the option of dropping back to the tracks – but then it would be a long, long walk back to the car – and anyway, Tunnel Road was just over the ridge!

As we gained the top, the next ravine looked familiar, and we were sure it was the big rocks at the bottom of Tunnel Road – but suddenly there was no road and the cliffs over our head were higher than any we had ever seen on that road! It seemed, at that moment, as if we were far at the bottom of a well with no way to climb out! No reason to panic. It was still before noon. We should take time to look closer at the plants and things, but our mind seemed obsessed with getting out! Standing knee deep in stinging nettle, we felt trapped and envisioned being there all night. Even the relative closeness of the railroad didn't help.

We maneuvered up over the rocks through laurel and brush and shuddered to see a huge oak tree recently split full length by lightning. Finally gaining the top of the cliff, we knew then just where we were coming out. The lay of the land was familiar. We'd be on the road in a minute. But once again, the road wasn't there! We continued over yet another ridge, and in the distance we began to hear a brook. This was immediately puzzling for there was no large brook where we thought we were. Then the light dawned. That was Doubleday's Brook ahead and not the one we had crossed when we found the orchid! Of course we were not coming to Tunnel Road for it was still far beyond this brook. Somehow all of southwest Rowe has the same type of terrain with huge rocks and cliffs alternating with ravines and small dells – each one looking essentially just like the next.

We had tramped across a whole mountainside of totally new territory which we would never have done if we'd had our wits about us. This certainly was not the way we would bring anyone in to search for orchids! Then we were mad at ourselves for covering all that territory without taking time to really investigate things. Perhaps there had even been more orchids. We followed along the truly familiar hillside along Doubleday's Brook and with great relief, joined Tunnel

Road just below the little drive overlooking the clay pit. We consumed all of our bottle of water as we climbed one more hill to the welcome car at the Cressy turnout. It was just three o'clock.

Finally relaxing (or was it collapsing?) on the car seat, we reflected on our lucky day – a Wild Side hike during which we actually found a rare and endangered species in Rowe! We had found the orchid, in blossom, and hopefully with a little clear thinking and map study we could come up with a less horrendous approach to the area! We could hardly wait to get home and make the call to announce our rediscovery and set up the date for the Natural Heritage trip. It was planned for the following Monday the 18th of August, and there came our second Wild Side hike this month.

* * * * *

Neither Hurricane Charlie nor predictions of heavy rain kept Bruce Sorrie from driving out from Boston to spend the day orchid hunting in Rowe. We were also joined by Al Plante, geologist-naturalist, from Adams. Barre Hellquist was on vacation in New Hampshire and would have to forego this trip. Our final decision was to truck in past Soapstone quarry by four-wheel drive, and walk up the mountain from there. This proved quite possible, although a bit hair-raising driving over the rocks and through a deep mud hole, and Al had to get out and remove several trees. An old wood road led up the hill, and we started off from there on foot, crossing one brook and then another in a deeper ravine. Once out of the logging slash and onto New England Power property, the going was steep but not as rough as we had expected. There was lots to see and investigate. Al tapped rocks and gave a running geologic report while Bruce recorded plants in his notebook. We immediately knew we were out of our element entirely – always having to ask, "But what's the common name?" as both men spouted Latin with the greatest of ease.

"Look at that stand of Goldie's fern!" we shouted to a chorus of "Dryopteris Goldiana." It was, indeed, a lovely colony of this fairly rare large dark green stately fern which we have found before in that general rich soil area of Rowe. Then there was Asarum canadense, Panax quinquefolium, Viola pubescens, Sanicula trifoliata, Osmorhiza claytoni, and lots of Adiantum pedatum. With the exception of the black snakeroot, we knew them all by common name, but we had to check each find to be sure, for they were total strangers as identified by their Latin name! (If only our high school Latin teacher had made that class more appealing!) Mushrooms and more mushrooms were everywhere – the funniest being one species that had molded in the recent constant rains. They had all become little puffballs of white cotton scattered here and there on the forest floor. And then there were the earthstars – our very favorite!

When we spotted a landmark from our previous rampage through the area, we all began to search more diligently for the elusive orchid. Bruce made the first discovery – a clump of twenty or more! And on looking around we each found several singles and more clumps – one numbering over sixty, but growing so close together it was hard to count them. This is a strange little plant – growing in profusion in a small area one year and likely

disappearing entirely for the next several. The whole colony blooms on the same day, then, skipping a few days, other flowers all bloom together again. It is a plant of rich woods, living on leaf-mold and dead organic matter in ravines and at the base of slopes forested with beech trees. From first appearance above the ground to blossom may take only a week. Even if fertilized, the seed rarely ripens and the plant spreads mainly by its tuberous root system. It is also a delectable morsel for chipmunks and probably deer, which accounts for its often sudden disappearance. Although uncommon and rare, the plant ranges from Maine to Florida, west to Texas and north to the lake states. So there you have the life history of this now famous little Rowe resident. It's not for picking or for the perennial flower garden. It's much too fragile for that. But it is a plant to come upon in late August when you are walking through the beech woods. A plant to thrill you with its very presence on your path when you least expect that that is your lucky day!

And this had been our lucky day to be sharing enthusiasm with a botanist and a naturalist as we showed them where to find a rare orchid they had never seen before – and on the day it was blossoming! We have been excited with each new species found in Rowe – from the least weed to the most beautiful orchid – but it is difficult to impart just what a thrill it was to find again this rare and endangered little Triphora trianthophora. It almost inspires us to go back to school and really learn our Latin!   **9/86**

The Nature Conservancy later protected this area as "Rowe Rich Woods."

Thunder Mountain and Raycroft Lookout

Like a little Swiss village in the Alps, the miniature town of Charlemont lay before us in the valley of the Deerfield. We had been there on that spot before, many times, leaning on our ski poles, resting our knees or mustering our courage for the run below, but mainly just admiring that incredible view of the valley and the surrounding hills. Remembering... We could see, in the breathtaking stillness of a crystal clear December morning, the fresh new snow hanging heavy on every pine and hemlock, the mist rising from the river, and the sun highlighting the rugged rocky wall of Negus Mountain to the west in Rowe. We could remember the raw beauty of that valley as the cold January wind roared down the river and up the mountain, hitting against our already red cheeks and sending chills through our heaviest ski clothes. We remembered the damp cold under heavy clouds of a February afternoon as we watched an approaching snow storm gradually fill the valley with whirling flakes disguising the village below. We remembered the continuous rain freezing on our goggles one March day and the reward of bright sun the next morning, glistening on every branch and twig after the ice storm had transformed this valley into the most beautiful place in the world. And yes, we remembered the burning sun of an early spring day when we were skiing on mud and grass in our shirt sleeves and, stopping for a picnic by the "wine tree," watching a long freight train winding its way up through the valley. These were the memories that flooded our mind as we sat with a friend in the warm sunshine of a September afternoon at the top of the liftline on Thunder Mountain in Charlemont.

It had not been easy getting there! We could have climbed from the bottom in less time! We knew there was an old wood road near the top, where we had often seen snowmobilers stopped to watch the downhill skiers or cross-country skiers heading out that way. We had always assumed (and you know we've been wrong before!) that the wood road branched off from a short road to the base of the mountain just up the hill from the Plantation House on East Hawley Road. Well, we found a dirt road to the left (higher up in Hawley than we expected) and took it, but it went up and up and on and on – a lovely ride on a September morning if we didn't have other ideas in mind! High on the mountain we passed a stony road to the left, but by that time we thought we were totally wrong and kept on just out of curiosity.

"On the edge of Hawley" is a local expression, and we certainly were on the edge of some part of Hawley we never knew existed. This world is crowded, they say, but we found an awful lot of territory without a house in sight! We ended up in Buckland down through LaBelleville and back onto Route 112.

But we were determined! We had a nice drive back through Buckland Center and down along the River Road to the Plantation House where we finally had sense enough to stop and ask Paul for directions. "Go back up the same road," he said, "past the Temple, and up top of the mountain there is a small road to the left." So then we knew, and by the time we parked the car just off that road, it sure was good to get out and WALK! We were armed with jackets and sweaters but really needed neither for the bright morning sun had already warmed our path through the woods.

As we said before, we really should have started from the bottom and climbed the mountain on foot for it would have given us more sense of accomplishment. As it was, we were out on the open trails at the top before we knew it, and we hadn't even worked up an appetite. But our enthusiasm for the sights was just as great! Although we could close our eyes and remember every view, our partner had never been there so we were busy at the start, pointing out Adams Mountain and Avery's Camp as we looked down the "Thunder Tour" trail and off to the wild northeast hills. Now known as Berkshire East, the Ski Area will always be Thunder Mountain to us, its awe-inspiring trails then known by such names as "Thunderbolt" – our longtime favorite which now disappeared over the brink of the hill in front of us.

One of the amazing features of this mountain is the changing perspective from every outlook. As we climbed the trail to a new view above the chairlift on the "Folly," we looked down on the big red barn and all the houses along the seemingly flat Warfield Hill, a steep road up out of the center of Charlemont. A red barn certainly livens up the landscape, and with the glasses we could see tiny sheep grazing in the pasture. We found ourselves often standing on tiptoes or bending to peer here and there over or through the trees. The intervening years, since our avid youthful skiing life on this hill, had added greatly to the tree heights and density! But the view as it spread out in the valley, a thousand feet below, was still the same. Looking down the vertical "Liftline" trail from the top, we could still feel the sore spots on our feet from the old heavy tie ski boots, and the aches in our legs after we had spent an hour or so with the "volunteer packing crew" who used to pack the Liftline for more challenging skiing when

the other trails had become old hat. (This, of course, before the days of sno-cats that can really climb mountains packing trails.)

And so enough of the cold weather memories! Today was beautiful and warm. For 1986, it was one of those rare, clear sunny days with the fall crisp in the air and the leaves just beginning to show their glory. We chose a grassy spot to sit for lunch just below the top of the big chairlift, where we could look over the miniature village and up the wide valley of Tea Street fields to where the river must have its course hidden between the mountains, for it seemed as if Negus put up a formidable barrier to its passage. But water to feed its ranks must come down through every fold of the mountains and hills where the beds of small streams have molded their way through layers and layers of rock over eons of geologic time – directly in front of us toward Legate Hill was a perfect example, where the steep sides of the "Northwest" drained into a brook which in turn had carved out the "Basin." Seeing the wide fields on Tea Street jogged our memory even further back to our childhood. Our family left Rowe and "went south" for the winter, living several years along Tea Street, and we used to hike back and forth across those fields after school, climbing the hills along the back, trying to keep ourselves from being so homesick for Rowe! It was difficult to bring our mind back to today's lunch when, looking more to the right, we could see the top of King's Highway in Rowe and follow the path down over the ridges to Charlemont and the old buttonball tree near where lived the earliest settler, Moses Rice, in 1742. How many times had Rice followed that path he had made to our Fort Pelham in the wilderness? How many men and Indians had also trod that trail?

Ah, but it was time for lunch! Homemade graham bread with raisins, and our partner's homegrown cherry tomatoes were the highlights along with shared pears and peaches. What could be nicer on a September afternoon? While eating we noticed two or three pretty little stems of ladies' tresses orchid just below us in the grass. A rather prevalent flower this time of year, ladies' tresses have a delightful fragrance and a spiral of small white blossoms on each stem. Goldenrod and asters of all varieties decorated the landscape in every direction and the bees were busy with their honey-gathering. It was one of those days you wanted to put your hands behind your head and just lay back and watch the world go by. In the comfortable warmth of noon-day sun there was time to share stories, and we had a special one to tell.

* * * * *

Something very exciting had made our day the previous Sunday when part of our family had gathered at Portsmouth, New Hampshire for a whale watch trip. Those trips can be routine moneymakers for uninspired sailors, but we were only a short way out to sea when we realized we had a really special crew, including a naturalist who gave a running lecture about the whales and birds and was keeping track of all sightings. We encountered fin and mincke whales, a large school of dolphins, gulls, terns, petrels and even a couple of butterflies. But the crew seemed intent on finding us some humpback whales and when the captain heard from a fishing boat of sightings further out to sea,

he headed full steam ahead another ten miles and another hour out beyond the usual range to try and spot them. It was a perfect day with a sea like rippled glass. And, yes, we found the humpbacks – two, swimming and diving in unison and spouting the water and steam from their lungs – powerful animals making beautiful, deep dives in which they brought their tails (flukes) out of the water. The captain would draw the boat nearer as the two surfaced time and again after their deep water searches for food, which lasted three or four minutes. Another whale watch boat joined our circle as the mammoth animals seemed to be enjoying the attention. Then suddenly one whale breached, not fifty feet from our boat! An estimated fifty-five ton of whale, probably forty-five feet in length, came straight up out of the water until only its flukes were still submerged, and then slowly it twisted its white belly toward our boat and crashed back into the water on its back. What a fantastic sight! It had everyone on board, including the captain and the naturalist, almost speechless and then wild with excitement to have been at the perfect spot at the precise moment! It was a real thrill on the Wild Side, twenty-five miles out at sea!

* * * * *

That's right, don't get confused – those whales didn't rise up out of the Deerfield – we were just sitting on Thunder Mountain, after lunch, catching our partner up on our recent adventures. The faint roaring coming up the mountain wasn't a wave, but the tractor with Danny Denis, Berkshire East manager, mowing and grooming the slopes for winter. A friendly wave and a good word made us feel welcome. He apologized for the noise and went off to the far side to continue cutting. Our lunch was certainly properly digested, for we hated to leave that choice spot. Our second car was in the parking lot below, so when the time came to rouse ourselves, we meandered across the trails in a westerly direction, enjoying the sweet smell of fresh mown hay. As Danny crossed our path again, he stopped to chat and informed us that about one hundred and fifty hawks had been seen migrating over the mountain the day before. How we would have loved to see them! Danny also explained some of the new trails, and we were sorry to hear that so patient an instructor and beautiful skier had given up the sport, but fortunately, he now spends his life making the mountain a great place for others to ski.

We chose the slope still called "Minnie Dole" to wind our way downhill. This was one of the more challenging runs in the winter and was equally so in summer! This trail was named for Minot Dole who started the National Ski Patrol and was often seen here on the slopes back in the early days. Each turn of the trail brought into view something new in the village below. Crossing further to the left, we took a short climb back up to the top of the "Thunder Bunny" – a nice, easy, wide open trail. We could look back up the mountain to the old trail called "U-Mass" for the college ski team that cut and used it. It still seemed perfectly vertical and one more winter memory flashed through our mind. We always had more nerve than sense (or skill) in those days, and the one and only time we ever tried the U-Mass trail, we fell immediately and proceeded at some horrendous speed all the way to the bottom

– face first on our belly, landing deep in a snow bank! Unbeknownst to us our young son was nearby and the first thing we heard was his voice proudly announcing to his companions, "That's my mother!"

It was good to be older and wiser and walking on a pleasant September afternoon! Mount Peak and Mrs. Peak were the mountains to our left now, and it reminded us that they still remained a challenge since our childhood. We would climb them yet! The sun was well past the zenith as we started down Thunder Bunny slope, jumping the water ditches that carried the runoff to the side and provided good winter moguls for those skiers who liked them. All along the woods grew New England asters – those deep purple and sometimes rose-colored flowers that put even more beauty into our September and October landscape. We gathered a large bouquet of these asters – a treat to keep us smiling all through *Goal Post* week!

Mid-way down the hill, another treat was in store. The grass had been cut once and stunted them, but the short stems survived to produce a beautiful collection of deep blue fringed gentians. These we would not pick, for they only open in the bright sun, and the ripe seeds need to be scattered to the wind for the next generation of biennial plants. They are not rare, but they are not common either. And what's that blue spot in the wet soil further down the hill? A spring Violet? Sure enough, several of them! How's this for a prediction – "If the violets blossom in the fall, it means a winter will follow with so much snow they won't have a chance to blossom in the spring as the snow will cover them until summer!" We could only get away with a prediction like that "thinking snow" as we walked down a ski hill! (But take heed, the spring marsh marigolds are also blossomed in Rowe!)

There are never enough days like this in the fall, when you can go off hiking with a lunch and just drink in the beauty of autumn in New England! As we walked through clumps of black-eyed Susans and white snakeroot at the base of Thunder Mountain, we both began to feel a little cheated. We were at the bottom of the hill, and it was still early in the afternoon. Wondering how we could prolong the day a bit further, it suddenly seemed the perfect time to take a drive over to Florida Mountain for the short hike down to Raycroft Lookout. Great idea, we both agreed.

So many beautiful spots in this area would take only an hour of your time to go and see on a lovely afternoon. Why do we always put things off to another day, thinking we're too busy to stop and enjoy life? We had not been to Raycroft Lookout

for at least ten years. It's such a beautiful sight from there, looking directly over the deep gorge of the Deerfield, and the lower and upper Bear Swamp Reservoirs. All the hills of Rowe seem to be a real wilderness, totally covered with the loveliest carpet you could imagine. From the top of the hill under the power line, the view is unobstructed from Monadnock in New Hampshire to Greylock in North Adams and south as far as the towers on Massamet in Shelburne and Savoy. Down at the stoned lookout, the view is closer and more personal and one can see the rapids in the Deerfield and hear the rush of waters down the Fife Brook canyon to the west. We watched several hawks lazily riding the air currents of the valley, and saw the shadows lengthen to the east as the sun dropped toward the western horizon. A day and sights to recall, warmly, as the great snows of the coming winter drift themselves in every nook and cranny around us. **10/86**

View towards Rowe from Raycroft Lookout

Downhill on The Trails of History

We have been going steadily downhill all month. And it has not always been an easy descent – along the old military trail carved out of the forest by the soldiers on patrol between our hill forts; down the early road built by settlers in the hills and valley of the upper Deerfield River; or by way of the near vertical drop of the "Immemorial pathway of the Mohawks to the land of the Pocumtucks." But descending along these paths of yesterday has been a great way to appreciate the glorious month of October and pay appropriate homage to those who have trod the trails before us.

Historical Society scouts starting the hike

The first of our adventures was on a chilly but beautiful morning (October 11th) when we joined twenty-six other "scouts" and Katie, the dog, hiking along part of the military trail from Fort Shirley in Heath to Fort Morrison in Colrain – continuing the project of the Rowe and Heath Historical Societies which began last year with the Bicentennial trek between Fort Shirley and Fort Pelham in Rowe. Soldiers manned these forts from 1744 until 1754 when the hill forts were abandoned, but action continued at Fort Morrison and Fort Massachusetts in North Adams until this wilderness was made safe for settlement with the peace treaty between France and England in 1763, ending a series of what became known as the French and Indian Wars.

The beauty of a frosty morning in Heath delighted everyone as we gathered and looked off toward Monadnock Mountain in New Hampshire from the Smith yard on Hosmer Road. We had hiked the previous week with Mike and Sophie Coe to mark the trail from there to the Colrain School and had come to the conclusion that the scouts of 1986 should not be required to trek all the way to Fort Morrison on the busy, hard-surfaced highway. We would compromise with a bus waiting at the covered bridge. This morning, Newland Smith led us off down the trail by his field, and we soon crossed the power line, meeting up with the old road to Adamsville which had been the early military road from nearby Fort Shirley and later used by settlers until about 1800. Two old cellar holes are in the vicinity, but we did not find them, although we spent some time searching. This road had old stone walls on either side and followed a clear mountain stream which created pretty waterfalls over the numerous ledges. Wild ginger grew in the path, and we stopped to pull a root and smell its pungent odor.

The remains of old bridges twice took the road across the stream and further down, modern day loggers had installed a strange rectangular culvert to carry off one small brook. The morning sun was warm, but the frost was still beautifully etched on the red strawberry leaves in the shady spots. Woodland asters lined the path and fallen leaves made a carpet for our feet as the group stretched back in a long line of march. Civilization came upon us all too soon as we followed the road past a farm with turkeys and on down the hill. Here we had our only climb via a road to the right, which we took only to avoid the highway along the river where we judged the real military road would have continued. At the top of the hill, we followed a dirt road lined with maiden hair fern and the largest collection of sharp-lobed hepatica we had ever seen. This road will be a must when they are in bloom in the spring. Down past more houses, we were again on a main road which we quickly crossed in favor of a trek through the fields along the river and up an ingenious stairway made of tires into the Catamount Sportsmen's Club. Several surprised campers welcomed us to rest a bit around their picnic tables in the warm sheltered sunshine of the campground.

The wind picked up as we made our way out on the highway again and walked down toward Foundry Village, stopping by to see the newly cleaned Hezekiah Smith monument in the cemetery. Mr. Smith was one of the early settlers to venture into Colrain in 1768 when times became more peaceful, and several of us acknowledged our kinship with this pioneer. Our timing was perfect, and we arrived at the covered bridge to find Cleon Peters with the big yellow bus waiting for us. Even though our three hour hike had been mostly downhill, everyone was ready and glad to climb into the bus – including mascot Katie who chose her seat in the front row. We were taken on a tour past the Fort Morrison site and then delivered back to the picnic grounds on Hosmer Road where a little "rum" quenched our thirst as in times past, and Sophie Coe shared her delicious homemade bread and chicken soup. Did the scouts from Fort Shirley travel down our road and then along the river to Fort Morrison or did they climb and descend the steep mountains on the cross-country trail? This will forever remain speculation for there are no written records and even logic has to be questioned. But our feet trod some of the trail, certainly, and we all came back with greater respect for those early defenders of our homeland.

* * * * *

And after the soldiers had secured the land, the settlers rushed in. Land was cheap for those who could afford it and the General Court granted large tracts to men like Cornelius Jones, William Bullock, Samuel Pierce, Jesse King and Joshua Locke. In 1764 one Samuel Rice, son of Moses Rice of Charlemont, was given a grant by the General Court to build a road from Cold River to Hawley's Road on top of Clark Mountain. This road was completed in 1768 and ran from the junction of the Cold and Deerfield rivers up along the Deerfield to the junction of Pelham, where there was a ford to the east side of the river. From there, the road turned west again along the river to another ford on the level above Zoar Gap. From there it began the climb by a series of switchbacks almost a thousand feet to the top of the mountain (now in the town of Florida) where it joined Hawley's Road – the primitive trail vaguely parallel to the old Indian Mohawk Trail across and down the other side of the mountain.

The popularity of snowmobiles and trailbikes in recent years has led to the discovery and clearing of many of these old roads, and they thus have become good hiking trails that otherwise would have been lost in the debris of time. Rice's old road has been on our list for several years and fortunately a visiting friend prompted us to choose this adventure to keep us on our downhill trend this month. Leaving one car at the cemetery by Florida Bridge, we drove up the Mohawk Trail to South County Road in Florida. Parking by the familiar long, open field (Remember January's hike from there down Wheeler Brook?), we once again admired the wide open view of southwest Rowe – the Upper Reservoir, Doubleday's Cliffs, and all the wild land of Rowe's Neck by the Hoosac Tunnel. In the distance across two bends of the river loomed Raycroft's Lookout among the evergreens in Monroe State Forest where we took you on a short hike last month. We will spare you further raving over the view, for the greatest thrill that afternoon was right in the field below us. At least twelve large turkeys were quietly feeding at the lower edge. We watched them for several minutes and then like a flowing stream they headed up through a stone wall and into the woods.

The sense of anticipation is always great when we approach a new venture and today was no exception. What would be the course of this ancient roadway and what goodies would we find along the way? It was a lovely warm afternoon, and we started along the ridge of South County Road on Joshua Locke's three hundred acres. His grant from the General Court on April 26, 1771 read thus: *"A petition of Joshua Locke of Hubbardston setting forth that he served his majesty upwards of six years during the last War; the fatigues of which hath greatly impaired his health; that he*

is desirous of erecting a House of Entertainment upon Hoosac Mountain for the accommodation of Travellers which, he apprehends, may be of great benefit to the public. And praying that he may have a grant of some of the Province Lands in some commodious part of said mountain to enable him to erect and maintain such a House." The land was surveyed and confirmed to him the following year with the stipulation that he build his "House" within the year and maintain it for a period of seven years. Written history does not tell us just where the tavern was built but presumably it was within sight of our location at that moment and was a much appreciated stopping place for weary travelers – especially those having made the climb up the mountain.

On down by the curve near a small pond, our road went straight into the woods. We found the narrow path through a swampy patch which soon formed a brook along side the trail. Another brook from the hill to our right joined in and together they began the long tumble down the mountain directly across our path. Later, studying the map and looking at the hill, we could see where this small brook had created a large ravine on the north side of the hill. Someone had built a small slab bridge, but it had long since rotted and tipped, and we had to pick our way through the brook. The road then became a wide path and seemed to follow eastward some greater distance than we expected before the first hairpin turn started us down the other side of the ridge from the brook ravine. At the turn, another road went on up the hill. We puzzled for a moment, but knew our path must be downward.

Time out for mushrooms, ferns and other bits of woodland clutter which our friend was collecting for a winter terrarium. It made us more aware of all the little bits of beauty in the fall woods – twigs with delicate lacy white fungus along the bark, red checkerberries hiding under wintergreen leaves, little new Christmas ferns with their tiny socks attached to the stem, and everywhere the prolific woodland asters. The sun filtered through the bare birches and maples to reflect on the still tight, yellow-orange beech leaves as they rustled once in a while in a soft breeze. After a few switchbacks, we wished we had brought a pencil and paper to chart the course. In a few places the road would disappear under huge fallen trees, and it was difficult to decide if it continued down or again reversed its course. The true path was always found because the builders of the road had hauled rocks to bolster the downhill side. Steep it was! And here we began to wonder how logical its path. Had they roamed the mountain for the easiest grade or simply said "We'll build it here?"

On March 26, 1786, the road over Hoosac Mountain was again a subject to be considered by the General Court, and the committee for the sale of unappropriated lands in Berkshire County was authorized to pay *"one hundred and seventy-five pounds to such person as shall complete a good wagon road from the west line of Charlemont to the easterly line of Adams (now North Adams) and shall erect a good bridge over the Deerfield, said road to be completed by December 1787. The funds to be used for such payment to come from the sale of more lands in the area."*

Thus was built by Col. Asaph White what we now know as Whitcomb Hill Road and the first bridge across Zoar Gap. This lessened the traffic on Rice's Road until 1797, when Whitcomb Hill became officially the Second Massachusetts Turnpike, a toll road. Rice's Road then suddenly became popular as the "shunpike" – steep and winding as it was, it was free, and well used until the tolls were lifted in 1833.

Now let's get our heads out of the history books and enjoy our hike! Look up to the left – wow, what a cliff! It took a look with our binoculars to be sure the green stuff flaking off the ledge was really the lichen called rock tripe. Such huge pieces of it. We climbed off the trail and over the rocks and ferns to the base of the cliff to try to peel off a piece but they were all just out of reach. These woods must provide ideal growing conditions. Although ugly and leathery when dry, rock tripe can provide a source of food to chew if you are starving. What we saw today was fresh and green and rather attractive on the cliffs. The beautiful, evergreen spinulous ferns grew en masse everywhere while the more fragile species had been changed to a pretty brown.

We had come into a rich soil area and the maidenhair fern, not yet totally damaged by the frosty weather, added a lovely touch with its lacy yellowish tinge. Here, too, were the remnants of the more vulnerable silvery spleenwort fern, bent and dead and hardly recognizable. Scattered here and there a dry stem of blue cohosh berries added interest to the landscape. Looking like little ferns growing fresh in the wetter soil were new leaves of sweet cicely, creating confusion in our minds until the old dry stem of leaves and seed pods appeared still attached. It even took us several minutes to identify the tall brown remains of stinging nettle in a swampy patch. It is such fun to discover our woodland friends in all sorts of new costumes for the change of season.

When the road finally became a real brook, our pace slowed considerably as we carefully picked stable and dry rocks on which to wind our way down the hill. We wondered why on earth those old timers would risk ruining a wheel or wagon or maybe even a horse on this road just to avoid the toll. One more look back at the records, and we found out why. Col. White and Jesse King and their Turnpike Corporation were collecting thirty cents per four wheel vehicle with two horses! More horses passed for five cents each, and a man on a horse was charged seven cents. A hefty price for country pioneers of those days! Of course, White and King had to keep the turnpike in good repair and their account books up to date and ready for inspection by the Governor.

Once in a while, we could look across to Negus Mountain and see its long rocky spine as it traced down toward Florida Bridge and the large glacial boulders sitting prominently on its back. The noise of the machinery working on the new bridge gave us some sense of direction when we couldn't see through the trees. We reached several plateaus and declared ourselves almost at the bottom when the road took another turn, and we were descending once again. A loud squeal behind us on the mountain startled us, and we were trying to make out the species of bird when a trailbike suddenly started its motor and then the sound faded off in the distance. We judged the screech to be bike brakes complaining at the steepness four or five zigzags back up the hill.

The trail turned right across another brook and the worn path swung uphill to a level area beyond. Somehow this did not seem quite right, and we still could not see the bottom. But we had no intentions of bushwhacking! We would follow the path to the end where we expected to join the road just beyond the cribbing north of Florida bridge. Well, it didn't, and the further we went, the stranger it seemed. Finally, we started down and around a long, steep hill alongside a ravine. Across the ravine and higher up, there was an old stone wall enclosing a small level spot on the mountainside. This still fascinates us, and we must go back to investigate for it has to be part of the Luke Rice farm *just at the Florida line on the south bank of the Deerfield... with the torrent at the door*" that Thoreau describes as the place he found lodging during his trek through the Deerfield valley in 1844. Rice kept "*many cattle and dogs to watch them*" and this walled enclosure was probably one of his pastures.

Soon we heard the roar of the river below, and, as we suspected, we had followed a path that came out on the old road below the bridge. Then came the real surprise! The construction had made access to the road through the bridge impossible from the river edge! We would have to climb back up the hill and slide down a rather treacherous spot above the cribbing. Every hike has its challenge and as we said, this month's were all downhill. Of course, we lived to tell the tale, and it was rather funny as we looked back across the river from the car to see the trailbiker, having made the same mistake, standing puzzling as to how he was going reach the bridge.

* * * * *

Downhill on The Trails of History

Our last hike on the 14th followed the most ancient and intriguing path of them all, the old Indian Mohawk Trail – used since "time immemorial" to cross Forbidden Mountain. Originally, it was a path of peace and friendship between the Mohawks of the Hudson River to the west and the Pocumtucks of the Connecticut and Deerfield valleys of New England – the Iroquois and the Algonquins. It became a warpath, and in 1664, the Mohawks "swarmed across the mountain" and annihilated almost completely the Pocumtuck red men of our Deerfield valley. Other Indians and white men during the French and Indian Wars would use this trail, too, as a highway to Fort Massachusetts and the Dutch settlements to the west or in reverse to the commissary at Deerfield and the hill forts of Pelham, Shirley and Morrison.

It was the shortest line of communication for curriers with dispatches between the fronts on the upper Hudson and Boston. To our thinking, this was perhaps the most illogical path of them all – straight up the mountain! There was a more gradual route up the Cold River, but it was much longer and not nearly as exciting. The Indians were nimble of foot and probably wanted quick access to the lookout on Todd Mountain where they could see into the fields of Charlemont and spy on both rivers. As we have seen, the settlers would build numerous roads in the attempt to easily cross this mountain with a wagon. When such a road was finally accomplished in 1914, it was for cars, and would be known as The Mohawk Trail.

We started again on South County Road in Florida, bypassing Rice's road and continuing through one field into the next by an abandoned brown house. The trail entrance was at the top of the field and marked by a dark blue arrow of the State Forestry. It was a partly sunny day in the Indian summer of 1986, and it was a special treat to be in the woods on yet another adventure down our hills. The path followed around the high points of the hill, winding down the farther side through lovely open woods. Just as the path turned more to the left to follow the ridge, another trail came up to join from the hillside to the immediate left. This was the "road not taken" the day before when we made the first hairpin down on Rice's Road.

Laurel began to line our path and was thick ground cover all across the mountain. What a fabulous walk this must be when the laurel is in bloom! Large oak trees, beech, birch and ancient hemlocks predominated, and the fallen oak leaves often made us think we were on skates as we slipped and slid down the little inclines. The first views through the thick bare branches seemed to highlight the blue water of the Upper Reservoir of Bear Swamp. The outline of distant mountains could be seen through the trees, but it was difficult to focus binoculars on a particular speck which looked like a building. Something white and sort of tall caught our eye, and we jumped from one hummock, to rock, to tree root, first bending then standing on tiptoes to find a tiny, clear space through which to aim the binocs. When we were finally successful, the tall, white item became the cupola on Rowe School! We could see the playing field, Rowe's Bowl and the white flagpole with flag flying. Somehow, it all seemed very appropriate! And thinking on this... the site of Fort Pelham is on the hill west of the school, so it seems logical the Fort could be seen from this trail.

Also seen from the trail were Pelham Brook Farm, Floyd Veber's barn and the Dandeneau (Leger) house and perhaps more, but hunger pains were beginning to be felt, and we moved on across the ridge. Lunch was to be served on Todd, still a ways away. The ridge was a real razorback with spots where you could see both the Deerfield and Cold Rivers. It was sometimes difficult to get your bearings. Looking over two bends in the Deerfield, you'd swear the river was suddenly flowing backwards. At one point, we looked down on the white waters of Zoar Gap and just a few steps further on we could see the wide expanse as the river turned south from Beaver Island. Our path was certainly well-defined and worn into the earth and over the outcroppings of ledge. It eventually dropped down into the saddle, where the trail either goes on to the Todd lookouts or starts the descent down the mountain in the famous series of steep switchbacks only an Indian on foot could appreciate! We chose first the climb to Todd

Todd Mountain has two tops, and after admiring the first view back up the rivers to the west, we went just over the hill to a sheltered rock near a fragrant stand of sweet fern where we could look down on the Mohawk State Park campgrounds and see the sun once in a while dodge the clouds and shine on a stand of beautiful bronze and yellow trees accented by dark evergreens above the Cold River. Our homemade vegetable soup was thick with a garden harvest and, even though cold, tasted pretty good with the luscious sandwiches provided by one of our partners. Not exactly Indian

fare! The other peak of Todd overlooks Zoar, but the evergreen cover on that side is such that no lookout is possible and the enemy could pass back and forth through the dugway unnoticed. The view east toward Charlemont and the ski trails of old Thunder Mountain was well worth the climb.

Well, we started this story off on a downhill note, and here's the climax! The Indian trail from the saddle to the river drops six hundred and fifty feet in two or three switchbacks and several zigzags – the rest is vertical! The trail was wet with slippery oak leaves under a layer of acorns and we were on skids most of the way. The solution was often to sit down and slide. It was incredible to think that over this steep narrow trail had passed not only hordes of Indians but men with pack-horses, cattle, oxen, and soldiers ready for battle. Climbing these zigzags had been men as varied as King Philip, the Indian, with five hundred warriors in the 1660s going to the Hudson to look for allies and arms and ammunition, and in 1775, the newly appointed Colonel Benedict Arnold on his way to take command of troops with Ethan Allen and capture Fort Ticonderoga four days later.

The valley men marched over this trail to the Battle of Bennington in the Revolution, and some of the prisoners of war from Burgoyne's army were marched this way to Boston. Not until the building of the Turnpike in 1787, did traffic cease on this mountain trail. Today we passed over the long slanting cliff that had claimed the life of an ox, but history records no other casualties. We hoped we would not be the first! One section of the trail had conflicting blue arrows and we judged an extra switchback might be of recent origin (or did it indicate the site of the landmark dead hemlock – standing in 1909 and long since gone in 1986?). We were concentrating so much on our feet, we had to stop and think about looking up and out to the glorious color of the oaks and beeches surrounding us. And then we remembered to stoop and pick up another goodie for our friend's winter wreath. Did the Indians appreciate October days? And did the soldiers and scouts ever take time to look and enjoy? Or was life then only hardship and responsibility?

During these three carefree, sunny fall days of October 1986, we trod the trails of history, spanning from "time immemorial" to the present as we finally wandered back to the car parked on the Mohawk Trail. And somehow we, too, have become part of that history, if only by walking in the footsteps of time and keeping alive the memories of those who have walked before us.   **11/86**

REFERENCES:
Rowe Historical Society Archives
Notes of Percy W. Brown

"The Mohawk Trail," an address
by John A. Aiken
Pocumtuck Valley Association, 1909

"The Connecticut Valley Indian,"
by William Young.
Springfield Museum of Science.

Province Laws and Resolves
Massachusetts Records of the General Court.

"A Week on the Concord and Merrimack Rivers,"
by Henry David Thoreau

"Thoreau in the Mountains,"
Commentary by William Howarth

**Old Indian Trail up
Forbidden Mountain**

Racing the Sunrise on Adams Mountain

The morning light was just beginning to creep into our bedroom when we awoke with an urgent idea. It was mid-November, and we had been pondering where to take our Wild Side hike. November is always difficult because of bow hunting season when we don't stray far into the woods. And really, what is there to be enthusiastic about in November? Our idea, early this Sunday morning, was to race the sun and be at the Adams Mountain lookout in Pelham Lake Park when the first rays came over the mountain to waken and brighten the village of Rowe.

There wasn't time for breakfast. This was a real hardship to start with, as breakfast is our favorite meal, and we seldom take many breaths before putting on the coffee pot first thing in the morning. Instead, today we put on long johns and wool pants. With snow on the ground and recent cold temperatures, we weren't taking any chances. This was our first mistake, and we had our jacket tied around our waist as soon as our inner heater revved up on the first incline.

Rain had been predicted, but as usual something had gone askew with the weather bureau and old Mother Nature had done as she pleased. It was hazy with high clouds that could easily be pierced by the rays of sun soon to come over the mountain. Just as we started down the lawn, faint tinges of pink were coloring the heavenly canopy. Once we mastered the shock of getting up, it was invigorating and very pleasant to be outside on this crisp winter morning.

The first real snowstorm had come on Veteran's Day and given us about four inches of clean white covering, and our short walk along this same park trail on Wednesday was a memorable sight as we watched a real bright sun turn the world into a sparkling wonderland around the lake. We must tell you about that walk first, as we were following in our own footsteps today along the Williams Trail from Pond Road to the back side of the lake.

* * * * *

Deer tracks were our first observation, right across our own lawn. We have not happened to see a deer for several months and here they had been feasting right under our own apple trees that very night. A lone person had walked the trail before us in the snow, and we did not spend much time on the paw prints for they could be a following dog. Only when we cut through the brush to the Lake Trail did we begin to observe more carefully. What a glorious sight with every limb, branch and twig covered with all the snowflakes it could hold. We came onto the unmarred Lake Trail and headed back toward the dam. Tiny mice tracks made short little trails here and there, and then, suddenly, we came upon several snowmobile trails right out of the lake! But that's impossible!

The lake had only a thin skim of ice. After closer observation, the trails proved to be those of beaver. They must have had a desperate night realizing that, with the snow, winter had arrived and they were not ready! Various trees were freshly gnawed at the base and the ground looked as though brush, probably the abundant low hobblebush, had been dragged to the water. Looking out over the lake toward the channel, one beaver was still swiftly paddling across on an urgent mission as he passed four merganser ducks lolling around near the beach.

Racing the Sunrise on Adams Mountain

We were following more footprints when a long trough in the snow gave away their identity. An otter had been passing through his territory. They always seem to have such fun walking a ways and then taking a slide for the pure joy of it on a snowy morning. Just as another cove came in sight, the sun peaked over Adams and provided orange stage lights to highlight all the snow-laden trees along the shore. Making the final turn toward the dam, we looked out across the lake and saw the lone Canada goose who has been living here for nearly a month, shunning other flocks that might have accepted her on the flight to warmer lands. Geese mate for life and become very depressed when their partner dies. Perhaps this poor bird is still in mourning and will not leave the site of happier times. Along the cove by the dam, the otter had crossed again and disappeared into the water, in search of a good tasty fish for breakfast. We stomped across the bridge below the dam and down along the brook under the hemlocks which were quietly shedding a few sparkling flakes into the morning breeze.

* * * * *

Ah, but all that was on Wednesday. Today was Sunday and we were starting out along the same Williams Trail to climb Adams Mountain. The landscape was pale by comparison. Patches of ground had begun to show through, and the trees were bare and grey. Nevertheless, we were on our way once more. New boot prints beside our own previous ones cluttered the trail and made us glad that others were appreciating our park, except that today we had wished for something fresh and wild – undisturbed by human feet. Soon we could look up

and see our destination through the trees – a white patch of open ground on the mountain above. The trails, we knew, would make walking easier, but if we bushwhacked straight up, it probably would take less time in our race with the sun, and tracks, if any, would be animal.

Anything is possible first thing in the morning! We should have known the territory. Our favorite hiking guide had raced us up this way several years ago, and it wasn't easy then! We were soon out of breath and tugging at our long johns which seemed to be restraining our knee action, but the race was on and we now had to make the lookout by sunrise or the whole point of this endeavor would be wasted. Thinking back, it was a competition with ourselves. We were out to win but we had no opponents – except the quickly rising sun. Once in the woods above the Sibley Cabin Trail, the white patch on the mountain seemed to be getting further away. The more we climbed the further it was!

Traces of rusted old woven wire fence told us that we were along Emory Sibley's old sheep pasture. Our earliest memory is of sheep bleating on the mountain when we were little and had to go to bed before the day was done. No time now for memories. Duck under that branch, swing around that tree, climb over that log and continually wipe the cobwebs off your face. What were spiders doing out stretching webs across our path at this time of year?

Up and up we went, following a deer trail here or a porcupine trail there. And in spite of the hurry, we had to take time to look at the dried Indian pipes, a deer rubbing tree, and catch our breath and rest our aching knees. No aerobic class or nautilus equipment could make our heart beat any faster or stretch our muscles to a greater extent. Water – if only we had brought our trusty bottle of water. We stuffed our hat in our pocket and started off again – still out of breath!

Going gung ho straight up to the lookout, it was hard to put on the brakes as we approached the mass of downed trees, brush and rocks on the steep hillside just below the clearing. We were already into the mess before we stopped to realize we should have gone around! But was there time? We crawled over a rock, under a big fallen tree and then up on a log that might carry us over some brush. The end was in sight, but there were still great obstacles in the path. Frustration! Standing up on the log, we realized we hadn't really looked back to see how high up we really were. We were surprised to see the view for we were looking at it through the very tops of the trees, and in a few more feet we would be in the clear. The tiptops of the mountains to the north were pink with the rising sun – but they were obviously in Vermont. We still had time to make it before the first rays hit north Rowe!

Running to the left, we stumbled face first in the snow. Oh well, no harm done! A quick brush off and we were climbing over the rocks and pulling ourselves up the hill by small saplings along an animal path heading just where we wanted to go. Sweet success!

Looking down on Pelham Lake from lookout on Adams Mountain

We made it! Slowly we turned around and watched the line of pink come down Potter Road just above the Dennington house and across Round Hill above Bill Brown's. We wanted to sit down, but we were too tired to find a rock under the snow. And any distraction might make us miss this curtain rising on Sunday morning in Rowe.

With our coat and hat back on, we actually shivered as we cooled down from the inside out. Using binocs, we began to check out things more closely, especially in the direction of our own house. Was anyone up cooking bacon and eggs? Wow, were we hungry! Gradually smoke began to rise from chimneys where folks were stoking up their morning fires – the Alixes on Middletown, Russ Jolly on Pond Road, the Galvins in the village and someone, probably Dick Taylor, in the pines over on Hazelton. A goodly column of smoke rose at first, then seemed to settle down to even burning. More people must be up and cooking breakfast. The sun had now made its way to the top of Middletown Hill.

It was deer hunting season in Vermont and every so often you could hear a volley of shots in the distance. Dogs, too, were up and barking vigorously at various attractions in their yards. Scanning the horizon to the west, we could see Raycroft Lookout right over Sparky Truesdell's house with Whitcomb Summit tower and the mountain rising beyond. Our great, great, great, grandfather, Thompson Smith, lived on that mountain about 1850. Wouldn't it be fun to go back in time and see for a day what life was really like for the families who settled these hills?

Our camera was in hand, ready to snap a picture as the sun hit our own red barn, but a strange thing happened. The sun shown on the lake and on Quinn's yellow house over the hill, but seemed to avoid our house. Studying the situation, we could see the rounded shadow of the mountain projected on the landscape. This time of year, the sun rises almost directly out of the top of Adams Mountain, as seen from our kitchen, and the house remains in shadow longer than places in the lower village. An early morning jogger was headed up the Pond Road and cars were beginning to buzz up and down the roads as if someone had pushed the switch on a miniature animated scene.

Still waiting for our picture, we found a limb to sit on and, looking out over the town, our eyes followed two brooks up their valleys. Pelham, draining into the causeway pond from the north as it passes down by the old Pelham Fort, makes a wide trough in the land. Further west, Shippee Brook's source seems to be on quite a wall of land that rises westward to meet Round Hill. Its valley is long and narrow. A group of oaks stood out as a darker landscape just above the lake, and pines seemed to engulf the Hazelton Road area. Yes, we are still surrounded by wild, unsettled country!

We took pictures of the red barn in the morning sun and the panorama in all directions, but we knew they would only show a flat blue/grey land, doing no justice to that lovely, Sunday morning scene. With our mission accomplished, we started our journey home.

This time we would go by the path – or would we? It was slippery going up the hill to follow the snowy path over shiny leaves back to the main trail up Adams. We kept looking back at the view just in case we had missed anything. The trail from the lookout is on the side hill under spruce trees, where we soon picked up the animal super highway. We have invested in a shelf full of track books and always go out in the first snow with the greatest confidence that we can identify anything. But there is always a hitch. Snow conditions distort tracks quickly or a few flakes in a flurry can cover them. Today the tracks in soft snow made no imprint on the leaves below. The only sure thing was that the woods were alive with wild creatures and this made us happy.

As we approached the main trail above the notch, small animal paths seem to converge from everywhere and go over the hill to the left. We heard strange noises off down the other side toward Davis Mine. It didn't take long to recognize the voices of a flock of turkeys. Unfortunately, a jet overhead soon drowned them out. Noise pollution! At the top of the notch, more tracks went off to the left and, under the hill, we could see a huge tumble of rocks we had never been aware of before. Off we went.

Porcupines monopolize areas such as this, but some of these tracks were larger. Although we could make no positive identifications other than porky, the tracks and trails were intriguing. Big rock slabs had broken off the mountain and piled against each other, creating wonderful caves. We climbed over and through the rocks like a kid in a new playhouse. All kinds of hiding places nestled in this condominium complex and several holes had ice crystals on the outside and very warm air escaping from within. Lots of our wild friends certainly lived there, but try as we might we couldn't rouse a one. Evergreen polypody fern covered the tops of many rocks and green moss and grey lichens made lovely patterns on the stone.

Reluctantly, we wandered down the hill. The land became almost level for a spell under the sudden vertical rise of the mountain. We tried to visualize that land as the early cleared pasture it once had been. Heading down around to the left, we eventually came back onto the trail near the shelter. Under the cathedral hemlocks, we stood in awe for a moment as the rays of morning sun came streaming through the branches.

And so, early this Sunday morning, we had won the race with the sun and been rewarded many times over with sights and sounds of the Wild Side. Now, if only the bacon and eggs are ready! **12/86**

Giant's Causeway Coast, Northern Ireland

Take two aspirin and keep on hiking

Take two aspirin and go hiking in the morning. That has long been our remedy for a bum knee during the holidays. Maybe we were done in originally with that hike down Trout Brook back at the end of November. The muffler of the car certainly was, but we'll tell you that story later.

Lack of light, the new theory is, makes people depressed during the holidays, which come, of course, during the darkest time of year. And December, 1986 has been one of the cloudiest and dreariest months in a long time. We needed to get out under the sun! So on the rare beautiful day before Christmas, we took the two aspirin and called a friend to go hiking in the morning.

Our pace was unusually slow, favoring the knee, but that gave us more time to look and enjoy. We started at the foot of the Switching Station road and hoped to reach the Bear Swamp Upper Reservoir. The sky was deep blue with the character of each tree silhouetted against it. The lifting arms of a big white birch mingled with the lacy maple branches, while smooth pure blue-gray beeches still holding some of their orange leaves grew in a row in front of the curly, shiny bark of the yellow birch, whose hair was full of dry catkins. Our body seemed to soak up the light and warm sunshine like a sponge. It was good to be alive on such an ideal winter day.

The big old glacial boulder loomed on the hill above us as we passed the ledges dripping with melting snow in the morning sun. Streaks of

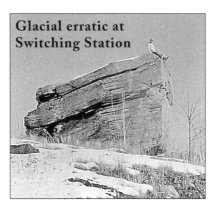

Glacial erratic at Switching Station

white quartz created pretty patterns in the rocks. On the hillside, old dry goldenrod made many winter bouquets in the snow and the huge electric wires over our head were playing their own music as they gracefully looped from pole to pole, reflecting the bright sunshine.

Up and up we went, knowing that it would be on the downhill return that we might be in trouble with the knee, but who could turn back on such a delightful morning? We would roll back down the hill if necessary!

Animal tracks are always a puzzle, but there were a few human tracks that baffled us along the roadside as well. Something that looked to be a cross between a snowmobile, snowshoes and a man's footstep made a path in the snow west of the road while in the road was the trail of narrow runners like a sled but much too wide apart. Who or what made this trail, we couldn't quite fathom but "it" had also been accompanied by a dog.

The first view from the top of the dike is always exciting, looking off to the mountains of Savoy and Florida across the Deerfield and then to see where the water level is in the reservoir. This morning it was very low, with hardly a ripple for the air was unusually quiet. We searched for birdlife but nothing seemed to be about. Turning right we followed the road around the edge peering down at the cattails in the ice of the little swamp on the north side and wondered if all the spring frogs were settled comfortably in the

Bear Swamp Upper Reservoir

Venus in the day sky but should have tried earlier before the clouds blurred the clear blue heavens.

Turning at the tower where the road ceased to be plowed, we now focused on the mountains north toward Pulpit Rock, where the bare rocks and cliffs stood out dramatically above the snow cover. With the summer foliage gone, the lovely tree barks of the small birches and cherries along the ridge beside us created a picture for any artist. We stopped to investigate anything that took our eye, actually trying to prolong an otherwise short hike.

mud for their long winter's nap.

Around the corner, the strange track (now more like unusual snowshoes very close together and a footprint) went down over the edge and disappeared on the open rocks where the water had been. Did this thing swim or walk on water? Looking across, the tracks seemed to come up out of the water into the snow and up on the road. It did look strange, but we surmised it was the snowshoe tracks of the New England Power Company man who checks the instruments near the tower. He had probably taken a shortcut and walked along the open edge of the water rather than going around the road as we were doing.

Stalks of mullen lined the inside of the basin and a gold beam of sunlight streaked across the water. The sun, although bright, was low in the sky even at noontime, as we were just three days past the winter solstice. Tomorrow would be Christmas and already the high thin clouds of the coming storm were moving in. We tried in vain to locate

Reluctantly we left the reservoir, standing and surveying the horizon for one last image to carry us through the next cloudy days. We inched ourselves down the first incline with our fingers crossed that the knee would hold out. It was good to reach the level road around the switching station, but suddenly in that seemingly sheltered spot we were hit with a good breeze coming at us from the northeast. The storm was coming.

As we limped down the last hill, we passed the spot where the fringed gentians bloom and under heaps of snow on the roadsides, we knew the roots of the first flowers of spring, the dandelion-like coltsfoot, were safe in the sand. We did not long for spring. It was a beautiful winter day, and we appreciated the change of seasons that after all IS the beauty of New England. Our battery had been charged by the sunlight and our spirits rose. It was a hike that should be tied with a big red ribbon and put under the Christmas tree with the tag, "To Everyone, from the Wild Side."

* * * * *

The day after Christmas we were very much worried about a real Wild Side hike when the bum knee had to say no to the gang as they went off to see the waterfalls back of the Hairpin Turn. (We promise to take you there in the spring!) But it was Saturday morning when our favorite hiking guide took pity on us and suggested that he could chauffeur us up into South Readsboro and around, and we could write about what we saw from the CAR! We ran for the aspirin bottle again and announced we were going for a HIKE!

Our flower-searching partner was ready and waiting and we took off for our favorite swamp. Even though the bushwhack to the old path is short, it was murder through the trees and hummocks with these snow conditions. One foot up, the next down through the crust to our knees, up again, two steps holding on top and down we go again. But summer or winter, the anticipation of life in the swamp always carries us in. Once on the old road, we picked up a snowshoe trail and the walking was somewhat easier. The hemlocks were especially pretty, still holding their burdens of fresh snow hardened by the freezing rain of Christmas day. And there along the old gravel bank were rabbit scats, little pellets here and there and the small bushes nibbled on the slant. Only one rabbit, perhaps, but even that is progress for they have been so scarce here in recent years.

Once in the open by the swamp, we headed like little kids to skate on the tiny pool in the corner outside the main beaver pond. The ice was clear and perfectly smooth and one long stride took you nearly to the opposite shore! Climbing up on the bank, we looked over the desolate frozen swamp full of old dead trees and might have been tempted to say no life existed there. But we knew better and walked out on the ice to investigate. This surface was frozen and covered with a crusty blanket of snow but there were open spots where the small brook current swirled to find an escape through the crevice in the sticks and mud of the beaver dam.

It was such a treat to walk across the water surface that we had looked across from so many angles in summers past, watching the nesting herons. Heading toward the dam we found open beaver and muskrat escape holes and scent mounds built up on the snow. Walking along the dam was tricky for often a step went deeper than expected and we came up with a wet boot. But not to worry. We found a new pair of warm waterproof boots under the Christmas tree, and we may never have to tell you about wet soggy cold feet again!

Open water was intriguing, and our partner was on her stomach arched over the dam looking closely for life in the water. Nothing could even be stirred up except one poor worm among the leaves. The tracks in the snow by the open water were well distorted from the heavy snow and rain, but the otter slides nearer the middle of the dam were unmistakable. They must be a happy-go-lucky lot! We picked our way across and looked at the greenery on the down side where grasses, sedges, ferns and mosses were bright green in the wet area where the snow had melted.

Heading toward the back of the pond, we detoured up over the beaver house and observed the few fresh sticks of food in the open water by the entrance hole. As always with an active house, the top had an air hole where the warm air from inside was escaping and keeping the snow melted. We followed some fairly traceable tracks and determined that they were probably mink from their size and four-in-a-row pattern. On close observation, the old dead trees were pretty rotten and ones we especially remember from other years have already fallen. Some of the numerous swallow nests in holes are now out in the open because the protective bark has rotted away. Twenty years ago, this had been a living spruce swamp and now it is a good example of the way forests change due to natural causes (beaver, etc.) entirely separate from any influence by man. We found the heron's nest still there but as flimsy as it looked in the summer. It has fledged several birds in the last three years, but the graceful tree with the high nest has gone.

Back by the entrance to the second pond, the water was again open and animal tracks including the otter were in and out and around. Something had bounded across the ice and torn apart a small stump and cleaned out what looked like a mouse nest. This perhaps had been a coyote rather than a fox. And then we came upon the tragedy. A nest was quite open at eye level in an old broken tree, and there was a dead bird on the nest. We picked at its few remaining dark feathers and bones to see if we could determine what it was and found three whole blue eggs under the bird. A mother had died while sitting on the eggs. Our sadness was abated somewhat to find on checking the nest/egg book at home that the bird was probably a starling and not the beautiful, high flying tree swallow we first anticipated.

A winter trip to the swamp always includes a session with the cattails! Take the dry brown top and with your fingers and carefully pull off a handful of the fur. It will come loose of its own accord and gently wrap around your hand, opening to light the softest and prettiest light brown fur mitten you have ever seen. It becomes an obsession to try just one more, like lifting the top to see the jack in every jack-in-the-pulpit you find in the spring. The cattail fluff scatters in the wind, where it sticks to your clothes and gets in your nose!

We stopped to soak in the blue sky and sunshine once more, listening to the gurgling open brook, admiring the gnarled old dead trees of the swamp, and marveling at winter in New England. With a last check around to be sure we hadn't missed some special treat, our eyes focused on several bits of witches' butter on a dead spruce. This bright orange fungus swells with rain and dries to almost nothing. Often it swells and freezes large for the winter. Take a piece of this home with you and you will have a natural magic show for your friends.

The dried sedges and grasses of the swamp were lacy against the white snow, and we each picked several for a home bouquet. Not wanting to carry them in our hand, we stuck them in the sleeve holes of our vest with the flowers draping over our shoulders. Thus we marched back through the woods looking like a strange clan of soldiers with epaulets.

* * * * *

And now you are still asking what happened at Trout Brook? Well, that was back when we said yes to any trip offered by our trusty guide, but this time he got himself in the doghouse! It was to be a long hike; we could see that from the geodetic map. Savoy, Hawley and Charlemont and a drop in elevation of thirteen hundred feet down a wild ravine. Somehow we should have realized going with four guys who knew the route from previous trail bike rides that we flower seekers wouldn't have a chance.

We really shouldn't say much about the muffler because our guide's intentions were good. He was trying to get us as far back as possible on the old road off Harwood Road in Savoy and then up the old logging road that was rutty and icy but nearly passable. It was just that it was our car and he was driving and there were six of us weighting it down! Wham! "Looks like we hit a rock in the road." "Stop immediately!" "O.K., O.K.!" "How's it look?" "Fine, no problem." "Are you sure?"

Then came the marathon race! Anyone bring the stopwatch? Down, down, down. Down brook beds, down rocks, down hills, down ravines. Wet feet, tired knees, out of breath. "Hey, wait a minute. Look at these ice patterns, look at the way the water has carved a trough in the rock, look at the blue color of the brook, look at the silvery sunshine on the branches, look at all the deer tracks, look at these bear claw marks on the tree, look at the waterfalls. Oh never mind! What do you mean you are going to stop and eat rock tripe? We brought turkey sandwiches!"

Someday we must take you on a nice leisurely Wild Side hike down Trout Brook in the Mohawk Trail State Forest. It's wild and beautiful country and about as far from civilization as you can get. It comes out just this side of the State Forest Campground on the Mohawk Trail where you can sit on the guardrail and collapse at the end.

"So who's going way back in there for my car? We're not walking another inch! You're kidding, not with the BMW? Hey, watch out for rocks!"

The muffler? Well, what do you say to the garage mechanic who asks, "Do you have any idea how you got such a huge dent in your muffler?"

"Big dent? Say, that reminds me. Do you have any aspirin? My knee is killing me!" **1/87**

Hiking guide Rob pointing out the rock tripe

An Old Sport with Newfangled Equipment

The whole affair culminated with Super Sunday, but it had nothing to do with football although it was a giant step for us and the darn things tossed us like a bucking (Denver) bronco.

It had been brewing for a few weeks, our firstborn son nagging us to try cross-country skiing. There was a feeling of deja vu, only the tables were turned, the day he packed us off to Clark's Sport Shop in Greenfield and outfitted us with the proper ski equipment. We had done the same to him as a child, persuading him to try downhill skiing and finally dragging him off to the ski shop for his first outfit. Saturday morning the 24th of January 1987, it was our turn to be the persuadee.

And we were not even allowed to sit and admire our equipment while we built up our courage. The crew was going out that very afternoon. How could we say no? But hadn't anyone looked at the temperature? It was about five degrees with a wind chill factor of minus fifty! No one seemed to care. Our introduction to cross-country skiing was to be around the lake via the beach and, appropriately, to the Williams Trail and back to Pond Road. We parked the cars at the school and walked to the beach road.

Never, ever, ever have we been as cold as we were facing the wind walking down Pond Road! Our face and hands ached, and we couldn't imagine how we would ever warm up walking on skis. The wind whipped across the lake and hit us directly in the face and hands. We wiggled fingers, clapped our hands and threw our arms around in the air, ski poles and all. Our persuader took pity on us and exchanged gloves, and then the trail started up hill. It was a whole new ball game from there on.

Actually, the whole thing took us back to our childhood when our old long skis had beartrap bindings which you could unhook on the sides and walk along, picking up your heels. This fancy cross-country stuff was just an old sport rediscovered by the younger generation! Many a time we have skied up across Uncle Emory Sibley's field so we could get a long ride back down. Likewise on the wide windy flats of Tea Street in Charlemont, we skied back to the hill, herringboned up to get a fast ride down through the trees. But these new skis are like matchsticks instead of rugged and solid and heavy like the old ones. And we must admit that this fearless old lady was actually scared to death on the first downhill!

Once across Pelham Brook and in the trees, we lost the wind and the uphill climb stirred our inner fires so we really began to enjoy the new adventure. The first thing we learned was that those fish scales or whatever they call the bottom surface do not allow you to walk straight up hill as we had been lead to believe. We had to struggle, herringbone (not so easy today on skinny boards with these old joints) and finally side step, which seemed to be referred to as cheating. The men were breaking trail and this was no easy job with a couple feet of new snow and lots of drifts. And on the climbs, our ski poles would sink out of sight providing no lift at all. Fearing that the conditions would discourage our further participation in and enthusiasm for the sport, our three companions kept repeating the good news that these were the very worst conditions we would ever encounter on cross-country skis! At that point our fingers were toasty warm in the borrowed gloves, and we had no complaints at all.

The woods were pretty with heavy snow on every limb, but the trees groaned and moaned with the weight as they swayed in the wind. "*I talk to the trees, but they don't answer me*" was an old song from the musical "Paint Your Wagon." Today the trees were talking to us, and we could only listen to their melancholy words. There had been just enough rain with an earlier storm to coat the branches and somehow make the new snow stay put instead of blowing off in the wind.

A fox trail followed along the path and wove in and around the trees, finally turning up toward the rock condominiums at the base of Adams Mountain. Friend fox would surely find some mouse morsel for dinner there or perhaps with a full stomach he, too, was returning to his snug den among the boulders. Not a deer track could be found. Because of the deep snow, they must be yarded up in some sheltered spot. A pileated woodpecker had tapped out a few test holes in a tree under one of the park trail signs. Was this his form of protest at human intrusion?

It was late afternoon and the setting sun streaked through the trees in our favorite Cathedral Woods in the hemlocks by the shelter. And then came our first real downhill. Quick and fast, and we made it without disgracing ourselves. The next one would be a different story. Along the level we tried to practice the correct stride but with the deep snow it took all our skill to maneuver along without being smart.

We thought that the longer downhill run would be fun, just like old times. We always did stand too straight on skis and when we breezed down the slope, trying to keep in the tracks and turn the corner at the same time, down we went over backwards. Trying to get out of the predicament gracefully didn't work. There was nothing to hang on to. We were sitting down between our skies and if we tried to put our hands down and push, they disappeared to our shoulders in snow. Rolling over wouldn't help for we'd end up with a face full of snow. Were we okay, they enquired? Of course, we were okay, we just couldn't get up! Once again they were saying, "Don't worry, this is the worst you'll ever have to go through." We tried to tip forward to get on our knees but the skis slid further ahead. By this time, we really felt foolish and somehow got our pole connected with the solid ground and with super human effort stood up once more, skiing off as though nothing had happened. But we knew downhill on cross-country skis was not going to be our strong point.

One last clever maneuver was required to pass our first test. It involved crossing Pelham Brook on the narrow bridge that had built up an even narrower pile of snow. On the tiny downhill approach you had to have perfect aim for this tightrope or you would be in the drink. We all made it safely with a few yells and squeals. Back on Pond Road we got our sea legs again by shedding the boards and running up Middletown Hill.

The next day was Super Sunday and what a glorious day it was. Blue sky and sunshine, calm winds and fifteen degrees, but we were committed by then to *Goal Post*. The usual last minute had arrived. There was a phone call (it's amazing how fast the word gets around!) asking us to go cross-country skiing. Regretfully we said no rather emphatically. We had already said no to our gentle persuader who was at our side still determined that we not spend the day in the house (our own performance coming back to haunt us!). After all (we were weakening) what should come first, our own pleasure or the *Goal Post?*

A half hour later we were in Heath with the crew of nine – ten, if you count little Simon who was being pulled on a neat Norwegian sled complete with windshield. The starting point was at the Fink house at the top of State Farm Road that goes down and then up into the Cook State Forest. This road is not plowed in winter but there was a good snowmobile trail to follow. We knew it was to be a long downhill run to start with. "Just snowplow to keep yourself from going too fast," our guide instructed. Sure! "How do you snowplow," we wondered, as our speed seemed to exceed what we thought of as fast, when the trail is a foot deep and two feet wide? We held on to our poles for dear life and knew the only way was forward, come what may. Those were pretty shaky old knees under us, but we bent them and didn't stop until the uphill trail absorbed our speed and we came to a halt.

Then the fun began. We had to climb. That took energy and we were soon shedding our mittens and unzipping our coat. But the climb was not as bad as we had anticipated. The skis glided along and we sort of got the hang of lifting our heel instead of picking up the ski. The hotshots raced on ahead and we seemed to be able to keep up with the others. But there was no smelling the flowers. This was serious business and you had to stay on the trail and keep going. When we did catch up with the hotshots who were resting, they went flying on ahead, leaving us in a flurry.

It was a glorious day and what a treat to be out in the woods! Although we look back fondly at our exciting days of downhill skiing, it did seem nicer to go on the cross-country trails away from the cold lifts, icy hills and the ever present crowds of people. This was a quiet sport with just the brushing of the ski on the snow and the happy laughter of our own crew. It was strenuous and easy all in one. Good exercise coupled with the joy of being out on the Wild Side. What more could we ask? We had a strange feeling we were already hooked.

At the top of Christian Hill, we came to the plowed road from the other end and had to blaze a trail through the field or climb the bank. Here we picked up another crew member and Bear, the dog, who insisted on running back and forth, keeping track of front and rear flanks, almost upsetting our apple cart each time! Continuing on another trail, we wound our way up by the Panel Hill Cemetery in Halifax, Vermont. In the open field there just past the state boundary marker, we stopped for refreshment of one sort or another that appeared out of various backpacks and took a photograph or two. From there on top of the world someone had a plan in mind, and we reversed directions. The long gradual uphill was a delight on the way back as we breezed along the downhill and enjoyed again the long stretch of level where we tried to practice long strides with much greater satisfaction than the day before. We began to believe what they had told us... that frigid trip around the lake in deep snow was probably the worst introduction to cross-country skiing we could have had.

An Old Sport with Newfangled Equipment

Somehow we must have known that all this was coming. We were terribly out of condition, and the first free day we had had the week before we called a friend to go for a short walk on Dell Road. It had been another cold day with high clouds beginning to hide the low afternoon sun, but it was good to be out again and we just kept going. Our short walk took us all the way around the loop to 8A, Number 9, Cyrus Stage and back to Dell Road – five miles at least! Walking in the snow was like walking on sand, and it exercised strange leg muscles to keep going forward. We realized on Super Sunday those were the same muscles we needed for cross-country skiing!

Back down State Farm Road, we met two snowmobiles. We got out of the path, but then wondered who has the right of way in that case. It must be like a sailboat and a motor boat – natural power should have had the right of way. But then there is the story, "Here lies George. He had the right of way and took it." Best we had gotten out of the way!

Eventually we took a trail off to the right, which is a loop road and would bring us back at the bottom of the hill below the cars. Those snowmobiles had evidently just come this way for this trail had not been opened on our way up. They made our return much more interesting, and we were glad we hadn't given them an argument about the right of way after all. It seemed like a long, long climb to the top or perhaps we were getting tired! But the best was yet to be.

Once at the top, it was a long gentle ride to the bottom through snow-covered evergreens and open hardwoods. We sailed down the path, just steep enough to be exciting and wide enough to keep control. The wind went through our jacket and was luxuriously cool to our overheated body. Rounding a corner we recognized our location as passing by the old Newton cellar hole on the "Old Farm" where our Dad had lived as a young man, and we wondered if he had ever sailed down this same road on a pair of barrel staves.

How many times today had we looked up to admire a deep blue sky, or the long shadows of the trees on the snow, or the crispy orange leaves of the beech trees, or the lovely clumps of snow on the dark evergreens, or the wild footprints in the snow, or the rays of sunshine thru the forest? It was a Super Sunday in every respect. The crew was gathering at the bottom being joined by each member as they came flying down the last hill overflowing with enthusiasm. Final refreshments were shared before we peeled off down the last slope and plodded up the hill to the cars.

Well, they say the Giants won the Super Bowl. We never did get to watch the game. We were too busy making up for lost time on the *Goal Post*. But it certainly had been a Super Sunday in our mind, and we'll not soon forget it – thanks to our persistent persuader who finally got us out on the trails! **2/87**

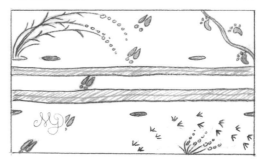

The Race Is ON!

Five, four, three, two, one, bang! And we were off! Two hundred and six cross-country skiers headed up the field like a giant wave crashing on the sand, creating rivulets which rushed to a point and then washed back out to sea as the skiers turned and made the loop, flowing downhill to funnel out across the roads to the trail with the greatest of ease. With suits of every color and texture from dungarees to the latest synthetic skins with spider web designs, it was quite a sight. But hey, let's get going. We wore a bib that carried a big number 96 and that meant we had finally mustered our courage and joined the race for our fourth day ever on cross-country skis. And by golly if Maggie hadn't pushed us in a snow bank, we might not have come in last!

Racer Nan and Bernie

That persistent persuader who recently got us into this sport in the first place took off for the mountains of Utah with his downhill skis and in parting, threatened us with humiliation if, while he was gone, we didn't show up for the Third Annual Cross-country Ski Race in the neighboring Town of Heath on February 8th. What was a mother to do? We knew Dick and Sue and Simon were going, but they were way out of our class. So we called Lenny and Cindy and Bob and Maggie and finally persuaded them to join us. We all agreed we were far from good enough to really race but were joining just for the fun of it. We pictured the five of us at the tail end of everything, plodding to the finish line or, worse yet, being picked up by the rescue crew when they came to sweep the trails... at least that was the talk as we waited for the race to begin. When the gun went off, the situation suddenly became serious competition.

We stood fascinated, watching the first uphill surge but suddenly realized that we were part of it and had to get moving. In spite of our reluctance to race, we, too, put our poles in the ground and with all the strength we could muster, pushed off with great strides. We never saw Lenny or Cindy again. We caught up with Sue for a minute, and just over the hill, Dick, having waited for the crowd to disperse and pulling Simon, age two, on the Norwegian sled, passed us and disappeared down the trail. Simon was already asleep. There should have been a prize for skiing with a handicap, but then the sled never seemed to handicap Dick.

After crossing the roads, we headed down the valley on a beautifully groomed trail. The sky was overcast but the temperature was ideal. Fortunately, we had been persuaded to shed a heavy jacket – a sweater and vest were perfect. The hat was too warm, but there was no place to stuff it once we were underway.

Will you look at that! Bob has not only passed us but that's him in the distance almost out of sight, and he's only been skiing since December. We never saw him again either! But old pro, Maggie, was still behind us, so we couldn't be doing too badly after all. This wasn't to be the sociable event we had all talked about... everybody meant business. The race was on! We kept going full force while our energy was fresh.

A cheering squad ushered skiers onward as we passed behind a house off Avery Brook Road. Our wobbly knees did a wide snowplow down the next hill, and we quietly congratulated ourselves for still being upright. In fact, we were rather enjoying the whole thing.

With all that downhill, we knew the up was coming sometime soon and suddenly there it was... definitely a herringbone hill that we had dreaded. Well, fortunately we'd had a good start, for here was where everyone would pass us. Margalee had been just ahead all this time, and she disappeared in the trees as the trail wound up the hill. We didn't dare take time to turn around and see where Maggie was. Out went our skis in a wide V and, taking a deep breath, up we went. About halfway we had to stop and breathe. Probably we had been holding our breath all that time. We not only had to stop, but we had to maneuver out of the way so other people could pass. Standing still, our heart was beating full force, and we were already thirsty. Our water bottle was back in the jacket we left behind.

But the embarrassment of being the old lady who couldn't make the first hill soon got to us, and we jumped back into the mainstream and continued the herringbone. It must level out around the next corner... It must, but it didn't, and fleeting questions crossed our mind on just why we were there in the first place, torturing ourselves in this manner. It had something to do with the upbringing of our children and their expectations of us now that the tables were turned, but we couldn't focus on serious thoughts just then. Several skiers passed us, but where in the world was Maggie? Maybe that's what kept us going... if we could only stay ahead of Maggie we wouldn't feel like such a klutz at this sport.

Whew, the trail finally turned, and there was the long gradual climb ahead. The only people we passed were those who had stopped to blow their noses. And there again was a problem... a drippy nose and how to extract a Kleenex from the pocket with gloves on without stopping. It proved impossible and we snuffed until the problem was too obvious.

We were finally making the long assent up the side of Burnt Hill, a place we had never been. We told ourselves that was really why we had attempted this race... a chance to finally see the view from Burnt Hill in Heath. And remember, it was to be a sociable trip where all five of us slowly crossed the hill enjoying the view together. So where was everybody?

The trail eventually came out of the woods and turned down around the edge of the wide-open section of Burnt Hill. Free at last was the feeling as we relaxed and flew down the trail, totally out of control and just missing a tree but enjoying every minute of it. When we came to a stop and had to push, we lifted our head and saw the dreaded herringbone coming up again. Thr route skirted us around the field, probably to cause less damage to the blueberry bushes for which this lovely hilltop was famous. The upgrade was on a slant and we saw that others had sidestepped it. This we tried at a great pace but got ourselves into the deeper snow and then had to change to herringbone to get back onto the path. In our haste and excitement from the last run, we fell forward with a belly flop in the snow between the wide-open V of our skis. Some falls are at least spectacular and accomplished with a flare. This one was downright clumsy, and we were covered with snow, but in a race you can't stop to brush off. You just get up and go... at least this early in the race.

Back on an even keel, we could look far across the hill and see the long line of skiers filing around a loop and up the hill to cross as silhouettes on the very top. It must have been at least a mile from us to the last skier in sight. Wow, that was a long ways off, but the finish line must be just over the hill for we had already gone miles, it seemed. Perhaps we haven't explained that the major goal of this race was a fifteen-kilometer run, with the finish line back at the field where we started in Heath Center. Those of us with big orange circles on our bibs (forty-six in all) were signed for half the course with a finish at the seven and a half K mark. We've been avoiding the metric system with the same fervor as the Latin names of flowers, but we did know that one-kilometer was somewhat less than a mile.

With a straight course now, we could think about taking longer strides and we pushed our skis along, remembering to pick up our heels as we went. Now that we were out in the open, there was also much more to see. A few real old, weather-beaten trees dotted the hillside and we wanted to stop and appreciate each one in turn but that would have to wait for next time. But look to the west now, there's Greylock looming so close and the back side of Adams Mountain and we could see we were slowing down and that would never do. Full speed ahead, the view would have to wait.

A nippy little breeze cooled us off as we crossed the field and doubled back to where the trail went straight up - herringbone up. As we went into it with gusto, we found that our legs were beginning to feel the effects of the last miles and our breath did not come back as easily. We had to stop and breathe once again - and we'd best take the time to find that Kleenex. In fact, why didn't we just slow down and take it easy and enjoy the view. We sort of half turned to face the west and look down the trail. Maggie! Where have you been?

Quickly using and putting the Kleenex back in our pocket, we took off in front of Maggie and both talked a blue streak up the rest of the hill. She had tried to climb a tree on one corner and fell and then had been stuck behind two sociable women. It was really nice having someone to ski with at last and we shared the joys of fleeting glances at the view. But we could see there wouldn't be any sitting on the stonewall for a time out. Maggie was pushing right behind us, and we talked without turning around. Then came the heavenly downhill, and we had visions that from that height the rest of the course would be downward. As usual we were wrong.

We were first down the upper section and turned back to watch Maggie make that run while waiting for those ahead to clear the course. She must have thought we were blowing our nose again for she flew right past us and disappeared around the hill. Well, so much for Maggie! And we took off down the hill with a little skate to gain speed... faster and faster around the corner. Oh no! Two skiers were down where the course became rough and there went Maggie right in our path. At the speed we had gained, it would be either a spectacular collision or the boondocks toward the woods where we would end in a heap of deep snow and never be able to get up. There was really no choice. We yelped loudly and crashed on our back, rolling in the deep snow.

"Maggie, wait!" we thought to ourselves as we looked up to see her taking long, determined strides across the flat. We finally stood up, brushed ourselves off, tried to wiggle our right arm up the back of our vest to dislodge all the snow we had scraped up, and reached for our poles as we prepared to go on. Something had happened to our enthusiasm, but then the end was near. A man in a ski patrol jacket was standing on the sidelines not far from the crash site, and we asked how much further to the finish. "Twenty minutes," he said. Unbelieving, it took another question from us as to whether he meant the seven and a half finish or the fifteen. Unfortunately, he was talking about the seven and a half and probably timewise it would be an hour for us. For some reason we didn't look at our watch and it was

probably just as well. The race was definitely not over.

From there on was a sort of downhill section but still we had to push with poles to keep going. Our shoulders were aching if we stopped to think about it... which we tried not to do. We remembered recently having been told that someday we would want to wax our waxless skis. Along this section we admitted it would have been an advantage but would have killed us on the steep parts! Looking on the bright side at that moment, what seemed like pretty darn good skiers were still passing us and this gave us courage that perhaps we were not such a slowpoke after all. It later only proved that what you don't know doesn't hurt you or that we sure weren't thinking clearly. Those skiers were the winners of the 15K going around the second time!

The terrain was woodsy again and for the first time we looked around a little. The hemlocks were pretty in the snow, rocks and ledges begged to be investigated next time, small brooks and wet spots made dark holes in the snow where water gurgled, and in several places, tracks crossed the path. The porcupine's trough was the only one we could recognize on the run. But mostly we remember the short uphills that were getting steeper for our tired legs and the blur of Maggie's red outfit further and further in the distance. The ski patrolman was following not far behind us, and we imagined that he was lolling behind sweeping the slopes and politely trying to wait for this poor old woman to make it. He eventually passed us and at the top of a hill was talking on the two-way radio. We were cheered that the conversation sounded routine and not a call for a vehicle to bring us in. Even as exhausted as we felt, we were determined to finish this race with dignity!

Mirages began to appear. There was a road in the distance with people standing around, and we thought we saw a small building. Ah, the finish line - and it was mostly downhill. We could see that Maggie was almost there. This had really been a great race and lots of fun, we thought, as we barreled down the trail and plodded up toward the road with a spring in our step. You tend to forget the bad parts when the goal is in sight. Hey, what's Maggie doing across the road climbing another hill?

"How's it going?" asked the friendly Heathen who was tending the road crossing. "Just great," we said still in a state of shock not only that that was not the finish line but that they had put yet another long uphill in our path. Twenty minutes, the patrolman had said. Maybe if we stopped to blow our nose it would kill a little time and the race would be over sooner. No, no... now we knew we were too tired to think straight.

Like the "little engine that could" we kept saying "I think I can, I think I can," and somehow reached the top of the hill. With the next down run, we were passing camps in the Mohawk Beach area. Whoops, here we go down off the road bank where big orange arrows pointed the way as we crossed a road and turned into the woods once again. Was this another mirage? Ahead we saw people and food, skis standing on end in the snow and a fork in the trail. Trusting the sight was for real, we veered left and mercifully slid under the seven and a half kilometer finish line proclaimed by a banner strung between the trees – one hour and thirty four minutes after the gun.

"Hey, Maggie, congratulations! But you only beat us by a minute! Bob, Cindy, Lenny! How'd you do? No kidding Lenny, one hour and fifteen minutes? Not so bad for an amateur!"

Shedding our skis, we helped ourselves to a large cup of cool water and an orange quarter offered by the race workers. We took half a muffin as we limped into the cellar where everyone was gathered, tired but exhilarated, and swapping stories like golfers at the nineteenth hole. Once we tasted the muffin we realized we had had no lunch, and quickly went back outside for the second half. By golly, there were still skiers coming under the finish line. We weren't the very last after all!

The Heath folks, hosting their third popular and very successful cross-country ski race, should be congratulated for their community spirit and cooperation. We know it has involved the time and effort of a lot of volunteers, and as your racing neighbors from Rowe, we send our enthusiastic appreciation for this winter event. Piling into Cleon's shuttle bus, everyone heaved a sigh of pleasant relief to be sitting down at last. We wondered to ourselves if we should phone Utah that night – but then, our persuader knew we'd do it or he wouldn't have challenged us in the first place. So what's to tell? Life needs a challenge now and then – especially in mid-February!

Farewell friends! Thanks for joining us. It was great fun just to see some of the Wild Side of Heath. And Maggie – all is forgiven! (But just you wait until next year!)   **3/87**

Way Down Mexico Way

"Now ladies, don't call me Loco Mexicano Capitan. S'or right," shouted the captain of our small boat as he revved up his Yamaha motor, waited for a huge ocean swell and shoved his boat into it as we all crashed through the hole under one of Los Arcos, the mammoth rock islands guarding the entrance to Mismaloya Bay. "Crazy Mexican for sure," we muttered under our breath, heaving a sigh of relief at having survived what seemed like a macho antic performed for gullible American tourists. We were supposedly on vacation from Rowe, the *Goal Post* and all the cares of the world, but there was no doubt about it... We were still out on the Wild Side!

Ramon, with his deteriorating twenty-six foot fiberglass boat equipped with a makeshift awning over the center seats and no lifejackets (what's one turista more or less?), had been hired for the day to take the four of us along the Mexican Pacific coast from Mismaloya to Yelapa (pronounced like jalopy), a distance of some thirty-five kilometers or an hour's boat ride at top speed. Crazy Ramon was the lesser of two evils. The alternate choice was a big trimaran (advertised as cruising under beautiful sails but always seen as a bare boat with motor) loaded to the hilt with new tourists each day as it passed by our cove at precisely the same time each morning.

Our breakfast had hardly settled back in our stomach from the last daring run through the rocks when we realized that crazy Ramon was going to do it again through the next rock. Our screaming, "Ramon, no!" was lost in the noise of the crashing waves. Only after the third go-through did we begin to appreciate the skill of this man of the sea and relax a bit to enjoy the strange, carved shapes of the conglomerate rock in the caverns. The water was very clear and aquamarine in color, with sudsy collections of foam from the continuous pounding of the surf. Today, as most days, blue sky and sunshine reflected on these restless waters of the Pacific Ocean.

When the initial excitement was over, Ramon cruised slowly around the largest island so we could see the colony of nesting brown pelicans in the dwarf trees and rock outcrops. It seemed as if every available space was taken, with two or three nests in

Heading under Los Arcos

each small tree. Some birds could be seen flying toward the rock with long vines or sprigs of tall grasses trailing behind them. As we watched the pelicans, Ramon was preparing the two fishing rods which he had brought to hang on the back of the boat for trawling. This was for the benefit of the avid fisherman in our crew, but there was nary a bite on either line.

Cruising back past Mismaloya Bay, we could get a good look at the ruins of the movie set from the Tennessee Williams play "The Night of the Iguana," filmed here with Richard Burton back in the late fifties. It was that movie and the developing romance of Burton and Elizabeth Taylor that made this place famous, taking it from a tiny cluster of fishing huts to a popular beach lined with hotels on one shore and villas on the hillside. We had hiked through the eerie, roofless ruins which stand crumbling on the hill and still wonder why such a lovely spot has remained undeveloped. Perhaps the ruins are still such a tourist attraction that they hesitate to completely destroy them.

As we headed down the coast at an enjoyable pokey speed, we watched the swells crashing on the rocky shore. Tiers of mountains rose one beyond the next until the highest were out of sight in the cloudy mists over eight thousand feet above the level of the sea. These were the Sierra Madre del Sur, part of the

Rocky Mountain chain stringing down the western side of the Americas. Spread with a variegated green mantle of vegetation, the mountainsides were lovely to look at but uninviting to hike, as we would find later in the week. Traversing the dense jungle required the use of a machete, the long wide knife seen in the hands of many men along the road as they went about their business of carving out the foliage to make farms or roads in this land. We recognized the distinctive leaf patterns of the various palm trees and the small banana plantations on the steep hills, but the rest of the greenery was strange to our New England eye and looked nothing like our own maples, oaks and pines.

Ramon with his small English vocabulary and we with even less Spanish did manage to communicate, and with much hand waving asked and answered each other's questions. He pointed out and described the tiny settlements along the shore, where for a moment, smooth sandy beaches replaced the constant rocky shore. Reached only by boat, some of these were native fishing villages and others were referred to as private villas of "rich Americanos." We turned down a

Nan pointing out Mismaloya Bay

chance to stop at one village "to see the native wildflowers" preferring to continue on to our destination. WE were afraid that the stop might be either a typical tourist trap or that something could be lost in the translation of "wildflowers." We shall never know what, if anything, we missed.

Looking back, we could now see the high mountains surrounding the whole Bahia de Banderas, at the center of which was the city of Puerto Vallarta. The name "Bay of Flags" dates back to the Spanish invasion of what was Indian country here in the 1500s. A squadron of pelicans passed us flying south, intent on some birdly mission. Perhaps they anticipated a school of fish in the distance where they could gather their lunch by high quick dives to scoop up the unlucky fish in their unique inflatable pouch beneath their long bill.

A rough sea over huge boulders guarded the entrance to the pirate cove of Yelapa. Another village reached only by sea, this one had grown to good size with grass huts, primitive stucco houses and some nicer villas on the steep mountainside rising from the sea. Very high up near the clouds were what looked like alpine pastures. With the binocs, we could make out grazing horses and burros. We also spotted the long white ribbon of the waterfalls for which the town was noted. As we docked on a small pier, children came running down the path carrying their large pet iguanas over their shoulders and shouting, "You want to take picture?" It was understood that for the privilege of taking a picture you would give them a few pesos. We declined the offer to handle those prehistoric-looking lizards and continued along a rickety walkway to the beach.

As we had arrived at Yelapa before the daily tourist boat, we were fair game for all the vendors and they descended upon us by the dozen. Rugs, silver, dresses, knit bikinis, and ladies selling pieces of pie which seemed to be the specialty of the area – pecan, banana, coconut, chocolate, and pineapple. We had in mind to first go to the waterfalls on the other side of the bay and were soon approached by several men offering horses or burros for the climb to the falls. Many animals were saddled and waiting behind the grass huts along the beach. One member of our party, from previous experience, promptly vetoed such mode of transport so we declined this offer also and proceeded to find our way on foot, taking off our shoes to cross the small river that flowed into the bay from the valley to the left. It looked to be imperative that we replace our shoes as soon as possible, for climbing the steep path up the hill we were on the burro trail, well peppered with you know what.

A small boy offered to guide us to the falls and again we declined, but he followed us anyway, pointing out with single English words the sights like the school and church as we wound up the mountain path through the village, across the front doorsteps of native houses and along the mountain stream, where the women were washing their clothes and laying them out on the rocks to dry in the sunshine. It was easy to get off the correct path and our little guide always stood at the intersections to point the way. Going up, we met many women hurrying down with tins of pies for the tourists. "When you come back you ask for Juniata. My pies the best." At one lookout point we could see that the daily tourist boat had already arrived in the bay, creating this sense of urgency among the natives.

The day was now very warm and humid, and it was a relief as we climbed higher to be under the shade of huge overhanging trees. Now and then we stepped over a lazy pig or dog basking on the cool earth or scared off a rooster picking his way along the path. Meeting an English speaking couple on the way down, we inquired how much further. "About five minutes," she said, "and there is a restaurant right by the falls." This sounded good, and we pictured quite a place as our little guide now watched closely to be sure we were able to climb up and over the rocks that seemed to be getting bigger and more numerous.

The tropical Mexican rainy season starts in early summer, so, this being March, we were in the midst of the dry time of year, as evidenced by the powder-like consistency of the earth and some brown foliage. The high waterfall that appeared around the next corner was also a victim of the dry season and produced only a veil-like trickle of water across the rock cliff, dropping into a round pool ringed with small boys ready to dive for the pesos thrown by tourists. The "restaurant" was a crude thatched shelter with makeshift chairs and tables to seat ten or fifteen. But it looked across at the falls and the pool, and we were glad to sit and enjoy a cool drink. Our small guide sat quietly in a chair nearby until we handed him a bill worth 500 pesos (about 50 cents) and he went gleefully back down the hill to latch onto another turista. The topic of our conversation was a mythical vision of how we could promote a tourist attraction in Rowe complete with a string of burros to take tourists up the mountain

to one of several waterfalls along Steele or Wheeler Brook or down the ravine above Beaver Island. Anyone want to sell pies or dive for coins? Heaven forbid!! Please, no turistas in Rowe to spoil our Wild Side. How sweet it is to come home to unspoiled friendly landscape off the beaten path of the world. But sometimes you have to go away for a time to greater appreciate your own backyard – even if you come home to find it still six feet under the snow banks of winter.

Back beside the waterfalls on the mountainside in Yelapa, we spotted a few ferns and took time to look them over, but, like all other wild things, we had to appreciate rather than identify them for there were no knowledgeable guides or reference materials. Our timing had been perfect, for when we started our descent the first of the mob of tourists from the boat began to arrive in all their outlandish attire and inappropriate footgear. And then we met those on the horses and burros, yelping and squealing that they would never do that again. It was a real circus you would have paid a peso or two to go and see – mostly our own compatriots, crazy Americanos.

Captain Ramon was back in a deck chair at the beach, relaxing with a beer (what a life!) and chatting in Spanish with his friends at the small outside restaurant behind him. The waves were rolling in on the beach and every so often he had to run out and jump in his boat anchored offshore and pull up the motor which had been jarred back in the water and was being beaten against the sand. After a swim of our own, Ramon joined us for lunch at his recommended restaurant. In spite of much dickering, fortunately we never did come to an agreement on buying a pie, but sampled one with a taste from a generous neighboring table and found it to be too sickening sweet for our palate.

The trip home was on an even keel at high speed. "Muchas gracias, Ramon. Usted es bueno capitan!" we all agreed upon parting. It happened that we were a day too soon to spot at close hand the killer whales which would come to play and feed near shore at Mismaloya the next afternoon.

Our lovely casa on the hill looked out over the bright blue water, but all week our thoughts had been in the other direction – up the mountain behind us. Beautiful as it was, we had been confined to our concrete quarter acre long enough. We had to get out on the Wild Side! We had started up the path twice before, going a little further each time, but always quickly returning to join the non-explorers patiently waiting for us at the car. This morning we were up before the sun, putting on long pants and sleeves and hiking sneakers, and as a last minute thought stuffed a plastic bag for goodies in our pocket. The outfit was not for warmth but for protection against the unfriendly foliage. Breakfast could wait. We had a mission in mind and closed the door quietly so as not to wake the others.

Walking up the steep cobblestone road was no easy task, and we were greeted by a dog in every villa on the way to the top where the mountain path began. Jumping over the wall and walking around the concrete water tank, we found the path to follow. Otherwise the stiff thorny jungle foliage and steep sides of the mountain would have discouraged us from venturing forth at all.

The path was steep, narrow and dusty dry as we quickly climbed up to the first lookout, where we were probably seven or eight hundred feet above and looking down upon Los Arcos and the whole gorgeous bay. What a lovely sight in the early morning light. The arches through which Ramon had taken us looked impossibly tiny for navigation from that height. Behind us was a "scrambled eggs tree" in full yellow bloom and down the hill, the first bird had a sweet warbler-like song. Other larger birds squawked here and there and seldom came in sight. Two large, striking black and yellow birds flitted within sight in the tree below and two more green parakeet-looking and -sounding ones quickly flew by. In the sky overhead, several turkey vultures were already riding the morning air currents. Some trees were lacy green with long pods hanging down and others looked dead except for occasional blossoms like monster witch-hazels.

Scratchy long grasses closed in the path as we climbed further up the razorback of rock to another high point overlooking the sea. A sandy spot was slippery, and we had to hold on to a burned tree stump swinging ourselves up to solid ground. The path continued, narrow but visible and occasionally there was recent evidence of machetes having been used for the cutting of a branch or bush. We were now into strange territory and we hoped beyond all else that we were not destined to meet the man with the machete. Two iguanas perched like statues on the rocks ahead but scuttled off quickly when we approached too close. We had seen four or five coatimondi (monkey-like raccoons) at a dump down in the valley and hoped to scare up some here. They may have been responsible for strange noises and rustlings in the foliage further on. The various growths were so thick it was hard to spot anything through the trees.

A small mat of blue lobelia-like flowers was often under our feet and dry, brittle stems of tiny, bright red flowers grew along the path. After going along a ridge we began to climb again. Now the path was totally closed in, and we had no view, but on either side of the trail the mountain descended abruptly. We tried to study the trees and remember them all, but each was so different and so foreign. A reddish grey squirrel was scolding us as suddenly the path took a turn down hill, and we stopped to remember that from afar we had seen a dip before the final approach to the top. Going down into a little dingle there were boulders and such heavy palm foliage that it seemed as if we were under a tent. The palm fronds must have been at least four feet across. Nearby in the trees something croaked like the sound of a raven. Curious to perhaps find a nest, we investigated but could not see one, and the sound stopped as we drew closer.

Out from under the tent we passed under a bare tree discovering that it had dropped acorns – the strangest ones we had ever seen. Looking up we found more on the tree. They looked for all the world like the long beak and head of a toucan bird. We put a sample in our plastic bag and from the other side of the path, pulled off some red, skin-like bark from another interesting, huge tree. Then the path was steep for a while and at one point we thought we had reached the summit. Feeling elated at our success, we stopped to cool off, for it was already getting hot.

Nearer the top, the trail passed through some tall grasses that seemed

to be wet with morning dew, and a strange growth like sphagnum moss covered an area where there might be a spring in the wetter season. Then, tall graceful bamboo plants appeared. We had definitely arrived at the beginning of the rain forest and even the soil underfoot was damp. At the peak, the land widened out to a small plateau where the path ended by a tall rock which we climbed. The view was not of the sea but in the other direction down over the village of Mismaloya and up the valley to the east, where the sun was not far above the horizon. Its rays streamed down through the morning mists. Echoing up the valley we could hear the crowing of roosters and barking of dogs as the village began its daily routine. Over our head, a huge termite nest looked like a strange burl overpowering a small tree. Behind us through the pathless jungle thickness where the mountain began again its ascent to the clouds, a tree was blossomed with bright red flowers. The foliage suddenly seemed to have softened and become more friendly – or perhaps it just seemed that way now that we had come to know each other, on the Wild Side of the Pacific coast in Mexico.   **4/87**

Willies and No Wildflowers

Ever have the "willies"? It's that sudden feeling of nervousness when you find yourself in a precarious situation or have to observe someone else on the brink of disaster. Your heartbeat is increased and your knees wobble uncontrollably. We had the willies constantly during this hike – no sooner would we get our feet on solid ground and our arms around a sturdy tree away from the edge, when our guide would be back down in the center of the cascade pointing to a new course up through the impassable boulders.

This trip had been promised since last fall, and we approached it with great anticipation, not really expecting the magnitude of sights and frights that were to come. When our favorite hiking guide raves about a new find, we should know from experience that it will be nothing to sneeze at. This time it was vouched for by the third member of our party who had also been on the discovery trek. With the advent of the rainy season, our guide had been itching to get home and gather the clan for the excursion to see these cascades. When the day arrived, he was afraid with every passing minute of blue sky and sunshine that the water level would be decreasing from spectacular to just great. After the build up he had been giving to us these many months, he wanted the sight to be spectacular. Believe us, it was. The only fault we could find was that it was not in Rowe.

If you have a geodetic map of the North Adams quadrangle, look in the town of Clarksburg, just north of the Hairpin Turn on the Mohawk Trail. The fine, blue line of Canyon Brook starts on top of the mountain in the town of Florida around the altitude of 2,250 feet. It flows south for some distance paralleling the Clarksburg line and then turns abruptly west at the 2,100 foot mark, crossing the line and dropping down Hoosac Mountain one thousand feet in approximately two-thirds of a mile. With statistics like that, the cascades had to be spectacular and their exploration could give most anyone the willies.

After numerous unsuccessful phone calls to several of you, we started out. You all seemed to be busy outside with spring chores and thus lost the rare opportunity to join our Wild Side safari on the morning of Saturday April 11th. Our crew remained at three. It was just past ten o'clock when we parked at the rest area by the Hairpin Turn and headed past the restaurant into the woods, inquiring of the man working nearby if it would be permissible to continue to the brook. With a very skeptical look at this female, he warned that it was pretty steep back there. "Oh, we've been there before," we announced (speaking for the guys, of course).

It was steep just going straight into the woods. With all the rain, the whole mountainside had become a waterfall of sorts and the moss on the ledges easily gave way, as did our footing on the soft muddy ground hidden under the leaf cover. When you lose your footing on a vertical hill, it tends to give you the willies right off the bat.

It was early spring and the trees were bare and the ground still brown with last year's leaves. An occasional, matted green Christmas fern punctuated the dullness. This reminded us to take time out for flower search, and we hung back a few minutes to scan the ground, calling to our partners to report any new shoots of anything, especially

One of the falls on Canyon Brook

off in the distance, we could hear the familiar croak of a raven setting the tone for the wilderness canyon ahead.

Before we saw it, we could hear it. The rushing waters of the endless cascades echoed on the rocks and grew louder with each step. And finally we could see the canyon as the hill turned in toward the steep depression in Hoosac Mountain. Here our guide headed down the hill. "Hey, wait a minute. You said we were going up." "Well, let's not miss any of it," he shouted as we slid down the mountain another hundred feet or so, finally turning right and descending to water level near a lovely wide falls that would have been worth the trip in itself. We nearly used up our roll of film right there, but we were soon warned that there was more to come and that the really big falls was right near the top. A quick look at the map and we could estimate a climb of at least 500 feet up – and looking up, we knew there would be no easy way.

We hardly had time to appreciate the first scene and rightfully say "cowabunga" before the upward trek began. Thinking

wildflowers. Huge overhanging ledges and rock hideaways distracted us on the way, as did the monster rocks on the mountainside that obviously had fallen away from the overhang. We quickly searched the rock surfaces for ferns and such but found nothing except moss and lichens. Then, somewhere back, it seems as if we bypassed the first falls and climbed the hillside on the right, no less precarious. But the general route was up the cascades, climbing over the rocks, hanging on to tree roots and sometimes just depending on luck and invisible skyhooks. It was the ravens that gave us our first breather. High above us, one by one, three huge, black birds took off from the rocks on the upper left and soared in the sky overhead. Had we disturbed their dinner consisting of some poor creature that had fallen to its demise from the high cliffs? Even though there was no mistaking their voice, it was startling to see them so close under the canopy of the treetops. We followed them with the binocs until our own balancing act midrock in midstream became too difficult.

For whatever reason, the amazing fact was that the rocks were not slippery. This probably saved us all from being carried out of the area in a prone position. Nevertheless, it didn't really calm the willies when we had to jump across a fast flowing cascade to what certainly looked like a slippery rock on the other side. Our guide went first and dangled a leg over the upper rock for us to grab onto once completing the jump. There was no turning back and the longer we stood mounting our courage, the wetter we became from the splashing cascade. The water was crystal clear and very cold. We jumped.

Each climb revealed a new arrangement of waterfalls, boulders and trees – all of which were worthy of admiration and exclamation. Mexico could take a back seat, this treasure right in our own backyard rated rave reviews. Of course, adding to the charm of the area was its wilderness location and inaccessibility to the general public. But the usefulness and power of the water had not gone unnoticed to someone in the past. There were remains of an iron pipe, twisted and discarded, that must have carried water somewhere at some time. Also some sections of large plastic pipe had been used in more recent times. We wondered why it had been necessary to lay the pipe so high on the mountain if used for water power at the base. The pressure must have been tremendous. But whatever projects they represented had been outsmarted by Mother Nature and the remains lie in ruins among mighty boulders tossed in the floods.

Looming over us to the left during the first section of the climb was a tremendous outcrop of bedrock that looked like a monster boulder which was about to give way and roll down the mountain. In another location where the water had carved a trough deep in the rock, we had to skirt the canyon walls and climb the hill. Our request to be alerted to growing things was ignored as both crewmembers tramped through a patch of wood sorrel whose green shamrock-like leaves were desperately trying to raise their heads to a new season. As the flume deepened, we pulled ourselves along the rock edge, willies and all. After that, even the other two brave ones were glad to lean against a solid tree and discuss the situation. You don't suppose they had a touch of the willies, too?

Along about this time, the brook split and twin waterfalls towered ahead. We would follow the left one. Again we were cautioned not to waste film on lesser things for the mighty falls was still high above. Debris had collected there against a rock at the junction of the two waters, and we were attracted by what looked like a small blue balloon stretched over a piece of limb. Reaching for it we soon realized what it was – a bloated dead frog. Strange item to find in such a fast moving cascade! Our guide knew the source of the righthand brook. It was a beaver dam on top of the mountain, and no doubt the recent flood had washed this poor critter out of his snug little pond hurling him downstream.

We often had to shout to each other to be heard over the constant roar of the cascades. This time when the message finally came though, one of our partners was pointing out the three-layered, hanging botanical gardens on the other side of the brook. Three huge layers of overhanging rock were completely covered with very healthy evergreen polypody ferns that, because of the slanting angle of the rock, seemed to be hanging downward. Quite an interesting sight. (Praises be, one of our crewmembers had finally noticed something in our department. Maybe next it will be a wildflower.)

We actually had done quite well so far, avoiding any mighty hanging on with our left shoulder, sore from bursitis. But there came a time when we switched to the left side of the brook. There we had the choice of surmounting a waterfall or pulling ourselves up by the tree roots on the left. We were not quite tall enough to tackle the waterfall climb and had to go the root route. We took it slow and said "ouch" a few times but finally made it, looking down on our other crewmember taking the falls route. With that accomplishment, our guide seemed to expect greater things of us. Perched on a lefthand high rock, he again dangled his boot for us to grab while our

other partner braced his boot midway up the rock for us to climb on. We tried but failed to grab a small tree left of center. Our left shoulder had rebelled, and we had to backtrack and go around on the hill. We couldn't afford many failures or we would be left at home next time. No harm done today though, for we were soon all back together in midstream where we could get our first glimpse through the trees of the mighty falls at the top.

This grand sight had been out of view from further down because it was set back at the end of what I would hesitate to call a level area. Let's just say the land ceased to be totally vertical for a short distance. Waiting for our reaction, the guys seemed a little worried that they might have been over zealous in their description of its grandeur. We assured them that we were not in the least disappointed. In fact we were overwhelmed by the entire length of Canyon Brook.

Now we were encouraged to take as many pictures as we could and both crewmembers suggested angles and offered to pose on rocks for perspective. Of course, in our haste, no photo would end up doing justice to the scene. We stayed back to take pictures while the other two went to the base of the falls and then we scrambled up to join them.

The old iron pipes still evident here and there must have come from the small concrete dam enclosing the pool at the base of the falls. Since its construction, a huge piece of the cliff on the left had broken off and crashed into the pool, almost covering the dam. The remaining pool must have been deep although no one offered to test it. The high falls dropped straight at first and then splashed on outcropping rocks, spreading the water to create a veil. The roar was deafening and a fine mist filled the air, quickly fogging the camera lens. After much calculating, the figure of 50' was agreed upon for the full height of the great falls. (You are free to argue this point.)

It was interesting to see just how high the water had been in the recent flood. On the upper left, a two-foot channel had been carved through the rock across from the top of the falls. In floods, the volume of water must be so tremendous that the down channel is filled and the surplus flows across to the lateral spillway through the rocks, emptying down over the bank and back into the brook. Enough floods in eons of time had carved the channel and had eventually been responsible for the breaking away of the large rocks now in the pool. As we climbed up and wiggled into this trough, we had a bad case of the willies again, expecting to precipitate another crash involving the very rock we were standing on. Across the way, our third member was obligingly sitting on the edge of oblivion by the top of the falls so we could use up nearly the last of our film. The resulting cockeyed picture tells more about our case of the willies than his position overhanging the chasm.

From here on, we had to detour on the hill around the very top but were soon back to the water that again had dug itself an amazing chasm through the ledges above the high falls. Finally, we reached a flat ledge where all began. Looking out through the trees from that point we could see in the distance the bridges in the center of North Adams. We had not done much looking back during the whole hike, so intrigued

Bob Taylor at Canyon Brook high falls

were we with what was ahead. It was here that we fished out the apples we had brought for a snack (not expecting this short hike to go into lunch time which was now long past) and although we had visions of a pleasant, relaxing break, we seemed to be eating on the run as our guide had already gone exploring further up the brook.

Canyon Brook continued on up the hill for a short distance and leveled out as it swung off to the left, where it appeared as a common ordinary brook unaware of the glorious cascades it was about to create. By this time, we must have been in the town of Florida for we were certainly on the top of the mountain. Our guide joined us, coming back down an old wood road that we all continued to follow out to the beaver dam from which the unfortunate frog had most likely been ejected during the recent storm. The waters must have been high and the beavers absent, for the dam had broken and the beaver house was left high and dry. The brook had made new channels in its fury to escape. The old dam was on the brink of the hill and looking down, we spotted two walls either side of the old streambed. There on the steep side of the mountaintop, some old settler had had a mill and the walls must have contained the water wheel. Ah, there must be a story there, and we wonder where we can find the answer. Perhaps someday in the Berkshire Registry of Deeds...

We followed along what remained of the pond and stopped to watch the bugs called water striders – or "water Rodgers" as one of our crew humorously quoted the nickname used by someone we all knew. Suddenly our guide stood still and said, "Listen to the quiet." The roar of the cascades had completely gone, and it was noticeably still after more than three hours down along the crashing waters. Here and there, the green leaves of goldthread rose above the leaf pack and some of them were so large, we had to dig down to find the gold root to be sure of their identification.

As we headed west through the woods, the hobblebush was almost impassibly thick, rivaling a stand of laurel. It was a ways out to the edge over the Mohawk Trail, but we finally came upon a good lookout point, site of a tower in the past, for there were two heavy iron pins in the ledge. This was at or near the joining point of Clarksburg, Florida and North Adams. We thought of Charlie Canedy, the photographer from Rowe who had taken so many of our old glass slides around 1900 and later developed the first tourist businesses along the Mohawk Trail when it was built in 1914. Charlie Canedy, so often photographing various falls on Rowe's brooks, had certainly not missed these spectacular waterfalls near his businesses on the Trail, and it was a good bet that somewhere there was an old postcard of same. We could almost envision having seen it now that we thought about it.

Finding no path from the lookout, we bushwhacked down the steep mountainside to the right and finally came out exactly where we had entered the woods in the first place, four hours earlier. Back on solid ground, we had no trouble at all shedding the willies that had plagued us from the very start that morning. It was a sudden and miraculous recovery.

A beautiful day with spectacular sights and adventures. One of our most memorable hikes, in spite of the willies, was marred only by the last words of wisdom from our crewmember, "By golly, we got through that one without finding a single wildflower!" **5/87**

A Red-letter Day

A real red-letter day, that's what we called it after the excitement was all over. The search had been on for several years, combing the town where the soil was rich and woodsy, looking for the showy orchid. In our mind, it ranked second only to the yellow lady's slipper which is still first on our list of "hope-to-finds." The showy orchid is not a particularly rare plant, just choosy in its habitat, usually preferring limestone soil. The purpose of our yearly trek to the old Whitingham lime quarry on Memorial Day is to see the showy orchids in bloom there. Somehow, we thought they ought to grow in Rowe and have been told by Rosemary Veber that she found them several years ago beside Steele Brook Road. As always, our red-letter days come when we least expect them.

It was Monday, May 11th, and we zipped through our morning responsibilities in anticipation of the arrival of a friend to join us for her first leek-digging trip. This spring ritual is a wonderful experience for it means a day in the woods when the spring flowers are at their height. And it means a picnic with the best tasting sandwiches you have ever eaten – the best because they are accompanied by big juicy raw leeks right out of the ground.

Leeks grow in several places in town, and we try to vary our itinerary each year. Although we had written of the ravine off Tunnel Road two years ago, it seemed like the perfect spot to take our two companions for this year's trek. This time we planned to go from top to bottom and return via the railroad to Florida Bridge where one car had already been left waiting. A hike down any part of Negus Mountain is steep and this one was not without its moments.

Our first mission was to purchase a supply of Avon SSS Bath Oil from Robin Reed. All the Conservation/Outdoor magazines seem to have high praise for this item as a black fly repellant, of all things, and we knew we would need something strong in the woods at this time of year. After parking the car in the Peck field, we soaked all bare skin with the oil and shouldered the knapsacks. Our faraway place had been invaded by loggers, and big machinery was in operation in the log yard on the west side of the road. New England Power Company officials feel they must harvest their forestlands for greatest profit, but it is often a sad day to see the resulting mess and erosion created by modern machinery such as bulldozers and skidders, as they change the shape of our gentle and delicate woodlands.

As we started down Tunnel Road, we listened intently for a field sparrow, a favorite bird of such wild and deserted mountaintop fields. We hoped they had not been chased away by the turmoil of logging. The chestnut-sided warblers were in abundance, singing on every side, always just far enough away to be out of view. Then, further down the road where the old fields become woods, the field sparrow sent forth his song from the far corner to the west. It doesn't take much to make us happy when we are out on the Wild Side.

The long beech ferns were coming up along the edges of the road, tipping over backward in their characteristic stance, and we stopped to examine a clump of corn lily leaves. We soon realized that none of us had brought a flower book and we spent the rest of the trip trying to remember that plant's other name – Clintonia. What the T.V. ad says should apply to our flower book, "Don't leave home without it!" Or the fern book, or the bird book, or the binocs, or the geodetic map! You'd think we'd have learned our lesson by this time.

The road was somewhat damaged by the recent floods, and we were glad to be on foot. We entered the woods across from the dike and meandered down to pick up the ravine brook that we were to follow. A bulldozed logging road to a lot across the brook had changed the landscape and another spur made a scar along the brook. If this continued on down to the heart of the ravine, we would sit down and cry.

A bitter cress was the first flower we investigated. One of our local cress plants, it grows in brooks or wet places and the leaves taste bitey and pungent. We should collect them for a salad sometime, but it's more fun just to sample them on discovery as we did today. We followed along the left side of the brook and already the mountain was rising above us. Every path of spring run-off showed signs of having increased to a wild torrent in the recent floods. Nature as well as man can be mighty destructive. But all was quiet and calm now, and the pretty little brook flowed gently around big boulders and rippled over small rocks and outcroppings of ledge. The stinging nettle plants were doing well all along the way, and we tried to avoid them as we crisscrossed the brook, looking at this and that on either side.

Small laurel bushes on both sides indicated acid soil until we reached the real ravine, where both sides became steep and the soil quickly changed to rich woods. Toothwort was our first clue of having arrived at our destination. It grew in a wet place on our side of the brook, and we climbed a little to admire its white flowers in full bloom. On the drier hill above were the leaves of the tiny yellow violet. With the blossom now gone, the prominent dark green rosettes of leaves have grown to three or four inches long, and it is always hard to associate them with those early spring violets that are one of the first blossoms to poke up through the mat of brown leaves, sometimes while patches of snow still lurk nearby.

Looking across the brook, we saw that the hillside was full of goodies, but individual plants and flowers for the moment all blended together in a lovely, variegated green carpet. Earlier in the spring, the bright green leeks would have stood out alone against the bare slope. We crossed the brook and admired things one at a time – the huge, red trillium almost gone by, the lovely, tiny white miterwort with fringed bells on single, dainty stalks with two opposite leaves halfway up the stem, the larger foam flower almost blossomed full, the weird blue cohosh now a perfectly respectable green, leafy plant with its purple and yellow flowers gone by, the somewhat similar red and white baneberry plants in bud, the downy, yellow stemmed violets everywhere as were the stemmed purple-backed white Canada violets, and the tiny, sweet white violets with their short, red stems, the light green lacy rattlesnake ferns up and producing their fertile fronds, the Dutchman's breeches gone by but the similar squirrel corn with its heart-shaped flowers occasionally still on the stalk, and the first flowering hepaticas gone by but already producing a new growth of shamrock-like leaves, soft green and velvet to the touch. In among all this were the leeks, long, darker green leaves now mostly lying on the ground with their flower stem and pointed red bud already formed. Leeks come up as soon as the ground is bare in April and after flowering, the leaves dry up and disappear very quickly.

Today the leeks were in their prime. Sticking our fingers down in the damp soil we wiggled three out from under the roots and rocks where they usually hide and washed them in the tiny waterfall on our side of the ravine. As we relished ours, we stood back, waiting for our friend's reaction to her first choice morsel of spring's greatest delicacy. Instant approval! Of course, she probably realized if she had spat it out in disgust, we might just have marched her back to the car at the top of the mountain!

Digging leeks takes time, patience and strong fingers and sometimes just the courage to give up and move on to the next patch, in hopes they are not so firmly rooted in the underground debris. We dug and visited for nearly an hour, each coming up with a good Baggie full, but as with blueberries you just want to pick one more. There are times when you wish you had brought a shovel or trowel but that really doesn't work as well as fingers – and if you don't break your nails and get them full of dirt, you haven't really experienced leek digging. And then there is the smell – the earthy smell mixed with the strong onion scent that stays with you for days. Well, at least for the rest of the hike. And yes, the taste stays with you, too.

Reluctantly, we moved on, noticing the considerable amount of natural windfall on the mountain. Larger trees had uprooted mounds of soil and tipped them downhill. The logging operation was within sight at the top of the ravine but hopefully would never come closer. Perhaps we get a little overprotective of Rowe, but we do have our favorite spots and this is one of them. As we roamed down toward the brook, we were careful not to step on the delicate, pinky fronds of the dainty and lacy maidenhair ferns just beginning to unfurl along with the larger and more open silvery spleenwort ferns, both of which are so typical of rich soil woods. At the brook, we all soaked our sore and grubby fingers in the cool waters.

From there on, the hill became steeper, and we had to watch our footing in several places. One spot in particular was a series of wet ledges that created wide steps down the hillside. The rock was covered with years of leaves and thin mucky soil. From past experience we knew this terrain was treacherous, and we skirted the whole area by going up the hill a ways and then back down toward the brook. We were looking for the cut-leaved toothwort but didn't seem to come upon any. The mountain and the brook were arranging themselves for the long and lovely waterfalls that are the highlight of this lower ravine, but first, the lingering smell of leeks and the anticipation of a gourmet lunch prompted us to give in to both.

Ordering the prize table at the fanciest restaurant wouldn't hold a candle to our chosen luncheon spot on the rocks, midway down the long waterfall. As we washed the leeks in the fast moving falls, the others opened their knapsacks and distributed the chicken and lettuce sandwiches. One bite of leek, one bite of sandwich. Out of this world! The music of the tumbling water, the beautiful streams of sunlight on the mossy-covered rocks, and the gourmet lunch made for an unforgettable dining experience. The leeks were so fresh and good that we even had to wash a few more to go with the last of the sandwiches. This was the highlight of the day, we thought at the time, not knowing what was yet to come.

Carefully traversing the hill around the steep waterfall area, hanging on to trees when available, we wound our way back down toward the brook, with cut-leaved toothwort on our mind. We passed more leeks and stepped carefully through the maidenhair

Showy orchid

fern. Suddenly there they were! Not what we were looking for, but showy orchids in full bloom. Two glossy, green leaves with a five-inch stalk of lavender and white blossoms that looked like miniature tropical orchids. We yelped with joy and fell on our knees beside them, at first not even noticing the large ginseng plant under our right elbow. The showy orchid was in Rowe after all!

It was exciting and we all gathered around to admire them. We looked around quite thoroughly and found only eight plants. Perhaps they had just recently established themselves or perhaps there was only a small area that met their fussy soil qualifications.

Yes, we finally found the toothwort, but we knew that was there in profusion somewhere along the lower ravine. Cut-leaved toothwort blossoms in late April with the Dutchman's and squirrel corn, and it had all gone to seed, the leaves now just blending into the background. The southern sunny exposure all along this mountain makes for an early spring, while we on the hilltop are still knee-deep in snow.

We eventually came down along the old wood road probably created by the Cressys and Pecks for logging with horses back before the turn of the century. On the brow of a small hill, we came out by a large rock and found again the old rotted fire hose lost and forgotten back in the 'fifties when fires on Old Smokey were an annual event.

We decided not to bushwhack into the thick blackberry brambles ahead, and we turned back toward the brook. And then things began to get a little hairy. Along the brook, it was steep, wet and mucky, and we had in mind meeting up with another wood road that we thought was a little higher up. Marching along with this in mind, we carefully led our crew across the vertical hillside, optimistically assuring them that it would be better on the old road. Our hairy crossing led to thick laurel and no road. We had to admit defeat and very carefully go sideways down to the brook and hope for the best.

As we were wondering how we could gracefully get our companions down through the mess of fallen trees and mud slides, our eyes caught the gleam of sunshine on the rails of the railroad tracks a stone's throw below us. Whatever the immediate problem, it could be solved with the end in sight. We heaved a sigh of relief – but we're still puzzled about what happened to that old road!

We shook ourselves out, rearranged knapsacks, and prepared for railroad walking. It was good for a change to be out in the sunshine, but railroad ties were never designed for walking as we always find out. Too close for a normal step, too far apart to take two at once, we gave up and tried the stony surface of the road alongside and then alternated between the two, wishing we had worn hiking boots instead of sneakers which translate every rock to the foot.

The recent storms had created a small landslide on the mountain and the mud and debris had been cleared from the track and roadway, but nothing to compare with the monster slides here in the 1938 hurricane when a train was demolished.

It was a long and rather warm hike back to the Florida Bridge area, but we were treated to some beautiful clumps of violets growing out of the side walls, a view with binocs over at the spot where real skunk cabbage still grows along the river, and looking back we could see the whole length of the ravine in the fold of the mountain where we knew lovely treasures were hidden away.

By the famed arched rock just below the Rowe line, we climbed down to the river, shed our shoes and socks and sat dangling our tired and aching feet in its cold but mighty refreshing waters. What a way to end a red-letter day! **6/87**

Arched rock in the Deerfield River

What Is So Rare As a Rainy Day in June?

What is so rare as a rainy day in June, 1987? We've had a sunny day June hike to Negus to see the lovely display of laurel, to ooh and aah over great patches of our favorite pink sheep laurel and to watch the turkey vultures making lazy circles on the wind currents among the puffy white clouds in the blue sky overhead. We've walked the railroad on a hot, sunny day to find new and different flowers of waste places and taken a detour up the mountain to be sure the beautiful stand of Goldie's fern is well and prospering. On a hot humid June day we've walked the old HT&W path under the cool shade of overhanging trees to the old dam abutments on the Deerfield and then worked up a terrible sweat tramping back on the vertical mountainside. And early one evening at sunset, we walked down the old washed out Davis Mine Road to the town line, crossed the rusty brook and climbed up over the hill to Rowe's southeast cornerstone, listening to the sweetest chorus of hermit thrushes and then enjoying the pretty sunset from the power line – after which we fought our way back to the car through the biggest and ugliest swarm of mosquitoes you could ever imagine. These were all our June hikes under the sun, but somehow they just didn't qualify as real Wild Side expeditions.

Today would be considered a miserable day if you were inside. No doubt you shivered as you went to the mailbox in the drizzle and fog, but after a month of sunshine, you would agree that we needed the rain. Looking out our window early this morning we knew that, at last, it was going to be the perfect day for Wild-Siding. There is among us a new young recruit to this business of investigating and appreciating our wild world, and we called her to join us.

And what better place to spend a drizzly morning than in the swamp? As we passed Pelham Lake, we were treated to the lovely sight of mists rising from clear, open water surrounded by soft green trees – a sharp contrast to the stark world for which we were headed. Starting in the woods at the Heath line, we were wet to our knees in the first one hundred feet, but we never noticed, for we were caught up in our friend's story of a summer adventure she had had kayaking off the foggy coast of Alaska, studying the harbor seal population. Our surroundings blended well with her story.

After crashing through the woods over fallen trees and branches in our haste, it was the webs of the funnel web-weaver spiders that first slowed us down and focused our attention on the world around us. On a sunny day we never would have noticed these thick, soft webs, but today they were covered with tiny diamonds of water, and as we looked around, we noticed many ferns held these funnels of various sizes, all with a spider lurking at the entrance of the tube, waiting to snatch its prey. A warbler sang close by, reminding us of how negligent we have been of our warblers this year and that we have taken little time to birdwatch and relearn their individual songs and costumes.

The underside of a willowy bush looked silvery in its coat of water drops and every piece of grass was highlighted with the same. A whole new world met our eyes – the world of a rainy day. It was a misty rain that fell gently and did not beat upon the flora and fauna of earth. Although it could be termed dismal and dark, in reality the world was soft and beautiful and delicate – deeper green from being wet. Everything seemed more alive and flourishing and the ground was spongy as our footsteps penetrated nearer and nearer the swamp. The well-hidden path to the first lookout was overgrown with hemlocks and drops of water cooled the backs of our necks as we stooped to pass under their branches. Quietly and slowly, we approached the water's edge from out of the trees so as not to spook any creature, but there is always a frog that gives us away with a loud squeak as he jumps back into the water.

Otherwise, all was momentarily quiet. And to the inexperienced eye and ear, one could declare the place cold and dead and move on. But we knew better, for we have spent many happy hours observing this swamp. First and foremost on our mind today was locating and counting the great blue heron population. A week or so ago we had seen two nests and counted four young in one and five in another – rather crowded housing by the looks, but we were thrilled to find so many. It took a few minutes today

with both of us using binocs to account for all nine, but yes, they were all there.

Moving out to the old gravel bank a little further around the swamp, we found several holes dug by recent nesting turtles and several broken rubbery eggshells where the skunks or raccoons had had a feast. We wonder how the turtle population ever expands – but then more turtles devour more baby ducks and geese, so that's the way of the world. High water and perhaps a slight raising of the beaver dam has flooded more of the gravel bank and it is wet and mucky to get to the back side of the swamp, but we were well soaked already so it really didn't matter. But the high water is also killing a lovely sheep laurel bush and will destroy some woodland orchids that grew in profusion along the edge. As we focused back on the swamp, three black ducks quietly paddled across our binocular view and another flew over our heads.

Checking the herons from all angles as we made our way around the back hill, we

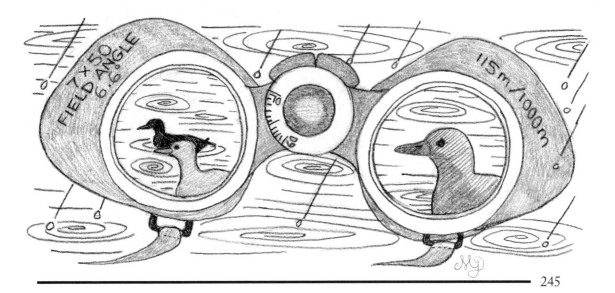

were just investigating the bank of calla lilies by the beginning of the dam when mother (or was it father?) heron came squawking over our heads and landed on the nearest nest, that held the four chicks almost as

big as the parent. We scrambled around the corner to get a better view of the young herons who all attacked the adult's mouth as food was regurgitated for them. One big smarty thought the little runt of the lot was getting more than his share for he/she turned on him and pecked at him until he was almost shoved over backwards. Drama in the swamp. Mother stayed for a couple

of minutes and then flew down to the water for a drink, after which she went off fishing again. The chicks seemed to be picking at the bottom of the nest for a while and then settled down to wait for more – all squabbling over for the moment.

Just as we started to walk around the top of the dam, the old bullfrog in the lower pond started to "chug-a-rum" and soon was echoed by several from all directions. We figured they were passing the word that two intruders were invading their territory. It was like walking a tightrope to cross the dam. One false move or loss of balance and we would have been up to our ears in cold, black water and mud. Each time we got a solid foothold, we would stop and look over the scene.

A bird on the little island ahead of us caught our eye and we watched it more closely as it bobbed up and down, walking along the edge of the grass. "It's an ovenbird," we said with great authority until suddenly it began to sing a pretty song far different than the "teacher, teacher, teacher" of the ovenbird. Then we knew its bobbing actions were distinctive and later proved it to be a northern water thrush – something new to us.

Nearer the middle of the dam now, we stopped for quite some time, just observing the eerie, mysterious scene all around us. Gray dead trees of all shapes and sizes appeared and disappeared as the mists rolled across the water. From high on the hill to the west, a sapsucker every so often loudly tapped on a dead tree. When the mists moved faster before a slight breeze, the water drops on the trees in the woods fell off, sounding like pouring rain as they touched the understory leaves and eventually making big plops of water as they hit the surface of the dark swamp. When all was quiet and the fog grew thick again, we could hear a train in the distance as if it was coming right down Cyrus Stage Road.

As we sat eating checkerberries, two nests of tree swallows kept us watching as the pretty blue parents gracefully swooped catching bugs for the hungry little ones in holes in the dead trees. Grackles were noisy from the treetops and cedar waxwings made soft zeeeeing sounds. Kingbirds flew close to the water, catching insects, and then lit on dead limbs to digest them. We nearly lost our balance looking at a large bird near the first heron nest. From the coloring, actions and size it was probably a red-shouldered hawk. We later heard it screaming off in the woods. When all was quiet again, the sweet call of the white throated sparrow, "We praise thee, O Lord," drifted across the swamp. The surface of the water was almost covered with the lily pads of water shield, with its little red flower in blossom.

We were stalling some, in hopes it would be feeding time at the second heron's nest, for every so often the young would start loudly talking among themselves and march around the nest with some flapping of wings as if ready to fledge. One nearly fell over the edge but seemed to know how to pull himself back. After a while they arranged themselves: standing with three facing one way and two the other as if resigned to waiting for a delayed lunch. Herons are very patient birds.

The fog rolled in again and the sapsucker loudly tapped in the distance and the bullfrogs talked. Then all was quiet. The herons rearranged themselves, flexed their wings and stood still. Somewhere, unseen, the beavers rested from their labors, waiting for darkness to come to inspect the new footprints along their dam. The blue flag had gone by and the swamp candles were just beginning to light up along the edges, where deer tracks were imprinted on the muddy shores. The various kinds of St. Johnswort were not yet budded. A whirligig scooted around and around the water surface, sending ripples in wide circles across the still water. The sapsucker tapped. The wind picked up quickly, clearing the fog and making a ruffled path across the water as the soft drizzle continued to wash our faces. The wind stopped – the fog collected again and all was quiet. The white throat called – the scene was mysterious, enchanting and hypnotizing. There was more life here than we could imagine. Each creature would have its moment on stage, but unfortunately, we could not stay for the whole drama to be enacted. We must move on, come back to reality, to the "nowness" of everyday life – to the *Goal Post* waiting to be composed and arranged on an inhuman machine.

When we finally turned our backs on the swamp, we realized we were shivering with the dampness and cold. A fast hike through the woods to the power line would warm us up, even though soaking wet dungarees would weigh us down. The lay of the land had been changed with recent logging operations. Our favorite hillside of spring beauties was covered with slash, but the corms would survive and come spring thousands of tiny, pink-striped white flowers would blossom unseen under it all. We followed along the swamps and saw violet leaves as big as maple leaves, the tops of every blue vervain nipped by deer and the golden ragwort going to seed but still making yellow patches among the lush greens. In the woods, the distinctive flat leaves of two big, round-leaved orchids caught our attention. Something had eaten the blossom stem from one, but the other was budded and would produce a cluster of greenish white orchids in the near future.

As we pushed our way out of the woods onto the power line, we were suddenly in the highlands of Scotland. Rugged mountain terrain appeared in both directions with low grassy and bush foliage, the fog hanging low. Another enchanted scene. Everything took on a magical quality. Each cluster of plants and grasses covered with water drops made a new pattern – new forms, new shapes, new colors – each glistening in the muted light. Stands of ordinarily, dull, ugly bracken fern had become patches of light green, sparkling lace. A late frost had killed the sensitive ferns and painted the tops of the cinnamon and crested ferns with rusty brown. These mingled with the greens created beautiful contrasts. A masked yellowthroat looked at us from the top of a bush and flew off singing, "wichity, wichity."

We climbed down the small embankment and waded through the wet foliage to the roadway. Soaked now to the waist, it did not matter if we took more short investigating trips into the bushes to see a silver everlasting or sample a juicy, wild strawberry or check out the carpet of white blackberry blossoms. The bears will have a feast here next month. Near the trail, two tiny spring bluets still survived near a rosette of transformed, wet velvet hawkweed leaves. Delicate grasses with pinkish tops were bent over like birch trees in an ice storm while stiffer grasses stood tall and green. We stopped to listen to a brown

thrasher at the edge of the woods. His twice-repeated phrases distinguished him from the more common catbird.

Often we turned back to admire and appreciate our sojourn in the Scottish highlands, which seemed to be rising higher in the fog behind us. The meadowsweet was all blossomed, and we took time to look with the hand lens into the faces of the individual, delicate pink blossoms that make up its rather nondescript-looking clusters. A treat on any day is this close-up view of a flower face. The next treat was a pair of birds that perched in close view. A brown female came first and then her flashy mate – a lovely blue indigo bunting. We then sidetracked to see an unlikely stand of cattails only to find that they were in an area of deep sphagnum moss. That it can hold many times its own weight in water was quickly proven as our feet felt cold water ooze over our shoes. We passed the old stone wall near the town line and finished our walk in Heath, finally coming to Number Nine Road and hoping the traffic would be light. People would be sure to wonder what these two bedraggled creatures were doing out on a rainy day.

By the time we reached the car, the enchantment was almost gone, for the sun was desperately trying to penetrate the fog. As we picked a yellow-fringed loosestrife beside the road, a winter wren flew into the tree over our heads and burst forth with his long, happy, musical song.

Stark, eerie, cold, mysterious, wet and yet a beautiful unforgettable day in June.   **7/87**

Free at Last!

Free at last! Free at last! That was our glorious feeling as we set out about nine this morning, July 27th. With the unusually hot, humid weather and the constant threat of thundershowers for most of the month, a Wild Side day had been hard to come by. We tried once, by ourselves, to walk down Tunnel Road to the old cellar hole past Doubleday's. It was humid and breathless, and we returned shortly after poking around and finding a hop vine, new to us, and a tall cluster of weeds from which we tried to break off a sample to later identify and ended up carrying back a four foot, five stalked plant, roots and all (motherwort, a big ugly weed!) because it was too hot to fuss with breaking a stubborn stem. With one empty hand left, we just couldn't resist pulling a small clump of orange day lilies that had been disturbed in the present logging operation. We don't like orange day lilies, but somehow after looking at the old cellar hole, the barn foundation and the old double-walled lane, all dating back to the early 1800s, we felt sentimental about the surviving lilies and would enjoy them just because of it.

All that was by way of saying our thoughts were lodged in the "Cressy Neighborhood" and when today dawned a perfect Rowe day, we called a friend to see if she wanted to spend the day climbing around a mountain in west Rowe. We parked the car at Doubleday's and set off down Tunnel Road, marveling at the cool sunny weather and our great good fortune to be out on the Wild Side. Birdsong stopped us immediately, and we listened to a happy goldfinch with his musical canary song, telling the world that it was his nesting season, later than other birds to correlate with the maturing thistle seeds.

Back at the cellar hole, we again found the hop vine twining around two trees and our partner did her best to try and shinny up the tree to extract some blossoms, but they were just a bit too high. From there, we intended to head west up the lane and out the woods road, but somehow we kept going up and to the right, first passing a spot where someone had dug an old dump and left fragments of a cut glass pitcher and broken bottle. Orange pieces of an old sock scattered in the area looked like tiny fungus growths but were definitely of a yarn consistency. We took time to dig around a protruding jug handle but found the jug also in pieces.

Moving on up the hill, we looked around, envisioning the land cleared and pastured with sheep as in years gone by. The area had amazingly level areas for being a sidehill farm and wonderful rocks and ledges. We hoped the children of yesteryear had enjoyed them as much as we would have. On the backside of one rocky knoll, a huge grotesque oak tree called us to investigate. It must have been stepped on by animals in its youth, a pasture oak, for it was squatty with many large, circular limbs. As we climbed down to walk around it, we discovered a beautiful, large, salmon-colored rosette – a mushroom "flower" – growing on its roots. Looking around, there were several others which had grown and decayed in years past. According to our books, it was probably a variety of sulphur shelf with white pores.

We really wanted to head back in the other direction but an old stone wall led us back to familiar ground on the old woods road to Doubleday's Cliffs. It seemed then best to change course from our original vague plan and circle the mountain in the opposite direction, heading for the cliffs first. Cliff country, for sure. We bypassed many ledges and boulders, some of which our partner referred to as black icebergs. The old woods road is fairly well defined, but we usually have been there in autumn or winter and at one point nothing looked familiar. A red-tailed hawk suddenly screamed at our intrusion, but we stood our ground and found ourselves in a good soil area covered with baneberry, blue cohosh with big green berries which will eventually ripen to blue, and lots of silvery spleenwort fern. One large, round-leaved orchid had blossomed full, withered and dried to hopefully produce more seeds and scatter this lovely flower.

After another sharp angle in the road

Large round-leaved orchid

up to the right, the territory became familiar again, and we then went left under the big cliffs. This was a mistake. We should have gone the usual route to the right and then up over the cliffs, for the vines, brambles

and bushy summer growth over rocks and dips made unpleasant walking. But we were soon through it and distracted by the various heights of the cliffs, hiding places in the rocks, beautiful ferns, and obvious indications that we were in bear country. Scrambling up the old roadway to the top, we seemed to be going faster and faster as one of us had mentioned lunch and, although it was early, it suddenly had sounded like a great idea.

The Upper Reservoir off to the northeast was full and shone bright blue in the morning sun as we arrived at the small level ledge which is the southeast lookoff point on the cliffs. We were ready to sit and enjoy this gorgeous panorama stretching from the reservoir, with Adams Mountain in the distance to the left, across the whole western green velvet slope of Negus, to the trails of Berkshire East rising in the background, the valley of the Deerfield in the center picture although the river was not in sight, to the long thin range of Forbidden Mountain, over which traversed the old Indian Mohawk trail, and finally across the hills of Florida to the peak with Savoy Fire Tower to the extreme right. What a day, what a treat, what a view!

The ants found us as soon as we opened the knapsack, but what would a picnic be without them? The lunch of cheese and tomato sandwiches with vinegared cucumber slices, thrown together just as we were leaving in case we didn't make it back by noon, tasted mighty good at eleven a.m. In trying to describe the view, we decided the trees on the mountains looked like varieties of moss with all shades of green, darker green in the distance, and definitely bright green sphagnum in the foreground. All through lunch, we watched the yellow jackets going

Free at Last!

The lining tower bolts in ledge

in and out of a hole in the bank below us, minding their own business until the very end. When they decided to investigate our food supply, we swallowed the last crumbs, put away the wrappers and moved to a new location while we looked up some puzzling detail in the flower book.

For the next lap of our hike, we definitely had a purpose in mind. Back in April, 1985, we had taken you "in search of lining towers," finding a tower on Florida Mountain and taking a hike to this area looking for whatever remained of a lining pole on Rowe's Neck – all used in 1866-68 for surveying of the Hoosac Tunnel. We had come close but never found the spot. The instigator of our search found the site himself the next day, but we have always wanted to see for ourselves.

We knew the lining pole was located on one of the spines of the mountain and we knew our last efforts were too far to the left, so we went over the hill and down more to the right coming out to an open ledge facing directly north toward the Lower

Reservoir Dam. Wrong again! But what a view... Raycroft Lookout Mountain and all points upriver. In contrast to the full and very blue Upper Reservoir, the Lower Reservoir was low and a brooding, dark black. Backtracking a little, we continued around the mountain. Remains of three or four old burned tree stumps puzzled us, for there have been no fires in this area that we can remember. It was soon obvious that we were crossing another rock outcropping, and here we followed it down the mountain a short distance. There they were – four heavy iron pins solidly in the rock – and the view? Standing behind the pins, we could read the "1877" carved squarely in the middle of the arch over the Tunnel entrance.

So this was the famous spot in Rowe (having sighted from five other towers over the mountain from the western portal) where engineers stood at times over a two year period and sighted into the black eastern portal of the tunnel bore and performed an engineering feat looked back upon proudly by the Society of Civil Engineers as an accomplishment of national historic significance. The discrepancy when the headings met was no more than 9/16th of an inch. The Hoosac Tunnel, four and three quarters of a mile long, was the longest tunnel in North America from 1873 to 1916.

With this mission accomplished, we continued to head around the mountain, hoping to rim the high plateau on the edge of the more dramatic dropoffs on all sides, finally leading back to the cellar hole on Tunnel Road where we started, covering a section of territory totally new to us. But first we came upon the open ledge facing the tunnel where we had come two years ago, thinking we had found the lining tower spot but not the rock pins to prove it. We could see now that the angle of view from there was not directly into the tunnel as it had been at the actual location.

We must mention that we did a lot of sitting on this hike. Each opening onto a different angle of view across the Deerfield Valley necessitated time to stop and contemplate, to enjoy, to share enthusiasm. Our partner was seeing these sights for the first time, and we were identifying points of interest as we remembered them. That's Pine Cobble, where we stayed too long on a hike one winter day and all had to slide straight down the steep side through the leaves and snow in a hurry to get someone home for work on time; that's Fife Brook canyon where there is a pothole you have to climb the mountain to see into; that's the brook ravine above the Tunnel with lovely twin waterfalls, where we climbed one day and were saved from oblivion by grabbing one very small tree; that white water is the

whirlpool under the railroad bridge where you have to be especially careful in a canoe; there is our red-tailed hawk soaring on the wind currents; there, along that straight stretch of river, is where we investigated the old dam abutments just last month; and that white spire on the mountain is the steeple of the Florida Mountain Church.

Progress from here on could be best described as meandering where the spirit took us, stopping to watch a flitting female redstart, to examine a new ledge, marveling at a section of comparatively level land again and keeping our eyes on the ground vegetation, hoping to find a choice new botanical morsel. One surprising find was all the very soft reindeer moss, actually a lichen. It was all shades of beautiful gray and gray-green and felt wet to the touch. Last night's showers must have soaked it well, for not a bit felt stiff and crunchy as we have always known it. Can it be that we have never seen reindeer moss after a rain? Growing high on the mountain in the wind, it probably dries out quickly.

We could have spent hours just looking and appreciating the reindeer mosses, lichens, clubmosses, ground pines and cedars, quartz outcrops and other odd shapes of rocks and soil as they created miniature landscapes on the ground in the filtered sunlight. On still another open ledge we stopped again, this time looking almost directly down on the railroad bridge. Here we had to eat our apples, giving us time to watch the puffy, white clouds creating shadows that played across the mountains, and we imagined them the monster shapes of flying dinosaurs.

Neat is often an overused word, but it did seem to apply to the huge rocks and ledges with their nooks and crannies and overlooks that made up the nose of the mountain overlooking the big turn of the river so distinctive to Rowe's unique, southwest boundary. Here was an amphitheater of rocks and stage that was just calling for the performance of some artistic event, or perhaps if we sat long enough on these rocks, the local animals would take the stage and entertain us. Instead, it was the remains of a blue bee, further up the mountain that caught our eye and enthused us. An unusual color, we have seen green bees and beetles and blue dragonflies, but this was an iridescent bright blue bee or wasp. We carefully brought him home in our jar and still have not been able to identify him by name, Latin or otherwise.

A natural square-cut white rock seat would have been fun to bring home but was far beyond our knapsack capacity. A piece of a beautiful unfamiliar grass should have come with us but at the time it seemed too dainty and pretty to pick. We had to dispense with any ideas that we were the first to traverse this sort of basin on the mountain when we came across a fireplace in the grass – a wonderful place to camp, whoever you were. We seemed to have come to the end of the plateau and climbed a bit, always curious about the next ledge. The tree cover was heavy toward the river now and there were no further outlooks. We came to a bit of level area and finally had to consult the map. To continue around at the same level we would have had to almost double back for a ways, so after consulting the compass, we decided to go down – a generally easterly course should bring us back to the cellar hole. We found lots of blossoming helleborine, an alien, dark

green-purple orchid and then a little mangy maidenhair fern. Somewhere in here, we expected to find more good soil plants and perhaps some ginseng, but none appeared.

After dropping down about two hundred feet, we came into what must have been the upper pasture for the Cressy farm – another wide level plateau where recent logging had opened the woods to brighter sunlight. A big iceberg rock graced the middle of the pasture and several piles of small stones indicated a farmer's pride in clearing his fields. When settled in the late seventeen and early eighteen hundred's, this section of Rowe was still a part of the unincorporated track called Zoar.

So, we came full circle on this glorious day, back to the old cellar hole. We looked again at the huge rocks in the barn foundation

Chuck Blackler Photo

Lower Cressy cellar hole

and wondered by just what means they were moved and appropriately placed so many years ago. And as we walked slowly up the hill to the car, we wondered about the next hundred years and what this now wild country and its old cellar holes and stone walls will look like for the next generation. **8/87**

High ledges, both of them, separated by only a hundred and fifty miles or so, but worlds apart in their sights and sounds on the Wild Side. To tell you about the first high ledge, we chose a choice perch on the second. To describe a quiet walk in the mountain woods among the sweet clear voices of the hermit thrushes, we traveled to the sea with our clipboard and pen and listened to the wild, lonely cries of the gulls. To take you to the mountaintop on a still August morning, we sat beside the ocean with salt air in our nostrils and a sea breeze rustling our papers. From the first high ledge, we could see the hills of Western Massachusetts, New York and Vermont, and from the second, we could see to the edge of the world.

Four years had gone by since we took our first hike to the top of Spruce Hill in Savoy Mountain State Forest in North Adams. We thought then that it would become an annual event, but the day must be clear and not too windy and free of sudden thunder showers for we could spend an hour and a half on the walk in, with stops for breathing on the steep climb at the end to attain the 2,566 foot height of its high ledge.

All summer, Spruce Hill was making its way to the top of our mental list of places to hike, and on the morning of August 6th our hiking partner joined us rather early after breakfast so we could beat the heat and humidity of our recent August afternoons. The trail starts on a sharp corner off Shaft Road in Florida, and we missed the turnout on the first try. The trail is well marked but not until you turn the corner a short ways down a dirt road in Florida State Forest. "Busby Trail" it says on a small sign on the right side. Large blue triangles mark the trees

ahead. We noted the appropriateness of the blue color that was there to guide, blending nicely with the wilderness surroundings, and did not disturb our thoughts, as florescent orange tends to do.

* * * * *

This morning, August 24th, we rose early and headed east toward the sea. Having spent the weekend in New Hampshire, we have found our perch here on our second high ledge, smelling the early morning salt air, in about three quarters of an hour. The sea is calm and the tide is dead low, unfortunately spoiling our chances to see the ocean's performance through the blowhole in the rocks nearby. There is not a cloud in the great blue sky to block the bright sun coming over the bluff behind our left shoulder.

Already the sea is busy with early morning traffic. Eight or ten Maine lobstermen are out checking their traps, whose buoys are scattered like polka dots over the blue waters as far as we can see. In the far distance south, against the light ivory color of the sky where it meets the sea, is the familiar landmark of Cape Neddick Lighthouse at York and further out at sea to the east, tall Boon Island Light stands against the horizon. In the near distance is the tourist shore of the Kennebunks and neighboring towns on down the coast toward York. Behind all to the southwest rises lone Agamenticus, the Indian mountain. We are sitting atop a long length of rocky cliffs about twenty feet above the water with a spooky stone and shingle three story house silhouetted against the sea to our left.

We focus the binocs on a busy green lobster boat circling yet another buoy and watch while a yellow-aproned fisherman catches up the buoy and on a pulley draws up the lobster trap to rest on the shelf on the starboard side of his small boat. With a rhythmic motion well familiar to him, he opens the trap, withdraws the lobsters (two) which he measures, pegs and throws in a large can full of circulating sea water – made obvious by the running stream of water through a tube off the port side. Then he reaches in the trap again and throws out other undesirable catches of what we do not know, but the gulls quickly gather around and fight over the goodies. Lastly the lobsterman withdraws a bag, which he refills with bait from another tank, refastens it in the trap, closes the cover and as he revs up the motor and slowly pulls away, the trap is pushed in the water, followed by its long length of rope and lastly his distinctive green and white buoy.

* * * * *

The air was still and the path well-used as we continued along the one and three tenths mile woodsy trail to Spruce Hill. Our knapsack was full and heavy on our back. For once, we had included all the equipment: binocs, camera, flower guide, bird book, maps, whistle, knife, first aid kit, compass, extra jacket, magnifying lens, and fruit. Actually, all we really needed was the geodetic map which showed our intended trail as a dotted line from highway to summit. The wood road passed the first power line and led into the woods once again, coming to a spot where a well-worn narrow trail branched off to the left. Although the blue arrows continued along the road, we were in a quandary to know which way to go. We knew some of the trail was used by motorcycles and thought perhaps the hiking trail was different. After

a rather long conference and map study, we made the decision to take the path to the left. You can imagine the expression on our faces when we very shortly found that the path was just a short convenient detour around a rather long mud puddle.

The terrain between the two power lines was fairly level and easy, and we found more blackberry bushes under the second power line than we had ever seen in one place before. Solid blackberries as far as we could see, mostly green berries with a few still sour black ones beginning to appear. What a bear feasting ground this was going to be in a couple of weeks. Back in the woods it was quiet except for the hermit thrushes who followed us just out of sight on either side. The climb was beginning, a gradual winding ascent through hillside farmland fenced and divided in the long distant past with the prevalent collection of large mountain rocks.

* * * * *

The shadow of a gull passes across our high ledge and its lonely cry above us is carried off on the wind. On the jagged rocks in front of the mystery house, ten black cormorants are sitting in a graduated row down the slope of the ledge. Two are sleeping, three are preening their feathers and another is fanning his wings to dry in the morning sun. The rest are looking out to sea, waiting. A few gulls have joined them, facing always into the wind. On the eastern horizon we can distinguish the outline of a large sailboat, skimming the edge of the world. When the wind is just right we hear the sound of the lobster boat motors as if they were here beside us. Another sailboat comes out of the harbor to the right under motor, trailing its dinghy. It's a beauty and we watch as it crosses our field of vision. Eastward a red lobster boat catches our attention. Three gulls are patiently riding on the back, waiting for their fair share of the discards. This boat is from Portland and the lobsterman picks up the red and white buoys. We watch with the binocs and see him extract three lobsters from the first trap. The gulls seem to know just the precise moment their handout is coming and they take to wing and are ready to dive, gulp and then scrap over anything extra. Back toward the harbor, three big, sleek white fishing boats come roaring out as if they are ready to take on the world. As we watch, they slow to a near stop and draw together as if in conference.

The sea is becoming noisier as it splashes against the rocks, and we realize the wind has picked up. We are restless, too, and need to walk around. We head toward the blowhole and remember that our son had warned us to be careful – when did the change occur from our telling him to be careful? Looking up, we see our shadow, greatly enlarged by the angle of the morning sun, looming on the rock that rises on the further side of the blowhole. It is rather ominous, and we decide to be careful after all. The seawaters restlessly splash back and forth below the hole. The spectacular power and glory of this phenomenon is not evident in the least this morning. We move on to other things, watching a floppy monarch butterfly chase in and about the rocks of the shoreline.

The triple fishing party is headed off again, one boat after the other about to round the green navigation marker out some distance. Climbing back up the ledge, we stop to watch two cold bumblebees just

sitting on the top of a pretty stem of yellow seaside goldenrod. A man and two small boys interrupt our solitude as they, too, climb over the rocks. We overhear them talking of how wet they got here yesterday, watching the blowhole in action. A gull has dropped a clam on the rock down by the water and another gull has swooped in and is noisily demanding his share. A cormorant is flying low over the water in a westerly direction. Cormorants always fly with such determination and purpose in their wings. This one glides in for a landing among the buoys and sits on the rocking water, obviously having had no real purpose in mind. The fishing boats are now headed three abreast in a southeasterly direction, full speed ahead, three white wakes trailing behind.

* * * * *

Spruce Hill soil must have been good for farming for it still exhibits the tendency to richness in the flowers it produces – wild ginger in profusion, baneberry, in berry now looking like its namesake "dolls eyes" and yellow jewelweed. We did not go far afield looking for plants, these being noticeable along the trail. Passing the old square cellar hole of the farmhouse, we stopped a moment to investigate and wonder who carried the harvest down its still intact cellar stairs down the hatchway in the back, who tended its fields and animals – probably sheep on this rocky mountainside – and what sort of women spent their days in its kitchen, and how many children were born within its walls?

The trail now could be termed steep, and we took it slowly, admiring the white birches, rock clusters and the jungle of ferns on either side. As we approached the summit, a total of

681 vertical feet from the car, each step was carefully placed and our knees reached close to our chins at times as we pulled ourselves up the rocky, rooty path, finally squirming between narrow ledges up to the eastern outlook near the top. We immediately sat down, partly to catch our breath and rest our weary bones and partly to unload our knapsack to find the binocs so we could rest our elbows on our knees and stare eastward toward Rowe.

What a view! In the foreground, across a wide valley, was the long eastern range of Hoosac Mountain, on the northern end of which the tower and buildings of Whitcomb Summit were prominent and to the south an inverted V of power lines draped down the side. Above this in the far distance was the long distinctive range of Todd, Adams, and South Mountain in Rowe, with only three houses and one roof standing out among the sea of green forest. The yellow Williams farm and open pasture could be seen to the left; the gray Krumm house stood above the surroundings toward the center; and above and further back were the white Corarito buildings and grounds on Dell Road. Looming high over all in the far, far distance was Monadnock Mountain in New Hampshire. We both looked at the lone roof among the trees more to the right of the others. It was a mystery which we sighted and discussed for several minutes until we spotted something moving, appearing and disappearing, above the roof – the flag flying high on its pole across the road from the Quinn house on Middletown Hill.

* * * * *

Obviously late for work, another dirty, white lobster boat chugs out of the harbor

and we can make out a "For Sale" sign in his window. The captain pulls up to his first buoy fairly close to shore and we can watch him without the binocs. Three men are in the boat, two in working outfits and one standing by in a heavy flannel shirt. Late for work, overstaffed and when they pull the first trap they throw back three undersized lobsters – no wonder the "For Sale" sign; they just aren't natives with a knack for the business. We are going to abandon our high perch now and walk up the rocks to the left and down to sea level closer to the eerie house. The three fishing boats, now only visible in the binocs, are still speeding toward the dropping off place on the horizon.

Looking behind us now, we admire the beautiful wild rose bushes covered with round orange rose hips and a few lingering pink roses. We hear the familiar "zeeee" sound of waxwings and finally spot them at the top of a nearby bush. A robin calls from across the road. Tiny heath asters cling to the soil along the rocks. The cormorants are still sitting in a row waiting for an inspiration to strike. We climb down the rocks, naturally broken in chunks, making convenient steps to the "beach" of large smooth pebbles. The tide is definitely coming in and the floating seaweed is swishing back and forth with each wave. We bend to look closely at the miracles of sea life – clinging barnacles and snails on the rocks. As we look up to watch the small flock of terns, the incoming tide washes across the tops of our sneakers and we move quickly to avoid the next larger wave.

* * * * *

Moving around to the topmost high ledge on Spruce Hill, we came out to the spectacular view of the Hoosac River Valley, across which looms Greylock, the highest mountain in Massachusetts. Stamford, Vermont and Clarksburg were to our right, and as we turned, Williamstown towers could be seen nestled in the trees between the high Taconic Range of New York State and the city of North Adams in the foreground. Down there along the Hoosac River was the site of old Fort Massachusetts and we knew Indian feet had climbed on our high ledge. Next in front of us was the bulky range of Greylock, with its rounded dome summit below which the white lime quarries of the Adams area seemed to be climbing up its back. Pontoosuc Lake off toward Pittsfield blended with hills and farms of the fertile river valley, and as we turned again to our left, we followed the southern ridges of the Hoosac Range, east of which Borden Mountain Fire Tower in Savoy sits atop its familiar pointed peak.

We are standing on top of the world; it seems, close to the fluffy white clouds in the blue sky. Free as a bird, we stretch out our arms and feel the heat of the noonday sun and the humidity of an August day cooled by only the slightest stirring of the trees far below. With a sense of accomplishment, we sit on our high ledge and share a lunch of cheese and crackers and cucumber slices in vinegar, and shiny red apples for dessert. Waxwings are "zeeeeing" in the bushes behind us.

* * * * *

We stand now on another high ledge, taking our last look through a clump of purple thistles against a blue sea. The breeze has freshened considerably, and we have zipped our jacket and cupped our hands over our cold ears. It is difficult now to tell the lobster buoys from the white caps on the water, and the waves splash loudly against the rocks. The lovely, silvery sea grasses are bending in the wind and the Queen Anne's lace whorls around with each gust. One last panning with the binocs – three lovely white sailboats are on the horizon, a commercial deep sea fishing boat is coming out of the harbor, a small Coast Guard boat is tied to the green navigation marker, the cormorants are still sitting, waiting patiently, "For Sale" is out there still looking for lobsters, another crying gull casts a shadow across our view, and the three sleek white fishing boats have disappeared off the edge of the world. We turn and walk up the road a short way to the car, returning a cheery "good morning" to at least ten members of another wild species – tourists on their way to our high ledge. **9/87**

An Irish Adventure with Finn McCool

Perhaps it isn't quite fair to say that we had been planning this hike since we were seven years old, but our desire to explore the area does date back to a fascination inspired by a favorite childhood book called "Wonders of the World." We still have the little three-and-a-half by five-inch blue and red book, well worn and frazzled, from which we memorized the pictures and dreamed of seeing the sights long before we could read the big descriptive words and understand the statistics. The world has changed considerably since that book was published and man-made miracles like a streamlined train, a China Clipper airplane and the Empire State building are no longer awe-inspiring, but the natural wonders of the Grand Canyon in Arizona, Mt. Vesuvius volcano in Italy and the Giant's Causeway in Northern Ireland still command awe and respect. Having been fortunate enough to become closely acquainted with the first two of those wonders in years past, it was now our good fortune to be nearing the site of the third.

"The Troubles" have kept many a tourist away from Northern Ireland in recent years, but once spending time there with other members of our spouse's family, establishing a new strong bond with relatives and their roots in County Fermanagh, we felt no qualms in exploring further north. From the cities of Maghera and Coleraine came three of our own ancestors to settle in Colrain, Massachusetts in the 1740s. As with all genealogical research, the results inspire one to become intimately involved with the local history and terrain of the "homeland." And so with great personal interest, we meandered north through the Sperrin Mountains and down onto the green rolling valley where sit the towns of Maghera and then Coleraine.

By this time, in the back of our mind, excitement was building as it seemed within the realm of possibility that we could visit the faraway site of that strange causeway of hexagonal rocks pictured in our cherished little book of childhood – and perhaps explore the area with the legendary Finn McCool himself. Little did we know that he was already there waiting for us.

Twilight and misty air were upon us as we drove into Bushmill on the northern coast and, as had been our habit, sought out the nearest "Farmhouse Bed and Breakfast" which happened to be high on the hill overlooking the west land side of the Giant's Causeway. Driving up the long narrow road to the farm we were suddenly faced with a wall of a hundred and fifty black and white cows with the farmer in his wellies at the helm, leading them down the muddy road to pasture after milking. We backed up and watched as they all turned in and the gate was securely closed. Just ahead was the farmhouse and although the road was muddy the cement courtyard and the house itself were immaculate. We detected more of a Scotch accent from these Northern Irish farm folks but always the same warm welcome.

Our dinner on that rainy evening was taken at the one remaining hotel in the area, built in 1836 when visitors first began to come in great numbers to see this unusual natural wonder of the world. The first hydroelectric tram in the world ran from nearby towns to this Causeway Hotel from the 1880s to 1949. The flavor of a century ago still remained at the hotel and the roast lamb was done to perfection.

We awoke just at daylight the next

morning and looked out on the foggy landscape, hoping that Ireland's changeable weather would give us something better by sunrise. As we stared at the white birds and sheep in the pastures down toward the sea, we became aware of the black and white river of cows that in total silence were again flowing back to pasture after morning milking.

Seated for breakfast in the large dining room of the farmhouse, an older man waited on us, recommending hot porridge for a chilly morning. This was followed by the usual plate of two sausages, two strips of what we would call Canadian bacon, two fried eggs, sunny side up, half a grilled tomato, a thimble of orange juice and lots of hot coffee. Bountiful plates of dark and light soda bread and pots of marmalade made up for the thin triangles of cold toast served in a lovely little silver toast holder with a handle that carefully separated the slices. Everything in Ireland was served piping hot except the toast!

Well fortified for the day, it was about nine thirty when we finally drove into the parking lot of the National Trust Visitor's Center for the Giant's Causeway. We saw a short film, looked at exhibits and heard again the legend of the Irish giant, Finn McCool, who was supposed to have laid the giant stepping stones from there to the island of Staffa in Scotland so he could walk across the sea and conquer his enemy.

We quickly checked the possibilities for exploration. The common means was a small bus down the mile or so road around the hill to the Causeway itself where you were free to explore the rocks. Or there was a two mile hike along the cliffs with a stairway back to the Causeway. Ah, that's it, we thought

without further questions. We'll take the high road and meet the others at the bottom, and we bundled up and headed out quite irrationally before anyone could object. We really wanted to see more than a tourist's eye view of this long awaited wonder, and having been cooped up in a car for several days we were ready for exercise. But there seemed to be some other force…

The weather had cleared but the wind was very strong. We appreciated our two sweaters and wool hat as we set off up the paved roadway that quickly led to a narrow dirt path. We followed down a dip and eventually up to the top of the cliff called Weirs Snout overlooking the ocean in a beautiful panorama of blue sea before us. There were walled green, green pastures and fields and, in the far distance, green mountains behind us. The Causeway? Well, there were rocks spilling out into the ocean far below the next "Snout" but they looked mighty insignificant as we stood looking down from three hundred feet above.

Back at the Center we had happened to read a derogatory remark attributed to William Thackeray in 1842. Being a realist, he had seen nothing spectacular about the rocks, was annoyed at all the tourist hoopla and was probably seasick on the small boat which he had hired to get a seaview of the Causeway. But we must admit that our first impression of that noted pile of rocks was somewhat the same.

However, we were in a gorgeous spot high on the cliffs, walking in the sea breeze and sunshine and we felt as free as the sea birds riding the air currents out over the water. We took a good look down from Aird Snout (of course, we didn't know the

An Irish Adventure with Finn McCool

name of this special lookout point at the time, for we had neglected to pick up the very detailed and useful trail map) right over the Causeway and examined the terrain in all directions with binocs, bracing ourselves against the stiff wind that tried its best to blow us off course. Going on, we very shortly came upon a path back down the cliff. This couldn't be the one the man had described. We certainly had not gone two miles and we could see the lower path continuing on around the next bend. So, as always, on we went with mounting enthusiasm. And as you well know, this has gotten us into trouble many a time before. But this time it seemed beyond our control...

Looking back, the Visitors Center, so prominent at first was now fading into the background and more protruding "snouts" appeared around the bends ahead. The path now skirted close to the cliff edge and was so narrow that we actually tried to concentrate on admiring the heather and bluebells beside the path on our right rather than looking down the three hundred foot cliff on our left. Out at the point, we took time to scan the Causeway with binocs and spotted the rest of the family on the roadway. We took off our hat and waved it in our right hand while we held the binocs to our eyes with the left to see if they returned our greeting. They did and we waved a little longer certain that they would be taking a picture of the speck on the clifftop for the *Goal Post*, but it never entered their minds

At least we had checked in, so to speak, and thus went merrily on our way. The path down must be coming soon, and we'd be back to the Causeway and join the others at the bus before noon. Other hikers were few

and far between, but we did chat with the next one coming toward us. He happened to be an American and we understood his answer. "No," he said. He was returning from walking further on some distance and had not seen a path down the cliff. The shadow of a doubt crossed our mind.

We walked on quickly now as the path descended near a cow pasture where we had to climb over a stile and follow the slippery way back up to the cliff top once again. New horizons came into view, mountains appearing from under the clouds, sheep in the next pasture, Rathlin Island out to sea and the ever-changing rocky coastline below, alternating coves with promontories. What a sight! We stopped a minute and gazed out to sea picturing in our mind just where on the globe of the earth we were standing – on the very tip of Northern Ireland looking north toward the western islands of Scotland. It was a thrilling feeling. But we did not linger long for we had begun to have a sense of urgency and fear that we were upon the Ulster Way, Northern Ireland's Appalachian Trail that might not return to civilization for many miles. By now we had certainly covered the two miles – but somehow we were not allowed to even think of turning back.

Never at home would we venture so far without out our trusty knapsack and water bottle, and we began to have a tremendous thirst. The muddy trail once again was pushed closer to oblivion by the pasture fence to our right and as the wind was forcing us ever closer to the edge, we stopped for a moment to pick our way more carefully, and in the process looked up to notice movement in the far distance. We found a secure foothold and scanned the distance with the binocs. People! Several gathered on the cliff top about three snouts down the coast. We studied them carefully and could just make out the ladderlike stairway from which they were emerging. Our feeling of great relief at knowing that there really was a return path was tempered by the distance we calculated it to be around the three snouts between here and there. We took off our hat and started off again with gusto, thinking that once at the stairs the trip back would be a piece of cake.

As glorious as the scenery was, we must admit that our car-bound legs were beginning to feel signs of strain and for sure we had already walked off the bacon and eggs! We had desperately wanted a hike and were thrilled to be where we were, but we had run off in a hurry, and now we were wondering just what we had gotten into and if the others were justifiably annoyed sitting in the car waiting for us. A sudden giant gust of wind pushed us from behind and the next hour was like walking on the breeze...

"Hamilton's Seat" the small sign read as we, at last, approached the point of descent. "Benbane Head," not another snout, we would learn later was the name of that particular headland, and the elevation was listed as three hundred and fifty feet. William Hamilton, it seems, was the first geologist to describe the area in 1786. We took a last look around, noting that the hikers we had seen climbing the stairs were miles further on, hiking the Ulster Way. Our watch read just twelve o'clock and we suddenly seemed to be at a high pitch of excitement...

With a feeling of great relief that we were finally at the turning point, we were heading for the top of the stairs when we heard voices and five happy young Irishmen appeared, four with pint Guinness stout glasses in their hands and the fifth who preferred Black Bush whiskey. We exchanged friendly greetings and surmised they knew not what they had gotten themselves into either. With the last one safe on top, we took our turn on the stairs and gulped on the first view down. Not only did we wish for a helicopter rescue, we considered it incredible that those lads had maneuvered the climb with partially empty glasses in their hands.

We had to put on our hat in order to hang on to the small rickety rail with both hands and proceed backwards down the wet and slippery narrow stairway three hundred and fifty feet above the sea. We think for once, without fear of being contradicted, we were petrified! But do you know what happened? We reached out and with giant magnetic force a large firm hand came down to steady us. Startled, we looked up to see none other than Finn McCool himself ready to guide this tiny mortal who had come far across the ocean to admire the handiwork of this Irish giant.

We should have known from the very beginning that it was the force of a giant pulling us toward this spot, but we never dreamed of such good fortune, even through all our years of dreaming of seeing this place. Looking down on the crashing sea below, our fears were gone, and we began to appreciate the fabulous geologic wonders of the Giant's Causeway Coast.

Once down the long winding stairway and safely on the narrow path that we would follow for the next two and a half hours, we stopped to shed one sweater and the hat, tying them securely around our waist. It was many degrees warmer under the protection of the cliffs. The path was perched about halfway up the cliffs and wove in and around the bays and snouts and strange basaltic rock pillars. This unique area was formed fifty-five million years ago when lava from underground volcanoes poured out of fissures and vents in the ground all over the Antrim Plateau of Northern Ireland and under the sea to Western Scotland and then solidified into hard basalt columns, some ninety feet high, often separated by reddish basaltic beds, creating a layer cake effect where erosion had occurred along the cliffs. (We obviously have to believe that all this happened under the direction of Finn McCool.) It is a giant geologist's paradise.

We walked carefully on the tiny, wet path and looked up in awe at the rocks precariously overhanging our head, confident that Finn McCool would stay their fall. But around the next bend we could see the path for a long distance and there was not another human being in sight. "What ifs" came to mind. What if we just couldn't make it any further? What if it started to rain and got foggy? What if we slipped off the path? Who would find us? Was that the wind or did Finn McCool just chuckle a bit at our lack of confidence?

Finally relaxing and enjoying it all, we checked the greenery and were sorry not to be able to properly identify anything except the bluebells and tiny pink herb Roberts, and now and then a yellow trefoil. White sea campion could often be seen in patches lower down the slope and we looked with binocs to be sure. Once in a while we were treated to a red campion that we had come to admire all over Ireland. Ferns and mosses often slowed

our progress as we stopped to appreciate some new collection. Looking out to sea, we judged the tide to be low but waves were still crashing against the rugged and jagged rocks eroded from the promontories.

Halfway around the next bay, we came upon the first flimsy guardrail on the path. It made us stop and take notice, for the trail so far had been hair raising enough and had no guardrail. What were we coming to? The path from here on seemed to be dug into rock with a vertical drop off into the water instead of slightly sloping. And low and behold, a couple passed us asking questions about the stairway to the top. We vividly described it to them but dared not promise that Finn McCool would go back and guide them. Now the path hugged the base of chimney top rocks as we made yet another turn into a new world of flowing basaltic columns called "The Harp," surrounded by a high semicircle of cliffs creating a natural amphitheatre.

Stopping for a moment to appreciate the splendor, we realized the strange force of Finn McCool was still calming our growling stomach, our parched throat and our aching legs – and giving us the sense that although we still had a long, long walk ahead he was there with a helping hand. We ceased to worry about the others; they would just have to amuse themselves with lunch and maybe even afternoon tea. Along the wall of rock beside us were specimens of peeling rock called "Giant's Eyes." We rubbed our fingers along their strange outlines and carefully picked our way along the trail. Here we began to meet afternoon hikers going with such zest in the other direction that they hadn't even seen Finn McCool standing behind us.

An Irish Adventure with Finn McCool

The next bend brought us into sight of the Causeway itself in the distance. The path gradually worked its way down to the shoreland that widened a bit back from the sea. Along the way, we stood beneath giant columns called "The Organ." As we stared up at their huge forms and shapes, we noticed a gigantic spider web hitched between the great columns. It took binocs to see the creature, white belly toward us, who had spun this appropriate giant web with heavier zigzag cross strands closing it near the center. It was our first wildlife except the sea birds, and the long black slug we were about to step on. Our trail then intersected with the "Shepherd's Path" to the first stairway, obviously the two-mile hike we had been advised to take before we knew Finn McCool had other plans for us.

And finally we reached the Grand Causeway itself and climbed up and out toward the sea on some of the 40,000 mostly hexagonal rocks, fifteen to twenty inches wide, that, packed together, formed the largest of the three causeways, stretching some 700 feet out into the sea. An incredible natural phenomenon lay before us as we turned and looked back up the Causeway to the "Aird Snout" high above – the exact view we had memorized from our little book of "Wonders of the World" so long ago. And to the right was "Weir's Snout" where we had first looked down upon what had seemed from there an insignificant pile of rocks. Thackeray had been very wrong, but perhaps he never really experienced the Causeway Coast by hiking with Finn McCool himself.

We passed up walking out on the smaller Middle Causeway to the famous "Wishing Chair" for after today, what more could we wish for? Rubbing our hand on one of the stones for good luck, we started up the long hill on the paved road to the Visitors Center seeing no bus carrying passengers. As we dragged ourselves up the last few feet to the yard, a friendly Irishman with a good thick brogue looked at our bedraggled being and said "Ah, you have walked down to the Causeway?" "Actually" we puffed, out of breath, "we have just walked the Cliff Trail to "Hamilton's Seat" and have returned by the lower trail and the Causeway." "Well, congratulations", he said quickly coming forward to shake our hand, "you did the big one." Yes, we thought, smiling to ourselves, it wasn't planned that way but Finn Mc Cool had certainly enticed us on the big one – things like that happen sometimes, if you are lucky, on the Wild Side in Northern Ireland.

Our watch said just two-thirty when we turned to bid a fond farewell to Finn McCool, but he had taken a giant step backward and was just disappearing in the fog and misty rain that had suddenly enveloped the entire Giant's Causeway Coast.   **11/87**

Giant's Causeway

Ah, November in New England

We had the best of both seasons, fall and winter, but in reverse order. Our first hike across the top of Rowe was along the border from the state and town line on Leshure Road following a compass line to the same markers on Potter Road. Our wildflower partner was in town and we had planned to check out north Rowe for any dry remains of late summer flowers. We waited one day too long in this year's crazy mixed up weather pattern and found the world a winter wonderland on November 12th. But then again, they say if you don't like New England weather, wait a minute. By the time we took our second hike with a friend just for fun on the 16th, it was Indian summer again.

The first real snow brought on the usual frantic search for the winter gear which we hadn't laid eyes on since early April. This always involves standing on a chair to locate the long johns and wool slacks on the top shelf of the upstairs closet, standing on our head in the downstairs coat closet to haul out the array of boots in the back corner behind the summer sneakers, and then the ritual of getting down on our knees to paw through the back of the bottom drawer under the swimming towels to pull out the winter hats and gloves. Then we suddenly remembered it's "bow season" (for deer hunting) and had to make a trip to the barn to locate our old red ski jacket saved somewhere for just this time of year. Having accomplished all this, it required time out for lunch before we could finally get under way for our first winter hike.

North Rowe always has a few more inches of snow than the rest of town and the powdery fluff reached between our boots and our knees as we jumped off the road and pulled ourselves up the small banking to level ground on Anne Carey's Tree Farm, so the sign said. Dry beech leaves rustled to attract our attention to their lovely orange/bronze shades as they clung steadfastly to the smaller trees, waiting for the more severe winds and snows of midwinter to carry them away to their final resting places. They always give their fate a merry chase for even when they finally depart their parent tree they blow in the wind and scurry across the crusty snow to temporarily lodge here and there in an animal track, only to dance off again with the next wintery gust, avoiding at all cost any brook or swamp where they meet their fate and sink to the bottom.

There is always something magic about the outside world after a snowstorm. You can sit inside and shiver with your back to the woodstove and moan about the traveling or you can put on your boots and go out in the woods and experience it! This morning we, too, had a hundred excuses, but once in the woods it was heavenly. A bright blue sky made a lovely backdrop for the variegated tree branches that formed a lacy canopy over our heads. And as we hiked further into the still fairly level woods, we came to the evergreens, all branches hanging heavy with the glistening new snow. Tiny hemlock trees looked like unopened white mushrooms pushing up through a blanket of white. We brushed our hands against one now and then and they seemed to happily shake themselves free and restore their branches to the upright position. The snow had fallen easier through the spruces but had collected on each little branch so the trees seemed to have long white fingers at the ends of their hanging arms. And then there were the balsams, handsomest of all, with white robes covering their bright green bodies. We reached for a small branch to smell our favorite woodsy fragrance.

It was time to check the compass again. "West 100 degrees North," the old deeds read when referring to the province line along the topside of the Myrifield grant. Lots more calculations would be needed to be accurate these days, so we weren't being real exact. Generally we faced west, raised our left arm toward the sun and could tell when we were way off course without mechanical aid, but we checked every so often to be sure. Our partner seemed to have an uncanny knack for direction ignoring both of our methods. Sometimes a wall of evergreens prevented us from going straight and we had to make up for detours. Some of the larger evergreens had become like wigwams and, as we walked around them, we always seemed to find the "door" and bent to peek inside to see who lived there. The snow must have taken everyone by surprise, as there were no signs of life whatsoever, no squirrel tracks, no rabbit tracks, not even a mouse had ventured forth.

Our course would cross the power line about midway and we seemed to arrive there sooner than expected, after stooping to go under some low hanging trees which carelessly dropped their fluffy white fur down our necks. The wide-open lands along power line rights-of-way are about the only places where we can visualize what the cleared pastures of "old Rowe" really looked like. We stood at the edge of the woods, looking up and down the lay of the land thinking of the boxes we had drawn on a map representing the plots of the early settlers. The Thomases to our left bought their 189 acres from Cornelius Jones in 1775 and the Taylors to

the west had a 98 acre piece acquired from Jones in 1777. It always puzzles us why the men built north/south walls but none east and west along this northern Province Line boundary. And do you suppose the women back then ever had time to enjoy a glorious winter hike such as this?

Once out of the woods, the wind picked up and we zipped our jackets. We probably could have spent the rest of the afternoon identifying the grasses and bushes rising above the drifted snow in those wide-open spaces, but fresh wildflowers are our specialty and their roots were now buried deep for winter. But admire the dry ones we did, sometimes using the hand lens to see things like the beautiful tiny five-sided seedpods in the brown cluster topping the numerous branches of meadowsweet. Then there was something looking like cotton grass, and the graceful stalks of fire weed with their curved, white, feathery seeds, and grasses resembling waving stalks of ripened wheat. One branch held the remains of a wasp nest with grubs still visible. Our partner put this in her pocket for later study, trusting that body heat and sunshine wouldn't activate the contents! All these goodies reminded us of that childhood poem by Robert Louis Stevenson:

*"The world is so full of a number of things,
I'm sure we should all be as happy as kings."*

There surely wasn't much more we could have wished for to make us happy on that lovely afternoon.

We crossed the power line on an angle north and entered the woods on the other side where there was evidence of woodcutting and downed brush. We had probably crossed onto the Dennington/Willey property. It looked like a great place for rabbits but nary a paw print. One vague, drifted set of deer tracks seemed to wend its way around a wet spot but we could not follow them. Our footprints were green as we crossed the wet area of sphagnum moss. Several wood roads crisscrossed our determined path but we resisted the urge to follow them, for we meant to stay on the Province Line all the way. From the map and the lay of the land, we knew we were on course as we approached the highest point in North Rowe – a small flat hilltop circled on the geodetic map as 2,100 feet and bisected by the boundary line between Massachusetts and Vermont on the old Province Line.

The hill was covered with trees and offered no view. The northwest wind was blowing in the tops of the trees as we headed over the hill that sloped down more to the north on the backside. As we started to descend, we chided our partner for leading us too far to the north. She argued a bit but then changed course slightly at our urging. We looked at another wasp nest in an old woodpecker hole high in a dead tree then continued down the hillside. Coming out finally at our destination on Potter Road, we were within sight of but somewhat south of the boundary marker. Our face was red, but our partner was good enough not to say, "I told you so!"

* * * * *

When Indian Summer returned in the next couple of days, we began to think about another hike in the warm sunshine. Monday morning dawned bright and early on we called another hiking partner to make plans. With

one car safely at our destination on Monroe Hill, we started off west under the power line on Potter Road at a little after eleven. It seemed more like spring with melting snow, running water and mud. Again the sky was bright blue but faded to white around the horizon, where high, thin clouds seemed to be collecting. This time we needed no jacket and could loosely wear a red vest and wool sweater. We were glad we had waited until Monday for this must have been a busy place on the weekend given the vehicle tracks and footprints along the well-used trail. The snow had melted considerably in the last few days and the land was a patchwork of white snow, green/gray grasses and bronze hillsides of dry hay-scented ferns.

Numerous birds were about this morning and our first treat was a pileated woodpecker calling loudly from a birch tree at the edge of the woods across the way. His bright red head flashed in the sunlight as his large black body flew off deeper into the woods. Then a few goldfinches flitted over the highline, off on a mission of seed collecting, and soon a large flock of evening grosbeaks gathered in the evergreens just above our heads. Blue jays here and there made their "hermit" calls, and we stopped for some time listening to two hawks, probably red-shouldered, calling from either side of the power line.

At the top of the first hill, we took time to look with binocs to the west and south identifying Bill Brown's house on Shippee Road in the foreground with the Foberg, Thoung and Sibley houses seeming to sit in a field just above. The third field and house directly on top was a puzzle. Then suddenly we remembered the answer to this puzzle from last time we were in that spot. It was the Taylor house on Petrie Road; we were seeing the back of it across the Truesdell field. The odd angle from which we were viewing created the mystery as roads, fields and houses took on a strange relationship. We consulted the map to be sure. With that problem solved, we detoured into the woods on the wood road that descended the hill at an easier grade. Chickadees, nuthatches and juncos could be heard in the trees surrounding us.

At the bottom of the hill, we crossed a couple of small brooks which make up the headwaters of Shippee Brook flowing south through town and finally joining Pelham between the Community Church and the Museum. The remains of old culverts were on either side of the trail, perhaps for a roadway of sorts in years past. While looking down the brook we noticed red berries on a small bush and examined them, coming to no real conclusion without their leaves but admiring their beautiful bright color against the snow.

A stonewall crossed our path at an angle on the hillside ahead and we consulted the map to see that it was indeed the boundary line of a parcel of the Monroe State Forest land sold to the state many years ago from the old Bolton farm. Spotting a cement post we climbed the hill and up on the wall. The post had a large "C" on the back that must mean Commonwealth, we finally decided. There was also an identifying circle sign on the tree behind. Standing on the wall and looking at the map, we could follow the boundary wall down the hill and across the power line to the woods on the other side. Old names came to mind: Capt. Goodspeed, George Bennett, Thomas Brown, Joseph Steele – all men who owned these lands and

may have built this wall so long ago, trying to tame this wild countryside.

The warm noonday sun made the wall a most pleasant place to sit, and we quickly decided we were very hungry. Sandwiches, crackers and cheese, apples and pears – all tasted like a feast and we left our cores for hungry animals to savor. A lovely spot, a lovely day in November, so different from the frosty winter wonderland of four days before! Perhaps if we sat quietly for several hours, we'd see our animal friends come by for their snacks, but we would have to leave that to our imagination for there was much rugged territory to cover before the early setting sun dropped behind the western horizon.

Across the top of the hill we came to the familiar junction where the old Readsboro Road crosses north to south and goes either way past near forgotten cellar holes of earlier days in Rowe when sheep and cattle kept these hillsides close-cropped and open. Sometimes we turn here and go down to Shippee Road on this old road, abandoned by the town in 1878, or sometimes via the recent snowmobile trail a little to the west, but today we were going to follow the power line down over behind Round Hill to Monroe Hill Road. Before starting this 500 foot descent, we took time to look west at snow-covered Greylock and the line of mountains to the west. And we also looked down at the ledges on which we were walking and knelt once to closely observe a tiny "Christmas garden" of dark green moss, light green lichens, greenish gray pixy cups mingled with red "British soldier" lichens. Perhaps because of its northerly exposure this particular power line from here down is alive with beautiful clusters of mosses and lichens.

Ah, November in New England

One of Rowe's many choice spots.

We have neglected to mention the wonderful collection of dry grasses and flowers, goldenrods, asters and ferns that have been all along our route. We repeated our newly learned verse, "Sedges have edges and rushes are round" to our partner and then we promptly found some of each. Perhaps we should take a very leisurely hike someday and sketch them all for later identification. *The world is so full of a number of things...*"

Our descent was more or less gradual as we picked our way down the first section of the hill, taking it in the center and bypassing a stony wood road that went into the woods on the north side. Eventually we came to the spectacular spot, the point of no return at the edge of the cliffs where we looked down on Yankee, Sherman Pond and up the river valley past the surge tank at Harriman and beyond toward the lone high rounded peak and basin in Readsboro, Vermont where hides that mystical place called the "freezin' hole." We took time to admire the view from all angles before we tried to find a way down. Although we had been at this point before, we had forgotten what we did next. We must have missed the entrance to another road around to the north. The cliffs were steep and we knew we must go around rather than down. Checking on the south side, we found another steep but passable old wood road and we waded in a patch of drifted snow toward the woods. With running water under foot we stepped carefully down the road, hanging on to each small tree available in the path. Of course, this path took much longer because

we were admiring all the intriguing rocks and bright patches of evergreen polypody, Christmas and spinulose ferns on the bare hillside above us.

Once back on the power line road we looked up to see the rugged "powerful" hill we had bypassed. It was quite a dramatic

sight; the mighty towers of two highlines perched on the brink above the cliffs carrying away the electricity being produced by nuclear power from Yankee Atomic's large white ball on the river below and by hydropower from New England Power's Bear Swamp powerhouse in the mountain just downriver.

Ahead, we had the choice between the road that dipped lower on the hill or another roadlike shelf that ran along the top. We chose the latter and had a fairly easy walk to the next highpoint. We stopped so often to admire another moss or lichen or dry bouquet or rock or view that the sun had dropped in the west and we were already in the shade. There was still a long ways to go but we just couldn't ignore things and hurry on. *"The world is so full of a number of things..."*

Then there were the elephants. On the next hill we rounded the mountain back into the sunshine, where huge, smooth gray rounded ledges looked for all the world like the elephants lounging in the low afternoon rays of the sun. The hillside was bare as we walked down the last slope into the shadows again where the cool waters of Lord Brook created a winter chill as we stepped carefully across on the rocks and through the remaining snow to the car. Winter in all its glory would surely return, perhaps even tomorrow, but in the meantime we had captured in memory a lovely November Indian Summer afternoon. **12/87**

The Deerfield River at Zoar Gap

Camp Marlynarotha farmhouse

Merritt Peck house

Thoughts For a Cold Afternoon

Today is December 30, 1987 and although the sun is shining brightly, the wind chill factor is hovering between thirty and forty below zero. After one trip to the mailbox, we considered it in our own best interest to remain confined to the fireside instead of venturing out on the Wild Side, as had been our original plan. To calm our disappointment, we looked for something interesting to think about. Ellen Peck Powell's recent letter was sitting there among the Christmas cards in the basket. Her letters always get us to thinking about something. This time it was place names.

Ellen's question from the last *Goal Post* was why the eight hundred or so acres belonging to New England Power "over west" were called the Ethier place when the Pecks had lived there so much longer. Well, we considered that a good question and began to think about it.

We wondered how many there are now who remember the Ethiers . . even though Leo returned recently and cooked the chicken barbecue for Old Home Day as he always did (and sometimes donated the chickens) when he owned a vacation home over on the Peck place. Out of sight, out of mind, you know. Of course, Nettie Peck was town treasurer for twenty years and school committee member for nearly as many years, as well as being active in all sorts of town and church affairs. The Peck family arrived in Rowe before 1850 and stayed around for at least a hundred years. The Ethiers were here give or take ten years but it was fairly recently. So what does one do? Is it the Peck or Ethier place?

At the beginning of the century the same place was known as Camp Marlynarotha, a summer camp established by Martha Peck and Arolyn Johnson. Perhaps the name matter could be settled by calling it Millinery Hill, as two maiden ladies had a hat shop there way back when. But then it might be confused with upper Middletown Hill that also had a hat shop. Even calling it Sunset Hill for one of the Camp Marlynarotha cabins could be confused with Sunset Hill and cabin on Middletown Hill. Actually, it could have been called Nuclear Hill for the area was acquired by the Power Company and considered as an alternative to the Charlestown, Rhode Island site for another atomic generating plant, but that whole project was cancelled along the way. So you see, deciding on the correct names of places can become a terrible problem.

Reading through the Historical Society Bulletins, one is struck by the number of changes in town through the years. In an effort to try to bring houses up to date in the 'sixties and 'seventies and refer to them by their modern owner, one finds in the 'eighties that that owner, too, has moved on and been forgotten and their name attached to a certain house is more obsolete than names of those longer ago, like the Pecks.

We kept a little notebook when Martha Henry was alive, in order to bridge our generation gap of house names. Martha referred to the Rice place below her Wells family farm but of course we knew it as the Jackman's and now it's MacLean. But sometimes that got confused with the other Rice place over west on the way to the Pecks. And now there are four Rice places in Rowe.

Then there was the Amidon place in the village that everyone knew as Aunt Grace Stanford's. It has been the Hazelett and

Hollis and Ruth place (Who were they now? Couldn't have stayed long as generations go.) and the Post Office. Martha Henry solved that house name once and for all when she referred to it as "the brick base" and there is no confusion to this day.

We remember the first house on the right going up King's Highway as the Clifford White place. Someone recently mentioned it as the Johnson house and it took a minute to register in our mind just where they meant. Now it's Hale. Actually it's probably the Moses Rogers place as he may have built it when he ran his corn mill in the 1790s across from the Burton place, or should that be referred to as the Newell or Sibley or Kemp house? It really is the Glass house... but a glass house across the pond from the brick base, you must be kidding.

Walter Miller, after living in town for a few years, asked when their place would finally be known as the Miller place instead of the old Schuler place, which was really the old Magnago place, but actually should be called the Bradley Newell place and is now the Johnson/Sprague farm. See what I mean?

Rick Williams recently bought the Litcoff place that we all know was the Lawrence Bolton place, but then the other Charles Brown's lived there and it really belonged to John Ballou who was postmaster in 1854, but it may have been built by Asa Foster II. Whose place is it anyway? Wonder if it will ever become the old Williams place?

Bob Sittinger lives on the Decker place but some of us still call it the Gregory place and any of the Woffendens know it as their home farm except the old house and barn are gone. Dennis May lives on the Dennis

Williams place but it was really the Ray Berry house and of course the old cellar hole belonged to Cornelius Jones and later became part of the old Ford farm, for which Ford Hill was named. Can't go much further back than that. Lou Beaumier lives in the Codrick house but of course that was the Leshure Estate and Camp Merryfield and there are still those who might remember the Edmund Wilson house before Will Leshure remodeled. And for goodness sake we wish the town would take the "s" off Leshures Road or put in an apostrophe.

Most any place in town could be called the John Woffenden place as he built or rebuilt so many. Take the old Day place for instance. John and Gladys lived there and the Lynchs and the Clements and the Coes and the Garys, but it's now the Reardon place. See how complicated it gets? On the other hand Jane Gracy lives on the old Day place for Stephen Day who ran the satinet factory where the fire station is. The Days and the Knights lived in that two family house, the Deverals in the little house on the north side and the Lords down in the house on the village green. Once again quoting Martha Henry's ditty for remembering house names: "Day and Knight in the same house with the Lord in front and the Devil behind."

Who has the rights of a name? How does one family name stay attached to a certain place? Well, the Cupples/Hageman place on King's Highway ought to be called the Stanford place for a while because members of that family owned it for ninety-eight years but people soon forget. And that could be the Moses Gleason place or the Post Office.

The Doubleday name has done pretty well for a summer home. Of course that is really the Sifton place and that's all it is these days is a nice place with the old house now fallen in the cellar hole. But if you really want to be technical, it is one of the three Cressy places. So where did Struck come in? How come the Knowlton barn still stands on the Soule property on Sibley Road on the old Isaiah Adams Lot? Couldn't that all be combined into one, do we have to remember four names? Then there's the old Todd place which became Rowe Country Club, but if you search the records it's located in the Streeter neighborhood. No, that's up north where Anne Carey built a new house. No, it refers to the old Todd place on Davis Mine Road. Actually, it is a cellar hole facing the Sabrina Rice Trail in Pelham Lake Park.

The Oliver place is really the old Davenport farm except for the Colton apple people who lived there first and maybe some of their old orchard can still be found. But that could be confused with the Van Itallie place that was also a Davenport farm out past the Devil's Elbow on Davenport Road. And then there is the other old Davenport farm that is on Brittingham Hill and is now the Pierce place. But everyone knows the Davenports live on Hazelton Road.

The Community Church parsonage is really the old Furlon house. Now that's cheating when they start moving houses around as well as changing their names! And didn't that used to be the Baptist Church? But Sparky Truesdell lives in the old Baptist church, which was moved from near the west school site and became the Kiley house. How about the brook that runs by the church? We old-timers all know that's the Ide Brown Brook. How'd it get to be called Shippee Brook?

Road names, too, are changeable. The old Bennington Road was the Whitingham Road and now is known as Potter Road because the Shields place where the Wylands used to live was the Potter place when the roads were renamed by Selectman Grant Hartshorn in the nineteen twenties. But really, Middletown Hill could have been Potter Road because Ambrose Potter had a tavern at the Alix place (which is really Fort Pelham Farm) back in the 1780s. But that was later known as the Doctor's house from Dr. Humphrey Gould who lived there although there are those of us who still call it the Wright place even though Miss Neal lived there and it is now Fort Pelham Wood Products sawmill.

Petrie Road was named for the Petries who lived at the old Amidon place which became the Bond place but the road ought to go back to the old name Taylor Road (from the old Taylor family whose cellar hole is by the old yellow rose bush further on in the woods) because the Ed Taylors and the Jim Taylors and the Dick Taylors and Bob Taylor have lived on that road for the last twenty-seven years and who remembers the Petries? Run through that one again. On the other hand, maybe it should be Truesdell Road because Sparky was born in the Amidon house.

We call the road west by the Unitarian Chapel, West Road because Auntie Henry always called it that as she sat in her low rocker by the south window, reporting that another car was "just going out the West Road," (That's when cars were few and far between in Rowe) but today they persist in calling it Hazelton Road for the family who lived in the Truesdell house now a cellar hole out by Laffonds. And believe it or not at the Laffond corner starts Tunnel Road and everyone knows Hoosac Tunnel is seven miles away, well maybe a little closer as the crow flies, and the bottom half of that road is discontinued although John Magnago got lost one day and made it down in a rented Dodge Aries back in 1986. At the bottom nearer the Tunnel there was Rowe's only so-called hotel, the Hoosac Tunnel House, operating during the construction of the Tunnel in the middle 1800s so I guess maybe it was okay to start Tunnel Road back at Lenny Laffonds which was the Essert place after the Quillia's sold out. Tunnel Road must have led to the real action in town down at the hotel in 1860.

The oldest name in Rowe is probably Pelham going back to 1745 when Fort Pelham was built and named after Henry Pelham, first lord of the British Treasury and prime minister of England under George II and he never even lived in Rowe. And neither did John Rowe of Boston for whom the town was mysteriously named when we had requested Exeter. And John Rowe never even gave the town the bell that tradition says he promised us. Then there is still Steele Brook named for the family of William Steele who fought in Shays' Insurrection and was considered a criminal by the town back in 1786.

Adams is a good old name for Adams Mountain. John Adams bought six hundred acres on that mountain from Cornelius Jones back in 1800. Jones founded the town and not a single thing got named after him. What did Adams do to have his name survive so long? Probably never even held a town office. I guess you have to have your name attached to something solid like a mountain. And the mists still rise up there

before a storm which, according to legend, is old John Adams putting on his night-cap indicating a storm is brewing. Well, you'll notice he's still up there watching out that his mountain doesn't get renamed after someone else!

Old cellar holes don't seem to change names. The sightly place for instance is still there but its lovely sight has pretty much grown up to brush. The Mountain Lodge of Masons was born there in 1806 but it's still called the sightly place. The Wheeler-Wilcox cellar hole is a substantial landmark for hikers and snowmobilers on the Old Readsboro Road. Not much danger that will be renamed. And Hosea's Cave down across from Joe King Hill is in danger of being forgotten but not renamed. Old Hosea was a tramp – one of the early homeless I guess you would call him but he liked his cave in the summer and had lots of friends who would give him a meal or two when he called at the door. That's the way it was in the old days.

Then there are place names in Rowe which everyone knows but that are not listed on any map. Take Skeeter Hill for instance. If you had ever skidded on Skeeter Hill you'd remember it down by the old Deerfield Glassine building on the river. And simply "the mountain" – there are lots of places in Rowe on a mountain but when the road crew is out sanding "the mountain" they are down on Monroe Hill Road. And take Joe King. There's a hill named after him because he lived at the Snively place. The road crew and the selectmen know where it is but you can't find that on the map and what's a newcomer to do when confronted with "Meet me at the watering trough on Joe King Hill?" And Rainbow Hill? Where's that? Everyone in seven counties knew where that was when there was a restaurant there back in the 'sixties but try and find that one on a map. It's listed as Brown Road. Well, that's pretty legitimate for Noah Brown built a place up there back when he bought the land in the 1780s. But there were other Browns on Middletown Hill where the Stickneys live on the Murray place. Oh well. And how about Tuttle's Flats? That's where they used to play baseball when Rowe's team was a hot item. No map shows that but there may be a few left who can still remember their own great winning play in a ballgame there.

And Browning Hill. Know where that is? It's on Zoar Road, which is nowhere near Zoar. It divides the upper and lower villages and was named for Mrs. Julia Browning who was a widow (and fondly known as a real character) and kept boarders at the Lehr house which recently was the Stanford house. Julia ought to be remembered. She knew where all the rare wild flowers were and brought bouquets of things like fringed gentians to grace the altar of the Unitarian Church on fall Sundays. The thought was nice but of course out of the sunshine the gentians would all close up and the flowers having been picked would produce no seeds and there would be that many less gentians.

How about Chalk Stone Road? Bet you never heard of that. But look back on some old deeds bordering Monroe Hill Road by the Massachusetts Talc Mine and see what the road is called. That one ought to be revived, it's so descriptive.

Julia Browning

Browning House on Browning Hill

Thoughts For a Cold Afternoon

We should continue Norton's Trail but that, too, has been forgotten. It was the path up over South Mountain from Fort Pelham to Rice's Fort in Charlemont. Norton was the chaplain at the forts and on August 1, 1746 he rode his horse over this path from Fort Shirley in Heath to Rice's and on over Forbidden Mountain to Fort Massachusetts in North Adams for his month's tour there. He was captured by the French and Indians when they destroyed that fort and he was taken captive to Canada. He returned after a year, only to find that his little girl had died and was buried at Fort Shirley in Heath. Let's remember Norton's Trail when we walk up over the old path to the notch on South Mountain instead of paying homage to the king.

One name that is just as well forgotten is Slab City. Rowe Village was known for years as Slab City. They say the name came from all the piles of slabs used as firewood at the old talc mill across from the museum. Slab City Club was an organization sponsoring square dances at the town hall not too many years ago. And another name to forget is Rowe Pond. In years back all the fishermen from around the area knew where Rowe Pond was. But please, it's now Pelham Lake. Pond goes with the word Mill, as in Mill Pond in the village.

Years ago, lots of men worked "down the mill" and everyone knew what they were talking about. Now the mill is closed and a lot of men and women work "down the plant." You know that "plant" that grows uraniums down by the river. Both these places are "down the bridge." Rowe has lots of bridges but "down the bridge" is the Monroe Bridge area, of course, and that is "down the mountain!"

Now let's consider the stores in the village. They started out with one built by Cyrus Ballou right there by the Margaret Barnard Memorial, then it became Uncle Ed Amidon's, only to give way to Ben Henry's, who sold out and it became George Rice's, after which was B. S. Tower and then William Janovsky. Before it got named anything else it burned one winter night. (We remember that because we had the measles at the time and were allowed to emerge from the required complete darkness to quickly look at the smoldering ruins from our front window.) Charlie Newell's store just over the hill from the old store was a neat place in our time and then it became Lynton Martin's and burned to the ground. For nearly forty years we got used to Bjork's Store in the lower village but then they retired and we had no store at all. Thank goodness the Lehrs named theirs the Country Store. Think how much simpler that would have been instead of remembering all those other names. Of course Rowe stores really started in the 1790s at the Old Centre with Ransom and Langdon before the Tuttles built Ford Hall but that's another whole story.

Thanks for listening on this cold afternoon and let's hope the wind subsides in early 1988 so we can get out on the Wild Side, maybe down in The Northwest (which is really on the south side of town) before all this nonsense has to continue. On second thought, maybe we should hike to Siberia. After all this strenuous thinking this afternoon, we've decided that the name for that area over west by the junction of Steele Brook and Tunnel Roads is now officially to be known as the Old Peck Place. Sorry Leo. Squeaky wheel gets the grease. **1/88**

It was too nice a day to be tax collector. The morning sun was streaming in the south window of our cubbyhole office at the town hall and business was brisk, but it was the twenty-second of January coming off the tail end of the January thaw. One shouldn't sit in the office and let that brief respite from winter go unnoticed. We vowed to finish business at noon and, before we could change our mind, called our hiking companion to join us twenty minutes thereafter.

As fate would have it, our last customer needed the most attention, and we were late to start which necessitated a very quick peanut butter and jelly sandwich eaten while we changed into warmer clothes and hiking boots. A late afternoon deadline to be back pushed our schedule even tighter, so another friend was persuaded to be our drop-off and pick-up chauffeur.

Three years ago on a beautiful fall afternoon we had started at the Zoar line and hiked to Vermont on Zoar and Leshure Roads, a distance of six and a half miles. Today, because the woods were treacherous with icy crust, we chose another road hike and, strangely, it measured the exact same distance, this time from the Heath line on Dell Road to Monroe Bridge. There was no turnaround at the Heath line and the little-used road was icy so our friend had to continue to Knott Road to reverse direction, promising to pick us up on the way back if the walking was too hair-raising.

Our watch read five minutes of one as we started toward Rowe picking our way carefully up the tire tracks on the slippery road. As always, it was a special treat to be outside on a lovely winter day and once underway we probably would have crawled on hands and knees before taking a ride as the car passed us a short time later. The sun was warm and the sky bright blue behind the lacy shapes of the overhanging leafless trees. Ice from the recent storm shown like a glass covering along the stone wall to our right but had melted from the tree branches in the warmer sun and breeze of yesterday. Today was cooler, probably in the twenties, but the air was still and our own feeling of warmth or cold fluctuated with the effort required on the ups and downs of the roads, tempered by the appearance and disappearance of the sun behind thick woods.

The first signs of life along this country road were chickadees in the evergreens on either side and animal tracks, enlarged beyond recognition by the ice, coming and going into the woods. A telltale pile of chips at the base of an old maple tree indicated a pileated woodpecker had been busy just recently, boring into the innards looking for a meal of ants and bugs. As we walked along admiring the shiny blanket of snow, it was hard to imagine the lovely stands of ferns, lady's slippers and partridge berries that carpet this roadside in the summer, all now well buried for winter – all except one. The dry stem and ragged remains of blossoms and seed pods of a very special beautiful large, round-leaved orchid by an outcropping of ledge now stood a bit on an angle but still reached above the snow to scatter its seeds in the wind. It was a pleasant surprise to find, in winter, the old friend whose health and growth we carefully check out each summer.

Dell Road climbs the hill from the town line to the Wayne driveway where it joins the old original road between the early forts, Shirley in Heath and Pelham in Rowe, and the main road between the towns when they were first incorporated in 1785. We always listen for echoes from the past and there were many as we traced our way from here to the Old Centre.

Coming out of the woods as we approached the Corarito house (or the old Cornish place) their wonderful western view opened before our eyes. Looking sideways at Todd and Adams Mountain to the left, the view extended across Rowe from Sibley Hill on Hazelton Road to the long expanse of new homes along Potter Road and then back to the hills around the Upper Reservoir and finally leaped the Deerfield to Whitcomb Summit Mountain and beyond where loomed snow-capped Greylock.

Somewhere there in between, we made out the open pasture at the intersection of Monroe and Ford Hill Roads by the Magnago house. If all goes well, we would be rounding that corner before our hike was finished. Looking skyward, we scanned the expanse to find the crescent moon and hoped for a sight of Venus in the daytime, but they had since separated from their close conjunction of the night before. Our elevation at that point was about 1,700 feet. We would drop a couple of hundred feet, climb and drop again, only to climb to new heights of about 1,850 feet at the top of Monroe Hill and descend finally to about 1,100 at the bridge over the Deerfield. Rowe is truly a hilltown.

Our first downgrade took us past the old Waste cellar hole on the left along that lovely stone wall and row of old maples then on to the level by the old Carpenter cellar hole on the right. The old road obviously continued on the left, between the two stone walls, but

that had been abandoned for newer paths. The corner field where Dell joins Cyrus Stage was full of interesting winter bouquets. The tall grasses had turned wheat brown and shone in the sunlight. The first clump of sticks was a variety of open milkweed pods, a few with white streamers still attached. Behind that was another clump of sticks looking like individual tall brown, dried chrysanthemums. These were at first puzzling and intriguing, and we had to brave the crusty snow and inspect them more closely. They still looked like dried chrysanthemums, but were really goldenrod bunch galls formed by a midge, which gets into the leaf bud and stunts the stem growth making the foliage bunch at the top like a flower. It also proves the goldenrod variety for this only happens on Canada goldenrod with a plume-like shape. The third clump of sticks was goldenrod stems covered with ball galls creating little onion-like swellings part way up the stems. These swellings contain the larva of the spotted-winged gall fly that overwinters in the galls. Both these galls are often found in colonies on clusters of goldenrod and these typical examples made for an interesting field of strange winter flowers.

Rounding the corner onto Cyrus Stage Road, rays of sun caught some remaining icy branches and many trees now sparkled in the woods. Our thoughts and eyes then focused on the tall spruce tree by the little cottage cellar hole where the famous painter, John Marin, spent the summer and fall of 1918, his renown evidently unbeknownst to the local populous. He saw and painted our Rowe hills with a different eye but these paintings are now worth thousands of dollars in New York art galleries, even the painting of the little red cottage right here where he stayed has a price tag of twenty grand. We passed by the spot and stopped further down to admire the tall, bare tamarack tree. We looked at it closely with binocs to determine if the things along the branches were cones. Spotting a downed limb in the snow, we climbed over the bank and broke off a couple of small twigs. Sure enough, there were tiny cones securely attached along the bare twigs. We had to stick one in our pocket to bring home for this week's kitchen windowsill collection. Further along, we took time to admire little bouquets of silverrod with blossoms still intact.

At the bottom of the hill, we continued on the wide-open road but looked across at the old Bates-Upson-Tuttle-Blakeslee (did we leave out anybody?) and now Grieco place. "Old Mowing," the sign called the house beside its neighboring pond. We thought of the little book written by the Upsons for their friends telling how they (from Detroit) bought this abandoned farm for a summer place back in 1935. It wasn't actually abandoned but that made the title sound better. Lots of work, sweat, love and enjoyment went into that old farm with the building of the pond and other projects connected with its ownership – lots of water has gone over their pond dam since then.

We walked on up the hill and looked toward Greylock once again. We stopped to count the young pines, hemlocks and spruces, all of which were vying to reforest the roadside banks through which this new highway had been cut several years ago. Descending yet again, we passed the site of the old East School house where the only trace of its existence is in the minds of those who fondly remember it. Our childhood memory has to do with hearing about an awful town row among the parents that stirred up animosities all over town. The school committee decided it was in the best interest of the town to close the East School and send the seventeen or so pupils to the Village School (of course, in those days it seemed to parents like sending their children to Timbuktu). The only effect on me, then a pupil in the Village School, was that our grade had to be moved over to the present Bjork house. As we remember, this arrangement lasted about two weeks when the school committee had to bow to public opinion and reopen this East School. Fortunately, the Great Hurricane of 1938 came shortly afterwards and took folks' minds off school problems. (It needed at least a hurricane to do that!)

Crossing Potter Brook couldn't help but bring to mind the annual spring war whoop from the recent younger generation in Rowe when the word was passed that "the suckers are running" and all took off for Potter Brook with baseball bats. Suckers are large trash fish and seem to be more than plentiful in this particular brook. This spot was also the site of one of the earliest sawmills in Rowe, as lettered on an old map survey dated 1793. Wonder if boys chased suckers back then?

This little corner of town also brought to mind another controversy having to do with a man who lived in a red house over on the right snuggled into the hill just past the brook. His name was George Whitefield D'Vys, and he was a poet of sorts and truly the imposter he was known locally to be, for he claimed to have written "Casey at the Bat." In our book collection we have a little black autographed paperback of his poems called "*Cheering Some One On,*" published in 1933. The following comes to mind:

Casey's Confession
"However did you do it, Jim?"
The fans still at me yell.
So I – to ease my mind a bit –
The secret now will tell.
Just as the pitcher raised the ball,
I saw a-back first base,
The sweetest girl in Mudville
With happy, beaming face.

I saw that she was watching me,
I strained to do my best,
I swung my bat with fearful force,
And – well, you know the rest!
But this I say in closing,
I'm sure beyond a doubt
Had I not seen that pretty girl –
I would have struck out!

Meanwhile, we are back in Rowe walking across town on a lovely winter day that was beginning to show signs of things to come. A mackerel sky had overspread the bright blue, and we stood for a moment discussing the technical difference between "mackerel" and "buttermilk" skies. This one definitely had the flavor of fish. "Tuttle's Corner" this spot was once called for the people living in the big farmhouse, now gone, and down there in the meadow was "Tuttle's Flats", the best ball field in town. Maybe there is more to that Casey story than we know.

But we must hurry on for as poet Robert Frost wrote, "*I have promises to keep, And miles to go before I sleep.*" The uphill now revved up our inner heaters and we unzipped jackets while climbing Ford Hill. Here we were jogged into remembering traveling down this hill the day, as an excited young kid, we were allowed the great treat of riding around the

mail route with old Will Upton in his horse and buggy. The hill was steeper then and a rutty, old dirt road. The horse had to travel slower and hold back, but was rewarded for his gentle efforts with a drink at the round stone watering trough in the middle of the triangle at the bottom.

We passed the Cornelius Jones cellar hole and wondered what he would have thought of the modern solar heat collectors on the May house nearby. Probably be would have been quite impressed, for he was an educated Harvard man. The surrounding woods may have been pretty much the same in Jones's day, for it was only during the farming era of Rowe life that the fields were cleared and used for hay and a wide open view of Pelham Lake was the special feature of this Ford Hill Road route across town. A little breeze had come up and the red Liberty Flag was waving a tattered tail in the wind as we passed by that newly restored triangle.

The Seven Sisters

On down the road, we noted the land where the old military route would have turned into Fort Pelham but we continued on the early route "to the meetinghouse." As we started round the great bend, we suddenly realized something was missing and stopped to look around. The Seven Sisters, those lovely seven white birches which had graced this road for as long as we could remember, were gone, a couple of years now at least, but they had been old friends and we missed them. We walked briskly through the Old Centre, the former village center of Rowe with stores, a tavern, the meeting house, a hat shop and various other amenities needed for a town of over eight hundred souls back in the 1820s and 1830s. Triangles at road intersections have a way of being lost in road widenings and one nice one here by Middletown Hill, said to have had the best wild strawberries in town, has been long gone to provide for faster (safer?) travel. From here, we would follow on a newer road for the old cross-town one of the 1780s dropped down Middletown Hill and turned west in front of the Alix house and later followed the west course of Hazelton Road. "Bernie" Williams barked and wagged a hello as we started down one more hill nearer our destination.

The low riding sun of winter was lost behind the evergreens on the left and the continuing slight breeze made us rezip the jackets. We skidded to the side of the road when a large oil truck slowly came down the hill behind us. It came to a stop and the man inquired directions to Readsboro. We described Monroe Hill and bridge, and he took off as if the light had suddenly dawned as to where he was.

Down at the bottom of this hill, we began our final ascent on this cross-town trek. In the dip by Shippee Brook we passed the old Center School now a livable cottage. Here they didn't move the pupils, they moved the whole school building from its perch further up the hill to a more secure location on the level, then it, too, was abandoned, but that was before our time.

It was good to see some more animal life about when Deb Larned's horse acknowledged our passing as he wandered on his well-worn snowy path. Further on we stopped to scan the swamp, but it was frozen solid and not even a beaver trail was evident. We thought of the open Upper Reservoir where, a day or so before, we had scared up two ducks and eight Canada geese. We wondered if they were our summer resident geese who had raised three babies at Pelham Lake. We had never seen them winter in the area before.

The farm scene as we approached the Spragues' was a highlight. Several Beefalo and whiteface Herefords with their heavy winter coats were milling about the barnyard and some were eating at the hayracks. The big old bull certainly had the characteristics of a buffalo only much lighter colored. Kathy's Morgan stallion was there, too. All were curious and turned to watch us as we enjoyed watching them. It was good to know that Rowe still had animals in such a friendly barnyard scene.

Pushing on, we looked along the roadside for any hint of the very early coltsfoot which blossoms here, but it would take more than the recent January thaw to stir its frozen roots. On attaining the Magnago Corner, we turned to look east and see the Corarito house and the open expanse of Dell Road where we had passed not so very long ago and congratulated ourselves on our progress. Taking a deep breath, we turned the corner onto Monroe Hill Road and continued up the hill pointing out the remains of a large wild clematis vine or old man's beard twining around a bush.

The air was definitely cooler with the sun behind the hill as we started our long descent down Monroe Hill. Chickadees were again numerous in the evergreens overhead and the view was toward Haystack in Vermont and the mountains surrounding the "freezin' hole" in Readsboro. Before the present road was rebuilt for the Yankee traffic, Rowe men working at the paper mill used to walk down and up this mountain every day in winter. That was back in those "good old days" everyone always wants to return to!

Skeeter Hill took us on the final downgrade to the bridge, and we checked our watch at just quarter after three. There were only a few minutes for us to watch the Deerfield water rush under the bridge and to look over the fast decaying paper mill before our chauffeur appeared around the corner. Pretty good timing, we thought, on a cross-town hike in this hill country. **2/88**

Conquering Stress

D o you ever wonder how many forms of relaxation there are in this world – expensive hobbies, sports of all descriptions and creative crafts enough to keep us all busy and relaxed? Well, we have to admit we have found yet another new and strange form of relaxation which makes us forget all our other stressful projects and deadlines and this therapy costs nary a penny. Like the song title, it is called "Blowing in the Wind." We practice this sport in a swamp, preferably while out on the Wild Side in winter.

We had just arrived after a three-hour drive from New Hampshire early on this February Monday morning, rushing home with an impending *Goal Post* deadline hanging over our head. Thoughts of sitting right down at the computer for the rest of the day didn't appeal at all! As we unloaded the snowshoes from the back of the car we had a great idea. How about a quick trip into our favorite swamp off Cyrus Stage Road? Checking the computer, fortunately we found that our fellow editor had things well under control, so we quickly bundled up and drove off with fewer feelings of guilt at neglecting our job for a few hours.

We hadn't seen a single snow flea all winter and in lieu of any other purpose, we started looking for them around big old trees as we bushwhacked our way to the old gravel bank road. We had gone this route many times but the snow was deeper than usual and we had to duck for branches we normally walked under, losing our hat more than once. After investigating several trees, we realized that snow fleas like warm winter days and although sunny, today was windy and cold.

Snowshoes are a wonderful way to travel and we always enjoy them with a couple of ski poles for balance. We would have had a better trip today if we had taken time to properly fix the harness across our boot; something was drastically wrong and one heel strap kept coming off. Because we were in a hurry, we continued to shuffle along without fixing it.

How many times had we circled this swamp in summers past to get a better look at the nesting herons or the Canada goose hidden on the beaver lodge or walked the tightrope across the beaver dam to save going downstream to cross the brook? Cold winter air had created a miracle. We could walk on water all over the swamp and admire the driftwood silver gray of the old dead trees with their grotesque shapes, each with an individual character, and most covered with silver and green lichens and moss. Now and then a group of red British soldier lichens grew out of a high stump. We could poke our fingers into the holes in the trees to feel the old nests of swallows, and best of all, we could stand right under the one remaining flimsy stick nest of the great blue herons and remember the young we had watched as they stood patiently waiting to be fed by big graceful parents.

We searched the bit of open water by the dam but saw no sign of life, no tracks on the frozen snow and no otter hole under the ice. If we did not know better, we could easily say this was a dead and lonely place. But we knew there was a multitude of hidden life under the snow and ice. We sidetracked up the hill a bit to examine new beaver gnawings on a tall ash tree. Back on the ice, we realized that we had bypassed the beaver lodge and had to go back and climb to the top and feel for the warmth coming up through breathing holes between the sticks. The warmth from the beaver family far down within was creating crystals in the snow, indicating that at least some inhabitants were alive and well in this seemingly uninhabited place. Standing straight, we looked around and felt like a child playing king of the mountain as we stood tall on the beaver house. Bending to fix our straps again, we noticed that there were faint tracks of a predator that had also recently checked the beaver family and marked out his territory by leaving a patch of yellow snow.

Moving on, we took the binocs to look closer at the wonderful old wolf tree ahead on the south shore. We always expect to see an owl perched above the large hole near the top or a raccoon licking his chops after a meal of fish, but have yet to spot any occupants. When there is nothing stirring here, this is a swamp of memories.

We can close our eyes and see the red and blue darning needles flitting across the water, and hear the birds in song, like the rose-breasted grosbeak who was so vocal one happy morning, and taste the wintergreen of the numerous fat checkerberries along the shore, or envision the blanket of pink and white spring beauties in blossom on the western hillside or remember the deer that to our surprise came wading up to its shoulders in the murky water and proceeded to browse, moose style, for goodies underwater or think back to the night the old beaver came swimming toward us as we sat quietly watching the sunset twilight deepen into a starry evening. A gust of wintry wind woke us from our spring and summer reverie and we shuffled on toward the upper pond, delighting in the myriad patterns of drifted

snow like the sands on the ocean shore.

The below zero temperatures of January and February had solidly frozen the ice and even the running water between the ponds had a heavy transparent sheet of ice too tough to be broken by the ski pole, which we poked on top to watch the water bubbles move like amoeba underneath. Usually there are many tracks here but today the area was barren of these signs, but only because the snow was also frozen and did not record the impressions of little feet. We realized this when walking further back among the cattails where there was a short section of soft powder snow full of the usual goings and comings of the local population.

And this brings us to the location of our very special playground, today enhanced by gusty winds from across the ice to the rear. It was to be like eating potato chips: you can't eat just one, or like blueberrying where you have to pick one more handful, or like jack-in-the-pulpits in the spring when you have the urge to lift the cover on just one more to see if there really is a jack inside.

The cinnamon brown flower heads of the cattails which one finds in abundance in most every swamp are the culprits of our addiction. They are usually out in the water, too far to tramp without boots. Winter ice creates the ideal situation and, of course, by then the cattails are mature and dry and ready to be blowing in the wind. There is a real knack to our sport and it does take practice to get just the right magic results. No matter the temperature, our pastime is best performed with bare hands.

We approached our first cattail sort of casually, trying not to show our excitement and enthusiasm. It takes a good grip to do

fingers and wrapping around your wrist. The inside of the cattail becomes the outside of your new glove with the most beautiful soft reddish brown color and soft consistency. As you stand amazed, looking at this lovely creation, it gradually continues to move and spread and, if you are lucky, like today with a gusty wind, it starts to blow away, winged seed by seed blowing in the wind.

Today the winds were special; we could raise or move our hand of fluff so it would catch the wind and spiral up in great cattail devils like the dust devils of western prairie lands or blow straight out in tunnel-like fashion, then suddenly another gust would whip the flying seeds (all 125,000 per blossom) en mass high into the pines along the shore. It was better than flying a kite, to see how the next one could be maneuvered to create the most interesting pattern. Once we were looking close at an especially lovely glove in our hand when a gust of wind from a cross-direction blew the whole thing in our face and we must have looked like the bearded wonder as the fuzz stuck to our chin and nose and eyebrows

Forgetting everything except the beauty and freedom of movement and the joy of watching each new unfolding and the bizarre design of our cattail seeds blowing in the wind, we played for nearly an hour. Suddenly coming back to reality, we sort of sheepishly looked around, hoping no one had been watching our childlike antics. Relaxed beyond words, we bent once again to secure our snowshoes and climbed up the bank toward home still looking for the elusive snow fleas along the way. **3/88**

it properly and, with one motion, split the blossom down the side, pulling it off the stem and quickly turning your hand palm side up. If the flowers heads are not dry enough, they come off as a handful of fluff and have to be discarded. Our first one today was a dud and we moved on to a choicer group to try again. If you do it just right, the amazing phenomenon happens – the cattail opens and, like magic, creeps across your hand forming a glove around your

Rushing the Season

Rushing the season was what it was, pure and simple. The Boston news had reported their local skunk cabbage in blossom and, not to be outdone by the city folks, we prepared to march on Rowe's only known natural colony on the Deerfield. (Alton Davenport has some skunk cabbage that he transplanted from elsewhere, but in his yard on top of the mountain, it must be still under snow, for he had promised to call us when it appeared.) Anyway, our flower-identifying partner was here from New Hampshire and we were itching get out on the Wild Side.

It was a cool, windy March 11th but the sun was shining and we knew that 1,000 feet or so lower down on the Deerfield it certainly would be spring and we dressed accordingly. Our partner still hasn't gotten thoroughly warmed up ever since!

We parked the car at the Thunder Bridge and started off up through Zoar Gap beside the railroad. The river water was flowing well and we quickly admired the arched rock and noted our passage across the town line into Rowe. There is a slight bend in the railroad that follows the contour of the mountain and as we emerged with a view straight up the tracks, there came a tremendous roar down through the valley, reaching a crescendo at the gap where we were. No train, no plane but just the wind raging out of the northwest and coming straight down the river slamming into the mountain west of the gap then whirling itself across the river nearly knocking us over in the process. We stood for a moment awe-inspired and fascinated as we shivered with the piercing cold.

Suddenly a passage in a book, the identification of which we cannot yet remember, came to mind, describing a strange wind condition in the gap at Zoar. We certainly had witnessed the phenomenon in person. The river, after many twists and turns, flows directly north and south here. Looking north on top of the mountain, one sees the dike at the Bear Swamp Upper Reservoir. This special wind from the northwest now whips across the water above, then quickly funnels a thousand feet down into the river valley. As we stood watching, sheets of spray like at the ocean blew off the river surface. Once in a while, a gust was in a slightly different direction and didn't get caught up in the funnel but roared and bounced off the mountaintops far above our heads. Then all would be calm and quiet for a few moments until another gust came blasting down the funnel.

If we were ever to stay warm, we had to move ourselves quickly and of course the skunk cabbage was there ahead, just pulling us along. As soon as there was level land along the river, we ran down the bank into the snow to explore the territory. A colony of beaver had taken up residence there and made several tiny dams along the side flow of high water from the river and some drainage from the mountain. With a fluctuating river level, the beaver must be in a continual state of confusion as to just what they are doing wrong with their dams. Several trees were white at the base where they had been gnawed. Instead of working until they felled one tree, they seemed to have tasted them all.

Just before crossing one of the dams, we stopped to admire nature's artistry in the patterns on the thin sheets of ice clinging to the edges of the little pond. Such fleeting beauty, waiting to be appreciated before it melts into oblivion! We searched the river edge where bare ground had appeared in the spring sun or been washed by the river but nothing growing caught our eye – except something overhead. We looked up into the blue sky to watch a red-tailed hawk riding the air currents. Once in awhile his pace was quickened by the gusty wind but mostly he stayed above the swirling funnel of air in the valley, his red tail flickering in the sunlight as he occasionally soared, dipping one wing downward. On the upper end of our little island, we stood at water's edge to watch again the flying white caps on the flat, rocky river. Up on the mountain to our right, we could see the scars of the various landslides that have wiped a great deal of the soil off the steep landscape, probably creating the islands of land where we were walking.

Crossing the water again, we came out on the open stretch where stood grotesque remains of sumac bushes on the bank of the river. Here we concluded we were not in skunk cabbage territory and climbed back to the railroad level, still keeping one eye on any bare ground along the river. Spotting a dry, three-pronged lily head with capsules, we made a mental note to return and check it out come July.

We knew just where we were headed. We had found the large leaves of the skunk cabbage one summer day after a hike down the ravine from Tunnel Road. We had walked a ways on the railroad, then dropped down to the land by the river just after Beaver Island. It was a jungle in the middle of the summer but after wading shoulder high in ferns, vines and goldenrod, we noticed some large leaves at our feet under a clump of alders. A little digging with our fingers and we readily identified our first specimen of skunk cabbage in Rowe.

Skunk cabbage is a strange plant, especially in early spring when the temperature is above freezing. Its new, emerging flower buds enclosed in a purplish spathe actually create heat to melt the snow around them, and as they progress, the heat may release chemicals which attract pollinators. The temperature can be a fairly constant 70 degrees inside the spathe or covering of the blossom! Undisturbed, a skunk cabbage plant may live indefinitely, and conceivably could be older than some of our ancient maples and hemlocks. Although no books tell us this, we believe skunk cabbage is a plant of lower elevations, as we have not found it along our mountain streams where what is locally referred to by old timers as "skunk cabbage" is really false hellebore, a very poisonous plant if consumed.

So you see why we were excited to finally reach the point of land where we knew this weird plant was waiting for us – or was it? The snow was deep and drifted but fairly solid as we climbed down from the tracks to the left once again. This area was full of brambles and we dodged them as best we could. The fertile fronds of hundreds of ostrich ferns stood above the snow like candles on a white frosted cake, each making a hole in the snow around its stem where it had rubbed when blown in the wind, scattering brown spores on the white snow. From this first vantage point, we could see the deep snow cover over the area where the skunk cabbage should be. Walking closer to the clump of alders, we saw a little bare ground where it was wet but the rest of the land was hidden under one or two feet of drifted snow! What's all this nonsense about skunk cabbage being 70 degrees and melting the snow? It's enough to make you lose faith in the guidebooks with all their Latin names!

Our partner roamed the area to see if perhaps we were in the wrong place, but we stuck to the alders and whacked our boot around squares of snow to cut off chunks lifting them up to see what was underneath. Finally we had to take off the gloves and freeze our fingers, digging under the snow. We came up with a solid rootstock of a fern and could see the tiny green fiddleheads, smaller than a dime, all furled and waiting for warmer weather. Our pawing in the cold snow and wet soil only elicited chuckles and head shakes from our partner, still shivering from the wind as she returned with her prize, a small beaver skull with its two long curved, brown teeth.

After a short conference, we concluded that even though other places sport skunk

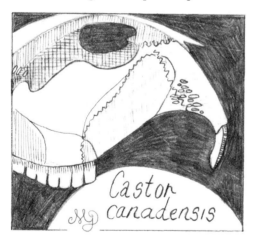

Castor canadensis

cabbage in February, we were still pushing the season to be looking for it by March 11th. Next week for sure!

We walked across even deeper snow, jumped a brook and came out a little farther

down on the railroad. This time we walked back on the snow-covered roadway. We soon discovered that it was a turkey super highway, covered with tracks all going in the same fairly straight direction until something interesting seemingly took their eye and the tracks would veer left or right or go in a circle, only to continue on in a forward direction. The turkeys must have passed by on a quieter day, for today they would be blown in the river for sure!

Water tumbling down a small ravine made by one of the early landslides, intrigued us and we stopped to look at the myriad of ice diamonds, shining in the sun. Climbing up a ways, we were fascinated by an ice chandelier formed by the splash of water on a rock that continually sprayed a fallen branch in the brook. It was obeying some law of ice formation in which hundreds of little balls were forming by enlarging around each drop on every twig and branch. It gave the impression of a beautiful crystal chandelier with the sun sparkling on every curve. A small log across the brook had homemade tallow candles of ice hanging all along its lower surface. Another intriguing law of ice formation.

The wind was at our back now, still roaring over our heads and blowing the spray off the river as we quickly headed home following turkey tracks etched in ice and mentally planning our strategy for the next skunk cabbage escapade.

* * * * *

It was a week and three days before the opportunity came again. In the meantime we had attended a rare plant conference in Sudbury and got all fired up for spring and summer plant searching and, having had lunch that day in shirt-sleeves on a warm, bare hillside, we had absolutely no conception that our skunk cabbage would still be buried in the snow.

Monday the 21st our newly designated plant photographer called to say that time's a'wasting and we'd better hit the trail to both the coltsfoot (found at the switching station last year on March 23 and already in blossom in Charlemont this year) and the skunk cabbage. We alerted our regular hiking partner and were soon all under way to the switching station by car. We stood, unbelieving with our mouths open looking up and down the roadsides at the snow. Not a coltsfoot shoot in sight. Foiled again! We headed south for the river.

The day was perfect, warm and comfortable — a world apart from our last trek along the Deerfield. We lingered, looking at the well-worn rocks with potholes in the river, which was exceptionally low, probably to accommodate the loader that was installing riprap under the span of the new Florida Bridge. We could look through the hole in the high arched rock and wondered why recognition has never been given to this interesting landmark. Rare plants and animal species are being protected, why not rocks? Nathaniel Hawthorne likened this natural arch to the "doorway to an old-world cathedral" back in 1838.

It was interesting to contemplate what the flow of the river might have been back before the power company dams. It probably was much like today, for a horse and wagon could easily splash across in several locations. We looked up at the mountain across the way to trace the steep route of the old shunpike up over Forbidden Mountain, used in the days when paying a toll to travel this easier route was costly to the early settlers.

We didn't waste much more time and kept marching enthusiastically on down toward the skunk cabbage. We had wasted time earlier this morning, looking for a small thermometer to check for this mythical 70 degrees in the skunk cabbage blossom, so, in addition to lunch, we sported two thermometers. We were well equipped, to say nothing of the photographic equipment to record the find.

Well, many good plans go astray. Let me tell you about our great picnic sitting on the rocks at the bottom of Ravine Brook. We don't need to belabor the point — the skunk cabbage was still under a foot of snow and even our digging of the previous week hadn't opened up any new channels. We were still rushing the season and we finally had to admit it. Even the pussy willows, which we picked, didn't really have much fur!

Lunch consisted of fat ham and cheese sandwiches with special mustard, pickles, oranges and some of those yummy Rowe chocolate chip cookies. What more could we ask for on a lovely March day? Not being one to give up easily, during lunch we were sure there must be early yellow violets on the hillside above, and we tried a little poking around, but it only convinced us that, as much as we tried to hurry it along, spring was yet to come!

Heading home along the railroad tracks, we contented ourselves by noting the bright green rosettes of the prolific weed, peppergrass, and chased a real live butterfly. We were also thinking that this time we'd go home and wait for that call from Alton. **4/88**

Is It Spring Yet?

It was a spur of the moment sort of trial run. April 13th should be too early for wildflowers but the weather had been warm and we were anxious to just get out in the woods and watch things grow. We planned to return at the end of April for our real Wild Side hike. But here it is the end of April with miserable cold rainy weather, and looking back, nothing is ever quite like the very first sight of all those spring goodies poking holes in their winter blanket of fallen leaves, pushing their heads right up into the spring sunshine, sometimes raising several dry leaves as collars.

Our hiking partner followed with her car, and we optimistically left one car by the picnic area just before the new bridge construction on the way to Hoosac Tunnel, then drove on, starting our hike just across the iron bridge and railroad on the Rowe side. It was a lovely day, cool but no breeze, and the sun was warm on our backs as we headed down the road along the tracks. The trees were leafless, so we soon decided the sun would be just as warm in the woods and took the short path up to the old Tunnel Road. It wasn't long before a clump of budded red trillium took our attention. These first appear distinctly pointed and gradually unfurl three diamond-shaped leaves, with the green bud remaining sharply pointed. When blossomed, the leaves continue to grow very large. That is the fun of this business on the Wild Side, trying to identify each plant and flower in various stages from its first appearance in the spring, to blossoming, maturity in its fruiting stage, and lastly, its dry brown stems and often seedpods of winter. Each stage is unique, beautiful and often very different from the previous one.

Rocks and ledges at the base of this mountain are spectacular along this old road and we took time to appreciate their varied color, created not only by the minerals in the rocks but also by their covering of lichens. Once in a while, we would put our hand on a huge outcropping and feel its texture and strength, sometimes finding garnets under our fingers. As we went up over the high point in the road, we could look down on a full river flowing swiftly over the rocks, muffling the sound of the approaching westbound train that suddenly appeared on the tracks just below us. After a few gondola cars went by, we realized that this was the special train we have wanted to see for years – the "Unit Train" of all gondola cars which goes weekly from the coal fields of West Virginia to the coal-fired electric generating station at Bow, New Hampshire. These destinations used to be stated on the front of the engine. We could not see the engine front from our high vantage point, so cannot state with certainty that the train still comes from West Virginia, but certainly coal for Bow, New Hampshire is still its purpose. We had always wanted to see the full coal train go by on Sunday afternoons, but now finally seeing it as the empty returning on Wednesday morning, was almost as good. The railroad is still a fascinating part of American life, right here in Rowe!

On over the hill, the good stuff soon came into view. There is an abrupt change in the soil from laurel-loving acid to rich and mildly limy nearer the old Soapstone Quarry. The first view was of the bright green leeks on every slope among the rocks and damp springs of the hillside. Spring just wouldn't be the same without this wonderful treat of sight and smell and heavenly taste of leeks right out of the ground. But between us and the leeks, we found more budded trillium, spring beauties blossomed in their finest pink and white, dainty leaves and tiny buds of Dutchman's britches and squirrel corn, and everywhere budded toothwort, which later will create a carpet of white blossoms. We always agonize over the Dutchman's britches and squirrel corn for the leaves look exactly alike. This time we thought the squirrel corn was a little purplish on the underside, or was it the other way around? The flowers are different and the heart-shaped squirrel corn is quite fragrant and has yellow corn-like corms at the base of the root. These plants are scattered, while the Dutchman's tend to grow in clumps. Both are lovely and totally disappear after blossoming and dispersing their seeds.

We looked for the small stand of narrow-leaved spleenwort fern and found the circular fiddleheads just unfolding above ground. It is such fun finding old friends in the same hideouts year after year. Which thought reminded us to look for the single plant of rare yellow trillium that was up and budded in its special place. After checking out all the favorite spots here, we just had to dig our first leeks. They have two long bright green leaves and way down in the ground, usually tangled around rocks or tree roots, is the succulent little prize white bulb reeking an oniony smell. After breaking several fingernails and getting our hands well worked in the dirt twisting the plant, digging and pulling, we loosen the bulb from its deeper, stringy roots and, if we are fortunate, pull it out whole! If we didn't have to work so hard pulling leeks, they probably wouldn't taste half as good.

After each of us acquired a good handful, we took them to the small stream to wash off the dirt on the leeks and clean and soothe our sore fingers. This early in the year, the leeks were quite small which we both agreed, standing there over the brook, made the flavor even more delicate and absolutely the most delicious morsel we had eaten since last spring! So it goes with the loyal cult of leek-lovers.

We went on up the brook, climbing over and around windfall limbs of winter and soon spotted our first yellow violets. Once we started looking, these tiny precious flowers were everywhere, blending into the pale orange and brown leaf cover on the forest floor. In the spring, the leaves are smaller than the tiny flowers but later in the summer, they can be spotted as large green patches of big leaves which one would never suspect as belonging to these dainty spring violets. We looked along the brook for the large dark fiddleheads of Goldie's fern but they were not yet raising their heads.

One of our most important reasons for this early spring trek was to see the hepaticas, which always win the race for early blossoming and are often gone by the time we venture their way. This does not always disappoint us, for their later soft, new growth of fuzzy leaves is almost as lovely to behold in a large clump as the flowers. We climbed the special hill and found them all again – a few already dropping petals. We admired each new cluster of white blossoms and especially one cluster of blue ones. After this treat, we dropped back down the hill across the road to some of our most favorite spots and climbed over and around the rocks to see Canada and downy yellow violets above ground and budded, and weirdest of all, the blue cohosh that comes up a dark bluish purple with uncurling fingers of leaves and, yes, even blossoms of the same color with tiny yellow centers. In a few days you would see the cohosh and wonder what we were talking about, for it soon turns ordinary green with blue flowers. Just beyond the cohosh, we hurried on to see more lovely clumps of hepaticas, waving happy faces in the sunshine. Then, climbing around the huge rocks, we found the red columbine leaves in their own special places in pockets and on shelves of the boulders.

From there we followed our traditional route up over the rocks through more cohosh and trillium to descend through the leeks into a tiny rock dingle, where we found the heart-shaped green leaves of wild ginger unfolding over their funny, little reddish-brown flower just appearing at ground level. This always necessitates a tug to loosen a root to smell and taste its pungent ginger flavor. We searched for the delicate maidenhair fern but it, too, had declined to call it spring just yet. On the wall of ledge, we checked out the little circles of evergreen maidenhair spleenwort fern in the nooks and crannies and took note of the small section of fibrous asbestos in the serpentine rock. Looking close we found the first early-blossomed saxifrage, although the plant was hardly an inch high!

Up out of the dingle, we looked on the ground along another special rock to see the tiny plants of dwarf ginseng up and budded. The sun was so warm and the area so peaceful and inviting, we were happy to realize that it was lunchtime. We started to sit on a long fallen log then decided to climb a little higher and sit on a rock facing downhill. From there we were able to observe this lovely area of rocks, open hillside and the emerging loveliness of spring. What we were really anticipating was the ham sandwich stuffed with fresh leeks. Wow! Celery and carrot sticks and grapes from our partner's knapsack also hit the spot. We had brought along some tangy cucumbers in vinegar, which we usually appreciated on a picnic, but today they were too strong and not good at all in competition with the leeks.

As we sat munching, two red-tailed hawks could be heard screaming overhead, and we watched them through the trees as they rode the air currents high above. And then as a special treat, that tiny little winter wren which we love, burst forth in song in the gully below. These wrens seem to be getting more numerous for we have already heard a couple this spring. They always used to hide in faraway brook valleys. We sat so long enjoying the scene that our left leg went to sleep, and we had to get up and exercise, endure the limpness and then the prickles until we had the blood flowing once again.

The next adventure took us through the brambles back up to Tunnel Road to see if the large patch of white was really a rock or the unmelted river of ice it looked like. It proved to be just a lovely ribbon of white quartz. Once on the road, we walked up a little further to admire the highest section of ledges and noticed once again that these woods were bare of the good stuff. No green leeks outlined the rocks, but as we thought about it, this acid soil later produces lovely laurel blossoms, large clumps of blue and white violets, lady's slippers and other orchids, so we'd best not be too critical just because early spring is not its prime time.

Our destination, as you know, was to return to Florida Bridge, so we had a rather long haul ahead of us. We decided to brave more brambles and go cross-lots down the hill, picking up another old wood road also thick with brambles. The thorns scratched our jacket, caught in our hair and rubbed across our ankles as we tried to step on them. There is just no easy way to attack such things; one must just endure if you must pass their way.

Soon we spotted a tiny, funny-looking clump of green on the grassy roadway. Looking closer with the magnifying lens, we could see little buds on the leafy stems, all very tiny. We finally dug the clump, about an inch wide, with our fingers and stuffed it in our pocket. It must be something common (or we would not have removed it) like chickweed, but it intrigued us for some reason. At home, we put it in a little salt dish in water on our sunny windowsill over the sink (which is always full of strange things in pots of water) and were still mystified when our wildflower-identifying partner appeared on the scene. It was the first order of business to show her this strange clump and explain how we had spent the week trying to identify it. We were a little insulted when she burst out laughing. She explained that she had done the same thing herself before she identified these little budded rosettes herself in spring a couple years ago. As we said at the start, it is fun to see things in different seasons, in different shapes and forms beyond the familiar. So I will tell you that the contents of my little salt dish have grown and blossomed into a sweet little bouquet of bluets! Live and learn, on the Wild Side.

After the brambles, we came to a mass of destructive grapevines and then a collection of very large, old dry brown plants with rather hollow stems. It took a few minutes but we figured these out as old pokeberry bushes, which must have been huge. After this we passed through an old gateway in a stone wall, which went on off up the mountain. It made us stop and realize that this old Tunnel Road area was a thriving section of Rowe farms back in the 1800s. Now it is deserted except as trails for dirt bikes and ATVs, whose tracks were well in evidence as we rejoined the lower road toward the brook.

Rather than dropping through more brush to the railroad, we picked our way across the fast flowing, clear mountain stream and scrambled up the hill to the continuing old wood road along a nice section of open woods, again bare of any early spring goodies. At one point, we climbed further up the hill to check out the lay of the land inside an old three-sided stonewall section. These open woods at this height did sport lots of yellow violets. Once getting our bearings, we joined the road again and followed it to a familiar curving stone wall where we knew we could drop down to the railroad near Soapstone Switch. We had come up this gully many times, but going down on very slippery leaves was another matter. About halfway down, we anchored ourselves to watch another train, eastbound, rumbling across the Soapstone Switch below us and, seeming to gain speed, roared ever faster down the track rounding the great curve by Beaver Island. This one was full of new cars tugging at their chains as the big, open carriers bounced over the switching area. When the train was gone, we maneuvered down the rest of the hill by sitting and sliding our way to the bottom.

Once out in the open, we shook ourselves out, adjusted knapsacks and proceeded to meander down along the railroad, spotting

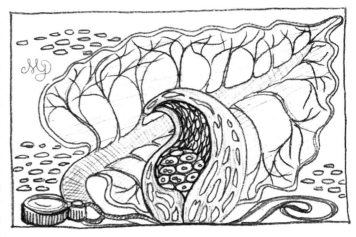

more Dutchman's and a good collection of cut-leaved toothwort at the bottom of Ravine Brook. Our partner was excited because she knew today's proposed venture was going to take us past the skunk cabbage site and, having been on last month's unsuccessful exploration in that vicinity, her curiosity was high, as was our own. As soon as the land widened out toward Beaver Island, we dropped down off the tracks along the river. One large stem and bent, pointed bud of false Solomon's seal was about a foot and a half high. They always draw our attention for they look so important, as if they were going to blossom into something very rare and special, when actually they are pretty but a dime a dozen! The rest of the land was rather dry and barren, and even the prevalent ostrich fern was still hiding its fiddleheads. More brambles slowed our pace but we soon were near the special stand of alders scanning the ground for skunk cabbage.

Well, by golly there it was at last! Very unimpressive blossoms only four or five inches high, blending well into the muck from which they were growing. We had been off our expected location by only a few feet. We immediately stuck our finger inside one blossom to feel its unique warmth, but it was as cool as the air and the texture of the blossom was a bit dry. We concluded that sometime in the three weeks between our March 21st visit and today, April 13th, the Rowe skunk cabbage had already done its thing about warming up, attracting insects and getting pollinated. It was now gone by. We were disappointed at this and our partner was totally unimpressed with the blossom size. We both had had big imaginations in this respect! The leaves, we know for sure, do grow very large. We counted the plants and found nine or ten, only half of which had blossoms, the rest being just a pointed spike of furled leaves. It was also interesting to find in close proximity shoots of false hellebore that along our hilltown brooks is often erroneously also referred to as skunk cabbage. Again we live and learn something new by observation, on the Wild Side.

Homeward bound along the tracks, we enjoyed the bright blossoms of several red maples near the river and took note of the little beaver ponds now flooded with high water. At the bridge, we were greeted by several kayakers preparing for an afternoon of fun and videotaping at the Gap. "Oh," they said spotting our binoculars, "you've been birding."

"Well, yes and no," we answered, "we've also been wildflowering and leeking, on the Wild Side." **5/88**

A Bear Story

«𝓣he bear went over the mountain…»

Well, it was really just a little gully, but hold on – we're getting ahead of our story.

You know by now that we have our favorite places at certain times of the year and that list of choice spots keeps getting larger as we find new treasures in the woods and fields of our local hills and valleys. You also know that we are partial to Rowe, but when it comes Memorial Day time we have an annual urge to go over the border into Vermont and observe one of the loveliest hillsides in the area. Such a memorable sight gives us food for dreams on many a nasty, cold winter day.

May 1988 has not been very cooperative. Rain, rain and more rain has kept us inside and the threat of thunder showers has kept us close to home when there has been a small break in the clouds. Early one foggy morning, we did run over on the Peck place and chase halfway down the mountain to check an orchid we had seen earlier in the month. The buds were still not open, but were advanced enough for us to determine that we had found something new, Hooker's orchid, a much smaller version of the large round-leaved orchid with leaves that grow up instead of flat on the ground. This orchid, found among the laurel where

we never expect to find anything of note, only proves you have to keep your eyes open and mind alert or you'll miss a lot out on the Wild Side!

Monday, May 23rd, our deadline, had to be a good day or we would have to go out and sit in the dooryard and describe the raindrops for this Wild Side. After the early morning fog burned off in that strange, new light called sunshine, we packed a lunch and the usual paraphernalia in the knapsack and waited for the arrival of our hiking partner.

We were crossing the suspension bridge over the Deerfield to Harriman Hydro Station in Whitingham, Vermont just at ten-thirty.

Our first detour was to the lovely, blossoming lilac hedge on our left. Reaching up, we drew the lowest branch to our noses and inhaled that wonderful, fleeting perfume of spring. It took several whiffs to satisfy us before we proceeded along the driveway and climbed the bank to the road. Doubling back toward the station, we took our usual route, climbing another bank and ledge to the upper road. With this route we could check out that funny yellow lousewort or wood betony with its unusual, arched flowers and fernlike leaves that grows along the hill. As we passed behind Harriman Station, we admired its style with the four corner gargoyles and other architectural decoration of a bygone era – early 1900s. It was pleasing to see this gem of the past still generating power from the great reservoir of Harriman Lake behind the mountain, on whose side the huge, strange, dark surge tank loomed above us.

Along the road, we looked at the big leaves of gone-by bloodroot and the just blossoming, pink wild geraniums. But this is really the road of birds and we could have spent the next several hours chasing warblers with binocs. They sang loudly and often but hid nicely in the middle of new foliage. One should carry a tape of birdcalls instead of the picture book. We always come especially to see wildflowers – warbler identification often gets left for next time.

Our first treat was a Baltimore oriole, who usually sings on a high conspicuous limb but this one seemed to be especially pleased to sing and show off for our appreciation. The trees were full of birds, and all along the way, we were rewarded with various short musical notes and the almost continuous song of the red-eyed vireo. Off in the woods, we could hear the least flycatcher's incessant "chebec," bringing back memories of our high school geometry exam, which had to be taken with the background music of this constant chebec outside an open window.

Today was already warm and very humid. The water flowing over the mossy rocks of the little brook that comes down over a white limestone waterfall higher up the mountain, already sounded very refreshing as it sparkled beside the road in the sunlight. As we came out of the woods and walked around the upper road above the gravel bank, we stood admiring the lovely sight looking down the river, which becomes Sherman Pond, toward Yankee. The trees between us and the river have grown considerably, and now that the leaves are out, the full view is becoming obscured. We shall soon have to go higher up the mountain and over the waterfall to see this special glimpse of our valley. Fast growing, small trees are already covering the once open field, but the whole view with the field, mountainsides ahead and hills across the river, was beautiful with so many shades of spring green – some trees fully out, some still blossoming and others just unfolding. High above our heads, six huge, dark turkey vultures soared and floated and mingled with each other like a grand sky show in slow motion. Trees and birds and sunshine. What a day! And the real special flowers were yet to come.

By the time we crossed the field, identified a female rose-breasted grosbeak which was too big to be missed, listened to the witchity-witchity of several yellowthroats and the "very pleased to meet cha" of numerous chestnut-sided warblers, we had arrived at our destination at the bend of the river. Here a flourishing little community developed in the 1800s and at the turn of the century, a busy lime quarry. This area along the bed of the old Hoosac Tunnel & Wilmington Railroad is now a ghost town. Amid a rich jungle of vegetation one finds old stone kilns, stone walls of building foundations covered with moss, cement cisterns high on the hillside and the remains of various other unknown structures, all resembling certain Mayan ruins. The old quarry itself has become an enchanting grotto. Limestone soil is the special ingredient here producing such lush greenery and abundant wildflowers.

Turning onto the woodland path, it was suddenly a relief to be in the shade and coolness of the woods. But the bug attack came immediately, and all we have said about the blackflies not being as bad this year was suddenly complete misinformation! We stopped and doctored ourselves up with bug stuff but they still went for our neck just under our ears and tried to cloud our vision by swarming in front of our face. But it would take more than blackflies to blur our appreciation of this woodland paradise. Before starting along the path, our partner spotted a small blob of orange/pink fungus on an old decaying branch. We poked it to ooze out its inner contents and prove the identification of the appropriately named, "toothpaste" slime mold.

Then we entered the Avenue of the Miterwort. The fairly wide path turned slightly to the right and continued up the hillside, lined on both sides with that lovely little plant which has tall stems of tiny white snowflake flowers above the distinctive two opposite leaves part

way up the stem. These blossoms are not spectacular but very dainty and grow in clumps which, when growing on a rock back-lighted by a ray of sun, are lovely to behold. And one, even then, has no idea of the hidden beauty of the tiny individual, fringed flowers unless they are observed with a hand lens.

This avenue was also rich in flowered toothwort, foam flower, both red and white baneberry, Canada violets, downy yellow violets and numerous blues, along with the textures of unfurling Christmas and maidenhair ferns, budded Virginia waterleaf and lots of dainty sweet cicely, distinctive double-leaved stems of wild ginger, and here and there growing agrimony, all mixed with the now gone-by flower and huge leaves of the red trillium. Before we reached the top of this first level, we were both on the ground looking to be sure that the plant before us was a long-bracted orchid – only the second one known in this area.

Foam flowers

Conrad Frey Photo

"Look! Here they are," was the shout to our partner when we found the first of the showy orchids. They had seeded down much further than we had ever observed them, as we were still below the quarry. You might think the first of the lot would get the most oohs and aahs but today we must have admired and exclaimed over nearly every one. The showy orchid has four or five exquisite little orchid flowers less than an inch long on each stem. The hood on each blossom is lavender or magenta and the long lip is white. Sometimes you can find a rarer, all white one. This year some of the flowers seemed to be lighter colored than usual, perhaps because of the rainy weather. It was all the more reason to exclaim over a stem that was deeper purple. Showy orchids are not considered rare but they are very choosy about soil and prefer limestone, thus in our area they are not often found and should not be transplanted.

The old quarry is an intriguing place, with moss-covered, high circular walls full of pink-stemmed, long tapering fronds of bulblet fern. A little stream appears from nowhere out of the hill to the left and flows across the wide entrance only to disappear in the sand again to the right. The floor is strewn with hundreds of bulblet and maidenhair ferns, jack-in-the-pulpits and nettles along with toothwort and Canada violets. A center pile of marble rock pieces is also now moss covered. This time, the floor was somewhat cluttered with the windfall of a big tree and we wished we'd brought a saw and had the time to clear away the debris. Near the brook, small clumps of fragile fern clung to soil between the rocks.

We climbed up the usual steep path by the waterfall and, almost immediately, were among the showy orchids once again. It was a slow ascent from there on because it took time to admire and appreciate each and every one. But it was memorable time, for they were beautiful. We found our other long-bracted orchid to be blossomed and in good shape, and all the Goldie's ferns where they should be. Springtime names this fern, for the young, handsome fronds were a lovely, light goldish green.

Here, by an old road above a gully into which the brook must disappear higher up, is the well-remembered spot where we discovered and dug leeks for the very first time. It had been an early spring hike several years ago and we investigated the large patch of distinctive bright green leaves. Consulting the book and digging our fingers in the ground around the bulb – one whiff and we shouted "Leeks!" and have been a fan ever since. So today we stopped to pick just a few for lunch but the "diggin was easy" and we quickly filled our spare bag. Still following the orchids, passing fading Dutchman's britches and lots of maidenhair, we climbed the hill to one of the cisterns. From there we looked down another gully across such a lovely texture of ferns – ostrich, silvery spleenwort, Christmas, maidenhair, in between flowering foam flower and toothwort. Once again like the new T.V. ad says, "It takes time", to enjoy each and every sight.

And time had passed quickly, for it was already twelve-thirty and the flat top of a small stone structure on the brow of the hill was the ideal spot for lunch, even though we sat in wet moss and had to stand in the breezes to dry later on. Our view through the trees overlooked the river to the north. Just before sitting down, we watched a beautiful male rose-breasted grosbeak, a bird the size of a robin, black with white under parts and a lovely rose patch on his throat. He was singing such a happy song to us that we felt welcomed to his hilltop. Shortly after opening our sandwiches and pickles and cleaning off a few leeks with a paper towel in lieu of water, we spotted something dark in a tree not far in front of us. With the binocs we could clearly see Mr. Grosbeak sitting on the nest and singing for all he was worth! What dinner music! And such joy expressed! He sat all during lunch and then we saw him fly away. We looked around for mother to take over the duties but then we were distracted by some other event. Later, we focused back on the nest and sure enough, mother was there, snuggled comfortably in the sticks while father could be heard in the distance still singing. Getting up to leave, we discovered that our foot had been hanging in six jack-in-the-pulpits growing out of the moss, and stepping off the stone, our partner called our attention to the leather-green pipsissewa surrounding it.

The pretty hillside of red-stemmed sweet white violets could not take the place of our disappointment at the loss of the large round-leaved orchid which has disappeared for the second year in a row – probably for good – from its special spot below the cistern. We have watched this one for several years and through several stages and have taken photographs. It was like missing a friend. Only the far off trill of a veery thrush took our thoughts in another vein.

We made the usual pilgrimage up around the next hill, where we observed several rattlesnake ferns, almost gone pink-stemmed

spring beauties with their tiny seedpods which we had never seen before, and off up on the mountain ahead, another batch of leeks which we had never noticed before. Then we went down again and up through the fern gully, where we checked the special narrow-leaved spleenwort and some of nearly everything you could name. Even the orchids started once again as we went off south through a beautiful hillside of maidenhair. It really is difficult to describe the delicate beauty of texture and color of these countless, emerging young fern fronds. Later in the summer, some of them may be old and dry and brown, but right now each one is lovely to behold and we stepped carefully between them not wanting to crush a single one. Here we are always alert for a possible bear, as we have seen much evidence, but no such luck once again.

The orchids continued occasionally up the hill and joined with the yellow, round-leaved ragwort just beginning to blossom. As we went down over the crest of the hill, we could hear the grosbeak singing sweetly behind us and we turned to see him in plain view on a maple limb. Was this our nesting father telling us once again of his happiness or just some happenstance stranger? We liked to think it was our friend saying "good-bye and come again to our woods." We started straight down the hill and began to think the trees had really grown thick since last year. Fortunately, we realized we had come over the hill further south and must retrace a few steps back, turning directly north to go around the quarry and see the rare walking fern. This large patch of fern still looked small, somewhat brown and not too healthy, as always, but the individual plants in the seams of the ledge further down looked larger and more prosperous. This fern "walks" with the tips of the long, pointed leaves taking root. These leaves were hardly two or three inches long and can grow to several inches where the limestone rock is richer. Nevertheless, this was our first and only discovery of this fern in this area and we check it carefully on each visit.

The return trip down Miterwort Avenue was a little sad, for we always hate to leave this enchanted spot. A large mass of the yellow mushroom witches' butter caught our eye and we collected a glob. This is fun to have around, especially a piece on an old stick. It dries almost to the point of invisibility and then literally blossoms out when immersed a few minutes in water. The ovenbird was singing loudly as we came out of the woods into the more humid, hot, hazy sunshine. Thinking the excitement was all over, we strolled on homeward back toward Harriman, appreciating the breeze from the water and hoping it wasn't blowing up thunderclouds.

Near the last gully before the field, we stood quietly for a minute concentrating on listening for the towhee we thought we heard in the distance. The quiet produced the sound of heavy rummaging in the woods in the gully. Realizing it was bigger than a chipmunk, we ran toward the opening where we could see through the trees and as we did the rummaging grew louder and more determined. We arrived at the viewpoint just in time to see old bruin scurrying up and over the hill. It was not an especially large bear and we thought it might be a mother with cubs but none were in sight.

A bear! At last! In all the years we have been hiking the woods, this was the first bear we have come across. We are sure we heard one getting itself out of the swamp one day a couple years ago, and we have been hot on one's steaming trail a few times, but have not laid eyes on the beast in the wild. Wouldn't you know we'd have to go to Vermont to see the real thing!!

Well, it took us a few minutes to discuss that one, and we were still looking off on the hillside, hoping but knowing the bear was not really sitting up there watching us. It was just about that time the fisherman, a neighbor from Readsboro, came up out of the gravel bank and was as surprised to see us as we him. He said he wasn't expecting two young ladies to be coming out of the woods. (We knew right off that he was not familiar with the Wild Side.) He thought that that area was his territory and didn't know anyone else ever bothered to go in there. He was going to fish the brook and, seeing the bugs still circling our heads, he said he wished he'd used some bug juice. Fortunately we had some left to share.

We, of course, told our bear story and wished him luck in seeing it, too. He announced that a real big one had been reported further up the mountain in Whitingham. After visiting a few minutes, we went on our way, looking for sandpipers in the gravel bank and wondering what kind of a report that fisherman was going to tell his wife about the strange wildflower ladies he met on his fishing trip. It probably would be better than a bear story! **6/88**

A Hike in the Wilderness

The whole trip into the WILDERNESS was daughter Sue's idea.

She dreamed it up on a dull, cold winter day in March and presented it gradually to her unsuspecting parents as merely a family outing come some hot July weekend. Half listening as we read the Sunday newspapers we both readily agreed thinking that anything that far in the future was sure to be a great idea. Why argue about July in March?

Then a few days later came her phone call saying we had reservations at one hut and three out of four in the other; they'd put us on a waiting list for the fourth. Would we put our check in the mail for the deposit?

"Whoa, wait a minute, what are you talking about? Huts? Trails? Backpacks?"

"Our July week-end hiking in the White Mountains, don't you remember? Lonesome Lake and Greenleaf Appalachian Mountain Club Huts."

"But how do we get there?"

"We hike the trails, of course. It's a beautiful WILDERNESS. You'll love it."

"But with a couch potato and a baby!!?"

"Dad and Chelsey will do just fine; we'll all take it real slow and easy."

"But what if there is a thunder shower?"

"Oh, Mommmm."

The check went in the mail, the calendar was marked and our thoughts concerning our July commitment again went off into space. After all, there were four *Goal Posts* and Old Home Day before we had to give it any further consideration.

Time sure flies when you are over fifty! *Goal Posts* and Old Home Day came and went in a flash and the following Monday we woke up to the fact that the time had come to PREPARE for our safari into the WILDERNESS. Sue sent us each a carefully thought out list of what we should take. She also called to say our fourth reservation was assured and we could now do the "long" hike to Greenleaf Hut.

"How long?" I asked.

"The pamphlet says it's 2.54 miles and should take 2 hours and 20 minutes."

"Anybody, even Dad, can hike three miles, that's just around the square in Rowe." (We knew, of course, that not all miles are alike!)

"See, I told you we could do it. Den and I hiked in to Lonesome Lake when I was pregnant. It's only 1.7 miles and takes about an hour, might be a little longer with Dad not used to hiking. He IS still going isn't he?"

"He hasn't said no."

"Great! We'll see you Thursday night."

I took off for Gleason's Camping supply in Northampton to buy some essentials, namely sleeping bag liners for sheets (blankets supplied, they said), plastic water bottles, rain ponchos (not AMC approved for windy NH mountains, we later learned), and a new pair of lightweight hiking boots and socks (I thought better of wearing my usual sneakers).

Thursday afternoon was a hassle, packing knapsacks and then the back of the car with all the paraphernalia we had "better have with us just in case we needed it." We joined Sue and Den and baby Chelsey at their Deerfield, New Hampshire home by dinnertime. THEN we sat back and read some of the AMC literature.

"Due to the high elevation of Greenleaf Hut (4,200 ft.) and exposure, hikers should be prepared for very severe weather" – into the

knapsack went the wool sweater, hat, mittens, long johns, and ski outfit. (Temperature at the moment close to 90 and extremely humid!)

"Wear long pants" – out came the shorts.

"Lightweight shoes for after hike comfort" – in went more socks and the sneakers.

"Sturdy boots, well-broken in…"

"What do you mean you bought new boots? Don't you know that is the worst thing you can do before a hike? You'll be sitting beside the trail moaning and groaning."

"Hey, does that sound like me? Okay. Then let me worry about my own boots. You haven't exactly worn yours out sitting on the couch!"

"But I've had them for years!"

"Come on guys, let's get under way. It's already nine a.m. and Chelsey is ready for a nap."

Eighty miles north, the four-lane superhighway goes right through Franconia Notch and the traffic on Friday morning was not bumper-to-bumper but continuous and speedy. To get to Lafayette Campground on the west side, we had to go to the Cannon Mt. Tramway exit and reverse direction. The Old Man of the Mountain was just above us. You would swear he was shaking his head but maybe it was just the vibration of all the traffic. We parked (there was one space left) halfway between the trailhead where we would start today and the one tomorrow. There was again a rearranging of the knapsack contents. The bird book was left behind but the flower book was included in a separate case with the binocs and the bug juice. It was HOT and HUMID but we did not remove the "severe weather items" for after all, why would they warn us?

The first real shock was shouldering my knapsack. Wow, was that heavy! Nothing like our little green "Wild Side" one with a flower book and a bottle of water. Sue saw the look on my face and decided to trade packs, tightening up the new shoulder straps so I "looked perfect" but felt as hunch-shouldered as if I had a terrible case of osteoporosis! No one else seemed to complain and Den shouldered Chelsey in the red frame carrier loaded with diapers and baby food. Chelsey was happy as a lark. Grampa donned his hat and knapsack and soon found an ideal walking stick that made him look like the perfect Appalachian Mountain climber – except for the extra hundred pounds he carried just above his belt.

Our procession started at eleven, crossing the Lafayette Campground west onto a well-worn trail. I had to do something to shake my knapsack into a comfortable position so started off ahead at a good pace covering some little distance of fairly easy walking. I soon pulled off the knapsack and sat on a rock above a brook basking in its cool dampness and waiting for the others to catch up. Chelsey was already asleep with her head rolled to the side in total relaxation. It was a beautiful day with clear hot sunshine and we were glad to be under the trees on a woods trail. At a third of a mile, really feeling the heat, we readily agreed that we would all take it slow and easy.

At the first switchback, the trail started to climb in earnest and we stopped often to sit on a rock or to let other hikers pass in one direction or another. Chelsey was always admired and commented upon by each passerby. We talked of lunch for nearly an hour before we finally stopped on an appropriate

A Hike in the Wilderness

Sue and Chelsey at Lonesome Lake in the background - Mt. Lafayette

log and rock and prepared for a meal. We had bought a fresh loaf of bread at a bakery on the way (now slightly squashed from the full knapsack) and had a good slab of cheese and some apples. I passed around hunks of bread and cheese while Sue mixed up Chelsey's flaky food in a paper dish. The baby, released from her choice seat on high, was bent on crawling and climbing and would have been far up the trail or over the edge if left alone. The longer rest, free of the knapsack, was probably more welcome than the food. Although we were fairly high on the mountain we knew we weren't in the WILDERNESS yet for we could still hear the buzzing of cars down on the superhighway.

We finished lunch with a handful of trail mix and started on. The loss of one loaf of bread did not lighten my load and I slung the pack over one shoulder to start. 100% difference without the pack high on my back! We loosened the straps, more on one side than another and carried the pack low which brought my shoulders back out of the hunch position. Sue raised her eyebrows but I said "To each his own," and climbed on in greater comfort. The steeper climb began with another switchback to the left by the ravine of the same brook where we had first stopped. The trail was rocky, and well worn down through the last hundred years of hikers on this, a section of the Appalachian Trail.

The final assault was up and around a ferny glen with a few big old trees and mossy boulders. Then the path dipped downward to the right and the bright blue waters of Lonesome Lake shone through the trees. Several trails converged near the water's edge and we stopped to admire the lovely sight of the blue lake surrounded by mountains. Tucked in the trees on the opposite shore, we could see the AMC Hut that was our destination. There was still some distance to cover but the trail was on the level and often rose on half logs above the mud of the lakeshore. Our spirits were high at having achieved our goal in a little over three hours.

A Hike in the Wilderness

But lonesome it was not! Other hikers were going and coming and as we neared the Hut lots of people had gathered to sunbathe on the dock or swim in the lake. We decided that checking in was our first order of business and we climbed the rugged path to the large cabin with long bunkhouse ell, behind and in front of which were two more bunkhouses. A "hut" it was not! We were assigned to the lower bunkhouse and quickly found our separate room with two double-decker bunks.

After a change of clothes and the donning of sneakers (bathing suits for Chelsey and Sue), we gathered on the dock. Chelsey loved the water and I thought it would feel great, too, but it was just so comfortable relaxing there in the sun looking across the lake to the far Franconia Range and high Mt. Lafayette.

Having studied our small copy of the trails map, I was pretty certain I could pick out the ridge where we were destined to climb to Greenleaf Hut on the western flank of Mt. Lafayette the next day. With our elbows on our knees and our binocs in hand we could make out people on the trails to Mt. Lafayette, and with a little scanning of the ridge below could see people passing an opening in the trees which must be the trail to Greenleaf Hut. The truth of the matter was plain to see – that trail had to be steep and would be the longest and steepest 2.5 miles we may ever climb! (But best we don't draw attention to that fact!) Two A-10's roared through the valley just at eye level above the trees. WILDERNESS? We rolled over, used a sneaker for a pillow and fell sound asleep on the dock (actually the helicopter landing pad!).

Supper was promptly at six and everyone pitched in for KP duty, setting tables for the 46 guests ranging in age from Chelsey at eleven months to some well-seasoned hikers in their seventies. Families with children seemed to predominate, including some young folks with no discipline or manners, as we would learn upon retiring later on. The meal started with good old-fashioned barley soup that was delicious. Then came the fresh homemade bread, cabbage and carrot salad, roast turkey with sauce and pasta. We were stuffed to the gills and expected to pass up dessert when the apple cake came along, irresistible and scrumptious.

The evening program at eight was to be a tour of the services used to run the hut: water, sewage, garbage, cooking, storage, etc. We knew the water came from the lake since the well had failed (even the mountains are very dry) and that the sewage smell from the flush toilets did not improve the warm night air. The WILDERNESS was obviously getting too crowded. The amazing thing we did learn was that the staple goods are brought in twice a season by helicopter and that the fresh supplies are carried up twice a week on the backs of the "Croo" who work at the huts for the summer. More power to those enthusiastic young people! We took a few very short hikes on the trails near the Hut, identified water lobelia and pipewort at the edge of the lake and saw a lovely, bright pink wood sorrel in the woods. Not even lasting until lights out at nine-thirty we were all in bed by eight-thirty and fell asleep to the voice of a Croo member giving the tour of the compost heaps and the screaming, racing and screen door banging of the children in the next room.

A Hike in the Wilderness

We dislike people who go places and do nothing but complain, and we do not mean to give the impression of doing just that. The Appalachian Mountain Trail System and Huts are great and have been for the last hundred years, and it's amazing how many people are taking advantage of them. We enjoyed every minute of our trip, but it did open our eyes to what's happening on this "superhikeway" in the WILDERNESS and if we sound critical, our only intent is to convey life like it is, or like it was on July 15, 16, & 17, 1988.

Much to Sue's surprise (having greatly worried), Chelsey never peeped during the night as she slept with her mother in the lower bunk. The chorus of white-throated sparrows woke me at daylight and I heard Grampa go out the door for an early morning walk along the lake to see the sunrise, but I just turned over in the upper bunk and luxuriated in the cool morning air and another hour of sleep. Even then, I was up and ready (wearing my wool sweater) long before the appointed hour of seven o'clock breakfast, and I walked down and checked out the sky toward Mt. Lafayette. High clouds had rolled in to lessen the heat of the sun but the mountaintops were still clear. It already felt like a day of afternoon thunder showers and I wanted to be safely across the valley and up in the Greenleaf Hut, not on the trail, when this happened. I tried to be subtle in suggesting an early start. The other fearless folk, in turn, were a bit subtle themselves when they did not repeat to me the whole weather forecast posted at the hut at 8 a.m.

Those of us that weren't trying to feed Chelsey (without a high chair) were on morning KP again, setting tables. Big bowls of hot cereal were delivered to each of five tables, along with all the orange juice you wanted and lots of hot coffee, tea water and cocoa for the kids. It was hard to believe that these great meals are repeated day after day for new visitors all summer in these high mountain huts in the WILDERNESS! Crispy bacon and scrambled eggs were joined by heaping plates of freshly made Sally Lunn. The Croo acted out a skit about the perfect hut guest who carries out his own garbage, folds the hut blankets properly and leaves a generous tip for the Croo.

We were packed and under way shortly after eight. Sue re-traded knapsacks and carrying my own I spent the return trip going over in my mind everything that could be removed to lighten the pack, changing my mind several times. The lake was still as glass and reflected the ridge and high mountain where we hoped to be by afternoon. Thinking statistics: we were at 2,765 feet, the trail would drop to 1,450 feet by the car and climb the other side to 4,200 feet. That's a lot of footsteps but surely the trail would be a series of switchbacks and not straight up – or would it?

The descent from Lonesome Lake was not bad at all, even though Sue and I favored our often-troublesome downhill knees and Grampa talked about his inherited not-too-sturdy Williams knees. Den with Chelsey (who had not a care in the world) was in the best shape and probably would have been halfway up the other side if released on his own. The scene at the car was pretty humorous. Everyone dumped their pack and rummaged in the trunk for new or different items, changed clothes discretely in the car or helped Chelsey get a little assisted walking exercise on the nearby bike path. Grampa found a cool spot on the lawn and took a rest flat on his back. Our own ideas of "Let's get going before the showers," gave way to "Let him rest if he wants to before we tackle the other side," and this eventually came to "It's going to be a long hike and we don't want to be doing it in the dark!"

But these thoughts were not expressed and I let nature take its course concentrating instead on the contents of my own knapsack. Necessities: weightless sleeping liner, toothbrush (paste too heavy), tiny lip balm tube, rain poncho and lightweight windbreaker. The wool sweater went in and out several times and finally stayed in (that severe weather warning still echoing in my ears), and we had to include the full water bottle. I was wearing long pants (you can always roll up the legs), a Rowe t-shirt and a short-sleeve overshirt (which shortly went back in the pack as being too warm) and binocs slung over my shoulder. Gone were the long johns, sneakers, two hats, gloves, change of clothes, flower book etc. etc. The pack was light and rode nicely low on my back. The only problem that developed was that I obviously had room to spare and each of the others in turn mentioned that their what-cha-ma-call-it or other could fit in my extra room. No dice! "You expect me to take your extra shoes when I don't take my own?!

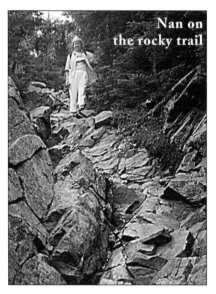

Nan on the rocky trail

You can go barefoot! My new hiking boots are so comfortable there is no problem wearing them day and night!"

It was eleven o'clock, as yesterday, when, fully outfitted, we headed east for the underpass below the superhighway and took the dirt trail called "Old Bridle Path." No warnings were posted in red on the trees; "Amateurs keep-out," "Couch potatoes will never make it," or "No one under fifteen allowed." Simply a notation that read, "Greenleaf Hut 2.54 miles." The wide path took a gentle incline along a small field and soon entered the woods. The sound of water was appealing and we pictured a cool hike up along the stream, but another "Falling Waters Trail" parted our company to the right over the brook on a wooden bridge. Our Bridle Path Trail soon turned left and that was the last we saw of water.

We must have gone for half a mile on a decent gradual path that gave us high hopes that those old horses must have known what they were doing. The first real switchback turned the trail slightly more uphill and then leveled out. The old trail description, which I had copied and carried in my pocket, told of a sharp left turn where you had a good outlook toward Mt. Lincoln and was the halfway point. Having climbed and stopped and climbed and stopped for about two hours it seemed as if we must be near this point and we asked the next set of down hikers how far to the first opening and view. They stopped and thought and thought and finally said "quite a ways."

With this news, we all became terribly hungry and soon found a widening of the path and a big rock to lean against and stopped for lunch. We got out of the path just in time to let pass a crazy hiker running down the trail, jumping from rock to rock. One false move and he certainly would have a few broken bones but he was pretty sure-footed in our sight. WILDERNESS chipmunks began to appear over the rock and ran back and forth around us, expecting their accustomed handout from these beings that keep going through their territory. We munched on Nabisco crackers and cheese packets and finished up the bread and cheese, throwing only our apple cores to the beggars who immediately ran off with them.

It's hard to remember where the trail really began to climb. We were up along a deep ravine a couple of times and made slow progress through and up over the rocks. Each group of hikers that passed gave us an excuse to step to the side and lean against a tree for a moment. We were not in a hurry; we were not in any hurry at all. In fact we were beginning to say out loud a few previously thought but unspoken words about not really expecting this trail to be so difficult and long. The halfway quote really puzzled and worried me until finally I realized that the description from which I had been reading was almost twenty years old and the trees could have grown up in the view. We had to be past the halfway point and this gave me renewed courage.

It was very hot and humid and our couch potato was actually doing very well, although soaking wet with perspiration, probably having lost at least five pounds by this time. We were all a bit worried about him and perhaps stopped more often than necessary until he accused us of plotting to favor him and marched off up through the rocks while we genuinely needed a rest. If only we had worn shorts, the hike would have been more comfortable for all. The trail had swung to the left and we could begin to see sky through the trees, but every time we thought we were coming out in the open, the trail, now just ledge, went around another corner and on up the mountain. No horse could ever maneuver this bridle trail in 1988!

When we finally could see sky above, the stunted evergreen trees beside us were just high enough to keep us feeling as if we were deep in an open ditch. Our first real clearing to the north and east opened up a view of Mt. Lincoln and Lafayette across steep and really wild Walker Ravine. This superhikeway, so crowded with people, really was in the middle of the WILDERNESS and one would not want to venture out of sight of the trail – that's when amateurs and experienced hikers alike can easily get into trouble.

The second sight from this first opening was toward our destination. The razorback ridge on which we had emerged continued on for at least half a mile, at the end of which rose, straight up, a knobby peak behind which rose a second and higher knobby peak, blending into the ridge on which we assumed Greenleaf Hut was located. It looked like two more hours at least. (Actually it looked like forever!) When our ledgy ditch did open out onto a rock ledge, there were twenty people having a picnic. It gave me a real case of the willies to look over the edge into the ravine and I made no bones about telling our crew to stay away from the edge (at least while I was watching).

On and on and on, even hotter now out in the open, and we were glad when the trail finally dipped down into bigger trees. Here we all sat on the grass beside the trail and tried to stretch out for a few minutes in the cool shade. Our trail description said of this point, "...and then begins the rather steep climb to the hut." What did they call the trail so far? It had already been the steepest thing we'd climbed since the top of Monadnock back in our youth. But we must admit that, steep or not, at least there was the semblance of a trail to follow and this didn't take quite the real breathless energy of some of our bushwhacking Wild Side adventures up and down the mountains in Rowe!

Up and around the next ledges, we came out in the open and saw our first good view to the south and west. Far, far away across the valley perched high up in the mountains, was Lonesome Lake. What a sense of accomplishment to think that we had hiked all that distance! The next down hikers were carrying a small boy in a backpack. They had started shortly before we did this morning, going up the Falling Waters Trail, across the high ridge over Mt. Lincoln and Lafayette, stopped at Greenleaf Hut and now were already part way down the trail back! Oh well, they were young and experienced! And then passed a young female Croo member from the hut carrying the tall wooden back frame on which she would return with 95 pounds of fresh food and supplies. And we thought our pack was heavy! She would probably be down and back before we reached the hut! Hey, now, let's

not get discouraged. For real out of shape amateurs we were doing okay!

The next sight was really incredible. We turned the corner and saw the trail heading straight up through the rocks as far as we could see. We heard the hikers ahead of us shout loudly in the distance "Oh, no!" as they turned another corner. Would we ever make it? Luckily at that time we didn't know that there were five or six more stretches just like that! The old trail description mentioned a place so steep that an easier path had been made to the right. The easier path was out in the open, straight up the face of a ledge. We climbed it, keeping low to the rock and not daring to look back until we felt a firm footing on soil at the top. We got the willies again, looking back and seeing Chelsey riding high on Den's back as he climbed the ledge. She will have no fear of heights! What a fabulous view on three sides!! The great WILDERNESS – full of PEOPLE. We could see the heads of many hikers coming and going along the ridge where we had just come, and across the ravine up on the high peaks, little stick figures were moving in both directions. If we had taken time with the binocs, we could have seen the new group of hikers sunbathing on the dock across the valley at Lonesome Lake.

Thinking we were doing quite well for the circumstances, we asked the next down hikers how far to the hut. "Oh, about an hour and a half!" We must be taking two steps back and only one forward, for a half hour later another group told us the same thing! Understandably we took more rest periods and each step brought our foot at least to knee level on the next rock and sometimes we had to grab onto trees to hoist us up another notch. (Even Sue, the great promoter of this whole expedition, admitted to being tired.) The good part was that at the slower pace, there was time to observe the woods, full of spinulous ferns and a lovely carpet of blossoming wood sorrel, even on the moss-covered rocks. Corn lilies and trillium were prevalent under the evergreens and sheep laurel was just in blossom beside the trail. Bunchberry leaves were numerous and the flowers were still in bloom as we neared the upper elevations. White-throated sparrows accounted for the major bird population, and an occasional warbler and frequently a winter wren seemed to be following us.

By some miracle we reached, at last, the grassy opening where we had watched hikers appear and disappear as we had looked thru binocs from Lonesome Lake. It was sort of a time of rejoicing, picture taking and self-congratulations. A little further on, a man stopped to talk saying that the hut was just up the path, ten minutes at the most. Wow, that put the old adrenalin in my veins and I took off with gusto, arriving out of breath up on the level far ahead of the rest. I threw the knapsack down with such satisfaction thinking that I had arrived and the hut was just there a few steps ahead. I put one foot up on the bank, leaned my elbow on my knee and just stared into the soft mossy woods. After a few minutes I came to and realized that I was staring at sweet little flowers that I had never seen before but knew them by name as a twinflowers with two pink, drooping, bell-like blossoms. Den was next to arrive on the scene and verified my identification and later Sue called me to look at "this cute little flower." You always remember where you first saw something and now twinflower will be especially remembered.

The bad news was – the hut was not there. The path continued on, heading a bit downhill and then another up one of these long rocky uphills. After being so sure that we had arrived, it was hard to muster up any energy to continue. Sue took over from there on, sprinting up the rocks and waiting at the appropriate spot to announce that the hut was indeed right there in the open, a bit under the hill from the crest, which was covered with krummholz, the stunted evergreens at tree line. The land dropped down in front of the hut to the small, pond lily-covered Eagle Lake, then rose straight to the summit of Mt. Lafayette. Looking at my watch, the hour was four-thirty. We had been five and a half hours on the trail. We all felt a tremendous sense of achievement but were particularly proud of the perseverance and determination that got our couch potato to the top! (Or was it? We found out later it was his "I'll do this if it kills me so Rick will have to pay off that $25 bet!" frame of mind!)

The accommodations at Greenleaf Hut were two bunk rooms either side of the kitchen and main room. We assumed, with the Ladies room on one side and the Men's on the other, that we had to separate. Sue and I found bottom bunks on our side and Grampa and Den got third and fourth tiers on the other. We assumed wrong. The dorms were coed, twenty people per room, modesty to the wind. So great was our jubilation at reaching the Hut that any sense of being tired quickly vanished and we all went back outside to enjoy the sights. I was looking at the tiny, white diapensia alpine flowers growing around the rocks and fragile grass and watched Chelsey crawl and climb to her heart's content. The weather had cleared and there was promise of a nice sunset. My Rowe t-shirt attracted the attention of a former Rowe Camper and we chatted.

The supper gong rang none too soon, for we were all really hungry after our day's journey. The soup was minestrone; the meat was roast beef with gravy and fancy rice, fresh broccoli and a crisp delicious salad. Dessert was a chocolaty brownie that we couldn't resist. After supper the choice was the sunset or a lecture on the "Uses of Spruces". We chose the sunset and started to walk down to Sunset Rock some distance over the hill to the west. Grampa, who we all expected to be in bed, was leading the pack down the trail. It wasn't nice to laugh but when he turned his ankle because of loose boots and went head first into the krummholz, it was pretty funny.

Fortunately, no great harm was done except to dignity and we continued down to a choice rock overlooking Profile Lake, Cannon Mt. Ski Area and mountains beyond mountains into Vermont under the setting sun. To the southwest, we could see far-off Lonesome Lake now all dark in the evening twilight on the east side of the Kingsman Ridge. Far below us in the valley was the Old Man Profile. A small airplane flew down the valley a thousand feet below. The scenery was spectacular and the sunset lovely as that red ball of fire finally dropped into the bank of clouds on the horizon. A small crowd had gathered to watch this WILDERNESS exhibit and we talked and listened to a variety of comrades as we hiked back up the hill to the hut.

Compared to the noisy talking of several adults until well after lights out, Chelsey's one loud yelp around midnight was nothing, but it embarrassed Sue and she grabbed her up with a couple of blankets and went out to sleep on the common room floor where she expected to be alone. Two other transient hikers had come in for the night and rose up with flashlights and helped her settle in. Chelsey, all by herself still sound asleep in the middle of the common room floor, looked pretty cute when we arrived on the scene near breakfast time. It was best Sue had moved out, for the ruckus started in our dorm about four-thirty a.m. when the resident cat and a visiting dog (no dogs allowed on the trails or huts) were growling at each other across the room. We could have slept through the animals but the "in command of everything" woman on my top bunk had to join the chorus and try to talk them out of their natural instincts. WILDERNESS?

Hot cereal, omelets, banana and chocolate chip pancakes, and lots of juice and good coffee got us off to a great start for our eight a.m. departure under heavy hanging clouds. Asking someone to take our picture by the hut sign would produce the final proof of our expedition (along with our new hut t-shirts). We again needlessly worried about downhill knees and thunderclaps and made it back to the car in three hours flat.

Three cheers for couch potatoes and long live the WILDERNESS!!   **8/88**

Den, Chelsey and Sue, Nan and Jack

Music in the Valley

"*Was there ever music sweeter...than the coming of the train?*" This quote from a poem by E. A. Fitch of Wilmington, Vermont sentimentally describes the HT&W Railroad as it echoed through the hills along the Deerfield when he knew it back in 1892. We wax sentimental about the old line, too, which actually isn't so many years "long gone." We can remember in the days of our youth when a trip to Pulpit Rock was at least a weekly occurrence in the summer and was never quite complete unless we could watch the old steam engine of the Hoot, Toot and Whistle pulling a small snake of cars up or down the Deerfield valley nearly a thousand feet below. Our history lesson to newcomers wasn't quite accurate in those days, for we referred to the line as a quaint narrow gauge track and never learned until years later that it had been changed to standard gauge back in 1913!

For those of you unfamiliar with the area, the HT&W was a twenty-four mile line of track from the junction with the Boston & Maine at Hoosac Tunnel to the village of Wilmington, Vermont, a climb of 790 feet or a rise of thirty-three feet to the mile and precariously perched along the eastern bank of the Deerfield River – as spectacular a train trip as boasted by many a noted western line. Six miles of this track from Hoosac Tunnel to the Vermont line at Sherman was in the Town of Rowe. This section was the first to be built, with the first train steaming upriver to Readsboro on July 4, 1885, and the last section to be used when the last train came down the valley on August 2, 1971 – a span of 86 years of constant and profitable use. Its builders were the Newton Brothers of Holyoke, who discovered large stands of timber in these hills for their paper mills on the Connecticut River and soon developed several wood-using businesses in the Readsboro/Wilmington area.

Actually today, September 16th, 1988, we had another idea in mind and the walk along the old HT&W track was to be a means to an end, but that old, sweet music of the bygone trains echoed in our mind. We parked the car near the Monroe bridge and started down the old track bed, now overgrown with blackberry brambles, brush and weeds from seventeen years of abandonment. The ground underfoot was wet with mountain drainage even after a dry summer and there soon appeared telltale signs of the washouts and landslides that plagued the little railroad. We stopped at a Joe Pye weed-looking flower which wasn't Joe Pye weed at all and agreed to stop and examine it further on the way back. It was such a lovely day we wanted to be on our way. Amid the brush, there was a worn path probably used by fishermen, and we followed it, ducking under small trees and crouching over to go through the tunnels of leaves, putting our hands in front of our face to catch the cobwebs before they dragged across our face.

The gorge of the Deerfield was on our right, a jumbled collection of rocks and boulders well-washed by the floods of time. The music of the tumbling waters lulled us along and when the river widened out a bit, the sun sparkled like silver upon its waters. A perfectly lovely afternoon to be out for a hike on the Wild Side, and we thought "What is so rare as a day in September" was an even more appropriate phrase than the same for June. There won't be many flowers, our partner said at first, but then looking around, the land was covered with asters and

goldenrod of all descriptions, white snake root, boneset and deep blue closed gentians. They were not the dainty flowers of spring or the lovely flowers of summer but the showy, sturdy, extravagant display of fall, the ones that can withstand the touches of early frost and keep smiling in the warm fall sunshine on into November.

The old railroad bed meandered inland away from the river when the land flattened out a bit and then pulled back close to the embankment where the mountain rose up directly from the river bed. Sometimes a heavy stone wall had been built on the side to keep the mountain solidly in place and these rocks were now overgrown with ferns and moss and liverworts, all loving the dampness of the dripping waters and the coolness of the shade of overhanging trees. Now and then a huge tree had toppled across the path and we had to climb over its numerous limbs and branches or sit upon its back and throw our feet over to the other side. Stopping to watch the flowing waters through the trees, the old Robert Lewis Stevenson poem came to mind: *"Dark brown is the river, golden is the sand, it flows along forever with trees on either hand."*

We often peered through the trees to get our bearings and see how far downstream we had gone. Actually, we were looking to be opposite the outlet to Dunbar Brook, for in that vicinity was the old original river crossing and road up the mountain used by early settlers from "the Gore" (Monroe Four Corners area) when they wanted to go to their village and meeting house which, of course, back then was in Rowe. What a mighty steep and muddy trip that must have been to come down off the mountain on one side, cross the river and climb even greater heights on the other. The only alternative was to go through South Readsboro, cross the river at Sherman and travel up through Lime Hollow and down through North Rowe to get to the meeting house at Old Centre by the intersection of Middletown and Ford Hill Roads. Is it any wonder those old settlers soon petitioned the town to have the lands across the Deerfield set off from the rest of Rowe? The Town of Rowe more or less gave those settlers their independence in 1803, and the area west of the Deerfield was incorporated into the Town of Monroe in 1822. This old road has fascinated us for many years and there may be a description in the old country records. Today our only purpose was to find the remains of this road as a preliminary to some day following it up the mountain.

"Is that a train coming?" "No, just a helicopter overhead." Think back to the days when passenger trains really did chug along this track twice a day, and people from Wilmington and Readsboro could board the train for Hoosac Tunnel, catch a train through the tunnel, spend the day in North Adams and return home the same night. Sometimes the train was delayed because a big boulder had rolled down the mountain onto the track or a tree had fallen in its path. On those trips, the line became known as the "Hold Tight and Worry." And on some occasions the passengers probably thought they needed "Hot Tea and Whiskey" to complete the journey. Think of the excursion trains that carried six and seven hundred people up and down this spectacular valley. There were many hair-raising trips in the line's eighty-six year history but there was never a passenger lost. Unfortunately, that was not true of all the trainmen for some of the engines they ran were real killers.

Rounding another corner of the mountain, we were then headed south and the warm fall sun penetrated through our sweatshirt that had felt good in the cool woods thus far. An opening now gave a lovely view far down the river, and in the distance we could see the power lines climbing the mountain by Bear Swamp lower mountain entrance. We had often looked in the reverse direction upriver from one of our favorite spots at the top of that power line. Now we were actually down there beside the river, and we couldn't help but keep calling our partner's attention to the lovely sparkle of its waters on this September afternoon.

The terrain changed a bit; the mountain receded to our left creating what had been an open, sloping field. It had been deepened and scraped for clay or fill during the building of Bear Swamp but the scarred surface had been planted to various types of quick growth, pretty but not necessarily native to our hills. One would never know now what had transpired. Many of the small trees were silver-leaved autumn olive with red berries, and as we looked around, it was obvious that old bruin thought they were quite tasty, for he had trampled the grass around each tree, pulling down and breaking the brittle limbs to clean off the berries. We kept to the high ground near the river where it became a beautiful park with moss-covered ground punctuated by lovely blue-green clumps of ground cedar, each plant with its dainty candelabra of cones. This was the kind of place to stretch out on the moss, look up at the deep blue sky, watch the lazy vultures circling over the mountain and wish that the month of September would last forever.

Further on, we found ourselves in the midst of a great stand of pink lady's slipper leaves, their distinct dry seed pods at the top of tall stems, each pod attached under one pointed, dry, triangular bract. This would be a lovely sight in May! Here the edges of the riverbank had well-hallowed troughs now and then, and we at first thought they were fishermen's trails to water level. Later we decided that they were indeed fishermen's paths but made first by beaver that had climbed the bank to chomp on succulent trees in the field. Several remains of beaver houses could be spotted along the river as we began to search the shoreline for the outlet of Dunbar Brook. In addition to flowers, fall mushrooms underfoot often took our eye and attention. Mushrooms of every color and description littered our path. At this point, it was hard to decide whether to look up and watch the breeze ruffling the trees on the bright yellowing mountainside, or to look ahead down the lovely sparkling river with its occasional overhanging early-turning red tree, or just to kneel on the moss and examine closely an especially pretty mushroom.

The trees along the trail began to thicken as the mountain again curved back toward the river. We walked along a ways and although there was no sign of Dunbar Brook, we had a hunch and ducked between the trees off the path and closer to the rising mountainside. Here, as expected, we spotted the vague outline of a road climbing south around the hill. We climbed up and with a good imagination could trace the path of the one hundred and eighty year old road to Rowe. Although little was left to convince anyone that this had once been the main thoroughfare into town from the west, it was exciting to have found any part of it once again. This much we had discovered some twenty years ago and periodically have given thought to looking further. Hopefully, on our next quest our energy and time will take us up the mountain. Fortunately, our partner convinced us that the way home today was back along the Hoot, Toot and Whistle before we got too Hungry, Tired and Weary.

It is amazing how quickly one can find the way back home when it has seemed so far in the "going and exploring" direction. We bypassed the top branches of the largest tree across the path and went inland around its stump. Back once more on the rail bed, we tried to visualize the huge 175 ton nuclear reactor arriving via this route to Yankee Atomic in the late 'fifties and the spur line that put it right in place under the containment building. As the mountain pushed us to the river again, we also tried to picture the destruction to this railroad just fifty years ago in the September 1938 hurricane when a tank car went into the river from Deerfield Glassine and the tracks were broken by landslides and washouts in 103 places between Hoosac Tunnel and Readsboro. But in spite of looming financial problems, the HT&W was rebuilt and back in business just over four weeks later. The tracks as far as Yankee would be rebuilt one last time, in order to accommodate the power plant construction material traffic and this would put the line back into the black financially for a few years. After eighty-six years, the demise of this railroad came in 1971, when customers narrowed down to only Deerfield Glassine, and occasionally Yankee. Profits finally did not justify continuance and

soon New England Power Company was to build Bear Swamp Pumped Storage Power Plant downriver in its path.

Remembering having seen on the way in an interesting plateau of land toward the mountain, we climbed the bank and found ourselves under the cool pines at the bottom of a fern-covered rocky mountain. Here again, the mushrooms were delightful, along with the deep green of the marginal ferns and the thick cover of spinulose ferns. Something bright orange along a log took us on the run up the hill. A huge old log well decayed and mossy, was covered with sulfur shelf or chicken mushrooms. These polypores look like little bright orange shelves with yellow edges. What a sight! The colors of nature are often far brighter and prettier than anything man-made.

Back on the path and nearing the end of our line at the Monroe bridge, we were wishing we could have been a frog in the mud on the night of the big raid back during Prohibition on March 24th of 1923. We could have watched, in the dead of that Saturday night, a train of the HT&W coast up these tracks with no whistle and no lights and pull into the Monroe Bridge station here with twenty-five state police, federal prohibition agents and deputy sheriffs, who had recently been tipped off to the existence of a well-known prosperous distilling business in the quiet little town of Monroe. Ten houses were raided, much incriminating equipment and liquor was confiscated and eight bootleggers were summoned to court before the troop, mission accomplished, re-boarded the train and left town as quietly as they had arrived. This final reverie took us right past the Joe Pye weed-like plant and we still don't know what it was.

* * * * *

Still thinking road and not wanting to waste a sunny day, we took off on the spur of the moment alone on the following Monday from the top of Monroe Hill tramping through the woods to the old wood-road out to the power line. Here we stopped on a log to catch our breath and remember how beautiful the woods had been with the leaves slightly yellowed, the larger ferns a gorgeous brown and the smaller New York ferns that lovely creamy white they take on after losing their chlorophyll. Big boulders and surface rocks beside birch and beech were highlighted by streams of sunshine and set off by neighboring hemlock evergreens. The ground under foot was spongy and gave a spring to our step. The day was warm and hazy, in fact it was humid and hot by the time we finished.

We just wanted to cruise around the top of the mountain and see if there was any evidence of the road there. We bushwhacked beyond the power line and came out on a perfectly good wood-road apparently well-used in recent days. It took us past a monster rock cliff and into a dip down over the hill. From there, we followed a path which we surmised went out to the Monroe TV antenna, further to the north than we wanted to be. We ventured partway and returned to explore a little more of the area where the old road went down over the mountain. We came to no real conclusions, except to prove our theory that this road would have to be traced from the bottom up.

Curiosity took us down another logging road and we walked around a bit to become more familiar with the lay of the land and appreciate the sights and sounds and smells of a fall afternoon. We were hot and tired when we arrived back at the top edge of the power line, and headed for the same log to sit down. We took a long drink of water and were content to just settle back to look and listen. The bees were humming in the goldenrod and asters and we detected the faint unforgettable smell of goldenrod honey. A pair of towhees flitted and chirped in the low bushes. Since we didn't often sit on our hikes, we thought perhaps we had gotten old and decrepit and someone had kindly pushed our wheelchair out here and left us alone to spend a quiet September afternoon. We must have been very tired or were we dreaming? No one seemed to appear to push our chair back out, so we eventually stood up, shouldered our knapsack and reluctantly started for home.

Just before we entered the woods, over the hill echoed the sweet music of a train as it came with a hoot, toot and whistle out of the Hoosac Tunnel and down the Deerfield valley. *Was there ever music sweeter...than the coming of the train?"* **10/88**

**Old postcard view from Pulpit Rock
showing the Deerfield River and HT&W railroad track**

Old Davis Mine

Walking the Road at Old Davis Mine

We weren't rambunctious enough for a real strenuous hike even though we had been dreaming of finally taking you up one mountain and down the next to make up for leaving you stranded in the house now for so long. It is amazing how housebound you can get without a real Wild Side hike every month!

It was December 30th and we had to do something interesting and fast before the New Year was upon us. For a change, the weather was lovely blue sky and sunshine, although the low angle of the sun left many a spot in darkness behind a hill or a clump of trees. Our hiking partner was available and we settled on southeast Rowe, the general Davis Mine area. It was a two-car trip so we wouldn't have to retrace our path. The first car was left at the "Devil's Elbow" and the other we parked by the old sugarhouse just over the line in Charlemont on Tatro Road. From there we reversed direction and headed back into Rowe.

At the town line, we gazed across the open field and brook ravines into Heath, noticing many more buildings poking up through the trees than there used to be. Bill Wolf's red house was still visible and, as always, from that we could get our bearings. The lay of the land dropped into two brook valleys that made small ravines in the foreground before the gorge of the deeper Davis Mine Brook. Behind that rose a high ridge to which we could sight across a line and pretty well tell under which clump of evergreens Rowe's southwest boundary corner stood. We were now on a section of land that was added to the town at incorporation in 1785 and not part of the original Myrifield parallelogram purchased by Cornelius Jones in 1762. Before

continuing on, we admired the deer tracks in the soft mud of one of the few remaining dirt roads in Rowe.

We started off at a good pace but there was always something interesting to admire or investigate at the roadside – dry seed pods, lycopodium poking up through the snow, or the lovely color of the tree barks in the afternoon sun. On the left was a group of bushes looking like high bush blueberries with beautiful red tops and a couple of moosewood trees with upper red shoots. They looked so spring-like that it was hard to believe we were just a little over a week away from winter solstice.

The Williams hunting dogs were aware of our passing by and sang out with a chorus of howls. Rounding the big bend in Tatro Road we turned abruptly south and down the hill, where winter shade had kept more snow in the woods, and ice on the road surface. We stepped carefully even though it had been well sanded, and climbed onto the roadside when we heard a truck approaching from the rear. It was Ralph, the UPS man, who was as surprised to see us as we him, and he stopped to bid us a cheery good afternoon.

We crossed Maxwell Brook, whose headwaters drain the east side of South Mountain, and continued on through the woods – a lovely section of road with the sun highlighting the evergreens and the still remaining beech leaves. It was hard to envision the person or persons who had thrown out their lunch bag here, a soft drink can there and a beer can across the way.

Quite a wood cutting project was evident behind the Lively's and we were greeted by their two Dalmatians as we rounded the corner north onto Davenport Road. Maxwell

Road into Charlemont bent around to the south, where the town line marker was in sight. Passing the house and looking up to the left, we could see the back side of Adams Mountain, and we soon went down in a dip to cross Tatro Brook which drains the east side of Adams. Someday we must follow these brooks to their source on the mountainside, but not today, for it was too nice and easy just meandering along this pretty road through the woods.

Coming out into the open by the power lines, we marveled at the open fields. It was good to know that someone was still using the land. Looking to the east, a broad-wing hawk was making lazy circles over the hill and on down out of sight. Its white under parts were quite evident against the sky. Another unnamed brook crossed our path and we looked down to see its sparkling clear waters.

The precise spot we are not sure of, but somewhere going up the next hill we crossed the old line into the original Myrifield grant. Off in the woods, down near the road below Davis Mine, there is probably an unnoticed pile of rocks that marked Myrifield's southeastern corner. More open fields and old apple trees brought us to the old Davenport farm. Looking at one apple tree by the road we did a double take, for one lonely apple hanging on the tree looked for all the world like a red-breasted robin perched on the limb. On up the hill to the left, the lacy branches of large clumps of white birches were lovely against the blue of the sky.

Then came in sight the old Jonathan Davenport barn, solid and rugged as the day it was built in 1895 by Alton Davenport and Mary Sibley's father and uncle when they were boys in their early twenties. The wood all came from the farm, was cut by crosscut saw and dragged out by sled with oxen and a team of horses. Unique in design and built to last with a slate roof, the barn is topped with a cupola. Any boys in their twenties today want to tackle a job like that from start to finish with oxen and old-fashioned tools?

Down another dip to cross a second unnamed brook that originates in the swamp just below the saddle between Adams and Todd Mountains, we then climbed the hill by the sheer glass, icy driveway to the Soviecke house. Now in a new location, this building had once been the Davis Mine schoolhouse and if its walls could only talk, what stories it might tell of bygone days and children of Rowe!

At the corner, we opted to continue straight along Davenport Branch, where Pelham Lake Park now joins this road on the left. At the top of the hill, it was evident again that the land was being used, for the fields were open on both sides. When the road turned, we continued straight down the lane that was the old road. The Rice dogs announced our arrival in the neighborhood as the road swung down along the barnyard fence where Bob's two dapple-grays and a red cow greeted us. We stood admiring the horses and wishing there had been a good snowfall and we could go for a sleigh ride.

Carefully stepping over the electric fence (we didn't test it but treated it as live!) we continued into the field and down by the old Boullie place. Once again, we thought back and wished we could have been walking here ninety years ago when Davis Mine was in its heyday and hundreds of people lived in this now quiet neighborhood. The mine buildings were down over the hill, past the main road, and life would have been bustling even on a December afternoon. The driveway down to the road, being on the shady side, was crusty and we walked gingerly all the away to safer ground.

We had done all this in just an hour, and as we approached the car we both said it was much too short. The sun was still visible through the trees and we still had energy to spare. So we took the first car back to the second car at the town line and walked on down Legate Hill Road in Charlemont. The hazy views to the south were dramatic as we walked up past the old Pearson farm driveway and on down the hill. With binocs, we could see the skiers on Thunder Mountain (Berkshire East to newcomers). The fields of the old farm were still open, but houses have sprung up everywhere. We couldn't blame folks for wanting to build there; the view was spectacular.

We found it easy to trot down the hill but realized at the bend that retracing our steps back to the car would be uphill all the way and perhaps we'd better turn back. The sun was lowering to the west as we slowly climbed back, stopping to chat with Verne Bissell, who was taking this relatively warm afternoon to paint some bare clapboards on the old house he was remodeling.

We exchanged greetings with some other afternoon walkers who had stopped to rest on a porch. With the sun now behind the hill and the air taking on the early evening crispness, we arrived at the car well satisfied with our afternoon's venture on the Wild Side of southeast Rowe and northwest Charlemont. **1/89**

Searching for "The Birches"

Tuesday August 13, 1912: We four (Charles, Florence, Percy and Corinne Brown) started about 9:30 for the western quarter. A lovely drive up hill and down hill. We met Mr. Peck with mowing machine on top of the hill. Put the horse in Cressy barn and tramped to "The Birches", about 3/4 mile. A lovely view of valley, river, R.R., tunnel, etc. Had a sumptuous lunch and used the spy glass to good effect. Got away about four.

* * * * *

Sunday March 19, 1989: About 9:30 we (NNW) drove our car over to the Peck field and walked down the old Tunnel Road to the Cressy cellar hole and then tramped through the woods looking for "The Birches." Found many paths, saw lots of birches, and enjoyed many lovely views of the river, but only from up behind "Doubleday's Cliffs," about 3/4 of a mile beyond Cressy's, could we see the tunnel. Curiosity satisfied and having brought no lunch, returned to the car about twelve.

* * * * *

The more things change, the more they stay the same. Seventy-seven years have come and gone between the writing of those two paragraphs. The former was an entry in the diary of Charles Brown, father of Percy Brown, who spent about thirty summers in Rowe at the Brown cottage, Rocky Knoll, on King's Highway. This particular entry was repeated almost every year, but only in 1912 was there a clue to the exact location of one of their favorite spots, simply called "The Birches." The clue was the word "tunnel." Many spots along the western ridge could qualify for "the birches" with a view of the valley, the river, railroad and mountains, but only from that western end of the ridge above the big bend in the Deerfield could one see into the East Portal of the Hoosac Tunnel.

After our winter spent more on the inside than the out, we were anxious to take off to the hills for a Wild Side hike and, although it was the day before the first day of spring, we knew from experience that the wildflower season in Rowe had not yet arrived. One advantage of our inside winter was time, at last, to carefully read the Brown diaries for any new insights into Rowe's olden times and history. The yearly reference to a tramp to "The Birches" intrigued us and we just had to go and do likewise, although I'm sure we did not follow the original path.

With this crazy winter of ice and no snow, the bare brown, icy ground has often been treacherous for hiking, but the recent warm days have melted the ground cover of ice and settled it into depressions, making flat-topped skating rinks that will become vernal pools for the spring frolics of our amphibian population. On the mountainsides, great glaciers of ice still pour down the stream beds and over the ledges.

Arriving at the Peck place Sunday morning, we wished that Merritt Peck had been there with his mowing machine this last summer, for the fields are fast growing up and soon the clear view to Greylock will be obscured with limbs and branches. As we slung the knapsack over our shoulders, a robin was singing happily in the maple tree over the stone wall, giving us our first sure sign of spring. The first view from our car was also of a row of maples clustered with spring sap buckets along the old dirt Tunnel Road.

To the west, Greylock loomed white with yesterday's high mountain snow flurries. The only scar on the horizon was around the Florida church steeple, once standing tall and bright among the tree-clad hills, now is located near the clutter of Florida's highway department buildings, perched in a new clearing on that mountainside. In the nearer foreground, but still in the far distance, stood the rounded hill locally known as Doubleday's Cliffs. We knew that was to be our destination and did not give a second thought to the burst of energy and knee bending that this winter couch potato would be required to muster to achieve it and return. Enthusiasm and curiosity always take us a long way before we realize what we've gotten ourselves into.

Starting off down the dirt road, it was rutty but frozen and we skipped along in great shape thinking of the many lovely seasons when we have passed this way, observing the unfolding, long beech ferns and flowers of spring, watching the warblers and listening to the thrushes of summer, breathing in the sweet smells of autumn and basking in the riot of color produced by these maples along the roadside or feeling the brisk, cold winds on our face as we descended this ski trail of winter. Today, neither winter nor spring, the sky was blue, the sun was bright and warm, and the ground was bare except in occasional shady spots. We stopped to look up through the limbs of the overhanging maples to the tiny red buds against the sky and through the poplar branches to their emerging pussy willow tips. What a glorious day to be alive, to be free and to be out on the Wild Side!

As the road turned a corner and leveled out a bit, ice still blanketed the surface. We avoided it by walking in the brown grass along the edge and carefully stepped over a big glacial ditch which flowed off to the side. The corner just before the dike view had survived the winter well – but come to think of it, it is the spring rains that raise havoc with dirt roads and spring is yet to come. Another long flat section of ice in the next shady spot required that we carefully negotiate its surface. We did so with arms outstretched for balance and quickly saved ourselves in the midst of a few slips and slides. The road showed evidence of winter use, and in the next low spot, the deep ruts were filled with ice and we had to walk the frozen rim of the ruts like a tightrope. Once back on dirt surface we looked in vain for the old leaves of the hepatica plant that grows along there somewhere. In its rightful time, it always blossoms but we never seem to locate the plant between times.

Next came the tiny rushing brook that flows from the mineral spring on the hill. I'll bet the road crew nowadays doesn't even know about going over there for their spring tonic (and I certainly wouldn't recommend it!) but in days long past, it was as much a spring ritual for them as the first mess of dandelions. Here a strange stone wall comes to an abrupt end at the top of a ledge and then continues on the lower level. Up a small hill and off to the left is the start of the Cressy pasture. How pretty it must have been when the view was open and one could see across the river valley.

Coming up, also on the left, was a jumble of stone walls indicating the old Cressy barn foundations. We stopped a moment and in our imagination went back those seventy-seven years to 1912 and watched Charles and Percy Brown hitch their horse and buggy in the barn while the ladies shook out their skirts and prepared for the tramp to The Birches. Now our question is, which way did they go? They never mentioned passing the cemetery, so we presume they took off west of the house across the lawn – an amazing spell of level ground for these hills. Of course the recent excavation of the clay pit has changed the landscape considerably. The question was, did their path go straight back and then along the ridge or did it cross the clay pit area in a more direct route to connect with still traceable old roads behind the Doubleday house? We guessed the latter to be the true course, but not being able to reconstruct the clay pit, we chose the former for our tramp today.

We entered the woods across the old ell foundation of the Cressy house. It's always sad to think of such a lovely, big old, two-story house being reduced to an abandoned cellar hole. And even that has been gradually robbed of its prize flat stones – for sentimental reasons, our own stone fireplace displays one of them. The yard remained basically level until we got back to the clay pit road. Crossing this recent road, we again entered the woods on another wood road, probably dating back to an old stone house whose remains are still visible further on. At the base of the hill, we opted for a climb to the ridge. Even though our knees quickly objected, we wanted to be sure we didn't miss any spot that could possibly have been the site of The Birches.

Like gray hairs on our own head, this old mountain is covered with white birch trees but all seem to be of the young variety – fifty maybe, but not one hundred years old. The southern shoulder of this mountain wall is particularly rugged with boulders, high cliffs, ledges, outcroppings, valleys and summits of all sizes, shapes and intrigues, while its northern flank over the river is vertical. On such a ridge it is never hard to find a path. Deer seem to love the edge of the world and their trails are always overlooking the greatest heights. We followed one after another, stopping often to admire the view through the trees or to marvel at the rock formations where we would have been perfectly happy to sit and while away the morning and afternoon. Someone else had been looking for deer here too, for in a rather level shelf of the mountain on a tall tree had been constructed a deer stand, complete with ladder.

That was our first sign of civilization; the next was soon to come. We climbed another hillock in our gradual ascent to the cliff top and came out on the wide-open flat ledge we remembered as being so beautifully covered with a carpet of reindeer moss, lichens of green and gray hues. Today we quickly noticed that places had been dug up and the shallow brown earth below was showing in spots. Were the bears out already this early digging for grubs? Not hardly. Closer examination revealed the symmetrical pattern of a tire track! Invaded by civilization! Looking around, we could see the trail leading up to this summit lookout. But what can be traversed by an ATV can also become a hiking trail and perhaps, without the dread of bushwhacking, more people can again climb the heights and spend an afternoon among the birches, enjoying the dramatic western view toward Raycroft Lookout on the opposite mountain and Bear Swamp

Searching for "The Birches"

View toward Rowe from Doubleday's Cliffs

a slippery icy top in the center. Boiling out and over the bank was a heavy cascade of ice flowing down the mountainside. Without hardly trying, we could have sat down near the edge and gone flying down through the trees to the river! We remembered doing this on an icy porcupine trail on Adams Mountain back in our youth. The idea was exciting as we stood on the edge hanging on for dear life, but we thought better of it in the end and continued our climb on bare ground to the summit.

Sure there were birches on top as there had been birches all along the ridge, but somehow here on the western heights they seemed more in clumps, more the way we had pictured them sheltering the Browns as they enjoyed their picnic that Tuesday afternoon back in 1912, and on so many other delightful-sounding afternoons during their memorable summers in Rowe. And climbing out on the rocks we, of course, could see the tunnel entrance tucked in the mountain across the river valley. "Prospect Rock" they had also once called the spot. There were many prospects on this western promontory of the mountain, many small shelves of land with birches and outcropping ledges with a view of the tunnel. All together, they add up to an ideal destination for a tramp and a picnic seventy-seven years ago

lower reservoir dam and power house on the Deerfield River below.

We started down the new trail but it soon went its own descending way, while we wished to continue up the ridge clinging to the backside where the footing was easier than over the long, jagged cliffs on the front. Every so often, we remembered to take a closer look at the ground and its variegated plant life in hopes of finding some exciting brown seedpod or dry leaf stalk that would signal something new on the hill. Once we did pick at some dried white leaves but concluded they were Solomon seal or the like and nothing of great importance. Spring and summer are the times for plant search, but you never know – the strange new flora in our life has always popped up at our feet when least expected and not when we are methodically searching.

The flat area just before the last real climb was a bit of a mountain swamp covered with pretty ice crystals on the edge and or today – very little has changed in that spectacular outlook over the valley and hills. Perhaps the diesel engine on a train instead of the electric switchers pulling a chugging steam engine out of the tunnel would be the only clue to the passage of time. And yes, with a spyglass one might question the stacks of shiny modern cars being transported by rail, but not much else would give cause for question. Except, of course, if there was a flyover of A-10s!

Doubleday's Cliffs is not new to us. It has been a favorite destination of ours for many years. But our special outlook is in the other direction, so we soon turned and scrambled back across the rocks to find our own little nitch atop the cliffs, where we settled down with our back against a tree. There we looked out toward Adams Mountain, the blue waters of the upper reservoir, on down across the length of Negus to Thunder Mountain in Charlemont, where we spotted the skiers with our own spyglasses, then on over the Deerfield valley, across to the ridge where follows the path of the old Indian Mohawk trail, and down this side of the mountain where zig-zaged the old shunpike when tolls were charged on a better road up the valley in 1800. Finally completing our semi-circle of open view, we turned westward toward Savoy Mountain with its distinctive spike of a fire tower.

This was our special spot high among the oak trees overlooking, a great wilderness. Everything was still except two tiny chirping birds that quickly flitted past and disappeared over our head before we could get up and identify them. We scanned the landscape from one side to the other with our glasses and stopped abruptly when we focused on the only bit of civilization (except the ski hill) in sight – a car in a field far away on a hill. We were so lost in our quietude and reverie that it took us a few minutes of study to realize that we were looking back at our very own car in Merritt Peck's overgrown field.

The sight of our car, hardly visible to the naked eye, caused a momentary panic in our mind. We suddenly realized we had to walk our already very tired body all the way back to that point! There was no friendly house where we could knock on the door and say, "Please drive me home." (Short of a dire emergency we knew we wouldn't give up and do that anyway!) We did wish we had thrown an apple in the knapsack, to say nothing of a good fat sandwich!

Near where we were sitting there was evidence of an old road up the side of the hill and we were curious to now look closer at it. Even though well built up with rocks on the lower side, it was impossible for us to imagine a horse and wagon making the climb, but then we are not really that familiar with horses or wagons. The fact that good-sized trees now grow in the middle distorts the picture somewhat. We have always thought this particular road must have had something to do with the erecting of the lining tower for Hoosac Tunnel, but no one has verified that assumption. The sad part is that there is no one left who can give us a firsthand answer. However, one thing of which we became fairly certain was that this was the western end of the Brown's trail to "The Birches."

We descended the road and tried to follow it along under the cliffs but had quite a time climbing over windfall, toppled rocks, brambles and vines all mixed together. This is a better spot to traverse during a winter of heavy snow, which fills the cracks and holes and mats the vegetation. With grumbling stomach, we looked up at the quantities of rock tripe that we knew we could consume if starving, but the situation was not quite that desperate yet. It was much more comfortable walking when the trail finally made the turn downhill, away from the cliffs and we settled into a most enjoyable stroll.

Finally coming out on Tunnel Road, we found ourselves in mud. The sun had thawed the dirt road and it was soupy, wet mud in places. We looked at the fallen remains of the little cottage where friend, Virginia Mosher, lived and then across to her father, Lloyd Doubleday's tumbling house and pictured it, even in our own memory, when the land was clear and the houses and lawns neat and tidy. We were looking at the house as we walked past, but because of the soft mud had to glance down and be sure of the next footing. It was a shock to see a fresh boot print and we quickly looked up and exchanged greetings with a man in camouflage jacket just crossing the wall to the right. Civilization is closing in, two hikers out on the same day!

Uphill was the name of the game from there on. Because of the open road, we tended to keep up a good pace but often had to stop and catch our breath and rest our aching legs. Out of shape and then some, we vowed to hike a little every day – after *Goal Post!* But stopping gave us a chance to appreciate the sunshine, the coming to life of the trees, the running ditches, and everything else about this lovely day on the Wild Side.

The last stretch of road was the softest, and each step an effort, so we finally climbed into the field, much too tired to even cross the road again and snitch a drink of sap from one of the buckets. It was an exhilarating feeling to look back at the cliff hill and to know we had achieved our goal and made it back to the car. In the words of Charles Brown after their tramp to "The Birches" on August 13, 1914, "What a view & What a Day!" **4/89**

Scratch and Sniff

"Scratch and Sniff" are often the instructions on a magazine page advertising the latest in new perfume. Some wonderful process allows the smell to be embedded on the paper and a mere scratch rewards you with a whiff of whatever magic formula they have manufactured for your pleasure and enticement. Now we have come up with a nifty, brand new idea for a page in the future May issues of the *Goal Post!*

As you anticipate our annual spring hike to leek country, wouldn't you be thrilled to think you were going to be able to scratch and sniff the smell of leeks as we talk about digging our hands down in the soil and pulling out one of those aromatic and tasty morsels of spring? Wouldn't it just put you right there in the woods, in the warm spring sunshine appreciating the arrival of a new season of growing things?!

Well, all right, if you don't like leeks, then just don't scratch. But we'll bet you would, just out of curiosity, and then you'd be hooked for life. Spring just wouldn't be the same ever again without your annual earthy whiff of leeks. And by golly, you wouldn't misplace that issue of the *Goal Post* either for that wonderful smell would just keep flowing out of that little patch on the page like steam out of a boiling pot, no matter where you hid it away. Why, we could probably sell thousands of issues of the May *Goal Post* and make our budget for the whole year, so unique would be its appeal!

So much for dreams. Come early April, our excuse is always the hepaticas. Their date for full bloom seems to be April 13th in the river valley, and as the date approached this spring, we watched the weather and our schedule pretty carefully. We'd all be busy right around the thirteenth so it had to be earlier. The weather was cold, it even snowed one day, and we kept hesitating. Finally, rather late on the cloudy afternoon of the 11th, two of us just couldn't wait any longer. We thought we had a third recruit but she wouldn't be convinced that flowers bloom in the valley when the cold wind blows on the mountaintop.

It is usually a whole new world down along the railroad track on the bottom of the abandoned Tunnel Road into the old Soapstone Quarry. It is protected from the wind, and the sun, when out, is warm and penetrating. One feels a sense of being in a faraway land, as you exit the car and shoulder the knapsack, always quite empty, of course, on this first spring trip to leave room for the leeks. If you are lucky, you'll watch a train chugging up or rolling down the valley to or from the Hoosac Tunnel. Today, all was quiet except some air traffic far overhead.

Such a sense of freedom to be out on the Wild Side! We can stay confined and busy just so long and then fortunately a *Goal Post* deadline looms on the horizon and we get out in the woods. But today we weren't even planning to take you along; we were just out for a hike, free and clear. But what fun is the first smell of leeks and the faces of the first little flowers if you can't share them with everyone!

The road was a little wet to start, and we jumped from leaf clump to pebbles and finally up on the bank until it was drier on the hill. When the road widened out to a level area, we detoured just into the woods to look for those bright green clumps of spring ambrosia. Looking ahead on the hill, we saw none, and disappointment loomed large. Then we happened to glance at our feet. We were standing in the leeks! Only about two inches high, they were hiding well in the leaf and grass litter. We poked a finger down beside the one nearest our left toe and took a whiff, just to be sure, then quickly dug the tiny green and white leek and devoured it, bits of earth and all. It's amazing how that first one can taste better and better each spring!

This wasn't our digging area so after our scrumptious hors d'oeuvre we moved on down the road, up hill and down again, by all those beautiful ledges, which we admire to the fullest every time we pass them by. In the spot where we usually hear a rose-breasted grosbeak, we stopped to watch a bird flitting in the trees. So many of our birds have arrived but are not yet singing, and it is hard to identify the ones we know mostly by song. This small greenish bird, in after thought, must have been a least flycatcher or chebek that we often hear but seldom see.

Where the road divides, we chose the upper course, just to see the area that is always covered with early spring beauties. The leaves were completely scratched up, as if someone had been raking and not a spring beauty was in sight. We looked closer and the turkey droppings proved our suspicions – the turkeys had been scratching to get the corms of the spring beauties! That is our theory, at the moment, pending someone informing us to the contrary. But it did disturb us. Spring beauties spread by the thousands, but if turkeys (who are also multiplying pretty fast) are digging for these, they will also be after the other rarer plants with similar underground goodies. The thought is almost enough to call on the town clerk for a bird-hunting license!

Down over the hill again, and then we began the climb, first through the brambles and then across the hillside, looking for the hepaticas. Still no spring beauties, but perhaps we were pushing the season as always. (No way! We've seen spring beauties beside piles of snow and the ground has been bare here all winter.) It was great to be out no matter what we found. And suddenly there they were – beautiful white hepaticas with sweet little faces and fuzzy soft sepals and stems. But no wonder we had trouble spotting them, they were hanging their heads down.

Evidently, the weight of the recent snow had caught them in full bud and bent their necks toward the ground. Of course, the rather cloudy cool day didn't help draw their faces skyward either. We climbed to the big round boulder and found all our favorite clumps in the same reverent position although once in a while one lone flower stood face up and smiled at us.

Climbing carefully around the rock was our usual procedure and in so doing, we found the columbine with small leaves just big enough to be recognized. The backside of the rock needs some clearing of old fallen trees and we had to climb down over branches finding underneath the first weird spikes of blue cohosh. The leaves, curled around the same color buds and stem, are a strange purple color in the spring. Out of the tangle we crossed to look at the beautiful long ledge draped with wet moss and in a little pocket of soil a lush collection of squirrel corn – well out of reach of the turkeys. A rather large depression is located in front of this ledge and walking across it, we always step gingerly, anticipating falling through some concealed hole down into the old talc shaft far below.

From there we went on up the hill where we both spotted one tiny yellow violet – so small yet so pretty, and so welcome in the spring. The toothwort was coming up bronze-colored and white buds were beginning to show. This too would turn ordinary green with the cohosh after a few days in the sunshine. The Canada violets were just tiny little bunches of green hugging the ground. Each favorite spot was visited in turn – our next one was the little dingle among the huge rocks and ledges. Here the leeks were higher and greener, the red trillium was sprouting up its pointed rocket head and the toothwort and cohosh grew abundantly. The dry maidenhair fern from last summer showed where to look for the new dainty fiddleheads, but it was as yet too early for them. But the evergreen maidenhair spleenwort on the rock was thriving in its pretty little rosettes. The dingle is at its best at a little later date, so we rubbed our fingers on a slippery piece of talc and poked on over the hill, where we climbed through the old bramble stalks and came out on the road by the lovely white quartz rock looking like a patch of ice sliding over the gray ledge.

We were headed for hepatica hillside down the road a ways, but the opening to the right looked inviting and we thought we could go down over said hill instead of climbing up from the road, as was our usual procedure. Well, one intriguing spot led to another and we just had to see what was over the top of the next hill, and the next and thus got ourselves up into a rather interesting basin with a stream running though and lots of wood roads that would have led us into all sorts of trouble if we didn't throttle the urge to look still further. The sun was shining intermittently and we could have spent the afternoon sitting on the ledges or listening to the brook, or examining several more outcroppings of white and reddish quartz, or just basking in the sun, far from our maddening schedule.

However, the sun was on its way into the west and we still had leeks to dig. The present problem was to get ourselves off the high hill and back to the road – always, as a matter of principal, without retracing our steps. We were pretty sure we had overshot hepatica hillside, and we had a vague notion we might be in slight trouble. The rocks on lower Tunnel Road are not just any old rocks, mind you! They are walls, cliffs, giant boulders, outcroppings, and ledges – rugged, high, dangerous and beautiful. You get the picture? And we love every one of them.

We headed down, never sure we wouldn't have to climb back up and go a different way. Closer to the brook, we were treated to that wonderful, cheerful woodsy song of the winter wren. Stopping to listen for a moment gave us time to plot our course. By then we knew exactly where we were and remembered how we got there last time – it had been up the ledgy waterfall of the brook, chasing some little white violets. There really was only one choice of descent, down around the ledge on the left where, hopefully, there was enough soil to hold our footing. Downhill on the waterfall would not be the best choice.

There are always enough distractions in the woods to take our minds off a precarious situation and we enjoyed the scenery, the greenery and a few feathered friends as we picked our way slip-sliding down the side of the ledge to the safety of firmer ground at the bottom by the brook once again. Here we identified the spot where Goldie's fern grows, looked at a few clumps of Dutchman's breeches and wandered back up the road to hepatica hillside, just far enough to enjoy the lovely blue hepaticas. By then we were tired, with just enough energy left to dig our leeks and beat the afternoon shadows back to the car.

As we slowly walked back down the old road, we looked up to the high ledges where we had just come down and were pleased with ourselves that we could both "still do that sort of thing!" And there on the left at the bend of the road, pushing up some heavy leaves, was the first and only spring beauty!

The leeks were probably some of the smallest we have ever dug, but the leaves were still tender and could be eaten, too. So we each dug our allotment, washed them in the stream, and headed home, pleased as punch with our afternoon adventure.

* * * * *

True to our New Year's resolution to really watch the spring flowers emerge week by week, we returned on the 17th for an all day meander over the same general territory. This time, we carried our lunch and ate our sandwiches with fresh leeks on a birch log with our feet in the hepaticas because they were so numerous. This was a glorious sunny

Favorite hiking partner, Mary Liz Snively

day, the kinglets were busy in the bushes and a pair of phoebes seemed to have taken up residence around the old quarry. We found the spring beauties where no turkeys had disturbed the ground and the little yellow violets dotted our paths. With knapsacks full of bigger leeks this time, we found our way back to the car in late afternoon. It had been a beautiful day to remember but nothing quite takes the place of that very first day in the spring when you taste the leeks once again! At the end of the road by the house, the little Hardison boy looked over the hill down at us and eagerly called, "Did you have a good time?"

"We sure did," we replied. "We always have a good time out on the Wild Side!"

Oh, by the way, did anyone try scratching the "S" in the box at the beginning of our story? **5/89**

The Lure of the Field Sparrow

When we first got out of the car, the towhee was so boisterous he dominated the area. Many birds were singing in the background but the towhee's repeated "drink your tea" drowned out even the loud ovenbird's yelling of "teacher, teacher." We stood and listened for several minutes, for it was the field sparrow we really wanted to hear. A visit to the old Peck place in spring and summer would not be complete without the faraway-sounding call of the field sparrow. We seem to be stuck in southwest Rowe this spring when so much more of town goes unexplored, but easy access and lots of goodies keep calling us back.

The Peck fields are growing up and soon the lovely, open meadows on this mountaintop will be just a memory. Hopefully, the field sparrow will not totally abandon the territory. Standing there today, May 25th, we began to think he had gone already. Our partner was closing up the car and collecting her knapsack while we listened to the myriad voices of our feathered friends. We had chosen this trip today especially to hear and see the birds along the old Tunnel Road to Hoosac Tunnel. The bird book, and not the flower book, was safely tucked in the knapsack – and you know by now how that works – we'll need the flower book on every turn.

We were still listening for the field sparrow. The numerous chestnut-sideds led the warbler chorus, a wood thrush joined in over the hill and a rose-breasted grosbeak sang in the top of a far-off tree. Having four pair of rose-breasted grosbeaks at our home feeder, their lovely plumage and song have unfortunately become commonplace, and we always hope the song is that of the less social and similar-voiced scarlet tanager. Our partner soon asked if we were ready. No, we responded, not until we hear a field sparrow. We both stood and listened. It was quarter after eleven on a lovely spring day with enough blue sky and sunshine to make the whole world glad.

The field sparrow song came first faintly from far behind us, down over the hill on Steele Brook Road, then another closer in the field across the road toward the reservoir. We listened to several choruses and then agreed that all was well and we could now start off on our day's journey. While writing this, we wondered how to describe the song of a field sparrow and took a minute to consult the Audubon Bird Book, which says, "Series of soft, plaintive notes, all on the same pitch, accelerating to a trill at the end." It lists the habitat as "abandoned fields and pastures grown up to weeds, scattered bushes, and small saplings." How better could we describe the old Peck farm?

Perhaps only the green of Ireland is greener than New England in spring.

Actually, our spring colors rival our fall colors, only now they are in shades of pastels instead of bright reds and oranges. Looking off toward Greylock, the mountains were a mass of soft shades of greens and pinks, perhaps a little lavender as the shadows played on the hills. Everything looked thoroughly washed and clean after yesterday's rain, and colors were crisper because they were still wet. Dark evergreens stood out on the landscape and tree trunks were more prominent under their dresses of bright green leaves. Ferns and new grasses on the ground came in every shade and shape.

Once headed down the road, we tried to spot the various warblers, but as always, we stood with the glasses, our heads bent back, looking up and searching as the songs came from here and there, always just out of sight. If we caught a fleeting glance, the illusive bird then flew off to deeper cover. We hoped that further down over the ravine we could look into the treetops at eye level and be more successful at spotting and identifying. For the umpteenth time, we vowed to learn all the warblers by song. Our partner did spot a yellow-rumped warbler and, seeing a flick of orange, we both focused on a redstart. Several chebeks (least flycatchers) were singing and an eastern wood pewee kept saying "pee-ah-wee." Whether or we saw the birds, all the songs were music to our ears on this lovely morning in May.

The long beech ferns on the banks were well up and not quite as tipped back as when they first appear, and the yellow corn lilies were starting to bloom. Further down the road, little candles of foam flowers rose above darker leaves and made pretty little patches in the wet spots, and we had to gently lift the cap on the first jack-in-the-pulpit to see its jack in a pretty, striped cup. All along, the new fronds of the Christmas fern (the one with the little Christmas stockings) were standing straight and tall, so much so that the first one fooled us into thinking it was a narrow-leaved spleenwort.

When the roadside became covered with the little blue-flowered gill-over-the-ground, we knew we were nearing the old Cressy place. By the cellar hole we stopped to smell the lilacs, which were still wet with the rain, and admired the full-blossomed old apple tree. The wet trunks of the numerous locust trees stood dark and gnarled in the woods behind the cellar hole. From here on down the hill, we watched for any evidence of emerging pink lady's slippers among the laurel and wild azalea bushes but found not a one. The timetable of all plants is a little off this year. A trio of lovely, large painted trillium had just started to fade but we stopped to admire them anyway.

At Doubleday's Brook, we looked at the tall gone-to-seed coltsfoot flowers with still tiny leaves, admired some flowered baneberry, which provoked a discussion as to whether the small flower head is the red or white-berried species, wishing, of course, that we had the flower book to correctly identify those along with the buttercups or crowfoot. High water always enhances a brook, and we looked downstream and watched the water sparkle in the sun as it raced down past the old stone walls. The yard of the old house (Cressy house number two, to go way back in time) was literally covered with leaves of the old-fashioned orange daylilies. Although not our favorite flower, we do have to admire that plant's longevity and persistence in covering the earth, and we always pause and wonder who planted the first one beside a long-gone front door. The New England asters were coming up well and abundant and we both remarked how we treasured the ones we had rescued from this spot.

From here on, the road was very muddy and we jumped back and forth across the ruts to find the driest footing. Far from being in the wilderness, this road shows signs of being well-used by sturdy vehicles. The walls and strange large built-up structures of rocks in the pasture here always draw our attention as well as the ledges on the upper side. We inspected the third Cressy cellar hole and walked back by the still sturdy old barn foundations where we found more daylilies and looked for the hop vine we had seen in previous years. It was there in a couple of places but fooled us with its rough stem – we again needed the flower book to double check that, as well as some plentiful bedstraw. Near the lane beyond the barn foundation was the remains of an elaborate shelter with shreds of plastic cover on the makeshift roof hanging in the trees. Nearby was the campfire circle. Like we said, this area is well used.

Looking forward to the next landmark, a pretty, old arched stone bridge, we meandered on down the road spotting a hermit thrush hopping along the ground flicking its tail. Of all the birds we heard today, not a single hermit thrush was raising its voice in song. We were soon at the junction where an old road crossed the brook to the right, and we climbed downhill a bit to look back at the arch of the old bridge. To our disappointment, the seeming great need to log the forest had spoiled something that had probably lasted as built a century and a half or more. The old stone bridge, well-built enough to have survived the ravishes of nature all these years, had been crushed by the weight of heavy logging equipment and the brook was now flowing over the top. Sometimes it's hard to understand why these old landmarks must be destroyed for the sake of convenience and a few dollars.

Turning our back on the sad sight, we watched a veery thrush investigating the tree roots and underbrush on the upper side of the road. Another of his kind was spiraling his song in the distance. The road began a more pronounced downhill course and turned to the right crossing the brook on another less attractive but just as sturdy and still-intact stone bridge, below which the brook dropped into a very deep ravine. It was from here on that we expected to look into the treetops and spot more birds. Well, the treetops had grown higher in the interim since we passed this way last, and it being half after high noon, the birds seemed to be quietly taking their afternoon siesta. We bemoan the tree cutting and then fuss when they sprout back in our view. This lower part of the old Tunnel Road was opened up by logging several years ago and displayed a lovely view across the river back toward Negus Mountain. Now the trees have sprouted and grown to some heights and the view is through leaves once again. Trees have crowded out the brambles and less sun has discouraged the large clumps of violets so prevalent on our last trip.

We had also forgotten just how steep and narrow this winding road really is. Still obviously four wheel passable, it must have been something for a horse and wagon to climb when those people from the Cressy Neighborhood drove back and forth to take the train at Hoosac Tunnel station. A winter wren burst into song and we enjoyed every minute of its long joyful serenade, again and again as it seemed to follow along with us. Not being able to see a view, we looked to closer objects and admired the rock tripe covering the ledges now beginning to loom on the right side of the road. The tripe had already dried from the rain and turned brownish black. Sometimes when fresh and wet it is a lovely green.

Now the monster cliffs rose up alongside the road in what is the most spectacular attraction on this highway in the wilderness. Beautiful ledges and high rock formations with mosses, ferns, rock tripe and lichens of every kind mixed with little gullies and valleys of greenery decorated, we could make out, with lacy herb Robert. A strange little waterfall comes out of one lower ledge and spews forth green and orange slime as well as clear water and one tends to say, "yuck" but ah, this is algae, natural and interesting, and not pollution by man. The jumble of rock chunks across the way were interesting and we speculated whether they were there because of the glacier or the natural breaking and cracking of a mammoth piece of ledge that had fallen from higher up. We concluded the latter. The big boulder just beyond had a huge, moss-covered tree stump squarely on the top.

Rounding the next curve was our clue to drop down to our favorite little dingle, where we knew we would find leeks for our lunch. It was now nearing one-thirty and we were both starving, but neither could bear to think of lunch without fresh leeks. Braving the brambles along side of the road, we picked our way through the brush down the embankment but shortly found ourselves in a veritable jungle, hardly recognizable from our earlier trip in April. The little yellow violet leaves were now large clusters of dark green, the cohosh was like a small sapling and the ferns were waist high. We ventured toward the dingle, passing the rock with dwarf ginseng and found only one little seed pod near the already gone-by toothwort. The bright green leeks – where were they? Withering already, as is their nature. The sturdy tall leaves were yellowing and mostly on the ground, and in several places we found the red bud of the flower stalk. Nevertheless, we dug down with our hands and loosened enough leeks for lunch but then realized that we were a long ways from the brook. We would have to use our sleeves or pant legs to brush off our hands and maybe a small jackknife to clean the leeks. One way or another, we'd have them for lunch.

Our plan was to pass through the dingle and eat by the rock on the other side, but the foliage on everything was so lush that we had trouble finding the usual entrance through the brush and had to climb down from the top. It was like being lost in your own back yard. But once there the columbine was just in bloom on a shelf in the rock and the stiff sprigs of tiny white-flowered miterwort just caught the afternoon sun, while the rosettes of maidenhair spleenwort had never looked so green and healthy. The wild ginger grew lavishly under maidenhair fern between the cohosh. The Canada violets scattered white blossoms through all. A jungle indeed, but a lovely one. We climbed across the stony hillside under the small trees and came out in a little more open territory, picking the first rock we could find as our picnic site. Wow, was that first leek strong! But good! Our breath will probably smell for three days. But there is nothing like fresh leeks with a sandwich, tiny tomatoes, carrot sticks and some of those good church chocolate chip cookies. After the second or third leek we found them less violent, and perhaps sweeter for their faint covering of good mountain earth.

After a long and enjoyable lunch break in this choice restaurant on the mountainside, we did a little yard work. An old rotten limb had fallen on our favorite hepatica patch, now completely taken over with Canada violets, and we lifted, pushed and shoved, and finally got the log away from the flowers. There underneath were the cutest clumps of the tiniest little hepatica leaves we had ever seen. They seemed to spring to life once the old log was removed from their heads. Before moving on, we explored a little in the immediate area, looking for the other columbines on the rocks and peering into an animal hiding place back in the dingle. The wet moss on the rock was beautiful, as were the emerging circles of evergreen spinulous ferns. Various bushes were blossomed, including the dangling flowers on the moosewood.

The afternoon hours were already racing by and we gathered our knapsacks and moved on down the hill, past the big old dead wolf tree, so unique with its stunted limbs sloping downward. Again climbing over brambles, we made it back to the main section of the road, where we doubled back to the brook. Here we had to check for the majestic Goldie's fern, which seemed scarcer, and the narrow-leaved spleenwort which was thriving. The jewelweed was well in evidence and would soon take over

the landscape, competing with the nettles. The brook was lovely splashing down over the rocks from high above the roadway. The profusion of April's bright green leeks were matted and yellow, soon to be gone without a trace, except for the strange red buds on naked stalks which blend into the surroundings and burst forth umbels of white flowers followed by black seeds in dry, round, sectioned seed pods.

We turned back down the road, headed homeward, except for our detour around the next corner to the leek patch where we dug our last supply for this springtime. A jeep rolled by and its occupants probably wondered what we each were doing on our knees on the hillside, and of course we wondered where they were going, driving up the old Tunnel Road into the wilderness. We washed the leeks in the brook, packed up and started on. A rose-breasted grosbeak sang over our heads and we got a good look at his flashy outfit. Nearing the end of the trail, across the way from some good rich soil we discovered a blossomed pink lady's slipper. A surprising find, knowing they want very acid soil and usually bloom nearer the first week of June, but contours change quickly and this growing season is unpredictable for sure. Out by the railroad crossing our car was waiting, hot but welcome.

Finally back on the mountaintop at the Peck field, we left our partner to retrieve her car while we opened our window and listened again to the song of the field sparrow. **6/89**

Life in the Combat Zone

Anyone attempting a hike this spring deserves a gold medal for combat. Yes, that even goes for those of you who walk to your mailbox to get the evening paper! The mosquitoes are taking over the world! We took a quick, late afternoon safari into the parkland off the Sabrina Rice Trail one day, enthused about the possibility of a new flower in that vicinity. We were ill prepared, as this was a spur of the moment trip, although we did have long sleeves and pants. Why bother to gum up with all that bug juice? Wow! We were no sooner out of the car than we began looking like a windmill – left hand swiftly batted to the right, right hand over our head to the left, left hand down to the ankles, right hand behind the neck.

We were bushwhacking off the trail, faster and faster, over this fallen tree, around that bush, through those low branches, left hand whamming our right shoulder, right hand swatting at our nose, when we went head first through a huge circular cobweb that stretched across our face. While both hands were occupied in wiping off the cobweb, the mosquitoes got the upper hand and, quick as a wink, summoned their friends, who all came like an attack squad of dive-bombers and just as loud. We wrapped our hands over our head and ran stumbling over moss, rocks and twigs, not daring to breathe. We could have been tramping on hundreds of rare and endangered and we would have never known! As it was, we saw nothing except a blur of green when we dared open our eyes. And when, for sheer survival, we had to take a breath, it required that we open our mouth and pant like a dog, swallowing seven mosquitoes on the first

intake. This induced coughing, sneezing and near choking, while our windmill started again, left hand over the right shoulder, right hand in a wide sweep left, right, up, down and sideways.

By this time, we had intersected with the Todd Mountain Trail, where we stopped to take stock of the situation. Not easily defeated when our curiosity is at its peak, we turned up our collar, buttoned the top button on our shirt, revved up the windmill and continued across the trail, where we began searching the more open ground for the little creeping plant called twinflower, nothing rare, just not yet on our Rowe native list. It seems that we do a lot of searching for special flowers, never finding what we are looking for but always coming upon that new discovery quite by accident when least expected. We seemed to have the upper hand with the mosquitoes for a moment and opened our eyes and quickly thrashed around the woods, becoming convinced that this was not twinflower territory.

The trail was now close by to the right, and we joined it, walking fast for some distance toward the lake. Finding nothing to our liking at this particular time, we turned back toward the car at Davis Mine Road. Near the old Todd cellar hole we skirted below it through ostrich ferns head high and nettle to our thighs, and were again attacked by the winged throng. We took off on the run as if chased by the proverbial bull in the pasture. Splashing though the mud back on the trail, out of the corner of our eye, we spotted a pretty little blossomed dwarf ginseng, one of our favorites, which should have been out a month ago but this was not the time to stop and admire anything.

For the last few yards across the stream, another legion of mosquitoes joined the already steadily attacking force and we held our breath, kept our mouth tightly closed and jumped in the car faster than a speeding bullet! Fortunately, a few rainy days followed and we had to stay housebound. Time to rebuild our courage before our next attack of curiosity took us to the woods again.

* * * * *

It came on the first cool, sunny morning about nine-thirty, when we found that we could bum a ride from Monroe Bridge, where we left our car, and headed back up to the trail out to the power line, starting by the old talc mine site on Monroe Hill Road. It was the right season and we were making our yearly search of new territory for yellow lady's-slippers, which only grow in good rich woods. They were native to Rowe back in the 'twenties, we have been told by several people. We have searched for the last five or six years to no avail. Of course, we have also been told that yellow lady's-slippers are particularly tempting to deer that may devour them to ground level. Nevertheless, the search will continue as long as we can walk! We've even thought of using a divining rod. Our Dad used to find water and dimes

in sand piles. We wondered if it would work on yellow lady's-slipper roots?

The cool breezy morning had abated the bug population but, just in case, we were well doused with all the remedies and carried more in the knapsack. The situation was actually quite pleasant for a change. We started off at a good trot, not wanting to waste time in familiar territory. Soon out at the power line, we continued across and entered the old wood road taking us out to the ridge. We stopped and looked at the high cliff rock. The sun was just highlighting its lovely covering of moss and ferns, and we couldn't resist going around and climbing to the top. It was great to be back in the woods, finding a jungle of plants, ferns and flowers all looking their beautiful best as the sunbeams streamed through the trees. We had so many directions we wanted to explore but we were trying to be systematic and cover new territory so we would know what might grow where.

Several times, we found the leaves of the large, round-leaved orchid but no flower stem on any of them. These are also susceptible to deer damage and especially slugs. All the ferns were fresh and green and lush, creating pretty scenes everywhere. We followed the path to the Monroe TV antenna garden and decided to go down the mountain to the left of this, for we had already done the bouldery right flank of that hill. We found red trillium but really nothing else to indicate the rich soil which might harbor yellow lady's-slippers.

Meandering back and forth across the hill, we found many mossy tumbles of rocks, a big balanced boulder probably dropped on the mountainside by the glacier and lots of huge old, old trees which had survived thousands of lightning storms, a few hurricanes and especially the woodsman's axe. Little dells and dingles appeared between the steep drops and we just wanted to settle down in one of them and enjoy the rest of the day. But we continued down, hanging on to small trees in the real steep parts and veering left around a small stand of hemlock that would later identify our location as we looked back from the River Road in Monroe.

Once down on the terrace above the river, we were back in familiar territory and did some searching where baneberry seemed prevalent, and then finally dropped down to the old HT&W track, weaving around recent landslides which would have raised havoc with the old railroad. Passing the steep path by the antenna line, we climbed the hill and immediately found the first real rich soil area covered with silvery spleenwort ferns, baneberry, trillium and all, but alas, no lady's-slippers. We tramped around a good bit, crossed the brook and followed an old road up the hill. Well braced with rocks on the lower side, this was the old road to the old bridge at Monroe, we finally realized, and we were excited to follow it up the hill. At one point, it made a hairpin turn and we decided to take what looked like a road slanting downhill. Well that came to naught, so we climbed the bank back up to the plateau, admired another glacial boulder and climbed to within sight of the guardrail on the bottom curve of Monroe Hill.

Now that we had our bearings, we decided to now follow the old road, which took off straight before that curve, back to see where it actually came down to the river. By this time it was getting near noon and the air had warmed considerably, plus, we were getting hungry (and maybe a little tired?). We traced the road back to the antenna line where we had come up but then lost it and finally gave up, carefully going down the steep path back to the track bed and out to the car. We had added an old road to our list but no new flowers, and we could sit at home with a geodetic map and visualize a little more territory on Rowe's western flank.

* * * * *

It was warmer and certainly buggier the morning we chose to make our annual spring inspection of the Pulpit Rock area with our hiking partner. The swamp pinks, or wild azaleas, were in full bloom and here and there a pink lady's-slipper. We stepped lively through the woods, doing a slow windmill, and had a little relief from mosquitoes out on the power line, where we admired, close and at a distance, the beautiful pinks which always seem to come back in spite of the vegetative spraying done periodically by the power company.

Taking the path into the woods by the little cairn of rocks, we followed it to the southern viewpoint over the river valley, just above the upper end of Bear Swamp lower reservoir. The mosquitoes had thickened through the woods but we endured, anticipating freedom once out in the open on top of the mountain. Wrong again! The black flies, the lesser of the two evils this year, suddenly recognized the human scent and surrounded us, and we were both frantically doing the windmill act there on the cliff. Creeping along the rock were three gypsy moth caterpillars that we quickly sent to their doom. The view was spectacular, as always, and we managed to

stay long enough to enjoy it along with our snack of crackers and cheese, the crumbs of which the ants carried off in great style.

Moving along the path toward the pulpit, we came to another lookout spot and found that, with a small change of direction, the wind was blowing toward us and we were suddenly bug free. What a blessing! Here we enjoyed the northwest view so familiar from old Rowe postcards that showed the river, open farmland and the rail line of the old HT&W, which we can well remember with a train chugging up the valley. Today the view has changed, only to reveal even wilder country. The old rail bed has grown in but is still traceable, the farmland has been set to trees, most of the river goes down through a visible canal and the old farms on the mountaintop across the river have long since been abandoned and grown to trees. We lingered here for some time, enjoying more pinks and investigating some vivid orange branches on a couple of shadbushes. Feeling like kings of the mountain, we admired the panorama up and down this spectacular valley, bounding Rowe on the west. From there we bushwhacked back to the power line, feeling that going on to the actual pulpit area would be just too much beauty to absorb for one day.

* * * * *

The last hike of the spring season was another annual trek this time to see the laurel on Negus Mountain. My, how that has grown up in the last few years! Up the well-washed rocky approach one has to go a ways on top before there is an opening to the west and up another hill for the full perspective on the Deerfield valley. In the blueberry days this was all open and you would have had a wonderful view, as well as a pail of berries by this time. The road is well-used by recreational vehicles. If they would only have respect for the landscape and carry out their trash instead of leaving behind cans, plastic cups and wraps, and broken glass. Perhaps one of those vehicle owners could go in some day with a large garbage bag and spend a few minutes doing a Boy Scout good deed in picking up the area and carrying out the trash of those who would desecrate our lovely mountaintops.

From start to finish, the laurel was beautiful with some as bright pink as we have ever seen and other bushes snow white. One tends to look at the bush, but it is especially rewarding to look at individual blossoms with a hand lens if possible. We hiked the path to the second peak and then down the open slope, seeing the ground covered with just fading bunchberry blossoms, a little sheep laurel mostly gone by and laurel, laurel everywhere, some in bud and others full out. The pretty cedar lycopodium had lots of brown from winterkill. A few of the blueberries were blossomed but they were not loaded, by any means. Tall yellow hawkweed and bristly sarsaparilla all added to the texture and hue of the lovely carpet woven into this mountainside.

Although it was before noon, the day was already hot, very humid and buggy. We had come early to avoid the predicted afternoon thundershowers, but the dark clouds were already massing just to the west. We had planned to have a snack, from our partner's knapsack, here while quietly enjoying yet another spectacular view, but better judgment pushed us back up the hill and on our way. The first hill was within a good fast hike to the car, so we stopped there and enjoyed our crackers and cheese and delicious fresh radishes while watching the storm clouds gather between Greylock and us. In the distance the water in the upper reservoir off to our right was full and smooth as glass, nicely reflecting the surrounding rock cliffs on the backside. On other days, we would probably have found excuses to sit and enjoy the scene until a train came whistling out of the tunnel and into view snaking down the valley and around the big bend at Beaver Island, but today soft, tiny raindrops again sent us on our way, never ceasing our windmill action until we were safely in the car.

If only all this acid rain would kill mosquitoes instead of trees and fish! **7/89**

Top of Negus looking toward Bear Swamp Reservoir

A Wild Side Here, A Wild Side There

"A fine kettle of fish" it has become when we've acquired such a reputation as hikers that neighbors and friends won't even stop and offer us a ride home when we are desperately dragging ourselves (behind the rail so we wouldn't get killed by the fast traffic) up Joe King Hill, one of us with knapsack on our back and the other carrying a baby in the Snugli, having climbed the mountain, traversed the ridge and slid down the vertical southern slopes, picked our way through the logging slash to finally come out at line bridge where we were sure someone we knew would take pity on us and give us a ride back up the mountain to the car at the Refuse Garden! Not one of you! (And you know who you are!)

Of course, we had only intended a short fifteen minute hike to find that stand of coralroot we had seen three years ago right beside the path. Things are disappearing on us these days (or our memory is fading with age) and the coralroot was nowhere to be found. "Maybe up over the next rise or just beyond those trees," kept us pushing on in spite of our partner's howls about, "How are we going to get down with the baby?" We extolled the virtues of the gorgeous view at the end of the ridge, which would compensate for our floral failure, and would you believe that had disappeared, too! Two hours later, when we had finally come out on a steep but fairly passable logging road all was forgiven when our partner spotted the large pale corydalis that we have been seeking for several years now.

So there we were, exhausted and hot, with an unaccomplished mission, and you all thought that we were just out looking for flowers along Pelham Brook. It was a great hike – wish you had been there!

* * * * *

Going into "The Swamp" (off Cyrus Stage Road) is always a treat, and we'd love to get up early every morning and spend at least an hour checking on life there. This particular hike was probably our reward for being confined with the August *Goal Post*. We always head for the woods to relax from the deadline pressure and get our eyes readjusted from the little square screen. This morning, the narrow-leaved gentian was in blossom, fewer plants than usual but equally as pretty, and the woods were full of lush ferns of all kinds. Near the water's edge, we stood and counted blue heron nests. We had missed a few weeks and the birds had long since fledged, all thirteen young that we had previously counted, we hoped. Four nests were there, one had disappeared. Scanning the water and logs, we counted five herons fishing or just standing, preening their feathers. The gray of their feathers and the gray of the old dead trees matched perfectly and only movement proved a heron for sure. One more flew in gracefully on its long flapping wings and glided up to the top of a hemlock tree behind the swamp. You can nearly always tell when herons are in the area because the tops of the pointed hemlocks are bent over from the weight of the birds roosting there.

Several Canada geese were lounging in the water near the herons, and a few ducks passed by as we watched with binocs. Various frogs croaked strange tunes and beautiful red and blue darning needles flew along the water. Still concerned about the lost heron's nest, we decided to try to bushwhack around to the back of the swamp, not such an easy task now that the beaver have raised the level of the water and flooded our passage across the old gravel bank. We had on our wellies so we could wade in some water further around the edge.

Standing at another spot, we heard a noise in the water behind the shore trees. Remaining perfectly still we watched three otters, one adult and two little ones, swim into our view. The adult did a double take, turned around, went under and then stood up on his haunches and looked at us. The little ones followed suit and there were the three of them all in a row checking us out. Their expressions were definitely saying, "Come on in and play." They went under again and came up closer, under the log, around the tree, further away and back again. After this ritual for several minutes, they finally decided that we were no fun at all and swam off to torment the herons and geese. We sloshed around the next hemlock and came eye to eye with a young heron standing in the water. We froze and stared at the bird who was staring at us. We were both statues waiting to see who would blink first. The heron won, for we could not stand still for more than what seemed like ten minutes and we quietly backed off. The heron, undisturbed by our intrusion, continued its quest for food along the shore.

Bushwhacking around through the thick hemlocks and brush was rather a pain, but we finally freed ourselves in the open woods and climbed down to the brook, where we balanced ourselves crossing a small beaver dam above a waterfall. Blackberry bushes and ferns growing up among the logging slash made for difficult walking but we managed and found a good vantage point on the back shore. The first sight was two adult herons standing straight and tall side by side on top of the beaver house. For all our tramping, there was no clue to the disappearance of the fifth heron nest, no special pile of sticks in the water or even any traces of them on the tree. Probably too many heavy birds and a hard rain followed by a strong wind had done the damage, and all had sunk to the bottom of the pond.

That problem investigated, we turned and climbed the hill, hoping to find some botanical morsel to make our day. We searched under the beeches, thinking that this might be a good place for our rare tryphora orchid, but to no avail. Higher on the hill the slash, blackberries and brush were head high and we had to really concentrate on getting out of the place. We went toward the power line, and eventually down the hill along a marked property line. Nearer the brook, a beautiful doe bounded across our path. Several minutes later, as we approached the brook, we looked toward the opening in the woods and there stood the deer in silhouette looking and waiting to see just what we were going to do.

The sun was bright and warm out on the power line and we detoured off the path to pick a bouquet of pink fireweed. This always looks so pretty growing in big clumps and that is where it should stay, for we found it does not revive in water. We looked at the common meadowsweet with the hand lens and marveled, as always, at the beautiful and so seldom seen miniature world of flowers. Our bouquet now included meadowsweet, steeple bush and everlasting, along with some ferns for greenery. So many of our wildflowers we do not pick, and it is fun to be able to rescue a few weedy ones for the sheer pleasure of a summer bouquet. Out on Number Nine Road we found pretty pink milkwort, new to us but over the line in Heath and thus not an addition to our Rowe list.

* * * * *

Then there was the wild rafting trip on the Deerfield. Ten of the younger generation had gathered to go down the river and we were lucky enough to be invited and available. This is always a treat for us and today was to be the lower section of the river, where we had never been, from Zoar Gap to the rest area below the Route Two bridge.

Preparations always take longer than expected and it was rather late in the afternoon before we headed for Zoar. A few raindrops hit the windshield and we contemplated letting the crew go and being the rescue car at the other end, but the rain stopped and the crew assured us there was no weather problem. Two of us quickly took a car to the rest area and came back. Then there was a further delay, assorting eleven people in two canoes and the raft. We reserved a raft spot, as our swimming techniques are not the best. Three of the crew from Wisconsin stated that they were canoers and could handle one boat. Were they sure they didn't want someone more experienced in the canoe? With some good-natured bantering back and forth, the final answer was definitely no. And to prove their capabilities, they were the first ones in their canoe and off they went – immediately tipping over and losing one paddle in the swift current down the river!

No great harm done. Just some good

laughs at the three of them, now dripping wet for the trip, from the rest of us who could enjoy it dry, and one more, "Are you SURE you can handle it?" from everyone. The raft crew quickly took off and retrieved the paddle, returned it to the canoe in route, and the three ships sailed downstream on good high water. There seemed to be more "potatoes" to paddle around than upriver and lots of big boulders to admire. We thought of the train wreck here and how it scattered cars in the river and were glad the track was clear for the moment.

Always scanning the shore for flowers, we decided this crew would probably not allow us to stop for samples. The dominant flowers were lavender Joe Pye weed and yellow tickseed sunflowers. Looking up at the surrounding hills, their summits were pretty well hidden in the low hanging clouds and mist, creating a unique picture of the valley as we turned the corner and surveyed the situation at the junction of Pelham Brook. "Stay right in the deeper water," our captain warned and we paddled quickly to avoid the rapids.

The world from water level looked entirely different as we cruised down through the village of Zoar, past the site of the old Massachusetts Talc Company buildings, the old railroad station and all the other landmarks of an earlier age, including the long-gone farmhouse and cleared fields on the opposite shore. As we looked for a big boulder called Otter Rock, which we had once seen on a postcard, the view began to dim and our skin was suddenly cooled. It was misting heavily. As we approached the junction of Cold River, we tried to think of the old Indian Campground there on the flat at the base of the old Mohawk Indian trail over Forbidden Mountain, but it was hard to think in the rain. It was suddenly heavy, noisy rain with huge drops making thousands of big plops on the river surface. It almost looked as if the river was coming up in spouts to meet the raindrops! No one was laughing except the crew from Wisconsin, already wet, who were merrily paddling down under the railroad bridge.

Then it began to rain – we mean RAIN, DOWNPOUR, and FLOOD!! You could hardly see your hand before your face, much less the potatoes in the river. What an experience! Wouldn't have missed it for the world. But we did begin to wonder if we could bail the rapidly filling raft with our shoes. The beautiful fog hung low on the green mountains above our heads, distorted as we looked through sheets and sheets of rain. Washed foliage along the shore was highlighted by clean ledges dropping into the river. We thought of the river swiftly rising, making it impossible to come ashore at the appointed place. The Route 2 bridge gave us shelter for a moment but we had to dodge the surface drainage pipes emptying ribbons of water into the river.

As we paddled beyond the bridge, the rain subsided somewhat and we peered through the mist, trying to see the two canoe crews ahead. We began to wonder just where we were supposed to go ashore and what had happened to the others, when they all appeared on top of the big outcropping rock and motioned us into a cove just beyond. We're not sure, but we think the Wisconsin crew was the first to reach their destination. They had the biggest smiles and didn't look one bit wetter than the rest of us!

* * * * *

Swamps get in your blood after a while, and we set out for another one between Dell and Davis Mine roads one day, searching again for the elusive twinflower said to be along its edge. Having recently led our partner astray off Zoar Road, we hesitated to again give an opinion on the best route anywhere, so it was a joint decision to head out the old wood road across and slightly east of the junction of Sabrina's Trail and Mine Road. And sure enough, we forged ahead, dismissing our partner's occasional advice that we should take the left-hand fork instead of the right. Once in the vicinity of the brook, we recognized the territory and we knew we had overshot the swamp by a long shot! Fortunately, it was early in the morning and we both treated it as just more territory to examine for woodland treasures, none of which we found until we reached the beaver dam at the end of the swamp. But there was one hole in the ground which was large enough for a cellar hole but wasn't, looked like the start of a mine shaft but had no drill marks, seemed like a natural formation but had rocks piled around the outside. We investigated but it remains a total mystery. Just above there, we came to the interesting bouldery falls in the brook which meant we still had a good ways to go upstream.

Below the dam, we found marsh St. Johnswort and are still pondering bugleweed versus water horehound. We climbed up the beaver dam, trying to determine if the matted grass indicated beaver, muskrats or just what. The pond was full but the dam did not exactly look freshly cared for. We wandered around the edge, stopping often to observe the quiet beauty of a secluded pond in the morning sun. Large dragonflies zoomed over the water, and a flock of cedar waxwings talked softly in the trees. Off in the woods, a tree frog chirped and a kingfisher squawked loudly further up the pond. Grey dead trees in the water made homes and perches for birds, and fallen logs in the water floated with various coverings of mosses, grasses and flowers, their loveliness reflected in the still water. Along the shore, green sphagnum moss was red with tiny blossomed sundew and sprinkled with the pretty, shiny dark green leaves of goldthread. The new, light green leaves of creeping snowberry draped themselves over old rotten white birch logs and the evening's dew still sparkled on them in the morning sun. The red bunchberries intermingled with the blue corn lily berries, creating a beautiful carpet. Again, as we sat staring across the peaceful scene, occasional red, soft maple leaves gently floated down and took their place in the water.

Under way again, we had spread out a little, and were searching the area when our partner called, "Hey, what's this?" We both went down on our knees to examine a long runner with unfamiliar, small green leaves. Nearer the ground, our eyes soon focused on the little row of tiny, dry twinflowers with seedpods. The joy of discovery is such fun!

Then there was the rescue. Squatting in some sphagnum to look closer at the insectivorous sundew, we found a blue damselfly caught in the minute clutching hairs. It took some doing by our partner to free the insect without injuring it in the process, but finally the damselfly happily flew away without so much as a thank-you nod. A more dramatic escape was observed as we were again enjoying the pond view. The kingfisher was still noisy and busy upstream, and after a loud splash we observed the chase. A small hawk had evidently been chasing the kingfisher that was loudly protesting the idea and dived into the water to escape. One more go round and the kingfisher must have tired the hawk. It flew up in a dead tree for a minute or so and then off into the woods to look for smaller and easier prey. And so goes the morning drama in a hidden swamp.

* * * * *

Last but not least, was this year's August search and thrill of discovery of stations of Rowe's rare three bird's orchid (Triphora trianthophora) off on the mountain at Hoosac Tunnel. Our wildflower partner was doing her second year of count and study of this lovely tiny and very erratic little gem which may appear in one spot one year and be dormant for the next six or seven. Last year's count neared four hundred, while this year it took much searching to find sixty. Stems usually have three flowers and each flower only blossoms on one day, forty-eight hours, they say, after a drop in temperature. The whole colony blossoms on the same day. However, slugs and bugs can devour a stem overnight, so now you see one, and tomorrow you may not. Our main duty was at home babysitting, but on blossoming days our duties were relieved (thanks Deb!) and we got to go to the site.

What a thrill to search and finally find that first little flower peeking just above the leaf litter under a beech tree. Such a sweet, little white face, vaguely edged with pink. By looking with the glass, one finds little green lines and a touch of purple, in its throat. Such fleeting beauty is so easy to overlook. We would start our searches with such enthusiasm and finding only one or two new ones, would console ourselves by saying, "But if they were plentiful, we wouldn't be here searching."

* * * * *

Two particular days stand out in our mind other than that first day of discovery. One was the afternoon when we introduced a new wildflower enthusiast and photographer friend to an orchid he had never seen. After much debate on blossoming date, weather and so forth, we happened to pick the right day and he drove out to photograph our orchid. We promised a lovely sight, but one never knows with this strange little creature. The sun and shadows were especially pretty in the woods that afternoon but would the orchid be blossomed? We hiked the steep climb up the hill and almost held our breath as we approached the first site. And there it was, the first little orchid, with a wide open smile, looking up at us. Our friend was thrilled and went on to discover five new plants on his own. The joy of sharing is always a special treat.

* * * * *

The second day we shall well-remember was when we meandered up on the higher ledges, searching while our partner checked the flowers further over on another site. We had found the Goldie's fern and a patch of ginseng, but no three birds. Standing on a rock, we were surveying the hill when we heard a twig crack in the direction of our returning partner – then another crackle in the opposite direction. We stood still, waiting for whatever was about to invade our territory, when a bouncy little black bear came bounding up the hill, stopped and looked at us, sniffed and looked again and may have been there yet if we hadn't tried to quietly alert our partner with a "Suuuuuuuue," which the bear heard and decided he'd better make tracks in the other direction.

And those are some of our joys and thrills and rewards out on the Wild Side in August, 1989.   **9/89**

Three-birds orchids

Up and Over the Hills and Down Again

Like a dog looking for a place to lie down, we walked up and down Pelham Brook under the power line below Brittingham Hill, trying to find a place to cross safely on the rocks without getting our feet wet. The top of the old double cable line for crossing was still in place, but the bottom had long since detached and rusted on the ground. We were tired to the point of stumbling, and finally just picked the shallowest spot and walked straight across. It took about half way for the cold water to seep into our hiking boots and thoroughly soak our wool socks and then our aching feet. Bushwhacking through the briars and thick goldenrod up to the guard rail, we began to realize just how good that cold water had felt and wondered why on earth we had sloshed so quickly to reach the shore, now too far back down the bank to revisit. We took a last look up the mountain to the ledge where we had just spent such a pleasant time and checked our watch – 2:15 p.m. – as we unlocked the car.

The trip had started about eight-thirty that morning when we made a quick decision to go, taking advantage of a pickup at the bottom of Brittingham Hill, where we left the car, and transportation to Davis Mine, where we were dropped off about nine o'clock at the power line crossing on Davenport Road, a distance of about two and a half miles from our car, as the crow flies that is. But today it wasn't the crow, and we weren't flying. The elevations on our intended path would be roughly something like this, give or take a few feet: up 100 feet, down 100, up 300, down 150, up 400, down 400, up 50,

East Rowe power line

down 550, and up that last 25 with wet feet.

The bright October sun of Friday the thirteenth shown on a glorious world of autumn color, and we stood for a moment in the green field basking in the warmth (we were dressed in our winter best, silk turtleneck and wool sweater), smelling the newly cut rowen across the way and admiring the beauty all around. How lucky we considered ourselves to be free for the whole day out on the Wild Side! We had chosen this particular route, thinking it would be something different, a route we could follow without an exhausting bushwhack all over the lot, like we sometimes chase ourselves. Exhausting it would be anyway, and temptation would be on every side to follow a whim or a wood road or climb to the very top of any of the hills we were nearly on the top of. But this sun is getting warm, so let's start on our way.

The sun, being lower to the horizon this time of year, made the trees cast shadows across the trail and it was cool in the shade. We immediately started scanning the ground for its floral contents and stopped right soon to inspect a group of dry blossoms of the square-stemmed mint family. We slung our knapsack down and had our dog-eared Newcomb's in hand before we realized that taking time to further identify shriveled dry flowers and leaves would slow our hike to a crawl. We decided to keep our eyes open for the unusual and the general makeup of the land but not to take the time to satisfy our curiosity on every blooming thing. Besides this was a day to look up at the trees and the blue sky and not down at the ground. We came to a happy medium and did both!

From the top of the first hill, standing among the pretty fruiting ground cedar, we looked back at the road and followed the power line up the opposite hill, from which we knew could be viewed the wilderness of the old Davis Mine area, once a thriving village of 200 residents or more with mining shafts going down 1200 feet into the bowels of the earth and from which ore was hauled in Studebaker wagons by four horse teams down the muddy rutty road to the railhead at Charlemont. The very existence of this major mining operation is now hard to even imagine. Turning our back on that direction, we looked ahead into the small swamp of Tatro Brook tucked in the fold of the valley before the power line marched on up the next mountainside.

The little swamp proved interesting. We admired a bush of black alder, sometimes called winterberries, covered with bright, shiny red berries, which will last long enough to brighten up the snow scene. We tramped around in the deep, soft sphagnum moss and looked at all the little dry flower stalks of the round-leaved sundew. Spotting two little beaver ponds, we wandered into the woods on the left to give them a closer look. A sweet little siren song echoed from the top of the trees beyond and lured us quickly over the little beaver dam to the center island where we tried to spot the unfamiliar songster. We were about to tramp right through the water when suddenly all was quiet. Our ellusive little creature had flown without as much as an introduction or farewell.

We crossed the second dam and jumped the brook that had broken through. This was obviously not an active beaver pond. We climbed up onto the level and stood wishing we could explore further afield in the bright sunlit woods. Instead we walked back out, crossed under the power line and stood looking up the tiny brook on the other side. The basin it had scoured out sometime in the last several million years seemed far larger than today's trickle warranted, but Adams Mountain, which it drains, had been higher then by a few thousand feet, and a lot of terrain has washed down this sluiceway since then.

Having gone in the woods some distance along this brook, our attention then focused on an old stone wall to the left. We turned uphill to examine the rocks, thought nostalgically about its builders, climbed over and soon came upon a good wood road going north. Gosh, so many temptations to follow a new path. We must come back another day, although the soil looked basic acid and did not hold much intrigue for the rare flower search. We returned to the power line and trudged up the steep hillside. In the distance, we could hear the Williams tree hounds and were glad we knew of them, else we would wonder what manner of wild animals might be howling in the wind or resenting our intrusion into their territory. Switching to the cooler side of the hill for a while, we detoured into the bright yellow beech woods to look at an especially plentiful clump of beech drops, those purple-brown clusters of small branches which suddenly appear in the fall as parasites on the beech tree roots.

As we neared the top of the hill, we could look now further east into Heath across Rowe Road and up to Burnt Hill. The power line followed a straight swath through the trees, its long, graceful loops of wires reflecting the morning sun as they stretched from tower to tower and hill to hill.

We rounded over this high point and were above the site of another old turn of the century mining operation, the Mary Louise Copper Mine in the thick woods just below us. Although much smaller than the Davis, it too had a part in Rowe's early fascinating mining history. We could now look south over the Williams and Monroe homes, Tatro Road and an open green field through which the Rowe/Charlemont boundary crosses, and beyond that to the hills of Charlemont and Hawley.

On this eastern side of South Mountain, it was warm and sheltered and the exertion of climbing had warmed us up, too. The shade of an overhanging pine tree now felt good and we shed our wool sweater and rolled up our sleeves. We longed to bask on the ledge for the afternoon, just absorbing the lovely scene to recall on some blustery, cold winter day. Instead, we veered off into the north woods, wondering how far to the top of the hill and curious to see if anything different grew in these soils. More rocks and ledges seemed to be the only addition to the general terrain, and we decided to forego a climb to greater heights ever mindful that there was still much territory between us and the car. As we turned back the haunting sound of migrating geese reached our ears and we ran in circles, bending and tiptoeing trying to get a glimpse of them through the trees. It was a small flock flying low and may have been a local one just changing ponds for the day as we did not spot another V all day.

Back out in the open, we picked our way down over the ledges, stopped to admire a couple stations of polypody growing in rock crevices, detoured just slightly on a wood road and gradually made our way to Maxwell

View toward Rowe from top of South Mountain

Brook, flowing through the bottom of this valley. We easily stepped over this small trickling stream that sparkled in the sun as it dropped in little falls over the descending bedrock. The path ahead looked like a long climb, not only because it was, but because we were ready for a rest. However, we seldom sit unless it's lunch or a spectacular sight. These we knew were yet to come, and besides, we weren't too keen on the thought of lunch, which, because of our haste to get started, consisted of two dry granola bars.

Our pace slowed on this hill as we admired the myriad of dry seedpods of meadow sweet, goldenrod with galls, brown grasses with tassels and beautiful carpets of now cinnamon-colored hayscented fern. Mosses of every hue and texture, fairy cups large enough for elves and pink lichens were only a few of the treasures underfoot. Blue sky overhead and a wall of beautiful red and yellow trees on either side were all a joy to behold. Several outcroppings of flat ledge were covered with small stones, as if groups of children had left their marble games and run off to explore elsewhere. We looked closer at the crosswise troughs in the rock and wondered if they were glacial marks where water had run off on the slant of the hill. One especially pretty white quartz rock sat invitingly on the ledge, and we picked it up and held it for a moment trying to judge

View toward Negus and Greylock

whether we could tuck it in our knapsack. Fortunately, we put it back, realizing that the world is as full of white rocks as the seaside is full of pretty shells. The chirping of a bird had us standing still scanning the brush and twigs. Finally we spotted it almost before our eyes, a white-throated sparrow somewhat upset, we thought, at our intrusion. It was evidently only chirping season, for he never sang his lovely summer song of, "We praise Thee O Lord." Later we came to the conclusion he was not objecting to us but being a friendly guide, following us most of the rest of the way.

Part way up the next hill, we looked for the crossing of the old King's Highway or Norton's Trail, from Fort Pelham in Rowe over this mountain and on down to Moses Rice's at Charlemont, and from thence either over Forbidden Mountain to Fort Massachusetts or south to Deerfield This trail was used by the troops and scouts back in the French and Indian War in the mid 1700s and later by the early settlers of Myrifield. The road opened up to the right and we followed it back across the power line to see where it entered the woods on the south side. Still a well-defined but little-used pathway from the past, it was now full of soft, spongy sphagnum moss of lovely shades of green and soft reds.

The height we were gaining now opened up a gorgeous panorama back to the east. In the farthest distance rose blue

Looking over Zoar Road to West Rowe

Mount Monadnock in New Hampshire, and close by to the left, the rounded mound of Mount Adams was just above the trees. And something we had not noticed in passing was a large witches'-broom formation in the top of a pine on the previous hill. When we at last reached the wide summit of South Mountain, we looked for a large boulder on which we could enjoy the view, rest and have lunch. No boulders appeared on the grassy summit and we pushed on, crossing the north/south trail which leads into The Northwest.

From the western portion of the summit, we could now see Greylock to the west, the Mohawk Trail in Florida, Raycroft Lookout, the Gfroerer farm, Bear Swamp Upper Reservoir and Switching Station, and Doubleday's Cliffs. This was a long and lovely view but, as we remembered, not as spectacular as the lower one to come. We finally settled down on a flat, sloping ledge in the shade, for the sun had become quite warm. Turning to open our knapsack and retrieve the granola bars, we noticed that old bruin had passed this way some time ago in berry season and those children had left more of their marbles on this ledge. In a few minutes the chirping white-throated sparrow joined us. And do you know what? Those two granola bars tasted pretty darn good after all!

We did not linger long over lunch, fearing our joints would stiffen and we'd never get down off the mountain. Starting over the hill, we stopped to watch the wind as it blew from the west up the power line, stripping the trees of leaves and creating a regular red and yellow blizzard. There is a slight crook in the path of the line in mid hill and thus the full force of the ever-increasing wind did not hit us until we reached that point. The path on this west side was the roadway for logging operations and was wide and muddy, and showed to full advantage a quantity of deer tracks.

Once down in the lowest part of the gully, we spotted blossomed white snakeroot, which means good rich soil. We quickly detoured up the hill, encouraged by one small baneberry plant, but, in spite of a lot of traipsing up and down and across, we did not find anything else worthy of comment except lovely stands of Christmas ferns. We continued up the next hill in the woods and eventually through the trees, we could look back into the center of Rowe, seeing well both Quinn houses, the Boggs house, our own Sunset cabin, and the flagpole above Rowe's Bowl behind the school. Then came the dramatic moment when we came out sideways onto the power line at the spectacular top where we could finally look down and see our car, 500 feet below at the bottom of Brittingham Hill.

We dropped the knapsack, put our sweater back on and sat down on the high rock ledge facing a stiff wind and overlooking the world. What a spot! We could see all of Negus and the Steele Brook valley, Greylock and the whole Whitcomb Summit range. Only two houses were visible, the Gfroerer farm on Petrie Road and the top of Floyd Veber's on Zoar Road. If we moved way to the south side of the clearing we could see

the Rice and Pierce places on Brittingham Hill, the barn on Pelham Brook Farm and Sparky Truesdell's on Tunnel Road. The rest was wilderness. Ah wilderness!!

It took us a long time to study it all and comprehend the beauty of the glorious autumn colors, still mixed with much green. One of the loveliest sights was right beside us. The ledge on which we were sitting had a long streak of white quartz and the trees were bright reds, yellows and bronzes. We sat for many minutes, then got up and walked around to be sure we weren't missing any other view, then came back to sit again. The very strong winds increased the excitement of the spot and we basked in pure pleasure for some time. The white throat was still our companion, as was a tiny snake, who was also taking in the warmth of the afternoon sun on the ledge. This was quality time and, with the car in sight down below, we did not feel the need to hasten our departure. It had probably been ten years since we had contemplated on this spot and who could tell how long before good fortune might bring us back again?

We tended to lean into the wind as we finally picked our way down the mountain, and when the wind stopped suddenly and we stepped sideways on uneven ground, we rolled slowly over backwards and found ourselves lying low in the ferns looking up at the bright blue sky, something we had really wanted to do all day long.   **11/89**

Looking down on Lund Lodge, Alta, Utah

Nan with
bog orchid
at Alta, Utah

Cecret Lake - Alta, Utah

This Hike Was an EXPERIENCE

The other day a friend was sharing a story about leading a Boy Scout hike many years ago. He will always remember the remark of one small boy as they precariously crossed a ledge on a rather narrow shelf. The boy looked up at the leader and said with great enthusiasm, "Wow, this is an EXPERIENCE!" In the back of our mind we were already thinking that's just what we want to do with Wild Side, give the folks sitting at home an "Experience!" Believe me, this one turned out to be more of an experience than we bargained for and you can be glad you are experiencing it at home in your easy chair.

Although we have had two beautiful days of cross-country skiing recently, and one afternoon of trekking all over the front of Adams and Todd to prove that we were still alive after being confined with this winter's virus, none of these quite qualified as a Wild Side hike. We wanted to experience something different.

With the January thaw over and the snows of a continuous, four-day storm accumulated on the ground, we expected to have lots of lovely choices for a winter hike. But the weather has turned warm and the forecast is for rain. Today, January 24th, was predicted to be partial afternoon sunshine before downpours in the next few days spoil everything. At the moment of our decision to go at one o'clock, the fog was thick and the day was dark. This would have to qualify as an experience, for who in their right mind would don snowshoes and head west from our dooryard looking for a Wild Side story on a day like this?

Snowshoeing across the road, the large rocks in our perennial garden looked spooky as they loomed out of the mist. On coming closer, the multitude of deer tracks in the fresh snow led us to believe there had been a deer convention there last night. The pawing of the snow to the bare grass was fine, but when we discovered they had served our yew bushes, our lilac, our Rose of Sharon and several other flowering shrubs for the banquet meal, we felt less than hospitable toward our wild friends. We envisioned our garden this coming summer needing to be surrounded by a high prison fence topped with barbed wire, if we were not able to teach these wild creatures better manners.

Beyond the garden, we disappeared into the fog over the hill. We descended into the brush to check out a series of animal holes we had seen in the summer and whose occupants we have never spotted. Somebody certainly lives there, and had made tracks under last night's fresh snow but had not ventured forth today. We are still curious but do suspect a fox. Just before detouring down the hill, we had looked further into the woods and spotted what we thought was a new pileated woodpecker tree full of light-colored, freshly drilled holes. That was to be our next checkpoint but as we drew closer the holes moved side-ways – a beech tree was full of remaining yellow leaves and the darker tree behind was as whole as ever. Just an optical illusion.

Crossing the wall behind our Hermit cabin, we picked up a deer track and followed it through the lower field to where it went into the woods. We stopped a moment to enjoy the bits of dry, brown goldenrod flowers just sticking their heads above the snow, and the brown, fertile fronds of the many sensitive ferns along the swampy edge of the field. Deer tracks were everywhere in the woods, and we followed them until they seemed to be going round in circles and even under a low log. Here we checked the hoof prints to be sure, as we had always believed a deer would bound over an obstacle rather than diving under. Looking around, we saw lots of small saplings that seemed like plenty of food for a herd of deer and certainly wondered why they felt possessed to stray out in the open to sample our garden. I guess we all like a new restaurant and change of menu once in a while.

Original wall on Pond Road

Because of the fog, the woods seemed cozy with many little hideaways under the hemlock branches hanging low with the heavy snow. With the warming air, the snow was gradually falling here and there, and a motion or noise was not an animal but the snow clumps falling and the branches shaking themselves free. The deer tracks often went up to the hemlocks, where the animal had seemed to nose around, then turn and move on. Perhaps if we quietly took up a position on a rock, we could watch some of this activity but we had miles to go (although we didn't realize it at the time). Our general plan was to go directly west until we came to County Road in the general vicinity of the Wasko place and then, with our snowshoes

over our shoulder, hike the road back home.

We sometimes had to move quickly under the trees to dodge a snow shower and soon found ourselves ready to cross Hazelton Road, actually, not quite as far up as we expected, for once over the bank, we had to cross the little open brook. One jump in summer would have done it but the water was now about three feet below where we were standing clumsily on snowshoes, and the space between us and the other side seemed like a giant crevasse. Sizing up the situation, we put our poles down in the water and managed the leap to the opposite shore quite handily, much to our surprise.

Somewhere under the snow in this general vicinity, we knew there was a small pile of rocks, possibly undisturbed for over two hundred years, marking the northwest corner of the old hundred acre lot which included the present village and the valuable water power of Pelham Brook in the natural Mill Pond area – a lot whose north stonewall intersects the road by our house and, although missing on the steep pasture hill, continues as the southern wall in the field below. This particular lot has always intrigued us, for since Cornelius Jones sold it to Seth Howard in 1778, it has been bought and sold many times and then divided and sold many times again. These hundred acres, with the first road passing through the center, have probably seen more activity through the years than any other in town, containing the first grist mill and a saw-mill, the satinet factory, the old stores, a church, town hall and library and now the village green and municipal complex as well.

We crossed the old north/south stone wall and marveled at the ancient trees along the line, full of holes and hiding places for all sorts of small animals and birds. In the treetops, we could hear a flock of evening grosbeaks and an occasional goldfinch. Shortly, we picked up a snowmobile trail and followed south a short distance then discarded that idea as we wanted to bushwhack rather than follow a trail, knowing where we would come out – it seemed more exciting going our own way.

Ahead at the top of the brook bank could be seen the huge triangular boulder with its topping of snow like a pointed cap upon its head. This boulder is an old friend and we detoured a bit to pay our respects and inspect its crop of moss and rock tripe. Several years ago, we gave it the distinction of the largest boulder in Rowe but were proven wrong by that afternoon, and have since found another triple its size, reducing this one to third in line at best. We tend to stand and admire rocks and may have been there still, except that a heavy glob of snow from the high spruce above us fell directly on our head. When trees start throwing snowballs at you, it is time to get going!

The bank was steep down to Ide Brown Brook (somebody in the last fifty years or so has changed the name to Shippee brook) and we had to put our poles ahead of us and

inch along, making a couple of tight hairpin turns to lessen the angle. The brook was playing gurgling music as it swiftly flowed around the rocks and under large cakes of ice covered with snow. We chose a rather wide covered area and hoped our weight was evenly distributed enough that the rotten ice underneath would not give way in midstream. We crossed with no problem and soon came upon a mass of deer tracks, the first we had seen west of Hazelton Road.

The tracks seemed to go up along the brook basin, but we abandoned them to head west and up the opposite bank that was not quite as abrupt. We stopped a moment and thought how lucky we were to be out in the woods on a lovely, foggy day like this! Partway up the hill we noticed the telltale cone midden of a red squirrel and could hear his funny, muffled chatter. He must have been in a snow tunnel, for the chatter stopped as we drew closer and continued later as we drew away.

Now we came up into a more open, logged area, which is only penetrable after a good snowfall covers the slash, and we were able to cross over rotten piles of limbs which crushed to sticks as we climbed up and over. The only problem was extracting the ski poles, which tended to catch on stubs underneath the heap. Rocks, too, were covered, and we found ourselves teetering on top of one, ready to play king of the mountain with anyone who challenged us.

Up away from the brook, it seemed less foggy and almost bright but it was not from the sun just yet but from the grove of small beech trees with their bright yellow leaves still clinging to the branches. We pulled at one leaf and found that it was still

well attached and not about to fly away on the first breeze. The land was fairly level, as hill country goes, and we were trying to imagine how it must have looked back at the turn of the century when this was all open sheep pasture.

Here and there were various clumps of interrupted and cinnamon ferns with their gracefully arching stalks devoid of all leaves except for tiny, beige flags at the very tips. It was warm and we took off our gloves and hat and stowed them in a zippered pocket. In the process, we remembered our thermometer/compass attached to our jacket and decided to take a look. The thermometer read 38 degrees and the compass indicated a hair south of west in the direction we were going. Right on, we thought as we picked up a snowmobile trail for a short distance, then veered more westerly. Off in a tree behind us, a chickadee was practicing his lovely spring phoebe call. The birds, too, were mystified by this strange winter weather.

The fog was definitely clearing, and by the time we walked up the gradual rise to the high point, the sun could actually be seen though a very cloudy sky. The snow was becoming heavier, and each time we raised a snowshoe, it carried a few more pounds of snow like weights on an athlete's legs. Looking down in the snow, we spotted the empty shell of a beechnut and looked skyward to see many more still hanging on the high limbs. We also noticed that the leaves were all gone on the tall beech trees and only remained on the smaller new growth trees. Wonder why? Ah, and there's a squirrel track in the snow. Most small animals must still be buried under the blanket of snow and have not yet worked their way to the surface. We crossed a wall but were hardly aware of it as such. A trail soon paralleled the wall but we made sure not to take that one, judging it to be the north/south trail that would end at Zoar Road.

Crossing the trail, we started on the downward side that we expected to lead to the beaver swamp east of Wasko's. The first thing we noticed was more deer tracks and a well-nibbled low laurel bush. Laurel is poisonous to goats, which eat the same type of food as deer, and the latter should know by now what's good or bad. So there's another puzzle. Someone should write a guidebook answering all these oddball questions for which there are no answers elsewhere. As we went down the hill, the fog again thickened. We declined another path to the south but eventually did follow one going more our way.

We were descending into darker and foggier depths, and it seemed strange, for we didn't remember such a steep valley to the beaver pond. The air quickly cooled and we donned the hat and gloves once again. After stopping to investigate a real pileated woodpecker tree, we then stared into the fog, fascinated at the eerie atmosphere.

We trudged downhill for a rather long ways before giving the situation much real thought. It was a clearing in the distance that finally brought us down to earth with curiosity. As we came nearer, buildings and a fence began to appear through the fog. Where on earth had we strayed? It certainly wasn't Wasko's beaver pond. Two more steps and we stopped dead in our tracks. Dumpling Hill!! Joe Vadeboncoeur's place on Zoar Road. What a dummy we had been to follow that path. We were nearly a half-mile off course. Zoar Road? We didn't want to be there, we had been aiming for County Road!

Chagrined at our mistake, in territory which we certainly knew on a sunny day in summer, we turned right around and marched back up the hill probably at a pretty good pace judging that we were out of breath most of the rest of the trip. Nearly back to where we had picked up the path, we then recognized the territory and decided to drop down and cross the steep narrow valley of Rice Brook and head for County Road. Again, we took the bank in a series of hairpin turns. This brook was singing, too, and we wanted to sit down and rest and enjoy it for

a moment but now we knew we had miles to go, and the faint ache in our weary legs began to be noticeable. Before moving on, we did scan the brook banks for any sign of animal tracks but all was fresh and untouched snow, except where the trees had shed odd-shaped globs of snow or dripped little circles of melt water.

Somehow, the brook intrigued, us and we continued to climb north within sight of it. It wasn't long before we came upon a cross-country ski track where someone had evidently made their own trail through the woods down along the brook. It almost seemed as if they had been wearing shortie skis, as their turns around the numerous trees were close and sharp. This gave us something new to wonder about and momentarily took our mind off the ever-increasing effort it took to climb the rather steep hill, lifting each snowshoe piled with heavy wet snow. It finally dawned on us how smart that skier had been to travel downhill. Maybe we should have reconsidered that exit at Zoar Road; someone would have given us a ride and we'd be home by now instead of alone off in the depths of Rice Brook valley. Ah, but then we would never have had this EXPERIENCE, this struggle with the elements and with our own endurance! And besides, there was no way of giving up now, we had to get ourselves home.

Fortunately, we did not have our knapsack with goodies like a geo map because if we had looked at it, we would have seen that it was a lot further to civilization than we even anticipated at that precise moment. Rice Brook (so named for Sam Rice who settled on the present Wasko place back in 1700 something), after the beaver meadow, drops into quite a long, deep canyon and although we are quite familiar with the lower section, these upper reaches were new to us. We finally left the ski trail as it crossed the brook to the right and we trudged on.

But look ahead! A little canyon coming in from the left has two big boulders and an animal trail around and under the upper one. We took off like a spring chicken to investigate. Tracks in the rotting snow could be anything, but judging by the narrow shelter under the rock it must be a porcupine. We contemplated our next move and decided the easiest way ahead was to follow the tracks up the bank. A little past the rock, they curved around and we could then see them disappear into a much larger gap between the rock and the bank. Someday we are going to stick our nose into one of these hiding places and find somebody at home – maybe somebody we don't anticipate meeting face to face! That thought always occurs to us but hasn't stopped us yet. We, of course, had to climb up and stick our nose in this one. It was a high step but we could do it by pulling ourselves up by a tree. We made it, but had to try again, as one snowshoe was left behind. Once on top, we peeked in the hole and thought it a good place for a bobcat or something exciting like that, but our

better judgment said a porcupine, although we couldn't see anything alive. Standing on the edge of the hole, we reached down to re-strap our snowshoe. As we were doing this, we became conscious of movement under our right hand and there was porky, quills aloft, up from the depths investigating us! He evidently didn't like what he saw and disappeared into another chamber.

Well, that was a nice diversion, but the trek must go on. We seemed to be near an upper plateau, so climbed the remaining distance and gained fairly level ground. But looking forward through the woods, no field or farmhouse could be seen. We crossed a stone wall, inspected an old maple tree and continued to trudge along. How great this would be if the weather was seasonably cold and all this snow didn't pile up on our snowshoes. Having lost one shoe back there, it continued to give trouble and we were forever reaching down to put the strap back on our heel. Even on the level, we seemed to be continually out of breath and finally picked a small sturdy maple tree and leaned. How good this felt! After moaning and groaning for a few minutes, we looked around and once again thoroughly enjoyed the woodsy scene with its soft misty atmosphere. This restored our spirits and we eventually pushed on.

It seemed a very, very long time before we detected the yellow Wasko buildings way in the distance up to our left. The first thought was to head directly there and pick up County Road from their driveway, BUT – we began to rethink remaining distances. It looked at that moment like a long climb to County Road and an even longer walk home. If we continued as we were, crossed the beaver pond to the right and picked up the trail it would be just a hop skip and jump out to Hazelton Road, one side of a triangle instead of two. This theory was probably correct – we just forgot we weren't hopping and skipping with loaded snowshoes!

Our mind made up, we marched (would you believe dragged ourselves?) out into the open area, where several old beaver dams were evident but water was rushing through them all. We guessed it had been a few years since these were active colonies. We pushed through dense maleberry bushes, thick with tiny, five-parted fruit capsules, and then climbed over the first and second dams onto the more open former pond area. The ice surface was rotten near the running water and we stepped quickly, as we didn't need wet boots to add to our troubles. Scanning the few dead trees along the edges, we wondered if they contained any blue heron nests, but all trees were empty. Looking up the stream, we thought the next dam was solid and that it would be fun to walk up the brook to the road, checking for any active beaver dams along the way, but we anticipated that it would take more effort than we could muster and we'd best trot right across and pick up that trail to Hazelton Road.

The hill to the trail was rather short, as we had expected way back at the beginning of this safari, but the trail seemed to go on for a hundred miles, as we literally dragged one foot after the other, trying to shed the snow but with not enough oomph left to shake a shoe. About every third step, our strap came off again, but that was all right because we had to stop and rest about that often anyway! Even the smart little chickadees in the trees gave us no comfort as they flitted from limb to limb, reminding us even more that we couldn't flit anywhere. Many summer hikes have been long and hot and tiring but we never remember being quite so tired or ever truly wondering if we really could make it.

Eventually there was a fork in the trail with the right hand one going uphill. We were in no mood for climbing but decided that it must be the shortcut to the Jurentkuff's, where we could surely get revival refreshment and a ride home. Soon the West Cemetery fence peeked through the trees and we knew we were still west of the old Taylor (now Boras) house. We could see the plowed driveway in the distance, but to cross the lawn to get there looked like forever. Finally, in desperation we took off the snowshoes altogether and walked though the deep snow. With not enough energy left to put the snowshoes over our shoulder we dragged them and our ski poles at our sides. Looking back at the funny marks we wondered how someone else would interpret our tracks.

The plowed road was heaven and somehow we managed to put one foot ahead of the other long enough to get to Jurentkuff's, climb their stairs, fall through the door without knocking and crash into their kitchen chair. It was just four o'clock.

"Where in the world have you been this time on such a foggy afternoon, and what can I get for you?" Pearl asked.

"Oh, just out for a Wild Side hike, and if you please, we'd like a double bouillon and a ride home," we answered between sighs of relief.

And, as we finally relaxed with cup in hand, we were thinking that for an old lady, this really had qualified as an EXPERIENCE!　　　　**2/90**

Skiing on the Wild Side In the Mountains of Utah

"Lord of the Hills" was one of the songs sung by the Salt Lake City Mormon Tabernacle Choir during their 3,160th broadcast on Sunday morning, March 11, 1990. Perhaps no one else in the audience appreciated that particular song as much as I did, for I had been skiing in the high mountains of Utah for the last seven days. The song was an expression of the joy within me, thankfulness for having had the chance to experience the beauty of the western hills, the strength to ski their slopes, and to do this in the companionship of family and young friends.

With gratitude to a new friend, Helen Lund, it was indeed a privilege to be able to join her for this Tabernacle broadcast. On a stormy but beautiful morning on Temple Square we waded through fast-falling snow that was heavy and wet, creating an unforgettable picture as it clung to the blossoming flowers and trees surrounding the tall spires of the gray Mormon Temple. And in this Square could be experienced the spirit and character and accomplishments of the great man, prophet, statesman and pioneer, Brigham Young, who was born back in 1801 in our own Green Mountain hills in Whitingham, Vermont, neighboring town to Rowe.

Many of us have treasured records or tapes of the famous Mormon Tabernacle Choir, but it has always been a wish of mine to be there in person to hear them. The Tabernacle setting itself, with the great organ pipes, rounded ceiling and unusual lighting, is inspiring to those of any faith, and when the three hundred and twenty-five members of the choir silently rise in unison and burst forth in song the effect is truly awe inspiring. No less exciting was the organ

solo, "Fantasia in G Minor," by Bach. Their literature tells us that the organ, one of the finest in the world, has 11,623 pipes and 206 voices, with five manuals on the console. Not distracting but technically interesting was the chance to watch the filming by the various TV cameras, and the instantaneous blending of the images as seen on the large monitors at either side of the front. Especially moving was the choir's rendition of the old spiritual, "Nobody Knows the Trouble I've Seen."

Before our dash to the airport to catch my plane (which never did arrive, but that is another long story!), Helen gave me a quick tour of the "Beehive House," the well-preserved and lovely home of Brigham Young, where she has been a Sunday guide for many years. This stately mansion reflects the life and times of this unusual man, second president of The Church of Jesus Christ of Latter-day Saints as well as governor of the pioneer state of Deseret and in 1850, first governor of the territory of Utah.

My unexpected visit to Temple Square was the fitting climax to my fabulous journey to Utah. The whole idea started near the end of December, when a friend challenged me back to downhill skiing. After years of enthusiastic skiing (always with more nerve than talent) in my own youth and constant weekend and vacation skiing with growing children, I had given it up back in the early seventies (the dates are a little fuzzy for I did not write in my diary, "Today I have given up skiing,") when a bout with tennis elbow left little strength to plant a ski pole properly. In the early eighties, I did try it again, got new equipment and a pass at Berkshire, but never used it more than a few days. In recent years I have taken up cross-country skiing and fully expected the downhill equipment would become antiques "up in the barn." But the idea, once planted by my friend, of downhill skiing again didn't take long to develop. A couple of good runs down hills on cross-country skis brought back a flood of memories of all those exciting days at Chickley Alps as a kid and in later years at Thunder Mountain and Haystack. I was hooked again!

With courage and determination and, for once in my life a little fear, I packed the downhill equipment in the car (son Rick had come by and checked it out saying it was antiquated but safe) and by myself headed for a day at Haystack. If my knees wouldn't bend and I fell flat on my face then so be it. I would gracefully return home and openly admit to advanced age and rigidity, and privately shed a tear for what might have been. However, it was a blue-sky day and, for New England, unusually beautiful packed powder on the trails. All the conditions were ideal; the challenge was up to me. As I rode up in the chair my mind was a mixture of wild excitement and panic fear. The fear was probably not so much concerned with a broken bone but the fear of failure, of disappointing myself.

For the first run I picked a green circle "easier" trail that meandered its way around the outside of the mountain. I fell into a wide snowplow (now called a wedge) while I attached my poles. Gradually the V of the snowplow closed and I was on my way, slow and cautious at first, then gradually becoming braver, my knees bending, my skis skidding around the turns, my arms capable of planting a pole and un-weighting myself.

Hallelujah! From green circles to "more difficult" blue squares and then a shot at the "most difficult" black diamonds, I braved the slopes and, like riding a bicycle, it all came back. Having convinced myself that I could survive even a "black", I returned to the blue squares where I rightfully belonged. It was a great day!

Next, I joined Rick and wife Laurie and a group from Yankee on a ten-mile workout on cross-country skis at Somerset. Another perfect day in the woods gliding on soft new snow, but more importantly, although I did not realize it at the time, it was building strength in stiff old knees and legs.

Two days later Rick called with another offer for me to join Laurie and friends for a day at Magic Mountain. I hesitated. I had planned more practice by myself at Haystack. I wasn't good enough yet to join anyone else downhill skiing, I thought. He blew away that theory and I gratefully said yes. It was another perfect day with more challenging hills! We had some great runs and we all seemed to arrive at the lift at the same time. It did not appear that I was holding up anyone. That hurdle overcome, I relaxed and thoroughly enjoyed the day. I was psyched to ski and it probably showed in the silly contented grin on my face.

It was on a late afternoon ride up the chair with Laurie (I must have successfully passed some unknown ski test) when she popped the question. Would I like to join her and Rick, the three skiing Bernhardts (formerly of Rowe), and four other friends on their planned ski trip to Alta, Utah in three weeks? I hung on tighter to the chair to contain my immediate thrill and enthusiasm. I must be calm and think about this. Do they really want an old lady on their vacation? Could I possibly keep up with them on western slopes where I had always dreamed of going, especially to Alta? What a compliment to have your daughter-in-law extend such an invitation! What a reward for all those cold mornings years ago when I tied Rick's boots and drove him to ski lessons! A parent this lucky couldn't refuse. I was on cloud nine.

Rick arranged another half day for me with friends at Mt. Snow and that was the extent of my practice skiing. The next day I left for two weeks on the Florida Keys for some sun and sailing, always mindful that I must walk with vigor every day to remain in some sort of shape for the next adventure. What a study in contrasts this winter would be. And, oh yes, there would be a *Goal Post* to publish between Florida and Utah! But all missions were accomplished and I was finally headed west.

Airline arrangements for Utah at this late date were a bit iffy, and I had to take reservations for a day earlier and come back a day later than the rest of the crew. This turned out to have several distinct advantages. First, I had a good night's rest in Salt Lake City and a day to get used to the higher altitude. The morning after arrival on March 2nd I went out for a long walk along the highway, enjoying the view of the snow-covered mountains surrounding this beautiful city. High on an overpass I stopped and looked toward the city that clings to the base of the high Wasatch Mountains to the east. In view were the gold-domed state house and the six spires of the Mormon Temple.

I suddenly remembered my first visit to this city and quick figuring made it out to be thirty-nine years ago, I was a young girl, foot loose and fancy free, touring the country in a forty-nine Chevy with two other girls. I remembered the valley as crystal clear and beautiful, containing a small well-planned city. Then one could certainly understand the statement, "This is the Place," attributed to Brigham Young after he led the small band of Mormon pioneers from Illinois and first saw the Salt Lake Valley in 1847. Sadly, time, development, and industry have taken their toll.

In the early afternoon I rode the bus back to the airport and was soon paged by our earliest arrival and together we met the rest of the crew with their mound of baggage. Rick, who organized the trip, was busy with phone calls to the lodge and canyon shuttle. The shuttle van soon appeared and the ten of us piled in, with most of the luggage and skis on the roof. In less than an hour we were climbing into snow country up in Little Cottonwood Canyon, past Snowbird Ski Area and finally to Alta's upper parking lot. Here, the road ended in high snow banks and we unloaded and waited for our hosts, Gary and Helen Lund, to come for us in their two snow-cats, one large one with open body on the back for luggage and the little "Imp" just for passengers. They were soon spotted coming down the trail, and upon arrival there were welcome shouts of greeting from some of the crew who were old friends, having stayed at the Lund lodge twice before. Newcomers were introduced and immediately felt welcome. The Lunds do a remarkable job at remembering names! The sun was now shining after a gray morning, and as we chugged up to the lodge more gorgeous mountain panoramas opened to view. We said, "Wow!" more than once. The Lund's lodge is right on the ski trail called "Rock 'n Roll" off the Supreme lift, just below the steep and mogully "Lund's Hill."

First order of business was a tour of the double A-frame lodge. There were a smattering of house rules like, please conserve water and, no ski boots past the entryway. But that was where the boot warmers were so why take boots elsewhere? The Lunds are retired and live year round in one half of this heavenly hideaway. Seven of our crew were in the west side of the building, which had a large living room with spectacular view toward Devil's Castle, (the formation of rocky mountains rising over a thousand feet just east of the lodge) the dining area and kitchen, four bedrooms and a hot tub. Three of us slept in the lower apartment on the Lund side which was furnished in the interesting style of the old mining era, complete with old photos of the mines in the Albion Basin, and, of course, our own hot tub.

It didn't take everyone long to get unpacked and comfortable while watching the evening sunset and having a few snacks (and lots of water to ward off altitude headaches from dehydration for we were at 9,600 feet) and then a good spaghetti dinner. Our menus had been sent ahead and the Lunds had the refrigerator and pantry well-stocked for the week. Everyone took turns on the cooking and cleanup detail, and already appetites were mountain-sized! A Warren Miller ski movie on the VCR completed the evening and everyone turned in early. Before doing so, however, so I had to take a peek out the door and experience the enchanting sight of moonlight on Devil's Castle. Above the

mountains constellation Orion, star Sirius, and planet Jupiter were glistening in the clear air and the Big Dipper hung, handle down, behind the lodge.

Sunday dawned clear and everyone was up about seven, breakfasted, and out putting on skis by 8:45. Enthusiasm was high in all of us. One by one we peeled off the deck and down the snow-cat trail to the regular ski trail for the long and gloriously scenic run to Alta's Albion Lodge, where we got our tickets. We wanted to get back to the lift called Supreme near our lodge but from the bottom chose the wrong connecting lift. From the top Rick tried to remedy this, and first thing led us all down an open slope of that famous deep powder. Trying so hard to keep up with everyone and not be a drag, I also headed down through the powder. Leaning too far forward, my skis somehow made a wide V with the tails together, and I fell face first between them! Bindings let go, skis got lost in the powder and I was a snowman. Well that settles it; I'll spend the rest of the week in the lodge. Through the snow on my face I could see most of the crew way off on the trail to the lift. Rick, obviously feeling responsible, was patiently waiting at the bottom of the hill for this old lady. What an embarrassment to him, and how could I have failed so soon? With infinite patience he said it was no problem, and carefully led me on a packed trail around another route (probably thinking, "Am I going to have to look after her like this all week?"). By the time I was riding up the next lift with even more spectacular scenery coming into view, my embarrassment subsided and my enthusiasm returned with the attitude "So I was the first one to fall, so what? It will

Nan and the girls

speed and performance.

That first day before lunch we tried another area called Sugarloaf, with higher and longer runs but also longer lines on this a weekend day. After some great runs and with our stomachs growling, Rick led the crew on a cross country trek he thought would be an easy route back to and up the Supreme lift and on down to Lund lodge. Every hill turned out to be deep and steep; great for the experts who took it straight, but it was now Rick's turn to apologize to the rest of us for getting us in "over our heads."

It was quite a long maneuver back and forth, and sometimes, not having enough speed to go across the more level areas, we had to pole our way. At near ten thousand feet altitude, this required some effort and breath, raising our heart rates a good measure. Stopping every so often just to breathe was a necessity. During that run down Supreme my legs were wobbling and my skis were floating in strange directions. Lund lodge looked pretty good to all ten tired skiers. But it was amazing what relaxing without boots and a good lunch did for everyone. We were gung ho and back on the slopes in an hour. Needless to say the hot tubs were well used for aching muscles that night, and after a hearty stew dinner everyone was ready to call it a perfect day.

Boom, boom! Out of a sound sleep I sat

happen to everyone sooner or later." And I now proudly admit that in seven full days of skiing that was the first of only three falls!

The crew divided into three groups; five experts trying all terrain, four of us intermediates, and one advanced beginner. From the top of Supreme I was thinking I should start out very cautiously and headed down the easier route when Laurie called "Come on, you can do it." That was all the persuasion I needed to follow the rest to a long, wide, and steep but well-packed slope called "Challenger." It took only the first hundred feet or so of that trail to reawaken my skiing passion, and I loved every minute of those next precious seven days on the slopes, game to go anywhere (well, most anywhere!), although I considered it more surviving rather skiing over the big moguls and through deep powder. I really preferred the long, steep, but packed powder runs where you could loose yourself in the exhilaration of bolt upright in bed and watched lightning flash in the sky. A thundershower in March? A storm was predicted and this must be how it arrives in Utah! Later in the night I was conscious of the snow drifting against the window, and by morning a foot of new powder had fallen on top of the 100 inches already packed on the hills. It was snowing and blowing at the lodge when we set out for the ticket run in the morning, but by the time we arrived at the bottom the sun was shining and it was quite warm. More loud booming this morning was not thunder, but the ski patrol bombing the avalanche areas to make them safe for the day's skiers. The mostly unpacked hills made interesting skiing and we tried a little of everything.

Our advanced beginner decided to stay at the lodge for the day, and had the fixings for bacon, lettuce, and tomato sandwiches all set out for us when we came in for lunch. That bacon sure smelled good! In the afternoon the experts went off to new heights to enjoy the powder, and we went back to Supreme for some good runs in spite of the top being in a fog. A real turkey dinner, complete with stuffing, and more Warren Miller ski movies ended another great day.

The second snowstorm started falling that evening, and nearly another foot had accumulated by morning when we woke in a dense fog. This new snow was lighter and fluffier and a real joy to ski, even in the fog. But what a weird feeling it was skiing down the long trail to the lower lodge when in places you couldn't see ten feet in front of you. Today we decided to try the lower and original area of Alta, at the lifts called Collins and Wildcat. This involved taking a transfer rope tow across the valley and also required

a lot of poling and climbing to get to the lift line. This area is more popular, and even mid-week had a long liftline. Once in the chair we were whisked up into the dense fog. The only sign read, "All intermediates get off at mid-station." Well, Rick had said "top" so up we went. We could always sit down and slide! The fog was so thick that we could have been anywhere, but the snow underfoot was excellent and we had some of the best runs yet on these trails.

Near lunchtime we parted company with the experts and the four of us took a mid-mountain lift called Germania that would take us to the top crossover to Sugarloaf trails and thus back home. Again, in the midst of beautiful scenery we were in a fog. A few signs pointed the way but when, without fog, you could plainly see where you were going the signs stopped. We were in a real quandary, not wanting to go over the hill and find ourselves on an expert slope and yet seeing no trail and never having been there before we had no idea where to go. We asked some other skiers behind us but they said, "No, we're following you!" We finally turned downhill and a high mountain loomed up beside us. That at least was comforting as we weren't about to go off the edge.

Eventually a gully looked familiar and we came out onto the Sugarloaf trails. It was funny on another clear day to look over at the terrain where we had been so lost in that fog. After lunch, still surrounded by dense fog, we girls skied down and spent a few minutes buying new hats and postcards in the Alta ski shop then skied the rest of the afternoon on Supreme.

And there was the scene of my second fall of the week. A very large mogul popped out of the fog and sat me down on my behind for a brief moment, with no harm done. The Supreme lift closed at four and we had to be on it in order to get home, otherwise there would be a long slow climb back to the lodge. Hot tub and snacks went well for a start. Lasagna, French bread and fruit were a dinner hit with everyone. The crew was less tired this night and didn't retire quite as early. Some played Pictionary, while others read or listened to music.

"If it's Wednesday it must be Snowbird!" We had talked about taking a day to go down the valley to the neighboring ski area of Snowbird, and Wednesday seemed to be the appropriate day. Again it was foggy at Alta and we skied down to the base and took the shuttle bus to Snowbird where it left us three flights of cement stairs down from the ticket office and bridge to trails. We were out of breath for sure by the time we awkwardly climbed the stairs, already buckled in our ski boots and carrying our skis. It was still rather early and we were all able to get right on the aerial tram that carries 125 skiers in 8 minutes to the very top of Hidden Peak at 11,000 feet.

This was truly a "cowabunga spot," with a few "wows" thrown in. When we got off the tram there was blue sky and sunshine in all directions, and we skied around on all sides of the rather narrow summit looking at the view, taking pictures, and putting on an extra swipe of sun screen lotion. It wasn't more than ten minutes before the fog rolled up from the valley and obscured most of the view. This is the way the rest of the day went, some sun and some dense

fog in ever-changing patterns, but at least we had had that ten minutes of purely gorgeous scenery that we shall not soon forget. The descent was spectacular with a choice of deep powder bowls or packed powder trails, and our long run, dropping over three thousand feet down and across this mountain, was a real thrill. The next venture was up Mid Gad lift to a restaurant lodge on the mountain where we left our lunch knapsack. Then it was up and down the mountain on various trails with our only real complaint being the long lift lines and more people on the slopes.

People were everywhere when we made our way back to the restaurant. Although we had our lunch we needed to buy beverages and hoped to sit down and rest. The place was mobbed. Two of us found what we thought was an empty place and started our sandwich when two men came along and, in no uncertain terms, told us that those were their seats and we were to get out – chivalry is indeed dead in the ski lodge!!

The gang at Lund Lodge

Skiing on the Wild Side In the Mountains of Utah

We ended up eating on the porch standing up and resting our drinks on a garbage can. Oh how we wished to be back at low key Alta and especially at Lund lodge, for lunch! Alta is for the real skiers, Snowbird is for the tourists and there were far too many of them! However, one couldn't knock Snowbird's trails, their lifts with safety bars and foot rests and, the ultimate luxury, a box of Kleenex at the end of the lift line!

We spent a delightful afternoon. I went "Bananas," a favorite trail, as often as possible while the others experimented with some new mogul runs and the experts went their own way. On the last run we stopped by and rescued the knapsack, and then took the long traverse down across the mountain back to the base of the tram where we got the shuttle for Alta.

We returned the back way because the main road was closed on account of an avalanche. At Alta we bought one ride tickets for the lift half way up the mountain, where the Lunds met us with the snow-cat. The outdoor hot tub was popular that evening, with a few hearty souls having their pictures taken jumping in the snow! Spareribs graced the menu, and for entertainment the crew had fun watching a pine marten eating the turkey carcass and scraps we had put out. What he didn't finish the beautiful Steller's jay and chubby Clark's nutcracker carried off in the morning.

Thursday morning I was poking around the kitchen early enough to see the sun still behind our mountain but painting pink the tops of Devil's Castle and other high mountains. What a lovely sight. The weather broadcast said Salt Lake would be 61 degrees today so everyone dressed for spring skiing, leaving off the heavy sweaters and hats. We were early this morning and on the lifts by 9:30 when they opened. It was warm and sunny in the valley. This was going to be a great day on Sugarloaf and we were soon on that lift which has a vertical rise of 1,300 feet. Nearing the top, we entered another world! The temperature dropped to the low twenties, and the wind was a gale blowing snow so that we could hardly stand or see when getting off the lift. With fewer clothes and no goggles everyone was freezing. This run would have to be back to Supreme and home for more weather protection. Although cold, it was not foggy, and the trail surface was the best ever. The experts went cross-country through the powder. Laurie and I tried to cut over lower down and came out too soon on top of a deep powder hill. But after a few, "Oh no!s," it actually was rather fun and the lure of powder could be felt under foot. With another week and maybe a lesson I realized that I, too, might become addicted!

After a stop at the lodge for redressing we all headed for Supreme, where the experts took the steep trails down through the powder using trees for slalom poles. My kind of packed trails had opened up in a new area around under Devil's Castle and I was in my glory. The whole crew seemed to meet simultaneously at the lift line and swap stories about their runs. Everyone had the leftovers of their choice for lunch and we were back out on the slopes in an hour. After all, time was getting shorter and every minute had to count! At the end we were racing down the slopes to get that last ride on the lift, and today we just barely made it.

Our legs never really ached until that last run and it always seemed the perfect time to quit. This was really the day for the outside hot tub, and we all took advantage of it. Corn chowder and more leftovers were consumed with great appetite while we watched the biggest porcupine I've ever seen on the deck chewing on the old turkey neck. Porcupines eat trees but this one was eating turkey! The evenings were getting longer as some played Pictionary, watched TV, or read. Once again the clear moonlight on the snow and mountains and the sparkling stars created a memorable sight.

Friday. One member of the crew had to leave and she went off in the cat as we took the ticket run to the base. This was the last day of skiing for everyone but me and they all wanted to make the most of it. We went back to Sugarloaf and it was beautiful, packed and fast. As they say, "I skied my heart out," and by lunchtime my legs were really tired. By this time the sky had cleared and we all ate lunch in the sun on the deck, but it was a quick stop, for today we couldn't waste a minute. We spent a glorious sunny afternoon on Supreme and, while zipping down one run the very same mogul that tripped me before did it again, and I just didn't have the strength to resist. Down I went, ungracefully but with no damage and I decided to take that hill off my list! The crew was both happy and sad as they finally skied under the ropes and into the Lund yard for the last time – happy for having had such a magnificent week on the slopes and, of course, sad that it had come to an end. Hamburgers and salad tasted good, and we spent the evening talking with the Lunds, signing the guest book, and looking back at pictures of Rick and the Bernhardts on their previous trips here, and then the inevitable packing.

Saturday morning I was up at 5:30 making sure everyone was awake then fixed coffee and scrambled eggs. You could already tell it was going to be a beautiful day as they all piled into the two snow-cats with Gary and Helen at 6:40 for the trip down to the shuttle at Alta parking lot. It was certainly sad to see the crew leave without me, but then, I had another day to ski! Now knowing the area, I felt well at home wherever I decided to go. After cleaning up from breakfast I transferred my food to my own apartment kitchen, as there would be another crew coming in this afternoon for the main lodge. I dressed and was out early, stopping to enjoy all the views along the way down to the ticket booth on this lovely morning.

Even though it was Saturday morning I was first on both lifts and was soon at the top of Sugarloaf. They do an extra special job of grooming before the weekend and the trails were in perfect condition. Things were booming on Sugarloaf as the ski patrol was checking out the Devil's Castle area to open for powder skiing. Before long you could see tiny skiers climbing along the ridge and then making long spiral trails down through the steep snowfields. I swooped down the long winding packed hills with great abandon and then ducked under the ropes for a trip back up the lift. The crowd was so small that it was the third or forth trip before I had to come in yelling "Single?" for a partner to ride the lift. You meet interesting people this way. One young man was getting his Ph.D., in molecular biology and extolled the thrills of research all the way to the top. A girl was a third grade teacher down in the valley and skied Alta every weekend. Another man was a fighter pilot in the Air Force and, as a new skier, he admitted to being petrified on Alta's high chairs without safety bars.

It seemed as if each trip down was better than the last. The weather was ideal, blue sky and sunshine, much colder at the top of the lift, hot at the bottom. I was sure that I must be the happiest skier on the hill! What an EXPERIENCE! I couldn't have dreamed of a better vacation than to be up and out on the Wild Side, all day, for seven days in a row. And to top it all, to think that I was back downhill skiing after all those years, and that I could ski well enough to be here at Alta, Utah! To Rick and Laurie and the whole crew, you certainly knew how to make an old lady happy!

On the eighth run I cut across, up Supreme and home for a quick sandwich, and then a run down to the base ski shop for a few souvenirs. This shopping venture didn't take long and I was back on Supreme to finish the afternoon. By this time the next predicted snowstorm was approaching. The wind on top accelerated and the clouds began to roll in. Just before three I could see snow squalls in the mountains all around. I had had my full day with perhaps more runs already than on any other. It was time to quit and I took a long leisurely run, savoring every turn. As I swung around the ropes at Lund lodge, the snowflakes were falling on my head. By the time I stacked my skis and took off my boots it was snowing hard. Although I spent the evening alone, Helen and Gary checked on me and made sure I had all the comforts of home. After a soak in the hot tub, a good dinner, a fire in the fireplace and two VCR movies, I was ready to call it a day.

Sunday morning there were blizzard conditions as we climbed in the snow-cat at 7:30 for the trip back to the real world. The snow was blowing so hard that Helen had quite a time finding her way down the mountain. At Alta parking lot we changed to her four wheel drive Suburban and crawled down the canyon to Salt Lake City where there was no snow and a booming thunder shower greeted us. By the time we parked by the Beehive House the snow was falling in heavy thick flakes, which by then only added to the beauty of our walk to the Tabernacle broadcast. While at first I'd bemoaned the fact that I couldn't get airline reservations with the rest of the crew, my extra days turned out to be the icing on the cake, thanks to Helen who allowed me the extra day at the lodge and then escorted me to Temple Square. I said a fond farewell to her as she dropped me at the airport and, instead of going straight home I spent the night in Kentucky, but I'm sure you don't want to hear those gory details!

Here's to a dream come true – seven glorious days downhill skiing, on the Wild Side, in the hills of Utah!　　**4/90**

Snowflakes at Alta

"Truth is stranger than fiction," they say, and when you are well into this hike we have a little story to relate that will prove just that, but you have a long way to go before we get to that point.

Deciding where to take you this month has required some thought. We've twice tramped into the Ravine looking for our lost (temporarily, we hope) showy orchids, but if we wrote up those hikes you'd be frustrated along with us and might even have to dig leeks again, and we already decided to give them a rest this year. Then, there were our three interesting safaris by canoe across Sherman Pond into the old Wheeler and Wilcox farms above Yankee and to the Lime Quarry area just over the line in Vermont, but we've taken you there so many times before that we were looking for something new and exciting to record in Wild Side this month. However, we must admit that on one of those canoe trips it was pretty exciting to return to the launching-picnic area and find not only the picnic table but our car "out to sea," totally surrounded by a foot of water! The pond had risen way beyond normal limits and our partner was able to paddle us right up to the driver's-side door where we carefully stepped out of the canoe directly into the car and gingerly drove it out of the drink! You never know what new experiences await you when you're out on the Wild Side!

Well, May 15th dawned warm and clear and we set out for our designated May Wild Side hike, wherever it might take us, and left a note saying we were going "over west." How could we be more specific when we knew we would change directions at the slightest whim to investigate a bird or a rock or a flower? It was about eight-thirty in the morning when we parked our car just below the power line on Tunnel Road, and listened to the morning chorus of birds as we slung the knapsack over our shoulders. We didn't need the bird book; we needed a portable recorder with our birdcall tapes! We knew the wood thrush in back of us, the veery deeper in the woods, the rose-breasted grosbeak up on the hill, the chestnut-sided warbler at the edge of the woods, and the blackbird in the beaver pond, but there was a "zeet, zeet, zeet, zeeet" in the low brush that we knew was a warbler but not by name.

The dilemma was already upon us, should we use the binocs and search for the bird or our little magnifying glass to more thoroughly enjoy the flowers? The flowers won out and we stooped to pick a little bluet or "Quaker lady." How aptly named, for close-up it was one of the plainest flowers we have observed, simply four petals of light blue with a touch of yellow in the center. Not far from the pretty little clump of bluets was a plain old common wild strawberry in blossom. We picked this and held it under the glass. What a pretty sight! Five white petals with numerous dark yellow stamens surrounding mounded yellow pistils in the center. Two common flowers, now fully appreciated as natural works of art.

We headed west up under the power line, first looking for some lousewort. That's the terrible common name for wood betony that was reported to be around Deb Truesdell's old sugarhouse. We had only taken a few steps when a chestnut-sided warbler lit in the tree not five feet away, turned toward us and sang enthusiastically his song that the Audubon bird book interprets as saying, "very, very pleased to MEET-CHA!" Wonderful little personal things like this are apt to happen out on the Wild Side.

And speaking of Wild Side, we realized this spot was rather nostalgic, for it was in April 1982, eight years ago, when we took this short walk to the old sugarhouse and found a dead red-shouldered hawk and a pretty waterfall and decided to come home and write a little one-column article for the *Goal Post* and called it "A Walk on the Wild Side." We have been walking and writing on the Wild Side ever since but never back to this particular spot. A new beaver pond had expanded Steele Brook to the very edge of the fallen remains of the old sugarhouse and it really didn't look like betony territory. We would have gladly perched on an old beam and watched the doings in the pond for the rest of the morning, but as always we had a vague purpose in mind of going over the mountain to search for flowers down the slope overlooking the upper end of Bear Swamp lower reservoir. Fortunately it was early; we carried lunch and had the day to meander to our heart's content.

The same pretty little waterfall greeted us beyond the sugarhouse and as we looked up the brook we made out the remains of the old stone and cement dam used to make a pond for cutting blocks of ice in the days before refrigeration. The most recent geodetic map shows a pond in this location, but it has long since washed out. Old cellar holes prove that some of the earliest settlement in town was in this area and perhaps this may have been a natural place for an ice pond even back then. Looking at the old deeds there is an interesting note of trivia that this 190-acre piece of property was sold by Richard Mason to Ephraim Hill in November of 1780 for

"thirteen hundred Spanish milled dollars." The little stream, named for the Steele family who also lived here back in the late 1700s, still has a good flow and toothwort blossoms along the edges and beaver continue to dam its waters. It's soothing to know that the natural environment, if left alone, changes little even in two hundred and ten years, but something like the currency, well that is another matter.

Crossing the old pond bed took some leaps across several little channels, and we had partially wet sneakers before we entered the woods on the upper side. Wet, probably because we were distracted by two veery thrushes chasing across our view and trying to sing at the same time, a weird distorted series of half spiral notes resulted. Following the brook soon took us into a cathedral of tall stately hemlocks. We stopped in awe as one would upon entering such a place. The murmuring of the brook was the soft organ music and the rose-breasted grosbeak was performing the accompanying solo from his perch in the balcony tree on the mountain. The clergy had not yet arrived, but we could see the pulpit on a huge rock draped with green altar cloths of moss. Again, we could have been content to sit for an hour or so in the peaceful solitude of this woodland cathedral.

As the brook turned north we left its side regretfully and climbed up the hill into a stand of beech and maples, where we found patches of the fast-disappearing leaves of Dutchman's breeches and squirrel corn. These dainty ephemerals with similar leaves are a joy of early springtime. Little white and yellow pantaloon blossoms hang from stems on one plant and sweet-smelling white and pink hearts dangle from the others, but in a few short weeks they leave no trace of their springtime fling. These flowers grow only in rich soil and tell us to look further for their companions, the waterleaf and baneberry that we found close by. Ambling on up the hillside, free from much underbrush and carpeted with matted dry leaves, we admired all the rocks and ledges and as we approached one, a hermit thrush flew off her nest among the leaves. We carefully peeked over the nest to see the four, lovely, pale blue eggs, and then climbed the ledge to sit and await her return. She did not stay around and scold but disappeared from our sight, and we soon decided we best remove ourself and not let our curiosity cause cold eggs and a lost generation.

It was a short climb now out to the power line where we were suddenly knee-deep in brambles, emerging ferns, and grasses. Even though our arms and legs were covered, it took a few moments to survey the situation and determine the best route to avoid being scratched to bits by the brambles. The steepest route was elected, and we passed a flowering red-berried elder after the second try to get a foothold in the sparse soil on the ledge. From this small summit we joined the power line roadway, now strewn white with thousands of wild strawberry blossoms. There were easier ways, but we again chose the steep route to the top of the mountain above the power line and finally crawled on our hands and knees through a narrow, near vertical, gully and pulled ourselves up to more level ground where logging slash indicated some cutting a few years back. We walked over two-blossomed starflowers and picked out

an old stump upon which to rest for a few moments.

The birds were again in chorus, all competing with the louder grosbeak still joyously singing in the highest treetop. We were conscious of the red-eyed vireo who sings continuously, the chebek or least flycatcher down the mountain, and numerous warblers, especially the same "zeet, zeet" we heard previously. The woods were open and we soon had the binocs following the "zeet" from small tree to bush near the ground not far from our own perch. Ah ha, finally captured in view, it was a black-throated blue warbler, and we watched him for several minutes. The book says he says, "please, please, SQUEEZE me" but to us he was saying, "zeet, zeet, zeet, ZEEEET" and that's the way we'll remember him, for his call had been haunting us for sometime this spring!

Well, it looked now as though we had arrived at the jumping off point. We had planned to walk down the open power line on the back side of the mountain, but that was south of us a ways and we decided we'd find more floral prizes in the woods. But the evergreens behind us stood on a very steep slope with low-hanging branches under which the ground looked bereft of any goodies. So, instead of going down we turned north and followed along the ridge, trying to decide if this was what we really wanted to do or whether we were a little tired and secretly being chicken to hike down something steep that we must eventually climb back up. But then we thought of you, and how we'd have to make excuses if we quit now and how you'd all be disappointed. So we headed down ten feet or so at a time to where the woods made an abrupt change to more open hardwoods. But it was really the splashing of falling water that drew us quickly forward on the downhill angle. A pretty little brook came rushing out from behind the rocks at the top of the hill and couldn't help but create waterfall after waterfall down the mossy bedrock of this rugged mountain, as it tumbled to join the Deerfield over seven hundred feet below.

We were tempted to climb upstream just to satisfy our curiosity on where the water was coming from so near the top of the mountain, but as we stood there admiring the scene we began to focus on blossoming miterwort and foam flower, and this again indicated rich soil where we might find an orchid or some other goodie for which we were ultimately looking. We crossed the brook into white birch territory and immediately saw a tiny six-inch currant or gooseberry plant. We have recently been trying to learn the five or six varieties of these two plants that are easily confused, and thinking maybe, in the process, to find the bristly black currant that is on the Massachusetts endangered list.

We sat down on the ground, our reference book in hand, determined to make a positive identification. The little specimen was not blossomed and thus we ended as confused and uncertain as ever. As we sat there our eyes wandered toward the brook about five feet away, and there on the ledgy precipice on the opposite side was a large stand of the very same bushy plant obviously in blossom! We jumped up with great enthusiasm, magnifying glass and book in hand. It took only a moment to be sure we had found the bristly black currant, whose little off-white with a touch of pink blossoms with bristly

ovaries hung in racemes from very prickly branches with much divided leaves. And such a lush stand of this plant "of special concern" on the rare list! And what's more it was a new one for our ever-growing Rowe list.

It's times like this, when our editorial "we" is just me off on the mountainside and how we wished someone else was there to share the very special joy of discovery! (The next day when we called Bruce Sorrie at the Massachusetts Natural Heritage he checked and found that this was the first sighting of the bristly black currant in Franklin County since "1915, Rowe, on the mountain above Hoosac Tunnel." Were we in the very same spot after all these years?

There was no question now; of course we would go down the brook, just to observe the beauty of its waterfalls if nothing else. Also in the back of our mind was the fact that the bristly currant is an indicator plant for the territory in which to search for the even rarer Braun's holly-fern that grows with its feet near a cool stream. Below us, to the north of the brook, was a lovely area of wild ginger, miterwort, maidenhair fern, red trillium, baneberry and all those special spring plants of rich soil. We descended the mountain, crisscrossing back and forth a rather wide area, with searching eyes examining every nook and cranny but always returning to the brook to enjoy another view of a true waterfall spilling over a small cliff. So much beauty! We often had to stop and let our eyes focus on the larger scene, a carpet of spring greens with shades and textures of every hue and form. We had found our prize of the day, so how could we hope to come up with something more? After all, the fun is of the search itself, and the constant anticipation is worth the many hours in the woods of Rowe even if we come up empty-handed, as is most often the case.

The lower reservoir, viewed through the trees, seemed closer and closer. A long hungry growl came from our midsection, so we found a nice flat rock, climbed up, settled ourselves in a comfortable position, and opened our knapsack. We had reduced its contents to a bare minimum this morning so it wouldn't be so heavy on a hill climb, thus our lunch consisted of two thin granola bars and an apple. Our luncheon music was the song of the wood thrushes, punctuated by an occasional ovenbird and in the distance the mournful croak of a raven. This was the real world – the wild world of plants, and flowers and birds. What art gallery has anything as perfect as the magnified face of a tiny flower? What musician plays music any sweeter than the song of the thrush? There is a quote from Thoreau about thrushes included in the Audubon bird book: *"Whenever a man hears it (song of the thrush) he is young, and Nature is in her spring; whenever he hears it, it is a new world and a free country, and the gates of heaven are not shut against him."* As we munched our apple somewhere there in the wilds on the mountain overlooking the Deerfield, we were young, we were free and we were happy.

Reality set in our old bones and joints some time later as we calculated the considerable distance back to our car on Tunnel Road and decided it was time to head up the mountain. We would do it in a series of hairpin turns, thus reducing the climb and also covering more territory. There must be an orchid here somewhere! We couldn't resist heading a little further downhill before

making the first hairpin. We continued in good soil but seemed to have veered north on the mountain and climbed more among rock tumbles and boulders.

Eventually, straight up, there appeared a long cliff-type rock dripping water and covered with mosses. We love cliffs and boulders, and have to make the acquaintance of as many as possible. This one looked intriguing. Also, up to the left at about the same level we could see something man-made, what looked like a downed silver and blue balloon. Which should we investigate first? The cliff got our vote and we scrambled straight up the mountain, needing a tree now and then to pull ourselves to the next rise. Finally, standing in front of the cliff we were catching our breath and scanning its surface for ferns and plants. In the process our eyes dropped to the green just in front of our feet. There, in all its plain and simple glory, was a long-bracted orchid in blossom! Another new flower, an orchid, to add to our Rowe list! As it happened, on our canoe trip into the Lime Quarry yesterday we had rejoiced when our partner for that day had found a second long-bracted orchid there, but that was in Vermont. We had never found one in Rowe! The bristly currant was a more important find but somehow an orchid, no matter how plain, is an especially exciting discovery. (The next day Bruce Sorrie informed us that this orchid was also a pretty rare find and it may soon be on the Mass endangered list.)

Two "finds" in one day!! How could we be so lucky? But there we were, all alone, with no one to give us a pat on the back or say congratulations. We usually enjoy our solitary wanderings but it is such a special thrill to share a moment like this! We looked the area over rather thoroughly but found only the one orchid so we could not pick one for a herbarium specimen. Hopefully, more will be discovered later on if we can ever find this precise spot again.

With lingering excitement but still feeling a bit lonely, we climbed sideways up to the site of the balloon. We could see it had been a party balloon with lettering and had a long blue string that we tried to unwind from the small sapling. Finally we broke the string and pulled it loose. The back of the balloon was missing, but we could unroll it and read the front. It could have been a weather balloon, or it could have said "Happy Birthday" or "Get Well" but no. Today, here somewhere on the mountain above the Deerfield at this very moment of our lonely excitement at finding both an endangered species and a new orchid in Rowe, we happened to pick up a lost balloon which read, "Congratulations!" We broke out in one of the broadest grins you

have ever seen. As we said earlier, "Truth is stranger than fiction!"

Rocks and trees and flowers all added to our enjoyment of the rest of the mountain, and when we arrived at the top of the ridge our reward was the loveliest song of all, that of the hermit thrush. We stood and listened for several minutes to notes purer than those of the most accomplished flutist. Moving on northward, we investigated more ledges with vernal pools between them and emerging cinnamon fern fronds around the edges, and lovely little twin starflowers and dwarf ginseng in blossom on the drier ground. We seemed to be lured along the ridge until we were drawn out onto a wide-open ledge overlooking the river valley, the southern Pulpit Rock area view but somewhat further south on the ridge. Well, this was an unexpected treat. We rested on a comfortable rock and looked over the scenery with and without the binocs, and tried to judge just how far down we had been in the forest of trees covering all those goodies on the ground.

Back in the woods, we hiked north again to see a monster rock house with all sorts of apartments for creatures of the wild. We stuck our nose in a few holes and caves, and finally met up with the porky in charge who definitely didn't say, "pleased to meet cha." There ought to be a zoning bylaw against this animal taking up all the desirable cubbyholes in such a beautiful rock house, or at least the board of health should condemn his sewer system! Over the next rise we certainly found the highest cliff in Rowe! We were on the underside and went down where we could look straight up. Wow! Wait 'till we show this to that favorite hiking guide of ours who comes down from New Hampshire every so often and takes us off on the run to see some new natural attraction. Now, this certainly is one place even he has never seen!

Well, son number one burst that bubble by calling the place by name, "Dead Deer Cliff" and informing us they've known about it ever since they found a dead deer there many years ago. Later, while talking to our hiking guide on the phone, he described all those rocks and cliffs, and told us he had tracked a bear from Monroe Hill Road all the way over there through the rocks and down to the east/west power line after the first snow last fall. Well, it's our goal to someday find something mighty unusual, besides an orchid that he has never seen, in the hills of Rowe!

There comes a time when one has to turn homeward and we finally followed a little gully down the ridge and out onto the north/south power line, followed along for a while and then went into the woods on the upper end of Steele Brook.

Again, we found ourselves in a vaulted cathedral of hemlock woods with a carpet of goldthread's shiny new green leaves and a dusting of its white starry blossoms. Once more in awe, we stopped to quietly look and listen. It was late afternoon, vesper time, and the brook organ was again playing softly but the soloist was now a white-throated sparrow, whose clear sweet voice always says to us, "We Praise Thee Oh Lord." Amen.   **6/90**

Of Moose and Turtles And Orchids Blooming

As we sat eating lunch on the log in Peck's field, the towhee kept us entertained with his "drink your tea, drink your tea" and the red-eyed vireos were competing with the chestnut-sided warblers. The air was filled with song but our day was not complete until, from the distance off toward the woods, came the plaintive call of the field sparrow. We started a tradition several years ago of writing our July Wild Side from Peck's field, and although today we were not writing there we were thinking about it as we gazed off toward Greylock to the west. It was not the best of June days for the lovely white clouds were gathering too close together and the sun had a hard time peeking through, but it was not raining and we were lucky enough to be sharing lunch with an enthusiastic wildflower friend. The field was full of New England wildflowers – white clover, red clover, buttercups, white daisies and red and yellow Indian paintbrush or hawkweed, and yellow cinquefoil, and between them all the bright green June grass rippled in the very slight breeze. A little earlier we had spotted a turkey picking its way across the field.

It had been a rather unusual morning. At early light we had donned a raincoat, hat and our Wellingtons, and poked our way into the very wet woods beyond our perennial garden. It was still foggy and gray and rather eerie and primeval, as we entered the even darker woods under the pine trees. The object of our search may surprise you. A moose had passed that way last night just at the end of twilight. It had been spotted in the Mill Pond behind the gazebo and been seen walking up Hazelton Road and in the field around Quinn's. It finally went into our woods behind Stetson's. So we were looking for moose tracks and maybe even the moose itself, although that was pretty unlikely. We made our way down to the stone wall through a healthy clump of jacks-in-the-pulpit, and had to stop and investigate the remains of an old dump along the wall. Nothing whole was left, but it is always interesting to find these remains of bottles, blue canning jars, agate kettles and broken pieces of china, all part of another day, another era.

Let's see, we were looking for moose tracks. Well, none there in the sand along the wall so we cut across and up the hill through a nice stand of New York ferns. As we crossed the next stone wall along the path we could see the spaced hoof depressions in the wet leaves tracking north under the pines. Yes, there was no doubt he (or she) had passed this way. We followed the tracks a little ways until they went into the brush and then gave up, realizing that the animal might be in Vermont by now. We turned back and walked out toward the field and quickly did a double take. Through the trees there at the top of the hill was a big dark brown animal! But darn it, the horse picked up his head and proved right away he wasn't the moose!

A little later we drove around "the square," hoping that the real moose would be grazing in a field along the way. He was not, nor has he been reported to have surfaced anywhere in Rowe since then. But let's keep looking! On Ford Hill Road a rabbit ran across in front of our car. That was almost as unusual a sighting as seeing a moose, for with the fox population up and healthy, the rabbit population has been very low in the last few years. Completing our journey by the lake we had to stop and try to protect a huge mama snapping turtle trying to lay her eggs in the sand right beside the road. We picked some green brush and made a little barricade in the road in front of her, and went home to get something bigger. But when we returned she had gone back into the lake without completing her task at hand. At the beach, we found another smaller snapping turtle returning to the lake after her journey up the brook for the second day in a row. Nations rise and fall, but nature dependably continues its appointed rounds year after year. It is comforting to know that, as in the past, we can still report nesting turtles in our July Wild Side.

After all the other excitement this morning, we finally packed the lunch and set out to show our wildflower friend the gorgeous laurel on Negus Mountain which we had been raving about for several weeks now. The laurel on Negus has never failed us before and we have included it in many a July Wild Side, but maybe it has to happen once in while to give us greater appreciation of our treasures. This year the laurel failed us but nature was not all to blame as we soon discovered.

Probably because of some quirk in the weather, neither the swamp pinks nor the laurel put on much of a show this year. There was hardly a pink at Pulpit Rock on our annual May trip and the laurel there had very few buds, but we expected

Bunchberry flowers

Negus to do better. Instead of the usual bushes blossoming everywhere in the shade and in the sun, they were spotty, and we immediately missed some special very pink ones which we always admire. We'd hate to be the ones to lament the absence of railroad forest fires, but for those of us who remember the lovely open expanses of "Old Smokey" years ago, and how we used to breakfast and lunch there as we picked Roy and Kathleen Bent's blueberries, the scene has drastically changed.

As trees and brush will, they have grown by leaps and bounds and now one has to hike to the highest peak (and the scene of the most recent forest fire) to get the full effect of the dramatic view down into the Deerfield River Valley. We tried to brighten up the disappointment of not showing our friend a mountain of blossomed laurel by looking for the "needle in a haystack" little green adder's mouth orchid that grows there, but that too came up temporarily missing. But compensation there was, because the sheep laurel was beautiful and plentiful, and the treat of looking into the face of one tiny pink blossom with the magnifying glass was worth the hike. The bunchberry created a carpet on the ground along with cow-wheat, northern bush-honeysuckle and still-blossomed Canada mayflowers, so we had to pick our way stepping carefully lest we injure one of these.

Our tradition fol-

Of Moose and Turtles And Orchids Blooming

lowed, we gradually led the way down through the laurel and brush to sit for a while on the ledge, above a dramatic drop to the river. Actually, we had a little difficulty even finding that spot, for since last year the bushes had grown tall and wide and the landmark old white birches just below had given up the struggle and fallen to return to the soil beneath. The Deerfield was very low, and Beaver Island was connected to the shore on one side by a multitude of dry rocks instead of being surrounded by two channels of the river. As tour guides do, we described the highlights of the surrounding territory and pointed out all the nooks and crannies where the fragile orchids bloom. Even on a cloudy day we think "our" mountains put on an impressive show!

Loesel's twayblade

As we started the return trip our friend asked about a hole in the ground just above the ledge. We examined it closely only to find another and another as we climbed the hill. One reason the laurel was not putting on such a good show was that some of the smaller bushes had been removed, some of the real pink ones which we especially remember and have photographed in the past. Laurel on the sprayed power lines has been fair game, but somehow the laurel on Negus was sacred in our mind. As we descended through the tunnel of trees, a hermit thrush sang for us as we hoped he would, and when we came to the little open meadow a lovely full-bloomed laurel bush posed for our friend's camera. Negus Mountain wasn't so bad after all!

It was nearing lunchtime but we had one more adventure in mind. A quick trip to the clay pit and we might be able to point out a rather rare adder's-tongue fern and an orchid called Loesel's twayblade. The first excitement was flushing a woodcock as we climbed down the hill into the clay pit. As time was short we soon gave up the fern hunt (we know they are there in number, it's just a matter of finding them, usually later in the season), and concentrated on the orchid. It took a while but we found the very inconspicuous tiny two or three inch high plants in bloom. It was a joyous sharing of a new orchid on our friend's life list. One could wonder, how could anyone get excited about the tiny plant we were trying to photograph and check with the magnifying glass while down on our knees in the wet sphagnum moss! Perhaps we can liken it to the thrill of coming upon the record of a special long-lost ancestor if you are seriously working on your ten-generation genealogical chart. It's the search that adds spice to life, and the finding a bit of joy and celebration.

So this was the mood as we shared lunch on the log in Peck's field – a happy day with moose and turkeys roaming, rabbits running, turtles nesting, birds singing, woodcocks flying, and orchids blooming, and, yes, even a bit of laurel blossoming, on the Wild Side of Negus Mountain.   **7/90**

Everything comes up wildflowers in the Albion Basin at Alta, Utah. If you remember (Skiing on the Wild Side, April '90), I last saw the Alta area as I left it early on a blizzardy Sunday morning in March after a fabulous week of skiing. I had signed the guest book at Lund Lodge with a wishful thought about returning in July for the wildflowers. The skiing trip was a dream come true; how could anything top that? And to think that all that snow would eventually melt, and flowers would pop up by July was beyond our wildest imagination! But I had seen the Lund's pictures of summer and all spring the thought was in my mind, and by the end of May we did some serious wheeling and dealing. Son Rob would take a week of vacation and mind the two little girls while Sue (our wildflower partner) and I went west for some botanizing in the Albion Basin. Our search for flowers in Rowe has come down to the rarest and well-hidden specimens, and a recent camping trip to New York state opened our eyes to the joy of finding new orchids, ferns, and other wildflowers beyond our home base. Now, like birders, we are compiling our "life list."

I called the Lunds at Alta and made reservations and Sue contacted the Utah Natural Heritage Program to check in and seek advice. All systems were go for July 15th to the 22nd.

The alarm went off at 3:30 a.m. on the

**Brigham Young's stone
at Whitingham, Vermont**

15th, and we were under way by car to the Albany airport by 4:30. As we passed through Whitingham, Vermont we thought of the pioneer Brigham Young, who was born in Whitingham in 1801 and eventually led the group of Mormon pioneers by covered wagon from Illinois to the Salt Lake valley in 1847. What would he have thought of this modern day travel, leaving his native Whitingham at 4:45 a.m., stopping in Illinois, and arriving at Salt Lake at noon?! Well, as the day progressed we decided that it was probably best that Brigham Young didn't know how fouled up modern day transportation could really be. Airplanes have hydraulic problems, ticket agents can only process a plane load of passengers needing airline changes so fast, and busy airports can delay takeoffs for hundreds of reasons, thus causing other missed connections ad infinitum.

We finally met up with Gary Lund at Snowbird Ski Area about ten of nine that evening and, just as the sun was highlighting with rosy red the craggy heights of Devil's Castle and dusk was descending on the wildflowers, he drove us up the canyon road into the incredibly beautiful and colorful Albion Basin. At Lund Lodge, Helen had saved us some strawberry shortcake from the barbecue we were supposed to have arrived for in early afternoon. Half a day lost. We would more than make up for it before the week was over.

Monday dawned crystal clear and we were up early, in spite of jet lag and exhaustion from the hectic trip the day before. The mountains were pink again as the morning sun lit them with alpenglow from the top down. From the deck it was hard to know which to exclaim over first – the surrounding Rocky Mountains, often rising to eleven thousand feet or the mass of wildflowers carpeting every inch of ground around us. Sue had never been in the west, and for her the mountains took priority for the first few minutes. My own reaction was first to the "lay of the land" now that the snow was gone. Rocks and gullies appeared, as well as a whole summer campground with picnic tables and facilities that had been buried far under the snow. Lund Lodge is at 9,600 foot elevation and even the excitement over the scenery took some extra breathing.

Finally we both concentrated on the wildflowers and then it didn't take long for us to pack our knapsacks with reference books, note pads, hand lenses, water bottles, and such, and don hiking boots and hats to start out. Where to start was a major question, and we quickly identified white columbine, blue-green sage, white Jacob's ladder, blue lupine, and western brick-colored paintbrush on the small incline to the newly seeded ski trail just above the lodge. They were trying to grow grass on the trails, an alien plant to these parts where everything naturally comes up flowers!

Just a short distance off the ski trail, under two Englemann spruce trees, we dropped our packs, sat on the ground, and just studied the flowers. Gary and Helen told us later that they were watching us every so often, and began to think we would never get any further afield. But to us everything was new, some flower family members recognizable but the particular species was not, and we would have to use the lens and study the books to make the identification. A twenty foot square area could keep us busy for several hours, the variety was so great! One of the first really unusual flowers was a (from one to five feet) tall, stately plant with whorled leaves called a green gentian or monument plant. It had large sort of square green flowers with purple-spotted roundish-pointed petals and star-pointed sepals. How's that for a description? Near this was a tiny plant, hardly two inches tall, called a fairy candelabra, with dainty white or pink flowers needing a lens to be seen at all.

We would be engrossed in the excitement of identification and then suddenly realize the beauty surrounding us, and we would take time to exclaim and enjoy and marvel at the wonder of it all. Slightly over the hill nearer a watercourse was a patch of false hellebore. Ah, ha, at last we had something just like home – but on closer examination it was different, sturdier, and very seldom blossomed and locally called corn flower (oddly enough also called skunk cabbage, the same local misnomer as for ours). It was Veratrum californicum and not our Veratrum viride. And so it went until lunch time, when we returned with an already impressive list of discoveries in our Albion Basin quest.

With such a good morning start around home, we were eager to climb the heights. After lunch we headed up the ski trail and around the bend, reversing direction to scale the top of that famous vertical Lund's Hill where moguls rein supreme during the winter, and where now the red paintbrush surrounded by blue lupine is a joy to the eye. The altitude did not bother us climbing and we made slow progress, stopping for each new flower and each new perspective on the grandiose view down the canyon. A book back at the lodge, called *Alta Canyon Guide* and edited by Dale Gilson, described the area as *"a superlative place surrounded by superlatives,"* a *"west-facing break in the Wasatch range rising from 5000 foot elevation at the mouth (of Little Cottonwood Canyon) to over 11,000 feet at the top of the watershed (top of Albion Basin),"* with *"170 varieties of wildflowers that must sprout, grow, blossom, pollinate and re-seed between the melting of snow in June and the first autumn snows in October."* Our first day and already we had run out of superlatives to describe the scene, but we had a good start on those 170 varieties!

The high hills were mostly open, with a few Englemann spruce and skinny pointed sub-alpine fir in clumps here and there in the lower basin. The watercourses made deep canyons in the hillside. Under a fir at the top of a canyon, after identifying the interesting scickletop lousewort, we found our familiar sweet cicely. It was like seeing an old friend! Although we find it in cool wet shaded rich woods in the spring, this was in the sun in dry barren summer soil and upon examination once again it was similar but not our sweet cicely! We trudged up a well-remembered slanting and steep ski hill, and while Sue was still sitting mid-way pouring over the books to make a new identification, I meandered up through the trees (hardly to be called a woods) and came out in a beautiful alpine meadow full of flowers and holes! Ground squirrels make little holes but badgers make the big holes like these, so they told us later. Sue soon joined me and we admired the view, the flowers and especially the deep blue penstemon. A little farther on we found the pretty light blue flax.

Each rise and knoll took on a different hue and texture, and we had difficulty deciding which direction our fancy should take us. The beauty of the low, more orange paintbrush of the higher slopes took us off to the right of one of my favorite ski trails, and as we peeked over the brim of the hill the colors were overwhelming – orange, sulphur yellow, white, purple, deep blue, and all shades in between. No landscaper could have arranged the flowers around the rocks with greater finesse. The camera was clicking far beyond our planned film allotment. Sue was again in the books, checking out coyote mint, and I was scanning the area with the binocs. We were close-up across the ski trail to the eastern flank of Devil's Castle, looking up to where I remember seeing a small avalanche in the winter. The steep mountainside, rising almost a thousand feet, was now green, with patches of lingering white snow around which it was yellow with buttercups. I refocused on two patches of white on the very top and discovered two mountain goats, which we watched for several minutes. Wow! What a dizzying height they choose, and we wondered what they could possibly find to eat. Little did we know that day...

Later we crossed the ski trail and climbed over the low shoulders of Devil's Castle where we looked closely at the buttercups, took pictures of the snow, and were thrilled to find patches of the lovely and rather large Parry's primrose clinging to the rocks. But we soon discovered that beauty has its price, for the flowers have a powerfully foul odor! From there we meandered down the mountain and arrived home about six. There was time for a leisurely soak in the outdoor hot tub while supper was in the oven. Meals were consumed with reference books and specimens spread around us at the table while we tried to finish the more difficult identifications. The reference book we were advised to have was unavailable, in spite of the Lund's frantic search for us, and Sue had to make detailed drawings of some flowers for future positive identification.

Tuesday morning we woke refreshed from an "around the clock" sleep, and felt back to normal after the trip and a first day of rather strenuous activity. The sky was a bit cloudy this day, a front coming up from the south they said. We were out by nine and headed for moist territory, first along the campground road under the ski lift to Supreme. How many times we had taken this lift admiring the glistening snow cover underneath, never dreaming there were roads and campsites and FLOWERS. We stopped at the first little trickle of water and found some leaves which looked like wood betony, and then there was one with a strange looking stem of purple flowers. We were down on our knees examining it with the lens when the light dawned – it was the famed elephant heads plant, with flowers that look exactly like the head, ears and trunk of an elephant! Close by were the dark pink shooting stars with their unusual curved-back flowers like little rockets.

Orchids are, of course, a special find anywhere, and we were told there was only one variety here, so it was exciting when Sue spotted the first bog orchid in a spongy area along the stream further down the hill. The spike had several small orchids with side petals looking like a handlebar mustache. We took pictures and counted seven. Lower down, in a boggy area, we soon found hundreds of these white orchids along with the elephant heads. Huge rock formations sported whiskers of wild coral bells and we came upon our first fern, called a brittle fern and resembling our fragile fern. This bog also gave us yellow and red monkey flowers, acres of mountain bluebells, forget-me-nots, and a meadow of elephant heads under the Cecret ski lift. (Spelling of Cecret remains from old mining days.)

We eventually turned uphill and reversed direction toward home. We had wandered a long way, intrigued with new specimens and with each new sighting of an area more beautiful than the last. EVERYTHING was FLOWERS. Raising our heads from the ground for a moment, we found ourselves face to face with a buck mule deer with a nice rack in the velvet. We inspected each other and soon went our separate ways, with us finding a stray spring beauty beside our feet – recognizable, but again not our variety. Just before crackers and cheese on a big boulder in a high meadow, we found yet another fern, the stiff little cliffbreak hidden in the rock crevices. We soon realized that a steep canyon was between us and home, and we dipped down into it and gradually climbed the rocks on the other side after finding lots of new things.

We were just about to examine the shrubby cinquefoil when there was a modest clap of thunder from the dark cloud north of the basin. Up and over, down and around, hats flying, we nearly knocked down a startled geologist examining some rocks at the top of the canyon. As we came racing out of breath onto the Lund's deck, Helen said calmly that all storms go north or east and anything already in that direction behind the house was no problem. Well, maybe not, but we were glad to be under cover and it did rain for a few minutes before the sun reappeared. We ate lunch on the deck, and Helen came over with some sour cream and brown sugar for us to dip the huge big juicy strawberries that we found on our table when we returned. What a place to call home!!

Time we did not waste. Soon after our mid-afternoon lunch we were back outside, this time examining the hillside behind the lodge. Rather than staying together we tended to separate, each following an interesting lead. I found pyrola and more sweet cicely but didn't think it warranted Sue's inspection so meandered around and, being a little tired, eventually started back down the hill along a deep gully. Suddenly from the very top of the hill came Sue's shout, "Hey, Mabel, you have to come up and see this!" "Mabel" being my family nickname, I guessed she meant me and looking up, saw her standing much higher than I would have cared to climb a second ago. A "Hey, Mabel, look at this," can get me up or down most any hill, mountain, ravine or canyon and she knew it. The old tired knees climbed that hill in record time, but it took fifteen minutes to regain normal breath at that altitude. The flower was a pretty stem of long slender pinkish-white tube flowers. Instead of the mystery she thought it was, I happened to have seen a similar red flower called scarlet gilia and presumed correctly that this was a white variety. Having once caught my

breath, I began to worry about the dark cloud overhead, and even though we had arrived at a lovely mountain meadow of flowers my warning prevailed over Sue's protest and we started down. She took Lund's mogul hill, and I the next ski run to inspect on the descent.

The cloud, as Helen had said, went north and the evening was mostly sunny. We had an early dinner in preparation for a trip down by car a mile or so to the basin meadows with Gary to see the flowers in the light of the setting sun. Although clouds came and went, the scene was glorious. Gary gave us the common names of some of the flowers he knew, and we introduced him to some of our newfound flower friends by technical or Latin names and to the wonderful new world of blossoms through a hand lens. We eventually parked at the top of Sunnyside ski lift to overlook the fantastic field of flowers down which we had skied so many times in March.

We were introduced to the DYC's (darn yellow composites) and agreed that our list might not include all of these for, like goldenrods, they are very frustrating to correctly identify. After this special treat with Gary, we returned home to take our place in the outside hot tub with glasses of cold cranberry juice and Vivaldi for background music. We luxuriated in the warmth as the evening cooled and watched the sunset glow fade on Devil's Castle while making a game of matching stars to constellations as they appeared in the darkening sky overhead. It had been another perfect day.

Wednesday. We were once again up and out soon after breakfast. Helen had listened to the weather and said we must take an umbrella with us so it will not rain.

We tramped down the road through the campground to the lower meadow, and followed the brook into a wet area with more orchids and a profusion of every kind of plant including pink geraniums, blue beardtongue, white bitter cress and endless DYC's. After exploring the bog, we turned uphill through the meadows to the roads and climbed the hill toward the top of Albion ski lift. This brought back memories of the day I disgraced myself, right there many feet above the sleeping wildflowers, by taking a nose-dive in the powder snow on my first ski run at Alta. Today the clouds gathered and covered the sun, and we put on the sweatshirts only to remove them in the sun a few minutes later. The umbrella made a good cane for climbing side hills and was only needed briefly for a short shower of fine rain. From the top of Albion lift we viewed a different vista into the lower valley guarded by Mount Superior, and then watched a yellowbelly marmot scamper among the rocks.

Hare figwort and star Solomon seal were added to our list as we took the high road homeward though an avenue of roadside flowers, and following along the mountainside behind the house, we came across the lovely little elegant camas lily – elegant being part of its name as well as a good description. After a late afternoon lunch we actually both succumbed to a ten minute nap, and then visited with Helen and Gary while we waited for the clock to reach five so we could report in to the family back east. This accomplished, and our minds at ease that all was well with husbands and children, we set out again back to the ledge over the canyon where we had been chased home by the thunder the day

before. Here we discovered the small parsley fern with separate fertile leaves like our grape fern and, then, tucked in a dark crevice, the mountain holly fern that is listed as rare in the area. As we continued to climb gradually toward the base of Devil's Castle, Sue perched on a high ledge to check a flower, and then we sat fascinated as a golden eagle made many passes up and around the Castle rocks irritating the jays and nutcrackers.

Everything was especially rosy and beautiful in the afternoon sun, and we

Sue identifying a plant on the ledge

together "thanked our lucky stars" (and husbands) for this rare opportunity to be there in Albion Basin, free to hike and wildflower to our heart's content among such natural beauty as we never imagined was possible. It was eight o'clock before we wandered home reluctant to give in after such a pleasant sojourn on the mountain. The hot tub and supper completed another memorable day.

Thursday dawned sunny and we were out at ten hiking up to the boulder field at the base of Devil's Castle, where squeaks and whistles drew our attention to a friendly little pika running about the rocks. We climbed up over the tree-covered shoulder of the mountain where, in a very strange place, Sue found a lost ski pole. We looked up and down where the skier must have traveled and shook our heads, wondering if there were any stray bones scattered about also. Rather high now, we began finding small alpine plants, and were busy opening and closing our knapsacks for reference books as each new one was discovered. Sue found a long steep spot of snow and couldn't resist starting at the top and boot skiing, more quickly than she expected, down its length. She now has the distinction of saying that she too has "skied at Alta" but the conditions could hardly be called powder snow!

Behind the next snow pile above the new batch of Parry's primroses, Sue retrieved an eagle feather which went into the knapsack as a souvenir for a small child back home. I acquired the ski pole and found it a great help in maneuvering the steeps. Standing on the heights we were discussing the huge black cloud that had developed to the north, and Sue commented that this time she would hide under a ledge if there was a thunderstorm. I turned toward the cloud in time to see a fierce bolt of lightning streak down behind the mountaintop. Fortunately, there passed some seconds before the tremendous crash of thunder indiciated that the storm was not overhead, but not enough time for me to warn Sue. She let out a yelp forgetting all thoughts of hiding under a rock, and we both

flew down the mountain, tossing the metal ski pole to the wind. Believe me, it had been much easier to ski down those hills in winter than it was to run them at the same pace in summer! It's a wonder we didn't break a leg.

The race was not for naught, for another storm soon made its way up the valley from the west and we were glad to be safe inside to watch the strange cloud formations below the mountains in the canyon before the rain came down. With the low humidity the grass dries fast, and we were soon out again for a short ten-minute check on a flower which lengthened to a two hour hike before we returned at four. We had found pink pussy toes and a strange and pretty little purslane by the brook. In our haste to get outside we had left the screen door open, and an Audubon's warbler had come in and made himself at home. The catch was made with some netting and the bird was safely returned to the wild. Our evening was spent in further identifications, and before dark we watched two buck deer along the path above the lodge eating their way through the white columbine blossoms.

Friday was a special day. Young ten year old Jason, a friend of Lund's, had come to visit for a few days, and he joined the hike Gary and Helen had been promising us to Cecret Lake just over the hill from the Sugarloaf ski lift. We were looking forward to seeing this mythical lake that seemed to be hidden from all hills we had climbed so far. The trail was about a mile long and wove up and around the brown open ledges that were the base of those wonderful ski runs on Sugarloaf. We tried to interest Jason in flowers, and he was very patient and tolerant, but animals were much more to his liking and at one point he distracted us with a shout to see three marmots on the rocks. Fortunately, Helen was distracted instead by a bush which she thought was a blueberry and when stooping for a closer look found a strange red-looking stem which we had all walked right by. The inevitable "Hey Mabel" followed as soon as Sue took a look recognizing the orchid called spotted coralroot, for the first time the very same variety as our own large coralroot. The find of this second orchid was a special treat as the basin was known to have only one, the prolific bog orchid.

Cecret Lake was nestled in the folds of the hill and was as lovely a spot as the Lunds had predicted. After viewing, picture taking and temperature sampling by Jason who agreed that it was COLD, the crew started back via the high trail at the base of Sugarloaf and the Castle. Gary showed us a couple of the abandoned mines (mining was important here back in the early days as evidenced by roads, holes and piles of tailings all over the valley), and he regaled us with stories of the mine at Albion Heights, where the boarding house had been built against a huge rock cliff so it wouldn't be wiped out by avalanches. We peeked in the still snow-packed mine and admired the small wall the miners had built to hold back the mountain from the path. Near the mine entrances the little pikas had piled bits of greenery for later use as their food supply.

While we stopped to list the lovely little pink moss campion, "Mabel's Knapsack Saloon" served everyone cheese and crackers to stave off hunger pains until lunch. The alpine flowers soon became so numerous that Sue and I had to stop and investigate while the others continued on home. One of the sweetest tiny flowers proved to be an alpine lily. Farther down under a big ledge we found another tiny little flower and, although it is still on the questionable list, we think it is something with a terribly long name resembling Romanoff Suzuki, which became our pet name for any unidentifiable.

Helen had sandwiches for us on our return and, for once, we sat on the deck to eat, away from the usual stack of reference books. We seemed to be able to sit and stare at the beautiful mural of Devil's Castle as one would watch the ocean. The ground squirrels were entertaining and, being little fat chubby things, Gary called them potguts. They often sat up and whistled, seeming to want to attract our attention.

We headed out after dinner for another short walk and were gone for an hour and a half finding ourselves trudging back up to the lodge in the glow of evening long after the sun had set. We had gone down again in the meadow and crossed to climb the further hill where the flowers along the path were beyond description – an incredible sight in the setting sun. The path climbed high over the meadow, where we could survey the whole basin whose nooks and crannies were now beginning to be familiar territory for us.

On the way home we witnessed "drama on the highwire." A sparrow hawk had perched on the upper cable of the Supreme ski lift and several birds were chattering their disapproval, but a flycatcher with sort of rosy breast and flicking tail and considerable courage also perched on the wire right near the hawk, scolding and taunting and hopping closer and closer, retreating some and then going at the hawk again with all the threat he could imply in his agitated chirp. The hawk seemed unimpressed and we finally left before witnessing the final act. The hot tub soaked out all our aches and pains from a day of climbing and we slept like logs in the cool mountain air.

The weather on Saturday couldn't have been better, blue sky and sunshine, and we wasted no time in packing up for our last day of exploring and soaking up the beauty in Albion Basin. We took enough cheese and crackers and apples to see us through, and all the reference books, cameras and the last of the films which Gary had replenished for us after his trip to Salt Lake City. One of our spoken goals was the top of Supreme but, looking back, I think we both secretly wanted to climb Devil's Castle. We headed up Rock 'n Roll ski trail with gusto and then into the masses of buttercups surrounding the patches of snow on the shoulder of the Castle. Seeing these, the search for other tiny alpine flowers seemed to intrigue us both more than the showy waist-high valley flowers. One of the first finds were alpine pussy-willows hardly an inch high. We climbed up the tree line, over the rocks, through the lovely alpine valleys, and across to high ledges for a view down into the basin toward the lodge. It seemed that each upward

Nan climbing toward Devil's Castle

thrust was accompanied by a "Hey, Mabel, look at this," for Sue was definitely in the lead! We gave her a little flack every so often and many "be carefuls," but once on the way our goal was the same. We both really wanted to go to the top! Soon we were walking on all fours with our noses to the ground trying to make the final ascent on small slippery loose rocks among the very low floral vegetation that must be the goat fodder.

It was even difficult to retain a foothold when we did find a tiny new blossom. When we finally arrived it was at the exact spot where we had seen the goats a few days before. But we had arrived facing uphill, and when we tried to turn around it took courage and muscle. One false move and a tumble and we would have rolled hundreds of feet. At this point, little goat hoofs would have been far more secure a footing than our heavy, clumsy hiking boots.

We were a thousand feet above Lund Lodge and the outlook to the mountains far to the north and east was spectacular, and so was the view straight down to the ski run we had left an hour ago! What a sense of accomplishment for two girls who thought Negus Mountain was about as high as you could go! We literally crawled up to the base of the larger clifftop rocks to get something secure to hang on to and there we were, within twenty feet of the ridge where we had been told there was a narrow path across the top of the Castle. The temptation was great to complete the climb but we had reached a point beyond which even a "Hey, Mabel" could budge either of us! Good judgement, and admitted fear (we were petrified!), restrained our curiosity to look over the top!

Even sitting and enjoying our heavenly perch, once acquired, was tempered with panic and wonder at how in the world we were going to get down! It was far too slippery to retrace our steps. We would have to cling to the base of the highest cliffs and somehow work our way down along the slanting ridge until the downhill angle was walkable. To do this we had to sit on several patches of beautiful and stinky primroses that grew right next to the rocks and inch across some snowdrifts. Not even a sudden thunder shower could have brought us down any faster! And would you believe that, as soon as we got ourselves down to safer ground, we began to wonder why we hadn't gone that extra twenty feet!? But we had certainly been to the top and we were tired but happy!

Back down nearer the ski trail, in a long bank of snow we found two orange signs. The first said "Area Closed, Avalanche Danger" and the other "Do not Hike above the Level of this Sign." Fortunately there were a few shots left in the camera and we posed with "our" mountain heights in the background. From there we debated about Supreme, but not wanting to leave anything undone, we climbed again, this time along the road to the top of Supreme ski lift where we spent much time looking back to the Castle mountain and pointing out (and marveling) where we had been.

The view from Supreme was also spectacular but in different directions. We looked off the back to the Heber City valley surrounded by more craggy mountains. Climbing to the top of Supreme Point through gorgeous low flowers including the orange paintbrush, white phlox and low blue asters and a quantity of other small blossoms needing identification, we finally joined the path down the north side leading us to glorious views over Lake Catherine. We turned homeward at Catherine Pass at about 10,300 feet, and followed the (weekend populated) hiking trail back down to the meadow, through acres of flowers waist high and natural rock gardens beyond description. As we dragged ourselves up the road to the lodge in late afternoon we could hardly put one foot ahead of the other, but we couldn't have been happier. It had been a day to remember, one to climax a perfect week in which we had enjoyed glorious sights, hiked to our heart's content, and identified one hundred and forty-eight species of wildflowers! Under that famous Alta powder snow EVERYTHING comes up wildflowers!

Staying with the Lunds and skiing or wildflowering in Albion Basin, both ranked a perfect ten, five stars, or just plain super anyway you described it. Later four deer came across the trail in front of the lodge as if to say good-by and everyone gathered on the deck to watch them along with the whistling potguts running around the rocks, and the sun painted Devil's Castle a rosy pink for the last time.

The Mormon Tabernacle Choir sang "Blue Skies" and The Lord's Prayer on Sunday morning and the tabernacle was full. This was a special week in Salt Lake City for Tuesday, July 24th, would be a state holiday commemorating Brigham Young's arrival through Emigration Canyon with the Mormon pioneers. Of the valley he would say "This is the Place," and 143 years later we would agree wholeheartedly. And fortunately our return trip back through his hometown in New England went like clockwork. **8/90**

The Other Side of Wild Side

In keeping with our policy of telling it like it is, we present "The Other Side of Wide Side," or "The Anatomy of a Lousy Hike." For umpteen years now you have read all the nice things about our hiking around the countryside in the glorious spring, in the lovely flower days of summer, in the warmth and beauty of autumn, and in the crisp invigorating winter sunshine. Now we are going to tell you about one of those rare days on the other side of Wild Side.

It was Thursday, September 20th, the last possible day we could take our hike for this month. Firstly, we were irritated with ourselves for having waited till the last minute. Sure, we had been in the woods many lovely days this month but always in places we have told you about too many times already. We were waiting, we guess, for a whole free day when we could pack our knapsack with the usual lunch, guide books, lens, and binocs and, with an itinerary in mind for a long leisurely hike, enter upon the stage where there was the possibility of lots of new and interesting sightings to enthrall you with the drama and beauty of our natural world.

We had half planned to go the day before but when the morning temperature stood at 28 degrees we were in no mood to head out at 8:30. So it was Thursday or never. Our mood on Thursday morning was more on the never side as we hurried to catch a ride to the bottom of Monroe Hill. Having left our car on Tunnel Road near the switching station road we knew a lot of mountain wilderness separated those two points. And the weather was not cooperating one little bit. The sky was full of forbidding November-gray clouds and the wind was blowing a gale. We did not proceed willingly, but with single-minded determination like the ad for man making the fresh Dunkin donuts "we had to take a Wild Side hike."

Our plan was to start at the big curve at the bottom of Monroe Hill and go down over the old road to meet the old HT&W track line, where a bridge had crossed the Deerfield in the early days. Then we were going to walk down the old rail bed along the Deerfield to the upper end of the Bear Swamp lower reservoir and somehow find the outlet of the brook on which we found the rare bristly black currant last spring. Our purpose was to climb back up the brook searching for whatever and then over the hill by the switching station to our car. So much for the plan.

Clad in a heavy wool sweater, we climbed over the guard rail on Monroe Hill and disappeared into the woods. Goldenrod was the first flower to catch our eye and as we were making a special effort this fall to recognize the different varieties we stopped and retrieved our guidebook from the knapsack. After long deliberation and great frustration, as is always the case with goldenrods, we tentatively called it Canada goldenrod, which may or may not have been the truth. Again we were irritated with ourselves for not being smart enough to come up with a positive identification. Okay. So we would give up on goldenrods today.

As we put the knapsack back over our shoulders we stood looking at the terrain – to the right was the path we meant to take, but let's go left a little bit, just to see what's there. And so changed the course of our whole day. In the process of prowling around we came upon what looked like an old wood road and, of course, this aroused our curiosity, for we had never happened to come upon it before. The further we went the more intriguing it seemed, because as it started up the mountain the lower side was obviously built up with rocks, indicating a traveled road rather than just a wood road. We were a good distance up the mountain when we realized that we were committed to a new itinerary and no longer would be following the river route. This intrigue probably improved our outlook somewhat, but we knew in the back of our mind that something wasn't going to come out right.

As the road progressed upward it veered toward a tumbling brook. When the two came side by side the brook held the greater sway and we quickly climbed down its bank to enjoy the mossy rocks and waterfalls. We descended a ways before turning upstream, and as we did we noticed a rather healthy currant bush beside a large rock. We scrambled up the other bank to examine it closer. The finding of another rare bristly black currant, on a whole different side of the mountain than the one this spring, changed our outlook considerably. But wouldn't you know, after several months of procrastinating we had just the day before filed our rare plant report from last June's findings with the state Natural Heritage people, and the next day here pops up another specimen in a whole new place. You can't win in this world. We spent a little time looking around for another but this one plant seemed to be an orphan.

So now we proceeded up the brook with some gusto and enthusiasm, full of visions of finding all sorts of goodies. At each fork, and there were many, we had the hard decision of which to follow. We tried to stay with the larger trickle of water, but it became increasingly more difficult to determine the main branch. This tiny little brook was pretty, we had to admit, and even on this dreary day the golden-colored fall foliage of many plants mocked the absent sunshine. A stand of silvery spleenwort ferns lead us astray once while looking around for other traces of rich soil plants, but with no further luck we always returned to the brook. At first, we climbed the bank every so often to be sure the old road was still in view, but eventually we forgot about it and concentrated on the brook. When we checked again, the road had disappeared. We were not about to search for it.

We amused ourselves wondering the whole time where the source of the brook would prove to be, but when we found it seeping out of the ground on the edge of the power line on the top of the mountain, at the head of an obvious little valley, we thought, 'how dumb'. Where else in the world did we logically expect the source was going to be? So there we stood, shoulder high in goldenrod, briars, and hardhack on the power line, hundreds of feet higher than we had planned to be, having proved nothing at all. It was not until later in the afternoon when we realized that following the old road up the valley would have proved far more interesting. We had suddenly remembered a letter from Percy Brown, back in the fifties suggesting that we someday look for the (early 1800s) road that went from the "old ranch" out past the Truesdell/Hazelton cellar hole on down to Monroe.

We stood there stupidly, one leg hurting from stepping down further than expected in some brush that had collected on the brook, hot with a wool sweater in the momentary sunshine, and in a total dilemma trying to decide what to do next. We could follow the power line back to the switching station and call it a day – this option seemed to keep coming up high on our priority list – or we could bushwhack down over the mountain back to the HT&W rail bed where we were supposed to be – but then we would have to climb back up another five or six hundred feet for the second time. Why couldn't we just go home and forget the whole thing? But "we have to take the hike" or we won't have any Wild Side to write about. Says who?

Still with no decision, we climbed up through the mess of vegetation to the power line road and headed south. The wind was blowing the dark gray clouds around, and it was very hot or very cold depending on the appearance or disappearance of the sun and the velocity of the wind – neither particularly pleasant. We walked on, ignoring the goldenrod on all sides begging to be identified and then hated ourselves for our indifference. The asters we likewise ignored, exposing our prejudice against these beautiful frustrating creatures of the wild. Today was just not the day to bother ourself with such a painful occupation. We marched on, letting nature decide our course.

It was not long before the wind got to us and we headed into the woods again on the west side, half thinking we might try to locate that old road on the other side of the ridge that went down to the river by Dunbar brook. A short distance into the woods we joined the path out to the Monroe T.V. "antenna garden" past "Joe's cliff" where we detoured closer to look at its very green rock tripe and lovely ferns. Bear scat and trampled grasses around the blackberry bushes indicated we were not exactly alone in these woods, but even old bruin was ignoring us. Gee, why couldn't this be the day we came face to face and THEN we'd have a story for Wild Side! The wind picked up and the woods were irritatingly noisy with trees creaking and moaning, and we could hear the grinding and banging of equipment on the bridge project at Monroe.

At the proper place we headed left down the mountain, through a little ravine we had always wanted to explore. Right off, a group of rocks seemed to rule out this as the path of the old road. Cliffs and boulders drew us back up the mountain a little but nothing interesting caught our eye, so we headed down into a little plateau. On the way we slipped and fell backwards, sliding down against a log with our knees bent up to our chin. It was a slow fall and did no damage except bending our knees too tight and it took a minute or two to get out of that position and put our weight on them again. This, of course, did nothing for our moral. We looked around the plateau for the possible path of the road and, finding nothing, came to the same conclusion as many times before that we will someday have to find this road from the bottom up where there are still traces.

So we stood there stupidly, once again trying to decide what to do next. Somehow, we didn't want to go downhill, so the obvious would be to go across. We could traverse the mountain all the way at this height, exploring new territory without much climbing until we came to the brook in our original plan. We headed on in rather pretty woods with birches and maples and deer paths making superhighways for us to follow. These make for easy hiking, but are often lacking the goodies of the plant world for which we are always searching and upon which the deer have already feasted.

We have to admit that occasionally there were interesting things like the whorled asters, which seem to be especially attractive to slugs with many eaten full of holes, leaving beautiful leaves of lace. Mushrooms were everywhere – little tiny bright red ones, perfectly round bronze ones, multitudes of pure white puffballs all along a dead log, glossy blue and purple gilled ones, growths of coral like the sea, congregations of tiny white hats on brown grass-like stems, and then patches of the forbidding black chanterelles. We took time to enjoy the tiny little red eyelash cups through the lens. Should we have brought our mushroom book? No. Most all of them have no common names, and this was not the day to add frustration with Latin to our woes. And, with the strong wind it was no day to quietly sit beside a 'find' and check it out in a guide book. We tried to analyze what was so very wrong in the woods today other than the wind. Looking around, and thinking back to spring and summer, we realized it was greatly due to the absence of birds. Not a single bird was evident either by sight or song. The woods were lonely.

On and on we went, following one path after another or our own inclination. The way seemed to edge upward although we went up and down over many rocks and rills. When a break in the trees gave us a view to the south we came to another discouraging realization. The mountainside under and on the ridge beyond Pulpit Rock was so rocky we knew we couldn't traverse it at this level.

We would have to again either go down to river level or climb to the top and go along the ridge. From that present viewpoint we could not determine just how close we were to Pulpit Rock. What a lousy hike! We still hadn't seen anything worthwhile, and we had gotten into one predicament after another. We turned our course up in a series of hairpin curves, and marveled at a patch of real grass in a moister spot.

The only good news seemed to be the eventual sight of sky through the trees, indicating we were not far from the top of the ridge and it was not too long before we came into familiar territory on the highest point of land north of Pulpit Rock. We checked out some little pools between the rocks and spent some time looking over a larger swamp edged up against the huge outcropping of open ledge. Hopping the tufts of grass above the water, we stopped at one bush looking somewhat like sheep laurel but not exactly. We hoped for pale laurel and examined it well with lens in one hand and guide book in the other. Another disappointment! It was just un-blossomed sheep laurel.

Well, lunch on the high ledge would be fun. It was a favorite spot of ours with the view over the Deerfield valley. Trees blocked the view down to the river and it was always rather cozy sitting somewhere on the expanse of open rock that was often covered with delightful varieties of mosses and lichens. You guessed it. Today, it was miserable. Dark clouds just seemed to assemble overhead, and the wind was loud and annoying. We opened the knapsack and realized we had the soft yucky granola bars instead of our favorites, and the new fall apple was bright red but hard as a rock and nearly broke our teeth.

The Other Side of Wild Side

We shivered, threw the apple to the wind, slung the knapsack over our shoulder, and headed down toward Pulpit Rock.

Here, we decided to follow the outside path and the wind continued to literally blow us into the hill. We couldn't even stand still on a rock long enough to look at the view or try to spot the pretty mountain ash trees. Finally, we gave up that idea and retreated into the woods path emerging again at the rocks on the southern point over the lower reservoir. From there we had to climb up on the rocks ahead in order to continue along the ridge. This small change of direction subjected us to even stronger gusts of wind, to the point of being dangerous to our footing and balance there on the open rocks. So once again, totally defeated by the elements, we retreated to the protection of the woods, stumbling over downed trees and tripping on the vines clinging to everything. It was total misery for the next hour even climbing up over the spectacular "dead deer cliff." In the end, we came to the back side of the little swamp that created the water for the brook on our original itinerary. No amount of curiosity or persuasion could lead us down that brook now. From the swamp, we made a beeline for the power line and walked over the blossomed slender gerardia, past our very favorite white boulder, past the gone-

Southern view from Pulpit Rock area

by fringed gentians, and past the seven foot tall goldenrod. As we neared the switching station road, we did look for our recently discovered large clump of wild bergamot. And just to add to our mood of the day, it was gone! A big light purple bushy plant of the Monarda family was gone! No obvious hole dug, no branches on the ground, just gone! What a crazy world today.

It had been six miserable hours and an awful lot of mountain since we had climbed over the guard rail on Monroe Hill. As we almost ran down the road to the car, a junco flew across our path with a happy little chirp. It was certainly nice to know something wild and alive was about on this lousy day. It sort of brought us back to the right side of Wild Side once again. The world of nature was doing fine. It was just us who were having a bad day. **10/90**

In the dead of night we came winging in out of the darkness and landed in the middle of the galaxy of lights known as the Tucson Valley. If it had been moonlight and several hundred years earlier, before modern light pollution, we might have seen looming on the southern horizon the mountain peak called Baboquivari, the sacred dwelling place of the Coyote-like character, I'itoi, the Creator of the Tohono O'odham or 'Desert People' known as the Papago Indians. Instead, the valley was bright with civilization, and the creations of water-gulping modern man rose above the desert.

From Massachusetts, Pennsylvania, Rhode Island, New York, and Florida sixteen of us, nature-lovers of one sort or another, were gathering for a tour called "An Introduction to the Sonoran Desert" sponsored by the Massachusetts Audubon Society. Making eighteen in all, the two leaders of the trip were Tom Tyning and Don Reid. Don is a naturalist from Audubon's Wellfleet Bay Wildlife Sanctuary on Cape Cod and

well known to several in the group (and probably to some of our sixth graders who have gone on the annual Cape trip). He had spent two years at The Nature Conservancy's Ramsey Canyon in Arizona, and this trip was a sentimental homecoming for him. Tom is a master naturalist from Audubon, based in Pittsfield, enamored of the Sonoran Desert, and was well known as a previous trip leader to some of the participants. I had become acquainted with Tom fifteen years ago while a volunteer at the Science Museum in Springfield, and he later did a nature program for us at Bench Tool here in Rowe one summer back in the seventies. Our paths have crossed only a couple of times since then. Tom is a herpetologist and has just written a fascinating Stokes Nature Series book, *Guide to Reptiles and Amphibians*. Both men are excellent naturalists, with boundless infectious enthusiasm and a cooperative brand of humor that would sometimes make our sides ache.

To avoid a flight out of Boston I had

Baboquivari Mountain, Arizona

Saguaro Cactus

There I was introduced quickly to Gambel's quail, black-throated sparrows, curve-billed thrashers, cactus wrens, Gila woodpeckers and, always sitting on top of the most prominent branch, the handsome glossy-black crested phainopepla of the silky-flycatcher family.

There too, we were standing in a forest among the giants of the desert, the ancient saguaro (pronounced sah-WAR-oh) cactus. Dwarfed beside one of these multi-armed natives, one suddenly becomes deeply aware of time. Many of these giants are nearly two hundred years old, some reaching heights of fifty feet and can weigh twelve tons. Their accordion-like structure allows for expanding or shrinking depending on the moisture available. Companions in this desert forest are the cholla cactus and the barrel cactus, the dead-looking thorny ocotillo which leafs out almost overnight when it rains, the bright green palo verde, the hard-to-distinguish varieties of mesquite, ironwood and acacia, and the small ubiquitous salt bushes, all of which may act as nurse plants to shade the occasional seedling saguaro.

Completing the picture underneath all this were various dried grasses and a myriad of tiny dried spring flower branches and seedpods known as bellyflowers, so small one needs a hand lens to examine them. Arizona November, hot and dry, blue sky and sunshine, but not the season when all the picture postcard pictures are taken of spring wildflowers! But it was a long shot from New England's gray and cold and dreary November from which I was trying to escape!

It didn't take long for Tom to detect my tendency for wandering off the beaten path, and he continually warned me of

chosen to join Tom in flying from Bradley a day early. This arrangement gave me the great pleasure of having a few hours Saturday morning for my first explorations in the desert, with Tom as a private guide, before the crowd arrived. In spite of a late night arrival, we were up and out early, driving to Saguaro West National Monument to hike around a small artificial waterhole that attracted a variety of birds and animals.

snakes, which he dearly hoped to see but not necessarily wrapped around my legs! We had to settle for a tiny zebra-tailed salamander that scooted across our path with Tom in hot pursuit, only to be outwitted as it disappeared into the bushes. The few hours passed all too quickly as I tried desperately to absorb in mind the whole new world of life in the dry Sonoran Desert.

My afternoon was passed getting exercise walking the highways around the motel in downtown Tucson, while trying to comprehend the desert, the hot climate and life in a big city, which was almost as foreign to me as the desert. Tom and Don, with two vans, arrived with everyone from the airport about quarter of six. I was on hand to welcome the crew and look them over, trying to guess who would prove be the avid birders, who might be too squeamish to look at snakes, and who might possibly be a flower person like me. Personalities and interests began to show even at dinner, as we all sat around one big table and introduced ourselves. As the spontaneous banter between the two leaders began to unfold, we all knew that we were in for an unforgettable sojourn in the desert.

The Sunday morning alarm went off at 5:30, and six of us were up and out with Tom and Don to Gates Pass in Tucson Mountain Park before breakfast. Birders flushed the trees, binocs in hand, while I felt the urge to climb and met the sunrise part way up the dry and rocky slope. What a glorious thrill, to see the sun suddenly turn the dark mountain rocks to soft red and highlight each and every stately saguaro on the bajada. Others had already learned new birds by name, while I had simply enjoyed the calls and songs of unknown feathered friends heralding the start of yet another desert day. Our avid birder had listed four 'lifers' before breakfast!

The very best first introduction to the Sonoran Desert can be experienced and enjoyed at the Arizona-Sonora Desert Museum in Saguaro West National Monument. This is a wonderful combination zoo and museum for geology, desert and mountain habitats, trees and plants, with a special cactus garden, animals, insects and spiders, reptiles and birds including a great new hummingbird aviary. Established in 1952, this has been called "the most distinctive zoo in the United States." So it was only logical that this should be our first day's adventure, starting with a tour at 10 a.m. We had lunch at their restaurant and all managed to keep interested and occupied with exhibits until 4 p.m. What an experience, to sit in a large round screened aviary and have various species of hummingbirds whizzing by your nose! Or to listen to the lady panther yowl for her mate in the huge enclosure with beautifully fabricated mountain rocks, caves, and waterholes.

To end our first interesting day in the desert we were driven to a nearby hill, which we climbed to get a closer look at several Indian petroglyphs, drawings scratched on the surface (desert varnish) of rocks by the Ancient Ones, sons of I'itoi, from the mountain called Baboquivari. Standing on the hilltop, surrounded on all sides by the saguaro forest, we watched the surrounding hills turn pink and the sun, having risen so beautifully for us early this morning and now having finished its journey across the big desert sky, set behind the far mountains as we looked southwest toward Baboquivari. I'itoi and the Ancient

Ones were watching over us and as a sign, as the sky darkened into evening, They set their friends the Coyotes to howling around us. And as we listened, the first and brightest stars began to peek through the heavens. Day one of our tour in the desert had softly and beautifully come to an end.

Monday, by early morning twilight, half of us with Tom and Don made our way out of the city, north to Sabino Canyon in the Santa Catalina Mountains. Quick floods down the wash bring moisture to the canyon floor, and more and larger trees, including sycamores and cottonwoods, grow along the now dry stream bed. Flying specks seen against the early light of the sky proved to be a small cloud of bats. The object of our morning jaunt was to listen for and possibly find great horned owls, and they soon were heard calling from various hideouts. We listened and then tried to approach the sound, walking deeper into the canyon and finally down along the dry wash. Our birder was sent in as a decoy but even he could not locate the elusive owl and soon the hooting stopped with the brightening light of day. We continued to wander up the wash, looking into the woodpecker holes in the saguaro for the tiny elf owl often hiding there. The canyon banks grew taller, but one hole looked especially intriguing in a saguaro on top of the bank, and when Tom volunteered to climb up the bank I couldn't resist following on this short expedition into the unknown on the upper level. The owl was not at home, but the walk in the grassland yielded several flowers and my first fern, a purple cliff brake. It also gave us a better view of the morning sky beautifully aglow with the pink clouds of sunrise.

Once more back in the wash two other flower people, Betty and Kate, emerged and we joined forces looking for specimens, pooling our knowledge trying to guess their identification in the absence of proper field guides. We found another strange fern, and the fruit of the unicorn plant or devil's claw, much used in Papago basketry. Don told us to save our specimens. He promised help.

By eight we had rejoined the rest of the crew, eaten breakfast and were on our way north beyond Oracle to Mammoth, and later turning up into Aravaipa Canyon Road where things began to happen. No kid with a new toy could be nearly as happy and boisterous as Tom when he spotted a snake in the road! "Yeeee Ha!!" And he jammed on the brakes and jumped out. A road kill small diamondback rattlesnake. What more could you ask for? Everyone was out in a hurry, sharing the excitement and all wanting a closer look. Lots of brave people can examine a dead snake!

No sooner were we all back in the vans and underway again when a large live tarantula crossed our path. "Yeeee Ha!!" And Tom's performance was repeated with a little more difficulty as he tried to get the gentle, giant, hairy, three inch spider to crawl on Don's hand. A beautiful specimen and most everyone, except the lady who would touch nothing with more than four legs and me, handled the spider. It wasn't that I was chicken. I had already handled one back at the Science Museum years ago so why waste time doing it again. (Quite frankly I'd rather pick up a live rattlesnake!)

At another stop for birds it was hard to get people back in the vans, as they had fanned out and were enthusiastically

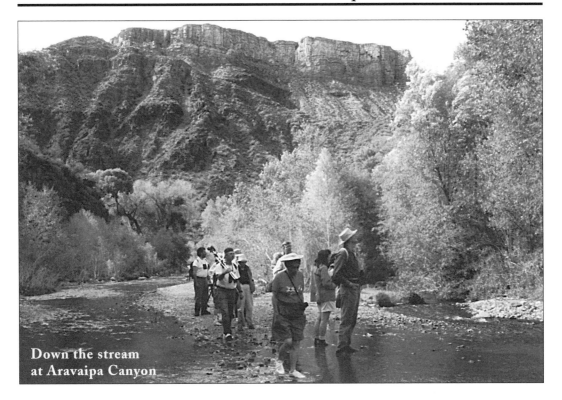

Down the stream at Aravaipa Canyon

looking at spiders, plants, and more birds and were well in the mood to search for further unknown treasures of the desert. Don lectured us on his topic of greatest concern – the destruction of the natural balance of the desert by grazing cattle – 'hoof maggots,' he called them with vengeance. Cattle have destroyed the native grasses and spread the seeds of the mesquite that grows thick and depletes the land of water for other inhabitants. Introduced grasses and damage from cattle back in the 1800s has changed some of the desert forever.

Eventually, after another half hour traveling a long bumpy dusty winding dirt road into an increasingly more beautiful canyon, and twice crossing a considerably

good-sized running stream, we arrived at our destination, the home of Tom and Debbie, who were caretakers and managers of the land owned or leased by The Nature Conservancy around the wilderness area of Aravaipa Canyon. Tom had been Don's old boss at Ramsey Canyon and the meeting was joyous. Tom explained to us the value of The Nature Conservancy's work with various agencies in protecting the precious watershed around Aravaipa Canyon.

We set out our picnic supplies on the table in the yard under the shade of lovely trees and enjoyed lunch, topped off with a big plate of Debbie's homemade brownies. I presented the new Tom with our bag of specimens and he, with the help of his field guides identified most of our flowers but not the fern. It would remain a mystery. In the midst of things someone spotted a golden eagle 'way high up near the mesa top. Everyone grabbed binocs and for a long time we watched the eagle swoop and dive and soar, seeming to be just having fun. We scanned the rocks for the bighorn sheep which make their home there but unfortunately this was their day on the other side of the mountain.

The main treat for the afternoon was a guided hike of a mile or more up the stream. We had been warned that it would be a wet trip, as most of it would be in the water. We wore hiking boots and the first leap from the bank took us in up to our knees. In the heat of the day the water felt great and with the dry air our clothes dried quickly when we were out along the bank. Birds were plentiful and I became well acquainted with a pretty black-throated gray warbler and the black phoebe and the voice of the canyon wren, but the birders were in seventh heaven with many more sightings. My binocs were spotting ferns on the canyon cliffs. There were many stops for interesting bugs or plants, and a few "Yeeee Ha's" from Tom as he spotted special beetles and butterflies.

Once, when we were watching some soaring eagles, someone identified hundreds of white-throated swifts so high up that they appeared only as tiny circling dots in the binocs. Later a blue heron flew in as if on cue and perched picturesquely high on a rock for all to see. In a more open area the crew seemed to slow down taking pictures and birding, but Debbie continued on and I followed, not wanting to miss all there was to offer. We finally sat, resting at the gate to the wilderness area waiting for the others to reach the destination, but only Peter showed up and he was on a mission to tell us the others had turned back after spotting two deer. As we meandered back down the canyon other stragglers joined us along the way, and all were collected by the time we reached the picnic table for a final snack and change to dry shoes.

We drove out of this green paradise just as the setting sun was highlighting the high mesa walls and turning the clouds to gold. We ate Mexican food on the way home, tired but happy, and were still able to enthuse at one more of Tom's "Yeeee Ha's" when he spotted a great horned owl sitting in the road. As for Don, his answer to one last quip from Tom on the C.B. was, "I'm just too tired to take any more humor!" And thus ended day two in the Sonoran desert country.

Tuesday was a day in transition. We were up for an early breakfast and out by eight on our way southwest to the town of Ajo, outside Organ Pipe Cactus National Monument. It was a long but interesting trip, with one general stop for cold drinks and a quick tour of an Indian crafts gift shop, where we were able to admire the intricate and artistic workmanship of the Papago baskets. Doug, the birder in the front seat, must have spotted a hundred red-tailed hawks! It seemed as if there was one perched on every third telephone pole across the desert. But there was always the possibility of it being a rarer breed and, every once in a while, there was an excited stop and all binocs focused on the bird in question. Our picnic lunch was saved until we arrived at the motel in Ajo and there we ate out under a ramada in the back yard. The shade was welcome, for it was hot.

Ajo had been a noted mining town, with the principal landowner Phelps Dodge Corporation operating a copper mine since 1917. The huge mile-across open pit mine was now fenced and silent as the company had shut down in 1985. There were still operations going on, as the company was obliged to cover their tremendous slag piles to keep the dust at a reasonable minimum, and eventually it would have to demolish the huge mining buildings. The company houses were selling cheap and the Chamber of Commerce was fiercely trying to promote the town as a retirement community. So far it still looked like a mining town although the company had created a lovely village green surrounded by Spanish style buildings and churches.

After lunch we toured the town, stopping at the little visitor's center overlooking the pit, and watching a film about the town, and looking at historical scrapbooks of the beginning of the mining operation. Next we visited a museum on the hill, where we pondered several rooms of artifacts of the old west and Ajo in particular. The attendant gathered us together, and in a great western drawl told us some stories of the old mining days. While others were still moseying around, I went outside and climbed up the hill scaring up a small rabbit. I was checking out the cactus and a few remaining wildflowers when I realized the vans were loading and I had to come flying down, this time following a path which led me astray on the other side of a wall behind the building.

The next adventure was a swing around a road, labeled as a nature trail, where we saw saguaro and more of the new organ pipe cactus. There was a stop where we could all climb a hill, walk the washes, or roam through the cactus spotting birds. I climbed the hill, and the first fascination was not nature but the airplanes over the military reservation and bombing range in the distance. Several fighters were climbing and diving and soaring much as the eagle had done yesterday. We all fanned out, with everyone investigating their own thing. Don later reported seeing a lizard and when Tom asked what kind he answered, "Oh, just an LGJ." This was evidentially understood between them as an unidentified "little gray job!" Two of the men wandered across the road and came back enthused with ore samples from an abandoned mine. From the top of the hill I had walked among the cacti on the back side and returned down through the dry wash. Seeing a BGJ on the bank, I was about to yell, but realized in time it was only the bare gray roots of the tree on top.

The evening of this third day ended with dinner at Dajo Joe's, where we all sat together at a long table. Don was the last to come in and without his usual smile he bent over Tom, saying, "We're in deep trouble!" There was dead silence as everyone's ears perked up for the details. It seems that when the sliding door of Don's van was slammed shut, as had to be done to close it, the door window shattered in a million pieces. The van was new, so the window must have been defective. All possibilities investigated, it was finally necessary for Don to drive the two or more hours back to Tucson, exchange the van for another, and drive back to Ajo. Hero of the evening, Don was rewarded with several bags of M & M's and candy bars from a grateful crew next day.

Wednesday, just as we arrived at the visitor's center at Organ Pipe Cactus National Monument, someone reached for one of the field guides on Tom's slanted dashboard. It came up orange and sticky with spaghetti sauce as did another, and another. It seems that Tom had brought Don home a spaghetti dinner, to be eaten in the wee hours when he returned from Tucson, and was unaware that the sauce had leaked out over all the books. First order of business was for Betty and I to take the books in and try to wash off the sauce without disintegrating the pages, and then leave them in the sun to dry. The operation was not a complete success, in fact, it was a real mess. And, come to find out, Don had been too tired to even look at his dinner, sauce or no sauce.

We all attended a short slide show about the park, canvassed the bookshop, and drank our capacity of water and filled our canteens. The orders of the day were to drive around the 53 mile dirt road called the Puerto Blanco Drive, with a guide book in which stops were numbered with a brief definition of the features of the surrounding area. We stopped for our first stroll where a large wash crossed the road. Everyone fanned out as usual and I decided to try walking up the wash. Tom, fearing that I might take off and climb a mountain, shouted that I should be back in ten minutes, fifteen at the most. Well, I was there but the rest were long gone, following Tom on the trail of snakes and lizards. I caught up with them and it was an eventful hour and a half producing a baby tarantula (thanks to Diane), some desert millipede cases which I came upon, a red velvet-ant which was really a wasp, a flying tarantula hawk (not a bird but a bug), and a small grasshopper with the beautiful rust and turquoise colors of the southwest. There were also many birds, various mammal burrows, and harvester ant holes with stacks of grass chafe which they discard near their holes after eating the rich seeds.

Lunch that day was under the ramada at Bonita Well, near the old creaking windmill which had been disconnected from its source of water but continued to turn with the breeze, a rather pleasant nostalgic sound. There was a loud "Yeeee Ha" from the well area and we all gathered around to become aware of the deadly bark scorpion Don had spotted under some old boards. Nearby a big saguaro was just growing its first arms (they have to attain the age of about seventy before they do this) with four or five little buttons just showing themselves. At other stops along the way we saw the rare crested form of the saguaro, the elephant tree, and a stand of the rare senita cactus. One of the most unusual areas visited for our late afternoon hike was at Quitobaquito Springs just over the fence from Mexico, where a running spring fed a small pond. There were the endangered desert pupfish, several ducks, yellow-rumped warblers and other birds, as well as cottonwoods and rather lush vegetation. What a surprising oasis in the middle of the desert! Perhaps the most spectacular sight as the sun was setting was the gathering of turkey vultures on the tops of the saguaros. Tom counted 113 and they were still coming in continuous numbers as we left. Probably thousands settled there every night.

A beautiful sunset behind the saguaros was our treat on the trip back to Ajo, and after another great meal and sociable evening around the long table at Dajo Joe's, a van full of us went out stargazing with Tom and Don back on the nature trail, behind the slag piles away from the lights of Ajo. Desert skies are bright and clear and Mars, especially, put on a great show, along with several stray meteors. Tom pointed out the major constellations, and the first thing that was hard to realize was the fact that we were far south of Massachusetts on this globe we call earth and the Big Dipper was out of sight! And, now that I think about it, the sun was far higher in the daytime sky. No wonder it didn't seem like New England November! And so closed the fourth day.

Thursday as we rose early the tiny crescent moon was bright in the eastern sky, and there was lovely earthshine on the rest of the moon. And we were all happy to see that the Big Dipper had been rotated safely back into our vision! After breakfast, the birders seemed to gather on the lawn of the village green where they were seeing all sorts of new listers, including a flock of cedar waxwings. There were those who claimed to have seen a Bohemian and those who took emphatic exception to this sighting. The creature didn't show its feathers again so I guess we'll never know for sure.

Leaving again, bag and baggage, we were headed for Kitt Peak National Observatory. This was an eventful day, with lots of "Yeeee Ha's" for white-tail deer and coyotes, and then a good close look at a javelina and a coati both crossing our path as the vans climbed the spectacular road up Kitt Peak. Here, too, we began to see the lovely red-barked manzanita bushes along the banks. The view was better and better and showed us so vividly the basin and range concept of the western geology. At the top, we watched an introductory film and had a guided tour of the huge Mayall 4-meter telescope observatory. The Mayall is the third largest optical telescope in the United States, contained in a building eighteen stories high. The mountain, chosen for its clear and stable atmosphere, contains eleven large telescopes, two radio telescopes, and three solar telescopes. The McMath is the largest solar telescope in the world, and in this we could see

The group at Kitt Peak

the image of the sun projected on a screen showing sun spots very clearly. The whole complex is the largest single collection of optical telescopes and instrumentation in the world.

The mountain on which the Kitt Peak complex is located is leased from the Tohono O'odham Indian nation "for as long as scientific research is carried on," and nearby one can see the sacred peak of Baboquivari looming above the desert, where I'itoi watches over this mountain belonging to His People. When first leased, astronomers were looking with their own eyes at the heavens, just as the Ancient Ones had looked in wonder for uncountable generations to the stars for explanations and created simple legends to answer the where and why of life and the universe.

The strange thing I learned on Kitt Peak is that these modern astronomers no longer "look" at the heavens. Instead, they are cooped up in a small room with a computer receiving data from the big computer which is scanning the heavens through the telescope. Every minute of telescope time is booked years in advance, and astronomers have to present detailed outlines of their research projects with only a few of those presented chosen and given a day or so at these facilities. Their technology and research has my great admiration, but is far beyond my comprehension. I seem to want to ask perhaps the same question as I'itoi, *"Has man not lost, in his reams of computer data, the truly magnificent wonder of it all?"* As I walked across the peak to the solar telescope, I watched the desert ravens soaring and diving and playing and looked down into a swarm of white-throated swifts. And then,

in reverence to the Ancient Ones, I stood for a long time looking off toward their sacred peak called Baboquivari.

Our lunch was at the picnic area down near the big radio telescope. Some of the birders walked down, listing a few new ones on the way, and even I saw the notable acorn woodpecker, which thrilled everyone with its appearance. New thoughts to ponder on 'heavenly' research and greater respect for the men who accomplish it, sunlight and shade, large rocks to climb and a gorgeous view in every direction, and a great lunch made it hard to say good-by to this exceptional experience on Kitt Peak.

We arrived at our new home in Green Valley in time for a swim and soak in the hot tub, and a leisurely dinner in the dining room. Those of us still wishing to stargaze in the clear desert skies went with Tom and Don to a country road away from the lights, and again located major highlights of the heavens and listened for owls and coyotes and other mysterious sounds of the night. And so ended a memorable fifth day.

Friday morning was rather special. We were up and out early heading for a wilderness road in the Santa Rita mountains, but most of the action took place before we even got to the real wilderness, although it was certainly out of the city. Don's van was first in the procession and at one point he pulled over, stopped, and got out. Tom pulled over, too, and as someone spotted some Gambel's quail down along a railroad track we all assumed that was why Don stopped. One by one everyone peeled out excited about seeing several quail, including some little ones. Quail seemed to be everywhere and as we looked up the tracks a road runner perched nicely on the rails, then ran along side and eventually into the bushes. Then several quail came one by one across the tracks. Then there was a wild "Yeeee Ha" as a bobcat was spotted walking along the tracks toward us. Every pair of binocs was on him, as was the spotting scope. He sat looking at the quail for a while and then disappeared into the bushes. Then, while everyone had turned in the other direction, he appeared again and sat closer for a long time on the rail, trying to decide if it was worth chasing quail for breakfast. Evidentially not, as he turned and crossed the tracks into the brush and disappeared on the other side.

Just before getting back in the vans we asked Don how he had happened to spot the quail, and he confessed he had just stopped to take off his jacket, as the morning was warming up so fast! The wilderness grasslands were a whole new softer-looking habitat where we saw coyote, pronghorn, white-tail deer and western meadowlarks. Our lunch was at a roadside picnic table and, as always, everyone was hungry.

The next treat in store was a hike with "Smitty" on the grounds of Fort Huachuca military reservation. This was to be a long, steep hike on a path up a mountainside where Smitty kept track of some rare and endangered spotted owls. It was great hiking, and I was happy to be seeing larger evergreen trees, stray wildflowers and some ferns – another purple-stemmed cliff brake, then an ebony spleenwort which gave away the limestone geology of the canyon, a woolly lip fern and another pretty little lacy fern which when turned over showed silver-white undersides covered with powdery fruit dots. Later identification at home from my trusty

Britton and Brown called it a powdery notholaena.

In the excitement of climbing, three of us had gotten somewhat ahead and had stopped to rest when a low, almost whispered, message reached us that the owl had been found lower down and we were to retrace our steps. We had walked right past the owl hidden in the branches of a tree. Expecting it to be higher up and somehow having in mind that it would be on the ground, I hadn't bothered to scan the trees. (Peter had spotted it ahead of Smitty and we all decided later that this had not been the correct protocol!) We all gathered around with binocs, cameras and spotting scopes and the large owl didn't seem to mind at all. The birders wanted to spend time observing, so it seemed the perfect chance to climb higher on the path. Betty joined me while we looked at flowers and ferns. Shortly after we felt that we must turn back we met Peter, once again rounding up the wanderers and ushering us back into the fold. The only disappointment of the whole trip was the spotting of that owl so soon and not being able to climb the rest of that intriguing limestone canyon!

It was impossible to persuade the few who had never been into Mexico that they really didn't want to go, so we drove south to Nogales and walked over the boarder for an hour of shopping, or haggling or whatever you call it. I bought some vanilla and called it a day. We had dinner in Nogales and drove on back to Green Valley finishing up our sixth day in the Sonoran Desert.

Saturday morning found us out early and back to Tucson, where we toured Saguaro East National Monument, stopping for several short hikes and one big "Yeeee Ha" when

Peter's sharp eyes again found the treasure, a small regal horned lizard. Seeing a few telltale diggings we searched for but did not locate the desert tortoise, endangered because cattle (and Don grumbled 'hoof maggots' again) have destroyed the weed plants rich in calcium which the tortoises need to survive. The Indians, the Ancient Ones, considered themselves part of the natural world and used its resources with respect. We began to understand how modern man in his greed is endangering everything, including himself.

The grand finale of the day came with the long looping drive up through the Santa Catalina mountains to Mt. Lemmon, 9,157 feet high, into the lovely breezes and smells of the Douglas fir, ponderosa pine, and Rocky Mountain white pine. From desert to the top we would experience all the zones of land from Sonoran Mexico to Hudsonian Canada. We learned a new term "hoo-doo," referring to a column of rock formed by erosion, and we would see many, many of these along the way. We lunched at a small restaurant on the mountain and then walked down the road along a small stream spotting more birds including the pygmy nuthatch, Steller's jay, and a dark-eyed junco, as well as a funny Abert's squirrel with long pointed ears.

The final stop was on top of the mountain at a ski area said to be the one farthest south in the United States. The trails in view seemed to be short and steep. There was time to hike, so Pamela and Kate and I headed for the top up a narrow road not really knowing where we were going to end up. After several switchbacks, we decided we'd better come back down a ski trail rather than try for the top at an unknown greater distance and

perhaps hold up the crew. The trails were rocky and full of small mammal holes, but we zig-zaged down finding in bloom the tiny fairy candelabra which I had seen in Utah. What a total contrast to the desert!

We couldn't have asked for a prettier sunset than the one that displayed itself to us on our return trip. Tom and Don made one stop at precisely the right time and behind just the right large many-armed saguaro and pictures were being snapped as if there was no tomorrow. Which was exactly the case. This was our last day in the Sonoran Desert and everyone would be departing at daybreak or soon thereafter. Dinner was another banquet around the long table, and the conversation was full of remembered sights and sounds and experiences of a very eventful, enlightening, and wonderful week in the Sonoran Desert, with special warm thanks and appreciation to two leaders who were responsible for it all! A big "Yeeee Ha" from everyone to Tom and Don who shared so much of their expertise and made us understand how fragile and beautiful is our natural world, a real Wild Side even in the desert.

It was shortly after one when our flight took off back to Bradley Field in cold and gray New England. But the warmth and joy and new insights of my Arizona trip will stay with me for many Novembers to come. As the plane rose off the runway and banked eastward, the last thing I saw out my window through the thick haze of the city was Baboquivari Peak brooding over the surrounding mountains and the encroaching civilization in the valley of the Tohono O'odham.   **12/90**

1991·
1992

Devil's Castle, Alta, Utah

Returning to Ski the High Mountain of Utah

It's beginning to seem like home, that cabin on the high slopes of Albion Basin at Alta, Utah and Gary and Helen Lund like part of our family. This was my third trip there in just over a year. In "Skiing on the Wild Side, April '90," you remember that, with a little persuasion I made the decision to face the prospect of senior citizen status by returning to my beloved sport of downhill skiing after nearly twenty years of inactivity. The culmination of this decision, and very little practice, was an invitation to join the younger generation on a ski trip to Utah. A "once in a lifetime" opportunity, I thought, never dreaming that my good behavior would warrant a second invitation. In the meantime, my wildflower passion surfaced and I told you about Lund Lodge and the Albion Basin in summer in "Botanizing on the Wild Side in Utah, August, '90." Now to ski the high mountains, once again.

The thoughts of Utah were exciting, but I had a few months to await the departure date. In the meantime, I have continued to roam the local woods and ski the eastern slopes but have sadly neglected our Wild Side stories in the last few *Goal Posts*. In December I celebrated my milestone of three score years by climbing Mount Greylock, for the first time fully and legitimately, from bottom to top and top to bottom. This challenge accomplished, climbing the highest mountain (in Massachusetts), has given me great confidence that I can continue to weather my senior years actively and joyfully, afoot or a-ski, on the Wild Side! The month of January was spent on the slopes of Mount Snow where skiing on a good cover of manmade snow still amazes me when I think back to the ice, grass and rocks on local trails twenty-five years ago. If Mt. Snow was good, think what Utah was going to be like!

In February, we deserted the north country and headed south in our motorhome, making visits to such places as Okefenokee Swamp where we went boating into that strange wilderness and saw, for the first time, the flower called golden club or "never wet," as it is locally known, because the water runs off the leaves. Hooded pitcher plants, which "eat" insects, were numerous, and in inspecting one I found a little tree toad sitting inside. What better place to find his lunch? Another day we hiked on Jekyll Island in Georgia, admiring the huge live oak trees hanging with Spanish moss and whiskered up and down with grey polypody ferns. And in the grass beneath one of these trees I found a new orchid, a lawn orchid, an introduced alien which is spreading through the south. We walked by the "Marshes of Glynn" made famous by poet Sidney Lanier, and saw a few herons and great egrets. And we walked the beaches chasing flocks of little sandpipers ahead of us, while barefoot we dodged the continual lappings of the Atlantic surf. But all this time in the back of my mind I was dreaming of the ski slopes in Utah.

Finally, we took up residence for a couple of weeks on the Florida Keys where we swam in the beautiful blue-green-turquoise waters and I walked the beaches in the warm sun and sand, marveling at the tiny perfectly formed seashells and the mysterious shapes and colors of other sea life. I observed but did not have the references to identify many local flowers and grasses. Some grasses, resembling tiny poinsettias, still fascinate me.

I knew the lovely orchid trees and bougainvillea and camellias, and did my best to distinguish the birds, such as the Louisiana heron, the little blue, and the reddish egret. Although some birds came in flocks and pelicans gathered around the fishing pier, the bird population seemed to be seriously diminished. And, when I flew north to Miami by small plane on my homeward journey, it took me over the Everglades, sickenly brown with drought due to man's greed for fresh water, agricultural production, and homes on canals. This, combined with a natural drought the last few years, is spelling permanent disaster for the Everglades. It is sad to see the destruction of this national treasure, the great "River of Grass" and wildlife habitat in southern Florida. Hopefully, enough conservation-minded citizens will find a solution before it is finally too late.

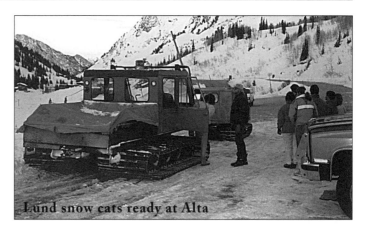
Lund snow cats ready at Alta

* * * * *

And so the year came around again to March, and the long-awaited return to Utah with "the gang." The departure day was anticipated with great pleasure. Leaving Rowe at five a.m., March 9th, we gathered forces along the way and six of us boarded the plane at Bradley Airport. Number seven joined us at the Salt Lake Airport, two had arrived the night before and two more came in at midnight, making eleven in all. Salt Lake City was bare and brown and people were playing golf. It seemed impossible that, within a half hour's drive, there would be eight to ten feet of snow five thousand feet higher up in the mountains surrounding Little Cottonwood Canyon. What a thrill

to see that breathtaking western mountain scenery especially on a sunny day in winter. And, this year, any sight of snow was a real treat!

We stood on one foot and then another for a very long time at the ski baggage counter at the airport thinking, the worst – lost skis – but they all eventually turned up and we headed for the shuttle bus to Alta. Gary was there to meet us with the snow cat in Alta's upper parking lot and, for the first minutes, it was a real old home day. The baggage was piled in the back of the cat and we piled inside, setting off on the two mile trip up the mountain where no car can venture between November and July. Part way up the cat began to spit and cough, and we envisioned a long walk up the mountain. After we all climbed out, Gary nosed into the innards of the machine and reconnected a wire on the fuel pump, and we were on the way again. In the meantime, we all had had a chance to breathe deeply of mountain air, admire Greeley Bowl from the bottom up, and just generally enthuse about our surroundings.

Swinging up into Lund's dooryard on

snow higher than the deck, I thought back to summer, and realized that the cat was sitting on snow eight or ten feet deep on top of a tiny canyon containing a rushing mountain stream. One would never guess! And there rising over all was the majestic rock mountain known as Devil's Castle, dearer to my heart since climbing to the top of its east flank last July. What a gorgeous spot to spend a week, summer or winter!

Helen was at the door to greet us by name with hugs and welcomes, and we immediately felt as if we were indeed coming home. Everyone was anxious to show our newcomers around and we repeated the rules, no boots beyond the hallway, and be careful of water consumption. It took the rest of the afternoon to catch up on the news with Helen, unpack and get comfortable and someone made the first batch of nachos for munching. When Gary came in from outside duties he and Helen gathered around my book of photographs from the summer wildflower trip, and I remembered all over again the unbelievable beauty and sheer joy of discovery of so many new wildflowers around the Albion Basin in July.

Then there was the happy reunion with the couple who had come in from Texas the night before. The girl, a member of the Mohawk Class of 1974, joined two of her classmates she had not seen in about twelve years, and a third arrived that night. They had probably all been together the last time in 1979 on our deck in Rowe for an Old Home Day picnic as a picture would later prove. Spaghetti always makes an easy supper the first night, but there are some people who just should not be in charge of cooking three pounds of spaghetti! However, the sauce was great and the garlic bread done to perfection, and the entertainment of the evening was watching a huge porcupine on the deck devour that monster glob of overdone gluey pasta. "Porky Pig" we named him and feared for his health when he didn't show up again for three days. Connections were missed and the last two arrivals were very late, but Gary was on hand to meet them near midnight and needless to say at that hour they had no welcoming committee among our ranks.

Sunday dawned a perfect day, and we were up and out early as the lifts opened at nine. One of the memorable features of our accommodations on the mountain was the morning ski run, two miles down, to the Alta Lodge to buy the daily tickets. Nothing steep, just a long sightly run down into the valley below. We all headed back up for Sugarloaf and spent the morning savoring the pure velvet underfoot with long curving runs in a variety of terrain. After getting a taste of powder, we were again led back for lunch as the crow flies across steep cliffs on unpacked slopes. It was a joy to watch the experts glide gracefully down through the powder. I did not handle it very well, but I was not as afraid of it as last year and, besides, the path took us across well-hidden Cecret Lake, where we had climbed in the summer and my curiosity got the best of me to see where it was hidden in the winter.

All the way I was raving about the lovely field of flowers we found here or the special beauty there by the rocks, but it was hard for anyone else to envision the huge rocks under the deep snow, to say nothing of a field of wildflowers! Lunch was in the sun on the deck, and we were soon back out on Supreme enjoying the afternoon. As predicted, storm clouds gathered by late afternoon and we looked forward to fresh powder during the night, but by sunset it had cleared. The outside hot tub was busy soaking aching muscles until it was time for our delicious stew dinner.

The weatherman had been correct about a storm, and early Monday morning it was snowing. The expert crew went off to Wildcat and by the time we were up on Sugarloaf, a good bit of snow had accumulated and skiing on the steeper slopes was heavy for this old gal and made my knees ache on every turn. But give up? Never! We went in for an early lunch and skied Supreme by the lodge until about 3:15, when the weather deteriorated into a total whiteout and we had to quit. The inside hot tub won out today, and we all made short work of a great shepherd's pie for dinner. The evening featured music and a VCR movie. Everyone had had a great, but tiring, day.

Tuesday was glorious! We were up early to see the rising sun gradually brighten the mountains from the top down. I went on the deck to take a picture and my nose quickly crinkled in the frosty air. The thermometer rested at zero! With this news we all dressed in the ultimate layers, but, by time to leave, the sun had warmed things to 20 degrees. Blue sky and sunshine, and mountains and bowls covered with fresh untouched snow greeted us on the run down for tickets. We all opted for Wildcat, which was a little further down the valley and entailed using a horizontal rope tow part of the way. When momentum stopped, you were dead in your tracks and had to pole, skate or somehow get yourself across the rest of the field and up a hill to the back of the lift line. This may

seem like an easy task but with awkward slanted downhill boots and short poles, and at 9,000 feet altitude, this takes extra effort, breath and heartbeats and can bring you to the boiling point on the coldest mornings. Some people gave up, took off their skis, and walked. We plodded along, stopping for breath every few steps on the climb, and finally arrived at the back of a huge long line waiting for the lift to start. After at least a half hour wait our turn came around, and thereafter the crowd spread out over the hill and the lines were minimum. It seems that new powder snow brings out all the skiers in the valley, and before the day was done every bowl, unpacked hill, and tree studded steep was patterned with the weavings of the tracks of these fresh powder enthusiasts, including a good majority of our gang.

But I liked my powder packed on the marked trails, and there was plenty of this. We skied there to our hearts content until our knees wouldn't bend any more. Going home for lunch was a trek – back up Germania lift, over the mountain to Sugarloaf, down to the bottom of Supreme lift, and up to the top of the mountain and half way down again to the Lund Lodge. It sounds like a long way around but lunch in the sun at home far outweighed any inconvenience or crowded ski lodge smelling of French Fries at the base. Lunch was short and we returned to Sugarloaf for the afternoon, prolonging our stay and barely making the last ride up Supreme at 4 o'clock closing time. This last ride is essential for it would be a long climb home.

We had each brought with us our cross-country skis and this seemed the perfect afternoon for several to try their skills at telemarking just above the lodge. The rest of us hopped in the hot tub and, although we were backed by a huge snowdrift, we could watch the antics of the skiers reflected in the lodge window. Those on the cooking team had the chili hot and ready early, and no one complained they weren't hungry. The game of Pictionary was the popular entertainment of the evening.

Wednesday was another beautiful day and the trails were packed to perfection. We had planned to go back over and try Germania, but Sugarloaf was just out of this world and we couldn't leave. Another new trail was opened and we explored this several times. When we bought the tickets at nine, some of us decided to go for a half day and finish with some cross-country skiing in the afternoon. We began to regret this as the day progressed, but by the cutoff time of one thirty we had had a full day of skiing with no lines on Sugarloaf and three wild runs on Supreme, rushing to use our ticket up to the very last moment. My knees were so wobbly on the last run down that I expected to spend the afternoon moaning in the hot tub! But lunch is a great reviver and we were quickly back outside, donning our cross-country equipment.

Now, cross-country is a whole different ballgame from downhill skiing. It requires fewer clothes, for you are well heated from the inside out, and it requires effort – great effort at 9,500 feet! In fact, we walked a ways up the hill before putting on the skis and climbing the packed ski trail to a suitable place to venture out into the soft deep powder in the basins and tree-lined hills toward Devil's Castle. We had a good workout up and down the hills, and it was hard to keep quiet about certain favorite spots where I knew

what was lurking under the snow drifts – basins full of mountain bluebells, hillsides of red paintbrush, clumps of white columbine, bushes of purple lupine, wet meadows of pink elephant's head and cream-colored bog orchids, and, hiding under that huge boulder a tiny pygmy saxifrage. We could close our eyes, think summer and see it all again!

When returning just before four we hated to go inside so sat on the deck, watching the last of the skiers come down the moguls on Lund's Hill. We were especially waiting for the last member of our crew to return after a late trip to the lower lodge. We watched and watched and when the ski patrol swept the slopes we knew the dreaded had happened; he had missed the last ride on Supreme lift. Our sympathy was wasted, for when he came up the trail sometime later, with his skis over his shoulder, he insisted the climb had not been bad at all. But please, don't let it happen to us!

Everyone else was relaxing inside with the usual plate of nachos, but I couldn't resist the outside hot tub. Bribing someone fully dressed to open and close it for me, I went out and climbed in, thoroughly enjoying a long soak, looking at Devil's Castle and all the lovely tall spruce and fir trees surrounding the cabin. The wind picked up but the cool breeze felt good on my head and shoulders, and it was a lovely sight as the snowflakes began to fall.

For dinner, baked chicken was another culinary hit. The men were especially good cooks! Porky Pig porcupine appeared again looking for a handout, as did a squirrel and the pine martin, but there were no leftovers tonight. Instead, we fed Porky cookies from our hand. We listened to the

Returning to Ski the High Mountain of Utah

evening weather forecast and, honest, this is what they said: "We expect a little bit of everything tomorrow and not much of anything. Listen in again at eleven to see if we have changed our forecast." "Unsettled" was the byword for such days and we had to admit it seemed to fit the bill.

Rick and Nan at Alta

Thursday at dawn our two Texans were departing, and Gary was up and ready with the snow cat at the appointed hour, but, alas, the rest of us were dead to the world until a more reasonable hour. Today was to be our trek to the neighboring, more glamorous (and more expensive), area known as Snowbird. Friends of friends had delivered us some cheaper ticket vouchers from the valley, and we were waiting for the first bus at nine. But, would you believe we pulled the same boner as last year and stood in the wrong place and watched the first bus circle around and head down the valley? Fortunately they run every fifteen minutes, but that's one ski run wasted.

Our ticket did not include the tram, but we tried everything else in a wide and interesting variety of high mountain slopes. Standing near a fir tree after getting off one of the lifts, the group was making some decision on trails when we spotted a squirrel looking very friendly on the lower limb. With the slightest encouragement he ran down the tree, across the snow, up the body, and onto the arm of one of our members. With no handout he

quickly exited, and ran back to his perch with a disappointed outburst. A Mr. Goodbar was produced and he lost no time in repeating the performance and, carrying away the piece, he sat in the tree munching the chocolate as if it were his everyday fare – which it probably was!

We all gathered back together to lunch on our sandwiches from the knapsack at the mid-mountain lodge and found a table outside, which was an improvement on the very crowded conditions of last year. As we ate, the clouds rolled in and it became quite chilly and snowy, the little bit of everything that was predicted. Afternoon skiing was in the falling snow and visibility was poor, but we skied our full time and made for the bus in time to get back to Alta for the last run home. This of course required a lift ticket which can be costly for the two or three lifts it took to gain our lodge. Several brave ones made for the lift believing that no one bothered with tickets at that time of day, and sure enough no questions were asked. Then two more tried and two more – until just us two honest ones were left. We thought we had to play by the rules and bought a book of lift tickets. When we offered them to the attendant at the lower lift he waved us by saying, "This one is on me!" I'm just not just sure I want to figure out the moral of that story!

Returning to Ski the High Mountain of Utah

It had always been said that it was a tough cross-country hike home from the top of the second lift called Cecret (a misspelling of the word dating back to the old mining days), so we decided this was the day to try it. We were warm by the time we reached the lodge, but it wasn't the dreaded hike we had anticipated. And, by the way, the weather there at Alta had been fine all day, just that much higher than Snowbird which seemed to always be in the real unsettled weather region.

Again it was too nice to go inside, so we all sat on the deck watching one of our crew make a ritual climb up to the top of Lund Hill for his daily challenge down through the moguls. While waiting, we all decided to act as judges, and filled out slips of paper with such numbers as 8.6 or 9.9 or 10, which we were going to hold up as he skied under the rope in front of us. It sort of backfired, as he had an apple with him and disappeared over the hill where he sat resting and eating for fifteen minutes, oblivious to the judges who were singing and cheering, clapping and calling his name, much to the mystification of the other passing skiers. But the performance, when it finally came was rightfully rated a 9.9. Corn chowder sure tasted good for dinner and blessings on Helen who appeared with a large pan of fresh-out-of-the-oven cherry squares about nine o'clock. Wow, Lund Lodge sure rates a perfect ten!

Friday had to come around, sooner or later and it meant our last full day of skiing. It had snowed during the night, and it was still foggy and snowy and very slow going down the long run for tickets. We all went to Sugarloaf, where the skiing was very mogully in the heavy new powder and this old gal felt like a real klutz getting down the upper hill by the skin of my teeth using my very first learned technique, the Arlberg method of throwing the downhill shoulder around into the hill. But hey, it works! And, I suddenly realized that I had not fallen once all week. This should not have come to mind, as then I began to consciously be careful so as not to spoil my record! And with those snow conditions and my gradually tiring knees it would take some doing to keep my record clean until four o'clock!

The experts took off for the powder bowls and we were able to watch a few of their runs from the lift. Some of them came back with whooping stories of avalanches across their skis and how they skied the noted High Rustler. As the avalanche story kept growing in size with the telling, and knowing that there had been some real whiteouts in high wind that morning, we were never sure if they really knew whether they were on High Rustler or not!

Lunch was quick, as the unsettled day was settling into blue sky and sunshine, and some of us wanted to make for Germania trails where we had never skied. This required a long circular traverse from the top of Sugarloaf and a good bit of poling, but we made it after lots of heavy breathing and an elevated heartbeat, to say nothing of the body heat generated. The view of the area was superb and we enjoyed the new trails from the top to the mid-mountain Germania lift. Unfortunately, so did too many others and with the long lines we would have time for only two runs and a final trip back to the top to head home down Sugarloaf. On the second run the clouds were gathering and by the time we were half way down there was such a whiteout we had to take it slow and carefully.

The homeward trip was not the pleasantest skiing of the week but perhaps, it was my most unforgettable. By the time we gained the top of Supreme on the last run, it was like night. I had my camera and with most of our crew there I decided to take a picture through the snow. I removed my glasses, took the picture, and then everyone else disappeared down the hill. It snowed harder. I tried to clean my glasses but it was a lost cause in the snow. I tried to ski without them and had to close my eyes, as the snow stung them so badly. The light was totally flat and I couldn't see the slopes no matter what, but I finally decided I'd best try with my eyes open. After a fashion, I cleaned my glasses by bending over and shielding them from the falling snow and then stood with them on for several minutes to clear the fog. Well, I could probably see a tree looming in front of me, but not much else. Fortunately I knew the trail but – it really was the most harrowing ski run I'd ever had and my knees were giving out besides. And then, foremost in my mind was the fact that I had still not fallen all week and no way was I going to spoil my record on the very last run, blind or not! The last hill was steep and full of moguls, and I took them blindly one by one. What a feeling of accomplishment (for an old gal) when I skied under the rope and came to a full upright stop on Lund Lodge deck. My record for the week was clean!

Saturday morning was bright and clear, and we had until noon. Most of the crew raced to be first on the lifts to squeeze in another morning of downhill runs. I decided this was to be my time to take one more safari on cross-country skis and see a little more of the territory at the base of Devil's Castle, where we had spent so many happy hours among the flowers in the summer. I walked higher up the packed trail, then skied off into the wild white yonder through the trees to the open basins and cliffs. What a glorious morning, as the sun highlighted the surrounding mountains. We climbed higher and higher, and finally, from the top of a ridge, we would go down a cliff on an angle through the trees to the basin below. Suddenly the clouds came in, the light went flat, and we could see nothing but trees and white. We groped along, desperately hoping our angled tracks would not start an avalanche down the cliff. Past the trees I attained more speed than I wanted, and suddenly the tails of my skis fell into a trough made by powder skiers out of Devil's Castle. Down I went over backwards, with my weight on my shoulders deep in the snow. Well, nobody's perfect! It took a few minutes to gingerly right myself without creating the dreaded avalanche, and I called to my partner not to make the same mistake. A few minutes later the sun was out, and we were exclaiming over the view and listening to our skis glide down through the most beautiful powder you can imagine, sailing right over a meadow of sleeping bluebells.

It had been a memorable morning to end another fantastic week at Lund Lodge in the Albion Basin at Alta, Utah. Gary and Helen sent us off with hugs and good wishes, and we all secretly hoped to have many more happy returns.   **4/91**

The Wild Florida Keys

As I passed the mirror this morning, the backward image of Adams Mountain and Pelham Lake caught my eye, reflecting the t-shirt I was wearing over my bathing suit. The recent report from Rowe had been of temperature at 10 below zero, but the thermometer here on our camper window stands at 80, a little warm for February in the Florida Keys. The image of Rowe hills made me a bit homesick, but knowing the winter there had, so far, been cold and almost snowless I went happily off to the beach.

The beach is at Bahia Honda State Park, the next key southwestward from our campground. Crossing the bridge between here and there, you can see the beautiful shades of blue, green, and turquoise of the waters of the Gulf of Mexico on the right and the Atlantic Ocean on the left, only a bridge width apart. The road into the beach winds through thick mangrove trees and other assorted shrubs, some in flower. We have slowly learned to be content with observation and appreciation without identification, for the botanical guide books for the area are few, very incomplete, and totally frustrating for anything but the most spectacular flowers such as bougainvillea and hibiscus.

The beach sands are white and the beach is a long curving strand. Today was especially hot and I barged right into the water, but the tide was going out and it took some walking along the coral to get to the deeper water. I was so warm I finally just splashed down flat out to get wet and cool, then proceeded walking to swimming depth. On cooler days, although the water temperature is in the seventies, it takes a bit more courage to get wet. There were no waves today but at other times they have come rolling in, bouncing us on their surface or tickling at our feet on the shore.

We are not in the wilderness. The beach is scattered with beings worshipping the sun, in various modes of dress and posing in all sorts of contortions. When not in the water, I prefer to hide from the sun in a cover-up and a hat and sit under the beach umbrella staring out to sea or, as today, watching a beautiful big cloud building high into the sky to the north. However, this inactivity doesn't usually last long before I cast aside my cover to be off for a fast hike down the beach, watching for shells on the sand, birds on the water, or an occasional blossom in the grass. The little flock of sandpipers drifts ahead of me and five or six pelicans are active in a school of fish, into which they make clumsy dives head over feathers, ending up in the reverse direction and usually swallowing a fish.

The beach and the swim are always refreshing, but I keep remembering that I promised you a Wild Side for the March *Goal Post* so I'm now back at the picnic table, under the awning, enjoying a delightful late afternoon breeze. And through the modern miracles of a portable word processor and a fax machine you shall have a reasonable facsimile of my promise.

Greetings from the Florida Keys! The sky is clear blue and I can see a circling group (do they call them a pod or a wheel?) of black vultures and one lone magnificent (they really are) frigate bird. A huge wave of terns just flew over, probably changing feeding grounds now that the tide is low. A little palm warbler flits around the ground and on the table, flicking his tail as he looks for crumbs. Behind me are two mauve bougainvillea plants in full bloom, a dark pink azalea, and a red double hibiscus. The latter is full of buds, and each prize blossom seems to last only a day. These native plants have all been purchased to enhance the tiny yard around our camper and, hopefully, will be included in the baggage returning north.

When we first arrived here I was fresh from the ski slopes, and it took a week or so to settle down to a new way of life. On one of the first days, I took a quick trip over to Big Pine Key to search out the Key Deer Refuge as a possible place to hike. I found something called the "Blue Hole," a water hole with a huge alligator lounging on the back side, but a sign said that you couldn't walk around there so I left. On the way out, I had to kneel down and examine a little flower that looked like a Florida version of our Cyrus Stage Road toadflax. The other tourists were giving me odd looks! I drove further down the road and found the parking lot for the advertised nature trail, but, not knowing its length, I decided to leave it for another day.

And that day was Tuesday, when I was again free to "do my thing." Returning to Big Pine Key, I first went out to the Deer Refuge Headquarters. The key deer are an endangered species – there are only about 300 left. They are a variety of our white tail deer but very small, about two and a half feet tall, and weigh less than 75 pounds. The authorities are trying desperately to protect them, but civilization is encroaching from all directions, and about 60 per year are killed by cars in spite of the enforced 30 mph speed limits in the refuge area. With no fences the deer often wander out to the congested shopping areas.

At the headquarters, I wanted to ask some authority about hiking trails. Dressed in my sort of trademark outfit of dingy old white pants and aqua long-sleeved shirt, heavy sneakers, and socks, I walked in and asked the woman at the desk if it was permissible to hike on the trails that I noticed going out from the parking lot. Her answer was, as she looked me over, "Well, you certainly aren't dressed for it." I stood back with my mouth gaping open for a few seconds, then explained that I do a lot of hiking in this outfit in Massachusetts and what, pray tell, is required in Florida? "Well, er, it's wet and muddy out there." My next question, "So?" (She obviously was not a hiker anywhere!) Finally, the head ranger came out, realizing I wasn't the ordinary tourist just out to spot a deer. (One tourist who came into the parking lot while I was there said to me, "Where's the deer?" I offered that they were probably off in the woods. He muttered to his wife, "You'd think they'd have one penned up so you could see it!!")

Well, I explained to the ranger that I was interested in plants and flowers, not necessarily the deer, and that I didn't want to go someplace where I shouldn't be, and I wondered if there were other trails than the advertised one, and was there anything poisonous? (Having recently made the unexpected acquaintance of a cotton mouth snake in North Carolina, I decided I'd better ask.) The ranger and several others were then very helpful and explained things, gave me the number of The Nature Conservancy for field trips, and explained the one poisonous tree to stay away from. Before I went out, the first woman called to me and said that if I really wanted a place to hike I should go out to No Name Key, park across the bridge, and walk to the end of the road. It was REALLY WILD out there and I'd certainly love it!

(More later!)

As I was going out the door a little old lady in tennis shoes called me aside to say that I was perfectly well dressed and I could go out "there" (she waved her arm in the general direction) and hike if I wanted too! Then, when I got in the yard, another young man called to me. He overheard the conversations and also assured me I could walk out "there." The only problem might be at high tide when some of the area gets very muddy. Said he was also from Massachusetts (a biology major) and was now working at the Refuge. He told me a little more about the area, and took me across the street to show me the poisonous tree and fully explained and showed how it had five leaflets on one leaf stem and what to do if I got into it.

So, after all this, it was getting on toward noon and I decided to go back and try the regular trail (2/3 mile) first and then decide what to brave next. The trail was under tall pines, through low palmettos and many other bushes. A few glassed signs along the way told mainly about the deer and the man who started the refuge, but nothing about the plants. The first thing I noticed were the ferns – large dark wiry green ones and some lacy bracken almost as tall as my head and other assorted low ones, all sort of stiff and leathery. One bush had pretty little pink flowers, but there were no other flowers except some lance-leaved goldenrods with small unopened flowers. The vegetation seems harsh and noisy when the wind blows, especially the palmettos, but the tall pines are lovely and the walk wound around through all of this greenery. To my New England eye everything tended to look alike, except the poisonous tree which

I recognized immediately. I hope soon to join a Nature Conservancy hike with a knowledgeable guide and learn something!

I began to get hungry and very hot, as it was mid-day, and I didn't venture too far on the side paths. One path was supposed to go to a hummock, a small rise in the ground, hardly discernible to an eye expecting a hill! I went a ways and returned, a little fearful of getting lost until I had done the whole regular trail. I meandered along the rest of the way, seeing nothing new, not even a key deer. Once back at the car, I decided I needed lunch and drove back to the center for a bite to eat. The usual trusty granola bar was missing from my knapsack.

After lunch I debated whether to venture out "there" in the mud, but I succumbed to curiosity and decided to try that WILD No Name key. Driving out, I finally crossed the bridge from a well built-up area and expected great things. The bridge was full of fishermen, and beyond was a long straight tar road with no view and no shade. I decided to drive it first. Big cement trucks were going in and out the first side road. Wild? It would have been scorching to walk in the sun, and there was nothing interesting to see except the side of a road with a good bit of traffic.

At the very end of the road there was a large clump of the alien Australian pines and a glimpse of the ocean. Ah, I thought, a nice place to get out and walk. I had hardly stopped the car when over the bank out of the muck and garbage on either side, came about twelve begging raccoons! I thought at first I couldn't even get out of the car, but soon another car came and the raccoons took off after that one as a better prospect for a handout. I got out, shouldered my knapsack,

The Wild Florida Keys

locked the car, and prepared for a nice hike. BUT, by the time I reached the water, I was nearly sick to my stomach with all the garbage and litter everywhere. I took one look at the water, which was lovely, but I had no desire to follow a garbage trail.

I got back in the car and, by this time, at least ten other cars had come by and turned around in the WILD country! A little ways down the road, away from the raccoons I pulled over to the side to get a drink out of my water bottle. When I looked up, a little toy buck deer was crossing the road in front of the car! A little later down another road a deer was on the grass at the roadside, and would have come up to my window if I hadn't driven on. The deer are so tame and friendly they hardly seem like wild animals. It's little wonder they are endangered. And thus ended my wild expeditions for that day! Some other day I'll return and explore those

muddy trails, and my white pants will be dingier than ever, but maybe I'll find some real WILD country out "there."

The seashore across the highway from the campground is full of tiny shells and various wonderful creatures of the sea which I examine with awe and wonder on my early morning hikes. There I watch the big old sun rise right up along the flat edge of the earth, sending a gorgeous ribbon of red light across the water. The wading birds are just catching their breakfast and the mocking bird is still singing, having serenaded the campground all night long!

But the wildest experience of all here in the Florida Keys, the one demanding the greatest bravery, is the crossing, on foot, of Route #1, trying to dodge the steady stream of high speed traffic, even at dawn! Back home, the quiet countryside of Rowe will seem like heaven, even at ten below zero. **3/92**

Sailing the Wild Bahamian Seas

It was a Wednesday afternoon in late February when we returned from the beach at Bahia Honda, in the Florida Keys, and found a note taped to our camper door. The note said that a Don Ruth would call us at nine the next morning at the campground office. We had been hoping for just such a message. Last October we visited Don and Jane Ruth in their new home in Washington, North Carolina, and made vague tentative plans to join them for a few days while they were spending the winter sailing in the Bahamas. They had been out of touch on the high seas since before Christmas, and we took off for vacation in the Keys at the end of January, so chances were slim of joining forces, but there was the message and we were excited.

Don and Jane Ruth and family were residents of Rowe, in the "brick base" on Zoar Road, for several years in the late sixties and early seventies, and Don started sailing with the likes of a rowboat, a broom handle, and a sheet on Pelham Lake. While sitting there waiting for a summer breeze, he dreamed of someday owning a real

"The Beauty"

sailboat with an ocean to sail on. This dream gradually came true after they moved to Green Bay, Wisconsin, and had a day-sailer on the Great Lakes. They graduated to a twenty-eight foot wooden ketch called "Beauty" and we joined them for two great weeks gunk-holing in the North Channel of Lake Huron in 1976. They eventually upgraded to a thirty-five foot ketch called "Snowbird" and both retired in August of 1989. They headed south through the Great Lakes and canals on the boat, where they lived aboard for two years until moving into their new house last fall. But, after three months ashore, they were itching to hoist the sails once again.

The call came the next morning from

Sailing the Wild Bahamian Seas

Great Harbor in the Bahamas and Jack and Don made plans, which were finalized that afternoon, for meeting at Nassau Yacht Haven on Sunday. Advised that voter registration cards were not enough, there was a mad hassle for passports to be sent from Rowe, and luckily they arrived at noon on Saturday. A small American Eagle plane took us from Marathon to Miami, and another on to Nassau, flying over the beautiful turquoise blue/green shallow waters surrounding the some seven hundred islands comprising the Bahamas, which lie off southern Florida and extend on down to the tip of Cuba. There is much to-do this year in the Bahamas about Columbus as they are celebrating the 500th anniversary of his landing at San Salvador Island in 1492. We were in Nassau in time to have a fun reunion with Don and Jane over lunch, which included conch sandwiches and Kalik beer, native fare of the islands. At the boat we met Mickey, their springer spaniel, who was definitely part of the crew, if not the Captain herself.

With the afternoon to be spent in Nassau we soon went hiking, first boat gawking among the many yachts at the docks and then out on the street. We walked up over the high bridge across the harbor to Paradise Island and, of course, had to investigate the glitz and glitter of Merve Griffin's Paradise Island Resort and Casino. Walking through the gambling hall we dunked a few quarters in the slot machines, winning a few cupfuls and feeding them all back, for no financial gain, but we considered that the price of our admission to see how the other half lives. The beach in the rear was inviting, but mobbed with tourists, many from the five tour boats in the harbor including the huge

Fantasy of the Carnival Line. We all looked forward to the next day, when we would be far from the maddening tourist crowd out on a lonely island. Our first night on the rocking boat, we slept like babies in a cradle tied to the dock.

Monday morning, Don and Jack were attending to boat things, while Jane and I went shopping for fresh food with an edict from the Captain to be back and ready to sail at ten o'clock. Leaving at that time would have us out among the dangerous coral heads, with the noontime sun at the best advantage for spotting them under the water. (What, no buoys? Not in the Bahamas! Hmm?) Looking for fruit and vegetables, we went to the local market, which had recently been moved from under the bridge to far down the docks "to clean up the area to make it more attractive for tourists." Business was poor and the locals were upset, and wanted to return to the bridge area where their wares could be seen.

After this, we walked a long distance to the grocery store at a new mall. We had several heavy grocery bags, but were still looking for fresh fish. A native offered to drive us to a fish market and we accepted, but, being Monday the fish had not arrived. We thanked our benefactor and chose to walk back, but soon regretted our decision, for the bags were heavy and we were further away than we thought! But it gave us a new flavor of the island, walking by strange trees and flowers. We passed an ancient pink hotel, overgrown with trees. It must have been something in its day, probably back in the 1880s. A large wrecking crane was poised over one end of its sprawling layout and it would soon be history, although nothing moves that quickly in the Bahamas.

The lines from Snowbird were tossed off the dock, precisely at ten o'clock, with all aboard. It was interesting motoring through the harbor and seeing the local traffic of water trucks, both motor and sail, which go back and forth to supply all the out island settlements. We were headed east-southeast, about thirty-five miles, to the string of islands known as the Exumas. Don's Loran, a system of long range radio navigation, was working well, and he could plot our course precisely on the chart. About noon, we went through the Yellow Banks of coral heads with a bit of anxiety, watching for and avoiding the dark spots in the water. Because we were heading into the wind, the Captain opted for motoring all day instead of sailing, so we could be sure of arriving at the top of the Exumas before nightfall. Cruising out of sight of land, on beautiful blue waters under a tropical sun – wow, who could ask for more? The Loran beeped to say we had arrived as we approached the entrance to the small natural harbor on Allan's Cay (pronounced key), just about five o'clock.

A few other boats were already settled in, and when Captain Don found a suitable location First Mate Jane went into action, dropping the two anchors. Once settled with lines secure, Don recognized the neighboring boat as friends from back in Green Bay, Wisconsin. It's a small world. The first order of business was always to take Mickey ashore, so Don and the dog and I climbed down in their little red dinghy for a short motor to the beach. The first sight was disillusioning to me. There was a large pile of those lovely pink conch shells which all the shell shops sell (imported from somewhere) in Florida, but which are endangered and illegal to pick up alive in Florida. These shells on Allan's Cay had been discarded after the conch meat (a staple food in the Bahamas) had been cut out, but the disillusion was with the fact that they had all turned a dirty grey-black with rough surfaces instead of retaining that beautiful smooth polish with lovely shades of pink. We would see mounds of these shells wherever we went.

I quickly climbed a little hill and looked for flowers. The vegetation was much like Florida, rather leathery and harsh. Any flowers were on bushes or trees. Don soon realized that, next time I went with him walking the dog, he needed to bring along a leash for me, too! But I returned when called and we took Mickey, relieved and happy to have been free for a while, back to the boat, for she was barred from the next expedition.

We all climbed back in the dinghy and motored across the harbor to a small beach and were met by a strange welcoming committee on this deserted island. About fifteen iguanas of varying sizes, from a few inches to a foot or two, suddenly appeared from under the bushes and came toward us from all directions like a pack of baby dinosaurs. Unfortunately, they were used to being fed by visitors and came expecting a handout – which they did not get from us. Wild animals should be wild. But they certainly were amusing. Wearing only boat shoes, and Jane with bare feet, we all carefully walked around on the rough coral to the back side of the little hill and found a lovely curved beach with incoming waves on the ocean side.

Ah, a place to take a good quick hike, and I did. Then we all disappeared in various directions exploring the island. Jane tried the rocks with bare feet but retreated to the beach. I climbed the rocks and followed breaks in the bushes to the top of the hill where there was an abandoned house, minus its windows and roof, but with a gorgeous view in all directions. Once inside I could hear the voices of Jack and Don coming up the front side. Unbeknownst to them I was already there. I stood just inside the doorway and, as they approached, a large iguana crossed their path and came into the house, almost across my feet. Then I stepped forth from the spooky doorway, and they both let out shrieks Jane could hear back on the beach! Just a little fun on a deserted island. Well, not totally deserted – there were about fourteen other boats anchored there with us that night.

A beautiful Bahamian sunset was the backdrop for a delicious stir-fry dinner aboard. The First Mate also doubled as a great short-order cook! The evening was windy, but the stars were brilliant. In the darkness, some strange birds began flying around making equally strange peeping and squawking noises, almost as if they were feeding young, but we could not see them and they were nowhere in sight during the day. We heard these same creatures at night, on several islands, and never did solve the mystery. Everyone was tired (not from exertion but just from fresh air and enjoyment), and we turned in almost with the daylight. My bunk was forward under the open hatch where I could lay gently rocking, looking up at the stars.

Tuesday morning we were up with the sun, chores done, and ready to go. Jane and Jack hauled in the anchors and Don maneuvered us out into the open sea, where we had to go out about three miles to avoid shallow waters before heading south. The Loran was out of reach of its towers and navigation was in the hands of the Captain. The wind was right, and we were in no hurry today, so the sails were unfurled and the motor silenced. What a way to go! We took turns at the wheel and it was a challenge to stay on course. We eventually headed back toward shore, and navigation was by visual spotting of landmarks along the long low row of islands. Very light blue water meant a sand bar, and we found one of the only marine markers, a wooden stake with a gull sitting on top, marking the end of the sandbar along the entrance to Norman's Cay where we were headed. After lining up gaps in the islands and spotting two large white buildings we sailed flawlessly into Norman's Cay harbor – a delightfully beautiful spot.

Back in the late 1970s, Norman's Cay was reported to be the smuggling headquarters of the Columbian Medellin drug cartel, with bribes to the Bahamian government – headquarters through which 70% of all illegal marijuana and cocaine was entering the U.S. Norman's Cay has an ideal snug harbor and a small landing field. The facts of the story are sketchy but, at some point, there was a raid and all the property, houses, boats, and cars were destroyed, including an airplane shot down and still laying on a shallow reef in the harbor. There are said to be two or three occupied houses on the far upper end of the island, but nothing by the harbor. The remains of what must have been a lovely resort and small settlement are trashed and abandoned. All boaters obviously check all these things out

The downed plane at Norman's Cay

holes in the sand next to the dinghy and not wanting to move. Mickey, you see, is diabetic, and she was obviously having a reaction (peaking, they call it) and needed food quickly. Don jumped in the dinghy and went to get some Karo syrup and dog food. In the meantime, Mickey was shaking with some sort of seizures and could no longer hold her head up. I stayed with the dog and Jane ran to some boaters on shore to see if they had any food, (they didn't) and we were shouting to Don to hurry. It seemed to take forever and we thought sure the dog was gone. But Don arrived and Jane put the syrup on Mickey's tongue, and after a bit the dog could lap it herself and gradually sat up and then stood and ate her dog food. Within fifteen minutes she was running around as if nothing had happened!

Jack and Don were anxious to go see the downed plane, so they took off in the dinghy and Jane and I took another long walk around. With lots of exercise we were all happy to settle back on the boat, watch the evening sunset, and count about the same number of fellow boaters anchored in the harbor as last night. Pork tenderloin made a great meal and we happily turned in at 7:30! There were great thoughts of spending the evening reading, but one by one the lights went out and finally only the anchor light kept watch over a tired and

as the chief entertainment on Norman's Cay. There are no "No Trespassing" signs, but supposedly there are friendly Bahamian police who appear once in a while.

Arriving about 2:30, we immediately went ashore, dog and all, and investigated all we could find with lots of speculation. After a good hike around, we returned for a swim on our own private beach, enjoying the calm water and warm sunshine. But then Mickey, who had been racing circles around us, began to act strangely, digging happy crew soon rocked to sleep on the gentle tide.

Rain in the night roused us long enough to close the hatches, but did not keep us awake. Daybreak on Wednesday was beautiful once again. Jane and I were determined to go ashore early, before it was too hot, and take a long walk down the road we had seen yesterday. We must have walked a couple of miles by just going around the next bend, over the next rise. We first walked through a grove of cool Australian pines, and then along the end of the cement and grass runway, across which we could see a small bungalow and hear a generator running. We assumed that must be where the police stay. We could see another house 'way up on the hill and sort of made that our destination, but once there everything was overgrown and we couldn't find it. But there were strange walls and depressions in the coral, as if relics from settlements long ago. It was a long, hot walk back, and the swim was heavenly. We felt great with all the exercise. Don had been getting his exercise scraping barnacles from some instruments under the boat, while Jack supervised the operation.

Jane packed a lunch and Don and Jack joined us in the dinghy for a trip out to the plane, where we tied up to the propeller. Don swam into the plane and waved to us from the cockpit, and Jane did some snorkeling. Not being a great swimmer I had a pail with a glass bottom, and could kneel in the dinghy and look over the side. There was a fairly good-sized brain coral growing on the wing of the plane, which gave us some idea just how long it had been there. Then we headed back to a tiny island with one lone palm tree. After checking out

the coral and flora, and taking some "rescue me" pictures, we all sat under the tree and had lunch. What a gorgeous spot and what a beautiful day!

Then the excitement began. We climbed back in the dinghy, which was, we estimated, loaded nearly to its 800 pound capacity. The wind was blowing and the waves were apt to splash over the side, but we were in bathing suits so that didn't matter. We went around to the open ocean on the east side and on up along the shore to an inlet. The tide was receding, and we had to get out and walk the dinghy to shore over the sand bar. We pulled the boat ashore and explored. Don and Jane went snorkeling along a reef, Jack climbed the hill to take pictures, and I explored the nooks and crannies of the coral along the shore, hitting the jackpot when I found a beautiful king helmet conch in the sand.

We were all so busy doing our own thing that no one had looked skyward to the northwest. Any black cloud rouses my fear of being caught out in a thunder shower (so, some people are afraid of snakes), and I called to Don to check out the weather. There are no weather reports in the Bahamas, so you sort of take what you get, which is usually pretty good except when a front goes through. The cloud did look ominous, and, eventually, Don gathered his troops and we hauled the dinghy (containing the remains of lunch, pail and snorkel equipment, a large conch shell, and a camera) across the now larger sand bar so we could get into deeper water to go around the upper end of the island and back into the harbor to the boat. Getting into the dinghy from deeper water was not always a graceful operation, and we had a man overboard before setting off.

Maybe we should have saved a little time and not spent so much of it laughing at that episode!

The cloud came closer and grew darker. I watched for a telltale flash but didn't see any. Then, the wind really began to blow fiercely, and it was questionable whether the motor could move our heavy weight forward before we were blown backward. It was barely holding its own. The waves were high and splashing over

Captain Don and First Mate Jane

the sides, which of course were very low in the water. Never mind being blown out to sea, we were going to sink! The cloud now looked like a long black spiral – could it be a waterspout? (I am prone to worry under these circumstances!) The water level inside the boat was about the same as outside and added more weight to the already laboring motor. I grabbed a snorkel mask and tried to bail, but it was a lost cause as the waves were splashing so fast. Then the motor groaned and stopped. We had run aground in the middle of the harbor! The other three got out and dragged the dingy forward against the wind. I stayed, getting a free ride while trying to hang on to the floating equipment. My eyes were smarting with the salt. The cloud was overhead, the fantastic blue water was ugly grey, the wind was wild, and we were soaked although it was not raining. They finally pulled us to deeper water and all climbed back in. Some time later there was a joyous shout when we reached Snowbird. It had been an EXPERIENCE! Even Mickey was happy to see us.

Once aboard, we could see the black cloud retreating to the southeast and clear sky to the west. While we dried off and gathered our wits together the rain started, and it was a mad scramble to zip the top and sides on the cockpit. It rained in sheets out of the blue for maybe a half hour, then the sun returned and we went ashore for a lovely late afternoon swim. Clam spaghetti and salad, with lots of laughs over the crazy events of the afternoon, made the day complete and we gladly repeated our early bedtime schedule.

Thursday was another perfect morning, and Don and I went ashore early with the dog and a bag of garbage. The dump was a ways down the road and Mickey was thrilled to have a walk. At the dump we found all sorts of things, including part of the airplane. From there we went down a path out to the water on the outside of the island and walked along the rocks looking for shells and flowers, and even found still another section of the plane. Soon we realized we had walked as far as the runway so we decided to return down the center and connect with the road back to the beach. Again, Mickey was exploring everywhere, and running circles around us and even up to the little bungalow where we could now see the sign that said something about Bahamian police. I was looking for flowers, and we weren't paying much attention to the dog, when we looked over and saw that she was being accompanied toward us by a somewhat official looking young man with a gun! We exchanged a friendly greeting. It is sometimes hard to understand these people with a strange accent, but we soon got the message that he wanted to take our names – for what reason we still don't know. Don asked if he had a pad and pen with him, but he said we needed to come with him back to the house. How do you argue with a gun even if it is wrapped in a friendly voice?

Then followed another EXPERIENCE that we will not soon forget. We climbed the steps of the house and were ushered into the deepest, darkest, blackest hole you can imagine. Alone, I would never have set foot inside! There was no light, except for a ray or two through a dirty window mostly covered with a broken shade. When our eyes adjusted, we saw the hulk of another tall burly man getting some sort of breakfast on a filthy stove. He did not speak. In the corner were two very messy, dirty beds, and in the center a table full of boxes, dirty dishes, and what-have-you. Our young man brushed aside some junk, found a crumpled pad, tore off some pages to a clean sheet, and asked us to sit down on some broken-down chairs. Is this how you are arrested in the Bahamas? And what awful thing had we done? Don tried to ask, but the man just

mumbled something about keeping track of people in case they found something wrong. Wrong with what? The place couldn't be any more trashed than it was. Pencil in hand, he asked for our names, addresses, birth dates, and the name of the boat. We again asked if there was some reason we should not have been walking where we were and the answer, I think, was negative. I ventured to ask when the drug raid had taken place. The policeman did not know, he said, he was new there and too young. Duty done, I guess, he, gun in hand, escorted us out and all the way back to the beach, again very friendly but with no real explanation even of why the police were there in the first place. Could there still be "something" in those two large white metal barns off the runway? We were glad to escape in the dinghy and sail away from this eerie island paradise.

We motored out of the harbor and then had a great day of sailing, with Mickey on one lap or another, very much part of the crew. It was cloudy, but the wind was steady and we made our way south to a place called Warderick Wells, the Exuma Land and Sea Park. The entrance was tricky, between some rocks and into a beautiful harbor, with deep water around the edge and a sand bar in the middle. We anchored among a few other boats, along the far edge near the beach by the lone building, the park headquarters. Don, Jane and I went ashore with Mickey and explored the building, asking a few questions of the woman on duty. She was very pleasant but knew nothing, having been there only three weeks. But she did show me the library, where they had a wonderful collection of reference books on the local flora, fauna, and sea creatures, probably due to the British influence in the early years. What a place to spend a few weeks, hiking, observing, and studying the references.

We looked at the trail maps and learned that there are all sorts of hiking trails. Some of the trees near the building are marked with identification, listing such strange names as Joewood, strong back, rams horn, seven year apple, poisonwood (Ah, that I knew from the Florida Keys), wild dilly, pearl necklace, milk berry, and long-leaf blolly.

We went down on the beach and followed a winding trail, mostly on sharp coral, through the bushes and low trees and open dry mud flats. My boat shoes were not the thing to wear, and Don finally broke a strap on his thongs. As it was impossible to return barefoot, he had to snitch a trail marker ribbon to hold his shoe together to get back to the boat. He took the dog, and Jane and I continued on to an interesting causeway, where there were remains of an elaborate salt-trapping operation of years ago. Having been warned by returning hikers that the trail was "for mountain goats" from there on, we decided to turn back and try tomorrow with better shoes. At some turn we missed the trail (was it because of a missing trail marker?) and had to bushwhack across mud, rocks, and through sharp thick underbrush out to the beach by the boat. Yet another lovely sunset concluded an exciting day.

Friday's leisurely breakfast was spam and eggs on the deck. We were out by ten to hike the trails properly equipped, but it was already very hot and we knew right off that we would not attempt the two hour hike to the ruins on the lower end of the island. Instead, we retraced our path from yesterday and climbed the small hill for a gorgeous view in all directions – the water color displayed every hue of blue and green. Don, Jane, and I continued down the "mountain goat" trail out to the high cliffs, with crashing waves on the ocean side, while Jack had something else in mind. On our return to the top of the hill we could see him far out in the water, back down by the causeway, having explored some old ruins there and, then, had spotted a large sea turtle, which he was following out to sea in hopes of getting a picture.

Back at the beach, we all went out in the dinghy to overlook the Sea Garden through the glass-bottomed pail. What a lovely sight, with waving fronds of vegetation and various corals of all different sizes, shapes, and colors interspersed with very colorful fish. A whole new incredibly beautiful world is waiting under the sea. Back on shore I further explored the labeled trees, Jack talked with

Jane and Nan on the hiking trails

someone at the park headquarters and Jane and Don went back out to the Sea Garden to snorkel. Later, we watched a big sailboat come in with an obviously green crew, taking a couple of hours moving around while trying to find the right place to anchor. Although out of fresh food, Jane rustled up a great rice and chicken dinner from the boat supply chest. It is hard to remember which sunset was the most spectacular or which night the stars were brightest, but that night was lovely.

Saturday, February 29th, Leap Day, A Day To Remember. Venus and the crescent moon graced the pre-dawn sky, and from my bunk I could stand up through the hatch and see it all. We had breakfast with the sun, and Don, Jane and I took Mickey for a morning walk around to another beach. The tide was low and we had to walk the boat

quite a ways to shore. The purpose of this excursion was to follow a tradition carried on by all boaters in this harbor. Rising above this beach was a small bare nameless hill, with what looked like some weird structure on top. We climbed the hill and added our contribution, a bottle with cover, containing a picture of Snowbird and the date and our names. The tradition was for boaters to leave some identifying souvenir marking their stay at Warderick Wells. Some of the dates went back to 1979 and what an assortment; including everything from clever carvings to rusted dinghy motors.

The view from there was spectacular in the early morning sun. Little did we know, until the next day, that Jack, back on Snowbird, was learning some momentous news concerning Rowe. He was being sociable with the Captain of a neighboring

The hill of souvenir contributions at Warderick Wells

boat, Common Sense, from Boston. In the conversation, the Captain said he was not really from Boston but from Plymouth. Jack's reply was that we were from Rowe, and we have a nuclear plant, too. "Oh, no you don't," said the Captain, "not anymore." He went on to say that his radio had faded in and out, but that he had heard something about the word "permanent." Jack decided not to break the news to us until further verification.

We departed Warderick Wells, with regret, and had a beautiful day of sailing down the Exumas to Staniel Cay, where we arrived about four in the afternoon and anchored behind the first of three huge coral rock islands. Staniel Cay has a small settlement with a few amenities. We hiked the roads, and Jane and I found the two little stores where we bought fruit and a Miami newspaper. We felt we had been out of touch with the world except for whatever Jane had been able to hear on her little short wave radio, usually from the BBC or Voice of America, which she listens to with earphones when she goes to bed.

Meeting up with Jack and Don, we decided to make reservations at the tiny local restaurant and they went off to do so. Jack had seemed overly insistent that I should go back to the "Yacht Club," another tiny building, and call son Rick back in Rowe. Did we have a new grandchild yet? So Jane and I found the one phone on the outside of the building, with the number to reach AT&T written on the wall in pencil. It worked and I reached Rick, who confirmed that they were still awaiting the birth. "But," he said, as I stood looking out on a lovely sight of sailboat masts, blue water and a setting sun, (You always remember where you were when you hear something of major importance) "have you heard the BIG news?" "No, what?" "Yankee has closed permanently." And when I waited anxiously for Jack's return to break the news, his first comment was, "So it's true?" and we then heard his story of Warderick Wells that morning.

As we were standing absorbed in "Yankee" talk, someone yelled that the Snowbird dinghy was in trouble, and we all rushed to the stony beach where the dinghy was taking a beating in the rising tide. Back on the boat we relaxed and waited to return for dinner scheduled at seven – way past our usual bedtime, so we all had coffee to stay awake. The wind had picked up and we got a little wet returning in the dinghy for dinner, but the lovely sunset sky as seen through the boat masts was a sight to remember. I shall somehow always think of that glowing sunset as a fitting farewell, after 37 years, to "Rowe Yankee." Dinner was excellent; grilled grouper, salad, beans and rice, and ice cream as a surprise for dessert. The voyage back was in the dark under bright twinkling stars, with an occasional wave slapping into the dinghy. We headed for a faint anchor light in the distance, and climbed aboard Snowbird to find a happy Mickey waiting for her cookie.

Sunday morning after breakfast, Don announced that he was going ashore to "walk Mickey and Nancy." Not wanting to sit when I could be walking, I usually went ashore whenever the dinghy left and thus joined the ranks of the dog that needed exercise. We had a nice hike out by the airport, with Mickey investigating all the smells and me all the flowers. I was surprised to find quite a few, the most prevalent being bushes of purple nightshade and some pretty yellow thistle poppies. We came back by the dock, where a long wall had been made out of conch shells and another huge pile of discards lay by the water. We returned the dog to the boat and got the glass-bottomed pail, and I had a

Captain Mickey

wonderful tour over the reef surrounding all three rock islands. Although I had been in glass-bottomed boats before, this was a much more personal introduction to the fascinating world below the sea, and I certainly appreciated Don's patience in transporting this non-snorkeler in the safety of the dinghy!

By the third rock, we realized that the tide was low and it was the perfect time to explore the Thunderball Cave. We raced back to get Jack and Jane, and they outfitted me with a water-skiing jacket. The cave was famous for being filmed in the James Bond movie of the same name. We anchored the dinghy on a rock and could walk part of the way, and then swim, into the cave. The jacket gave me great confidence, and I was the first one inside the huge domed room with three holes in the top through which sunbeams came down in streamers. Under water there were lovely coral formations, and where there were holes to the outside you could see hundreds of colorful fish in the light, mostly yellow and black sergeant majors

and bright blue angel fish. We must have spent over half an hour there with the place to ourselves, investigating all the nooks and crannies. When we finally swam out we were surrounded by at least ten other dinghies full of people. This was the main attraction at Staniel Cay and all the boaters were taking advantage of the low tide. At high tide you have to swim underwater to get inside. Back in the dinghy Don was nursing his foot, as he had cut his heal on the coral. Hopefully, the blood had not attracted any barracudas to the area!

In late afternoon Don, Jane, and I took Mickey through rough water 'way across the bay to a beach near the open ocean. The tide was rushing in and the top of the water was pointy, like the surface of the exposed coral rocks. I hung on to Mickey, for she was anxious and I was sure she was going to jump overboard, but they say she never has. On shore we investigated a large house being built, everything is obviously very slow in the Bahamas, and then walked up a high rock hill where we could see the open ocean with huge waves crashing on one side and the harbor with Snowbird, a speck on the water, in the other direction. There were several rock cairns around, so I decided to build my own and gathered loose pieces of coral, topping the two foot cairn with a dry root.

Sailing the Wild Bahamian Seas

This was for good luck and a wish to return someday to Staniel Cay.

Monday was another delightful morning, graced with the early view of Venus, Mars and the crescent in the east. Don and I took Mickey ashore, but with his sore foot Don stayed and threw sticks for Mickey on the beach and I took a quick hike, promising to be back in exactly fifteen minutes. Returning we passed a big sleek black sailing yacht, "Liberty" from Newport, which had just tied up at the dock. As we prepared to get under way, we sadly realized that Staniel Cay was the turning point in our trip, and this morning we were sailing north on our return.

It was another beautiful day to sail and we went thirty-eight miles north to Highbourne Cay, spotting a dolphin on the way. The navigation into the harbor is "look for a stick with an X on a rock and line it up with a pink church," but you don't see any of this until you are right there. It takes a good Captain to read the sea color and avoid the sand bars and the coral heads!

Highbourne Cay has a small snug harbor, and this time there were several big yachts to maneuver around in a small space. We anchored precisely with the expertise of Don and Jane, who are old hands by now, even though the shouted commands back and forth are sometimes not heard or misinterpreted! Several big "real money" power yachts were in the harbor, and we watched the formalities of paid crews waiting on the every wish of the owners. We were more than happy to be on Snowbird! One of the last boats coming in was a small sort of home-made sailboat with a loud bellowing man at the bow and a little old lady following his instructions at the wheel. They must have been sailing all their lives and were "characters" who seemed to be known, for there were friendly welcomes from other boaters. We went ashore, where there is a good dock and facilities but only three or four other houses scattered on the island. We all walked up the hill and down a ridge road where we looked out to sea, again with waves crashing on a rocky shore reminiscent of the Maine coast but with the loveliest blue-green water. The sunset performed again, but those strange night birds were not around.

Tuesday morning, Don walked Mickey and Nancy for the last time. We went back up on the hill and then down along the beautiful crescent beach on the ocean side, where we looked at shells, coral formations, plants and the large waves rolling on shore – one of the loveliest spots in the Bahamas, I'm sure, or was it the realization that this was our last day in the Exumas? Mickey was begging for a stick toss, and Don threw a couple just as we were leaving. We didn't realize until we were back in the dingy that the waves had given her a blanket of fine sand. Back on Snowbird Jane had to give her a scrub bath to get the sand off.

The thirty-one mile sail back to Nassau was windy and exciting. It was so difficult to hold the wheel that I had to give up my turn with aching arms, after only half an hour shift. Keeping the wheel on a steady course so that the sails would hold the wind and move that big vessel forward was a great challenge, all part of the fun of sailing the wild winds of the Bahamas – a privilege one doesn't come by often unless you are lucky enough to have good friends with a sailboat, who seek you out in mid-winter and have a message left on your camper door. **4/92**

Our main purpose was a return trip to Ginger Hill on the old HT&W track north of Yankee near the Vermont line, but perhaps the third-hand report that someone had seen three bear cubs in the same general area was what really prompted our hike on May 21st. We'd been dawdling on a hike a couple of years ago, and by the time we discovered that rich soil spot and quickly named it Ginger Hill it was 'way past time for us to be home tending to business. We vowed to return and investigate, hoping some hidden botanical treasures were there among the hillside crop of healthy ginger leaves.

This year the bug season arrived with vengeance, and we knew we'd have to go out early while it was still cool to beat the little critters. Hot weather was also predicted for today but we'd be home long before that. We parked at Yankee and were walking up the hill by the old visitor's center at 7:15. It was a beautiful morning and we were at the top of the hill along the outer fence in no time, slightly breathless with our early morning enthusiasm. Already we were nipping the large water bottle from the knapsack.

Starting down the hill on the back side, we had to walk on a carpet of tiny northern white violets in the moist grass and mosses. A yellowthroat sang "witchy, witchy, witchy" along the little brook below and a flicker called from the power line ahead. Other birds sang in a general happy morning chorus, background music for the unfolding scenery which still featured the soft pastel green and pink colors of spring. Near the bottom of the hill, there was a beautiful patch of foam flowers with their pointed white candles standing above the mass of green heart-shaped leaves. What a wonderful world this is! And what could

be nicer than having the privilege of taking a Wild Side hike in the woods?

The day we discovered Ginger Hill we had come across Sherman Pond by canoe, so it has been some years since we have approached the old Wheeler property around the Yankee fence. In the meantime construction work has been done to tame the small stream on the east side and it is now well stoned on the sides, with the scars healed and violets and grasses and sedges growing among the rocks. We rock-hopped for a ways but soon decided to climb up into the woods, where we picked up a wood road obviously used recently by trail bikes. It was difficult not to be distracted by the various small brooks which begged to be climbed and investigated. We admired the red trillium, the smooth yellow violets, and the budding baneberry, but kept our internal Loran fixed on Ginger Hill.

We were not in new territory, but certainly our memory had not retained the picture of the stone walls with huge rocks that surrounded this old Wheeler farm. Higher up the mountain in the Wilcox pasture is a memorable wall, but somehow we had forgotten the extent of the walls here. Even the little brooks were walled along the sides. What an incredible amount of work, probably with oxen. The town is full of old stone walls, but these walls seemed beyond reason and must have been built by a man who found it a lifetime challenge to clear the land and just loved to build walls! Chipmunks chattered loudly all along, and must have found the nooks and crannies of the walls a wonderful hiding place. We looked at the emerging fern fronds of several varieties adding lace and texture to the scene.

The old Noyes Wheeler house

Rowe Historical Society

Crossing the brook, we were welcomed by a chestnut-sided warbler and an oven bird at the old Noyes Wheeler cellar hole and yard, now so grown with trees it was almost hard to imagine the scene of fish fries and picnics that Cliff Sibley had described the day we hiked in here with him several years ago. He had been a kid again, recounting episodes from his childhood when he spent summers here on the farm. The young stock was pastured high on the mountain, and one of Cliff's jobs was to climb up and salt the cows, a happy job he remembered in detail. The red trillium and yellow violets, foam flower, miterwort, and baneberry were blossomed while the wood nettle and jewelweed were fast taking over.

Admiring the even stonework of the old foundations of the house and barn, it seemed far different than the bulky odd-shaped boulders of the surrounding walls. Among the leaf litter, the seedpod of a spring beauty stood out and we stooped to examine it. Things look so different at various times of the year, and it took a minute to realize what had happened to that early little pink and white spring flower. Seeing several rattlesnake grape ferns, we took a little time to look for the daisyleaf grape fern we had once identified here. But, once again, we reminded ourselves we were out to discover new things on Ginger Hill, and almost had to close our eyes to get ourselves headed out to the old HT&W track bed.

Sherman Pond was like glass through the trees, and another option would be to go out and sit along the shore and watch for bird life. *"The world is so full of a number of things"* or choices this morning that, yes, we were *"as happy as kings,"* and we knew that the day would pass all too quickly! A rose-breasted grosbeak sang in the trees overhead and we enjoyed the song, even though they are so common at the birdfeeders in our yard. We wish we could hear and see a scarlet tanager, which sounds much like the grosbeak. They are rarer these days, and the last one we can remember seeing was several years ago on a hike high on the mountain above here in the Wilcox pasture. Ah, we become aware of the red-eyed vireo song. He is such a constant singer and seems to follow us everywhere. His song blends with the breeze. What a happy bird!

Walking was easy on the track bed, except for all the violets and bluets underfoot and an occasional wood betony. A little white flower had us on our knees in a hurry, but it was only a dwarf raspberry. Ferns, wet green mosses, and lots of early saxifrage decorated the rock cliffs along the path. On one level place above the rocks, a large stand of curved false Solomon's seal peered down at us. We recently hiked with a botanical group in New York State and the botanist referred to it as Solomon's plume, which far better describes this lovely arching plant. Nothing should be false something else, it should have an identity of its own! And still the vireo sings on. We often went to the edge of the bank to see what was growing there, looking hopefully for a lily or two, but it's probably too early for them to be above the other foliage.

When the cliffs subsided and the hillside was a little more open we watched for the location of Ginger Hill, but we didn't want to investigate it yet. Our plan was to go to the Vermont line and work back so that we wouldn't miss anything. Ginger on the bank toward the water gave it away, but we marched on to the line. Somewhere along the steep part of the hill there were scars and evidence of a landslide of years past. These were frequent major perils in the early days of this railroad. "T'sweet, T'sweet, T'sweet, Toot, Sweet" was our interpretation of the warbler we were hearing so often. Finally, we stopped and retrieved the binocs from the knapsack and identified a pretty redstart. It takes some time to identify most warblers, but the redstart is flashy orange and black. Our personal goal

is to be able to recognize warblers by their song, as it takes away so much flower time chasing these elusive birds! And still the vireo sings on.

The state line rock appeared rather suddenly beside the brushy path. It was tempting to go further, but we vowed to stay in the bounds of Rowe. After a long chug on the water bottle and readjustment of the knapsack we looked at the mountain and began our climb. Of course, we didn't intend to climb very far, but one curious thing led to another and we were soon quite far up but on the slant heading sort of across. "I Want To Go To Sleep," said the black-throated green warbler flitting through the trees overhead, always just out of sight. And, if we thought about it, the vireo was still singing, too!

The plants varied, but gradually the red trillium and baneberry was joined by kidneyleaf buttercup, blue cohosh, sweet cicely, toothwort, and lots of miterwort standing out as the sun came over the hill and backlighted its thin spike of tiny flowers. We never tire of looking with the hand lens at this the daintiest flower in the woods. Then a mass of smooth yellow violets preceded the first maidenhair fern. And there was the first clump of ginger! Looking around we knew we had indeed arrived on Ginger Hill! There were all the lovely spring flowers of the rich woods. The squirrel corn and Dutchman's had already gone to seed, and the leaves were turning yellow and would soon disappear for another year. The maidenhair fern was pinkish and the early fronds of the maidenhair spleenwort were a bright light green. Wow! What a garden of treasures hidden on the mountainside! The plantain-leaved sedge (fondly known by our own Latin nickname, Carex parmesan) was blossomed and prolific in the rich soil.

Just below a stand of hemlock trees, we followed under the open face of a long ledge across the hill. The mosses were lovely and there were lots of little fragile ferns and saxifrage sitting in the crevices. What a pretty sight! And there is a rosette of maidenhair spleenwort, and more, and more! We only have two other stations of that fern in town. We hardly had time to enthuse over the fern when we spotted a healthy blossoming bristly black currant growing in the ledge! Double wow! Although we have found a good bit of this plant growing all along the steep western boundary of Rowe, it is a plant of special concern on the Massachusetts rare plant list and will require a report of its location to the Mass Natural Heritage Program. And besides that, it has pretty racemes of light pinkish-purple blossoms and it made our day. We continued to hunt for the impossible, like walking fern or ebony spleenwort or perhaps a showy orchid.

We recently had the fun of identifying the strange green violet in New York, so we tended to stoop and investigate every similar looking clump of vegetation, but we really believe they do not grow in Massachusetts. This ledge had been so interesting we climbed up and over and doubled back to do it again.

As we continued along under more cliffs, a bird was frightened out of her nest on the ledge. It looked for all the world like an ovenbird's nest under some overhanging ferns and grasses, and we assumed that was what flew out and was noisily voicing her objection in the tree behind us. We stood on tiptoes on another rock but couldn't quite see into the nest so we decided to step away a little distance and be quiet to see if she flew back. As we concentrated on the bird, it didn't really sound like an ovenbird, and as a matter of fact the only agitated birds around were a pair of juncos. Sure enough, that's what flew off that little oven nest. We could hardly wait to get home and look up juncos in the bird nest book…"Junco nest is commonly on ground under concealing weeds and grasses; often on slope, roadside bank or rock ledge; in tree roots, under fallen tree or log." It's such fun to discover these things for yourself out on the wild side!

It always comes as a surprise when hiking in this area and thinking you are the only person for miles around, when suddenly a voice comes booming out of the loudspeaker at Yankee, calling some Joe Dokes who is wanted somewhere else than where he is at the moment. You kind of think "big brother is watching you," and you'd better not step on any flowers! We continued down through the ginger, the Canada violets, and more toothwort, and when we got about half way down we decided we should go back across the hill to see if we had missed anything in the middle. Our stomach growled once, and it was time to sit a minute and consume the emergency granola bar in our knapsack for we hadn't planned on being out for lunch! Still basking in the pleasures of the morning it took some minutes before we realized that we were eating with one hand and waving like mad with the other – the bugs were awful!

Lunch break was short and even that little stop made us realize that we were a little tired and still had miles to go. We don't ram around the hills quite as fast as we used to and sometimes we have to consider the consequences if we let curiosity take us an extra mile in the opposite direction! However, today we were going to go back across the hill, up and down, to the town line again. We just might have missed something important! It had also become very hot and we had to shed one layer and carry it in the knapsack, put on a layer of bug juice, and take another swig from the water bottle, which really dictated just how much further we could go. We thought nothing of drinking out of the nearest brook until a few years ago when our granddaughter had giardia. We haven't tasted any delightful bubbling country water since then!

As we started up the hill one foot didn't seem to lodge in the niche where we were trying to put it, and we looked down to see that we had been stepping on a small ginseng plant – another item on the Mass special concern listing. We unwrinkled its leaves and apologized, and decided we hadn't done terribly much harm. Looking around, it seemed strange to us that with all this rich woods there was not a single leek in sight! Back at the state line once more, we felt that we had mission accomplished and headed back down the track bed, promising our aching legs, sweating body, and buggy hair that we would go straight to the car.

But what good are those promises when something interesting turns up! Somewhere along the path we veered off up the hillside again, listened happily to our first hermit thrush of the season, and bushwhacked our way down to the Wheeler place again. We followed up the brook a ways, crossed, walked on top of the big stone wall, and marveled at how it climbed right up the hills. Then we followed another brook up a ravine, but gave up as it seemed to be totally devoid of green plants under the dark canopy of overhanging hemlock trees. We crossed a knoll and tried the next brook, which was more promising with a few jacks-in-the-pulpit. Somewhere up one of these brooks is a nice long waterfall over the ledges. Should we look for it? By this time we were around on the south side of the hill and it was very hot, and well after noon. We were finally persuaded to call it a day.

The old wood road lead out to the power line where we meandered down through the brambles. The final hill looked enormous and we took it slowly, one step at a time! But there were the foam flowers again and those pretty white violets, and before we knew it we were on top, resting a minute and finishing the last of our large bottle of water. No bear cubs, but lots of ginger, a couple of rare plants and the beauty of spring flowers beyond description. And do you know, when we really listened, that red-eyed vireo was still singing! **6/92**

The Wonder of it All

Pure guilt shoved us out the door this morning. Guilt, because we have had some beautiful hikes this summer and fall, and we have left you all at home and enjoyed them just for ourselves. By now you must be really stiff, sitting so long and waiting there in your rocking chairs, so it is high time you stretched your legs and joined us climbing a mountain.

This has been one of the most beautiful autumns in many, many years. The early trees were at their height near the 12th, and some of those leaves are still hanging on. The bronze oaks and yellow beeches in our Deerfield River valley are glorious just now, and the woods are carpeted with gold. We started off this morning, October 27th, before the sun was over the mountain in Zoar, and by the time we reached the railroad bridge at Hoosac Tunnel it had disappeared behind a cloud bank. The wind was blowing from the northwest and we added another layer of clothing and a hat when we got out of the car. Who would want to hike on a day like this? But come on along and try it anyway.

Our plan was to cruise the mountainside, up behind the old HT&W track bed, between the railroad bridge and the Bear Swamp dam. Why? Just to see what is there, so when we look that way in passing we can visualize the landscape of rocks and ferns and flowers hiding under that solid canopy of trees. And, perhaps, discover a treasure or two in the plant world. The tide was just rising and coming splashing down the river, swirling into whirlpools at the big bend. We looked down from the bridge and watched gay colored leaves floating like little sailboats tossed on a windy sea. We were already in another world, enjoying the great outdoors. Fortunately, we came back to reality and decided we best not wait for a train whistle to scuttle us off the bridge in a panic.

On the other side, skeletons were everywhere. The tall, slender, bare arms of the once pretty yellow sweet clover towered over all. The stiff straight artemisia still held some dry leaves with white undersides. The Queen Anne's lace doilies had all made bird's nests, and the bush clover was reduced to several brown clinging dry heads. The thimble weed thimbles had all gone to seed, which was easily dislodging on the west wind. Pearly everlasting was shedding its white fluff and leaving heads of pretty little straw flowers. The Canada goldenrods almost all sported ball galls on

Railroad bridge at Hoosac Tunnel

their stems, recycling themselves as winter homes for insects. The viper's bugloss, stiff and gray, took us a moment to recognize, while the leaves of the tansy were as green as summer. We could have been happy walking the tracks back to Zoar, making a game of trying to recognize old friends of summer in their winter garb. But the mountain beckoned, and we responded, with forward steps along the old track bed as it turned off the mainline and headed upriver.

Before we got too comfortable on a path, we turned into the woods to bushwhack up the mountain. While still on the level, we contemplated looking for the foundations of the old hotel that used to be here on the flats at the end of the railroad line before the tunnel was completed, but we could come back for that search someday when we didn't have the energy to climb mountains. Laurel was our first obstacle, but we seemed to find deer paths through the shoulder-high bushes and gained the first ridge. Expecting to find nothing of interest in the acid woods of laurel and oak, we were overjoyed to come upon a beautiful moss and lichen garden covering rocks and soil. Perhaps it is the leaching chemicals of the bedrock and underground water which create the ideal conditions for hundreds of varieties of mosses and lichens of every hue and texture. The grey reindeer moss was soft and pliable instead of the usual crunchy, and the deep green poodle moss carpeted the rocks. Each little plot of mosses was a miniature landscape, some with hills of light-colored fern moss and individual dark evergreen haircaps towering higher. On our knees we examined these scenes with the hand lens and looked into the deep crevices of a primeval world, or into a fairyland of

pixie people with pointed hats.

We climbed on an angle up across the mountain, and were soon in a new territory with far less moss and no laurel. The soil had changed and so had the plants. Instead of laurel and oak, there were maples and beech and white birches, and underfoot the Christmas fern was everywhere. The large leaves of goose-foot maples scattered here and there covered the evergreen leaves of spring foam flower. Small bushes of maple-leaved viburnum had a few black berries, but their leaves, still fresh, had not yet turned their typical fall pinkish color. We touched the softness of their furry leaves.

The mountainside was steep and, looking down, we could see directly into the rushing river now sparkling in the reappeared sunshine. The old track bed must be tucked in under the mountain at this point. We continued to climb carefully on the steepest parts. Once we braced our foot against a rock which gave way and we slipped downhill a small distance. Our leg hurt for a minute, but no harm done, and we wisely moved on more cautiously. Shortly thereafter, we spotted a deflated party balloon on the ground. In the past, they have been uncanny in their appropriate messages to us off in the woods. ("Congratulations" right after we had discovered a new orchid etc.) Well, this one displayed a teddy bear saying "Get well soon!" Oh my goodness, were we supposed to have broken our leg on that last slip? We don't think about such things!

There continued, more or less the same sort of territory, with lots of evergreen marginal and spinulose woodferns and stockings enough on the Christmas ferns for every child in America. Then came large trains of rocks, tumbling down the mountain with more wet mosses and wonderful rock caves for the animals. Each boulder had a toupee of polypody ferns, and one rounded rock had layers of sphagnum moss like a child's winter hat folded around its face. We headed up instead of sideways to check out these new rock friends, and found some more wonderful moss gardens with polypody fern forests in the center and lots of gone-to-seed wood asters and blue-stemmed goldenrod. Hearing the familiar croak of a raven, we stopped and leaned against the uphill side of a tree and watched while it rode the air currants high above the tree tops. A blue jay screeched below in the valley and the leaves all around sang with the strong northwest wind.

Light through the trees ahead exposed a long rocky ridge and we climbed with enthusiasm, for we knew this was the site of one of the lining towers for the surveying of the Hoosac Tunnel – surveying accuracy which made history in its day. This tower had been just a pole and we have seen, still in the rock, the heavy iron bolts which kept it solidly in place. We climbed out on the open ledge and, sure enough we could look back directly downriver and into the black hole of the tunnel, now hidden somewhat by trees down there. There too was the small blue speck of our car, and we realized how far we had come and that we must return the same distance. For the return, we knew, we could always drop down to the track bed path but at the moment it was several hundred feet below us. Overhead was bright blue sky and sunshine.

It was a slow climb up the cliffs as we found different moss and lichens and several varieties of lycopodium, all of which had to be examined and admired. Higher up, there opened a wider view out upon our beloved wild valley and glorious bronze mountains. Upriver, we looked at Bear Swamp dam and into the lower reservoir, and across the deep dark ravine which is Fife Brook to see Raycroft Lookout in Florida. Downriver, the houses and church steeple high in the town of Florida loomed over the tunnel, and others were scattered in the valley along the river. What history has been made in this deep, quiet valley of the bending river!

Going up the rock we veered to the back side, where we were fascinated with the vegetation and convenient shelves for climbing. Other times, all there was to pull us up on the bare rocks were the low blueberry bushes, which seemed to be anchored very firmly in the ledges. We knew the lining tower site was just over the high rocks to the right, but on consideration we decided we didn't need to see it again. This new side of the mountain looked inviting for our descent, and we knew if we climbed in the other direction we would retrace our steps downward in familiar territory. For this decision we were rewarded with more incredible rocks and ferns and mosses. One spot was a lovely garden of polypody and lycopodium, mixed with the little stems of the Canada mayflower's red berries. No Christmas wreath was ever prettier. The soggy leaves and graceful bare candelabra stems of a patch of clintonia gave us pause for a moment, as it always does, tricking us momentarily into thinking we have an orchid.

We drank in the scene, lovelier still as it was among pure white birches. We finally had to force our steps downward. The hill

The Wonder of it All

was very steep, and we kept going further across on the pretense of looking for an easier way, but really wanting to see just one more beautiful rock formation capped with greenery. All this beauty, and so seldom seen by human eyes! The hill below was a jumble of rocks and bright green spinulose ferns. A downy woodpecker was our sole companion as we picked our way, hanging onto trees which sometimes gave way with the sudden weight. We climbed over rocks and slid into holes between rocks, and sometimes just let go and slid on the carpet of leaves. We did veer to the right, and nearing the bottom, came upon a large ravine. It had a slight dripping of water, but no brook, and we wondered if this might be an old landslide path but it seemed too deep. Near its edge the Christmas ferns seemed to multiply, the foam flower increase and then there were a few fronds of the delicate maidenhair fern, a bit light but still green. We looked about for the other rich soil plants, but found nothing more except the large tell-tale leaves of the linden tree. But we knew there were secret underground treasures, just waiting for the warm breezes of spring.

We made our way down the last few feet and leveled on the old track bed, beside the gouge made by past flood waters of the ravine. Turning downriver, we walked briskly for a half hour on the path back to the bridge, stopping now and then to investigate a plant, or to gaze at the river and remember the valley from the water level of a lazy raft in summertime. Our memory was full of beautiful sights and, forever, when looking at this mountain we will recall the rare hidden beauty of those rocks and moss gardens and ferns. Oh, *"The world is so full of a number of*

things, I'm sure we should all be happy..."

The drive back along River Road is always a favorite, winter or summer. Years past we remember it as the road where you were guaranteed to flush up an indigo bunting or a scarlet tanager or an oriole – all scarce items recently. Today's sighting was even more memorable. Coming over one of the humps there in the middle of the road we saw a large fisher, an animal we had never before seen in the wild. It stood for a moment in the bright noonday sun and then ran across and up the bank. A beautiful richly-colored dark brown animal, and a rare treat to see. We couldn't help but think that that was our reward for tipping you all out of your rocking chairs and enticing you up and down the mountain on the Wild Side. Thanks for sharing "the wonder of it all." **11/92**

Welcoming Winter

Welcome winter! A snow storm of three or four inches has blanketed the earth and put all the flowers to sleep. They may kick off the covers once in a while, before their deep winter sleep, but for all purposes they are happily bedded down until spring. New England's changing seasons are a treat to the spirit. The glorious fall was with us longer than usual this year, and the silver tones of November are just beginning. We are slowly learning to appreciate the silver grays of this month, having been for all these many years highly critical of the month of November.

This afternoon, November 18th, we took to the woods. We had purposely waited for the predicted sunshine, but the cloud cover remained heavy and perhaps it was all the more beautiful – a Robert Frost type of day, when *"the woods are lovely, dark and deep."* With a couple of hunting seasons in progress the safest territory was Pelham Lake Park, and we entered on the Williams Trail off Pond Road. Immediately, we were in another world, with the snow hanging on the evergreen trees and every little twig. The beaver dam on Pelham Brook was full of icicles, and the brook was gurgling as it slipped down over the icy branches and circled around the rocks in the big curve under the foot bridge. We climbed the hill into the "big mowing," now a tall pine forest where once we rode on the hay wagon as a child.

We soon picked up tracks, but it was hard to determine their identity because they went through the snow to the leaves below, and thus there was a depression but no "print." However, we soon found evidence of the double hoof of a deer. Later, another set of deer tracks were intriguing, as they seemed to indicate an adult browsing and a young one more actively jumping and playing around. In one place they had ruffled up the leaves above the snow, digging for something. Looking up, we could see the large beech tree which was providing them with their winter snack of beech nuts. The trees were a constant Christmas card picture, especially the small snowy hemlocks among the young beeches, which retain their leaves well into the winter. We stood still and realized that there was not a breath of air stirring, not a bird singing. It was absolutely quiet – except for an

Winter on Middletown Hill

occasional clump of snow, which became too heavy for a limb and dropped to the ground in a white veil of fluff as it came apart on its descent.

How lucky we were to be in the woods! We planned to continue on to the Saddle Brook Trail, up and over Todd Mountain, and come back the Sabrina Rice Trail. But what track is this crossing the path ahead? A trough through the snow, with two paw prints every so often. We knew at once, but it seemed too good to be true – an otter! It was headed toward the lake, and we immediately changed direction and followed it through the woods, up, over, and around. But the trough seemed to stop at a large tree. Had we been misled by a porcupine? We looked up and saw nothing in the tree. There were several tracks going on from the tree but no trough and it was mystifying. The lake was not far and we pushed out through the brush to the Lakeside Trail and, sure enough, there was the trough coming out of the woods straight into the water. The animal must have walked higher, instead of plowing in a trough for that short distance. We went to the water's edge but couldn't see the animal anywhere. Although the tracks were fresh he or she could be under the ice, or by now long gone on to the next waterway in their fishing rounds.

We continued around the lake, admiring the view and checking all the seedpods and dry twigs and ferns, trying to learn the winter identification of all our summer friends in the plant world. With their change of garb through the seasons, this is quite challenging. Past the "horse tree," where our granddaughter played while on a hike this summer, we swung up the hill on the trail, back to our original destination, and continued on toward Todd. The woods had now become predominantly hardwood and more open. We stopped and listened again. Not a sound. This was the spot where we remembered, one moonlight hike near mid-night, when we had heard a rabbit, presumably caught by an owl, suddenly scream into the night silence, and then coyotes took up the chorus in the distance. What a scary treat that was! Silence does not mean lack of inhabitants, as proved by the number and variety of tracks in the new-fallen snow. Lots of squirrels had hopped here and there, with little holes in the snow where they dug for a nut. Tiny trails of mice, voles and shrews to and from holes in the snow or under dead trees, told us that the blanket of snow was covering not only sleeping plants but a whole village of inhabitants, very awake and active.

In the peaceful quiet we began to hear a soft musical sound, and came to one of the little streams that works its way down the mountain from springs near the ridge. We stopped to look at the ice patterns and listen to the trickle as it gained momentum on the steeper lower side. Here was a place for animals to refresh themselves, and deer tracks came to the edge indicating they had done just that. The trail toward Todd followed along a little larger stream, called Saddle Brook, which made a small ravine up the mountain.

We looked at trees and tried to identify them. Tiny brown T's scattered on the snow told us that there was a birch towering above, which had scattered its seeds in an earlier breeze. The lovely green stripped bark of the moose maple was not hard to miss, and some still had their seedpods hanging in long

Welcoming Winter

bushwhack exploring, but with such a late start we decided to keep to the trail. Evergreens now predominated with the shells of several huge old trees, home perhaps to the owls we hear in the evening off on the mountain. It's darker still, and quiet, as we climb around through these

clusters. Lower to the ground we examined the hobblebush, already sporting its tightly packed brown leaf buds and flower clusters for next season. Here and there was a bright green spot where an evergreen spinulose fern peeked above the snow. What a fascinating beautiful world we live in, and how often we stay inside, bemoaning the weather on such a dark cloudy day!

Near the top of the ridge the deer had scuffed up another large patch of leaves, and here we found an oak tree telling us that lunch today had been acorns. The open area was covered with ferns and not many trees leading us to believe that, here, bedrock was quite close to the surface. We passed a ledge and looked at the little mouse tracks running along the base.

The trail soon turned left toward Todd. This ridge looked inviting for some further

trees. Wouldn't it be fun to just sit on a rock and observe what goes on here? There were different tracks now. One set, coming from the far side of the mountain, seemed more cat-like without the claw marks. Could it be a bobcat? Down the backside a straight line of tracks looked more like a fox, but obviously two animals were following the same path, for once in a while one of them would make a detour – perhaps they were coyotes. It was fun to speculate, but we wish once in while these mostly nocturnal animals would cross our path in broad daylight.

The top of Todd Mountain is a lovely place with its open ledges, grasses, small trees, and several old apple trees. We looked at one whose trunk was all but gone, except one live shoot still persisting. We thought of the famous painter, John Marin, and the pictures he painted when he spent a

Welcoming Winter

summer in Rowe in 1918. Several from this spot showed Pelham Lake, and one was northward showing Haystack. It must have been much more open then and what lovely views there would have been, for even now, on a clear day, one can still see the surrounding mountains and valleys through the trees.

We headed down the back side of the mountain where the evergreens began again, spruce, hemlock, and pine. Many of the oldest trees have fallen, some victims of lightning strikes. One big old dead tree has fallen over, but is being held up by neighboring trees. Here we found a real porcupine trough with the wavy foot prints and quill marks, not to be mistaken for the otter slide. This side of the mountain is steeper, and we sometimes had to go sideways to keep from sliding down the chute. We often just stood, looking around, marveling at all the woodsy sights. Little bushes of beech drops stood above the snow with the tiny flower pods slightly curved downward, creating a pretty dainty pattern. Then the various lycopodium looked like little Christmas trees topped with a crown of snow. One of the most unusual sights was a clump of marginal wood fern, the five evergreen fronds spread out laying flat on the snow, making a perfect five-pointed green Christmas star.

Once down on the Sabrina Rice Trail, we decided to go toward Davis Mine Road and look for the seedpods of some of the plants we knew in the rich soil there. We had seen a small hop vine last year and especially wondered how it had done, but searching turned up only the ubiquitous bindweed vines and a few dry ostrich ferns. A car passed by out on the road and we realized that it was the first real sound, except for the brooks, that we had heard all afternoon.

Heading back toward home (*"promises to keep and miles to go before I sleep...,"* Frost), we marveled at the height of some the trees. When you are a child everything looks big. Then, when you return to a childhood spot later on, things seem so much smaller than you remembered. Later in life you observe, over a period of time, the actual growth of trees. This is what we were realizing along this old trail. In our lifetime these trees had grown tremendously. What do you suppose they looked like, back in the teens when this was a bridle trail, passable by horse and carriage through the covered bridge over Pelham Brook?

Passing through the more open woods again, and looking up, we felt the soft mist on our face. The heavy cloud cover was shedding a little moisture, making the next path under the evergreens even more *"lovely, dark and deep."* Here, one or two chickadees were talking quietly as they flitted among the branches. Arriving finally under the "Hemlock Cathedral" near the shelter, we stood in awe of the majesty of those wonderful tall trees and found peace in the absolute stillness of the earth beneath them.

Thanks for joining us on our tramp today. Have a wonderful happy holiday season and, remember, that some of the most beautiful gifts in life are experiences and sights which sometimes make no sound and are always free, out on the Wild Side. **12/92**

1993·
1994

The Deerfield River with Mt. Peak and Mrs. Peak, Charlemont

Fireweed

Pink lady's slippers

On the Wild Side in the Florida Everglades

Destruction and damage are not the words to use when talking about the effects of Hurricane Andrew on the Everglades in southern Florida. The correct word is change. Destruction occurred to the man-made objects, the buildings and the board walks, but what happened to the environment was change, a natural event which has occurred predictably with hurricanes over thousands and thousands of years, and has kept the Everglades the wonderful, mysterious, and unique environment that they are. Hurricanes are a necessary event to flush out the bays, prune the mangroves, and topple tall trees to allow the understory plants to flourish. The greatest danger now from hurricanes is that they will blow in the seeds from alien ornamental plants man has used to landscape homes in the Miami area. If these trees, such as the fast-growing Australian pine, the melaleuca, and the Brazilian pepper-tree, really establish themselves, then they will overpower the native species and destroy the whole fragile natural ecosystem of the Everglades. The forests of melaleuca, are fast approaching this category.

I was fortunate to be able to join a trip to the Everglades, in January, sponsored by Naturethics of Amherst under the leadership of two very special people, Tom Tyning, master naturalist from Audubon and author of the Stokes book "Amphibians and Reptiles," (Remember Tom from the Arizona trip, December, 1990, Wild Side?) and John Green, free-lance interpretive naturalist and noted nature photographer. These two men make an unbeatable team, with a combination of enthusiasm, tremendous knowledge of birds, beasts, trees, plants, reptiles, and butterflies, balanced with great personal concern for the environment and a bantering humor that keeps you with a constant smile on your face and often doubled over in a real belly laugh. My first introduction to the Everglades was about twenty years ago, and all I seem to remember were the mosquitoes. I looked forward to this new trip with great anticipation and deeper appreciation for all things on the Wild Side – even mosquitoes – have their place.

The Florida Everglades are a giant "River of Grass," fifty or sixty miles wide, that gently slope at the rate of two or three inches per mile, draining Lake Okeechobee (second largest fresh water body in the lower forty-eight states) and its watershed southward for one hundred miles to Florida Bay, covering millions of acres with a unique ecosystem like no other in the world. A section, 1.5 million acres, about one seventh of the total area, was established in 1947 as Everglades National Park, second largest national park in the continental U.S., to protect and preserve its varied and unique biological features. It has since been declared an International Biosphere Reserve and a World Heritage Site. The settlement of Flamingo at the very southern end of the Park would be our destination for the trip to explore and experience this national treasure.

But first, we have to understand that this national treasure, teeming with life, is in deep trouble. Man, in his greed for water and land, has upset the natural order of things and threatened all species, including himself. As Florida was settled, there continued a great effort to dry out the swamps and create more land for development; thus were built canals, dams, and dikes, not only to drain the land but to channel the water to the coastal cities. More than sixty percent of the wetlands present in 1900 have now been destroyed. The Tamiami Trail and canal were built across southern Florida, creating an effective dam stopping the natural flow of waters through the Everglades, and opening up the area to even more exploitation. Agricultural businesses grew in this new fertile soil and even more water was siphoned off, but destruction of the natural water base of these farmlands has led to the once fertile soil slowly drying up and blowing away, at the measured rate of over five feet in sixty years! Now, the runoff from the pesticides and fertilizers on the farmlands is changing the chemical makeup of the waters that do succeed in seeping into the Everglades, and is promoting the growth of choking algae and cattails. The western portion of Florida Bay is already a "dead zone" from lack of refreshing waters that normally drained from the Everglades and made this area a rich hatching grounds for lobster, shrimp, and stone crabs. There is even danger that water from this dead zone may be killing the beautiful and delicate coral reefs of the Keys. Drawing down the reservoir of water in the Florida aquifer is also changing the balance of pressure that holds back the salt water, and there is great danger of man polluting his own lifeblood, the natural fresh water in this great aquifer.

But there is a small ray of hope. Man has at last admitted his own excesses and become concerned. Congress has extended the Park boundary to the east to protect a good bit of the Shark River Slough, where there has been a 93% decline in the nesting bird populations. The State of Florida, the Park Service, and the U.S. Corps of Engineers have finally agreed to cooperate on water management. This is a small step to solve

a large and serious problem. They say it would take at least one billion dollars – and goodness knows how much political clout – to fully restore the Everglades.

And so, on January 14th my car and I were dispatched from our camper at Homestead, and while my partner drove on down to our winter quarters on the Keys, I headed southwest to the Everglades National Park. The devastation at Homestead was incredible and made the damage at the Park seem minor. The main headquarters at the Park entrance looked bombed, but the downed trees in the pinelands had somehow faded into the landscape and were already covered with the green of new undergrowth leaves and vines. However, several sections of boardwalks along the road were just scattered pieces of lumber. As I drove along, the land soon opened out into that wonderful expanse of sky and saw grass and sparkling water. Water? This was January, and the Everglades were supposed to be in their dry season. This year natural rains were keeping them unusually wet.

Although on the edge of the temperate zone, the Everglades live by tropical laws with two seasons, wet and dry. During the months of April to October the rains come, measuring an average of sixty inches per year. The glades come to life, fish hatch and feed on the lesser organisms, the grass and plants grow, and the animals thrive. Then in the winter months things dry out, and the fish, the alligators, and the birds congregate in the few remaining gator holes, or "solution holes," as they are called. This is the time certain birds like the endangered wood stork nest – when they know they have a concentrated supply of fish for their young. If the dry season does not happen as planned, and they know they cannot easily find food enough for a growing family, they do not nest at all. Amazing how smart our "dumb" animals are. From these natural fluctuations the bird and animal populations have survived for thousands of years, but when the Corps of Engineers artificially lets water out from their dams when it is not normal there is danger of alligator nests being flooded, or the apple snail eggs being washed away instead of hatching to feed the endangered snail kite and other birds. One thing affects another, all the way up and down the intricate food chain.

Driving down that forty-mile stretch through the glades to Flamingo, I was thinking of all these things that I had heard and read, while enjoying the beauty of this land so foreign to my New England eye. I stopped several times to sample the roadside flowers and breathe the warm moist air moving slowly across the waves of saw grass as far as the eye could see. Only small tree islands, called hammocks, were visible in the otherwise flat terrain. All of the Everglades are less than eight feet in altitude above sea level. I went over Rock Reef Pass where a signboard gives the elevation as three feet.

In my slow drive to the Flamingo area, I was passed by only a couple of cars, and I began to picture the area as far from the maddening crowd. What a shock to first come upon the marina parking lot full, of cars with boat trailers. These waters are a mecca for fishermen. Then there are the other tourists. The line of double story motel rooms seemed full as did the recreational vehicle campground. Somehow I always have the mistaken notion that all the wild places in the country are made for just me (and a very

few chosen others)! As I swung around to the lovely tenting ground right on Florida Bay, only it seemed sparsely occupied. I decided to set up shop in our group campsite and then spend the rest of the day poking around. One group from Antioch College was already camped, but it was difficult to determine where the other two group sites were since the office had specifically told me they were boldly marked. After walking around the area, I determined that the first priority was to find a dry site! Much of the area was over-the-shoes wet. I found a nice little palm tree on a rise about an inch or so above the water and lugged out my possessions across the field from the car. Having spent only five or six nights in a tent in my entire life, this was to be a rather new experience for this senior citizen!

The tent went up in short order and I was quite proud of my accomplishment. By this time it was very hot, and I took out my beach chair and sat under a palm tree nearer the shore watching the birds and reading my book, *The Everglades, River of Grass*, by Marjory Stoneham Douglas, a pioneering conservationist who has spent her lifetime of nearly a hundred years working to make the world aware of the treasurers the Everglades hold and of the urgent need for their protection.

When pangs of hunger set in, I drove over to the main building and found a coffee shop, where asking for iced coffee seemed to prove that I must be from New England. After lunch I checked out the marina, and then set off to explore Eco Pond near the campground. The high platform looked over a small pond with a variety of birds. I found a loop trail and walked around, stopping at another low platform and watched the herons, ducks, and other birds whose identity I did not yet know. The pond was surrounded with the narrow-leaved cattails far taller than my head. It was cool in the shade and I enjoyed the trek, hearing the quick thrashing of an alligator but not seeing him. Looking for a longer trail, I drove up the road and found a side road that looked inviting. Here I was introduced to several of the zebra butterflies, on trees and shrubs that today all looked alike to me. Before the week was over I would know some of them by name.

Late planes and lost baggage delayed the rest of the crew until after sunset, but finally I spotted lights in the cabin and went in to meet Susan, the cook from Drumlin Farm Audubon Nature Sanctuary in Massachusetts and Clarissa, a teacher from Connecticut, one of the participants who was not a tenter and would stay in the cabin. They were both old hands at Naturethics tours. The cabin would be headquarters and mess hall. Sue was already at work whipping up a big chicken dinner. In previous years this Naturethics tour consisted of twelve to fifteen participants, but because of the hurricane uncertainty this year there were only three of us with three staff - wow, what a ratio. I took the flashlight, and headed back to the campground to meet Tom and John and be sure my tent was in the right place. With them was Tony, a professor from Vermont, the other member bemoaning the loss of his luggage and tent. He would have to share the cabin for the night. My tent was too far from the appointed spot and I would have to move closer the next day. Dinner was delicious and plentiful (Sue was always cooking for a least fifteen), and we had a fun evening getting acquainted. The first night in the tent was a windy one, but I slept like a log. When I tramped across the field to the facilities during the night, the mosquitoes attacked en force, but as a reward for enduring them I was treated to the sight of a gorgeous moon and brilliant starlight glittering on Florida Bay.

The first morning I was up early and took a walk around Eco Pond hearing a barred owl and several catbirds. Sue had a big pancake breakfast ready at eight and, soon after, we took off in the small van to check out the ponds along the road. Our pace was slow and relaxing with lots of cameras, tripods, and telephoto lenses and, of course, the constant use of binoculars. There were shouts of excitement when, at our first stop at Coot Bay Pond, there was a large alligator basking on the shore just begging to be photographed. But Tom was quick to give us our first lesson – don't get too near the alligators! They may seem sluggish, but in truth when hungry or disturbed they are mighty quick and have powerful jaws.

Two smaller alligators were discovered behind some trees. Scanning the pond, we counted ten more swimming slowly in the sun. A green heron sat quietly in the mangroves. A flock of snowy egrets flew over, and then we were alerted to several white-crowned pigeons eating fruit in the tops of the trees. Each new discovery was introduced with such enthusiasm by Tom and John that we always felt we were observing something very special. Driving along the road with Tom was another experience! He was always spotting some form of life and, with a yell, would suddenly apply the brakes and switch into reverse. Sure enough, there would be a mud turtle or a dead snake or a cotton mouse or a rabbit for us to examine. Road kills were numerous.

Our second pond that morning was little Mrazek Pond, alive with all sorts of birds – green herons, a kingfisher, white ibis, great blue herons, little blues and the tricolored, anhingas, and cormorants. We tried to keep them all straight in our mind, who had the black legs and who had the curved bills. Overhead, we watched the circling kettle of black and turkey vultures. Another quick stop along the road was to watch a passing V of white pelicans accompanied by an endangered wood stork. The real highlight of the morning was at West Lake, where we spotted a small crocodile who was sunning himself on the shore and obliged by opening his white mouth several times while we were all photographing. The much more numerous alligators prefer fresh water, while the fewer endangered crocodiles tolerate the more saline waters along the shoreline. They can be told apart by the much slimmer nose of the crocodile. Seeing this crocodile was very special, for it was the only sighting of one all week.

After a late lunch at the cabin, the afternoon was spent with a couple more stops on our way to Homestead for supplies. At the famous fruit stand "Robert is Here," just outside the park, we were treated to a thick key lime milk shake. Yummy! We saw more of the destruction and piles of debris in the city, and Sue did the grocery shopping for the week while others stocked up on more film. There was a lovely sunset through the palm trees as we made our way back to Flamingo for dinner and the outside evening program of slides on a huge screen and discussion of the Everglades by a park ranger.

We all crawled in our tents that night with weather reports of storm clouds gathering and tornado warnings! Never mind the tornadoes, but please, no thunder storms during the night. My tent had been moved closer to the others and well secured. My beach chair fit nicely in the tent and with a flourescent battery light I could actually sit comfortably and read before retiring. Another very windy night and the tent stayed put, but at dawn flashes of lightning and rumbles of thunder far to the north rousted me out of bed in a hurry. By the time I was dressed and safely in the car, the storm had receded further north, and I considered a walk around Eco Pond, but the sky was still rather ugly and I thought better of it and went to the cabin. There was a quick rain during breakfast, then clearing, but storm and tornado warnings persisted all day.

The first event of Saturday was that Tony became quite ill with stomach problems, and he was down for the day. The rest of us went off as usual to check out new spots at Nine Mile Pond, with its special variety of alligators and birds, and then made a stop at West Lake again but the crocodile was not in sight. We then did the board walk out around and into West Lake, seeing warblers, gnatcatchers, and several butterflies. We had a better look at the mangroves and how they make new soil at the water's edge and identifying distinguishing features of the arching down roots of the red variety, the up-shooting pneumatophores of the black, and then the white, which grows further back on slightly higher ground. Along the boardwalk I began to hear more songbirds than I was seeing and, looking to John for answers, I realized he was softly whistling through his teeth and imitating the songs of all sorts of birds, with even more on request once the secret was out. What a talent!

Saturday afternoon got pretty exciting! We were in the marina parking lot, watching a flock of black skimmers and some laughing gulls, and then went up to the main building to see the exhibits. From the open but covered walk-way we watched the ugly storm clouds to the north, while the sun shone where we were. A south wind was keeping the storm at bay, but as we watched the high flying flag the wind changed, the clouds drifted overhead, and the rains came suddenly and with force. We watched for a while, then all went in to the shop and had tea while waiting for the storm to subside. It outlasted tea and we did the gift shop and gathered on the benches on ground level, outside but still undercover. Tom and John were talking with a young couple, and we later learned they were Joanne McMullin and Wes Russell from the Shelburne Falls' area. They had been kayaking from Turners Falls, Massachusetts to Flamingo since the end of October! What a story!

The flooding rains continued, it must be two hours by now, and then came the real storm, with thunder and lightning. I was sitting on the bench against the wall with Tom, and I wonder if his arm is still black and blue where I grabbed him when the big flash and crack came right by the building. Everyone was tingling. All I could think of was, "What if I'd been in the tent?" Oh well, I wasn't, so why worry? Suddenly several people were saying that the lightning had struck the ground light which illuminates the flag right outside on the lawn. Sure enough, flames were leaping up from it. Everyone was

shouting when Tom suddenly told us to look at it with binoculars. It was raining so hard that the light was reflecting on the splashes, looking for all the world like red flames! Eventually the storm passed, but the only way to reach the tent that night, and most of the rest of the week, was to roll up the pant legs and wear boat shoes.

Sunday was a nice day and Tony was back among the living, but Clarissa wasn't up to par. We headed for Royal Palms and the Anhinga Trail. All trips involved stops at previous areas, always with new discoveries. We learned of the underlying limestone of the area, and how the "tree islands" are formed on slight rises of land and then surrounded by small moats where the tannin from the leaves has dissolved the limestone. The "cypress domes" grow in other depressions where the limestone has been worn down. At Royal Palms, in the northern section of the park, we listened to the ranger program on alligators, and learned that the Anhinga Trail was closed because of the total destruction of the boardwalk. The water course by the building was full of herons and several alligators, with some lovely cloudless sulfur butterflies nearby.

That evening, with the usual abundance of food that Sue was preparing, Tom and John felt free to invite guests and we hosted a camper friend and the two kayakers from Massachusetts. Let's hope the West County News latches onto their story. It fascinated us, and we hardly gave them time to eat with all our questions. A ranger program concerning the Everglades food chain continued the evening. During the program, a raccoon climbed way up on top of the huge projection board and stole the show. Later we took one of many night "road runs," and spotted a grey fox, a raccoon, a rabbit and a funny meandering opossum, as well as several false alarms on road kills. The most spectacular sight was at Nine Mile Pond where we could see eight sets of red eyes shining in the darkness – an interesting feature of alligators!

Other then getting to and from the tent (I admit it took a little courage on a cool morning or evening to put on cold wet boat shoes and slosh through cold water, batting mosquitoes) everything was pretty dry inside except for where the heavy dew soaked in when something was against the side. However, quit the grousing; I could have opted to stay in the cabin but preferred a tenting experience. So, it was Monday already, and there were special plans for the day. I was up early for a walk around Eco Pond, and identified a white-eyed vireo and watched and listened to the moorhens.

Our plans were for an all day canoe trip in Florida Bay out to a sand bar near a place called Snake Bight. This was a feature for which I was really excited. The day was perfect, with lots of sunshine and little wind. We rented two canoes, with Susan and John in one and Tom, Clarissa and I in the other. Tony declined the trip and went instead on the park sponsored tour of Florida Bay in a large sailboat. The first treat was to watch, at close range, the large gathering of white pelicans on a sand bar. What beautiful birds, and about twenty inches taller than the

White Pelicans

brown pelicans. The brown, an endangered species, make a spectacular dive for fish while the white swim along in a line and encircle a school of fish, scooping them up in their big pouches. The brown pelicans nest in Florida, but the white are migratory and nest in Utah! Most of the water was very shallow and John had his tripod set up in the mud beside the canoe. Overhead was lots of activity, and we watched a particularly lovely sight of a flock of black skimmers flying over. Several ospreys were in the air, and a nest was in view on top of a high tower. Also, an immature bald eagle obliged by displaying to us its flat wingspan in contrast to the nearby vultures with a definite upsweep in their wings.

Snake Bight was about three miles out, and what a sight that was, with thousands of birds feeding on the sandbar. The water became so shallow we finally had to stop and just sit and watch. The shore in the background was totally white with pelicans but the sandbar had everything – ibis with their long curved bills, the lovely roseate spoonbills, snowy and great white egrets, Caspian terns, and skimmers and herons of all varieties, as well as small shorebirds by the hundreds. What an incredible sight! One of the things we learned was about the "plume hunters" at the turn of the century and how they decimated the bird population. Men would come out here and kill (by gun or dynamite) birds by the hundreds, just to get the few feathers of their breeding plumage to sell for hat decorations. Through the efforts of the Audubon Society, laws were finally passed to stop this slaughter. We watched one large flock of terns flying in formation, dipping and curving and turning in total unison, and as they did, their feather colors would flash across the whole flock, disappear and flash again with another turn. And, several V's of white pelicans flew over us each time in total quiet except for the eerie whir of the wind in their wings. White pelicans show black wingtips when they fly, making them especially attractive in the air. In the shallows ahead of us, we were watching a reddish egret engaging in its special kind of "canopy feeding." The bird runs around with its wings spread to create shadows for the fish to hide in, and then snaps them up. Tom was videotaping, and the scene certainly begged for appropriate accompanying music!

What a day that was! We returned late afternoon, tired and hot but with such elation over the sights and sounds we had experienced. Tom and John have been coming here for twenty years, and still their excitement and enthusiasm runs high. Before dinner Tom had promised to take us to the scene of a daily miracle of sorts – the lovely unfolding and sudden fragrance of the large white moon flower buds. Each flower, opening at dusk, withers and dies by the next afternoon. About six, we set up cameras near the vines by Eco Pond and waited, and waited, and waited. Nothing was happening, as the sun set and Venus shone like a diamond through the pale orange and pink sky. Tom assured us the flowers had opened by six the night before, and we all said, "Sure they did!" After lots of kidding we had to give up and go for dinner about seven-thirty. On the way to the tent an hour or so later, I checked by flashlight and found all flowers open and smelling very sweet! You have to be at the right place at the right time – and that makes all the difference in this world!

Tuesday morning's early breakfast and packing lunch sandwiches was sort of on our own. Susan the cook had become sick (stomach cramps and total exhaustion seemed to continue to be the symptoms of this short-lived and evidently contagious ailment), and she had spent the night in the cabin, now being called the infirmary. She would not be joining us today. Well, everyone else could get sick, but not me! This was the day for Shark Valley, about an hour and a half drive out of the park, up around Homestead and partially across the Tamiami Trail. This gave us a chance to see, first hand, the canal and four gates that regulate the flow of water into the Glades, and the buildup of cattails on the north side. Part of the area is Indian Reservation, and they cater to the tourists with air boat rides and alligatorburgers. The air boats, banned in the park, are very loud and do lots of damage to the area where they are used.

This was a great day, starting with a tram ride out through Shark River Slough to an observation tower. We saw deer, a bald eagle, many wood storks feeding, a glossy ibis, alligators, and turtles. The tower gave a great overview of the area, which looked like the African savanna. We had lunch back under a shaded picnic shed, and then walked about a half mile each way up and back along a road with canals on either side. Here were alligators of all sizes, including many small baby ones hardly ten inches long, some of which were stretched out on rocks or lily pads. We heard limpkins and saw purple gallinules. I walked beyond, to a short trail in the shade, where I saw gumbo limbo trees with their shedding red bark and strangler figs, which take root on a host tree and proceed to drop roots and strangle the tree.

Swamp lily

The sun had been very hot along the road and I longed to find a place to sit in the shade, almost ready to stretch out on the ground when I found a bench. Wow, why was I so tired? I sat for quite a while, then walked back rather quickly, fortunately meeting Tom and asking him for the keys to the van. I opened the windows; it was very hot, and I stretched out on the seat and went to sleep hoping stomach cramps didn't mean anything! It was late afternoon by the time we headed home and we were to have dinner in Homestead. Food, who wanted food! By this time, Tom admitted that he wasn't in tip top shape, either, and we both had chicken soup for supper. Tom seemed to perk up after supper, and we did all the usual roads checking for wildlife. All I wanted to do was get back and, finally, after going hither and yon, I thought we were on the road home but realized the last glow of the sunset was on the left side of the van. I couldn't help it

when I blurted out, "Tom, why are we going north?" It was just a bend in the road, but I was thinking we were off on another back road chase that I would have enjoyed on an ordinary day. They wouldn't let me forget this remark the next day! By the time we got to the cabin I knew I was too exhausted to wade out to the tent, and asked for my turn in the "infirmary" now that Susan was better and ready to go back to her tent. They said I was in a dead sleep on the couch in less than five minutes. Fortunately, all things pass, and the good night's sleep totally revived me with a little holding back on too much food the next day. John stayed well and everyone else recovered in a short time, but poor Tony got the blame for bringing us "his" bug.

Wednesday, our last full day, and there was still so much to see and do. Not many flowers bloomed in January, but there was one swamp lily that could often be seen among the saw grass and this morning we set out for a wet hike to photograph them and investigate a tree island. I wore my hiking boots and the water was sometimes nearly up to my knees. We were walking on the jagged limestone that was covered with the ever present collection of soft brown algae and plankton called periphyton. This is the stuff that dries out on top during the dry season, but like a sponge, holds enough moisture underneath to keep alive the small organisms and fish eggs waiting for the summer rains. Growing among all this was the saw grass, actually a sedge with sharp teeth along the midrib. It took slow and careful walking not to step in a hole, and most of us were juggling cameras, tripods and binoculars. We found a lovely lily with three blossoms but, with quite a breeze, it was difficult to photograph. Other flowers included scattered tall white arrowhead, yellow composites, and one pretty tiny purple blossom fallen and floating in the water that proved to be a water willow. At the small hammock we found the dwarf cypress, with new needles evidently having re-grown since the hurricane.

In the midst of things Susan let out a shriek. She had seen a snake in the water! Now, Susan is a calm and cool-headed naturalist from Audubon and not afraid of snakes, but for some reason this one had startled her. Then she was suddenly totally embarrassed by her actions, but it was too late. Tom had heard her, and the betting is that she may never outlive the kidding about that incident.

Heading on, we made a quick stop at Paurotis Pond. We had been told there was an alligator there that people had been feeding. Sure enough, when we drove up to the water an alligator turned, came swimming toward us, and stayed put, watching us just off from shore. People think it is such fun to feed a wild animal, but then it becomes tame and causes problems for other people, and eventually, the animal has to be destroyed. And this alligator will

be very apt to attack someone, now that it expects food from people.

Next, we stopped at a cypress dome near the road and again walked through the water to its inner jungles. The hurricane had toppled big trees, but it was not bad, and we could walk and climb into the deep dark depths, where we saw many yellow bladderwort flowers growing in the water, lots of ferns and other vegetation on the upturned roots of the big cypress, and many epiphytes or air plants called wild pines on the trees. There were also several orchids, but unfortunately this was not their season to be in bloom. Tom spotted a barred owl and John went back for his camera equipment, as he had never had the chance to photograph a barred owl in the Everglades. Susan redeemed herself somewhat by finding us a baby water moccasin near the road.

Next stop was at Royal Palms, where we had lunch and walked the Gumbo Limbo Trail. For those who had seen this before, the effects of the hurricane were evident – a deep dark trail under big trees was now an open trail among fallen trees covered with pretty blue morning glory vines – still interesting but quite different. Back near the water were two large brown water snakes which held everyone's interest. At the gift shop I bought a popular video of the Everglades, for which John had helped with some of the photography.

The last two stops were especially interesting. The first was at Mahogany Hammock, where there were some downed trees but the boardwalk stayed intact, and we hiked out across the saw grass and periphyton where I spotted a small purple bladderwort and several apple snails in the water. In the woods was a treasure chest of trees, epiphytes, Boston ferns, butterflies, birds, dragonflies, and the remains of the oldest mahogany tree in the country. This great old tree, covered with resurrection fern and epiphytes, had lost several huge limbs, but was still impressive. Nearby, we watched several anoles, one of which was the Cuban brown displaying his bright red dewlap under his chin. In the distance, we could hear the limpkin again, although they are usually a bird of the night. The biggest attraction along the boardwalk was a female pileated woodpecker, high up in an old dead palm tree, cleaning out a nesting hole. John in his enthusiasm, would easily talk about certain birds as tourists would go by asking questions. Everyone was most appreciative of his knowledge and willingness to explain. But, having corrected a rather pompous woman who had identified a red-bellied woodpecker as a flicker, John was trying to explain the difference when the woman walked off saying to her companion, "Well, at home they are flickers!"

With wildflowers being my first love, I was always searching for them, although I didn't expect a January trip to produce many. Florida flower reference books are not very complete, and new finds are frustrating anyway, but I had found a new book and when we made our last stop in the pinelands I could have spent the day! The pinelands are just a bit higher in the limestone, and the area has numerous sinkholes which are wet while the land underfoot is dry. Natural fires set by lightning are a necessity in the pinelands, to keep hardwoods from sprouting and the saw palmettos from taking over the understory. The ashes probably have some effect on the flowering plants, too. We found many blossoming varieties among the grasses and ferns, and I could usually be found sitting on the ground flipping pages beside a new specimen. But there were other treasures, too. The rare and beautiful endangered Atala butterfly was spotted, and we watched three cavorting around trees. The caterpillars only feed on the rare cycad, coontie, and we could not find one of these but they must be close-by. The butterflies stayed in sight for a long time, displaying their lovely black, with iridescent blue spotted wings and bright red bellies.

And so with another great dinner, an obliging corn snake to examine alive, a perfect and almost dry final night in the tent, and an early morning hike, we broke camp after breakfast. It would take a long time to digest all that we had seen and done but it had been a wonderful experience, learning about more of the diverse wonders that are out there on the Wild Side in the Florida Everglades.

I took my leave first and poked into all the familiar ponds on my way out, lastly stopping on the main highway to save a snapping turtle from becoming a road kill statistic. As I was buying a papaya at the fruit stand just outside the park, the van with my companions went by, tooting and waving farewell. After safely depositing the others at the airport, Tom was headed off to pick up an Audubon group for another tour of the Everglades, and John was staying in the Miami area for a month, giving environmental programs for area school children. I'm sure the enthusiasm and knowledge of those two men will continue to inspire both young and old on the Wild Side! **3/93**

In a Patch of Fireweed

"*In a Patch of Fireweed*" is the name of a book we have read by Bernd Heinrich, a field biologist and professor at University of Vermont. He has now become a favorite author, with other books on such things as bumblebees, owls, and ravens. The fireweed book title came to mind as we were sitting on Negus Mountain on a beautiful May morning, trying to identify a patch of rather pretty, dark, pink-stemmed plants with bright pink stripes along the mid-vein of the leaves. They looked like nothing we had ever seen before. But, we know that things are mysterious in the spring when they first pop out of the ground, like the ghostly dark purple stems of blue cohosh and the big dark scaly fiddleheads of the Goldie's fern, or the sharp-pointed green spike of a jack-in-the-pulpit. And come fall, plants will turn into odd contraptions like the "doll's eyes" of the white baneberry, or the large three-cornered seedpod of the tiny bellwort flower called wild oats, or the beautiful sectioned seed cup of the marsh marigolds. Plants keep you guessing all through the seasons. But knowing all this didn't help at the moment. We sat there staring at the pink stems, and wondered and wondered.

It was a lovely morning to be out on the Wild Side. We had packed a granola bar and an apple and were set for the day. We had recently seen what seemed like acres of a lovely little pink flower called gaywings, and we are bound we are going to find them hiding somewhere in Rowe. Such searches can become quite fanatical if they don't immediately produce the object. Gaywings are getting into this category. We had found them over the line in Heath a number of years ago, and just expected it would be

only a matter of time before stumbling upon them in Rowe. Five years or more later, and we are still searching more fanatically than ever, just after we have seen them with their lovely orchid-like bloom in other areas. All this is by way of explanation as to why we were sitting on Negus on this bright spring morning. Gaywings grow where the soil is thin in oak woods or on mountain-tops – but they also grow in the valleys in deep rich soil, so there you have our dilemma. Today we wanted to try the mountain.

It was rather early when we drove "over west" and passed two turkeys in the back of Sparky's field. They were so still we backed up and put the binocs to them to prove they weren't decoys, as this was turkey hunting season. Sure enough, one head finally went down to pick at the grass and the other turned to the side – they were real, and not a hunter in sight. We were a little leery about being out in the woods in any hunting season, but with only a couple of days to go of this long turkey season we decided it would be okay and we'd probably have the woods to ourselves. Our first stop was in Peck's field. With great anticipation we were going to hear one of our favorite birds, a field sparrow. Ever since we can remember, there has always been a field sparrow calling in Peck's field. We stopped the car, got out and listened, and listened, and leaned against the car and listened, but no field sparrow. Was it too early in the season? Has something happened to all our field sparrows? Are they being driven out by all the che-beks, who seem to have made a big comeback? The chestnut-sided warblers were alive and well, as were the red-eyed vireos, the redstart, and the yellowthroat, all happily singing their hearts out. If those gaywings hadn't been calling, we'd have stayed there all morning, waiting...

It was cool enough so the bugs were not yet activated, and we started up Negus hill at a good pace. Early in the morning we can do quite well, and anticipation of a great day always helps. We were greeted by the chirp of a towhee and then the familiar, "Drink you tea," of his song. At least we can still say there is always a towhee on Negus. The view has almost totally grown in on the first hill. We stopped to watch a writhing mass of tent caterpillars emerging from a tent in the low crotch of a little cherry tree. Actually they were quite pretty, grey-blue with blue dots, and a light stripe and lots of brown fuzz around their feet. How's that for a scientific description? Some of them had fanned out and were devouring the cherry leaves. We took the hand lens and at close range watched one little creature chew away at the greenery.

Some of the swamp pinks were in full bloom, and they seem to be so dark pink this year, and, what a fragrance! We were climbing up around a large ledge the other day and suddenly, as our head came up into the breeze, the air was literally heavy with the sweet, sweet smell of swamp pinks. Climbing a little higher, eight or ten bushes in full bloom came into view surviving in a bit of soil on the south edge of the ledge.

The laurel that is so beautiful on Negus was not yet in bloom, and so much of it has been removed through the years. We made the usual detour out through the small field and gave it a quick once over for flowers. We were not lingering, for we wanted to spend time further over in new locations.

It was such a good feeling to be off on a mountaintop. Someone has said that paradise is half way between heaven and earth, on a mountaintop. How true! The last part of the climb was steep and a little muddy, and the road certainly looked well-used. Almost at the top we were looking forward to sitting down and enjoying the view while we caught our breath. But... Oh no, there is an ATV with a camouflaged canvas cab sitting right on top of the mountain. Turkey hunters for sure. Now what do we do? We really didn't want to be in the line of fire or, worse still, mistaken for a turkey. (Some city folks have proven they don't know the difference!) Should we leave a note, saying there is a hiker in the woods? No, they probably wouldn't be back to the vehicle until noon. We decided to just go about our business, but it just wasn't the same.

Constantly on the watch, we walked out to the front or west side of the mountain and admired the always gorgeous view of our beloved hills surrounding the deep Deerfield valley. We stood, instead of sitting, and draped our pink jacket over our shoulders. Soon the quest for flowers took our attention, and we admired the blue-green ground cedar, the scattered dainty star flowers, and the large blanket of bunchberry with its flowers recently opened and still more green than white. They will turn into bright red berries by fall. Of course, there were blueberries galore, and honeysuckle and mats of sheep laurel not yet in bloom.

We wandered down a ways, and found the orchid that had intrigued us last year when it was only a seedpod. It could have been one of two things, a large round-leaved or pad orchid, or a smaller Hooker's orchid, and we were anxious to prove it one way or the other. Sure enough it was still there, growing well with a good-sized stem with buds. We could see at once from the leaves that it was a Hooker's orchid. Nothing to see, really, except with a hand lens when the blossoms come out, but a native orchid none the less and very particular about its habitat. For being a mountaintop Negus is very wet, and mosses and liverworts thrive.

We remembered the odd red maple-leaved viburnum we had seen other years down over the far side, and we climbed down to look for it and got sidetracked with last year's dry pinweed blossoms. Suddenly, we heard a turkey call quite close, and looking up the hill we could see two hunters silhouetted against the sky. We called and waved, relieved to have made our presence known, and went about our business. Looking up a little later, we saw one of the hunters was closer, holding a gun on his shoulder and looking down at us saying something. It was then we recognized our fellow townsman, Junior Veber. He was out early, hunting turkey with his granddaughter, and was certainly surprised to see a woman way down over the hill on Negus Mountain at that early hour of the day. We climbed up the hill and joined them for a few minutes, much relieved to know who it was and confident that they knew what a turkey looked like! We swapped stories and a few laughs for a few minutes, and watched a turkey vulture circling in the valley, and then parted company.

From there on, the day was relaxed and joyful as we wandered over the mountainside. We found the viburnum, and then began to see the plants with the dark pink stems. Now we could sit in the midst of this plentiful plant, with our book, and try to solve the mystery. With so much of it, we ought to be able to guess the logical answer, thinking toward summer and knowing pretty much what grows there. The view distracted us and we found ourselves daydreaming and looking off into the distance. Like the proverbial light bulb going off, the answer came to us. We were sitting in Bernd Heinrich's "patch of fireweed!" And, we remembered the lovely garden it creates in the summer sun.

Climbing down as far as the fire of a couple years ago had burned, we investigated all the nooks and crannies for some new plant that might be clinging to this open and exposed rocky mountainside. Nothing new appeared, but the view was steeply dramatic as the Deerfield seemed to bend right under us. The myriad shades of spring green of the trees accented with the shadows of drifting clouds, the blue of the sky, and the "dark brown of the river" all combined to give us a wondrous world to behold. A raven called and we watched as three of them swooped and glided and played on the thermal currants. A veery thrush sang from the lower woods. As we turned in toward the mountain, the sun was backlighting the most beautiful collection of fruiting mosses on the ledges above. How lucky we were to have all this beauty to appreciate, just for a morning walk on the mountain.

From the road up Whitcomb Hill in Florida, you can look back at Negus and see a depression between the mountains that looks like a glacial cirque. This has always intrigued us and we've wanted to investigate. The area was between the peak I was on and the next one, more or less over Zoar Gap. We started into the woods and found brush and rock cliffs, but somehow we swung down on trees and came into a lovely wooded area full of healthy interrupted ferns, some already reaching shoulder height. Starflowers and Canada mayflowers carpeted the ground, along with Solomon's plume and wild oats, but nothing spectacular greeted us. We climbed on an angle and eventually came to the laurel wall. We wanted to be out in the open area and knew we had to penetrate that wall, hopefully without crawling on our hands and knees as we have done at times in such places. Laurel grows thick and bushy and doesn't like intruders. One secret is to find deer paths which will usually take you laterally where you want to go, but the deer will also have munched any succulent plants you might have wanted to find.

We came out in the more open area covered with low bush blueberries, and stopped on several rock outcrops to admire the views, now at a different angle. It was a long climb to the top, but each new vantage point was inspiring. The plant cover remained the same, with nothing unusual except a pretty patch of red columbine on the rocks near the top, definitely not gaywings country. From there on the new growth of the false foxglove was everywhere, and some of the tall old seedpods remained. This peak of Negus has also grown in, and the view is through the trees looking over the Zoar valley on one side and the Gap and off to Florida and beyond on the other. This is a memorable spot for us, thinking back to the morning, many years ago, when we walked out here with friends in an early morning fog and sat here on a rock in the sunshine just above the top of the fog, with only the peaks of the mountains showing like islands in a white sea. What a strange and beautiful experience.

Today, we decided not to follow the path back across the top of the ridge, but to go a ways down the back side where there might be more fertile and rich soils. Rocks and ledges always attract us, and we stood looking down at a peculiar upturned one trying to decide if it was worth the climb down to investigate. Suddenly our eyes focused on a fern growing in the crevice. Down we went in a hurry. Our reward for the day! Not a gaywings but a new fern for Rowe. Of course we had lightened our knapsack and left the fern book in the car, but we tentatively made the identification of a rusty woodsia. We took a couple sample fronds and, not having seen that fern before, we will need someone else's botanical expertise. Wow, anything new is fun but a new fern is really special.

We came back up to the ridge and spent some time looking at a lot of small saplings deciding they were young shagbark hickories. The mother tree is further over on the mountain. Shrubs in bloom were black chokeberries and hawthorns, and on the ground a few pink lady's slippers were already displaying their lovely moccasin flowers. On a small ledge in the sun we finally sat for our lunch break. It was long after twelve, but we had been so occupied and happy in our quest that food was far from our mind. A hermit thrush was singing now, not far behind us. Perhaps another day, another time, there will also be gaywings and field sparrows. **6/93**

A Goal Achieved, Fifty Years Later

Looking ahead, fifty years is a long time. Looking back, fifty years ago seems like yesterday. So in retrospect it was only yesterday when we were about twelve years old and living on Tea Street in Charlemont during the winters. We had been doing this for several years in order to get away from the harsh winter conditions further north in Rowe! We spent a lot of our free after-school time hiking across the long meadow behind the house, and up the side of the rather steep mountain across Legate Hill Road. If there was snow, we would cross-country ski to the top of the hill at the end of the meadow and ski down the then open slope. We often looked across the Deerfield River to Mt. Peak and wished we could climb to the top of that real mountain, but we could not do it alone. We also wasted a lot of time being homesick and wishing we were back in our own hills of Rowe.

During this particular winter in question, a young friend of the family often visited during his college vacations to take advantage of the skiing and hiking in our countryside. The previous summer he had been my first hiking partner and taught me the joys of hiking and climbing. We did not begrudge his solo jaunts, or want to join his Greylock climb to ski down the old Thunderbolt trail, but the day he climbed Mt. Peak and came back with stories of the view and tiny pond on top, we were really envious and determined to climb that mountain ourselves. (Having teased to go in the first place, we had been put off with the fact that we probably couldn't keep up with him on a real mountain climb.)

To pacify us, there was a vague promise to take us up there someday – probably after we got out of our bratty kid stage. That Mt. Peak day never came, although we learned to keep up and enjoyed many other hikes with him in and around Rowe hills the following

summers, establishing our lifelong love of hiking. But in all the succeeding fifty years, we have never driven through Charlemont without a glance at Mt. Peak (it's sort of hard to ignore) with thoughts of how we would someday climb that mountain. Memories come to mind of the day we rode down Tea Street, on a stretcher in the back of an open station wagon, as a "casualty" in an air raid drill during World War II. As we recall, the rescue crew arrived with no stretcher and we, reporting to have a broken back, had to take them to the barn to look for a board to use as a stretcher. We distinctly remember riding uncomfortably down Tea Street, amusing ourselves looking back at Mt. Peak, and wondering if, maybe, we would get to make the climb that spring. Now, they are about to commemorate the fiftieth anniversary of that war, and we look back and realize how unnecessary those blackouts and air raid drills were in those days.

We'd look up at Mt. Peak as we daily rode our bicycle from school up that cold and windy Tea Street, home for lunch and back and home again at night most of the winter, until real ice and snow covered the road. We'd think that, maybe, we were getting our legs in shape for the big climb. Of course, having never climbed a real mountain, Mt. Peak loomed pretty big in our young mind.

Then, there were our many years of skiing as an adult at Thunder Mountain and standing on the high slopes looking across the valley to Mt. Peak, and its companion Mrs. Peak, and thinking the same thoughts. And, rafting down the Deerfield, there was Mt. Peak rising as a wall near the end of our journey. When will we get to climb that mountain? It became sort of a mythical place in our imagination.

Knowing our desire, in recent years even our own children have made similar promises to take us up Mt. Peak for a birthday hike, but again the occasion never came. One son even had the nerve to go up without us! At one time or other we have climbed most other mountains in the general area, a lot of them by ourselves, so why not Mt. Peak? Well, we don't know, somehow it just never happened, and we continued to drive through Charlemont looking up its thousand-foot height above the Deerfield and dreaming. For some reason no other mountain presented such a strange challenge, going back to that day fifty years ago when we teased to climb it in the first place!

As those fifty years passed we began to worry a little, especially recently, that maybe we'd never fulfill that dream. Spring would come and go and we'd then think we should wait until the leaves were off in the fall to see more through the trees, and so another year would slip by. Winter snows would show up an old wood road angling up the mountainside, and we knew the climb to the top would be fairly easy. This summer as our old joints got stiffer we knew we MUST climb Mt. Peak. We knew that if the day ever came when we couldn't and we hadn't, life would be miserable in our rocking chair.

When the day finally arrived in early November, 1993, it was an ordinary day, partly cloudy, quite cool, and rather hazy. With fifty years of days to choose from, this was not the most perfect one but it was available and we were ready, no matter what (except maybe if there were predictions of thunder showers). We did not anticipate a long hike and packed the usual apple and granola bar for lunch. Even our trusty Newcomb's Wildflower book was left behind (November, No Flowers). But there was a small plastic baggie for mosses, our newest passion this summer and fall. Unlike flowers, mosses quite often take a hand lens, and even a microscope at home, to make a positive identification. So, instead of getting down on our knees with Newcomb's before a new flower, we gently take a small specimen of the unknown moss home in the baggie, hopefully having labeled its habitat and location. Moss is a new challenge (we've purposely skipped over grasses and rushes and sedges) for our mind, and our eyes have been opened to even more beauty and variety in the natural world around us. Now, instead of just "pretty velvet green," we see texture, size, fruiting capsules, shades of color, and tiny leaves. And mosses can be found summer and winter, from Maine to Florida.

We drove to the bridge in Charlemont, crossed the river and turned north on the River Road, parking the car a little past an abandoned house. We were excited, and full of anticipation, as we put on the knapsack and closed the car. The old wood road seemed to enter the woods just above where we had parked, but it had grown in thick with blackberry briers and small saplings. We had started up the hill into the woods when we were stopped in our tracks, realizing that there was a "No Trespassing, No Hunting" sign beside us on the tree. We do not make a habit of crossing these boundaries without permission, but on closer look the sign was not signed by the landowner, as it should be to be legal. We were not hunting, and this was such a special hike that we were sure most anyone would understand our need to

finally "trespass" on Mt. Peak! How awful if it was really off limits after all these fifty years. We still do not know the landowner and we certainly hope he/she, or they, "forgive us our trespasses."

A well-trod deer trail followed the road up the hill and helped us weave our way through the briers, although we were caught and scratched many times and, once in a while, found the bank rather than the road more passable. We had started off with such enthusiasm and speed that we soon found ourselves out of breath, and stopped to lean against a tree. We were high enough so that the river and the village of Charlemont were already below us as we gazed through the trees into the haze. The old road seemed well established, and we wondered if it had existed in the past long before the logging of some twenty years ago. Ferns were brown with frost, but here and there an aster still bloomed and several odd bluets still raised their tiny faces. Mosses were everywhere and bright green with the slight dampness. Most mosses fold up their leaves when dry and crisp and become less noticeable or brownish. When wet they open their leaves full and, of course, more green shows up, making a lush carpet all over the rocks and forest floor. Stooping many times we finally made a pact with ourselves not to stop and look closely at mosses until the return trip down the mountain. After all, our main objective was to climb to the top of the mountain.

At a certain height the road split, and we decided to veer off even more to the west and first climb the summit of Mrs. Peak. The woods were quite open, with hardwoods and little underbrush and lots of rocks and ledges as the going became steeper. We noticed immediately the numerous brown fronds of maidenhair ferns and the bare stalks with blue fruits of the blue cohosh, and knew that this must be good rich soil where the ephemeral spring flowers would abound. As we climb in and around and up over rocks and wet banks, it always surprises us that so often just where we are about to place our boot there seems to have been a step already taken by someone else. This happens in other woods, too, and we presume they are animal tracks of one kind or another, as what other human would be so foolish as to bushwhack in this exact spot?

Although it was chilly and we crunched on spaghetti ice in places, we took our jacket off and tied it around our waist. Climbing sure revs up the inner heater. We couldn't help but break our no mosses promise several times, so the ascent to Mrs. Peak was slow and meandering. A change in tree cover from hardwood to spruce and hemlock defined the ridge of Mrs. Peak. The western side of the mountain was definitely acidic, and laurel grew thick in the openings between the trees and rocks. We came out into the open on the west side of Mrs. Peak and climbed the high ledge. Wow! What a view! We were looking up the Deerfield River valley, past the peaks of Zoar and on to the wall of Negus Mountain. Over the meadow of upper Tea Street loomed the Northwest and the Basin, and somewhere up in there is the southeastern boundary of Rowe.

There in view, if we leaned forward a bit, was the house where we had lived on Tea Street, as the Mohawk Trail was there known. There was the highway (much less traveled in those days), where we were riding our bicycle that Sunday afternoon and when we came in, our parents tried to explain to a ten year old about the bombing of Pearl Harbor. There was the field where we skied for the first time, on a little pair of skis with one strap and a jar rubber to hold them on to our overshoes. We remembered our room in that house, and the little jar on our dresser where we saved every penny of our allowance and gift money so we could finally buy our first pair of ski boots at Avery's store for all of $5.00.

There were skates under the tree one Christmas, and an unusual ice crust formed on the snow once that winter. It was thick enough to skate on all across the field. And there beside the road is where the big red barn used to stand, and we remembered the cold winter nights when we went out with our father to watch him milk the cow, and how warm and sweet the hay and the cows smelled. And we fed some of the milk to the big old pig under the barn, and dumped the pail of garbage and meal in the trough for his supper. We laughed to think of trying to outsmart the old rooster that always chased us when we went to gather the eggs in the hen house. And there was our cat, Rusty, who never failed to be in the window when we came home from school. We remembered, too, eating crackers and milk sitting by the cozy old kitchen wood stove, and the wonderful smell of the graham bread our mother always baked for the young man who came to visit and climbed Mt. Peak and wouldn't take us with him. Yes, fifty years ago was only yesterday.

The wind cooled us quickly and we put the jacket back on as we sat on the high ledge overlooking the river. It was a day of nostalgia, a day of rejoicing to finally realize a dream, a day to be happy and content. We lingered a long time on that ledge for many reasons, not the least of which was the fact that we were pretty sure it was the only open view on either mountain and we wanted to savor it well. After all we might not be able to return to that spot for another fifty years.

Climbing through the laurel, we went back into the woods and down the hill toward Mt. Peak. We were already back in the hardwoods again, maples and beeches and now and then an ironwood, and the hiking was easy as we started up the side of Mt. Peak itself. The whole mountain was moss heaven, especially on the ledge outcrops where a little water trickled down. In one place, a pileated woodpecker had been at work on a log and the ground was covered with chips. Nearer the top, a small gully appeared but there was no brook. We wondered if that was the outlet for the famous "pond" but, reaching the summit plateau, we couldn't find the pond at first. Cruising around the fairly flat area, we spotted water in a small depression under several large hemlock trees and knew that must be it. We looked for a ring of sphagnum moss near the water, but there was none. We wondered if it was just a collection of rain and surface water or if it was fed by springs. Without moss, we decided it was just surface water caught in a rocky, or perhaps a clay, basin. With all the talk of springs drying up, and having seen the change on Negus, we decided there were no springs here, but in a wet spring or summer there is probably a substantial little pond there under the trees. Anyway, our curiosity had been satisfied! Walking around a bit, we realized that the actual top of Mt. Peak was not at the pond

but a ways to the south where the land rose a bit higher, culminating in a small rock summit.

We reached that ledge hungry, but thinking it must still be before noon, as we had not heard the noon siren. Either it did not ring, or we had been so absorbed in reverie back on Mrs. Peak that we never heard it. Our watch now read one o'clock. Before we sat down to lunch we looked as best we could through the trees and could see the back side of Adams Mountain, the power line east of Pulpit Rock, Whitcomb Summit area, a farmhouse probably in Monroe, and mountains further north in Vermont. It was again a hazy view and we did not have our trusty binocs, because they are sadly in need of calibrating and we have not taken the time to send them off to the company. The view toward the center of Charlemont was almost totally obscured by trees.

It was with a great sense of accomplishment that we finally sat there on the very summit of Mt. Peak. It had been an easy and interesting climb. The satisfaction came from finally having done it after fifty years! We could now drive through Charlemont, look Mt. Peak straight in the eye, and smile. We did it at last, and we did it on our own!

Our usual lunch was delicious and, as we couldn't gaze off at the view, we began to look at the mosses and lichens on the ledge around us and interrupted our feast several times for a closer look. The wind was a bit chilly and our jacket was zipped. The sun, visible but behind a substantial cloud cover, was not shedding warmth. A red-tailed hawk screamed a few times and flew on up the river. Local chipmunks were scurrying around, and often curious enough to look at us for a moment. We left them an apple core and a few granola crumbs.

As we stood to leave our rock perch, we noticed that the tree in front of us had several initials carved in it, and we contemplated leaving our trademark, "NNW," but decided we were too old for such things. Our thoughts for our descent centered on mosses, and we soon found the rock moss, Ulota hutchinsiae. We're still having trouble learning the Latin names of flowers, but, with the mosses, we're starting with the Latin mainly because there are very few common names. And, we've discovered it's just as easy to learn Rhytidiadelphus as Rhododendron. On the way back to the pond area we spotted a dark moss on a dry rock and, on very close examination, saw tiny red "flowers," the capsules of a Grimmia – exciting, as this was our first discovery of Grimmia, even though it's a rather common moss. As with flowers, we will always remember where we first found certain mosses, especially when they have distinctive features that can be identified in the field. The chickadees were having a chirpingfest in the hemlocks by the pond as we passed to the east and down around the outcroppings of moss-covered rock.

Never wanting to retrace our steps unless necessary, we kept to the eastern side of the mountain, which was steep and quite wet underfoot. We lost it once and went sailing down a muddy embankment with the seat of our pants looking a little worse for wear. From the sitting position, we observed the plants a little closer and found that we were in rich soil once again. Among the brown maindenhair ferns we spotted what looked like a large violet leaf. We couldn't imagine what violet it could be, with such long leaf stems. Reaching down to take a sample leaf, a strong familiar odor wafted across our nostrils – wild ginger, of course! The rich soil should have clued us to look for it in the first place. In our defense, so many plants look vastly different at various times of the year, but the pungent taste of the ginger root was no different than when we enjoyed that first sample in the spring.

Curiosity and various distractions kept us meandering here and there down the mountainside, and we were never sure exactly where we would emerge on the road. Through the trees we could see one rock covered with greenery that looked thick, tall, and very different. A wonderful mat of Hylocomnium splendens! This is one of the few mosses with a common name, "stair-step moss," for its manner of growth, one stem above the other in step fashion. Although we had seen Hylocomnium before, this was the first in our area, and what an unusually large and beautiful mat it was. The fun of this discovery added to the joy of the day. And just as we could see the road through the underbrush, we changed course slightly to avoid a wet spot. But there in the dampness was another find, a species of Climacium, the little tree moss that we had never seen before.

Once again with apologies to Robert Lewis Stevenson, *"The world is so full of a number of things, I'm sure we should all be..... Happy!"* We will need another fifty years, at least, to learn and identify all the wonderful things there are out there "On the Wild Side!" Just think, if we had climbed Mt. Peak that day fifty years ago we probably never would have noticed the moss! **12/93**

The Night Walk On The Wild Side

Hi, my name is Arolyn and I want to tell you about our night walk on the wild side. Mabel, my grandmother, Chelsey, my cousin who is six, and last but not least me, all decided to go outside for a moonlight walk. Mabel told us to get into all the clothes we had because the temperature was zero. She meant just our warmest clothes but we misunderstood and got into ALL our clothes, six underwear, nine shirts and three pants. We pretended we were fat and we looked it. In fact we didn't even look like Chelsey and Arolyn!

It was beautiful outside with the moonlight shimmering on the snow. It was quiet and still. We walked out on the Williams Trail. The water under the bridge sang with the ripples. We knew that not many people would be out at that time of night.

We stopped every once in a while to listen to the brook near the trail and for any other sounds of nature. It was a magical night. We quietly talked about fairies and watched as the moonlight shone on the hemlocks and made beautiful shadows on the snow. It was so bright we didn't even bring flashlights. Mabel showed us an old tree that she had seen crawling with bugs one summer night. After a while we crossed over to the Lake Trail.

As we walked on it looked as if there must be a full moon. The new fallen snow sparkled with delight. I imagined that the fairies flew around and with their wands made the snow sparkle. There were footprints in the snow of a dog and a person. We could hear the lake booming. Mabel told us it was pressure under the ice, but I told her it was a sea monster and we pretended it couldn't get out. Mabel pretended, too.

We stopped in the open by the lake and saw the constellation Orion and the brightest star, Sirius, was just coming over the mountain. We came back by the dam and across the bridge where the sound of the water was deafening.

It was a long walk but that was OK because of the wonder and beauty of Mother Nature. I hope you, too, can go for a magical night walk on the wild side.

– Arolyn Williams, age 8

A Wild Eleutherian Adventure

Little did we know, back in the late sixties, that we would someday have some wild and delightful sailing adventures with our new Rowe neighbors who had bought the "brick base" down on Zoar Road, and we couldn't have imagined that the Captain would be none other than that man who first amused us so trying to learn to sail on calm Pelham Lake with a small row boat, a broom handle and a sheet. But sitting there on Pelham Lake, Don Ruth was dreaming, and those dreams became a reality when the family moved in the early seventies out to Green Bay, Wisconsin, and Don took up serious sailing on the Great Lakes.

Our first sailing trip with Don and Jane Ruth was in the mid 70's for two beautiful weeks, gunk-holing on the North Channel of Lake Huron in their twenty-two foot wooden sailboat, Beauty. Two years ago in April, after their retirement, we joined them for a wonderful trip in the Bahamas where they were spending the winter on their sailboat, now a thirty-five foot ketch called Snowbird. (Wild Side, April, 1992) When Jack and I were again invited to join the Ruths in the Bahamas this February, we knew there would be a rare adventure in store.

Already vacationing in the Florida Keys, we left at noon on February 16th by small plane from Marathon to Miami. The elderly-looking grey-haired woman pilot unnerved us a bit, but all went well. It was a nice day and we looked down on the green islands of the many Florida Keys, but then we could see first hand the awful encroaching algae bloom created because of the lack of fresh water from the dry Everglades. Man has destroyed

Snowbird

a precious natural resource there, and it is doubtful if there will ever be enough genuine concern, political agreement, and money to restore the Everglades.

At Miami we changed to a little larger plane, and soon were flying over Key Biscayne and all the hotels along Miami Beach. We crossed the Gulf Stream and a gentle and beautiful blue-green sea was soon sprinkled with some of the 700 or so islands of the Bahamas, particularly Bimini, the big island of Andros, and finally New Providence. Since we were there two years ago, the city of Nassau now has a big new airport, and from there it is about a forty-five minute taxi ride to Nassau Yacht Haven. Here we found Snowbird at the west dockage, with Captain Don and Mate Jane and mascot springer spaniel Mickey aboard. We all enjoyed cold Kalik beer while sharing lots of news of our families and the old hometown of Rowe. Later Jane and I took Mickey for a walk in the grass along the docks. Poor Mickey is old, diabetic, and ill and it was sad, as she once rivaled Don as Captain of the Snowbird!

As we sat enjoying the activity of the harbor and watching the "packet" which flew low over our heads and landed at the Paradise Island airport, every hour, bringing in the gambling crowd, Jane broke open some delicious smoked salmon they had been saving for a special occasion and then followed it with a great steak dinner. Wow, what a start. The boat lights are on battery and have to be conserved, and this promotes early retirement. We all found our niche and, with small reading lights, each relaxed in bed with a book or magazine. It was a delightful night with the gentle tossing of the boat, and I slept like a log.

Thursday morning, early (when you go to bed with the chickens you are up at the first crack of dawn) we had our coffee on deck discussing the weather – the all important topic on a small boat. With rain and wind on the increase, it seemed best to stay in port for the day. First order of business was to walk Mickey, and as always I went along for the exercise. Later that morning, to pass the time, we became tourists and took a bus downtown, where we decided to catch another bus for Coral Island. Men were hawking buses, as they are privately owned, and one assured us he had the bus for Coral Island. He did, we found out, if you wanted a long walk across a causeway in the ever increasing wind while the right bus went roaring past us several times!

Oh well, we needed the exercise. The tourist attraction there is called Coral World, with an aquarium, underwater observatory, turtle, shark, and stingray outdoor pools, as well as a tower overlooking the bay and a small restaurant where we had a good fish sandwich and watched the waves crash on the rocky shore in the high wind. We attended the feeding of the rays that half climbed the sides to get a fish. Their flesh felt soft and velvety as we reached to pet them. We spent most of afternoon really enjoying and appreciating the marine life of the coral reefs so well displayed there. Because of the deteriorating weather we eventually took a taxi back to the Yacht Haven.

We relaxed on the boat and wondered how much stronger the wind could become. Good baked chicken and rice well satisfied us for dinner. It was again to bed early but it was a fitful night, with great rocking of the boat and creaking against the dock. We woke up about one a.m., when the winds reached gale force (34 + knots) from northeast. Boats were wildly rocking, and the neighbor's genoa unfurled and was madly flapping against the lines. I carefully opened the porthole enough to be sure it wasn't our sail. Sleep was hard to come by after this and I was afraid I was missing the excitement, so I went up in the cockpit where the Captain was keeping careful watch as everything about was being violently tossed in the wind. Don finally went out and tied another line to keep us away from the dock. It was a wild night, and after I went back to bed I still wondered, just a bit, if we were going to have to abandon ship right there in dock! The old "packet" just kept on droning in, every hour, in spite of the gale winds.

Official weather reports are hard to come by in the Bahamas. Friday morning dawned calm and sunny and we were ready to go. But the once a day 7:45 a.m. weather report, from the "NET" (a private volunteer radio communication system of small boats), said there were still small craft warnings for continued high seas and winds. Looking at the weather it seemed foolish, but with those reports they must know something we didn't so the lines would stay tied to the dock for another day. There were a few rain showers and beautiful clouds. Don left early and came back with a dozen Dunkin' Donuts, his very favorite breakfast food.

Jane and I took Mickey for a long walk up the hill and around an abandoned house, where I looked for and found my first sample of moss on the damp steps. There was heavy traffic as we tried to walk along street with walls and no sidewalks. Back down by the Paradise Island bridge was where all the native fruit, vegetable, and fish outdoor stalls were located. Jane dealt with "Esther" and bought bananas, tomatoes, peppers, and oranges. We found yellow tail at a fish stand and asked the man to fillet a couple for us. Jane made the mistake of praising his filleting job, and he asked for a tip. People were either really afraid of the poor dog, going out of their way to avoid her ("Beware of Dog" signs seem to be a security measure around houses), or they wanted us to give Mickey to them. She was different and nicer than any of the native mutts.

We went back to the boat with the groceries, and I examined my moss with a hand lens and made a tentative guess (without my guide books) as to its species. After lunch we all took off for the Botanical Garden (my request, of course). Same bus as yesterday, with a short walk up the hill in the opposite direction. The garden looked ancient but was an old quarry developed as a garden only twenty years ago. There were interesting plants and trees, and I even found some more moss, but it all seems to be the same variety. Nothing was labeled, but they say there are some 600 species of flowering trees and shrubs on the 18 acres. It was located near the humane society, and we saw cages of dogs and one lone donkey. The area was pleasingly cool and quite enjoyable on a hot day.

The garden bordered old Fort Charlotte, built in 1789 by Lord Dunmore, and named in honor of the wife of King George III. It never fired a shot in battle. The fort had a waterless moat, drawbridge, ramparts, and dungeons, all of which we investigated. There was a fine view of the western harbor and we climbed to a large grandstand, built twenty years ago for the Bahamas independence celebration and the Queen's visit. There had been a daily light show for tourists, but the operation had gone downhill since and was no longer used. We could see all the cruise ships in port, spilling their humanity into the shops on Bay Street, each to buy yet another souvenir t-shirt or a straw basket (made in China or some place other than the Bahamas).

It was early evening as we walked back to downtown, past the Bungee jumping, and took a bus to the Paradise Island bridge, where we walked up and over the high arch and down to the wonderland of hotels and gambling casinos. Fortified with two $10 rolls of quarters I played the 25 cent one arm bandits, and squandered the first roll with not much luck. I had not intended to use the second roll but, hey, that can be considered just the price of admission to this glitz and glitter world. I opened the second roll and dumped it into a large Styrofoam barrel cup. I found a "friendly" machine, which paid off a little the first time I used it, so I grabbed a stool and started dunking the quarters. How easily one could become addicted! Lights flashing, whistles sounding, machines paying off to the bell clanging, and excitement that equaled a fire engine on the way to a five alarm city fire, all creating a sense of urgency to keep slipping in the quarters or dollars or whatever you are playing, winning a dollar here, five dollars there, now fifty cents, all after sinking goodness knows how many quarters in between.

Then there was suddenly a loud dinging in my machine and the quarters started to flow – all hundred of them! Wow! This was getting to be fun. I kept thinking with that payback I should quit while I was ahead, but

with all the pay-offs I had no idea what dollar amount was in my cup. By feel it was heavier than the two original rolls, so I kept going, winning and losing in turn until finally the other three, having played out their quotas and lost it all, had gathered around me to watch. At last I could see the sun setting through the tinted windows and decided it was time for us to go – I really would rather see the sunset from the bridge than waste another dollar at this tourist game.

I took my cup of winnings to the redemption desk, for counting and exchange for green stuff. She handed me back $45.75! That paid back my original $20 and gave me $25.75 profit. Sounded good, until I remembered that folks were winning $40 at Bingo some nights back at our campground. Anyway, it was fun to live like the rich and famous for an hour or so, and I didn't feel guilty at all! And, like all phases of life, the trick is when to say NO or at least No More!

The hotel was having some kind of get-acquainted party, and folks were lining up for drinks and hors d' oeuvres so we just joined in. The rum punch and very spicy conch cakes held us over while we walked back across the high bridge, watching the afterglow of a beautiful sunset and all the lights of Nassau and the cruise ships in the harbor. Jane cooked the yellowtail, and we went to bed and read. The weather here had been fine all day, but the open sea could have been as wild as they predicted, and we knew the Captain had made a good choice to stay in harbor one more day. What's more, we were having a good time. The tourist scene in Nassau can be a wild adventure, too!

Saturday dawned clear and fairly calm,

with an east wind. After listening to the NET weather report, the Captain said it was a GO for today. Don and I walked up to the Texaco station to buy five gallons of bottled water. The Nassau water in our tanks was sanitary, but tasted terrible, and we needed drinking and coffee water. On the way back, I speeded up and walked down by the bridge to get another dozen Dunkin' Donuts to keep the Captain happy.

Paradise Island Bridge and Jane on deck

We threw off the lines at 9:15 and motored out of Nassau on the west end, passing under the arch bridge and past the huge cruise boats. Don's friend Sea Bob radioed a friendly call from his boat as we passed. On the radio we heard something about a cruise boat coming in, and when we were nearing the harbor entrance we could see the big white hulk of a boat on the horizon. It looked as if we could make it out the channel before it arrived but, to be on the safe side, Don decided to wait and turned into shallow water nearer the shore. It didn't take long from horizon to harbor for the giant. Amazing, how they can find a place to tie up among so many other boats in the narrow channel, but these ships come and go every day. As soon as it was clear of the channel, we went on out past the lighthouse and followed the buoys into deeper water toward our wild Eleutherian adventure, leaving the tourist scene behind.

Once on the high seas Don checked the wind and found that our course was directly into it. Sailing would take a long time tacking back and forth over the thirty-five some odd miles to our destination, so he decided it best to continue with the motor and leave the sailing for another day. The swells left over from the storm were fairly high, and it was an exciting trip with a 360 degree view of deep blue ocean and, soon, no land cluttered up the horizon. What a way to go! I was fascinated with the cloud formations, especially the wavelike narrow lines of clouds which looked for all the world like a G clef waiting for music to be written. Then there were little patches of cat paw prints. Don's guidance system, the Loran, was not picking up the coordinates so our course was by calculation with charts and compass. And this proved to be "right on" as we spotted the two part wreck, a landmark as we neared the tip of the Eleuthera Islands. Jane's large delicious sandwiches sure tasted good along the way.

The largest Eleuthera island is 90 miles long and only 2 to 3 miles wide, with rolling hills, lakes, steep cliffs and lovely beaches and woods, said to be reminiscent of Scotland. They were first settled in 1648, when a band of 100 people from England and Bermuda was shipwrecked on the reef. Under the governorship of Captain William Sayle, these people, who became known as the Eleutherian Adventurers, set up the first true democracy in the western world. The island is now known for its farms, fruit, corn, and cows.

At 3:15, after a six hour trip, as we motored into Royal Island harbor, storm clouds to the east were dumping rain, and we saw a beautiful full rainbow which was visible over the island for almost an hour. That weather never reached us and we enjoyed a lovely afternoon. We learned from the caretaker, who helped us pick up a mooring, that Royal Island (a small island at the top of the Eleutheras) was the site of a fishing lodge and facilities built in the 1920s for the children of a wealthy British family.

On the top of the hill, overlooking the harbor, are the remains of a grey stone lodge with many bedrooms and various outbuildings for communal gatherings and cooking facilities. There were docks, stone staircases, and terraces, and a steep cement road to the dock area and also a long winding cement road to the dock facilities on the northeast, more shallow side of the island. All was trashed and overgrown and much destroyed by hurricanes. Nevertheless, it was a lovely remote spot. Recently, a couple has been leasing this deserted island and trying to build a yacht club with moorings, a bar, and other facilities. The moorings are there, but the state has not given the permits to charge, and in the meantime the couple has met with

a recent misfortune when the wife had an arm crushed in a boat winch. The temporary caretaker was looking after the moorings, the chickens, and milking a small herd of goats. Some work had been started to reclaim the land, but there was a long ways to go.

In the meantime, we were enjoying free mooring in a beautiful secure and secluded harbor draped with a lovely rainbow. We took Mickey, and all went ashore in the little red dinghy and explored the ruins, marveled at what it must have been, and got acquainted with the caretaker and the goats. I was glorying in some very small moss growing on the steps, and wrapped bits in a Kleenex.

Jane and I explored the winding cement road to the other side of the island and found a beautiful view of the many-colored ocean, and a strange destroyed square dock area too shallow to be for anything but very small boats. In the distance, the waves were breaking on the reef. We later learned that much of the reef surrounding these islands has been destroyed by greedy local fishermen, who spray Clorox around the coral to flush out the lobsters. On the way back I found more samples from a moss-covered stonewall. Even without the lens it looked like "Barbula," with the tiny twisted peristome, the one moss which seems to be most prevalent (but not abundant) in the Florida Keys and Bahamas. Moss, in general, seems to be rare in these parts.

Back on the boat, we donned bathing suits and swam and snorkeled off the boat in beautifully clean water. The back of this secure snug harbor had large cement piers where native boats from nearby islands have tied up during hurricanes. A spaghetti supper with red clam sauce was a highlight and, although we had been sitting most of the day, we were tired just from constant muscle flexing as we bounded through the water. The sunset was a joy to behold, and the stars had never been so bright. I got up, several times during the night to poke my head out the porthole above my bed to see the reflection of the heavens and crescent moon on the still waters.

Sunday dawn arrived early or was proclaimed at the early hour of four a.m., by the roosters on the island, rather sweet and rustic music for Sunday morning, the like of which I really haven't been aware of since long ago when a certain Don Ruth kept chickens in the old spotting shack up behind the Rowe library. He never knew his roosters crowed, because from his house under the hill he never heard them while their voices carried sharply across the village and right up Middletown Hill!

Having gone to bed so early we were up at sunrise, a beautiful calm day. Don and I took Mickey ashore and walked the road to the far side enjoying tropical smells of blossomed trees and flushing a flock of white-crowned pigeons along the way. I gathered more moss on the old wall, finally taking a small rock covered with fruiting stems. The caretaker checked by all the boats to see if anyone had scraps for the chickens. I offered the grapefruit peels for the goats, and they were gladly accepted.

We bid farewell and left at 10:30, hoping someday to have the good luck to return to this lovely snug harbor, and hoping also that development would not spoil its appeal. Out past the rocks at the entrance we found a perfectly flat sea, like a mirror reflecting the clear blue sky. How many moods the sea had shown us already. We motored an hour or so across to Spanish Wells on St. George's Cay, a self-sufficient fishing community of people who claim direct descendance from the Eleutherian Adventurers, and also from the Loyalists who sought refuge at the end of the American Revolution. The Spanish, back in the 1600s, said the wells here had the sweetest water in the Bahamas, thus the name. Few people leave this community, and few newcomers join them. The people are very religious and, on Sundays, they are either at church or staying quietly at home.

We were told to contact Edsel Roberts (code name Dolphin) for a mooring in the channel. He told us on the radio to pick up a mooring and he would see us in the evening. Don skillfully maneuvered the narrow channel full of fishing boats and through town to the farther side, where we picked up a mooring with a large orange ball, hoping it was Edsel's. He seemed to be a jack of all trades, with moorings, fishing trips, snorkeling, and as a local pilot for boats going through the reefs on the outside. From the radio we learned he was a busy man and in person he rushed by in the early evening, all dressed up standing in his dinghy, to collect our fee. He stayed long enough to say he was Welch and on his way to church.

Once safely moored, we all climbed down in the dinghy and went ashore to explore Spanish Wells and find a restaurant for lunch. We walked along Main Street, finding everything closed and quiet. At the far end of the village we saw a large boat in dock, and Jack recognized the New Shoreham II, a small tour boat of the American-Canadian

Caribbean Line that we had toured while it was in Marathon a couple of years ago. It is unusual because it has a retractable pilot's cabin and was designed to go through the Erie Canal. The boat had planned to sail that morning, but they were waiting for the steward to come back with some local fish. The dock restaurant was closed and we wandered up over the hill in search of whatever there might be, hopefully, food. We suddenly encountered traffic and cars full of well-dressed people and we judged that church had just let out. Everyone on the island must have been there!

After walking a good distance, we finally caught someone getting out of their car and asked for a restaurant, and they directed us to "The Generation Gap," a local teenage hangout that happened to be open on Sunday. We were the only ones there and had a good lunch, with lots of very sweet tea. With a hankering for chocolate we decided on a hot fudge sundae, which came with good home-made ice cream but lumpy cold chocolate. We got a little local information from the waitress, who had not been far from the island in her young life.

The most notable event in recent history had been the destruction from Hurricane Andrew in September, 1992. Across the street had been the well known Spanish Wells Beach Resort, a motel-like resort facing a beautiful crescent beach with shallow water going far, far out. We crossed the street and toured the totally devastated buildings and it was incredible to see the damage well beyond repair. Jack had gone ahead and we spotted him far out on the beach, in water hardly up to his waist.

Walking back the loop to the boat, Jane and I explored an old cemetery with the same family names repeated, over and over, through a long span of years. Somehow, as we came around the corner to where we left the dinghy, the Snowbird seemed to be missing. More or less an optical illusion but it gave us a start. We investigated a house with a bakery sign on the open door, but knocking got no response. Spanish Wellsians just don't do business on Sunday. A doctored up canned stew from the ship's storehouse, and various side dishes, made a welcome meal as the sun put on a spectacular display behind the other boat masts.

The night was not such a good one. We were moored across from the refrigerator of the fish packing building. It was noisy all night and we were awake and up early. Once again, the Captain took the dog and me for our morning walk, and we did the loop, again dodging the far too many cars and motor bikes for so small an island (but the cars were more understandable when later we learned that, with a short ferry crossing to the main island of Eleuthera, one could drive the ninety mile length of the island). On our return we checked the bakery, for there was a strong smell of baking bread, but again no luck. The event of the morning was watching the men from the outlying communities come into Spanish Wells for work, riding in small boats loaded with twenty or more men crowded together, with the rim of the boat riding at water level.

Today would be a day to remember! We motored the short distance across to Current Cut, timed to arrive at this tricky narrow channel between Eleuthera and Current Islands at slack tide, about ten-thirty. When running, the current can be as high as 4 to 6 knots or more depending on the wind. The seas were very calm in crossing, not glass like yesterday but very smooth and shallow, and we could make out starfish on the bottom. We found the Cut quite easily but once entering it everyone seemed a bit tense, for we knew there was some precise navigating around coral rocks and shallow sand.

There was a road on the left hand shore, and a car driving along stopped and watched us. It seemed rather ominous. Was he waiting to watch us go aground? Don had passed through here once before but in the opposite direction, which is just as precise but perhaps a little easier to judge. The charts say something like stay in the channel until passing a sunken rock (obstacles in the Bahamas have no markers!), then swing right and hug the large rock outcrop and go, carefully, through shallow water along the shore for some distance before heading out to sea. The chart neglects to warn one to HUG the north shore when going through the Cut!

The Captain was doing nicely, and all seemed to be going well past the local mailboat dock. But, perhaps it was there that things began to go wrong. Perhaps the Captain was unconsciously veering away from the dock, and concentrating on turning by the big outcrop looming in the western center of the cut. Perhaps one of us distracted him with a comment or question. Who knows how these things happen? Suddenly instead of 20 feet, the depth sounder registered three feet, and before a split second decision could be made to slow speed and turn back into the deeper channel… wham! We hit with enough momentum to wedge us on the coral for sure.

After several choice words, the Captain took stock of the situation and churned us this way and that, forward and back but nothing worked – so close to the deep water and yet so far! The good news was that it would be a rising tide in a few hours and there was nothing to do but wait it out. We were listing to starboard slightly, but not bad. Jane got out the snorkel equipment and surveyed the area reporting back on the whereabouts of the deeper channels, but they were obvious by the color of the water once we stood up and looked around.

After a while a small boat came along side and a young man told us he was sorry he couldn't help us as he was "going to sea," but he would tell his father and someone would come and help us when the time was right. Thus we had nothing to do but relax (although I doubt that the Captain did), and wait and watch the natives unload boxes of bananas at the dock. Eventually the mailboat, called Current Pride, docked and was being loaded with the produce. It was a good-sized boat, and so was the big fishing boat that came through in the opposite direction. The channel was wide enough and deep enough, you just had to stay in the channel! In the midst of things, a big sailboat approached the Cut and madly radioed to "the boat in the middle of the Cut" to inquire why we were there and what they should do. Don explained and gave the one important piece of advice not on the charts, "HUG the left shore!" and the boat sailed on through with no trouble.

We looked at the colorful fish around the boat, and watched as the tide finally changed and rushed under the boat in the opposite direction. About one-thirty, a man came by in a boat and advised putting out an anchor to keep us from being carried in the wrong direction when the current became stronger. With doom and gloom he talked of ten knots and how other boats had been in trouble here. Don took the anchor out in the dinghy and dropped it back toward the entrance although he questioned the wisdom of this as it might hinder us once we were loose. But the locals must know...

Then the Captain had an idea, and asked the man to "give us some waves" that would raise our boat up while he revved the engine and tried to get us loose and headed back toward the channel. Each wave helped a little, and after the third or forth "go by" and with the rising tide we suddenly came loose and, just as Don suspected, quickly winching in the anchor was no small task. It was nip and tuck, with Jane and Jack both pulling furiously with much shouting by all. The most important thing was to get off the rocks, and the anchor was almost up when the Captain yelled, "Let it go," a big loss with heavy chain and all, but with the rushing tide we would have gone back on the rocks in a split second if it took any longer. Jane yelled for a fender to mark the anchor rope before letting go the last of the line. Somehow, I

was able to race forward with one, and Jane tied the fastest bowline knot she had ever done and let it go, hoping it would serve to save the anchor. In the same instant, Don was gunning us out of the small channel and into the main stream, heading back to the entrance where we had come in. We all took a deep breath and let out a collective sigh of relief! And, looking back, we could see the floating fender marking the anchor line.

Jane quickly anchored (they carry three anchors) the boat in the lea of the island, and Don prepared the dinghy (It's old, patched and needs air before each use – people don't steal that kind, Don says!) for the trip back through this now roaring current to pull up and retrieve the lost anchor. To me this

Captain Don goes to retrieve the anchor

seemed like a daring venture, and I had visions of his being swamped and having to swim for his life. (A not-very-good swimmer thinks this way!) My only advice was the life vest I handed him. For my peace of mind or his, I wasn't sure, but he tied on the vest and set off – but it still seemed like too daring a rescue. There were three sets of eyes watching as he rounded the comer out of our sight, and not much conversation while we waited, and waited and watched, as the current poured faster and stronger through the narrow cut. It was some relief to see, through binoculars, that there were some other small boats in the area that might come to his rescue if anything drastic happened, but they didn't seem to be offering any help beforehand. A whoop went up when we finally spotted the tiny red dinghy come into sight, fighting its way against the current but making slow progress in our direction. Mission accomplished, Don had retrieved the anchor. We were all of one mind, "Let's go back and spend the night at Royal Island."

A couple of hours later, Jane picked up our old mooring and we were snug back in that lovely harbor. Our wish to return had come true much sooner than expected, but we hadn't anticipated the circumstances creating our good fortune! The second try for "Current Cut" could wait for another day. Don and Jane took the dinghy and went snorkeling in the far comer of the harbor, Jack joined them on a trip along the shore, and I had a good swim off the back of the boat safely within reach of the ladder. Just before sunset, Don and I and Mickey went ashore for a brisk walk by another old road along the shore and, coming to a wall, we assumed it surrounded the main grounds and we

tried to imagine just what this estate looked like in its heyday. The sun was setting with beautiful colors as the dinghy headed back to Snowbird. After well-deserved "sundowners," Jane's concoction of spam and eggs, peppers, onions, and potatoes tasted gourmet to us all, especially when we suddenly realized we hadn't had any lunch!

It had been quite a day! I suddenly had more understanding of the sea, and sympathy and feeling for those early sailors, like the Eleutherian Adventurers, shipwrecked on uncharted reefs. Our lights were out early in all three cabins. Fortunately, our exciting and scary day had had a happy ending, with no more harm done than the creation of a good "remember when" story for future years and an Eleutherian EXPERIENCE to be duly recorded in the ship's log.

I woke up several times during the night, not because I was sleeping poorly but because the moon was shining in on me through the open hatch. I knew there was a beautiful sight to be seen by standing up in the bunk and looking around outside at the water reflecting, in perfect stillness, the stars, the moon, and the trees on shore. By sleeping, what could one dream that was more lovely than this?

The roosters crowed before dawn again, but we were in no hurry to arise. The slack tide at Current Cut would be an hour later today and we needn't get there too soon. But we had our coffee with the sunrise, and admired another perfect day with a fresh breeze that predicted good sailing. Captain Don took his two charges (Mickey and me) to shore for our morning walk, and we went down the old cement road to the far side of the island, where I admired that special sweeping view once again. If I had been building on this island, I would have put the lodge on that side of the hill. Because of the vastness of shallow water in the foreground there seemed to be a wider horizon, the blue-green color of the water more intense. Even leaving Royal Harbor for the second time we still hoped to return, but not for the same reason as yesterday!

The pass through Current Cut (hugging the north shore!) was a breeze, with only a few anxious moments going over the known shallow water along the eastern shore. Turning out to sea, it became progressively deeper until we were over the "tongue of the ocean," where the water is said to be 1,000 fathoms deep. Another sigh of relief as we turned southeast, aimed for Governor's Harbor, far down the shore of the Island of Eleuthera. The sun was bright, the wind was perfect and the sails were soon hoisted and the motor silenced. We were sailing at last; fast, smooth and exciting, and the Captain let me take the wheel for the first hour or so. This was really living! Jack and Don rigged some fish lines to troll behind the boat, but no disappointment was expressed when there were no fish to clean. I watched the ever changing fair weather clouds, we all did some reading, and generally relaxed and enjoyed a perfect day on beautiful Bahamian seas.

It was late afternoon by the time we dropped the sails and the anchor in the large open anchorage at Governor's Harbor. Don,

Nan at the wheel

Jane, Mickey, and I went ashore in the little red dinghy. We were anchored a long way out and it took a while to reach the shore near the center of town. We planned to look the place over, walk the dog, and hopefully find a good restaurant for dinner this evening, to give Jane a break from galley duty. The few stores were closed by this time, so we walked up the hill in the direction of a restaurant sign.

Don and Jane stopped to talk with someone and I went on up to check out the restaurant, which proved to be nearly a mile away over the top of a steep hill. Yes, they would be open at seven, but it was not very nice and I was sure we wouldn't want to walk that far before and after dinner. There were some expensive homes on the hill, with views overlooking the harbor. And, farther down on the beach on the back side, was reported to be a busy Club Med. Returning, I found another advertised restaurant, but they seemed to have no intention of serving dinner. Well, we would find something. The town seemed quite prosperous, with one stop light at the bottom of the hill, a grocery and liquor store and several gift shops. The police were dressed to the hilt like those in Bermuda.

Don took Mickey back to the boat and picked up Jack. In the meantime, Jane and I walked around the harbor to an area called Cupid's Cay, where it is said the Eleutherian Adventurers (early settlers) had

Don and Mickey in the red dinghy

their first headquarters in 1649. Some of the remaining buildings date back two centuries. We admired an old stone Catholic Church, which had a carillon playing lovely chimes. It was celebrating its hundred year history. Further on was a big old white wooden Methodist Church in very good condition, in contrast to some of the local abandoned buildings. We walked around the harbor, passing a couple of local restaurants but they didn't look worth investigating. Meeting Don and Jack back at the landing place, we almost decided to go back to the boat for dinner, but Jack suggested we make one more inquiry at the police station.

The Harbor Hotel, they said, one of those Jane and I had ignored on our walk. We had been enjoying a lovely sunset as we made these decisions, but it was dark by the time we headed for the restaurant. (There is very little twilight this far south.) Jane and Jack walked, and I went in the dinghy to show Don where to go. Fortunately there was some beach and we dragged the dinghy up on shore in time to join the others and walk on to the restaurant. It looked dingy,

but inside there were several full tables. The friendly waitress suggested the local rum drink, Goombay Smash, followed by conch chowder, fried grouper, rice and salad – an Eleutherian adventure in eating!

The moon was out among some clouds as we walked back along the dark road to the dinghy. I still regret that we did not go into the Methodist Church on the way back. The doors were open, showing a well lighted lovely old white church decorated with vases of red roses, and the choir was in rehearsal. I'm sure they would have welcomed an audience. It was a slow dinghy ride back to the boat with four of us, but we were enjoying the moon and stars. Just as we had all safely climbed back aboard Snowbird, a rain cloud scudded across the sky, and the heavens opened up. It poured heavily as we scrambled to pull down the flaps on the cockpit canvas. What timing!

After the rain, the sky brightened, and I again rose up several times during the night to poke my head up through the hatch to observe another lovely tranquil scene. What seemed like dozens of roosters crowed, well before the dawn. After breakfast Don and I took the dog ashore on Cupid's Cay dock and walked down past the hotel where we had dined last night. It still wasn't a place you would choose in the daylight. Later we all went ashore to do some shopping, walking, and sight seeing. I spent time trying to find the bakery, and after several inquires walked down a few streets and just followed my nose. I bought some fresh bread and some honey dipped donuts for the Captain. We agreed they were a much meatier donut than the Dunkin' variety. With bags of groceries Don and Jack went back to Snowbird, and

A Wild Eleutherian Adventure

Beautiful Bahamian Seas

Jane and I went to see the inside of the old stone church and then looked over the old gravestones in the churchyard. I found some orb weaver spiders and we spent time looking at their intricate web patterns. Lost in time we looked up, and Don was cooling his heels at the dinghy on shore wondering where we had disappeared. Jane ran through the field to buy ice at the last minute, and I ran ahead with our apologies to the Captain.

We were soon under way, and had a beautiful sail on down parallel to the long island of Eleuthera to a navigation point called "The Fix." I had fun watching the clouds again and there was a huge ring around the sun. Old sailors could have read the sky and told just what this would bring in the way of weather. Again, with the Loran not working, the Captain had to guesstimate the location of the Fix, and line up landmarks with an offshore obelisk marker (unusual in the Bahamas) on a sandbar a few miles away. This would give us a bearing on the Davis Channel going to Cape Eleuthera and our destination, called Powell Point.

The channel is surrounded with ever changing sand bars, and the depth marker went down from 3 feet to 2 feet to aground three times in spite of the crew watching the color of the water. But, slowly aground on sand is no big problem and we were soon free each time. Clouds made patches of water look deeper blue than the depth would warrant, and it took all four of us on the lookout to re-find the main channel. Definitely not the place to cruise at night.

Continual trouble with the Loran convinced the Captain and mate it was time to purchase the newest navigating technology (GPS), based on precise satellite signals. Shifting sand bars, however, would still be a menace.

Once around Powell Point, the water was deep and the path was direct into the Cape Eleuthera Marina, a small harbor with docks. Once the lines were secured, Mickey was in a hurry and made a jump for the dock. Her front feet landed but her back ones didn't, and as I was right beside her, I grabbed her harness and kept her from falling into the water until Don could reach her from the dock. She loves the water but that just wasn't the place to go swimming. Later leg problems showed she may have been injured in this impulsive leap.

Cape Eleuthera has quite a story, only a portion of which we learned. It was known as the "nicest resort in the Bahamas" until abandoned about thirteen years ago. There are at least fifty double cottages scattered through the palm trees, a swimming pool and large cabana, restaurants, club houses, four or five double tennis courts with the rotting nets still in place, an eighteen hole golf course, airport, beach cabanas, trails, and the marina – all except the marina are trashed, overgrown and very, very sad. A large sign says, "Coming Soon, Hyatt Regency Hotel," and there are drawings on how the area will be restored. It's owned now by an organization called "Landquest," and they have one man who comes in daily to take care of the marina where you can get fuel and water. It is also the base for the US supply boat which services the US Submarine Fleet at some point out in the ocean. There is one occupied condo complex and a few private houses near the marina and a road leading here from the rest of Eleuthera, but all else is abandoned. What a shame!

But what a place to explore. We walked a little near the marina and watched a lovely sunset from the shore before Jane whipped up a pork chop (Bahamian special) dinner, complete with sauerkraut and applesauce. A near full moon rose over the marina and I went for a moonlight walk along the elaborate dock complex. Perhaps it was the great abundance of those little biting gnats that closed this resort. They were awful, and the evening was very still. Jane put up the mosquito netting on my hatch, a welcome relief, but it prevented me from bobbing my head out during the night to look at the scenery.

This was such a nice spot, and there was so much to explore, that we were all glad to settle in for another day. I took my morning walk along the road to the eastern shore, where there were the remains of many rustic beach cabanas and a tiki bar and barbecue area. The road crossed a channel from the harbor, and wound back through the trees to the marina. Some of the cottages were along this road, but so overgrown that they could not be reached through the brush. Upon returning, the others were ready for a hike, and together we explored some of the cottages surrounding the old pool full of ugly green water. Bougainvillea, hibiscus, orchid trees, and various other flowers blossomed in profusion among the jungle of overgrown lawns.

At one point I made a detour down a road that we thought led to the golf course. It was overgrown but passable, and I found some moss growing in the moist area under the trees. Passing an abandoned and trashed golf cart, I knew I was somewhere near the course, and came out to a narrow fairway covered with low brush and weedy flowers and vines. If I had not known it had been a golf course there certainly were no clues, except the cart, and even the sand traps were covered with vines. I crawled through the brush under larger trees and made out the second fairway. I wanted to follow this to the end, but there was the feeling of being in a maze, and I thought I'd best retrace my steps while I could still find them. I did try to bushwhack through the woods and perhaps join the others on the road, but the woods proved impassable. At this point, I heard someone yelling something and repeating the same thing not too far away. I thought perhaps it was Jack, but thought it best not to answer in case it wasn't. Not being a golfer I hadn't recognized his attempt at humor shouting "Fore."

Once back on the road there was no sign of anyone, and I walked up and down several roads in what was getting to be very hot sun. I eventually went out to the beach, and kept following small paths and a long trail down through the cool Australian pines to another harbor for anchoring. Although from different directions, we all got back about the same time ready to relax and cool off. I took a pillow and found a shady spot on shore under a coconut palm to read *Natural History of the Senses*, by Diane Ackerman. While reading her chapter on hearing, I was quite aware of and enjoying the wind singing in the sail lines of the several boats in dock. Later, Jane delivered me a delicious sandwich and drink. What service!!

In the afternoon we all went out to the beach to swim and snorkel. Jane is a fish and loves to snorkel and swims all over the place – Don, too. Jack tried it and was enthusiastically trying to convince me to join in. After tangling in the flippers and choking on the mouthpiece, I had had enough! The thing that fascinated them was a huge hole that had been excavated out of the ocean, probably for fill for roads. It was eerie, standing on the edge and looking down into the deep blue hole, and I didn't get too near, for it seemed as if some mysterious force would pull you right to the bottom. I swam and played in the shallow water, and looked for coral and strange shells on the shore. What a beautiful spot and a glorious day. On our return there was a huge 100 foot French sailboat in the harbor, and we all had to do some boat gawking.

In the early evening I took a walk out around the marina to the tip of Powell Point, where I could see the obelisk a long way off and not close to shore, as it had seemed when we came in. On a little sandy beach I looked at the strange tracks of many tiny sea creatures that had been walking there. So much to observe, so much new to learn to keep life interesting wherever you go! A big round moon looked down on us as Jane served hot dogs and beans and a bowl of chocolate pudding for dinner. We retired early, having had a strenuous day of exploration and exercise. The pesky little gnats ate us alive and there wasn't a breath of air, but who could complain in such a beautiful place! Poor old Mickey was not doing well today and seemed unable to walk very far, although her heart had been set on chasing sticks in the waves.

In spite of the bugs it was sad to leave this spot, for there was lots more exploring to do, but we were headed for Norman's Cay in the Exuma Islands, which was a favorite on our sailing trip two years ago. I took a final walk around the old tennis courts and, in places, had to retrace my steps because of the overgrowth. Don moved the boat to the fresh water dock and the caretaker started the pumps. Mickey had a short walk, then sort of collapsed, and did not seem anxious to get back on the boat, so they left her in the shade while getting the water. All got aboard, the lines were thrown off, and the Captain was turning the boat toward the sea when someone remembered Mickey! She was still sleeping quietly in the shade, unaware that we were leaving her behind.

We had a perfect sail for most of the day, covering some thirty odd miles. The only wildlife was a tropicbird with a long graceful tail sitting on the water, and a frigate bird flying high. Once in a while, a flying fish would make a long fast pass across the water. Around the horizon in the distance, clouds were building higher and higher, beautiful to look at but threatening thunder showers with the coming front. With Norman's Cay in sight, we were searching for the landmarks to steer by when I noticed how black the bottom of the largest cloud had become, poised just to the south of Norman's. Looking closely, I spotted a dark line hanging down, and with binoculars we could make out the spiral swirling of winds that had the potential of reaching the water and becoming a dangerous water spout. What if it came in our direction? How do you race around something like that, now that we were coming into more shallow water with sand bars and coral heads? Never mind the water spout; it certainly looked

as if we were running into a huge rain and thunder shower! How could we ever find the rocky entrance to Norman's Cay in a blur of rain?

What is there about this place? This is where we got caught out in the dinghy in a storm the last time we were here! Weather changes very quickly. The spout lengthened and shortened several times and to our great relief finally disappeared, but the threatening black cloud remained. Finally approaching the coast, we sailed up and down a couple of times and began to wonder if we had the wrong Cay. Somehow, in veering away from the storm, we had overshot the entrance to the north. The Captain turned south, and we followed the shore until landmarks lined up properly and the boats in the harbor came into view as the charts described. Then we sailed on in and found an anchorage among the other boats, numbering about twenty-five by nightfall. By this time the dark cloud had blown away from us and the sun was bright and warm, and we took the dinghy in to shore so everyone could have a short walk. A lovely sunset was as red as the clam sauce on our good spaghetti dinner back on Snowbird. It was the night of the full moon and we all slept well, with the boat gently rocking.

A pancake breakfast gave us a good start for Saturday. We all went ashore and I first took a walk up the road, but when I could hear the diesel generators near the airport I was leery, remembering our brush with the local authorities (for what reason they never would explain) in that neighborhood on the last trip. Norman's Cay had been a resort back in the seventies until the druggies took

Captain Don climbing the mast

around the old dock and Jack insisted that I try the snorkel equipment again, which I did, walking around looking at various colored fish rather than swimming (I am a poor swimmer, side stroke on one side). I'm sure that if there was something spectacular to see I would give it my all, but in the meantime I am not too comfortable with the "face in the water, mouth full of rubber sort of thing." Jane came back all excited about seeing a good-sized barracuda.

Returning to Snowbird we were ready for Jane's big tasty sandwiches, had naps, and read. Later in the afternoon we again climbed down into the dinghy, and went across the harbor a long way to the beach on the southeastern side, on land called Wax Cay. The water was shallow and we saw several rays. Nearer the shore there was another dark spot, and as we neared we could make out the outline of a shark about six feet long, and we chased him a bit to get a closer look. The tail came out of the water and he swished around, then swam off. In the clear and shallow water we could keep track of him for some time. We later identified him as a Black Tip Shark. How exciting!

We landed the boat and all went looking for shells and whatever along a beautiful sandy beach. I climbed the rocky hill and was rewarded with a gorgeous overall view of the whole area. What a paradise! Jane found a pink angel wing shell and we all collected several sand dollars. The water was filled with baby queen conchs of all sizes. Jane went snorkeling, Don walked down along the beach, Jack went swimming and walked out on the long sand bar, while I investigated this and that and finally climbed the rocks again, finding some tree snails but not a bit

it over. When the U. S. authorities came in, the area was demolished and a drug plane was shot down and still remains, decaying in the bay, creating an interesting artificial reef for the fish and marine growths. Planes still come and go at the airport and I presumed something was still being protected. We all had a lovely morning at the beach, which is especially nice here. Jane went snorkeling all of moss. Don came back up along the heights and we looked at a tree with hard fruit that we both knew we had seen on the last trip at the National Park at Warderick Wells (we planned to go there tomorrow), where they have a lot of the trees with identifying tags. Later we remembered this tree as the Seven Year Apple.

It was treacherous coming down off the embankment, for it was hard sharp rock that sometimes broke off with your step. I climbed back down and went back to the dinghy for the camera, and climbed the hill again to record the spectacular view. By this time I was very hot as the sun was strong, so I found a cool spot under the Australian pines and sat until the others were ready to call it a day. It had been a memorable day all around, and we settled in for a sundowner and dinner glorified with another prize sunset.

The wind came up during the night and, by Sunday morning, the boats were swinging with the tide and the wind. We eagerly listened to the NET weather and it did not sound good. There was a front coming through. The anchorage at Warderick Wells is popular, and now by reservation only on the morning of entry. If nothing is available there are a few moorings outside, but they are poor holding in rough weather. It seemed best to stay put once again. Another boat that did go out reported on the radio that they made it but it was "no picnic."

The wind increased, and the more we listened to reports the more we wondered if we would even make Nassau by Wednesday, as planned. How would we notify the airline and friends meeting us in Marathon? Oh well, why worry now?

Captain Don had some communication with our neighbor, his old friend, Sea Bob. The neighbor on the other side was a Canadian boat called Maskoka with an older couple, very nervous sailors always fussing with their anchors and lines. Later on shore I had a walk and investigated the ruined houses while Don and Jane talked with some folks from the island, who told them that up at the other end there are some vacation homes and one man has his airplane in the big hanger at the airport. People come and go by plane rather than by sea. They didn't learn if they still keep a police force on the island, but I guess it's not as spooky as I imagined. An osprey usually sat on the radio tower, and once in a while we were conscious of its call and could see it flying over the harbor in search of fish.

Because of the rough water we spent the afternoon on the boat, reading and talking and listening to the marine call radio. And that's where all the action was! A fishing boat called in for help for another boat, Blue Streaker, reported to have three aboard, had lost the use of its motor and had no radio. The stranded man's name was Basil. The fishing boat was low on gas and had to get his catch home to the refrigerator, so he couldn't help. We monitored the communication with BASRA (Bahamas Air-Sea Rescue Association). They do not come out unless the boat is sinking or there is a matter of life and death. So, they asked if Basil wanted to notify someone at home to vouch for a commercial rescue. The word came back, "yes," and the name of the man's father was radioed. The next communication was most interesting and Basil learned the awful truth on how people feel about him!

BASRA reported that they contacted a woman who answered at the father's home and she said, "As far as we are concerned, Basil can stay there for all we care!" So, if no one would vouch for paying for the rescue, Basil would have to sink or swim. That gave us much food for thought and humorous speculation for most of the afternoon! Basil was anchored off Beacon Cay at the top of the Exumas.

I walked when Don took Mickey to shore, and with the wind it was a splashy wet ride back to Snowbird. One of the attractions of the day was watching two windsurfers from one of the boats. Wow! They would zip across the harbor, turn on a dime just before the rocks, and whiz back again. Sure looked like fun! Don opened the coconut we had found at Cape Eleuthera and we made pina coladas out of the milk which was clear instead of milk, and we ate raw coconut for hors d'oeuvres. Jane made mac and cheese with Vidalia onion sauce for dinner. By night there were twenty-nine boats holed up in Norman's Cay. It was a windy night and, for the first time, I crawled out of the front bunk and slept in the more stable galley as the boat was rocking from bow to stern instead of sideways. Captain Don was up a good bit of the night checking on the anchors, which seemed to be holding well, and our relation to other boats did not change.

Monday dawned a sunny but very windy day, so much so that I refused the dinghy ride to shore with Don and Mickey. The wind was reported to be 28 knots. Maskoka was still fussing with anchor lines, but was talking on the radio about moving to another harbor. A poor idea for today!

We again spent much time listening to the radio reports and reading. In the afternoon, an odd-looking boat with reefed sails came sailing all around the harbor, close to other boats, rocks, and over very shallow places. We at first thought they were in trouble and looking for a place to anchor, but finally assumed that they had a special boat and were excellent sailors, just having fun in the wind and showing off their skill, as agile as the windsurfers. They passed close to us and all three crew members waved and smiled.

Much later that day as the seas became rougher another boat called for help. It was a Frenchman, who spoke little English and finally had to say "May Day" to get attention. With the help of a French Canadian boat in our harbor as translator, he told BASRA about what turned out to be Basil, still marooned at Beacon Cay and looking for help. When the message was finally understood, BASRA told the helpful Frenchman in so many words to forget Basil and certainly not to risk his own boat. The poor Frenchman thought he was still being misunderstood and repeated the problem. He didn't understand how they could ignore a call for help but BASRA, it seemed, had no mercy! Later still, someone from the neighboring cay said they would go out and check Basil, "in the morning if the seas were calmer." And so the saga continued and poor Scoundrel Basil in Blue Streaker was still up a creek without a paddle. It must have been pretty scary by this time!

Don and Jane had a wet ride to shore with Mickey. I hated to be chicken again but decided to stay behind, not wanting to risk the possibility of having to test my fragile swimming technique in these winds and waves! It was another uneasy night, and sometime along we were all up observing the weather and realized that Maskoka had pulled anchors and was moving precariously among the boats. They looked to be in trouble in the high wind, trying to make their anchors hold in a new place. Both the man and woman were on deck. What could be their problem, as the anchors seemed to be holding in the previous location? Now they seemed to be in a worse predicament. Finally I went back to bed, too tired to watch their antics any longer, but bracing for the jolt when they were blown into us.

At the first look around Tuesday morning we didn't see Maskoka, and then someone spotted her aground and tipped badly way off in the shallow water. How did they get there? Must be they roamed around during the night trying to find an anchorage, and went aground. Strange sailors! There was an early call from Sea Bob, who offered to go with Don to help Maskoka put out an anchor so they wouldn't be blown further on the sand when the tide changed. When the men got there the couple was asleep and seemingly unconcerned, just waiting for high tide to float then off. Sea Bob persuaded them they must put out anchors. Another boat joined the effort and between them they got the anchors set, but the men were never sure just how Maskoka felt about the whole thing – maybe as dubious about anchors as Captain Don at Current Cut. They did learn that the man had been in the water for some time last night, trying to untangle his lines. Maybe the men should have minded their own business, but that was hard to do when you saw a boat aground and half tipped over in the wind. Too much help for Maskoka and not any for Basil!

We listened to the NET weather and decided today was the day to make the dash back to Nassau, as another front was coming and the next window might not be until Thursday or Friday. In boating you are at the mercy of the weather, and deadlines or plane reservations are incidental. Our trip to Warderick Wells as planned would have to await another time. Quite early, our lines were pulled, and Captain Don took us nicely out of Norman's Cay, past the rocks at the west entrance and along the more than four mile sandbar until a small post in the water signaled it was OK to turn north and set the Loran (which was working this morning) on Porgee Rock at the entrance of Nassau Harbor. We motored with the sails unfurled and flew like the wind up, over, around, and down the ten foot swells and white caps coming at us from the starboard side. An exciting day to be on the water. We wondered how Basil was enjoying it, for no small boat would venture out to check him in the high winds today!

We got into Nassau by 2:30, but it took a turn around in the very strong tide and wind to locate and get into the slip in the east docks at Nassau Yacht Haven. The dockmaster came out to grab the lines so Mate Jane was spared, fortunately, for the tide was low and the dock was very high. Before any of us could get off, Jack tied a fancy rope handle on a pole to make something to grab on to while we hoisted ourselves up to the dock. Jane and I walked to the grocery store. We had planned to go out for dinner, but everyone was tired and decided it would be more relaxing to eat in. A fine steak dinner ended the day.

Wednesday was a nice day, and we took

Don and Jane on the Queen's Staircase

66 stairs, one for each year of the reign of Queen Victoria, and an artificial waterfalls alongside covered with real moss growing on the rocks. At the top of the hill we looked over the ship-shaped old Fort Fincastle, built in 1793 and then took the elevator up the 126 foot water tower to get the most fantastic view yet of the whole of Nassau, harbor and surrounding ocean. We came back and found Jack well steeped in interesting local history, and we hated to inform him he had missed two of the best attractions in Nassau. We took the bus back to the Yacht Haven and settled in for the evening, with the most gorgeous sunset yet as backdrop.

Our plane reservations were early on Thursday morning and we said our good-byes and were in the taxi by 7:30 on the way to the airport. The clouds were black over the ocean and we ran into a lot of gusty wind. Our taxi driver informed us that on the night of the gale force winds in Nassau Harbor, the weather front had spawned an unusual tornado in the neighboring Berry Islands, destroying many homes.

The buffeted small plane rides back to Miami and Marathon were no fun at all, but we had such happy memories of our sailing trip with Don and Jane Ruth that those few minutes in the air were soon forgotten. Come to think of it, don't you wonder whatever happened to Basil? If you should sail off on a wild Eleutherian adventure, take time to check out Beacon Cay in the Exumas and see if Basil still needs help! He may just have learned his lesson by that time.   **4–5/94**

off by bus for downtown and had lunch at a garden restaurant, which was quaint until a quick downpour came through the open roof terracing. We moved inside and enjoyed a native fish meal. Later, we walked on the upper street away from the tourist crowd and decided to stop at the Nassau Historical Society. The nice lady told us the Queen's Staircase was just up the hill, so we left Jack in the museum and Don, Jane, and I walked up the hill. The long narrow cut in the coral was overhung with trees, and at the end was a staircase of

D-Day Revisited

Do you remember where you were fifty years ago when the momentous events of D-Day, June 6, 1944, were announced to the world? Were you aware that the greatest amphibious assault of recorded history was taking place? Do you remember it now in any detail? Unfortunately for me, I remember the news of the Pearl Harbor attack in 1941 vividly, but anything concerning D-Day has gone from my mind. I recently found my old diary (with scanty entries) and it places me giving the Gettysburg Address at the Charlemont Memorial Day observance on the 30th of May, and on the stage of the Charlemont town hall on June 9th graduating from Charlemont Elementary School Eighth Grade, but June 6th is a blank. And there is no mention of war. From the summer entries of 1944, it seems to have been a glorious time for a young teenager in Rowe – lots of young people, hikes, picnics, swimming, social gatherings for meals, cards, games, sing-alongs – but no mention or concern for the history-making events taking place in Europe.

Soldiers were far from my thoughts back then. But there was one soldier who has always remained in my memory. I was ten years old when he was drafted in early 1941. He boarded in Charlemont with our winter neighbors, the Gilberts, whose daughter was a pal of mine and we spent much time playing at each other's houses. The young man's name was Thomas Neary, Jr. He probably had been specially good to us little kids, finding us a piece of cardboard when we wanted to slide on the back hill or fixing our roller skates when we had a problem, for I can remember being at a gathering the night he left for service and recalling it as a sad emotional experience.

Although we were not at war, I knew there was danger involved. His whereabouts in service has been lost in my memory, if I ever knew, but I do recall the pang in my heart when the white cross with his name on it was put up on the Charlemont town hall lawn after Christmas 1944. And, although I really knew nothing more about him, it has been hard through these fifty years to pass that prominent white cross (there are now five of them) on the Charlemont town hall lawn without thinking about that farewell gathering for Tommy Neary.

D-Day and all the events of the Normandy Invasion have come to life for me during our recent three week European tour commemorating its fiftieth anniversary. There were thirty-five of us, and we did most of the traveling through several countries by coach. It all started in London with Churchill's Cabinet War Rooms, and we marveled at the antiquated communication equipment, then on to St. Paul's Cathedral, where the American Chapel pays tribute to the 28,000 American men killed while on active service in Britain, and finally to the Imperial War Museum to view tanks and jeeps and planes and a very realistic underground foxhole.

The trip continued on to Portsmouth and a tour of Southwick House, Eisenhower's headquarters, with the original huge wall map showing the sea routes of the planned invasion termed "Operation Overlord," and the room where Eisenhower made the decision to hold the invasion off for one day because of bad weather. Then, early on June 5th, he made the final decision, committing into battle for "The Longest Day" 176,000 men, 11,000 warplanes, 600 fighting ships

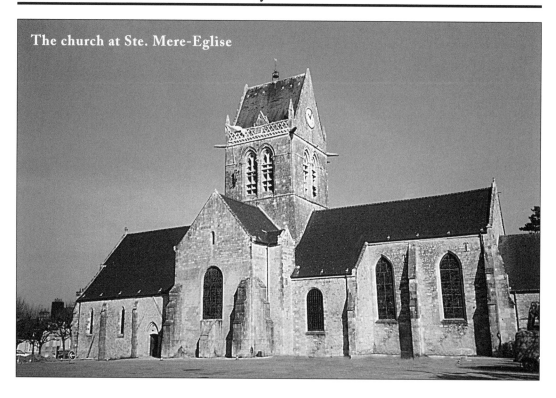

The church at Ste. Mere-Eglise

and 4,000 transports, and 50,000 vehicles from motorcycles to tanks (these numbers vary with each story, so this is approximate) with the now famous statement, "OK, Let's Go". The figures listed are for D-Day itself; there were all told three million men with their equipment and supplies waiting for their turn to cross the channel.

From Southwick House, we went on and visited the D-Day Museum where the famous Overlord Tapestry is displayed – 272 feet long in 34 panels three feet high, appliqué and embroidery, realistically depicting the massive and sometimes gruesome events of D-Day.

Our calm and easy four and a half hour voyage by ferry across the English

Channel to Cherbourg gave us time to reflect back on that awful stormy day fifty years ago, when so many seasick men faced the horrendous challenge to penetrate the fortified German "Atlantic Wall" in the fight to liberate Europe. We spent a couple of days in the village of Bayeux, the first French village liberated by our troops, and took time to view the 11th century Bayeux Tapestry – 230 feet long and twenty inches high, wool embroidery on linen, depicting the other famous channel crossing, when the Normans took England under the leadership of William of Normandy in the Battle of 1066. This, of course, was the inspiration for the Overlord Tapestry. Both tapestries are magnificent and memorable pieces of artwork of great historical significance. (See Smithsonian, May 1994.)

In the city of Caen, finally wrested from the Germans some six weeks after its expected capture on D-Day, our stop was at the "Le Memorial", a museum dedicated to peace. This is located on a hill said to be made of the rubble from the almost complete destruction of the city. This is the location in a Memorial Garden for the future "Wall of Liberty," where will be inscribed the names of all American veterans who served in the European Theater of Operations. Also, a very dramatic movie on two side by each screens – one side German army film of D-Day and the other Allied films. The horror of war came to life on both sides.

The first to arrive in France on D-Day were the 13,000 British and American paratroopers who landed behind the German lines. We visited Ste. Mere-Eglise, where so many of those paratroops were slaughtered before they hit the ground and one got hung up on the church steeple, playing dead to avoid being shot again. Nevertheless, the American flag was unfurled at the Ste. Mere-Eglise town hall at dawn, the first flag to be flown on French soil on D-day. The local museum displayed one of the gliders that brought in so many troops and equipment, and a C-47, the transport workhorse of the Army Air Corps. Pictures showed the German defense against these gliders, fields full of poles, named Rommel's asparagus, designed to smash the gliders as they landed, and they proved very effective.

It was the beaches themselves where Americans landed that awful day, beaches code-named Utah and Omaha, that left the most lasting impression on me. With our group were veteran men and one woman WAC who came in on those beaches, not on D-Day but not long afterwards, and one doctor who was on the ship Bayfield offshore, tending the returning wounded. At Utah Beach we walked down "Rowe Road." Named for a fallen soldier, the sandy road cut through the dunes where the troops fought their way up that day, only to find that the Germans had flooded the fields behind.

Pointe du Hoc was next, a high point where a daring group of American Rangers scaled the 100 foot cliff to destroy the enemy fortifications that were such a threat to both beaches. The field was full of bomb craters where the Allies had tried to penetrate with bombs the German Atlantic Wall of concrete bunkers and gun emplacements. Omaha Beach was under a long high embankment which had been much more heavily fortified than Utah, and the casualties there were great, 2,000 that first day, some 300 or more drowning in the tremendous tidal currents before they reached the beach. Mines and great steel X's, called hedgehogs, to puncture boats, and barbed wire lined that beach on D-Day. All told there were 9,000 American, British, and Canadian casualties on D-Day, the "Longest Day."

On the plateau bluff overlooking Omaha Beach, where the troops finally gained their first foothold after unbelievable obstacles and losses, lays the Normandy American Cemetery, the final resting place for 9,386 of the 37,000 Americans killed during the three months of the Normandy Campaign. At this cemetery, the Normandy veterans of our group participated in a very moving wreath laying ceremony. Many of us walked at random through the crosses, reading the names of our gallant young men who gave their lives, and we spent a quiet moment in the chapel reflecting on their sacrifices. The cemetery is beautifully designed and immaculately tended. A hike down to the beach area, now laced with well-worn paths and steps, gave us some personal experience with that hill which took such effort, and claimed so many of those lives, fifty years ago.

This very memorable day on our tour ended at Arromanches, at the start of three beaches where the British and Canadian troops landed and fought their way ashore on D-Day. They were known as Gold, Juno and Sword Beaches. Here we could still see the remains of the "Mulberries," the huge concrete boxes that were engineered and built in England and dragged across the channel by the British, to be sunk as breakwaters to form an artificial harbor for unloading the vast supplies needed to back up the invasion.

On the way back to Bayeux, we stopped at but did not enter the huge somber German cemetery with all their black crosses. Men there were buried four to a grave, and most of them are unknown soldiers. The German losses were said to be between 400,000 and 500,000. It seemed wrong not to pay our respects there, too. So many of the common German soldiers were either very young or very old, and most of them were fighting because they were forced to do so. Our war was against the Nazi Regime and its followers, the High Command, not against the German people as such. It's a shame so many good men on both sides have to be sacrificed because of the ambitions of tyrants.

After capturing Cherbourg, the Allies went on to Caen and Ste. Lo, with miserable slow fighting through the hedgerows. Finally, with the liberating of Falaise on August 21, 1944, the Battle of Normandy had reached its objectives, and three days later the Allied troops entered Paris. Our tour took us through Rouen and its lovely Gothic Cathedral, to Giverny and the magnificent gardens of Claude Monet (where we were caught in a thunder shower resembling German bombardment!), and finally to Paris and the Arch of Triumph, where the lucky soldiers who made it took time for celebration and posed for pictures, now duly preserved as historical momentos in museums. But the war was not over, as many would soon learn.

Our tour continued on to Reims for a visit to the school building where the Salle de Reddition, or surrender room, was located at General Eisenhower's final command post. Here the German high command surrendered on May 8, 1945, ending the great and costly struggle for the liberation of Europe from Nazi oppression. Later that day we made a stop at Verdun, and the World War I National Cemetery and Memorial to one of the fiercest battles of that war. The Ossuary of Douaumont was built in memory of the 400,000 French soldiers killed in the nine month Battle of Verdun. The number of men killed in these wars was staggering, and really beyond comprehension, as was the path of destruction from these battles for freedom. Why can not man learn to live in peace?

Luxembourg was the next country we visited, stopping first at the Statue of General Patton, larger than life, looking out across the hills, pistols at his side, and just about to raise his binoculars. He was the hero who re-liberated Luxembourg and brought relief to the besieged forces at Bastogne during the Battle of the Bulge. On December 16th, the Germans staged a last ditch effort with a swift and unexpected counterattack through the Ardennes, across the northern half of Luxembourg into Belgium aiming for Antwerp. The resulting bloody conflict became known as the Battle of the Bulge. The museum at Bastogne, Belgium where we visited had an unusual theater presentation of the battle with actual pictures and lighted maps showing the progress of each side. Patton's army had quickly marched from the Saar region of France, and arrived just in time to save the day for the Allied forces surrounded at Bastogne. By January 25th, the German threat was eliminated outside their own borders. The large star-shaped monument to the American Military is on the top of the hill, and carries the names of all the US states.

Now known as the Hamm Cemetery, this battlefield burial ground in Luxembourg became the permanent resting place for 5,076 Americans who gave their lives for freedom. Our veterans on the tour again laid a wreath at the monument at the top of the cemetery, near where General Patton is buried beside his valiant men. The two flag poles carried the American flags at half staff that day, honoring the late President Richard Nixon. This cemetery was a peaceful quiet spot surrounded by flowering bushes and woods.

Nan on Rowe Road at Utah Beach

As before, I took time to walk down among the white marble Roman Crosses and Stars of David, and when I returned back up the hill meandered here and there, reading the names of men from various states and of various ranks. I followed no particular row, and at one point veered a little left so as not to interfere with some workmen cleaning a stone.

The next name I read seemed incredible, impossible to come upon among five thousand white stones. The sight of this grave brought immediate tears to my eyes. The name read:

THOMAS J. NEARY, JR
S SGT 328 INF 26 DIV
MASSACHUSETTS
DEC 26, 1944

So Tommy Neary, whom I had known so long ago, had died at the Battle of the Bulge. He was killed by a sniper, I was told, when, last week, I discovered that his sister was Ethel White, who lives by the Chickley River in Hawley next door to the old Neary family farm. She said Tommy lived for a day after he was shot and might have been saved, but they were surrounded by Germans and could not get medical assistance. Today he would have been 78, but instead he lies peacefully in Luxembourg and is remembered by a white marble cross at the Hamm Cemetery, and a white wooden cross on the town hall lawn in Charlemont, Massachusetts, and by a once little girl who has never forgotten him.

From Luxembourg, we crossed the border into Germany itself, with a stop by the site of the famous Remagen Bridge, the only bridge that remained intact across the Rhine River and was captured by the Allies and thought to be "worth its weight in gold." Having been severely damaged by the Germans, it collapsed ten days later, and now all that remains are the abutments, one of which is a Peace Museum where we visited. This day ended with a lovely afternoon cruise up the Rhine River among the steep terraced vineyards, ancient castles, and quaint villages far from the scenes of war.

Nuremberg was next on our itinerary and our notable stop was at Zeppelin Field, the huge parade ground where Hitler held forth at giant rallies and scored chilling victories over the minds of his countrymen. One of the famous photos of the war was the shooting off of the big impressive swastika on top of this stadium. It was an eerie place, as most of us climbed the moss-covered steps and stood on the selfsame podium.

On we continued to Munich, capital of Bavarian Germany, where a nice young German man served as our guide for the city tour. As we were leaving on our own to visit the Nazi concentration camp at Dachau, he said, "Please go with an open mind. We are a new generation in Germany now." It was a sobering afternoon, looking at the remaining buildings and then at the pictures of real people imprisoned there. Heinrich Himmler, Police Chief of Munich, established the camp for "political opponents" in March of 1933. It would become a reservoir of slave labor and, for the German SS, a training ground for murder. Overwork, malnutrition, disease and medical experiments took its toll. Mass shootings were common, and others were shipped out to the gas chambers. More than 200,000 prisoners went through the concentration camp at Dachau. The total number of deaths cannot be ascertained. The camp was freed by American soldiers on April 29, 1945, and it has now been established as a memorial to the victims of Dachau.

One of our last pilgrimages from Munich was through the heartland of Bavaria to Salzburg, Austria, where we glimpsed the first of the Alps and had a day at leisure in the old and fascinating city of Mozart. On return we visited the lovely area of Berchtesgaden National Park, made famous as the location of the summer vacation homes of Adolph Hitler and all the other top ranking Nazis. We drove up the mountain road, to the General Walker Hotel at the center of the old Nazi complex. At the very top of the mountain, still under snow, we could see the

"Eagles Nest," Hitler's mountaintop lookout. Taking my usual hike around any new area to check out the flora and mosses, it was rather ironic to find here a large patch of forget-me-nots. The last day of the official tour took us via the old town of Rothenburg and on to our final destination at Heidleberg, on the Neckar River. At a gala dinner we relived the memorable days of the trip and said farewell to and promised picture exchange with our companions on this unforgettable D-Day anniversary tour.

Heidleberg was personally exciting and interesting for us, as Jack had been stationed there as a young MP in the US Constabulary with the occupation army in 1947. On our own, we visited the Grossdeutschland-

Hamm Cemetery and the grave of Thomas Neary

Kaserne where he was housed. It is now called Cambell Barracks and is the headquarters of the US Army in Europe. We spent some time comparing old pictures with present day buildings, and in the process met several military people. It was a coincidence that one of the officers was in charge of public information on all Fiftieth Anniversary Commemorative Events for D-Day at Normandy, including the visits of the president of the United States and other heads of state. He gave us some interesting reading material and posters, which you will see along with other displays at the Rowe Library during the month of June.

Our final good fortune of the trip was being able to locate a German friend Jack had known in Heidleberg forty-seven years ago. It was a shock out of the blue for her, but when the cobwebs of time cleared she remembered. We spent a delightful afternoon with Irmgard and her husband, Nick, touring the heights around Heidleberg, and as a guest in their home, exchanging remembrances and getting to know each other. After all the devastating sites of D-Day and reminders of World War II, the friendliness of these Heidlebergers brought home to us the fact that our two great nations, Germany and America, have put World War II behind them and united in friendship and peace.   **7/94**

Jack at Heidleberg, Germany

Bear Scat and Fringed Gentians

It has been a long time since we've taken a Wild Side hike together in the hills of Rowe. We went out on the spur of the moment the other day, not really prepared to take you all along, but it was such fun that perhaps we can reconstruct the trip from our ever more rapidly failing memory. We always prided ourselves on not taking notes on our hikes but, perhaps, the time has come.

It was a long hike, and we weren't really sure we'd make it back once we got started. Our car had a dead battery, so our better half dropped us off at the switching station gate on Tunnel Road at noon and said he'd pick us up at Monroe Bridge at three. We planned on bushwhacking over the hill and down to the river then following the old HT&W railroad track bed back to civilization. As soon as the car was out of sight we wished we'd given an alternative pick up spot, just in case we couldn't, for some odd reason, make it that way. Oh well! Starting to climb the hill, on tar road, we realized once again how out of shape we are, and how we should hike a little every day instead of such monstrous hikes every so often! And our hikes alone (Who else would go with us?) are seldom on a path!

Going up the hill, once out in the sun, we saw all the fringed gentians in bloom beside the road and a few spiral white orchids called ladies' tresses. What a wonderful sight! Remember William Cullen Bryant's apt description in his poem,

"To A Fringed Gentian"
"Then doth thy sweet and quiet eye
Look through its fringes to the sky,
Blue - blue - as if the sky let fall
A flower from its cerulean wall".

Fringed gentians grow in sandy disturbed soil, and are a biennial and do not bloom a second year. (Transplanting is useless, and picking destroys the seeds for blooms the year after next. And what's more they close their lovely petals once out of the sun and become very nondescript. Enjoy them where they are on a bright sunny day and leave them be!)

Turning in at the power line, the stately tall goldenrod was way over our head and full of bees. We savored the familiar smell of goldenrod honey. The leafy stems were even bending over the path and making a tunnel in places. There was also lots of everlasting, and a few closed gentians, a pretty flower in itself when not seen in close proximity to its fancy cousin. We hoped there might be some blackberries left, but they seemed to have been picked clean and well tramped down by one non-human animal or another. We passed our favorite very large white quartz boulder, and wished again it would by some miracle land in our front yard. It was ice cold to the touch, as are all white rocks.

As the path dipped down we took a left up into the woods, arriving exactly where we wanted to be, in a little swamp that feeds a brook which goes down the other side. The swamp was only slightly damp and the brook was dry. Chipmunks were having a heyday scurrying around, and chickadees discussed the weather and our intrusion into their territory. We picked our way through the mud, admiring and trying to identify the bright green moss on all the fallen logs. We had come this way especially to see the bristly black currant, by the brook just over the ridge. It is listed as of "special concern" by the Massachusetts Natural Heritage, although Rowe seems to have a goodly share. We thought we had found a new site elsewhere, but the plants were mostly eaten and we weren't just sure. We thought perhaps seeing these plants again would improve our search image, but now we're still not sure and will have to wait until spring. The flowers are unmistakable.

This hillside is such a treasure of rich soil plants, and must be beautiful in the spring. There are lots of white birches and today the sun was filtering through their yellowing leaves, making delicate shadow patterns below. We veered toward the brook to inspect a mossy cliff but, with no running water, some of the moss was already turning brown. We remembered it with a lovely waterfall over the ledges in previous years. We again crossed the hill, admiring the white baneberry doll's eyes and one of our favorites, the graceful arching blue-stemmed goldenrod. Further down we stood at the bottom of a cliff, trying to spot the long-bracted orchid which we have seen there for several years. We thought it had disappeared, but finally found it bent over, with the seedpods straight up. Gone by, it could be confused with the common helleborine orchid but those seedpods hang down. Glad this one is still there, as it's the only one of its kind we have found in town. As always, we spent some time looking for more plants, but there still were no obvious ones.

From there on we just meandered downhill, following our curiosity back and forth, re-acquainting ourselves with all our boulder friends with polypody hats and robes of moss and lichens. All the good rich soil stuff is there, including wild ginger, and we found a nice healthy panax quinquefolius in full berry, another plant of special concern in

Massachusetts. Mushrooms of every size and hue added color and intrigue to the landscape. Near the bottom, we knew there was an old wood road of sorts and anticipated following it upriver. Reaching there, we found that there had been a good bit of logging done in the area – it was difficult to tell how long ago. It's hard to imagine how they got the stuff out of there, as it is so steep back up the mountain. The road went out to the power line and probably connected down to the Bear Swamp tunnels road across the dam, still pretty steep territory. Unfortunately, we were not investigating in that direction today.

We could see the lower reservoir through the trees, and the strange deep circular ravine below us where we had been once before. Today we followed the wood road, stooping many times to look for "bug on a stick" moss, as the disturbed dirt seemed the ideal place, but no luck, or it was just too early in the season to see the tiny bright green capsules growing out of the protonema. We could have spent hours looking around that area checking out all the little mossy glens and looking for new plants, but it seemed best to keep going. Monroe Bridge was not just around the corner, and little did we know what we might find between here and there.

The road was brushy, but passable, with mud in places before it turned more uphill. We finally came to an old fence, something to do with the reservoir, we presumed. We climbed between the wires and continued on around the hill for a short distance, until there seemed to be solid brush in the road but more daylight beyond. We pushed through the brush and found ourselves on the high edge of the old rock quarry, with a drop of umpteen feet just beyond the toes of our hiking boots! Shivers ran up our spine and we backed off a bit. Then we stood there, feeling foolish that we didn't realize we would have to pass this old quarry where they cut back the mountain to get rock for the lower dam. Looking over the situation, we then wondered how on earth we were going to get by it! A turkey vulture was floating high above, ready just in case we didn't!

Our options seemed to be to climb half way back up the mountain and go around the top, or we could drop down along the river. But, if we went down and couldn't find a place to get through, we would have to climb back up to the top anyway. By that time it would be late and our chauffeur would be at Monroe Bridge, and we would be walking back home from the switching station in the dark! The quarry seemed to have been cut in layers, and there was a jumble of rocks and brush. It looked impassable, but we decided to keep to the original plan and go down until we could find a passage. Finally, it looked like a shelf, and we headed down into the unknown through a tangle of alders and, twice, came to another drop which we couldn't possibly manage. The way out began to seem hopeless. Trapped in a quarry!! Now what do we do? Maybe we could swim the river, but that was far down below, and would probably bring us to a high fence on the other side and then what? (Of course, one crack of thunder and we would have climbed right up the rock face at the back of the quarry!!)

From still another brink, we could now see a sort of ledge up to the right, so we punched through the trees and came out more or less in the open, under the back wall of the quarry. Here we could cross, but on the other side it looked like the same problem of drop-offs. There seemed to be one possible way, by climbing up a little and heading into the brush on the mountainside. We fought the poplar trees on the edge and broke through to woods. Walking over another fence, we assumed this and the last one were meant to surround the quarry when it was dug twenty years ago. Here, we immediately came upon a deep brook-less ravine and had to go down and up steep banks, but we were back on land, so to speak. In hindsight, this ravine and a couple more we encountered must have been the old landslide sites, of which there are several from the 1930s, along this mountain. Now we want to go back and investigate them!

Beyond the ravine, the trees opened up and we came out into the remains of an old field. Here, in the first opening, we saw a sight that would warm the heart of any nature lover. Here, far from the maddening crowd, a lovely clump of fringed gentians growing right beside a large heap of fairly fresh bear scat! Rare beauty amid signs of wilderness wildlife! Wow! (Well, the bears are coming pretty near civilization these days, but it was a nice thought.) The old field must have little soil left, for there weren't many trees, but lots of gentians, black-eyed susans, asters, everlasting and goldenrod, and grasshoppers. It was remote, mountains surrounded us, and we felt like just laying out there in the warm fall sunshine, looking up at the puffy white clouds through the fringes of those lovely gentians and hoping, perhaps, Mr. Bruin might pass by. At a respectable distance, of course! Dream on.... The trek so far had taken more time than anticipated, and we knew we had a long way to go. There was no time to indulge ourselves in such pleasantries today. We had a watch in the knapsack, but purposely didn't look at it. What could we do anyway if it was already three o'clock?

The rock quarry at Bear Swamp

The rest of the trip was a series of ups and downs over rocks and through brush on the mountainside often following well-worn deer paths. It always amazes us when out in the wilderness, looking for a spot to place our boot when climbing, and finding what surely seems like a recent human footprint (depression in the moist earth) in that very spot. We suppose bears with large paws must climb around the hillsides much as we do. We could finally drop down on the old railroad bed, and this was brushy but passable, full of spider webs in our face as we walked, so we broke off a leafy branch to hold in our hand ahead of us to clear the way. Once in a while, we wandered back up on the mountainside to investigate something interesting. The leaves were so thick on the trees along the river that, for a long time, we had no idea where we were in relation to things across the river.

Eventually the territory began to look familiar, as we had walked down river a few times in the past but never as far as the quarry. The old road was still visible, across from Dunbar Brook where it had come down from the hills of Monroe, crossed the river, and went up the mountain to Rowe to

the meeting house back around 1800. Difficulty in travel up and down this deep valley was the major reason why Monroe people soon petitioned to separate from Rowe, but it did not come about until 1822. There has been a lot of water down the Deerfield since then and a lot of changes in this valley, but the mountains stand as solid and reassuring as those old pioneers saw them. (Perhaps the folks settling in Monroe more aptly considered them forbidding in 1800!)

When the territory became familiar, we anticipated still another hour to get back to Monroe Bridge! Of course, when we came to the walled part along the path, the moss was so thick and inviting that it again delayed us while we collected several samples to bring home in the trusty box in our knapsack. And, nearer the river, the sun sparkling on the water swirling around the big boulders took moments of quiet appreciation.

No new discoveries today, but a lovely afternoon in spite of the anxious moments trapped in the quarry. And we know in our heart that where there is still bear scat and fringed gentians, there will be a Wild Side in Rowe for a long time to come. We walked out of the woods at Monroe Bridge to see our chauffeur slowly pacing up and down, but, surprisingly, it was only 3:25.

Thanks for joining us! **10/94**

1985
BICENTENNIAL
TREK

Mike and Sophie Coe at Fort Shirley marker

511

As a final contribution to the 1985 Bicentennial celebrations of Rowe and Heath, the Historical Societies initiated a hike to trace the Old Military Road between Fort Shirley in Heath and Fort Pelham in Rowe. The last patrol on this route was probably in the fall of 1754 when these two forts were officially abandoned in favor of fortifications along the more accessible and vulnerable trails in the river valleys. The Military Road was then a lonely path through the mountain wilderness of tall virgin forests, wild beasts and skies often darkened with flocks of passenger pigeons. But the hardwood trees would have put forth the same golden glow of autumn colors, and several of the ancient maples along today's path were certainly the very ones observed as young saplings by the scouts on that last patrol in 1754 as the men kept an ever watchful eye for the lurking enemy. That this was still dangerous country was proven by the massacre of Moses Rice in Charlemont the following year.

The appointed day, Saturday October 12, 1985, dawned bright and frosty. Those who were up before the sunrise had time to appreciate the beautiful sight of the crescent moon beside the planet Venus while they ate an early hearty breakfast and made their luncheon sandwiches. Decked out in several layers of clothing, twenty-one of us gathered in the field across from the Newland Smith house in Heath at 8:30 a.m. - an early hour, but then we had miles to go before lunch. The warm morning sun encouraged some shedding of flannel shirts at the start as we posed for a group picture for the annals of history. Guy Silvester came by with a promise to sweep the road crossings for any stragglers, and Cleon Peters arrived with the big yellow school bus to transport us the first mile and a half or so down Hosmer Road to the Fort Shirley path. There Mike Bakalar from West County News met us with camera in hand and recorded our first steps into the wilderness, but declined to follow as camp photographer!

Gathering in the tall weeds and ferns around the stone marking the swampy site of Fort Shirley, we listened to a brief history lesson by Dr. Michael Coe, President of the Heath Historical Society and Yale University Professor - our local expert on the history and excavation of the forts. We pause here in our narrative to acquaint you with a bit of that history.

During the years of struggle between France and England in the new world, the war known as the "French and Indian" or "King George's" broke out in the 1744. That summer the Massachusetts General Court, in defense of its western colonies, ordered and funded the erection of a cordon of forts to run on a line recently surveyed by Timothy Dwight two miles south of the northern boarder to extend from Hugh Morrison's fortified house in Colrain to the Dutch settlements. Governor Shirley appointed Colonel John Stoddard of Northampton as Chairman of the Committee to build these forts. On July 20, 1744 Stoddard wrote to Captain William Williams: "You are directed to employ soldiers under your command to erect a fort 60 feet square, houses 11 feet wide with roof 12 feet high shingled, mounts 12 feet square, 7 feet high, located about five miles and a half west of Morrison's on Dwight's line, and to find suitable places for two or three other forts the same distance apart."

The first of these forts, Fort Shirley, named after the able Governor, was erected on the ground where we were standing, and Mike pointed out that the site had obviously been pinpointed on a map and not chosen for its ideal location. One of the largest expenditures at the fort was for flooring, probably to keep them up out of the wet terrain. (In ten years this fort was to be listed as badly rotted.) Fort Shirley, a substantial structure, was finished in three months and by October 30, 1744, Capt. William Williams was in residence and in charge. It is assumed that scouts then began their patrols to the east and west thus establishing what was to become known as the "Military Road." In the following year as many as 350 soldiers "in the line of forts" were under the charge of Capt. Ephraim Williams, Jr. stationed at Fort Shirley. In 1747 Gov. Shirley decreed "keep a constant scout from one blockhouse to another and give proper advices and signals of the appearance of the enemy". Historian Josiah Holland mentions "scouts, assisted by companies of trained dogs."

Mike now led us a short ways behind the fort site to where a white picket fence surrounded a small gravestone and told us the story. The grave belonged to little Anna Norton who died at the fort in 1747 in the seventh year of her life. Anna's father, Rev. John Norton, was chaplain of the forts and with his wife and two daughters came to live at Fort Shirley in February 1746. On one of his appointed rounds, Rev. Norton left Fort Shirley and went via Fort Pelham to stay at Moses Rice's house (by the buttonball tree) in Charlemont on August 14, 1746 and from thence to Fort Massachusetts in present day North Adams the next day. This was

unfortunate timing for Fort Massachusetts was attacked and burned by 800 French and Indians on August 20th and Rev. Norton and others were taken captive to Canada. When he finally returned to Fort Shirley a year later to collect his family, he found little Anna had died and been buried nearby. Perhaps it was he who took the time to carve the small headstone to leave on his daughter's grave. (The memory of Rev. Norton also remains in Rowe with the name "Norton's Trail" or King's Highway referring to the still traceable Military Road which he traveled south over the mountain.) Anna Norton's original hand-hewn gravestone was removed to Williams College in the 1880's by historian Dr. Arthur Perry (a small marble one was left in its place) but the White sisters of Heath arranged for the return of the original in 1906. Now the original is safely in the Heath Historical Society and Mike explained the making of the exact replica.

Heading west, we crossed the ditch circling the Fort. Dug in the early days in hopes of keeping water away from the fort area, it had been to no avail as the ground remained wet and seepy because water moves slowly through the dense substratum of hardpan soil. Our trail followed a line of blue pieces of t-shirt carefully torn into strips by Sophie Coe and hung on branches. Mike, Sophie and I had pre-hiked and tagged a likely trail the preceding Friday on a very foggy rainy day!

The lay of the land was fairly level and wet until we crossed a small stream surrounded by muddy sphagnum moss. Then we began to climb along an old road up to the power line where we came out of the woods into the gorgeous blue sky and sunshine of a perfect October day. Looking off to the north, ski trails could be distinguished on Mount Snow in Vermont. The open pasture, scattered with low juniper and barberry bushes, was currently in use evidenced by the close-cropped grass and dark brown pancakes of "you know what" that had to be carefully stepped over and around! We learned from Sophie that the flavor of gin comes from juniper berries and that the bright red barberries are good for sauce and beautiful jelly. Old stone walls and foundations led us to a mammoth cellar hole under ancient maple trees. Two huge square chimney foundations were centered in the cellar hole and someone offered the information that this was the "Spooner Place" - having burned sometime before the turn of the century. What a wonderful old house it must have been, high up there on the hillside with a commanding view north and probably west in an earlier day. But we were following a trail used long before these settlers tamed this fair land. Scouts had walked this Military Road every day during those years 1744-1754 and, although they never met the enemy on this trail, they walked in fear for their lives as Indians had done their bloody damage in nearby Charlemont, Colrain, Bernardston, Deerfield, and further west at Fort Massachusetts.

After examining the Spooner remains, we climbed over and under the fence onto the abandoned west end of the Oxbow Road. Walking south for a very short distance, we entered the woods along an old east-west stone wall. The tagged trail from the previous week went into the woods farther north but had led us, by compass, into brush and eventually logging slash.

This we planned to avoid and hoped to pick up our "blue trail" further on. We couldn't have picked a nicer day to be in the woods. The pine trees had recently shed their needles and with the red and orange layer of autumn leaves made for a continuous carpet under our feet. After a stand of evergreens, the woods were fairly open with young growth of beech, maple and birch. The New York ferns had turned a lovely whitish tan accented with the dark evergreen of the spinulous ferns and an occasional small clump of crested fern where ground water moistened the surface. Along in this area everyone seemed to spread out looking for the "blue trail" and an eventual shout of "over here" gathered everyone along the appointed path, except, we discovered, for Jack Williams who did his own exploring continuing along the wall hoping to find same positive sign from the long distant put to verify the trail's location.

Although there are many records from this historic period, there are no primary source maps or descriptions of the exact location of the Military Road. For the Heath portion of the trip we were fallowing the recent "Costello map" which drew the path directly west from the fort to the power line then dipped it more in a southwesterly course to meet Ben Road on the straightaway. There seemed to be no physical evidence whatsoever of a road in this first section although the route was perfectly logical. Any path, though much used for ten years and then totally abandoned, would disappear in far less than the 231 years in our wet New England soils where trees grow, drop leaves to build up new soil, fall uprooting dirt so rains can create new water channels. In Rowe, we would totally disagree with the Costello Map.

"The Mohawk Trail, showing old roads and other points of interest" by the late David L. Costello, a retired state highway engineer, was published in 1975. He states: "I have plotted Timothy Dwight's line on the maps. The line was the means of locating much of the Military Road between Fort Morrison and Fort Pelham where many traces of the old trail can be found near or south of Dwight's line, as a section of the present highway and other areas such as abandoned roads or trails. This line, together with old maps and legendary information, leads me to believe I have located the old Military Road from Massachusetts in North Adams to where it crosses the boundary into Vermont in Bernardston with very little deviation from its original course." Although this work represents a great deal of research and tracking and is probably basically accurate on most trails, it does not quote any new sources, and we question just how he arrived at his location of the Shirley-Pelham portion of the trail.

Once down the hill we came out of the woods along a small brook by a fireplace and cleared site where a cabin had burned and then went south on the old section of Branch Hill Road to the open horse pasture on Ben Road. The sole occupant of the pasture came over to investigate our intrusion and got a little frisky kicking up his heals. Suddenly the hoof beats were close behind me, and I quickly made an ungraceful leap over the fence catching a pant leg on the barbwire. Fortunately the event was more humorous than serious! Clyde Churchill, one of our most senior members and an old hand with farm animals, quietly talked to the horse and held his attention while the other hikers crossed to safety.

Regrouping again, we took off at better speed on the tar surface. Recent historians

Clyde Churchill

seem to agree that this unusually straight section of Heath road was originally built upon the old Military Trail. The red and gold maples there were especially beautiful. Nearing the west end of Ben Road, Clyde, with a tall walking stick, took the helm and led us a short ways up 8A and then up the hillside to the west following his sap line to the famous Churchill Reunion ball field and picnic grounds hidden away at the top of the hill. From there Clyde had cut and marked a trail up over the dome of the hill passing an old small mining prospect and several apple trees in the area of the old "Ellis Farm." The crew followed Clyde, single file, Indian style, and he eventually delivered us to the old road from Rowe to Heath which becomes part of Knott Road. We had pre-hiked this the week before and tagged a steep trail further south which in the end did not seem logical. Knowing our hesitation, Clyde, in the meantime, had come to our rescue with a new trail. This led through fairly open and rich woods where we found maidenhair fern and the lingering blue berries of blue cohosh.

Once on Knott Road we followed it north past the old Hamilton place (now Leuchtman) through two pasture gates which Henry Leuchtman carefully opened and closed for us and continued on the well defined wood road which is reputed to be the earliest road between the towns. Once over the line in Rowe it became more grown-in and brushy but still discernible ending between two stone walls by the Wayne house and onto the present Dell Road. We pause again to catch up on further history of this trail.

Colonel Stoddard in the fall of 1744 had evidently commissioned Capt. Moses Rice (the first, in 1743, to settle with his family along the Deerfield in Charlemont) to build the second fort five and a half miles to the west of Shirley. Rice had drawn the timbers from Charlemont (why not Rowe trees?) but had not completed the fort for there is another communication from Col. Stoddard to William Williams on March 6,1745 which said in effect: "If in ten days Rice doesn't give his word that he will finish the fort, take your soldiers and do it yourself!" Fort Pelham, (a palisaded area 12 by 24 rods which enclosed about an acre and a half of good dry ground with a well, a single

story two-room barracks with one chimney, a two-story quarters presumably for the officer, and an underground magazine surrounded by a two-story mount) never as elaborate as Shirley, was built that spring and although tradition says Moses Rice built it, it seems more likely that the soldiers finished the job. In the direction of Dwight's line westward from Fort Pelham appears the canyon of the Deerfield River, and thus it was impractical to establish a road or build a fort in the next five or so miles. The old road near Pelham from the Alix house on across Hazelton Road follows precisely on the Dwight line to the end at the Laffond house. This could hive been a spur of the Military Road where scouts checked a lookout near Pulpit Rock above the river   and returned. To continue west, the Military Road was "Norton's Trail" south over the mountain to Rice's and then west over "Forbidden Mountain" following the old Indian "Mohawk Trail." In 1745 the final fort (on the design of Fort Shirley) was built near the Hoosac River and called Fort Massachusetts. (The location is in present day North Adams behind Friendly's in the Price Chopper parking lot.) This fort saw much action and was rebuilt after the first attack.

Back on Dell Road the crew spread out as individuals or small groups each walking their own pace, talking, observing and in general really enjoying a beautiful fall day in the now very warm sunshine. The route continued bearing left along the walls of the old road where Dell joins Cyrus Stage, then down the hill to bear straight through the cut to Old Cyrus Stage and past the old Blakeslee house (now Grieco). At the bend of the present road we kept left to again pick up the old road through the woods coming out at the corner by the East Cemetery. From there we followed the present road up around the corner and on Ford Hill Road past the site of the Cornelius Jones house and the Liberty Pole.

Our Rowe route differs with the Costello map from the point of entering Knott Road. Mr. Costello drew a trail from there across to pick up the old road between Dell and Davis Mine, and from the Mine Brook up through a natural "glacial melt-water channel," crossing Mine Road and circling around Todd Mountain some south of the present park trail, skirting the lake and the causeway pond to Fort Pelham. On the map this looks like a good fairly direct route, but in reality the lay of the land would have been very unlikely. It encounters steep rough sections and a great deal of swamp land including the whole section around the lake which back then was "the great swamp." Staying on the high ground of Dell Road makes better logic, and it has the following documentation.

In Percy Brown's History of Rowe, a section on roads has the quote: "The earliest road in Rowe was without any doubt, a rough cart path or bridle-way over the mountain from Charlemont to Fort Pelham which bore the name of King's Highway and today is called Norton's Trail. The second road was probably the road to Heath, following in general the trail between Pelham and Shirley. It is likely that at first the western terminus was at the house of Cornelius Jones. The old Heath road led straight on easterly from Blakeslee's over the hill down by the Hamilton place." Clearly this indicates Cyrus Stage Road and Dell Road following the

old route over the hill to Knott Road by the present Leuchtman place.

In Arthur Perry's *Origins in Williamstown* written in 1894 he describes Fort Pelham: "That the main opening into the parade of the fort was, undoubtedly, on the north side, along which, at some distance further north, on account of a head of a swamp in the direct line east and west, the military road from Fort Shirley certainly passed in a northerly curve to the west, the straight line being resumed about a half mile further on". Although this is a bit confusing it indicates Fort Pelham was approached down from the north which would indicate Ford Hill. It stands to reason, in our mind, that Cornelius Jones would have built on this old Military Road when he came as the first settler eight years later.

And so we continued our trek down Ford Hill Road and turned south into a newly marked trail (white t-shirt this time) by a stone wall on Historical Society property slightly east of the North Cemetery Road. There we inquired of Clyde Churchill (favoring a bad knee) if perhaps he didn't want to rest on the wall and be picked up there by bus. The answer was prompt and definite. He had never been to the forts before, and he never expected to make this trek again in his lifetime. He had joined us from the start, and he expected to finish with us! And he did, amid cheers!

The "white trail" crossed a small brook where the road might have done so and climbed a gradual slope through dry brown hayscented fern past the old Wright sugar house to the "north entrance" of Fort Pelham grounds. We had probably walked nearly seven miles, and the time was 1 p.m. At an enjoyable pace we had completed the trek in four hours, stopping now and then to learn a bit of history, to contemplate the lay of the land or to remember the scouts who patrolled in this "dangerous country" during that ten year period so long ago.

And finally at Fort Pelham site, we remembered Mike Coe's recent talk at the joint Bicentennial Historical Society meeting. He had said that the fort excavations by University of Massachusetts, and later under his direction by Yale University students, had produced artifacts such as Tippet clay pipes, English salt glaze china tea cups, fancy mermaid cufflinks, two-tined bone handle forks and even the parts of a pressing iron showing that the men and families stationed there were just typical Englishman in another land. In spite of hardships and danger, the Forts were English farms in the wilderness and not ragamuffin outposts. Even the animal bones in kitchen middens indicated the food consumed was typically English. Also with us on this modern trek

had been Richard Morris from Yale who is analyzing, by computer, the account books at Deerfield pertaining to these forts. He had earlier reported to us that alcoholic beverages made up 11 percent of those purchases studied so far. In some mysterious fashion, there had been delivered to Fort Pelham (presumably from the commissary at Deerfield) a supply of "rhum" (cold Coors and wine) for the twenty-one "scouts" who in 1985 had patrolled the old Military Road from Fort Shirley to Fort Pelham for the first time in 231 years - and reported a few settler's cabins but no hostile Indians.

Cleon was there to escort us to the bus waiting down the path on the Pond Road, and we were carried back to our starting point to enjoy our sandwiches on the perfect rock across from the Newland Smith house. It had been a glorious day, and we each sat looking off toward Monadnock feeling more intimately involved with local history and a very personal sense of accomplishment. ✳

Cleon's bus waiting on Pond Road

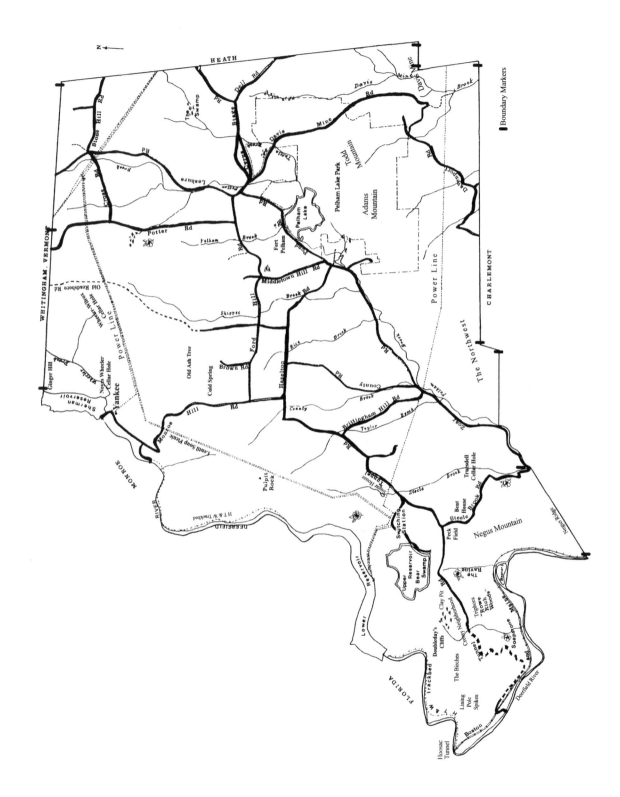